WOMEN WRITING
IN INDIA

Regional Language Editors

Afeefa Banu, *Urdu*
Vidyut Bhagwat, *Marathi*
Vijaya Dabbe, *Kannada*
Jharna Dhar, *Bengali*
Jancy James, *Malayalam*
S. S. Kalpana, *Tamil*
Shirin Kudchedkar, *Gujarati*
K. Lalita, *Telugu*
Jayanta Mahapatra, *Oriya*
Mukesh Srivastava, *Hindi*
Susie Tharu, *English*

WOMEN
WRITING
IN INDIA

600 B.C. TO THE PRESENT

Volume II: The Twentieth Century

EDITED BY SUSIE THARU
AND K. LALITA

THE FEMINIST PRESS
at The City University of New York
New York

Published 1993 by The Feminist Press at The City University of New York,
311 East 94 Street, New York, N.Y. 10128

Library of Congress Cataloging-in-Publication Data
(Revised for Volume 2)

Women writing in India.

Includes bibliographical references (v. 1, p. 522–529) and index.
Contents: v. 1. 600 B.C. to the early twentieth century — v. 2. The
twentieth century.
1. Indic literature—Women authors—Translation into English. 2. Indic
literature (English)—Women authors. 3. Indic literature—Women
authors—History and criticism. 4. Indic literature (English)—Women
authors—History and criticism. I. Tharu, Susie J. II. Lalita, Ke.
PK2978.E5W57 1990   891'.1   90-3788
ISBN 1-55861-026-X (cloth : v. 1 : alk. paper)
ISBN 1-55861-027-8 (pbk. : v. 1 : alk. paper)
ISBN 1-55861-028-6 (cloth : v. 2 : alk. paper)
ISBN 1-55861-029-4 (pbk. : v. 2 : alk. paper)

Permissions acknowledgments begin on page 624.

This publication is made possible, in part, by public funds from the National
Endowment for the Arts, the National Endowment for the Humanities, and
the New York State Council on the Arts. The Feminist Press is also grateful
to Ellen Bass, Janet E. Brown, Jean Barber Bucek, Johnnetta B. Cole,
Creative Graphics, Inc., Helene D. Goldfarb, Jane Gould, Elaine Hedges,
McNaughton & Gunn, Inc., Deborah Light, Joanne Markell, Gloria Naylor,
Nancy Porter, Margaret Schink, Myra Shapiro, Barbara Sicherman, Domna
Stanton, Gloria Steinem, Alice Walker, and Genevieve Vaughan for their
generosity.

Text design: Paula Martinac

Cover design: Lucinda Geist

Cover art: Detail from *Grieved Child,* 1980, oil on canvas, 48″ × 48″, by
Nalini Malini, from the collection of Vivan Sundaram.
Reproduced by permission of the artist.

Typeset by Creative Graphics, Inc.

Printed in the United States of America on acid-free paper by McNaughton &
Gunn, Inc.

For all the writers
we have not been able to include,
for the many we do not yet know about

CONTENTS

PREFACE

We began work on these volumes with the premise that critical assumptions, historical circumstance, and ideologies generally have been hostile to women's literary production and have crippled our ability to read and appreciate their work. In the two volumes of *Women Writing in India* we have attempted to make available for English-language readers in India and around the world a group of works that together will illuminate the conditions in which women wrote; bring more significant women's writing to light; help us reevaluate writers who were reasonably well known but had been misunderstood or dismissed; give us a sense of the themes and literary modes women drew on and made use of; and help us capture what is at stake in the practices of self or agency and of narrative that emerge at the contested margins of patriarchy, empire, and nation.

When we began work we were repeatedly warned, often by reputed scholars, that we would find few significant women writers in Marathi or Kannada or Urdu literature. One of the editors had been teaching courses in Indian writing in English for several years, little suspecting that the nineteenth or early twentieth centuries would hold such gems as Cornelia Sorabji's autobiography, Pandita Ramabai's letters or memoirs, Krupa Sattianadan's novels, Rokeya Sakhawat Hossain's utopian fiction, the many pieces that first appeared in the influential

Indian Ladies Magazine over the first two decades of the twentieth century, or the memoirs of such independent political thinkers as Muthulakshmi Reddi. Even the celebrated Indo-Anglian poet Toru Dutt, whose work invariably found place in syllabuses, was usually presented as a brilliant, but protected, upper-class child-poet, who died early of consumption. Rarely did students learn that, like her uncle Romesh Chunder Dutt, she was a nationalist and a passionate republican; that she was widely read in the history and literature of the French Revolution; or that she had translated speeches made in the French Chamber of Deputies around the time of the Revolution for Indian nationalist journals. Hardly ever is it mentioned, in the context of the literature classroom, that Sarojini Naidu was called the Nightingale of India as much for the rhythm and modulation of the speeches she made during the Independence movement as for her delicate verse.

We began, therefore, somewhat tentatively—hopeful, but uncertain. We read against the grain of literary histories, taking special note of writers who were criticized or spoken about dismissively, and controversies that involved women. Social histories, biographies, and autobiographies, we found, often provided information that literary histories had censored. From these we learned about debates in which women had intervened; about wives, companions, and mothers who "also" wrote; about the prostitutes of Benares who had written a *Shraddanjali* (a collection of elegies) when a famous Hindi writer died; about a women's *kavi sammelan* (poets' meet) organized by Mahadevi Varma; about Vai Mu Kodainayakiammal, who in the early 1900s bought a publishing house, which then published her 115 novels and many works by other women writers, as well as the journal *Jaganmohini,* which she edited. To our surprise we found that the early twentieth century, commonly considered a period when the women's movement was at a low ebb, had been a high point of women's journalism. In almost every region women edited journals for women (though clearly men also read them) and many hundreds of women wrote in them. Our list soon included the testimonies of Buddhist nuns from the sixth century B.C., rebel medieval poets, sixteenth-century court historians, many unknown women poets, novelists, and polemical writers of the nineteenth and twentieth centuries, and several published memoirs.

Confident that there was a great deal more to be discovered, we began to travel through different parts of the country meeting scholars, women writers, and feminist activists—and it was only as we talked to these people that the project actually took concrete form. We found ourselves slipping past the disciplinary gatekeepers we had first come up against, and searching out, or being directed to, a whole range of other people: historians, sociologists, activists, as well as writers and critics outside the mainstream, who shared information about little-known writers, told us about major works, and discussed what they considered dimensions of cultural history that helped us understand both the cultural economy in which women write and the politics of canon building as it affected women. In most languages, the literary canons had been established in the early 1950s, shortly after Independence. They were therefore charged with constructing an imagined community and sculpting the new citizen. But, as the section introductions also point out, the relation between articulations of the women's question and the discourses of an emerging nationalism was a very troubled one. Critics whose major concern had been to establish the universal dimensions of a literature that was at the same time also authentically "Indian" seemed to have had little interest in probing such unsettling configurations, or asking what these tensions implied for the woman writer or for literary form. They did not ask why, for instance, the central fictional relationship had changed between the 1880s and the 1920s from that of husband and wife to that of mother and son. Or what were the urgencies condensed in the recurring figure of the Hindu widow in the nineteenth-century texts. Neither could they ask, therefore, how this figure had been transformed in the twentieth century by women writers such as Nirupama Devi, Subhadra Kumari Chauhan, Indira Sahasrabuddhe, or Bahinabai Chaudhari, and why. Critics did not seem interested in how the question of the education of women into citizenship and identity, as fascinatingly broached in Chandu Menon's *Indulekha*, 1889, and in Rabindranath Tagore's *Ghare Baire* (The Home and the World), 1916, had been recast by Indira Sahasrabuddhe or Rokeya Sakhawat Hossain. No one asked what it meant for a writer to live in times and in situations where she was doubly "Other"—as woman and as colonized person—even in her own vision. Yet these are complexities in the cultural fabric that must be recognized if we are to approach the elusive nature of an identity that emerges at the margin, or understand the peculiar tension between public and private realities that underwrites women's writing.

Neither politics nor women's issues, nor indeed literature, feature in the introductory essays in forms traditional scholarship is familiar with. The essays recast and renew each of these disciplinary clusters. In addition, as they explore empire and nation in terms of transformations in imagined communities and imaginary selves, they point to the structural connections between women's issues and public politics and between these and the literary texts.

The more than 140 authors included in the two volumes of this project were selected from an initial list, itself selective, of over 600 writers. The detailed research into the literature of each of the eleven languages represented here—Bengali, Gujarati, English, Hindi, Kannada, Malayalam, Marathi, Oriya, Tamil, Telugu, and Urdu—was done by different scholars, each working in one of these regional languages. The scholars searched through archives and spoke with writers and critics before they made the initial selections. They also did the substantial original research for the biographical headnotes. Many of our most exciting discoveries were made at this stage. Each of us has different anecdotes about tracking down books and information, about surprise finds, and about unlikely people who helped us out with crucial details. Once we had searched out the information about the writers, we ran into the problem of actually locating the texts. Libraries had often not acquired the books, and even when they had, the copies were badly preserved. The pages were moth-eaten, the paper faded and brittle, reproduction sometimes impossible. S. S. Kalpana had to copy out entire texts by hand. Susie Tharu found one archive had just sold some nineteenth-century titles she had been looking for as junk. All Jharna Dhar could locate of Mokshodayani Mukhopadhyay's satiric poem was a long extract, quoted by an indignant literary historian. At other times we were luckier. Many of us found copies of early texts with individuals—women and men—who had carefully preserved them. K. Lalita discovered to her delight that the Saraswata Niketanam, an old library in the small, out-of-the-way town of Vetapalem, had a rare collection of early twentieth-century books and journals. Afeefa Banu located a fifty-year-old private library in Hyderabad that had maintained a special interest in women writers. Once Vidyut Bhagwat had convinced the historian G. B. Sardar that her project might be worthwhile, he made several priceless suggestions. Then she met Geeta Sane, who had just turned eighty and was overjoyed to find a new generation searching out her books. It wasn't long before Vidyut learned about a whole group of women writers unheard of in the corridors of the Marathi literary establishment. K. Lalita had almost given up in despair when she located handwritten copies of Tarigonda Venkamamba's poem's in her aunt's prayer room. Though Venkamamba's work had found no place in public systems of distribution, it had been kept alive in an alternative mode, as it was handed across from woman to woman. The translator of Mary John Thottam's "Lokame Yatra" (Farewell to the World), who knew the poem by heart, told us he had never seen a printed copy before, but his mother had had a handwritten copy, which she kept in her Bible. Jancy James discovered that the "ghost" that appears in Lalithambika Antherjanam's story was the ghost of a real woman, and tracked down the early twentieth-century newspaper reports of her trial. Shirin Kudchedkar unearthed clearly feminist stories and poems by writers who were not commonly regarded as feminist. Vijaya Dabbe came up with extraordinary selections from Kannada *bhakti* poetry.

Gathering information for the biographical headnotes was an equally challenging and adventure-filled task. We located and interviewed contemporary writers, but finding out about little-known authors who had died in the forties or earlier was unexpectedly problematic. There were few biographies we could draw on, little formal documentation, and almost no criticism. Occasionally we came across memoirs or could piece together letters kept by a relative or a friend. Sometimes we learned about writers' lives from published interviews, preserved by writers themselves or their friends, but dates and bibliographical information began to seem something of a miracle. Small presses often didn't record a date of publication and on occasion even children could not tell us when their mothers had been born or their major works published. Sometimes the writers themselves were depressed or reduced to penury and didn't have the space or inclination to keep copies of their own books. Ashapurna Debi could not remember when she had written the story she wanted us to translate for this collection. What a contrast it was to learn about box after box of Cornelia Sorabji's papers neatly labeled and filed in the India Office Library in London!

The physical problems we ran into were compounded, at more levels than we had imagined, by conceptual ones. Conventions of representing a life vary—historically across periods, but also spatially across a culture. The carefully preserved biographies of Buddhist nuns with which these volumes open, for instance, provide information about their previous lives and record the occasion on which each nun attained enlightenment and subsequent release from the cycle of birth and death, but tell us nothing about the rest of their lives or their other compositions. In keeping with the conventions of eighteenth-century Telugu court literature, Muddupalani traces her poetic lineage, naming as her mentors her grandmother and her aunt and telling us about her literary achievements. About her other experiences we know almost nothing. Much of the information we were able to glean about the important nineteenth-century novelist Krupa Sattianadan was from speeches made at a memorial meeting held shortly after she died. Colonial administrators cited her life as testifying that education or intellectual achievement did not destroy the modesty or sensitivity natural to women. The Indians who spoke at the meeting considered her novels important because they demonstrated that education had in no way alienated Krupa from her roots in Hindu society. Most of the headnotes therefore carry this double mark, some more interestingly than others, of the "standard" forms of our present-day investigation and the biographical imagination our sources represented.

A few observations about translation. Formulations that set up the problem of translation as one of judging how faithful a translation has been to the original, or how well it reads in the target language, divert attention from the fact that translation takes place where two, invariably unequal, worlds collide, and that there are always relationships of power involved when one world is represented for another in translation. We have been very aware that in India, when we translate a regional language—Tamil or Oriya, for instance—into English, we are representing a regional culture for a more powerful national or "Indian" one, and when this translation is made available to a readership outside India, we are also representing a national culture for a still more powerful international culture—which is today, in effect, a Western one. We have tried, therefore, in the translations (not always successfully) to strain against the reductive and often stereotypical homogenization involved in this process. We preferred translations that did not domesticate the work either into a pan-Indian or into a "universalist" mode, but demanded of the reader too a translation of herself into another sociohistorical ethos. We have taken pains, therefore, to preserve the regional grain of the work, and to create a historical context that might open the text up for a materialist and feminist reading.

On the whole we have required that a reader use the context a story or poem provides, which the other pieces and the introductions fill out and complicate, to make her way into the writer's times and the writer's world; we are asking that a reader—in India or abroad—learn slowly, as she relates to the objects, the concerns, the logic of the worlds women have inhabited over the years, to *live* a mode of life, and not just read about it. We have therefore kept the glosses to a minimum, presenting them only when we felt the information was difficult to locate and crucial to an informed reading of the text.

Unfortunately we have had to leave some important selections out because the translations "failed." For volume 2, we wanted to include the work of Krishna Sobti, one of the leading contemporary Hindi writers, but she writes in a dialect translators felt would be difficult to render into standard English and uses an earthy, lewd diction. Standard forms of English, sanitized as they have been over the last two hundred years, just did not stretch into anything that resembled the scope of Sobti's idiom. Very reluctantly we had to abandon the effort to translate Balamani Amma, a major Malayalam poet of the 1940s and 1950s, because her grand, public verse about motherhood presupposes an ethos we found difficult to recreate in the context of a few poems and a short biography. We are also sorry we were not able to include a story by Qurratulain Hyder, a leading Urdu writer, because of disagreements over the translation.

Considerable discussion went into deciding how Indian-language words would be transliterated into roman script in the body of the book. We began by developing a system of transliteration that was subtle enough to capture regional differences without becoming so elaborate that it would alienate an ordinary reader. Since each Indian language has sounds that others do not have, and we wanted the translation to retain the mark of the original regional language, this was no easy task. Vasanta Duggirala, who helped us with this task, had to go over each headnote and each piece with someone who spoke the standard form (not always easy to identify) of Gujarati, Malayalam, and so on. When we had finished, the page looked like one in an Orientalist or anthropological text. Since anthropology and Orientalism were colonial disciplinary contexts into which our book might so easily be assimilated, we had deliberately and consistently strained against those currents when we made the selections, did the translations, and wrote the headnotes and introductions. We were, to say the least, unhappy about that effect. So were the editors at The Feminist Press. We then talked the problem over with several people in India including publishers and editors. Most people in the trade seemed to think that the kind of elaborate transliterations Indological studies had established as a norm were not really necessary or useful. As far as we know, few readers vocalize words when they read. New words are "recognized," visually, but not necessarily formulated aurally, even as a sort of mental image.

We also found that there were many words, in fact a great many more than we had originally envisaged, that appeared in common English and American dictionaries and therefore had conventional spellings. A great many other commonly used words were in the process of acquiring such standardized spellings, *akam, dalit, kisan,* and *hartal,* for example. We finally decided that we would keep the use of Indian-language words that did not appear in the *Webster's New Collegiate Dictionary* to a minimum, and spell other words as they would normally be spelled in newspapers and journals published in India—without diacritical marks or combinations of letters that seem strange in English (such as -*chch*-). In one sense we might be regarded as taking the initiative in standardizing the spelling of these words. The same idea underlay the decision to italicize an Indian-language word the first time a reader meets it, but not later. What we had gained as a result of all this was a "reader-friendly" page that did not look like an Orientalist text. What we had lost—and we are sad about it—was the variety of the regional languages.

We have provided, for a reader who wants to pronounce the writers' names and the titles of works correctly and is willing to take trouble over it, an appendix in which the names and titles have been systematically transliterated.

It must by now be clear that when we made the selections we were not just looking for uncontroversially "well-formed" works or indeed simply for an individual writer's "achievement" that would appeal immediately across time and space. We looked more specifically for pieces that illuminated women's responses to historical developments and ones that gave insight into the dimensions of self-fashioning and the politics of everyday life as they affected women. We paid special attention to writers we thought had been underestimated or whose work ought to be far better known. Given these perspectives, it is not surprising that the writers whose work we found most significant were often not the ones that traditional critical establishments had singled out for praise.

Not all the texts or authors, therefore, were chosen for the same reasons. We might have included one piece because it was moving, another because the writer was already very well known, another precisely because she ought to be better known, or represented a class or other group whose creative activity is rarely taken into consideration in traditional literary histories and the canons they construct. Yet another might be raising an important issue, dramatizing a typical conflict, or representing a formal development.

It goes without saying that the collection is *not* exhaustive. Very regretfully we had to exclude Assamese literature, which has a long and distinguished tradition of women writers, and were not able to work on women's writing in Punjabi, Rajasthani, Kashmiri, or Sindhi. Our collections of Urdu, Bengali, Tamil, and English writing would have been richer had we envisaged the project as including writers from Pakistan, Bangladesh, and Sri Lanka, but space considerations precluded the inclusion of many possible works. We would have liked to include in volume 2 an extract from the Telugu writer Ranganaya-kamma's (b. 1939) *Janaki Vimukti* (Janaki's Liberation), 1977, but could not obtain permission to do so. Since the work of those who wrote in English would be more easily available to the reader, we included only rare pieces from the nineteenth and early twentieth centuries in English. This means we have not presented major contemporary figures such as Attia Hossain (b. 1912), Anita Desai (b. 1937), Shashi Desh-pande (b. 1938), or Meena Alexander (b. 1951). We would have liked, had space permitted, to introduce, in many more oral autobiographies, the voices of peasant women and women workers. We have too little material by dalit writers and nothing that represents the tribal traditions of resistance and celebration. We hope *Women Writing in India* will inspire future volumes that can make available more of this rich literature.

ACKNOWLEDGMENTS

No book of such scope could have been written without the support and cooperation of the many people who helped us in more ways than we had thought would be possible. We would like to thank all those who argued with us, introduced us to writers, unearthed biographical information, helped us locate rare books, put us up, fed us, and—most of all—shared our excitement. For any omissions we might inadvertently have made, we sincerely apologize.

Nirmalya Acharya
Hari Adiseshuvu
Wajid Aktar
Sukirat Anand
Madhavi Apte
Sumati Ayyar
Mohammad Abdul Aziz
B. N. Sumitra Bai
Kamakshi Balasubramanian
Samik Bandopadhyay
Shukla Banerjee
Ram Bapat

Shakira Begum
Leelavati Bhagwat
Sukumari Bhattacharji
Ashutosh Bhattacharyay
Salma Bilgrami
Brojendra Nath Bondopadhyay
Chittaranjan Bondyopadhyay
Sondeep Bondyopadhyay
Vaddera Chandidas
Narayan Chandran
Priya Chandrasekhar
Enakshi Chatterjee

Ratnabali Chattopadhyay
Girish Chandra Chaudhary
Raghu Cidambi
Susan Daniel
Kalpana Dasgupta
Usha Datar
G. P. Deshpande
Abburi Chaya Devi
K. Sita Devi
Deepa Dhanraj
Tilottama Dhar
Susannah Driver
Narain Singh Dubey
Vasanta Duggirala
Arup Dutta
Lalitha Eapen
Nissim Ezekiel
Shailaja Ganguly
B. Gayathri
Mamani R. Goswami
Yogendra Nath Gupta
Dibyendu Hota
Hridayakumari
Akhtar Hussain
Qurratulain Hyder
Susan Jacob
Gigy Joseph
Svati Joshi
Usha Joshi
Yusuf Kamal
Y. Kameswari
Kalpana Kannabiran
Lakshmi Kannan
Anuradha Kapoor
Geeta Kapur
Abid Ali Khan
Ahmed U. Khan
Deepti Khandelwal
Komali
Kondapalli Koteswaramma
Rambhatla Krishnamurthy

Durgadas Lahiri
K. Vijaya Lakshmi
T.S.S. Lakshmi
B. Lakshmibai
Utukuri Lakshmikantamma
Marjorie Lightman
Yasmeen Lukmani
Runu Mahapatra
Uma Maheswari
Swapan Majumdar
A. A. Manavalan
Celine Mathew
Bina Mazumdar
Jaya Mehta
Vijaya Mehta
Rama Melkote
Taki Ali Mirza
Sunita Misra
Aditi Mukherjee
Sujit Mukherjee
Romoni Mohan Mullick
T. Muraleedharan
Banda Muralikrishna Murthy
S.R.J. Muthukrishnan
Shama Narang
Vadrevu Narayanamurthy
Anupama Niranjana
Tejaswini Niranjana
Evashisha Nongrang
Joanne O'Hare
V. Padma
Mrinal Pande
Ayyappa Pannikar
P. Parvathy
Deepa Patnaik
B. D. Phadke
D. D. Punde
Ashraf Rafi
Chudamani Raghavan
N. Raghavendrarao
Sitaram Raikar

Ashish Rajadhyksha
Polapragada Rajyalakshmi
Nita Ramaiya
V. Ramakrishna
Chekuri Ramarao
Vakati Panduranga Rao
Abburi Varada Rajeswara Rao
R. V. Seshagiri Rao
Shanta Rameshwar Rao
Roopkamal Rastogi
M. Ravinder
N. G. Krishna Reddy
K. Sajaya
Tarun Sannyal
Saomi Saran
G. B. Sardar
Sannidhanam Narasimha Sarma
Saral Satapathy
Nabaneeta Dev Sen
Jyoti Seshan
Syed Ali Shafee
Tanuja Shammohan
D. P. Sharma

Veena Shatrugna
Nilima Sheikh
Gulam Mohammed Sheikh
Syed Sirajuddin
Krishna Sobti
Souda
K. Srikumar
Rajendra Kumar Srivastava
R. Srivatsan
K. Subramanyam
R. S. Sudarshanam
S. Sivapatha Sundaram
Vivan Sundaram
Suvarchala
Rajsekhar Thakur
Thomas Tharu
J. P. Vasandani
Vattikonda Visalakshi
Uma Viswakumar
Volga
Rajendra Vora
Rajendra Yadav
Robert J. Zydenbos

Anveshi Research Centre for Women's Studies, Hyderabad, for housing this project and for providing a context for discussion and exchange.

Central Institute of English and Foreign Languages, Hyderabad, for granting Susie Tharu leave during which the initial work on these volumes was done.

And special thanks

to Maitrayee Mukhopadhyay, Vasantha Kannabiran, Meenakshi Mukherjee, and Jasodhara Bagchi, colleagues and friends, who never failed to respond to the many demands we made on them, and treated this work as if it were their own.

to Florence Howe, who has been so much more than a publisher, and who made the process of editing an instructive and genuinely stimulating one.

to Shoshanna, Shamuel, Diya, Vithal, and Jim, who not only put up with our enthusiasms, our anxieties, and our despair through the years in which the book became a permanent guest in our homes, but also made it feel welcome.

WOMEN WRITING
IN INDIA

INTRODUCTION

What was the point, we were sometimes asked when we began work on the two volumes of *Women Writing in India,* of putting together an anthology such as this? Why did we think women's writing was different or that it called for special attention? Weren't women writers as much victims to social ideologies about the subordinate status of women as men? If we were arguing that women writers had been marginalized and their work misrepresented or misjudged, how did we suggest they should be read? Our answers to these questions have changed over the years we have been working on these collections, often because we learned a great deal, not only from the erudite and generous writers and critics we met in unexpected places, but also from our most skeptical interlocutors.

I

In 1910, when Bangalore Nagaratnamma reprinted the classic *Radhika Santwanam* (Appeasing Radhika), she was quite certain why she wanted to present the work of the eighteenth-century Telugu poet Muddu-palani to the reading public again. "However often I read this book," she wrote, "I feel like reading it all over again."[1] And as if that were not reason enough, "since this poem, brimming with *rasa,* was not only

---

[1] Bangalore Nagaratnamma, "Afterword," in Muddupalani, *Radhika Santwanam,* ed. Bangalore Nagaratnamma (Madras: Vavilla Ramaswami Sastrulu and Sons, 1910), p. 80.

1

written by a woman, but by one who was born into our community, I felt it necessary to publish it in its proper form."[2] The word *rasa* literally means "juice" or "essence." According to classical aesthetic theory, in a well-formed work of art all the nine rasas, or basic emotions such as joy, anger, or sexual pleasure, are evoked in fit measure to the subject at hand. In Nagaratnamma's judgment, *Radhika Santwanam* had achieved that rare balance: it was filled—to the brim—but not spilling over. Even Muddupalani's harshest critic, Kandukuri Veereshalingam (1848–1919), was forced to admit that "there is no doubt that this woman's poetry is soft and melodious, and that she is a scholar, well versed in the literature of Sanskrit and of Telugu."[3]

Nagaratnamma had first found mention of Muddupalani's name in an early commentary on the Thanjavur period of Telugu literature. The authors had spoken about Muddupalani as a great poet and had quoted some extracts from *Radhika Santwanam*. She tried to get hold of the original and finally managed with difficulty to locate a copy. It was poorly printed and difficult to read. Friends who learned about her interest sent her another edition, with a *vyakhyanam,* or commentary, appended, but it was only when she came by the manuscript that she realized what a perfect creation it was: "as adorable," she writes, "as the young Lord Krishna."[4]

The pleasure of the text was clearly the principal impetus for the new edition, but Nagaratnamma was also dissatisfied with the editing and the printing of a version of Muddupalani's poem put out in 1887 by Venkatanarasu, who was a classicist and associate of the Orientalist lexicographer C. P. Brown. Venkatanarasu had not included the prologue in which, as was conventional in classical verse, Muddupalani proudly traced her literary lineage through her grandmother and her aunt, and gave an account of herself and her not inconsiderable standing as a poet in the court of Pratapasimha, who reigned between 1739 and 1763. He had also omitted the *charanam,* or concluding couplets of several poems, and left other couplets out completely. Besides, the printing was poor and there were many orthographic mistakes. "I have compared the manuscript with the published edition," she wrote, and

---

[2]Ibid., p. iv.

[3]Kandukuri Veereshalingam, *Andhra Kavula Charitramu* (History of Andhra Poets), Vol. III: *Adhunika Kavulu* (Modern Poets) (Rajamundry: Hitakarini Samajam, 1950; 1st ed. 1887), p. 142.

[4]Nagaratnamma, p. ii.

"have prepared a new version."[5] If we were to look today for a precursor for these volumes of women's writing, we would locate one in the *Therigatha,* an anthology of lyrics composed by the Buddhist *theris,* or nuns, in the sixth century B.C. But for a figure who anticipates our critical initiative, we must surely turn to Bangalore Nagaratnamma.

Nagaratnamma was a patron of the arts, a learned woman, a musician, and a distinguished courtesan, and she approached her editorial task with confident professionalism and admirable feminist partisanship. But neither she nor her publishers, Vavilla Ramaswami Sastrulu and Sons, who Krishnaswami Aiyangar, professor of Indian history and archaeology at the University of Madras, spoke of as "one of the oldest and most reputable publishers in Madras . . . doing very useful work by issuing correct editions of Telugu and Sanskrit classics," could have been quite prepared for the furor that followed the publication.[6]

Muddupalani's poem had already aroused some controversy. Kandukuri Veereshalingam, father of the social reform movement in Andhra and a novelist himself, had, in his definitive history of Telugu poets, scornfully dismissed the poet as "one who claims to be an expert in music, classical poetry and dance," and denounced her work in no uncertain terms. "This Muddupalani is an adulteress," he wrote. "Many parts of the book are such that they should never be heard by a woman, let alone emerge from a woman's mouth. Using *sringara rasa* as an excuse, she shamelessly fills her poems with crude descriptions of sex." That is not surprising, in his view, because "she is born into a community of prostitutes and does not have the modesty natural to women."[7] The poem, he concluded, was pernicious.

Nagaratnamma retorted equally sharply. Perhaps, she wrote, Veereshalingam considered modesty natural only to women. "He can denounce a poet because she is a 'prostitute' and he claims that she shamelessly fills her poems with crude descriptions of sex. But if that is so, it should be just as wrong for men who are considered respectable to write in that manner. But, [as everyone knows] several great men have written even more 'crudely' about sex."[8] Her spirited de-

---

[5]Ibid., p. iv.
[6]Krishnaswami Aiyangar, Note appended to Government Order No. 355, Home, Public, Confidential, dated 22.4.27. "Petition of V. Venkateshwara Sastrulu and Sons, Sanskrit and Telugu Publishers, established 1856." Hereafter cited as Petition, 22.4.27.
[7]Veereshalingam, p. 143.
[8]Nagaratnamma, p. iii.

fense was of little avail, however. The government translator Goteti Kanakaraju Pantulu also declared that parts of the book were objectionable. Once he had translated the sections he considered improper into English, the British government was convinced that the book would endanger the moral health of their Indian subjects. In 1911, Police Commissioner Cunningham seized all the copies, and the government charged Nagaratnamma's publishers with having produced an obscene book.

The order met with considerable resistance. The publishers sent up a petition denying the charge, which was also directed against eight other classics they had published, though *Radhika Santwanam* was clearly the most "objectionable" one. It was "unduly straining the language of Section 292 of the Indian Penal Code," they argued, "to suggest that ancient classics that have been extant for centuries, could be brought within the meaning of the section." The petitioners respectfully submitted "that classics in all languages and in all lands contain passages similar to those that are now complained of and would come equally under the purview of this section, if construed in this manner."[9] Other pressures were also brought to bear on the government. A conference of pandits and scholars was held under the auspices of the Telugu Academy of Letters, and its members submitted a resolution to the government claiming that "such proceedings were inexpedient and undesirable and highly detrimental to the preservation and progress of Telugu culture."[10] Several distinguished scholars added the weight of their standing to the appeal. Peri Narayana Murthy, a well-known lawyer, who, like Vavilla Venkateshwara Sastrulu, was also involved in nationalist politics, argued for the publishers.

Despite these efforts, the petitions were dismissed, as was the plea that the case should be heard by a judge who knew Telugu. The British government banned the books. The publishers were allowed to bring out totally expurgated editions of some works; others could be reprinted with the offensive sections deleted; but all copies of *Radhika Santwanam* were to be unconditionally destroyed. The tree of Telugu literature, Nagaratnamma's publisher wrote, had received an ax-blow.

Much to the chagrin of the government, the books clearly continued to circulate. On March 3, 1927, the Vavilla Press in Tondiarpet as well as its shop in Esplanade was raided again. The police also raided a bookshop in Rajamundry and even tracked down two readers in Sri-

---

[9]Cited in Petition, 22.4.27.
[10]Petition, 22.4.27.

kakulam who had ordered copies by post. In an indignant letter of protest, written shortly afterward, Venkateshwara Sastrulu agreed that copies were being circulated. But he had taken care, he said, to sell the unexpurgated editions only to scholars. The versions that were being commercially circulated had been modified as required by the government. Each of these works, he argued, had been written centuries ago and occupied an important place in Telugu literature. It would be a travesty of justice if they were regarded as coming under the purview of Section 292 of the Penal Code. Prof. Krishnaswami Aiyangar endorsed these claims. "It is possible that the extreme purist may take exception to a verse here and a verse there," he commented, "but having regard to the genius of these languages, such a complete expurgation would be impossible without sacrificing the substance of the work. . . . It is hardly necessary to do so, however, as these passages hardly jar upon Indian feeling or sentiment."[11] All the same, the colonial government banned the books again. It is interesting that in the petition they filed in response, the publishers make no mention of *Radhika Santwanam,* although they contest the seizure of the other books.

Only with the support of a nationalist leader and spokesman for Andhra Pradesh as influential as Tanguturi Prakasam (1872–1957), who had just become chief minister, were the ban orders withdrawn in 1947. It had been a battle, Prakasam said, for pearls of great beauty to be replaced in the necklace of Telugu literature. Permission was also granted for Nagaratnamma's edition of *Radhika Santwanam* to be republished, and the Vavilla Press brought out a new edition in 1952. When in the late 1980s, our curiosities aroused by the harsh dismissals of Muddupalani's work in almost every contemporary literary history, we searched for a copy of her poem, it was difficult to find one. Critic after critic assured us that her work was obscene and simply not worth reading, though many of them had never seen the text.[12] Students of Telugu literature, even ones sympathetic to women, echoed their judgment. The ban on *Radhika Santwanam* had been lifted with the winning

---

[11]Petition, 22.4.27.

[12]Yandamuri Satyanarayanarao's comment is an exception: "These epic poems are well-formed works, complete with all the nine *rasas.* If we look at them with our present view of women, they might appear low and unrefined. That is the inadequacy of our culture, and not that of the epic or the poet." (*Saradadhwajam Thanjavur Rajulakalamloni Telugu Sahitya Charitra* [The Flag of Scholarship: The History of Telugu Literature in the Thanjavur Era] [Hyderabad: Sahitya Academy, n.d.], p. 231.)

of Independence. But the symbolic release of Telugu culture from Imperial bonds did not address the cultural economies of gender, class, caste, or literature that ensured that the book would continue to be decreed out of existence ideologically.

Radhika Santwanam and the history of its reception provide us an entry—unsanctioned, illegitimate, and therefore also subversive—into many of the major ideological conjunctures of the last 250 years of Indian history. This text and its author have been relegated to the marginalia of cultural history and excluded from the literary canon, but remain nonetheless to structure the strategic closures of both institutions. Almost as if by design, Muddupalani's person, her writing, and the misadventures of her text provide us a perspective with which it becomes possible to tease apart and display the *processes,* each partial and over-determined, through which cultural authorities were fashioned and secured as they were drafted into the emerging historical projects of empire and of nation. In the discussion that follows we trace the changing economies of gender, caste, and class, serviced in turn by transformations of literary taste as well as by altogether new notions of the function of literature and the nature of the literary curriculum that determined the fate of *Radhika Santwanam* and many other women's texts.

There is no evidence to suggest that Muddupalani's work was attacked or dismissed in her own times. The autobiographical prologue conventional in such works indicates that she was a respected poet and also accomplished in music and classical dance. It was not customary for male artists to dedicate their writing to a woman mentor, but Muddupalani records with pride that several works had been dedicated to her. She speaks of her beauty and of her learning with the directness and self-confidence of one who has never been required to be apologetic or coy, and records instances when she herself expressed her appreciation of other poets with gifts and money. If the honors and rewards bestowed on her by Pratapasimha, her royal patron, can be taken as the response of a contemporary reader, there can be no doubt that her work was truly appreciated in her own times.

The Thanjavur court, which provided the context, and the audience for Muddupalani's compositions, was famous for its patronage of the arts. The period is spoken of as the golden age of Telugu literature. Music, dance, and literature flourished, as did painting and sculpture. Many of the kings in this powerful southern dynasty were also scholars and poets, and the evidence we have suggests that there were several eminent literary women at the court. Ramabhadramba and Madhuravani, for instance, both composed poetry in three languages and were experts in *ashtavadhanam* (the capacity to attend to eight different intellectual activities at the same time). Ramabhadramba was also a historian and left behind accounts of the political and military events in Raghunadhanayaka's reign. She documents the presence of several women composers in the court. Muddupalani herself traces her literary heritage through her grandmother and her aunt, who were both poets. Unlike upper-caste family women in her time, as a courtesan Muddupalani would have had access to learning and the leisure to write and practice the arts. She would have owned property and expected and enjoyed a functional equality with men. Obviously, the esteem in which Muddupalani was held and the acclaim her work received can be attributed as much to the contexts, literary and social, she drew upon as to her own talent.

Developments in literary form suggest a changing society. Even Muddupalani's harshest critics comment on her scholarship and on the diction of her poetry, which subtly shifted the rhythms of classical Telugu verse closer to those of the spoken form. Other writers of her period were extending established courtly forms to criticize rapacious landlords and describe the everyday lives of craftspeople. No doubt nourished also by the social and political changes associated with the medieval movements of artisanal rebellion, commonly spoken of as the *bhakti* movements, which began in these areas around the eighth century but extended well into Muddupalani's times—the Alvars and Nayanars (of what is present-day Tamilnadu), the Virasaivas (of Karnataka and Andhra Pradesh) and the Varkaris (of Maharashtra)—was the growth of literatures, secular as well as spiritual, which extended the contexts of courtly literature as they drew for their themes on the everyday lives of the artisanal classes.[13] These movements brought into the scope of literary language a whole new *technical* vocabulary based on their expertise. Secular prose narratives had also begun to make an appearance.

Radhika Santwanam was a *sringaraprabandham,* a genre associated in the history of Telugu literature with the Thanjavur era. Epic poems in this genre usually retold, with significant transformations of plot, atmosphere, theme, and worldview, the story of the divine lovers Radha and Krishna. The principal rasa evoked was sringara, or erotic pleasure. Muddupalani's composition, which captures moods and tones of voice with a rare humor and subtlety, is one of the formally and linguistically more sophisticated

---

[13]See Vijaya Daheja, *Antal and Her Path of Love* (Albany: State University of New York Press, 1990), for a useful account of the Alwar saint Antal and her poetry.

works in the genre. But what must have drawn Nagaratnamma to her work and what strikes us today is Muddupalani's remarkable subversions of the received form. Traditionally in such literature, the man is the lover, the woman the loved one; Krishna woos and makes love to Radha. Though Radha is invariably portrayed as longing for him, the narrative has as its focus his pleasure. Not so in *Radhika Santwanam,* where the woman's sensuality is central. She takes the initiative, and it is her satisfaction or pleasure that provides the poetic resolution. With a warmth unmatched in later poetry, Muddupalani celebrates a young girl's coming of age and describes her first experience of sex. In another section, Radha, who is represented as a woman in her prime, instructs her niece, Iladevi, in the art and joy of love. Radha encourages her to express her desire and to recognize and value her pleasure.

Some of the most startling and unusual verses in the epic, however, come from the section that gives the poem its title. Though Radha encourages the liaison between Iladevi and Krishna, she is herself in love with Krishna and cannot bear the separation. She calls him names, accuses him of ignoring her, and demands that he keep up his relationship with her. Krishna responds warmly and appeases her with sweet talk and loving embraces. What makes the work so radical today, if not in its own time, is the easy confidence with which it contests the asymmetries of sexual satisfaction commonly accepted even today, and asserts women's claim to pleasure. In fact Muddupalani transgresses today as much in her attitude as in her themes and her person.

What made a work that was unusual but relatively uncontroversial in its time so dangerous and unacceptable two centuries later? When Nagaratnamma reprinted the poem a little over a century after it had first been written, Victoria was queen of England and empress of India, and major political and ideological shifts, which affected women's literary production and consumption, had taken place. As the British established their commercial and military authority over India during the second half of the eighteenth century, the old rulers were overthrown or marginalized, and the earlier centers of trade and administration lost their importance to the new port cities. By 1799, all revenues from the Thanjavur kingdom went to the British. Those driven to destitution as a result of these changes were principally artisans and craftspeople, but poets, musicians, architects, scientists, indeed scholars and artists of all kinds who depended on the patronage of the courts were deprived of a means of sustenance. Large numbers of women artists, mainly folk singers and dancers, who depended on wealthy households for patronage, but also court artists like Muddupalani were driven into penury and prostitution. What was to become modern Indian literature was largely produced by an English-educated urban middle class.

Important ideological changes, which also served to discredit such women artists as Muddupalani, were taking place at the same time. Increasingly over the nineteenth century the respectability of women from the emerging middle classes was being defined in counterpoint to the "crude and licentious" behavior of lower-class women. Decent (middle-class) women were warned against unseemly interaction with lower-class women and against the corrupting influence of the wandering women singers and dancers whose performances were laced with bawdy and a healthy disrespect for authority.[14] As we shall see, the sculpting of the new respectability was one of the major tasks taken on by the social reform movement, which set out to transform a traditional society into a modern one. Artists, such as Muddupalani, who had been respected figures in royal courts and artistic circles came to be regarded as debauched and their art as corrupting.

A similar process of class differentiation, on the basis of (among other things) redefined sexual mores for women, had taken place in Europe during the late eighteenth and early nineteenth centuries as the new bourgeoisie inscribed its identity on the bodies and souls of women and the proper lady was born.[15] Indian women's sexual propriety, however, was also to be vindicated under the glare of the harsh spotlight focused right through the nineteenth century on what was described as the moral degeneration of Indian society. Bureaucrats, missionaries, journalists, and Western commentators of various kinds filed sensational reports about Indian culture, and made authoritative analyses of Indian character, which was invariably presented as irrational, deceitful, and sexually perverse. The thrust of these descriptions was usually quite clear: the situation in India was so appalling that it called for intervention by an ethical and rational power. The British quickly persuaded

---

[14]Among the other books banned at the same time as *Radhika Santwanam,* for instance, was a sixteenth-century text, Ayyalaraju Narayanamatya's *Hamsavimsathi* (The Twenty Swan Stories), a colorful and somewhat bawdy work, which represents the culture of the artisan classes, and which the publishers described as comparable to Boccaccio's *Decameron.* The collection of twenty stories, they point out, presents "twenty different handicrafts and professions, and [is] intended to give the readers a picture of the life and manners of the sixteenth century." The text contained several technical terms now lost to the language. Petition, 22.4.27.

[15]See Cora Kaplan, *Sea Changes: Culture and Feminism* (London: Verso, 1986), pp. 31–50.

themselves (and the huge profits remitted to imperial coffers no doubt hastened the process) that India was the white man's burden and their government essential to its salvation.

Equally important to our understanding of what made a work that was so well regarded in the mid-eighteenth century unacceptable by the early twentieth century is an appreciation of the new curricular and ideological services literature itself was being pressed into. British colonial administrators and political thinkers, Thomas Macaulay, John Stuart Mill, and Charles Trevelyan among them, were agreed on the need to shape an Indian subject who would be able to not only understand their laws but also appreciate their efforts. The "greatest difficulty the Government suffers in its endeavours to govern well springs from the immorality and ignorance of the mass of the people . . . particularly their ignorance of the spirit, principles and system of the British Government," one administrator reported.[16] "The natives must either be kept down by a sense of our power or they must willingly submit from a conviction that we are more wise, more just, more humane and more anxious to improve their condition than any other rulers they could have," another observed.[17] Indian literatures, they were convinced, contained neither the literary nor the scientific information required for the moral or mental cultivation so essential if good government was to be desired and appreciated. Only suitably selected and carefully taught English literary works, thought of as embodying a "secular Christianity," could be entrusted with the fine-grained transformations of thought, emotion, and ethical sensibility necessary if the moral and political authority of the British was to be recognized, and a sense of public responsibility and honor to develop.[18] Imperial interests clearly underlay the fashioning of the literary curriculum—a fact that becomes all the more significant when we realize that English literature was taught in Indian universities several years before it was

---

[16] W. Frazer, Letter to the Chief Secretary, Fort William (now Madras), 25.9.1828. H. Sharp, *Selections from Educational Records,* Vol. I (Calcutta: Superintendent, Govt. Printing, India, 1923), p. 13.

[17] Minute of J. Farish, 28.8.1938. Quoted in B. K. Boman-Behram, *Educational Controversies of India: The Cultural Conquest of India under British Imperialism* (Bombay: Taraporevala Sons and Co, 1942), p. 239.

[18] Gauri Viswanathan, "The Beginnings of English Literary Study in India," *Oxford Literary Review* 9, 1987, pp. 2–26. The author quotes the evidence of Thomas Macaulay and Charles Trevelyan, *Parliamentary Papers,* Vol. 32 (Great Britain 1852–53).

in Britain. Readers critically trained to "appreciate" such carefully se-lected "canons" of English literature would probably have found not only *Radhika Santwanam* but the culture and the society that sustained the writer to be reprehensible, even dangerous. Gradually, as the new powers staked their claims over the land and over the minds of the people, not only individual works but whole literary traditions were delegitimated and marginalized.

Colonial restructurings of gender and the curricular institutionali-zation of literature both worked to undermine the authority of Indian literatures and undercut the societies that gave rise to them. On the face of it, Orientalist scholarship, which "retrieved" and put into cir-culation many classical Sanskrit and Persian texts, would appear to have reauthorized Indian literature and reaffirmed the significance of an Indian tradition. But, as we argue later, it was a highly restructured version of the past that emerged in the Orientalist framework. Scholars like Max Müller popularized the idea of an idyllic Aryan community, which was a learned, highly disciplined and ascetic one, governed by a sacred (and priestly) order. After this golden vedic age, they argued, Hindu civilization had declined. Historians have pointed out that the Indian past, reconstructed and reempowered by such scholarship, was not only the idealized paradise untouched by the disturbing changes taking place in European society that the Romantics longed for, but also a brahminic one in which the Indian society and its history was reduced to what could be found in the ancient sacred texts. One of the consequences of reaffirming the high brahminical image in the context of a history that was ostensibly in decline was the marginalization of the more recent literatures as well as the literatures that emerged from historically changing, nonbrahmin and secular contexts. Since these literatures often treated divine figures such as Radha or Krishna with familiarity or irreverence and undermined traditional hierarchies of caste and gender, Orientalist scholarship paid little heed to them, or, as Venkatanarasu and Brown did when they reprinted *Radhika San-twanam* in 1887, these works were trimmed and recast. It is interesting that they excised not only the verses they considered sexually explicit or obscene but also the *peetika,* or colophon, in which the woman writer traced her female lineage and spoke with confidence, unusual for later times, about her achievement as an artist.

There are other angles to the story. The cultural history of nineteenth-century India is commonly presented as a battle between the social reformers, who are considered modernizers charged with the interests of women and the "lower" castes, and the traditionalists, who are considered opposed to the movements for reform and in favor of the preservation of a traditional society. Figures such as Nagaratnamma and the cultural forces she represents, who are neither "modern" nor "traditional" in the sense that the modernizers represented tradition, are obscured by these categories, which also reduce the complex and heterogenous forces at work to a simple dichotomy between the progressive and the reactionary.

In the public records of Madras State, the years 1911, in which Nagaratnamma's edition of *Radhika Santwanam* was published, and 1947, in which the ban on the book was finally rescinded, are marked by major events in what had come to be known as the "anti-nautch" campaign. "Nautch" is an anglicized corruption of *naach,* an Urdu term for dance. Begun in the early 1890s by Western-educated social reformers, the campaign set in motion a process that transformed the traditions in which Muddupalani and Nagaratnamma trained and worked. Activists wrote extensively against what they considered the degradation of women and the major threat posed by *devadasis* (temple and court artists)—often derogatorily referred to as "nautch girls"—to the purity of family life. They demonstrated outside the homes of those who continued to support private performances, and repeatedly petitioned the governor and the viceroy. Finally, in 1911, a government despatch was issued desiring "nationwide action to be taken against these performances."[19] The splendid public rituals in which young women were dedicated to the deity in the temple declined with this despatch. During the twenties and thirties, with the support of the Self-Respect movement (an antibrahmin and broadly anti-caste-discrimination movement led in its important initial stages by E.V. Ramaswami Naickar [1879-1973]), the campaign took a more radical and democratic form, demanding that the devadasis' right to their property be protected and their children entitled to the same rights as those born "legitimately." In 1947, the bill prohibiting temple dedication, first introduced in 1930 by Muthulakshmi Reddi (1886-1968), herself the daughter of a dancer, was finally passed. In contrast, reforms that concerned upper-caste women—child marriage, widow remarriage, and dowry—received reluctant and tardy support from landed groups who formed the backbone of the Congress party. All the same, undeniably

---

[19]Amrit Srinivasan, "Reform and Revival: The Devadasi and Her Dance," *Economic and Political Weekly* 20:44, 1985, pp. 1869-1876.

set up as norm, even in the discourses of the Self-Respect movement, is the virtuous domestic woman.[20]

Almost simultaneous with the extradition of the dance from the temple and from the household of the private patron was the recreation of the art, and especially of the now maligned *sadir* (solo) performance associated with the Thanjavur court, in a sanitized new mode as the national dance form, Bharata Natyam. Rukmini Devi Arundale and her painstaking work at the Kalakshetra in Madras is commonly credited with this achievement, but initiatives to "revive" this dance tradition were supported by many in the Congress party and the Theosophical Society, both of which were dominated by the upper castes.[21] Rukmini Devi herself was selected and groomed by Annie Besant (1847–1933) and other leaders of the Theosophical Society to be the vehicle for the "World Mother." In the 1930s, strongly backed by the Theosophical Society, she emerged as a "public figure in the field of dance and 'national' culture in general [and as] . . . the champion for India's renaissance in the arts, specifically Bharata Natyam, its women's ancient spiritual heritage."[22]

As an art form, the well-known dance historian Padma Subramanyam writes, sadir, which was based on the fourteenth-century *adavu* technique, had been appropriated into a degenerate Vaishanav culture and "the higher philosophical and religious content of the dance forms were replaced by a blatant sensuous approach."[23] If the "shock treatment" of banning the dance in the temples had not been given, "followed by the votaries of art venturing to polish it and rename it Bharata

---

[20]A good measure of the effect the anti-nautch movements had on the self image of these women artists is the contrast between Muddupalani's and even Nagaratnamma's confident initiatives and the self-recriminatory posture of Muvalur Ramamirthathammal who wrote *Dasikal Mosavalai* (The Tricks/Ploys of the Devadasis) (Madras: Pearl Press, 1936). "The reform campaigns forced the devadasis to acknowledge the moral supremacy of *grhasta* [domestic] values," Amrit Srinivasan comments in the article cited above.

[21]Among them was the Congress member E. Krishna Iyer, a brahmin and a practising lawyer, who toured the south singing the patriotic songs of Subramanya Bharati and, after 1925, taking on female roles and dancing in the sadir style. In 1931 Krishna Iyer precipitated some of the most acrimonious battles with the Self-Respect movement over the issue of dance. See Sunil Kothari, "History: Roots, Growth and Revival," in *Bharata Natyam: Indian Classical Dance Art* (Delhi: Marg Publications, 1979) pp. 23–29.

[22]Srinivasan, pp. 1874–1875.

[23]Padma Subrahmanyam, *Bharata's Art: Then and Now* (Madras: Nrithodaya, 1979), p. 85.

Natyam, we would have lost a gem just because it was thrown into the slush."[24] To Bharata and the Natyashastra she attributes a quite unambiguous function in the revial of the art: "From the state of prohibiting ladies from dignified familes even witnessing the art, the pendulum has now swung to the other extreme where the practice of the art has become a status symbol. *How did the magic take place? Perhaps the main strategy was the association of the name of the great sage Bharata with the art.* The same content and form of the sadir got re-established in the name of Bharatanatya."[25] The dance critic Sunil Kothari attributes the revival more to the personal charm and the chaste sensibility of Rukmini Arundale: "Endowed with great beauty, possessing great taste and high aesthetic sensibilities, she removed the unpleasant elements from dance. She . . . devised . . . *padams* [steps or movements] with spiritual import and contributed in removing the stigma of eroticism. Bharata Natyam no longer remained base or vulgar. In that particular context it was necessary to bring back its devotional fervour."[26] Arundale herself spoke of her dance as part of "India's basic philisophy . . . a classical art [whose] classicism endures in the village, in the temple, in folk dancing, in group dancing, dance dramas and individuals."[27] Within the span of twenty years *sadir* and its lower-caste practioners had been replaced by a sanitized, ancient, almost mystic dance-force, which provided the spiritual basis of Indian femininity and nationhood.

A reader might still want to ask why, if the ban on *Radhika Santwanam* was lifted in 1947 and the book reprinted in 1952, copies could not be found in the late 1980s.[28] Why, she might want to inquire, is the book still condemned by most literary critics? The lifting of a ban imposed by the British was clearly a nationalist act. But the interests of empire and of nation are not always in contradiction. As we will repeatedly find, the institutions of literature and the issues of gender and class that the book, its author, and its history raise remained illegitimate.

---

[24]Ibid., p. 76.

[25]Ibid., p. 76 (emphasis added).

[26]Sunil Kothari, *Bharata Natyam* p. 28.

[27]Rukmini Devi Arundale, "Spiritual Background," in Kothari ed. *Bharata Natyam,* p. 16.

[28]We have, after combing through libraries in Hyderabad, Rajamundry, Vetapalem, Madras, and Thanjavur, located a copy of each of the 1887, 1911, and 1952 editions. The palm-leaf manuscript is not available even in the famous Saraswati Mahal Library in Thanjavur.

The story of Muddupalani's life, her writing, and the misadventures of *Radhika Santwanam* could well be read as an allegory of the enterprise of women's writing and the scope of feminist criticism in India, for it raises, in an uncanny way, many of the critical questions that frame women's writing. These include questions about the *contexts*, structured and restructured by changing ideologies of class, gender, empire, in which women wrote, and the conditions in which they were read; questions about the *politics*, sexual and critical, that determined the reception and impact of their work; questions about the *resistances*, the subversions, the strategic appropriations that characterized the subtlest and most radical women's writing. In Nagaratnamma's efforts to reprint Muddupalani's poem, we encounter not only an episode in the unwritten history of feminist criticism in India but also the hitherto invisible questions of the woman reader and her requirements for the literary text. That the narrative should take in the historical span of the two volumes of *Women Writing in India* is a bonus. Patriarchies, reconstituted in the interests of Orientalism, imperialism, the Enlightenment, nationalism, among other forces, provide the horizon within which the text articulates its feminist challenge. We move from the precolonial times in which Muddupalani wrote through, in Veereshalingam's and Prakasam's responses, the social reform period and the period of high nationalism into this moment, when we read both the original text and the controversy that surrounds it anew, engaged as we are in the unusual text we are preparing.

II

Given the dominance of English as a world language, and the political economies not only of publication but also of the circulation of knowledge, the principal feminist critical traditions we have access to in India are the American and British ones. The work of the French theorist Julia Kristeva has been available in translation for some time now, but the writings of other French thinkers such as Hélène Cixous or Luce Irigaray have become available in English only recently. Their work, however, is still not widely circulated, and has not been influential. (Our knowledge of Kenyan, Latin American, or Soviet feminist criticism is sadly limited.) Though the early work of the Marxist Feminist Literature Collective and of the critic Cora Kaplan are exceptions, British feminist criticism, which is, broadly speaking, more Marxist and more theoretical in inclination than its American counterpart, has steered clear of engagement with women's writing, possibly because it was difficult to reconcile the privileging of women's "voices," which underwrote the early initiatives, with the idea, which several British theorists have explored, of female subjectivity or selfhood as also ideologically constructed. British feminist critics have chosen instead to focus on questions of representation and genealogy.[29] Strictly speaking, of course, neither Cixous's concept of *écriture feminine* (feminine writing)[30] nor Kristeva's notion of femininity as marginality[31] is concerned with *women's* writing.[32]

Solitary figures such as Virginia Woolf or Rebecca West apart, the involvement with *women's writing* or the idea of retrieving a lost tradition of women's literature has actually developed only over the last twenty years and *has been largely an American one.* Since this is the work that is also most easily available and most easily assimilable into existing critical paradigms, it has seemed very attractive to many feminist scholars and to sections of the literary establishment in India. We have therefore chosen to focus our attention on it.[33]

---

[29]See, for instance, Rosalind Coward and John Ellis, *Language and Materialism* (London: Routledge and Kegan Paul, 1977); Rosalind Coward, *Patriarchal Precedents: Sexuality and Social Relations* (London: Routledge and Kegan Paul, 1983), as well as the important work done in feminist film theory by Laura Mulvey, Claire Johnston, and Annette Kuhn. In America Catherine Gallagher and Gayatri Spivak in cultural history and Teresa de Lauretis and others in film theory have taken up related issues.

[30]"Most women are like this: they do someone else's—man's—writing, and in their innocence sustain it and give it voice, and end up producing writing that's in effect masculine. . . . The fact that a piece of writing is signed by a man's name does not in itself exclude femininity." Hélène Cixous, "Le Sexe ou la tête" (Castration or Decapitation?), trans. Annette Kuhn, *Signs* 7:1, 1981, pp. 41–55.

[31]"What can 'identity,' even 'sexual identity,' mean in a new theoretical and scientific space where the very notion of identity is challenged?" Julia Kristeva, "Women's Time," trans. Alice Jardine and Harry Blake, *Signs* 7:1, 1981, pp. 13–35.

[32]For a useful assessment of these theories, see Gayatri Spivak, "French Feminism in an International Frame," in *In Other Worlds* (London: Methuen, 1987), pp. 134–153.

[33]Our discussion of American criticism would have been greatly enriched had we learned earlier about Hazel Carby's path-breaking work on black women writers: *Reconstructing Womanhood* (New York: Oxford University Press, 1989). Carby's analysis of black women novelists proceeds from a theoretical position closely related to the one we have developed in this essay. Her argument traces "ideologies of womanhood as they were adopted, adapted, transformed to effectively represent the conditions of black women and it explores how black women intellectuals reconstructed the sexual ideologies of the nineteenth century to produce an alternative discourse of black womanhood" (p. 6). Though the rhetoric of sisterhood obscures this contradiction, ideologies of white womanhood too,

The interest in women's literature in American feminist criticism grew out of an earlier polemical moment, best represented perhaps by Kate Millet's *Sexual Politics,* 1969, in which attention had been focused on the images of women in mainstream literature. Disturbed by the sudden realization that women had invariably been represented in stereotypical ways by a literary heritage that claimed universality, feminist critics turned to women authors for alternative images of women. Women reared on the idea that great literature embodied, in some quasi-mystical, transcendent sense, a universally and perhaps eternally valid ethic were understandably agitated by what they now experienced as the masculine biases of the classics. Some critics spoke in terms of correcting a deficiency in the record, enshrined in the canon, of the culture's finest literary achievements. Others, especially those who wrote as teachers, were more concerned with the cumulative effect such literature would have on the reader-student's understanding and response to life, and emphasized the similarity between the images of women found in popular literature, in advertisements, or in children's literature, and those in the canonical texts.

Literary texts, Mary Anne Ferguson's widely circulated anthology demonstrated, commonly cast women in sexually defined roles.[34] Women were mothers, good submissive wives or bad dominating ones, seductresses, betrayers, prim single women, or the inspiration for male artists. In Ferguson's scheme of things, these were clearly regarded as *false* images of women, which she counterposed in the concluding section, "Woman Becoming," with fictional accounts, by women writers, of women's working lives, their relationships with each other, their struggles, and their aspirations. She assumed, in keeping with the empiricist basis of her criticism, that women's writing would reflect women's *real* worlds and their real experiences, and much of the most persuasive feminist criticism of the early 1970s worked from the same principle. Although it is difficult for us to share her assumptions, we

Carby points out, were "sites of racial and class struggle which enabled white women to negotiate their subordinate role in relation to patriarchy and at the same time to ally their class interests with men and against establishing an alliance to black women" (p. 18). We are extremely grateful to Florence Howe for having drawn our attention to this important book.

[34]Mary Anne Ferguson, *Images of Women in Literature* (Boston: Houghton Mifflin, 4th ed., 1986; 1st ed., 1973).

must acknowledge with admiration that her collection, and other efforts that followed, did locate several women writers whose portrayal of women was clearly more complex and less stereotypical than that of the canonized fathers.

It is to this critical moment, and the initiatives it led to in publishing and curricular reform, that we owe the "rediscovery," not only of formerly undervalued works such as Charlotte Perkins Gilman's *The Yellow Wallpaper* and Susan Glaspell's *Trifles,* but such classics of women's working-class literature as Agnes Smedley's *Daughter of Earth,* Rebecca Harding Davis's *Life in the Iron Mills,* and Tillie Olsen's *Tell Me a Riddle,* as well as the extraordinary work of the black novelist and folklorist Zora Neale Hurston.[35]

An equally powerful propelling force for the turn toward women's writing was the growing realization that critical estimates of women's literature were invariably prejudiced. The tendency in Western culture, Mary Ellmann argued in an important early book, was "to comprehend all phenomena, however shifting, in terms of original and simple sexual differences; and . . . classify almost all experience by means of sexual analogy."[36] What she called "phallic criticism," or the criticism practiced by male academics and reviewers, extended this mode of thought by sexual analogy to criticism when it was faced with a woman writer.

> With a kind of inverted fidelity, the analysis of women's books by men will arrive punctually at the point of preoccupation, which is the fact of femininity. Books by women are treated as though they themselves were women, and criticism embarks, at its happiest, upon an intellectual measuring of busts and hips.[37]

---

[35]Charlotte Perkins Gilman, *The Yellow Wallpaper* (New York: The Feminist Press, 1973); Susan Glaspell, *Trifles,* in *Plays by American Women: 1900–1930,* ed. Judith E. Barlow (New York: Applause Theatre Books, 1985), pp. 70–86; Agnes Smedley, *Daughter of Earth* (New York: The Feminist Press, 1973, 3d. ed. 1987); Rebecca Harding Davis, *Life in the Iron Mills and Other Stories,* ed. Tillie Olsen (New York: The Feminist Press, 1985); Tillie Olsen, *Tell Me a Riddle* (New York: Dell, 1976); the excellent collection of work by Zora Neale Hurston, *I Love Myself When I Am Laughing . . . And Then Again When I Am Looking Mean and Impressive,* ed. Alice Walker (New York: The Feminist Press, 1979); Zora Neale Hurston, *Their Eyes Were Watching God* (Urbana: University of Illinois Press, 1978).

[36]Mary Ellmann, *Thinking about Women* (New York: Harcourt, 1968), p. 6.

[37]Ibid., p. 29.

Ellmann's witty exposé of "phallic criticism," elaborated a decade later with equally devastating aplomb by Joanna Russ,[38] demonstrated, with example after hilarious and infuriating example, that the critical establishment had been unjustly hostile to women writers. Writers who were widely read and critically acclaimed in their own times had, over the years, been so discredited as to be forgotten or even damned. Others, such as Virginia Woolf, had found a place in the canon but only after the radical, political edge of their work had been blunted. Clearly feminist works such as *A Room of One's Own,* 1929, and *Three Guineas,* 1938, rarely feature in critical discussions, though her experiments with the stream of consciousness technique are well known. Yet others, and Emily Dickinson is a commonly cited example, never received the serious attention they so richly deserved. Feminist critics soon pointed out that the problem was much larger in its scope than the prejudice of male critics. Subsuming the female into the category of human was a political act. With its universalist assumptions, literary criticism systematically obscured questions relating to women as writers, women as readers, and the representation of women in literary texts. Besides, questions relating to the social, historical, and ideological contexts in which literary production and consumption took place, which were crucial to an understanding of women's literature, had no legitimacy in such criticism. Feminist critics also pointed out that the "ideal reader," privileged by critical modes that stressed the universal, was white, upper-class, and clearly male and that the reader addressed by the canonical texts bore the same social imprint. In fact, the focus of disciplinary interest had become so restricted that what were regarded as classics could be read, to purloin a phrase from the American critic Nina Baym, as "melodramas of beset manhood."

By the late 1970s, three major book-length studies that set up women's writing as a new disciplinary field had appeared. Serious work on the tasks of writing feminist literary histories and evolving critical paradigms sensitive to the issues at stake in the study of women's writing had begun. In the earliest of these books, *Literary Women,* Ellen Moers admitted to an initial reluctance to separate writers on the basis of gender, but cited three reasons why she began to think otherwise. First, the astonishing results such separation does produce. Second, the realization that "we already practise a segregation of major women

---

[38]Joanna Russ, *How to Suppress Women's Writing* (London: The Women's Press, 1984).

writers unknowingly," and third, a better understanding of women's history.[39] Implicit in the second reason is the recognition of the covert politics of subsuming women into the category of human, but restricting at the same time their importance within it. But more important, we feel, is the realization that existing critical practices had a hidden political agenda and that a politics could only be challenged and undermined politically, however much the critical decorum might discourage such unseemly behavior. It might have been difficult to construct theoretically tenable reasons for dealing separately with women writers. But the political value of such a move was undeniable.

Moers argued that women's writing was actually a rapid and powerful undercurrent distinct from, but hardly subordinate to, the mainstream. Women writers, she demonstrated in her chapter on literary history with impressive lists compiled from their letters and other private papers, read each other's books and even kept up an international correspondence. Their writing therefore drew upon women's experiences but also on a literary subculture of women writers that the mainstream was hardly aware of. In fact, Moers's book touched on almost every theme that was to be elaborated and refined in the subsequent discussion on women's writing in America: the exclusion of women writers (who had been misread and misjudged by the literary establishment), the need to find new strategies to open up canonical texts for feminist readings, the idea that a knowledge of feminist history was crucial for an understanding of women's writing, and the suggestion that women writers had shared a subculture that they often secretly kept alive. It had all the components of a rousing argument: evidence of gross injustice countered with a tradition of secret solidarity and resistance.

Elaine Showalter's meticulously researched *A Literature of Their Own,* which came out a year later, covered much the same conceptual ground. But Showalter took issue with Moers's characterization of women's writing as an ongoing international movement and emphasized the transience of female literary fame. Though the "lost continent of the female literary tradition [had] risen like Atlantis from the sea of English literature," each generation of women writers had found itself, she claimed,

---

[39]Ellen Moers, *Literary Women: The Great Writers* (New York: Doubleday, 1976), p. xv.

in a sense, without a history, forced to rediscover the past anew, forging again and again the consciousness of their sex. Given this perpetual disruption and also the self-hatred that has alienated women writers from a sense of collective identity, it does not seem possible to speak of a "movement."[40]

Showalter set out to trace "the female literary tradition" in English fiction from about the 1840s to the present day, working not so much on the continuity of that tradition as on the identity it found in resistance. Any minority group, she argued, finds its self-expression relative to a dominant society.[41] She posited three major phases that she claimed were common to all literary subcultures. First, a phase of imitation; second, one of protest; and third, "a phase of *self-discovery,* a turning inward, freed from some of the dependency of opposition, a search for identity."[42] Showalter's own political biases probably make it difficult for her to acknowledge the theorist and revolutionary Frantz Fanon as the best-known source for this thesis about emerging subcultures. What is also obscured as a result is her transformation of Fanon's theory, domesticating an idea of revolutionary action to a liberal-conservative one of self-discovery and individual fulfillment as the goal of literary endeavor. Phases one and two in Fanon's argument about the emergence of a national culture from colonialism broadly coincide with those Showalter posits, but in Fanon's third phase, which is a "fighting phase," the artist "composes the sentence which expresses the heart of the people and becomes the mouthpiece of a new reality in action."[43]

A Literature of Their Own is, all the same, an important book, for Showalter provided women's writing with the kind of careful scholarly attention it had probably never received in the academy. She repopulated the period whose literary history she felt was marred by a residual "Great Traditionism" with many little-known writers, and deftly reopened the case for writers who were widely read and well regarded in their time but had been subsequently forgotten. We find it quite astonishing, however, that although the period covered by

---

[40]Elaine Showalter, *A Literature of Their Own: British Women Novelists from Brontë to Lessing* (Princeton: Princeton University Press, 1977), pp. 11–12.
[41]Ibid., p. 11.
[42]Ibid., p. 13.
[43]Frantz Fanon, *The Wretched of the Earth,* trans. Constance Farrington (Harmondsworth: Penguin, 1967; 1st ed. 1961), p. 179.

Showalter's book coincides with the age of high imperialism, neither Britain's colonial "possessions" nor the complicity of Englishwomen, writers not excluded, in the ideologies of class and of empire are seriously dealt with. In part, as we shall see, Showalter's own schemes replicate an imperialist design.

In two articles published a few years later, both reprinted in a widely circulated 1985 collection of feminist criticism, Showalter developed a theory of women's writing. Feminist criticism, she argued, could be regarded as functioning in two distinct modes: "feminist critique" and "gynocritics." The former is concerned with the woman "as the consumer of male-produced literature, and the way in which the hypothesis of the female reader changes our apprehension of a given text." She coined the term "gynocritics" for "scholarship concerned with woman as the producer of textual meaning, with the history, themes, genres and structures of literature by women."[44] Feminist critique is essentially political and polemical, with affiliations to Marxist sociology and aesthetics, whereas "gynocritics is more self-contained and experimental."[45] Showalter's own separatist inclinations become clearer as she extends her argument. "If we study stereotypes of women, the sexism of male critics and the limited roles women play in literary history, we are not learning what women have felt and experienced," she writes, "but only what men have thought women should be."[46] She is herself interested, like the historians and anthropologists she quotes, with the newly visible world of "feminist culture," which she argues will provide a setting and the rationale adequate to recovery of a tradition of women's writing. The problem is understood as analogous to that faced, say, by American literature as it sought to consolidate its independence from British literature and establish itself as the cultural arm of a new and sovereign nation. The idea is developed in a later essay, "Feminist Criticism in the Wilderness," where she reaffirms her distance from the Jeremiahs of feminist critique, who protest too loudly and whose concerns, according to her, do not remain strictly feminist.[47]

In their influential analysis of the major Anglo-American women

---

[44]Elaine Showalter, "Towards a Feminist Poetics," in *The New Feminist Criticism,* ed. Elaine Showalter (London: Virago, 1986), p. 128.
[45]Showalter, "Towards a Feminist Poetics," p. 129.
[46]Ibid., p. 130.
[47]Showalter, *The New Feminist Criticism,* pp. 243–270.

writers of the nineteenth century, *The Madwoman in the Attic,* which came out in 1979, Sandra Gilbert and Susan Gubar set out to explore anew a "distinctively female literary tradition" and develop a theory of "female literary response to male literary assertion and coercion."[48] The focus of their attention was "female literary creativity," conceived of in their argument as a kind of essence, struggling to find its way out of the strictures that contain it. The study charts "the difficult paths by which nineteenth century women overcame their anxiety of authorship, repudiated debilitating patriarchal prescriptions, and recovered or remembered the lost foremothers who could help them find their distinctive female power."[49]

Patriarchal ideology in the nineteenth century, Gilbert and Gubar argue, thought of the writer as one who in the image of the Divine Creator *fathers* his work; the pen, they demonstrate, is invariably imaged as phallic. Women could not, therefore, both write and remain feminine without transgressing the norms set up by patriarchal authority. Thus, the woman writer is faced with a double burden. She has to confront these myths of creativity, but she also has to work past the ideal of the "eternal feminine" that was set up as inspiration and complement to the male. This ideal was a combination of angelic beauty and sweetness: passive, docile, selfless. But, the authors point out, "to be selfless is not only to be noble, it is to be dead. A life that has no story like the life of Göethe's Markarie is really a life of death, a death-in-life."[50] Behind this frozen angel lurks the monster woman who has a story to tell, and she is one of the terrible sorceress-goddesses such as "the Sphinx, Medusa . . . Kali . . . all of whom possess duplicitous arts that allow them both to seduce and steal male generative energy."[51] If such a proudly masculine cosmic author is the sole legitimate model for all early authors, and women are by virtue of their sex defined as angels or monsters and denied the autonomy to formulate alternatives to the authority that has imprisoned them and kept them "from attempting the pen," what are the options open to the woman

---

[48]Sandra Gilbert and Susan Gubar, *The Madwoman in the Attic: The Woman Writer and the Nineteenth-century Literary Imagination* (New Haven: Yale University Press, 1979), p. xii.
[49]Ibid., p. 59.
[50]Ibid., p. 25.
[51]Ibid., p. 34.

writer?[52] Gilbert and Gubar provide an answer, which they develop through the seven-hundred-odd pages of the book.

> Women from Jane Austen and Mary Shelley to Emily Brontë and Emily Dickinson produced literary works that are in some sense palimpsestic, works whose surface designs conceal and obscure deeper, less accessible (and less socially acceptable) levels of meaning.[53]

The woman writer projects her uneasiness about literary creativity onto the emblematic figure of the madwoman, who, like Bertha Mason in Charlotte Brontë's *Jane Eyre,* is "usually in some sense the *author's* double, an image of her own anxiety and rage."[54] It is principally through these dark doubles that female authors both identify with and revise the definitions of femininity and female authorship that their culture proffers. But the woman writer is also engaged at another level with "assaulting and revising, deconstructing and reconstructing those images of women inherited from male literature, especially the paradigmatic polarities of angel and monsters."[55]

The theoretical perspective, which we have summarized here, is really the weakest and most whimsical part of this energetic book. Their sparkling style, apparently never at a loss for a meaningful turn of phrase or a surprising metaphor, is a constant pleasure. Not least among the achievements of this widely circulated work is that it uncovers in women's writing formal strategies of such complexity and depth that they live up to the academy's most stringent New Critical demands. In this sense *The Madwoman in the Attic* has probably done more than any other single work to provide feminist criticism and women writers with a "respectable" berth in the academy, not only in the United States but in any other country in which English (or American) literature is studied.

Yet, as they naturalize a "female literary creativity," Gilbert and Gubar fix—and universalize—women and literary creativity in the image of the high subjectivist aesthetics of nineteenth-century Europe. History or geography can only touch their schemes tangentially as incident or as locale. Patriarchal ideology seems to bear no relation to class, race, or empire, and once it enters the literary text it has a life entirely independent of its counterpart in the world.

---

[52]Ibid., p. 13.
[53]Ibid., p. 73.
[54]Ibid., p. 78.
[55]Ibid., p. 176.

III

Over the last decade and a half, American feminist criticism would seem to have arrived at a framework for the study of women's writing. Tasks have been assigned, themes located, areas of debate defined, and women's writing authoritatively established as an object for disciplined investigation. The confidence of having drawn up no less than a world picture of the history of women's literature rings through the introduction of Elaine Showalter's 1985 collection of essays. "Since 1979," when *The Madwoman in the Attic* was published, she writes,

> insights have been tested, supplemented, extended, so that we have a coherent, if still incomplete, narrative of female literary history, which describes the evolutionary stages of women's writing during the last 250 years from imitation through protest to self-definition and defines and traces the connections, throughout history and across national boundaries of the recurring images, themes, and plots that emerge from women's social, psychological and aesthetic experience in male-dominated cultures.[56]

The claims are awesome; the tone, one that colonized peoples have heard on many earlier occasions. An anthology of women's writing compiled, as this one was, in the late 1980s inherits a space—conceptual and political—opened up by these critical initiatives but also shaped by their assumptions. The metaphors we have used state the case too weakly, too neutrally. Feminist criticism has not merely developed a methodology to study a phenomenon that already exists: women's writing. Feminist criticism has actually shaped a new discipline and in the process created, as the object of its study, a new field: women's writing. There's no denying that women have written, or, to put it more accurately in the context of this anthology, that women have created literature in the past. But as those artifacts are studied as *women's writing,* which is charted as an area of study and sculpted into a tradition, they take on a significance that is a contemporary invention. As a discipline, "gynocritics" has designated its archives, forged its tools, asserted its authority, and made its political alignments.

There are several reasons why artifacts from "other" cultures might find hospitality in the space created by this new discipline: its self-proclaimed international scope, the increasing self-consciousness among Western liberals about the ethnocentrism of their white middle

---

[56]Showalter, *The New Feminist Criticism,* p. 6.

classes, the wild celebration of pluralism that postmodernism decrees, and the growing multinationalist scope of industry and commerce ensure a ready welcome, at several levels, for other cultures. Yet the assumptions of this criticism as well as the mode in which it extends a welcome to other literatures make it difficult and compromising terrain for an anthology such as this to enter or negotiate, and we feel the imperative to frame this critical moment and examine in some detail the disciplinary politics of gynocritics as it affects a project such as ours. It is a disturbing step, this, for we are as aware of our solidarities and the need to consolidate them as of our differences. But we hope as we engage critically with the bias of its feminism, and the political agenda hidden in its aesthetic, that we will also open up questions for Western feminism itself and make new, more self-conscious, more risky, and more radical, solidarities possible.

There are several dimensions along which a critique of the discipline as it has established itself might be developed. We have chosen, however, to pick out four major strands in its conceptual weave and tease out the implications of bringing them to bear on the study or reading of women's literature in India. We investigate, first, the idea of loss, which underwrites so much of the "recovery" of women's writing; second, the notion of release or escape, which tropes itself into a feminist poetics in works such as *The Madwoman in the Attic;* third, the problem that arises as the concept of experience, which in feminist practice has a critical, deconstructive charge, is uncritically conflated with an empiricist privileging of experience as the authentic source of truth and meaning; and finally, the hidden politics of what some strands of Western feminism have set up as women's real experiences, or female nature itself.

Notions of "loss" and "exclusion," for instance—lost women writers, lost classics, exclusion from the canon—are always underwritten by a dream of wholeness or completeness. A lost or excluded object can be recognized when it is found, and restored to the place from which it was missed. When it frames the problem as one of loss or exclusion, therefore, contemporary feminism sets up its present and the aspirations that stem from that as a covert norm against which the past is measured. Indeed, what gynocritics actually locates as it raids the past or picks its way through other cultural wares (and even the histories of other peoples) are the scattered fragments of its own dream. As it enumerates the themes and sets up the agenda for women's writing the world over, therefore, the present-day concerns of Western feminists are writ large to encompass the world, and the world collapses into the West. When women's literary history, for instance, culminates in what Showalter categorizes as the "female phase" turned in on itself, seeking its identity, history becomes a plot that finds its resolution in the current aspirations of Showalter's form of feminism.

If we ask the questions—apparently illegitimate, because the criticism seems to take for granted that the answer is such common knowledge that it does not even need to be stated—who has lost these writers, or rather, to what cause have they been lost, several answers suggest themselves. At one level they are obviously lost to feminists today, lost to a tradition of women's writing, lost to literary studies, lost to the reader's experience. But more significantly they are missing from another, more deeply embedded cultural institution that has over the last century or so provided literary studies with its legitimacy. It is this institution feminist scholars must invoke when they voice their grievances. In so doing, of course, they reaffirm its authority and align their concerns with it. These writers, the unstated argument is, are lost to the select company of great (male) writers whose works were charged with the task of providing post-Enlightenment Western society in general, and the nation in particular, with its ethical capital. In other words, even as the feminist act of recovery establishes a historical legitimacy for women's writing, it consolidates the hold of a (liberal) humanism and with it the political imperatives that underwrote the setting up of literary studies as a major agent of that ideology. In a recently published study, Gauri Viswanathan, for instance, argues that "humanistic functions traditionally associated with the study of literature—for example, the shaping of character, or the development of an aesthetic sense or the disciplines of ethical thinking—are also essential to the process of sociopolitical control." Drawing on evidence from parliamentary debates and educational policy, she demonstrates that "literary study gained enormous cultural strength through its development in a period of territorial expansion and conquest."[57] Other commen-

---

[57]Gauri Viswanathan, "The Beginnings of English Literary Study in British India," *Oxford Literary Review* 9, 1987, pp. 2–26. Viswanathan argues that the growth of English as a discipline in England took place somewhat later in the nineteenth century, and had as its basis "a shape and an ideological content developed in the colonial context." A reader might enjoy the following extract from a toast proposed in 1846 in Edinburgh by Thomas Macaulay (1800–1859), the British statesman and historian who was the principal architect of English education in India and the important spokesman for literary studies in Britain: "To the literature of Britain, to that literature, the brightest, the purest, the most durable of

tators have explored the process through which the discipline was institutionalized and its imbrication in the shaping of gender and class. The story of its establishment as a humanistic discipline in the "mother country" and that of its more nakedly dominative functions in the colonies are closely meshed.[58]

Gynocritics forces open the doors of a literary sanctum where only male writers—and that too, only some male writers—seemed to have rights of entry, in order to let a few women in. The unwritten rules that once debarred them are cleverly exposed. But the deeper political commitments that govern the teaching of literature are not subjected to serious theoretical scrutiny. Neither the legitimacy nor the function of the sacred monument itself can be radically questioned by those who wish to restore its fullness and thereby endorse its authority.

Structurally, the idea of "release" is not dissimilar to that of "loss." When it asserts the presence of a repressed female creativity struggling over the last two hundred years or more for release, which is recognized at last by the feminist critic and restored through her reading to a female literary tradition, *The Madwoman in the Attic,* for instance, extends the reach of the authors' present-day feminist consciousness to a point where it is naturalized and enshrined as female nature itself. The scope of what they conceive of as women's bondage or imprisonment, however, is clearly laid out. The "release" is to be principally

---

all the glories of our country, to that literature, so rich in precious truth and precious fiction, to that literature which boasts of the prince of all poets and the prince of all philosophers; to that literature which has exercised an influence wider than that of our commerce and mightier than that of our arms; to that literature which has taught France the principles of liberty and has furnished Germany with models of art; to that literature which forms a tie closer than the tie of consanguinity between us and the commonwealths of the valley of the Mississippi; to that literature before the light of which impious and cruel superstitions are fast taking flight on the banks of the Ganges; to that literature which will in future ages, instruct and delight the unborn millions who will have turned the Australasian and Catfrarian deserts into cities and gardens. To the literature of Britain, then! And wherever the literature of Britain spreads may it be attended by British virtue and British freedom!" Thomas Macaulay, *Miscellaneous Writings,* vol. 3 (London: Longman's Green and Co., 1880), pp. 398–399.

[58]See Chris Baldick, *The Social Mission of English Criticism 1848–1932* (Oxford: Clarendon Press, 1983). Francis Mulhern in *The Moment of 'Scrutiny'* documents the deep complicity of the Leavisite tradition, often thought of as humanist in contrast to the formalism of American New Criticism, in the ideologies of the Tory middle classes in Britain (London: Verso, 1981).

from "male houses and male texts." A further qualification sharpens the focus: and "escape" through ingenuity and indirection may turn for its metaphors to the other paraphernalia of middle-class "women's place."

> Ladylike veils and costumes, mirrors, paintings, statues, locked cabinets, drawers, trunks, strong boxes and other domestic furnishings appear and reappear . . . to signify the woman writer's sense that, as Emily Dickinson put it, her life has been "shaven and fitted to a frame," a confinement she can only tolerate by believing that "the soul has moments of escape / when bursting all the doors / she dances like a bomb abroad."[59]

In the process, all women's writing, or at least women's writing that merits serious literary attention, becomes feminist in the precise mode and to the precise extent that the authors themselves understand and experience feminism. Their reading gestures toward history. The subtitle itself indicates the focus as a specific period, the nineteenth century, and the text makes mention of earlier periods. But the past is a collection of intense, more or less univocal moments in which the authors identify the themes and concerns of contemporary American feminism. The paraphernalia of a European middle-class woman's place is regarded as an adequate metaphor for all women's worlds. Other times and other places are only a feature of dispersal, not transformation or change. Gender subordination imaged in these domestic, middle-class terms defines the entire scope of the woman writer's world, in which, as Gilbert and Gubar image it, there appears to be only the fundamental antagonism repeatedly played out in its primal tune: that of a monolithic, unchanging patriarchy, which would seem to have no connections with other hegemonies, say, of class or race, and an equally fixed and resilient female self: "The striking coherence we noticed in literature by women could be explained by a common female impulse to struggle free from social and literary confinement through strategic redefinitions of the self, art, and society."[60]

The idea of a natural being straining for release echoes the Rousseauist formulations of the Enlightenment. But in Gilbert and Gubar's argument, there is a significant reversal of the priorities set up at that time for the emerging bourgeois male. It is a reversal disturbingly reminiscent of the radically different and unequal programs the En-

---

[59]Gilbert and Gubar, *Madwoman,* p. 85.
[60]Ibid., p. xi–xii.

lightenment itself so confidently proposed for men and for women. The man was to direct his revolt outward against the Church and the king. *His* natural being, once it was released to enjoy the earth, which was his inheritance, would be governed by reason, which was also part of male nature. Woman, however, and it is important to remember that even the feminist philosopher Mary Wollestonecraft agreed on this, had to turn her energies onto her self. She had to refashion her nature to emerge as fit complement to the new man. The agenda for the colonies was structurally similar. In its most enlightened mode, imperialism regarded the colonized peoples as requiring a remolding, not of course to be fit complement to bourgeois males, but to be fit subjects for its rule. We will have occasion to return to this configuration from the point of view of the middle-class woman in India, and for the woman writer—the stresses it set up and the opportunities it opened up. But for the present it is enough to point out that, in Gilbert and Gubar's scheme, as the woman writer struggles for release, she redefines her self and with it the symbolic world of the literary text. As for society, that ghostly appendage does not seem solid enough to throw even a shadow on the imaginative world of the book.

The "last parable" through which this particular gospel of redemption explicates itself is that of

> the woman artist [who] enters the cavern of her own mind and finds there the scattered leaves not only of her own power but of the tradition that might have generated that power. The body of her precursor's art, and thus the body of her own art, lies in pieces around her, dismembered, dis-remembered, disintegrated. How can she remember it, and become a member of it, join it and rejoin it, integrate it and in doing so achieve her own integrity, her own selfhood?[61]

Like the messages on the sibylline leaves of Mary Shelley's story on which this "parable" is based, these fragments are written in several languages. Some of the scripts are faded, others unfamiliar. But they are inscribed on the elements of the natural world, bark and leaf, and on the secret inner lining of the female body, as Gilbert and Gubar quote Shelley: "a white filmy substance resembling the inner part of the green hood which shelters the grain of unripe Indian corn."[62] With effort, they can be deciphered. In Gilbert and Gubar's reading of Shel-

---

[61]Ibid., p. 98.
[62]Ibid., p. 95.

ley, these misunderstood, and therefore scattered, pieces of the woman writer's literary heritage rise now like a "lost Atlantis ... whose wholeness once encompassed and explained all those figures on the horizon who seemed 'odd,' fragmentary, incomplete. . . ." Here memory declares itself as an hermeneutic act, for as lost or forgotten works are "remembered . . . by the community of which they are and were members, such figures gain their full authority."[63] The cultural context for women's writing is a sort of female enclave untouched by masculinist assumptions and the woman writer is imaged as free from ideology. The mystic energy that attends the vision is invoked with a confidence that does not doubt its power to absorb the whole world into its project.

It is not surprising, therefore, to find that their equally monumental *The Norton Anthology of Literature by Women,* 1986, which is in many other ways a superb collection, places women from all over the world (who write in English) quite unself-consciously against the backdrop of Euro-American social history.[64] Even the idea that a sizable proportion of British or American society itself does not consider the history or culture of Western Europe as *its* past, that the history and culture of Africa—and not just of the slave trade—may be an important prehistory of the United States, for example, and that of India or the Caribbean of Britain, is simply suppressed. British imperialism is referred to—in one sentence—but it does not appear to have touched any of the women writers in a serious way. As the editors project it, the immediate contexts for women's writing are only the images of women in mainstream literature. But nowhere in the book do we find even an awareness that there are many "mainstream" literatures; or that women who write in English cannot so casually be gathered into the same fold; or that it is not the same essential female nature that is struggling, the world over, to free itself from male bondage.

Like Showalter, Gilbert and Gubar speak as if feminist "poetics" has finally arrived at its destination. Women writers, they indicate, can now set aside their palimpsestic plots and engage directly with their experience, as male writers whose full authority was never repressed have always been able to do.

Underlying both Showalter's empiricist literary history and Gilbert and Gubar's symbolic recreation of the woman writer's consciousness

---

[63] Ibid., p. 99.
[64] Sandra Gilbert and Susan Gubar, *The Norton Anthology of Literature by Women: The Tradition in English* (New York: W. W. Norton, 1985).

and her female literary inheritance is an assumption as deeply embedded in the practices of popular reading in the twentieth century (in India as much as in the West) as in literary criticism. Literary texts, the assumption is, express the author's experience and reveal the truth about his or her world, and as they do so, they provide us with access to the universal dimensions of human nature. As an aesthetic theory, expressive realism emerged in the second half of the nineteenth century, more or less in conjunction with the realist novel. It has been subjected to extensive critique in recent times, and its function, in shaping a reader, "cut to the measure" of the white bourgeois world, analyzed at several levels. The notion is, however, reaffirmed and given new life today by feminist critics who counterpose women's writing, which they choose to read as a transparent expression of women's authentic experience, to the stereotypes of mainstream literature, often spoken of as "male" literature, which is regarded simply as distorting the reality of women's lives.

Within feminist criticism, the idea that women's experience is a critical resource also draws its strength from the consciousness-raising groups that were so crucial to the development of feminist theory and feminist politics in the United States in the late sixties and early seventies. Several commentators have pointed to the similarities between the politics of consciousness-raising and those of the "speaking bitterness" campaigns of the Chinese Cultural Revolution.[65] The parallel helps us focus on dimensions of consciousness-raising that are often blurred over as the immediacy, intimacy, and spontaneity of these groups are highlighted. In fact, consciousness-raising was as carefully structured a political exercise as the "speaking bitterness" campaigns. It worked by challenging and recasting a dominant ideology's characterizations of women and interrogating authoritative interpretations of every dimension of social and personal experience. The focus was not, as it tended to become in literary criticism, on distorting stereotypes but on the wide-ranging strategies, social, economic, and psychic, through which mastery was exercised and subordination

---

[65]According to Florence Howe (in "Women and the Power to Change," written in 1973), Juliet Mitchell first noted the analogy in *Women's Estate* (New York: Pantheon, 1971, p. 62). Howe adds that there were also "several elements in the United States culture that allowed for the spread of such groups: the coffee klatch, for example, the quilting bee, and other forms of female social or work groups." Further, "in the southern civil rights movement, discussion groups, especially on the subject of racism, also provided a precedent." *Myths of Coeducation* (Bloomington: Indiana University Press, 1987), p. 172.

maintained. From the supportive contexts of the consciousness-raising groups, feminists confronted the institutions and practices of everyday life, and extended their micropolitical analysis into the domain of the family and even of desire. Women's experiences were used as a resource for critical discussion, making it possible for women to share dimensions of their lives they had earlier kept secret or felt too insecure to confront or even recognize. Groups encouraged women to focus on and articulate anger and dissatisfaction, and evolved through discussion new interpretations of their experience that questioned and rejected earlier modes of processing and making sense of what they had observed or felt. But these sessions were less a spontaneous outburst and more a reading against the grain, which was often so risky— socially and psychically—for the individual that they needed the combined resources of a group to make the "reading" possible. The new "feminist" significations that emerged were provided legitimacy through group consent and were consolidated and put into circulation through active and considered political or personal programs.

Not least among the achievements of consciousness-raising was the solidarity it generated among women who were closely involved in it, as well as the new self-confidence and sense of power it produced. Many women felt their lives had been completely transformed and that they had finally been "released" from the constrictions of patriarchal ideology. But consciousness-raising was also an extremely significant development in political practice. Though the politics of ideology and of representation had been discussed for well nigh a century, it was in the women's movement that a critique of culture first emerged as a viable political program. Consistently extended, this attention to the minute, everyday practices of subordination and expropriation has implications for the politics of class, caste, colonialism, ethnicity, and a whole range of other structures of domination that determine the lives of women—and men. But unfortunately the critical use of experience and the sense of release consciousness-raising generated were quickly annexed in several ways: most blatantly by a consumerism that addressed and orchestrated women's "freedom" in its own interests; but also by a powerful strand of feminist scholarship within several disciplines that naturalized and privileged the new "feminist" significations as they conflated the freedom they experienced, and their sense of having inherited the earth anew, with an essential—and visionary— femaleness. When the new validity women's experience acquired as a resource that could be drawn on for critical discussion was conflated with the empiricist idea that experience was the source of true knowledge, experience lost the critical edge it had acquired as a political tool. And to the extent that feminism accepted or promoted this conflation and the consequent valorization of female nature, it acquiesced to and even collaborated in the annexation of one of the most powerful political movements of our age into a dominant bourgeois humanist scheme of things. In ways that soon obscured the critical functions of consciousness-raising, many liberal feminists simply endorsed the authenticity of what were increasingly referred to in universalist and naturalistic terms as *women's* experiences. Liberal feminists invented a *female* tradition that was imaged as a lost city, submerged but intact, unaffected by history, waiting to be recovered, and they spoke of an essential difference between male and female. They argued for a privileged affinity between women and peace or women and nature, the body or the unconscious. When this popular strand of feminism set up its significations, won no doubt at considerable cost and in the thick of struggle, as a kind of covert norm, or began to think of these significations as "natural," or as constituting some sort of female essence struggling in the work of the woman writer to express itself, it effectively brought the critical politics feminist practice had so brilliantly designed and set going in the consciousness-raising groups to a grinding halt.

We believe that there are powerful alliances feminists of all classes the world over can make, and equally powerful alliances feminists can make with other oppressed groups if we accept the challenges held out to us. But since the kind of feminist criticism that naturalizes the experiences and issues of Western feminism in this way is so easily co-opted by the academy and so widely circulated among third-world scholars (while the more historically aware work done by feminist scholars is marginalized), we must explain in more detail why we find the subsuming of a critical method into a celebration of female nature so disturbing. We must also explore why it is that if we simply apply the theories of women's writing that have been developed over the last decade or so to women's writing in India, we will not merely reproduce its confusions, but compound them.

It might be useful, as a starting point, to unpack the concept of "reality" as it emerges in the work of the critics we have discussed, whether it is in the idea of "women's real experiences," which are transparently available in women's writing, especially in realist fiction and in lyric poetry, or in the related idea of a real or authentic female voice that can, if only we pay the right kind of attention, be heard in a woman writer's work.

In gynocritics the real is clearly invested with an oppositional force and with the sense of a knowledge preserved in the face of opposition, and is contrasted with "unreal" or "untrue" portrayals of women in the work of most male writers. The idea of the "real," therefore, carries the impress of a *truth* that emerges as the shackles of prejudice—or false consciousness—are thrown off. As one might have expected, the major contradictions middle-class feminists in the West experienced in the initial stages of the movement were those between the promises of freedom and equality that liberalism held out to them and the social and psychic determinations that limited women's access to these rights. Though the movement drew on many existing resources—theoretical and political—to develop a powerful and original critique of patriarchy, when the dominant strand in Western feminism articulated its own solutions to those problems, it did so in a way that only addressed the contradictions principally as women from such social formations experienced them. Other contradictions, which had their source, say, in patriarchy as it was historically constituted by class, by colonialism, or by caste, which would have shaped the subordination of a working-class woman in India—Bangalore Nagaratnamma, for instance—and determined her selfhood or subjectivity, were simply not addressed. Besides, even the contours of what might be more strictly defined as gender subordination were so normatively invoked that they could not accommodate other histories that shaped the contours of desire or of power. As a result, the shifting reciprocal relationships that determine women's worlds and female subjectivities are obscured. Further, the complicity of white women or middle-class women in the structures of domination are never subjected to informed or serious scrutiny. The myriad conflicts women came up against in their everyday lives were invariably woven into a fictional world or a "real" world in which an adequate "resolution" to problems was achieved as middle-class women uncovered the processes, material and ideological, that had "excluded" them from full citizenship in their society, and developed strategies to ensure their "inclusion."[66] Oppres-

---

[66]Betty Friedan's *The Second Stage* (New York: Summit Books, 1981) represents the anxiety to close the movement off once these initial demands have been met in its most intense and explicit form. Other closures are more subtle and more covert. See Susie Tharu, "The Second Stage from the Third World," *Indian Journal of American Studies* 13:2, 1983, pp. 179–184.

sions of class, of imperialism, of race, which for many women—white middle-class women not excluded—compound and reciprocally constitute those of patriarchy, were glossed over in a narrative logic that focused its attention exclusively on what it defined as *women's* concerns. Both the author and the reader such narratives assumed—and therefore produced and consolidated—as "woman" belonged to a social configuration the narratives took as norm. Of course, this was precisely how the narrative of the realist novel had a century earlier set up the world as home for its bourgeois hero. That world fell into place and acquired the aura of the real from the viewpoint of the white bourgeois male. Its objects were delineated from his perspective, in his image, and the world was ordered in his interests. Realism was an effect of his gaze. Only from his location could memory, actuality, and language achieve that perfect confluence which produced the "reality effect." But feminists who accepted a place in these frameworks and these narratives—whether in the passive sense of allowing them to take over and avoiding more risky initiatives, or in the active sense of choosing their allies—shortchanged feminism too.

We are not, of course, suggesting (what even a decade ago we might have easily been interpreted as doing) that feminism is only a white middle-class, or Indian middle-class, women's issue. What we are saying is that in the process of posing, elaborating, analyzing, and resolving questions of gender and projecting their resolutions as female reality, Western feminists from the liberal mainstream drew on a whole range of significations and inferential logics attached to them already in circulation, which constituted the common sense of their society. As they did so, they underwrote afresh their society's consensus about the "real" or the plausible. They questioned the ideological processes that endorsed their subordination as women, but they acquiesced broadly in the consensus on the significations of other cultural and conceptual objects, disciplinary commitments, feelings, tastes, everyday practices, and, indeed, narrative fragments of various kinds that were operative in their society and underwrote the politics of class, race, or imperialism, without subjecting them to the same vigorous critique they had extended to the social construction of middle-class femininity. Feminism drew attention in quite spectacular ways to the subtle strategies of power written into the shaping and differentiation of the feminine in the everyday practices of the family, of education, of the workplace, of the law, and of medicine and psychology. But feminisms that projected the results of this initial deconstructive move as *true* or *natural,* as essentially female, projected not only present-day middle-class subjectivities as normatively female but also the problem as they construed it, as the limits of feminism, and their present-day concerns as the great female themes. Such feminism inevitably aligned itself with the many splendored apparatus of power that liberal capitalism, which was also inalienably imperialist, developed over the not inconsequential history through which it established its "natural" dominions.[67]

IV

At one level the two volumes of *Women Writing in India* are a joyous retrieval of artifacts that signify women's achievement. At another, they represent a difficult and inventive moment in the theory and practice of feminist criticism. We have reread established writers and are introducing several comparatively little-known ones. There will be surprises—even for, say, Telugu readers in our collection of Telugu literature. In English translation, what we have is a stupendous body of new work. Judged by conventional standards, many of the pieces collected here are classics. Some have stood the test of time—biased and hostile though that test might have been. Others will not require unusually persuasive advocates to argue for their rehabilitation in the canons of Marathi, Kannada, or Urdu literature, or for that matter in an international canon of women's literature. Our collection might well provide an impetus for such a venture, but the refurbishment of canons was not the primary task we ourselves addressed. Had the recovery of literature, lost or damned in the conduit of male criticism, been our major interest, we might have translated different authors, made somewhat different selections, and used different working norms for the translations. We may not have felt the need to attend, as we did, separately to each of the regional literatures or work carefully through their archives and their histories. We would probably not have spent so much time dredging out information about the writers' lives, or attempted to reconstruct the changing ideological configurations in which women wrote and were read.

---

[67]For analysis of a replay of the liberal feminist problematic in the "new realism" of the late 1970s and early 1980s, see Susie Tharu, "Third World Women's Cinema: Notes on Narrative, Reflections on Opacity," *Economic and Political Weekly* 21:20, 1986, pp. 864–867.

We have not, then, simply tried to make good the loss for literary studies. The interests of that monumental institution as it stands are ones we wish to transform, not entrench. Neither do we claim that these texts, simply because they are authored by women, express women's *real* experiences or portray *real* women, or indeed that they therefore speak to women in other times, other places, or other social positions with an immediacy that affirms the universality of patriarchal oppression and the common experience of women. Women writers—critics and editors of anthologies no less—are clearly as imbricated in the ideologies of their times as men are; patriarchies take shape and are transformed in specific historical circumstances. Not all literature written by women is feminist, or even about women. Neither is the scope of women's writing restricted to allegories of gender oppression. Besides, even when the writing is specifically feminist, as most of the pieces selected for translation here are, opposition to the dominant ideologies of gender can be discomfitingly class or caste bound and draw on assumptions about race or religious persuasion that reinforce the hold of those ideologies and collaborate in extending their authority. Middle-class women, white women, upper-caste Hindu women might find that their claims to "equality" or to the "full authority" of liberal individualism are at the expense of the working classes, the nonwhite races, dalits, or Muslims. For, as we shall see, given the specific practices and discourses through which individualism took historical shape in India, these groups had to be defined as Other in order that the Self might gain identity.

Women writers may not be exempt from the ideologies that shape their worlds, but it does not follow, as some critics have argued, that there is no sense in which women's writing can be regarded as different or as warranting separate attention. Women articulate and respond to ideologies from complexly constituted and decentered positions within them. Familial ideologies, for instance, clearly constitute male and female subjectivities in different ways, as do ideologies of nation or of empire. Further, ideologies are not experienced—or contested—in the same way from different subject positions. What may appear just and rational from a male or upper-class point of view may seem exploitive and contradictory from a working-class woman's point of view. If we restrain ourselves from enthusiastically recovering women's writing to perform the same services to society and to nation that mainstream literature over the last hundred years has been called upon to do, we might learn to read compositions that emerge from these eccentric locations in a new way; we might indeed learn to read them not for the moments in which they collude with or reinforce dominant ideologies of gender, class, nation, or empire, but for the gestures of defiance or subversion implicit in them.

Readers trained in the appreciation of artifacts that assume and reinforce the power of the center, readers bred on the standard narratives of resolution, victory, or liberation and on an aesthetic designed to smooth over contradictions and celebrate authority (in both senses of the term), readers searching through other times and other cultures for mirrors that reflect their current concerns may initially feel insecure and disoriented as they find their way into texts that take shape at the margins. There will be few gratifications here to replace those domestic fires burning in polished hearths, few testimonies of liberation, or bugle calls that herald the nation or the revolution.

Women Writing in India represents a critical moment that requires us to strain against many earlier formations, but also one, we hope, that makes significant initial moves in developing an aesthetic that does not lessen discontinuity, dispossession, or marginality but dramatizes and clarifies it. It is an aesthetic that must undo the strict distinctions between the literary and the social text, abdicate the imperious functions it has been charged with over the last century and a half, and redesign itself to orchestrate contradictions and cherish the agonistic forms of insurgency and resistance. The promise it holds out is that of a critical practice that is by no means restricted to literature—or to the academy—but, in Gayatri Spivak's phrasing, fills the "literary form with its connections to what is being read: history, political economy— the world."[68] It is also an aesthetic that holds the promise of the many worlds that will appear as the old universalism fades and begins to look dull and simplistic; its self-confident posturing melodramatic; the tastes and feelings it nourished somehow decadent and sentimental.

What we have tried to do, therefore, principally in the section introductions, but also in the biographical headnotes, is to create a context in which women's writings can be read, not as new *monuments* to existing institutions or cultures (classics are, by definition, monuments), but as *documents* that display what is at stake in the embattled practices of self and agency, and in the making of a habitable world, at the margins of patriarchies reconstituted by the emerging bourgeoisies of empire and nation. The attempt is to search out the connections be-

---

[68]Gayatri Spivak, *In Other Worlds* (London: Methuen, 1987), p. 95.

tween political and cultural economies, for these are connections, we believe, that illuminate what is at stake in women's writing. Our introductions to the literature of the reform and nationalist movements in volume 1 place women's literary initiatives against the restructuring of patriarchy and gender that was taking place in the nineteenth and early twentieth centuries, initially with the establishment of imperial authority in India and later with the growth of the nationalist struggle. We have tried to capture the subtle reciprocal formations through which the contours of class, caste, race, and religious identities were redrawn. The texts in volume 2 have as their context the major reorientation in the social Imaginary that took place as the Indian state set up its authorities in the forties and fifties, and as new movements of opposition emerged in the seventies. Women's texts, we argue, challenge the new authorities in a variety of ways, but also often help consolidate the protocols of power.

Our stress is on what forms the grain of these women's struggles. How were their worlds shaped? we ask. How have they turned figures, plots, narratives, lyrical and fictional projects set up for different purposes to their use? With what cunning did they press into service objects coded into cultural significations indifferent or hostile to them? How did they tread their oblique paths across competing ideological grids, or obdurately hang on to illegitimate pleasure? What forms did their dreams of integrity or selfhood take? Most important, and this has been the major principle for our selections: what modes of resistance did they fashion? How did they avoid, question, play off, rewrite, transform, or even undermine the projects set out for them?

In other words, we are interested in how the efforts of these women shaped the worlds we inherited, and what, therefore, is the history, not of authority, but of contest and engagement we can claim today. But we also ask, what was the price they paid in these transactions, what did they concede, and how do those costs and those concessions affect our inheritance? Through these texts, therefore, we look back to a feminist inheritance more powerful and complex, but at the same time more troubling, than narratives of suppression and release might allow us to suspect.

LITERATURE OF THE TWENTIETH CENTURY

THE TWENTIETH CENTURY: WOMEN WRITING THE NATION

Women's texts from the nineteenth and early twentieth centuries, we suggested in volume 1 of *Women Writing in India,* are best read as documents of the writers' engagements with the reworking of their worlds that accompanied British rule in India. Much of the literature collected in volume 2 engages in the profound rearticulation of the political world and of imaginative life that took place in the forties and fifties with the birth of the Indian nation and continues, in many ways, to underwrite culture and politics into the nineties.

The beginnings of this enterprise in which culture and politics united in a singularly productive partnership can be traced back to the last decades of the nineteenth century, when the nationalist project first disturbed the advance of empire. But—and this is a major premise of our argument here—the idea of the nation, and consequently the task of creating an "imagined community" and sculpting a national identity, was significantly reformulated in the middle decades of the twentieth century.[1] Frames of mind and structures of feeling that underwrote

---

[1] We owe the phrase "imagined community" to Benedict Anderson, whose *Imagined Communitites: Reflections on the Origin and Spread of Nationalism* (London: Verso and New Left Books, 1983) can be regarded as having reopened the debate on nationalism in Western Europe and the United States.

disobedience, resistance, and revolt were carefully dismantled and oppositional energies were consciously diffused as the nationalist struggle
was closed off and the nation state began to establish its dominance. It
was in the forties and fifties that many of the myths, the institutions,
the discursive and narrative regimes that have secured the popular understanding of our history, our tradition, our identity, and our problems today—in other words, the popular understanding of what India
is, and what it means to live in this country or be an Indian—began to
take on their current configurations. The changes that took place in
these decades, we believe, set up the scenarios that underlay national
life until the late sixties, and further, the cultural conjunctures of the
eighties and early nineties need to be understood in the light of those
earlier configurations. There have been crises, implosions, redefinitions, and renewals. During the late sixties and through the seventies, for example, a variety of alternative visions challenged existing
institutions and articulated the grievances and aspirations of that
other India whose people had suffered loss of power and agency as
they were recast into the schemes of nationhood. The beginnings of
the most recent phase of the women's movement can be traced to
the early seventies. Through these years, but more clearly so in the
late eighties and as we write in the early nineties, the nation has continued to be redefined. Its story is being remade and affirmed with
a new urgency by politicians, religious leaders, administrators, corporate agencies, journalists, advertisers, television producers, filmmakers, and writers and artists of various kinds—both women and
men.

Gender, we hope to demonstrate, was intrinsic to these rearticulations of social and imaginative life in which women writers played an
important part. The women's texts in this volume—published from
the forties to the nineties—document the many-faceted and often contradictory configuration of the nation-in-process even as they shape it.
Not all of them are radical or feminist in any familiar sense of those
terms. In fact some of these writers clearly seek to manage the shift
into the modern from the side of the old order, staking at the same
time a not-so-conservative claim for women within the conservative
themes of nation, family, and tradition. Others interrogate and deflect
that order and its new incarnations, often in surprising ways, into more
egalitarian modes. Yet others stage what were, and continue to be,
some of the most fascinating and intractable conflicts and debates over
gender in India. Underlying the arguments within Indian feminism

today, and as crucial to an understanding of the women's movement as it is to an appreciation of women's writing in the seventies, eighties, and nineties, are the tensions and crosscurrents between the powerfully underwritten new "nationalism" and the resistances it encounters and engenders.

Political History 1947 to 1990: An Overview

1947–1968: The Nehruvian Years

The winning of independence in 1947 after a century-long freedom struggle that inspired anti-imperialist and human rights movements all over the world was accompanied by the partition of the country into India and Pakistan. Independence was both a climactic resolution and a determined beginning. India's "tryst with destiny," in the words of the thrilling independence day speech by the first prime minister, Jawaharlal Nehru (1889–1964), included the guarantee of political and economic self-reliance and a commitment to building a secular, democratic society. Political theorists point out that while the promises of economic independence were made primarily to the Indian bourgeoisie, and involved protection in international markets and support for indigenous industry, the promises of secularism and democracy bore a double mark. They could be read either as endorsing only the political and cultural changes that would support the growth of a self-confident, energetic commercial class, or as a commitment also to the egalitarian ideals of socialism and therefore to the people as a whole. The resultant tension characterizes the Indian state that, despite its obvious obligations to powerful business and landed interests, has maintained (at least at the level of legislation and of government policy) a commitment to social justice and equality. Among the first major legislative initiatives of the new government, for instance, was the Hindu Code Bill, which sought to create a uniform law ensuring women some rights to property and succession and treating them as equal to men in relation to marriage and divorce. As a result of strong opposition from the powerful right wing of the Congress party, and even from President Rajendra Prasad, especially on the clauses relating to property and inheritance, passage of the bill was delayed for three years. B. R. Ambedkar (1891–1956), leader of the scheduled castes and principal framer of the Indian Constitution, resigned because of the delay and what he considered to be the government's lack of commitment to its socialist principles. A somewhat modified version of the bill was eventually passed in 1955.[2] The 1951 elections were both the first elections to be held in a free India and the first to be based on universal suffrage. The Congress party was returned to power with the substantial majority it would continue to command until the late sixties.

Liberal and Marxist commentators seem agreed that the new government's international policy of nonalignment (neutrality in relation to world powers) and the protection it extended to indigenous industry and business embodied an unambiguous antiimperialist stance. Its domestic commitment to planned economic growth and state initiatives for social transformation—the Nehruvian heritage of the "mixed economy"—has aroused more controversy. The broad outlines of domestic policy were drawn up in the 1947 Congress Committee Resolutions on Economic Policy: to "evolve a political system which will combine efficiency of administration with individual liberty and an economic structure which will yield maximum production without the concentration of private monopolies. . . . Such a social structure can provide an alternative to the acquisitive economy of private capitalism and regimentation of a totalitarian state."[3] It also set down the principle that "land, with its mineral resources and other means of production, as well as distribution and exchange must belong to and be regulated by the community in its own interests."[4]

Liberal theorists read the policy as the "paradox of accommodative politics and radical social change" and as a creative and broadly successful attempt to "combine the goals of growth and reduction of disparities."[5] Its effects, they claim, are evident not only in the experience of the immediate post-Independence years, but also in the seventies and eighties. The economy, they argue, is growing, the system has held strong, and by all conventional indexes India is set for entry into the twenty-first century and a leading new role in the world. Others, and surprisingly the Gandhians and socialists seem broadly agreed on

---

[2]See Lotika Sarkar, "Jawaharlal Nehru and the Hindu Code Bill," in *Indian Women: From Purdah to Modernity,* ed. B. R. Nanda (1976; reprint, Delhi: Radiant Publishers, 1990), pp. 87–98.

[3]All-India Congress Committee, *Resolutions on Economic Policy and Programme, 1924–1954* (Delhi: Indian National Congress, 1954), p. 20.

[4]Ibid., p. 18.

[5]Francine R. Frankel, *India's Political Economy, 1947–1977: The Gradual Revolution* (Delhi: Oxford University Press, 1978), p. 3.

this, acknowledge the gains in food production, science, technology, and business, but consider the philosophy and practice of "development" to be severely limited, insensitive to the history and political ground of Indian society, and vesting too much of the responsibility for social transformation in the bureaucracy and other apparatuses of the state. As a result, they claim, the state has ultimately presided over a reempowerment of conservative forces and has worked in the interests of a world economic order in which the determining principle is profit for multinational corporations—tendencies evident in the crises that confronted the Indian polity in the eighties.

1968–1975: Widespread Disaffection

By the late sixties, contradictions evaded by the early post-Independence resolutions and gaps in the Nehruvian mixed economy began to show up.[6] Plans for industrial growth, agricultural development, land reforms, and social change based on the "best modern science can offer" met with technical problems that scientists had not envisaged and aroused antagonisms (often violent) from landed interests that planners should have predicted. Much to the frustration of the middle-class planners and the community workers whom the government had appointed, the rural poor resisted changes they did not perceive as working in their interests, making it also possible for those in power to blame their failure on the "conservatism" of ordinary people. Economic growth slackened. The government was not able to solve the problem of increasing urban unemployment, which left young people in the cities frustrated and insecure. Prices spiraled upward.

Commentators who regard the break with this early phase as having taken place in the late sixties relate it to widespread disaffection expressed at the time. Major peasant revolts emerged in several parts of the country, supported by students who left the universities to join agrarian struggles, as well as by urban intellectuals. In Bengal, Bihar, and Kerala, riots broke out over food shortages, while elsewhere workers went on strike for higher wages. In Bihar the Gandhian Citizens for Democracy movement called for "total revolution" and took up the cause of the agricultural workers against the priest-landlords of the temple at Bodhgaya. Among those who joined these protests with demands of their own were conventionally conservative groups of

---

[6]See for example Rajani Kotari, *Democratic Polity and Social Changes in India: Crisis and Opportunities* (Bombay: Allied Publishers, 1976).

teachers, doctors, civil servants, engineers, and students. Women, who had been relatively quiet on the political front after Independence, emerged in large numbers and not only took an active part in these movements, but demanded that women's questions be included on the agendas, and even formed separate women's organizations.[7]

An obviously disturbed government reacted with increasingly repressive measures, and in 1975 a state of emergency was declared. Elections were postponed, civil liberties guaranteed under the constitution were suspended, and for the first time in free India, censorship was clamped on the press. Hundreds of activists were imprisoned and movements were broken or driven underground, but the resistance continued and found new strength in the anger of the people over such issues as forced sterilization, slum "clearance," and city "beautification" projects. In 1977 the Emergency was lifted and elections were held. For the first time since Independence, the Congress party was voted out.

1977: A Turning Point

What we might regard as the third phase of the women's movement in India[8] emerged in the years that followed, years also important for the civil liberties movements and for struggles of other kinds. In terms of the strategies and coalitions of opposition that developed at many levels, but also in terms of a new sense of state power and its commitments, it was 1975, as much as 1968 to 1970, that ushered in a new phase. In fact, a broad consensus among political theorists regards the mid-seventies as an important turning point, although there is considerable disagreement about exactly what that turning point represents. Some commentators argue that the policies of economic liberalization of the late seventies and the eighties mark the arrival of a confident new Indian commercial class, with little need for protection, that had won the domestic battle against feudal or pre-capitalist forces and had sufficient control on the international stage to negotiate with the multinational corporations. Decentralization and the weakening of state

---

[7]An important new collection of articles that documents and analyzes women's involvement in these struggles is Ilina Sen, ed., *A Space Within the Struggle: Women's Participation in People's Movements* (Delhi: Kali for Women, 1990).

[8]Here we consider the nineteenth-century reform movements as constituting the first phase of the women's movement in India and the national struggle, the second.

mediation or control, they argue, is a logical corollary of this coming of age of Indian capitalism. The economic policies of the Congress governments of the eighties were formulated on this assumption. Left-of-center theorists acknowledge the relative vigor and independence of Indian commerce and industry—in relation to that of Latin American countries, for instance—but argue that by the mid-seventies both the economy and the polity had backtracked on the antifeudal and anti-imperialist commitments made at the time of Independence. While traditional landlordism may have been formally abolished, these critics point out, caste and communal conflicts and violence against women had increased. In addition, feudal power had reemerged as a significant force in the electoral process, and the Indian bourgeoisie increasingly were being forced to collaborate with multinational capital and make costly concessions to it.[9]

Analysts of contemporary culture and politics paint an even more alarming picture. By 1972, they argue, it was clear that the Nehruvian project had failed. The Emergency was a last-ditch attempt, in a changing international scene, to shore up the protectionist promises made to the Indian bourgeoisie. After 1975, world capitalism, led by Japan and the United States, made a concerted effort to break the power of national oligopolies, an effort that saw its most violent results in the overthrow of the Allende government in Chile in September 1973.[10] *The internationalization of markets, and the transformation of the Indian state essentially into a mediator in that process, required that the nation be imagined anew.* New forms of Indianness had to be invented, new identities forged for both state and citizen. The corollary in the cultural domain of the loosening of state control and the opening up of markets to private capital has been a centralized, "all-India" regime of cultural production that has created a hospitable climate for international capital and the markets it requires. This regime is discernable after the mid-seventies in literary production and in the massive expansion of the national press as well as in the narrative and visual languages endorsed by the most powerful medium of the times, television. We will return, later in this essay, to a more detailed analysis of this important moment in the cultural history of India.

---

[9]Sanjaya Baru, "Market Forces," *Journal of Arts and Ideas* 19, May 1990, pp. 53–60.

[10]See for example, Ashish Rajadhyaksha, "Beaming Messages to the Nation," *Journal of Arts and Ideas* 19, May 1990, pp. 33–52.

What Is a Nation?

Political analysts have pointed out that while the nation is undoubtedly the most important political unit in the world today, "nation," "nationality," and "nationalism" seem to lack coherence as concepts in political theory and are extremely difficult to describe or analyze.[11] Discussing the problem in 1941, shortly after the issue of a separate Pakistan first came up, B. R. Ambedkar argued that none of the attributes commonly regarded as forming the basis for the nation—race, language, and territory—actually suffice to create one. Nationality, he concluded, is a very elusive quality and can be understood only as a "subjective psychological feeling. It is a feeling of a corporate sentiment of oneness which makes those that are charged with it feel that they are kith and kin. . . . [N]ational feeling is a double-edged feeling. . . . [It is] at once a fellowship for one's own . . . and an antifellowship for those who are not. . . ."[12]

It is significant that the vocabulary Ambedkar drew upon—and many contemporary theorists would endorse his choice—is not that of political philosophy, but that of culture and of cultural politics, and that his focus is on emotional solidarity and subjectivity. For students of literature, the implications are extremely interesting. The making of the nation involves the shaping of a Self, but also, therefore, the making of an Other. The geography of the nation is not so much territorial as imaginative, for it deals with what constitutes a people or a community, with ways the land has been lived on and worked over, with boundaries that include and exclude, with centers and peripheries, with the organizing principles of the nation's "integrity" or cohesion, and with social institutions and affective spaces that can house, protect, and

---

[11]Partha Chatterjee, *Nationalist Thought and the Colonial World: A Derivative Discourse?* (Delhi: Oxford University Press, 1986), pp. 1–35, provides a detailed critical overview of the discussion. See also Anderson, especially pp. 13–14, and Tom Nairn, *The Break-up of Britain* (London: New Left Books, 1977).

[12]B. R. Ambedkar, *Thoughts on Pakistan* (Bombay: Thacker & Co., 1947), pp. 25–33. Ambedkar's secular reformulation of Ernest Renan's (1823–1892) now well-known thesis on nationalism is worth noting. He cites Renan as claiming: "A nation is a living soul, a spiritual principle. . . . The land provides a substratum, the field of battle and work; man provides the soul; man is everything in the formation of that sacred thing which is called a people. Nothing of material nature suffices for it." Benedict Anderson's notion of a cultural or "imagined" unity mediates interestingly between Ambedkar and Renan and is able to bring into focus the politics of this cultural artifact.

comfort. In other words, the imaginative geography of the nation deals with spaces whose laws we know and understand, as against alien ones that disorient or terrorize. The discourses of the nation encode belonging and alienation. They are concerned with subjectivity, but also with citizenship. Arguably, therefore, the "rationality" of the nation is not theoretical in the conventional sense of the word, but akin to the rationality of art. Literary and historical narratives, as well as various other imaginative artifacts, set up and consolidate the logic of the nation. Despite its disavowals, culture is also a politics and plays a key role in the shaping of civil society.

Cultural theorists have in fact suggested that the realist novel and film, both forms that emerged historically alongside the nation in India, as they did in Europe, developed the imaginative languages (the narrative forms, modes of address, conventions of character and emplotment, even the exact authority of the lyric voice) in which the nation (its imaginative geography, its political and moral legitimacy, its executive authority, and its citizen-subjects) was shaped. In fact, the "foundational fictions" of the nation can be regarded as preparing the ground for national projects that would be considered political in the more conventional sense. Mukesh Srivastava points out that Jawaharlal Nehru's *Discovery of India*,[13] perhaps the best known of the "foundational fictions" of the Indian nation, devises an unprecedented composite genre to write the story of India. History jostles with autobiography and social analysis in a narrative mode that draws on classic realism, but rewrites the imperialist logic of that form to create a legitimate space for the nation. The reader–citizen whom Nehru (who as "author" is himself also defined by his text) addresses is the new Indian-in-the-making.[14] Communities, like readers and viewers, are

---

[13]Jawaharlal Nehru, *The Discovery of India* (1946; reprint, London: Meridian Books, 1960).

[14]Mukesh Srivastava, "The Story of India: The Narrative Production of Humanism in E. M. Forster's *A Passage to India,* Jawaharlal Nehru's *Discovery of India* and Salman Rushdie's *Midnight's Children."* (Ph.D. diss., C.I.E.F.L. Hyderabad, 1993). See also Doris Sommer, "Irresistible Romance: The Foundational Fictions of Latin America," in *Nation and Narration* ed. Homi Bhabha (London: Routledge, 1990), pp. 73–98. Sommer argues that romance, emplotted as an emotional/erotic alliance between regions/races/interest groups and as the basis for the building of the nation-family, provided the foundational fictions of many Latin American countries. She takes off from a thesis earlier proposed by Benedict Anderson about the establishment, in realist fiction, of an "empty calendrical time" that can "accommodate an entire citizenry" (Anderson, pp. 30–31).

gathered and shaped through address. Identities and structures of feeling evolve in subtle reciprocal relationships. Worlds are laid out, peopled, and rendered plausible by narrative. Similarly, policies and programs define and construct their constituencies, and institutions their clientele. Welfare indexes and confers legitimacy on need much as a product gives birth to its consumer.

Three further observations are necessary here. They are somewhat cryptic perhaps, but will be discussed in more detail later. First, despite its own claims to the contrary, nationalism is not the awakening to self-consciousness of a nation and a tradition that already exist at some deep level. Nations, like traditions and works of art, are *made*—built, created, imagined.[15] The discourses of nationalism and its cultural languages suture over gaps and create what might be called a social Imaginary.[16] They draw on the past, and indeed might use ancient and "ethnic" or "indigenous" materials, but the structure and the politics of these traditions are contemporary.

Secondly, whatever its official discourses might proclaim, the nation (and its traditions) is constantly being recreated: contested, fractured, elaborated, redistributed, and *rewritten,* as new resolutions are negotiated or, as is more often the case, effected. Its closures, therefore—and

---

[15]For a perceptive discussion of this process, see Jayaprakash Narayan, *Nation Building in India* (Varanasi: Navchetana Prakashan, 1975), especially chapter 6, "The Concept of Nationhood," pp. 377–428.

[16]In Lacan the Imaginary signals a relationship of plenitude and rests upon a misrecognition *(méconnaissance)* through which the child identifies with the unified, powerful image of himself or herself that appears in the mirror. The "Ideal-I" of the specular image "situates the agency of the ego, before its social determination, in a fictional direction . . . which will only rejoin the coming-into-being *(le devenir)* of the subject asymptotically, whatever the success of the dialectical synthesis by which [she/he] must resolve as *I* [his/her] discordance with [his/her] own reality." In social relations this stage involves "a deflection of the specular *I* into a social *I*" as the ego replaces the "I" as the "subject" of the imaginary relation to the object, and is "experienced as a temporal dialectic that decisively projects the formation of the individual into history" (Jacques Lacan, *Ecrits: A Selection,* trans. Alan Sheridan [New York: W. W. Norton and Co., 1977], pp. 1–7). The making of the social Imaginary of the nation involves, in addition to the fictional synthesis of the citizen-subject, the securing of systems of representation that constitute its social world. The Imaginary, writes Ernesto Laclau "is a horizon; it is not one among other objects but an absolute limit which structures a field of intelligibility and thus the condition of possibility for the emergence of any object" (Laclau, *New Reflections on the Revolution of Our Times,* [London: Verso, 1990] p. 64).

that brings us to our third point—are never complete, never total. It is easy to forget, given the vocabulary of high Romanticism in which the nation is so often invoked, that these resolutions were contested and that they were, in fact, often shaped by the very disjunctures they sought to avoid, the very resistances they strove to contain.[17] The closures of government are strategic and always haunted by that which they write out of their schemes or delegitimate. It is important, therefore, as we attempt to understand the representational practices of the nation and the politics of gender implicit in them, to plot out the terrain as one that is constantly being re-formed, and, equally important, to conceive of the nation as a space in which meanings are battled over as they are composed. In distinct contrast to other critical efforts to define an ancient and timeless "Indian sensibility" or to locate the "authentic Indian,"[18] our attempt here is to understand the nation and nationality not as an essence, but as a *historically constituted terrain,* changing and contested, and its citizen-subjects as subjects-in-struggle, and therefore also always "in process." Only such a history, we believe, will help us appreciate what is at stake in women's writing and indeed in all writing on the margins.

---

[17]"The people," Homi Bhabha suggests, "are neither the beginning [nor] end of the national narrative; they represent the cutting edge between the totalising powers and the forces that signify the more specific address to contentious unequal interests and identities within the population" ("DissemiNation: Time, Narrative and the Margins of the Modern Nation," in *Nation and Narrative,* ed. Homi Bhabha [London: Routledge, 1990], p. 297). Though the idea of dissemination that he develops is uncomfortably close to that of cultural relativity, the reader will find that Bhabha's essay—and others in the volume—usefully extend the argument presented here, as do some of the essays in Eric Hobsbawm and Terence Ranger, eds., *The Invention of Tradition* (Cambridge: Cambridge University Press, 1983).

[18]The work of C. D. Narasimhaiah in *The Swan and the Eagle* (Simla: Indian Institute of Advanced Study, 1970) might be regarded as the urtext for this school of criticism, developed in the influential writings of U. R. Anantamurthy. See for example, Anantamurthy's "The Search for an Identity: A Kannada Writer's Viewpoint" in *Dialogue: New Cultural Identities,* ed. Guy Amurthanayagam (London: Macmillan, 1982) pp. 66–78.

The Forties and Fifties: Crucible Years

How then might we describe the crucial rearticulations that were taking place in the forties and fifties? Consider the writers with whose work this volume opens. Though their first major works appeared in the middle decades of the century, Rasheed Jahan, Ismat Chugtai, Indira Sant, K. Saraswathi Amma, M. K. Indira, and Amrita Pritam[19] and their contemporaries grew into adulthood in what was an earlier and distinctly different phase in the long-running project of nation-making. Right through the twenties and thirties a broad range of struggles sharpened the cutting edge of the nationalist movement and roused public opinion the world over against British imperialism. The major strength of the nationalist movement, however, derived from widespread popular or mass struggles that articulated a variety of discontents that the Congress endorsed and tried, with varying degrees of success, to orchestrate. Through this entire period there were peasant movements, tribal revolts, food riots, student agitations, industrial strikes, and campaigns of various sorts, each, we must take pains to remember, with varying investments in gender.[20] Indeed, from about the "autumn of 1930 onwards," the historian Sumit Sarkar observes, a broadly similar pattern emerges: "a weakening in forms of struggle associated with bourgeois groups or peasant upper strata (e.g. urban boycott and no-revenue) accompanied by sporadic and fairly widespread tendencies towards less manageable forms (no rent, tribal outbursts, popular violence)."[21] These picked up a momentum that, most

---

[19]See also Indira Sant, *Snake Skin and Other Poems,* trans. Vrinda Nabar and Nissim Ezekiel (Bombay: Nirmala Sadanand Publishers, 1973); Ismat Chugtai, *The Quilt and Other Stories,* trans. Tahira Naqvi and Syeda S. Hameed (Delhi: Kali for Women, 1990); and M. K. Indira, *Phaniyamma,* trans. Tejaswini Niranjana (Delhi: Kali for Women, 1989).

[20]For a history of the freedom movement that carefully records the heterogeneity of the struggles, see Sumit Sarkar, *Modern India: 1885–1947* (Madras: Macmillan, 1983). D. N. Dhanagare, *Peasant Movements in India 1920–1950* (Delhi: Oxford University Press, 1983) provides a more detailed and analytical account of the principal agrarian revolts. Ranajit Guha, ed., *Subaltern Studies: Writings in South Asian History and Society,* vols. 1 to 6 (Delhi: Oxford University Press, vol. 1, 1982; vol. 6, 1989) presents attempts to write an Indian history "from below" and to reconceptualize it in the process. These studies are of particular interest to students of literature as they often proceed from a textual and ideological critique of earlier historical narratives and are as vitally concerned with culture as they are with society and politics.

[21]Sumit Sarkar, p. 307.

historians agree, came to a climax in the countrywide Quit India agitation of 1942. By 1945 it was clear that there was no way in which a war-torn Britain could have held on to political power in India: "Who was that young madman," Winston Churchill is reported to have asked about Enoch Powell, "who has been telling me how many divisions I will need to reconquer India?"[22]

In many ways the forties were as difficult for the Indian nation as they were for the imperial government. Nationalist histories, many of them produced in the euphoria of the immediate post-Independence period, tend to tell the story of the triumphant progress of the Congress party–led movement to a climactic resolution. Cultural historians endorse the canonical story with a commitment that would put political historians to shame.[23] Such accounts not only rewrite the many rebellions that found articulation in the anti-imperialist struggle into the master narrative of the mainstream, but also suggest an exaggerated and essentially unproblematic continuity between the late years of the national movement and the early years of independence. As in the literary texts that fashion and rehearse this dominant nationalist narrative, a steady connotative pressure associates the liberation of the

---

[22]Paul Foot, *The Rise of Enoch Powell* (Harmonsworth: Penguin, 1969), quoted by Errol Lawrence in Centre for Contemporary Cultural Studies, *The Empire Strikes Back: Race and Racism in 70s Britain* (London: Hutchinson, 1982), p. 67. The British of course invariably spoke of "bestowing" or "granting" independence when India was "ready" for it. The carefully maintained image was that of a child, or perhaps a difficult adolescent, coming of age. In their scheme of things the central role was played by the "parent" country that guided various colonial territories to "responsible" self-government with a mature courtesy. The familial imagery, however, works more dangerously through the implication that there are natural, filial ties between the mother country and the newly adult nation that can and ought to continue.

[23]One might expect literary histories sponsored by the Sahitya Academy (the National Academy of Letters) founded in 1954 by the Indian government (their slogan is "Indian Literature is one though written in many languages") to follow this scheme, and without exception they do so. But, as our regional language editors also found, many other literary histories also take this narrative emplotment for granted. In a stimulating review article, Ashish Rajadhyaksha charges K. G. Subramanyan's *The Living Tradition: Perspectives on Modern Indian Art* (Calcutta: Seagull Books, 1987) with similar evasions: of seeking to "paper the divides over, to emphasise continuity above all else." Subramanyan's voice, he writes, "is that of a father figure whose reassurances I simply do not believe, which indeed, terrify me" ("Living the Tradition," *Journal of Arts and Ideas* 16, January–March 1988, pp. 73–86).

nation with that of "the land and the people" and in turn endows the indigenous state and its protocols of government with a "natural" authority.

Speaking for the People

The stress on resolution and continuity obscures the fact that the forties and fifties also signal significant disjunctures. If the early decades of the century had authorized the idea of a nation-people and their many struggles for freedom, the approaching climate of power demanded the setting up of a nation-state and a relationship between the ,state and "its" people that was designed for governance. The nation had to be restructured, rewritten. *Its story was no longer to be told, as it had been during the freedom struggle, from its many contested frontiers, but from its new center.* Different, often contradictory histories and interests were sometimes rearticulated, but more often were simply suppressed as the new authorities assumed the authority to speak for the people, and drew on the languages of science and liberal humanism in order to do so. A whole set of deeply embedded historical discourses, some of which we have described and analyzed in the introductory essays in volume 1 of *Women Writing in India,* were renotated as they were translated into the schemes of an ascendent nationalism. As we shall find when we discuss the literature on the Partition, or the texts in which the nineteenth-century figure of the widow reappears, literary and cultural narratives of various kinds played crucial roles in effecting this shift. But we need to ask what exactly is this "center" that assumes authorship, and who are "the people"? How are they constituted? And where do women come into the story?

Liberal political theorists acknowledge the realignment that took place in the forties and fifties, but interpret it as the logical consequence of the success of the freedom struggle, which they read simply as a conflict between *two* adversaries, India and Britain. In the liberal argument, therefore, the authority of the new indigenous state is implicit in the agenda of the national movement and the electoral mandate, especially a mandate based, as the 1951 general elections were, on universal suffrage, endorsed their entitlement to speak for the people. Marxist theorists offer a different analysis of the Indian state and its ruling elites. They acknowledge the strength of the new government's relatively anti-imperialist foreign policy, but consider the Indian state as representing not "the people" but a coalition of commercial and landed interests. The debate on the nature of the ruling elites, concerned as it is with assigning broad theoretical labels, does not take us far with the problem of analyzing actual effects, or understanding exactly how patriarchies were rewritten and pressed into service as the new dispensation was set up.

As far as the Congress leaders were concerned, by the early forties, the national movement had arrived. As we shall see in the accounts that follow, the troubled ambivalence that had marked the response of nationalist leaders when faced with popular initiatives settled into a remarkable singleness. Oppositional forces, even those that had found hospitality in the freedom struggle, had to be demobilized and contained. The bureaucracy, the police, and the army, no longer agents of oppression, but necessary arms of the new state, become "neutral."[24] Through a series of political and constitutional initiatives that included, as we saw earlier, a commitment to heavy industry, planned economic development, and modernization, the state became the custodian of the people's welfare, the articulator, through its policies and initiatives, of their needs. Questions of social design, development, and the distribution of benefits became matters to be dealt with through legal reform and centralized planning. Cultural texts of various kinds played a major role in effecting this reorientation—which was, importantly, a reorientation of the social Imaginary—and in giving shape and authority to the new, essentially upper-caste, middle-class, and male point of view of the agent-state. *The process might well be thought of as one of translation: the politically energized, heterogeneous articulations of the earlier period were rewritten into the quietist languages of social policy and legislative*

---

[24]There is no dearth of examples of this. The naval mutiny of February 1946, for example, is estimated at its height to have involved twenty thousand sailors and drew support in Bombay, for instance, from crowds who thronged to cheer them and merchants who threw open their shops, inviting the mutineers to take what they needed, as well as from many trade unions who downed tools in support. But both Gandhi and Vallabhbhai Patel were uncompromisingly hostile. Gandhi chided the mutineers for having "set a bad and unbecoming example for India," while Patel wrote, "Discipline in the Army cannot be tampered with. . . . We will want an Army even in free India" (Sumit Sarkar, pp. 423–425). Gyanendra Pandey quotes a letter in which the Congress high command reprimanded the chief minister of Uttar Pradesh for having inaugurated an exhibition that contained photographs of police atrocities. The letter read: "the caricature of official activities in the manner reported in the Press at a time when we are in office is open to serious objection. This is likely to affect the morale of the police force. . . ." (Gyanendra Pandey, ed., *The Indian Nation in 1942* [Calcutta: K. P. Bagchi & Co., 1988], pp. 14–15).

reform. These drew in turn on the languages of the social sciences, most significantly those of development economics and anthropology.[25]

In fact, we might argue (no doubt with some risk of oversimplification) that the disciplinary schemes—the authorities, assumptions, logic, and narrative urgencies—of anthropology and development economics acquired terrible new powers as they regulated the realignments of the nation-state intranationally in relation to "the people" and internationally in relation to global systems of power. The colonial embedding of anthropology, a discipline that emerged in the nineteenth century as sovereign European observers studied and documented native non-European societies and provided imperial authorities with the knowledge that empowered the management and exploitation of subject peoples, has now been widely analyzed even within the discipline. (A reader new to this debate might usefully pause to reflect on the politics of documentation suggested by this encounter.) Edward Said puts it with a force and eloquence that demand quotation: "The by now massed discourses, codes and practical traditions of anthropology, with its authorities, disciplinary rigors, genealogical maps, systems of patronage and accreditation have been accumulated into various traditions of *being anthropological.* Innocence is now out of the question of course."[26] As the newly independent nation turned to anthropology as the language in which it studied its people and devised programs for their development, it not only carried with it the baggage of imperialism but also reempowered it, reproducing in its policies similar authorities, a similar distance, and a similar manipulative intent. There were changes of course—a new "tact," new euphemisms, sometimes even new nationalist enthusiasms, but the strict regimes of the discipline displayed a singular durability.[27] Anthropology is at issue in

---

[25]See, for instance, Amiya Kumar Bagchi, *The Political Economy of Underdevelopment* (Cambridge: Cambridge University Press, 1982); James Clifford and George Marcus, eds., *Writing Culture: The Politics and Poetics of Ethnography* (Berkley: University of California Press, 1986); and Ronald Inden, *Imagining India* (Oxford: Basil Blackwell, 1990), for critical appraisals of such rewriting.

[26]Edward Said, "Representing the Colonized: Anthropology's Interlocuters," *Critical Inquiry* 15:2, Winter 1989, pp. 205–225.

[27]One of the themes that might be traced through Inden's *Imagining India* is the history and present composition of "anthropological tact" in a postcolonial world. For an analysis of the not-so-residual hold of imperialism on "indigenous anthropology," see Jurgen Golte, "Latin America: The Anthropology of Conquest," in *Anthropology: Ancestors and Heirs,* ed. Stanley Diamond (The Hague: Mouton, 1980), p. 391. The work of anthropologists such as M. N. Srinivas and

several texts in this volume—most poignantly perhaps in Baby Kamble's memoirs. The rush of exotic detail that describes the customs and beliefs of her people threatens to overwhelm her attempts to remember their political history and to articualte a self. In his "rational" daylight mode, the well-intentioned administrator-reformer in Mahasweta Devi's "Shishu" draws on anthropology and development theory to understand the tribals. The fears and prejudices that crowd in on him in the dark draw on the more "primitive," "irrational," discourses in which the people of the area have been written into the imagination of mainstream India. From the point of view of the tribals themselves, there is little to choose between the modern and the traditional.

Study after study has shown that the logic underpinning development action, even when focussed on women, is state-centered. In other words, the interests of the state and the classes it represents will take priority over those of the people. And when the state collaborates with global frameworks of economic, technological, and strategic growth, development programs ultimately serve the metropoles. Further, development programs have hidden agendas that exacerbate existing inequalities and leave women and other subjugated groups more marginalized than before.[28] We are only beginning to understand the global politics of the disciplines that told the story of the nation and underwrote plans for its development.

Even conflict is, as a result, contained within the well-modulated discourses of administrative policy, underwritten in turn by the social sciences. Not only, for example, is all other opposition neutralized when the principal conflict of the early years of independence is represented as one between the more socialist prime minister Jawaharlal Nehru and the powerful right-wing home minister Sardar Vallabhbhai

---

Andre Beteille, who have been extremely influential in the shaping of government policy and have, in the wake of the women's movement in the seventies, extended their interests to women, calls for critical analysis. See, for instance, M. N. Srinivas, *The Cohesive Role of Sanskritisation and Other Essays* (Delhi: Oxford University Press, 1989).

[28] An extended discussion of this is found in Maria Mies, *Patriarchy and Accumulation on a World Scale* (London: Zed Books, 1986). See also Gayatri Chakravorthy Spivak, "Feminism and Critical Theory," in *In Other Worlds: Essays in Cultural Politics* (New York: Methuen, 1987), pp. 77–94; and Susie Tharu, "The Myth of Universalism: Feminism and the Problematic of Civil Liberties," in *Indian Women: Myth and Reality,* ed. Jasodhara Bagchi (Calcutta: School of Women's Studies, Jadarpur University, 1990), pp. Tharu 1–14.

Patel, but the tension is reduced to that between welfarism and laissez-faire. As we will find when we discuss women's organizations, the political edge of the women's movement was blunted, and the movement itself contained, as the women's question was translated into one of electoral policy. A similar fate awaited the question of caste. The formerly untouchable castes were redesignated in the constitution as scheduled castes and a bureaucratic and ideological machinery was created to elaborate that redesignation and to put it into practice. In the process, the politics of untouchability, and the exploitation and oppression predicated on that politics, were translated into an administrative task that might be "attended to" by the relevant government departments. The *politics* of caste as well as the *politics* of gender were not only denied by the new dispensation; they were also contained.[29] Through its discourses and in the many institutions that were designed and set up to extend its effects, the body of the state absorbed the nation into itself. Imaginative artifacts of various kinds endorsed and extended these transformations as they set up a nation-space.[30] It is easy to forget, given the virtual explosion of these discourses and the aura of fulfillment in which resolutions "in the interests of the nation" were bathed, that the shifts that took place in the forties and fifties were carefully—even violently—wrought political and cultural effects.[31]

Nationalism: A Polyphonous Sign

Such resolutions were not totally new. Influential recent readings of the national movement suggest that their instruments were long in the making. As early as the twenties the Congress party intervened to support and orchestrate the discontent of the tribals, workers, and

---

[29]See B. R. Ambedkar, *Poona Pact: An Epic of Human Rights* (Jallander: Buddhist Publishing House, 1982) for a telling account of the costs of nationalism for the lower castes.

[30]For a critical analysis of Mulk Raj Anand's *Untouchable,* one of the most famous nationalist novels that deals with the issue, see Susie Tharu, "Decoding Anand's Humanism," *Kunapipi* 4:2, pp. 30–41.

[31]David Arnold titles his essay in Pandey, ed., *The Indian Nation in 1942* (Calcutta: K. P. Bagchi & Co., 1988) "Quit India in Madras: Hiatus or Climacteric?". Pandey's introduction to the collection and his essay, "The Revolt of August 1942 in Eastern Uttar Pradesh and Bihar" raise similar questions. Sudipta Kaviraj makes a similar point in "A Critique of the Passive Revolution," where he argues that "the Congress which assumed power in 1947 was not in many respects the Congress that won independence" *(Economic and Political Weekly* 23–27, Annual Number 1988, pp. 2429–2444).

landless peasants. Local revolts had therefore acquired national dimensions, but tensions also arose as these uprisings were deflected and recast into forms more acceptable to mainstream nationalism.[32] In a fascinating close reading of the political ferment in the Gorakpur District from 1921 to 1922, Shahid Amin charts the emergence of Gandhi (and by implication the nationalist struggle for which he took on an iconic value) as a figure in whom differently oriented accents intersected, or, to use Bakhtin's term, as a polyphonous sign. The nationalist press and local middle-class interests circulated accounts of peasant involvement with Gandhi as one of simple but touching reverence: "to behold the Mahatma in person and become his devotees" were the only roles assigned in the nationalist press to the *sadharan janata,* or ordinary people. In these discourses "it was for the urban intelligentsia and the full-time party activists to convert this groundswell of popular feeling into an organised movement."[33] Rumors about the Mahatma's extraordinary powers, of miraculous boons and punishments, were printed and tacitly endorsed unless they contained "dangerous" elements such as demands for the abolition of the rights of feudal landlords, or the reduction of rents or prices, in which case they were promptly disclaimed.[34] Gandhi's own speeches as reported in the nationalist press emphasized the need for unity between Hindus and Muslims but warned the people against taking the struggle into their own hands, using violence, or looting bazaars. Self-sacrifice and purification were of prime importance, and the people were to give up gambling, smoking ganja (marijuana), drinking, and promiscuous sex.[35] The peasantry, however, began to "look upon the Mahatma as an alternative source of authority," and notions of *swaraj* (self-government) appear to "have taken shape quite independently of the district leadership of the Congress party." The local peasantry perceived swaraj as a "millennium in which taxation would be limited to the collection of small cash contributions or dues in kind from fields and threshing floors, and [in] which the cultivators would hold their land at little more than nominal

---

[32]See David Hardiman, *The Coming of the Devi: Adivasi Assertion in Western India* (Delhi: Oxford University Press, 1987).

[33]Shahid Amin, "Gandhi as Mahatma: Gorakhpur District, Eastern UP, 1921–2," in *Subaltern Studies III: Writings on South Asian History and Society,* ed. Ranajit Guha (Delhi: Oxford University Press, 1984), pp. 2, 4.

[34]Ibid., p. 50.

[35]Ibid., pp. 21–24.

rents.[36] They drew on the spiritualized symbol of Gandhi as authority for what they regarded as just, fair, and attainable demands, while the *jaikar* (victory; adoration) of Gandhi often became the rallying cry for direct action when bazaars were looted and police stations were attacked.

A similar tension marks the spectacular Quit India movement of the early forties. The historian Gyanendra Pandey argues that Quit India was a popular nationalist upsurge that occurred in the name of Gandhi but "went substantially beyond the confines" envisaged by Gandhi and the Congress party. While at one level, Pandey writes, there seems to have been "widespread acceptance of the primacy of the Congress" and especially of the authority of Gandhi, at the level of popular political action the Quit India movement comprised a whole range of initiatives that "repeatedly challenged the notion of a necessary Congress leadership. These forces had their roots in the far from complete integration of the Indian economy, in the significant cultural divide between the elites and the masses and not in the least in long-standing traditions of militant resistance to class and state oppression in one region and another."[37] Indeed, as Pandey and others have demonstrated, from the twenties onwards, nationalist symbols such as Gandhi and the Congress party were constantly appropriated at the grassroots level by (often more militant) popular movements with their own priorities. These movements invariably forced the pace of events, transformed the style of Gandhian politics, and left their mark on the mainstream. But the phenomenon was never as widespread, as evident, or as alarming for a Congress leadership that had, so to speak "arrived," as it was in the Quit India movement. Not surprisingly, the nationalist leadership responded ambivalently. Even as they claimed the uprising as their own and took credit for it, they dissociated the Congress from what came increasingly to be spoken about as its "excesses." Pandey cites Gandhi as having declared that the events of 1942 were a "calamity" and that the people had gone "wild with rage to the point of losing self-control."[38] Jawaharlal Nehru regarded the

---

[36]Ibid., p. 52.

[37]Pandey, pp. 9–10.

[38]Letter to the viceroy written from jail, September 1942. N. Manserg, *The Transfer of Power,* vol. 2: *Quit India* (London: Her Majesty's Stationary Office, 1970) p. 1002, quoted in Pandey, p. 13.

movement as the greatest event in India since the Sepoy Rebellion of 1857, but wrote also that "the people forgot the lessons of non-violence that had been dinned into their ears for more than twenty years" and talked of the "impromptu frenzy of the mob." Pattabhi Sitaramayya, the official historian of the Congress party, commented that "the people grew insensate and were maddened with fury."[39]

The Protocols of Government

The phraseology, Pandey points out, "competes with [that of] any colonial lament over an uprising of the Indian peasantry."[40] Clearly it marks the growing distance between the leadership and the people. But it is also symptomatic of the questions of discipline, order, and control that covertly structured concepts such as "nonviolence," "self-control," "freedom," and, most particularly, "Indianness" (the genius of satyagraha, which is literally "persistence in the truth," we must not forget, was considered somehow essentially Indian) during the freedom movement itself. This structuring emerged more powerfully as the Congress shed its identity as an oppositional force and began to take on the controlling postures of government. The ambivalent responses of those who were, for several years to come, to provide the nation with leadership and direction, are embryonic forms of the tensions inherent in the institutions of governance and the languages of scholarship and the arts that were brought into play as the new Indian state consolidated its power and tried, not always successfully—and in the face of various resistances—to fashion the contradictions of the times to its advantage.

"Politics is war by other means," writes Michel Foucault (1929–1984). But what exactly were these other means? How do they impinge on our worlds today? How did those secret battles fare? How did they reinvent the subjugation of women? And how was this subjugation related to other agendas of government? The disputes between a dominant nationalism and peasants, industrial workers, the "untouchables," and minority communities, as well as the struggles of these marginalized groups etch out another map of the nation—and,

---

[39]Jawaharlal Nehru, p. 498, and P. Sitaramayya, *The History of the Indian National Congress,* vol. 2 (Bombay: Padma Publications, 1947), p. 373, cited in Pandey, pp. 13–14.
[40]Pandey, p. 14.

in turn, of the world. Women's initiatives—their labor, their movements, and their writing—shape the picture that emerges.

Engendering the Nation

Perhaps the most dramatic evidence of the shifts that were taking place, and their implications for women, are the events of the 1948 "police action" in Hyderabad State. The Indian Army had marched in to unseat a recalcitrant nizam who had refused to relinquish his power to the Indian government. (Much of Wajeda Tabassum's fiction—including "Utran" [Castoffs], in this volume—as well as that of Jeelani Bano, portrays the decadence and cruelty of these rulers and of the nobility in their courts.) The army turned its weapons almost immediately against the peasant movement that had given support to the nationalist struggle, but did not regard the ascendancy of the Congress a fitting resolution to its program. The politics of such initiatives, even when legitimated as being in "the nation's" interests, are clearly repressive. But more subtle is the widespread restructuring of gender that underwrote the consolidation of the national project. Recently published oral autobiographies of women who took part in the peasant struggle allow us to map this restructuring. "We were full of firm confidence," says Dayani Priyamvada. "[As we worked among the peasants] we began to appreciate what a new society would be like with equality for men and women. After the police action and the elections to Parliament, these dreams were smashed. Crushed like an egg. . . . After the elections you know how we were—we were like the proverbial blanket which, when asked, 'Where are you now?' replied, 'I'm lying exactly where I was thrown.' "[41] Whatever the designs of state or nation and their attendant patriarchies on the right or the left, Priyamvada's narrative carves out another space and sets up, in the very intensity with which she rejects the new resolutions and describes her feeling of annihilation and paralysis, the instruments for dissent.[42] It is significant that the story of Priyamvada's life, like that of Dudala Salamma of Quila Shapur (which is included in this volume), was not told until the seventies, when women's groups found it nec-

---

[41]Stree Shakti Sanghatana, *We Were Making History: Life Stories of Women in the Telangana People's Struggle* (Delhi: Kali for Women, 1989), p. 73.

[42]See also Vasantha Kannabiran and K. Lalita, "That Magic Time: Women in the Telangana People's Struggle," in *Recasting Women: Essays in Colonial History,* ed. Kumkum Sangari and Sudesh Vaid (Delhi: Kali for Women, 1989), pp. 180–203.

essary as part of their own program to search out this particular past that had been rapidly forgotten after the early fifties.

Other effects that accompanied the setting up of the nation-state were less obviously painful, but no less awesome, for they continue to form the very grain of everyday life into the nineties. The Committee on the Status of Women reported in 1974 that maternity beds constituted less than 17 percent of the total number of hospital beds and in general that no other beds were provided for women.[43] A 1989 study demonstrates how even these minimal facilities are culturally defined out of the reach of the large majority of Indian women, who are marginal to the whole system of medical research and technology. Very little has been done, the report notes, to understand the changes in women's health over the years and the complex maneuvers that the health care system demands of users. Hospitals, medical care systems, medicine, and medical education assume a standardized patient. Ideally this patient is separated from her social and psychological world and recreated (on a hospital bed, in a sterile atmosphere) as an object for the "science" of medicine. Peasant women, whose lives are only marginally acknowledged by such health care systems, use them only as a last resort. And when they do, invariably another woman, often the patient's mother, must make the difficult negotiations between her daughter's needs and a rigid alien institution. The need is urgent, the study concludes, "to understand why women find it so difficult and sometimes impossible to get access to and effectively use hospital facilities—what in fact lurks behind the familiar term 'absconders.' "[44] But the problem with medical care does not cease with access. A medical science that images its client as a well-nourished (Western) male, for instance, thinks of bone fractures as caused by force. It is not equipped, either conceptually or in terms of available technology, to deal with fractures common among less well-nourished older Indian women—fractures resulting from osteoporosis caused by long-term calcium deficiency and undernourishment. A health care system equipped to treat "fractures with tractions, pins and other operative procedures ... can at best put on a brave front and systematically evolve more 'effective' and 'sophisticated' measures to put women back

[43]Government of India, *Towards Equality: Report of the Committee on the Status of Women in India* (Delhi: Department of Social Welfare, 1974), p. 318.

[44]Veena Shatrugna et al., "Back Pain, the Feminine Affliction," *Economic and Political Weekly* 25:17, 1990, pp. WS2–6.

on their feet. But in the case of the recurring, even chronic fractures that result from osteoporosis, it is hardly an adequate response."[45]

The Partition

With the winning of independence in 1947 came the traumatic experience of the Partition. The many problems involved in the difficult history and politics of the relationship between the Hindu and Muslim communities were finally "resolved" in a decision to divide the states of Punjab and Bengal, in which the Muslims were a majority, to form West and East Pakistan (now Bangladesh). Thousands died in the terrible riots that erupted as refugees moved across the new borders to relocate themselves, and thousands more were left homeless and destitute. Some of the most powerful modern fiction, poetry, and films have dealt with the horror of the killings, the vulnerability of women, and the trauma of having, overnight, to leave beloved places and people. In *Subarnarekha*, Ritwick Ghatak's 1962 film, the tearing apart of a land and a history becomes a symbol for shattered dreams and for spaces that unhouse and outrage the self. He writes: "Literally, the problem I have taken up is that of the refugees. But when I use the word refugee, or displaced person, I do not mean only the evacuees of Bangladesh. . . . In these times all of us have lost our roots and are displaced; . . . in the beginning of the film one of the workers in the press says, 'Refugee! Who is not a refugee?' "[46] For many of those involved in the national movement, however, the Partition marked a failure—even a betrayal, etched deep by the pain and death that followed—of a national ideal, that of the integrity of the nation.

Writers and filmmakers have returned to the experience in work

---

[45]Ibid., p. WS–6. See also Shatrugna's "Experiencing Drudgery," which is a critical review of Patricia Jeffrey, Roger Jeffrey, and Andrew Lyon, *Labour Pains and Labour Power: Women and Child-bearing in India* (Delhi: Manohar, 1989), in *Economic and Political Weekly* 25:16, 1990, pp. 829–833. She writes: "The powerful colonial medical system had set itself the task of 'training' the *dais* [midwives] into the 'modern' and 'scientific' methods of delivering babies and this onslaught has continued for 150 years. . . . Though 'modern medicine' has sucessfully de-skilled the dai, there are no signs in Bijnor of the grand schemes of the health care system. The whole army of Primary Health Care (PHC), Maternal and Child Health (MCH) and Integrated Child Development Services (ICDS) personnel, so visible in bureaucratic plans and reports, are not to be found anywhere" (p. 830).
[46]Ritwick Ghatak, "*Subarnarekha*: Director's Statement, 1966," in *Ritwick Ghatak: Arguments/Stories,* ed. Ashish Rajadhyaksha and Amrit Gangar (Bombay: Research Centre for Cinema Studies, 1987), pp. 78–80.

after work, mesmerized by the anguish and savage irrationality of those times.[47] In her moving and widely translated "Kodunkatilpetta Orila" (A Leaf Caught in the Whirlwind), Lalithambika Antherjanam (1909–1989), whose "Praticaradevatha" (The Goddess of Revenge) appears in volume 1 of *Women Writing in India,* tells the story of a young woman, separated from her family and about to give birth to her first child, wandering through a refugee camp totally disoriented and crazed by fear and loneliness. Confounded by the pain of this young woman and the nightmarish savagery of the times, the narrative flails, for it does not have the resources to render her predicament, or indeed that of the country, intelligible. To put it more radically, Antherjanam's narrative—and this is a function of both its colonial genealogy and its present orientation—renders this crucial event in Indian history monstrous, irrational, intractable. All that the storyteller can do in the fictional languages available to her is lament the disruption of order, and as she does so, she cradles that lost child-mother and reinvents an older space, shared by the writer and the reader, in which a known and comforting ethical order holds.

Amrita Pritam, herself a refugee, turned to the eighteenth-century Sufi mystic Waris Shah, a poet loved by Hindus and Muslims alike and composer of the epic love poem "Heer-Ranjha" (one of the foundational romances of the Punjabi people), calling on him to speak from the grave:

> Once when a daughter of Punjab wept,
> Your pen drew out a million cries.
> A million daughters weep today,
> to you they turn their eyes.
> . . . .
> Heavy with venom were the winds
> that raged through the forests, poisoning
> the song of each branch into a snake.
> With sting upon sting the serpents
> struck a whole people dumb.
> A brief moment: and the limbs of Punjab turned blue.

---

[47]Films come most vividly to mind: in addition to *Subarnarekha,* Balraj Sahni's *Garam Hawa* and Govind Nihalani's *Tamas* deal with the Partition. For fiction we might turn to Kushwant Singh's *Train to Pakistan* and Saadat Hassan Manto's classic stories "Toba Tek Singh," "Tanda Ghost" (Cold Flesh), and "Naya Khanun" (The New Dispensation).

Threads snapped from their shuttles
and cut the song at the throat.

· ·

Branches laden with swings
split from the pipal trunk.
Boats stacked with goods
lost anchor and sank.

· ·

Only you can
speak from the depths of the grave
Waris Shah, to you I say:
add another page to your epic of love today.[48]

In some ways the most interesting figure in this poem is the "I," the poetic persona, female yet androgynous, whose lyric voice is saturated with national responsibility. Faced with the immense disorder that infects the world, the poet turns to Waris Shah in an ambiguous gesture that is at once an admission of her inadequacy and a clear affirmation of the writer as the bardic gatherer of a people. "We know the scene: there are people gathered round, and someone telling them a story. . . . They were not gathered before the story, it is the telling that gathers them. . . ."[49] Like Waris Shah, Amrita Pritam, too, gathers a people, for to speak is also to gather—and shape—an audience. She modulates a structure of feeling and binds her audience together into the unity imaged in her voice, to make the million cry today with the one. In a quick, bold gesture, sometimes read as feminist, that admits of no argument (and therefore also evades the contentious politics of women's place in this world), the poet peoples the land with its women: the daughters whose crying founds the community, and the women—at the spinning wheel, in gatherings, on swings—whose songs keep a sociality going. The task she sets out for herself as the country cries out for another gathering of its peoples forms the pivotal central stanzas of the poem (only a few lines of which have been translated here). In one she speaks of nature run riot and describes fields that have turned into graveyards, rivers flowing with poison, and winds heavy

---

[48]Our translation. A translation by Charles Brasch of the complete poem is available in Marian Arkin and Barbara Shollar, eds., *Longman Anthology of World Literature by Women 1875–1975,* (White Plains: Longman, 1989), pp. 626–627.

[49]Jean-Luc Nancy, *La Communauté désœuvrée* (Paris: Galilée, 1986), pp. 109–113, cited in Homi Bhabha ed., *Nation and Narration,* pp. 132–133.

with venom. The focus in the other is on the human world—a world of work, of play, of song and of viable human ties—that has been suddenly stilled. As in Antherjanam's story, the disorder is of impossibly monstrous proportions; the world has been denatured. However, to oppose the grotesque irrationality of the world in this way is also to imbue the poet-speaker (liberal, middle class, and, above all, nationalist) with a humane good sense, with moderation, responsibility, and a certain executive centrality. Only the poet (who, like the father-figure she invokes, speaks from a great, even magical, distance) can initiate the labor of salvage and reconstruction as she establishes a lineage and through her exhortation sets up the task for the nation—and a function for poetry.

Both of these important pieces stage a peculiarly post-colonial form of impotence that marks many of the texts enshrined in national(ist) canons today. Totally occluded, in fact delegitimated, in these moving (and to move, we must remember, is not only to shape the reader-subject affectively, but in the same gesture also to establish the value of that-which-moves him or her) texts that address the upheavals of the time, and in different ways take on the task of reestablishing an order, is the history and politics of the Partition and indeed the politics of gender that bears on it. Women, for instance, are pivotal figures in both texts, but they lose all marks of social difference and become emblematic of national spaces even as their worlds take on allegorical shapes. As they represent the Partition in "universalist" terms as outrage, and its effects as a metaphysical disorder that can be restored to equilibrium only by the artist (who is imaged as a magician-healer), these texts evade engagement with the specific conflicting identities and interests that comprise the event and address only what they designate as its effects. Consciously or unconsciously, such works lend the mystic authority of art to the project of mainstream nationalism, which becomes increasingly enmeshed in what we might call "mainstream internationalism." For the feminist reader today, texts such as these stage the powerful alliances through which the traditional languages of art and the new requirements of the nation-state rewrite and contain the question of women.

Women Writing the Nation

The forties and fifties concluded a long and grossly unhappy epoch of imperial dominance, but they were also a period in which new authorities were fashioned and consolidated, new repertoires of Indianness were composed and circulated, and a new imaginative geography was established. It is the ground laid out in these decades that has been extended, reworked, negotiated over, elaborated, and importantly contested right through the second half of the twentieth century. We believe that a feminist literary history must map the play of forces in the imaginative worlds in which women wrote, and read their literary initiatives not as an endless repetition of present-day rebellions or dreams of triumph, but as different attempts to engage with the force and the conflict of the multiple cross-cutting determinations of those worlds. Equally important, such a history should be able to read literary texts not merely as achieving aesthetic effects, but as addressing real tasks in a real world. It should read the schemes of the nation not only along their grain to comprehend and savor the resolutions they propose, but also against that grain to investigate those compositions. Women's texts force us to confront, even as they help us chart, the awesome historical texturing that situates and governs feminist initiatives in our time. Read thus, stories and poems that might otherwise appear to be concerned only with an existential agony or with spiritual endurance lay bare their politics, as do the universalist declarations of the autonomy of art that repeatedly appeared in the literary manifestos of the fifties. We find that these are engaged in negotiation, debate, and protest, invariably in areas that directly concern or are closely related to what it meant to be a woman in each historical moment.

As we shall find in the sections that follow in which we trace figures and themes across the century, the narratives of the nation drew on, but reinflected, powerful earlier articulations as they recreated the world. We focus on three long-running themes that will help consolidate our understanding of gender and the nation-in-process, and provide the narrative and analytical contexts for much of the literature translated in this volume and for the major break that took place in the seventies with the third phase of the modern women's movement. We will look closely at the Swadeshi strand of the nationalist movement and the questions of caste and communalism that emerge there; the Progressive Writers' Associations and the issues of gender and class raised in those contexts; and, finally, at liberal electoralism as it shaped the women's movement of the twenties and thirties. We try, as we trace these histories, to show how each sculpted the imaginary contours of gender. Our attempt is both to create a context that will bring women's writing—the themes that emerge, the formal languages that are forged—into the mainstream of the cultural politics of each period, and to provide the reader with a sense of the difficult but challenging terrain that the women's movement of the seventies inherited.

Swadeshi: An Interpretative as Much as a Political Contest

Though it was singularly short-lived and its political style later disparaged as "extremist" by some sections in the Congress party, the Swadeshi ("of-one's-own-country") movement (1905–1908) played a definitive role in the shaping of a national culture. Swadeshi was demonstrably as much a cultural as a political contest to represent, repossess, and inhabit a territory that had been meticulously and systematically alienated under colonial rule and to enfranchise an "Indian self." Colonial formulations were critically confronted in various domains as the imaginative contours of the country were refashioned and nationalist aspirations articulated. The politics of petitioning that had marked most nineteenth-century initiatives were rejected in favor of direct challenge and what was called "constructive Swadeshi": support for Indian industries, active village work, and a system of national education that emphasized regional languages and the importance of acquiring technical expertise even as it mounted a critique of the curricular and administrative priorities of colonial education. The reinscriptions that affected the meanings of everyday life were without doubt the most significant of the changes that took place, but the research that will allow us to trace those subtle shifts is yet to be done. However, even at the level of what might more conventionally be recognized as "culture," the achievements were impressive. History was reinterpreted, traditions invented. Existing festivals were charged with passionate new meanings and new ones were created; fairs were held; songs that drew on the forms and rhythms of folk poetry were composed; crafts that had almost become extinct were retrieved; and attempts were made to support artisans, to draw their products once again into the mainstream of national culture, and to renew village economies that had been badly hit by colonial rule. The aggressive publishing initiatives that Bangalore Nagaratnamma and the Vavilla Press took in the first decades of the twentieth century could hardly have been envisaged outside the contexts created by the Swadeshi movement. Painters who had for decades struggled to master the techniques of water color and oil painting as well as the proportions and perspective of Western art, and to represent Indian landscapes or figures within those visual regimes, now turned to various schools of indigenous miniature painting and to folk art for inspiration.[50] Poets drew on the imagery and meter of rural ballad singers, while the country settings of those lyrics merged with the romantic landscapes of Sanskrit literature and were infused with an unmistakable new authority as they were rehabilitated in the literature of the period. Philosophers, literateurs, political theorists, art historians, and indeed scholars in almost every field began to search for an essentially Indian genius, an Indian mode of perception and thought that was often structured in critical counterpoint to the "mind of Europe." As early as 1909 Gandhi had argued in *Hind Swaraj* (Indian Self-Government) that colonialism was an inevitable consequence of Western notions of progress and development. If the nationalist project in India was not to be limited to the replacement of one set of rulers with another—"English rule without Englishmen"—it would have to critically reconsider the goals and values of Western civilization, which were materialist, exploitative, and based on thoughtless contravention of the laws of nature.[51] Clearly what was being created in these inspired and energetic years was a new India that not only filled the measure of the political imperative of the time to the brim but also spilled over. As some of the texts in volume 1 of *Women Writing in India* indicate, and as we shall find in the discussion that follows, gender was a key dimension of that new creation.

Prominent among the discursive strategies developed by this emerging nationalism were ones through which a reformulated Hinduism—

---

[50]Geeta Kapur explores the significance of the earlier moment for what might be thought of as a new art history in "Ravi Varma: Representational Dilemmas of a Nineteenth-Century Indian Painter," *Journal of Arts and Ideas,* 17–18, June 1989, pp. 59–80. The result of Swadeshi initiatives in the visual arts is perhaps best explored in the writings of E. B. Havell, the enthusiastic British advocate of Indian art; Okakura Kakuso, the Japanese art historian who argued for a sort of pan-Asian indigenism; and the brilliant theoretician A. K. Coomaraswamy, who not only pointed out the inappropriateness of judging Indian art by Western Renaissance conventions, but argued that there are fundamental epistemological and ontological differences between Eastern and Western thought. For a sensitive and critical account of this movement see Subramanyan, *The Living Tradition.*
[51]M. K. Gandhi, *The Collected Works of Mahatma Gandhi,* vol. 10: *November 1909–March 1911* (Delhi: Publications Division, Ministry of Information and Broadcasting, Government of India, 1963), pp. 7–65. The critique of the Enlightenment and of modern civilization that was developed in *Hind Swaraj* and the metanarratives set up there would be returned to repeatedly by the nationalist movement and later by ecological, feminist, and epistemological initiatives.

one that soon began to be thought of even in secular nationalist circles as an "authentic Indianness" or as "the Indian tradition"—was set up as the ground on which a national identity was to be forged. Romila Thapar and others have pointed out that the past is very selectively drawn upon and that the historical experiences of religious groups are tendentiously interpreted when such imagined religious communities are shaped.[52] The ambiguities and contradictions of history are smoothed over into well-shaped traditions as the logic of present-day designs is projected onto a previous age. The evidence of history, these scholars demonstrate, has little part to play in the theaters wherein the past is conveniently redeployed into "traditions" that endorse contemporary political configurations.

Implicit in the establishment of the Indian tradition was the elaboration and endorsement of an Orientalist image of Indian society as essentially religious and, in the setting up of Hindu India as norm, an "othering" of Islam. Both tendencies drew on a logic that had been fed and fattened through many years of colonial rule. British administrators not only used religion as the basis for the analysis of Indian society, history, and politics, but also considered the religious predilections (nearly always represented as irrational, even bigoted) of the people as the explanation for a variety of "problems" that confronted the colonial government. These discourses had a double effect. They contained the threat that popular uprisings ("riots") posed to an administrative order and provided a reassurance that an enlightened government would always be necessary since the natives' primitive passions and incurable factionalism made them incapable of managing their own affairs. In distinct contrast to the master narratives of the Enlightenment, which were predicated on reason and progress, the singularly enduring master narrative for India was religion and antagonisms based on religious or "communal" identities.

These narratives were given a new lease on life by the nationalists. Aurobindo Ghosh's (1872–1950) pamphlet *Bhawani Mandir,* 1905, for example, envisaged the building of national unity through the "link of a single and living religious spirit" that could eventually *"Aryanize* the world,"* but would in the meantime "promote sympathy between the

---

[52]Romila Thapar, "Imagined Religious Communities: Ancient History and the Modern Search for a Hindu Identity," *Modern Asian Studies,* 23:2, 1989, pp. 209–231.

zamindars and the peasants and heal all discords."[53] In his 1917 treatise *Hindutva*, V. D. Savarkar developed the notion of the "Hindu Rashtra" which would not only fight the colonial rulers to restore Hindu self-confidence and pride, but also would embody the glories of an ancient Hindu civilization and contain what was described as the growing threat from an Islam that demanded transnational loyalties. By the mid-twenties, quite explicitly Hindu symbols, myths, and rituals pervaded the idiom of Congress nationalism.

Literary texts played a significant role in the growth of a communal mode of thinking. Bankimchandra Chatterjee (1838–1894), the Bengali novelist idolized by the Swadeshi movement, had referred to the Muslims as *yavanas* (foreigners) and repeatedly asserted that Bengal had lost her independence with the beginning of Muslim rule in the thirteenth century, and not in 1757 when the British won the Battle of Plassey. He "emphasised the harmful effects of Mughal centralization on regional life and liberally distributed abuse of Muslims in his later historical novels, particularly *Anandamath*, *Debi Chaudhurani*, and *Sitaram*."[54] James Tod's (1782–1835) tales of Rajput chivalry and honor and his accounts of the valor with which they resisted Mughal invaders acquired new currency as they were recreated in stories, poems, plays, and even children's books in nearly every Indian language. Muslim writers with similar ideologies soon began to glorify the periods and the figures denigrated in this way and spoke of the lost grandeur of Islam on a world scale.[55] The periodization of history proposed by James Mill (1773–1836) in 1817 was repeatedly drawn upon to set up a Vedic India, characterized as essentially Indian (and of course essentially upper-caste Hindu), which was contrasted to the medieval period of Muslim rule when the country had gone into material and spiritual decline.[56] Kalyanamma's (1894–1965) "Suryasthamana" (Sunset), in-

---

[53]Cited in Sumit Sarkar, p. 146.
[54]Ibid., p. 84.
[55]Ibid., p. 85.
[56]"The teaching of Indian history in schools and colleges from a basically communal point of view made a major contribution to the rise and growth of communalism. For generations, almost from the beginning of the modern school system, communal interpretations of history of varying degrees of virulence were propogated, first by imperialist writers, then by others. So deep was the penetration . . . that even sturdy nationalists accepted, however unconsciously, some of its digits" (Bipan Chandra et al., *India's Struggle for Independence 1857–1947* [Delhi: Viking, 1988], p. 411).

cluded in volume 1 of *Women Writing in India,* documents the aggressively anti-Muslim idiom in which some strands of nationalism were dyed, and reveals the powerful way in which women and the women's question were woven into that configuration. In that text, the Rajput warrior Raja Mansingh, who had given his sister Jodhbai in marriage to the Mughal emperor Akbar, is confronted one day by a woman (later revealed to be Jodhbai) who accuses him of having stained his sword with his mother's blood and of having betrayed the country and its women. She asks, "How could you sell a Rajput woman—brought up to worship her motherland, taught from a tender age to worship Lord Shiva devotedly—to an outsider in exchange for riches and power? Will you ever understand how that touch sears me?"[57] Communalism is not simply a prejudice that can be cast aside at will. It, like Orientalism and racism, is a kind of logic, a regime of truth deeply embedded in the cultural schemes of the nation.[58]

What was taking place in the twenties and thirties was not simply, as some nationalist thinkers have argued, the unfortunate hardening of hostilities and prejudices nurtured by the British policy of divide and rule, but a gradual (and political) reformulation of these religions, and of the subject-selves they interpellated. The historical beginnings of what is one of the most durable and adaptive configurations in recent history awaits inventive excavation.[59] One of the themes a reader might trace through the stories and poems collected in this volume is the new forms in which these questions appear in the literature of an independent India.

Subhadra Kumari Chauhan's (1904–1948) story "Ekadasi" (A Woman's Fast), also in volume 1 of *Women Writing in India,* for instance, can be read as an allegory about satyagraha and its essentially feminine,

---

[57]Kalyanamma, "Suryasthamana" (Sunset), *Women Writing in India: 600 B.C. to the Present,* vol. 1: *600 B.C. to the Early Twentieth Century,* ed. Susie Tharu and K. Lalita (New York: Feminist Press, 1991), pp. 395–400.

[58]Bipan Chandra et al. define communalism or communal ideology as a belief that all who follow the same religion have the same political, economic, and social interests, and that religious identity is therefore primary and more important than that of region, nation, or class. The interests of one community or group are initially defined as totally different and even divergent from those of another, and later as "mutually incompatible, antagonistic and hostile"—as Other. Bipan Chandra et al., *India's Struggle for Independence* (Delhi: Viking, 1988), pp. 398–399.

[59]Unfortunately, Gyanendra Pandey's *The Construction of Communalism in Colonial North India* (Delhi: Oxford University Press, 1990) appeared too late for us to make use of the genealogy of communalism that Pandey traces.

and equally importantly, essentially Indian power. But the story is also a conversion narrative in which the Muslim husband and the Christian doctor (both of whom are portrayed as sensitive, ethical, and socially responsible people) are moved into a speechless acknowledgment of the deep spiritual authority of this upper-caste Hindu woman who could marry a Muslim, but will not abandon her religion and its ritual fast even when her life is at stake.[60]

The figure Subhadra Kumari sculpts is the prototype for the lovingly etched upper-caste mother-in-law in Shivani's spirited story, "Dadi" (Grandmother), in this volume. But the distance between the two figures is critical and is emblematic of the renotation of the social Imaginary of the nation that took place in the forties and fifties. Subhadra Kumari's position is actively proselytizing, her creed one that she has to defend, its opponents people worth "assimilating" into the new imagined community, and the act of assimilation itself is thematic in her narrative. In Shivani's world the new incarnation of Subhadra Kumari's protagonist has acquired an uncontested authority. Tradition is notated as upper-caste Hindu, with a lightness of touch that suggests the mode is one that can be taken for granted. The deeply religious mother-in-law is portrayed not as representative of a powerful spiritual force, but simply as having a mature *good sense,* and a *human warmth* that her squabbling daughters-in-law have lost. The toys she crafts for her grandchildren and the games she plays with them are "traditional" but her intuitive sense of value, of education, and of child rearing is impeccably "modern." She is clearly more humane and certainly more secular than any other force the narrative acknowledges, and the reader identifies with her emotionally and intellectually. Though she hesitates to eat the food that the new cook of uncertain caste dishes up, when he is exposed as a Pakistani spy she is the one who rescues him from

---

[60]Narratives, both fictional and autobiographical, that describe conversion from Hinduism to Christianity—which nearly always was also a narrative that traced the transformation, or, more accurately, the *emergence,* of an ethical self—are among the first modern prose narratives in almost every Indian language. An interested reader might turn to Hannah Catherine Mullens's (1826–1861) *Phulmani O Karunar Bibaran* (The Story of Phulmani and Karuna), Krupa Sattianadan's (1862–1894) *Saguna,* or Lakshmibai Tilak's (1868–1936) *Smriti Chitre* (Memory Sketches)—all in volume 1 of *Women Writing in India*—and Pandita Rambai Saraswati's (1855–1922) *My Testimony* (Kedgaon: Mukti Mission Press, 1917) for examples of the more sophisticated women's texts in this genre. There is a sense of course in which we ought to read "Ekadasi" as a counterconversion narrative.

the uncivilized frenzy of the mob and hands him over, as the law of the land demands, to the police.

The protagonist in Manjul Bhagat's "Bebeji," also presented in this collection, is strikingly similar. Though her sons find her unreasonable and old fashioned, she has the sensitivity to realize and the courage to acknowledge that her "real" relations are the lower-caste people who live in the shack next to her house. Pratibha Ray's "Kambala" (The Blanket), also included here, can be regarded as belonging to this genre, as can many other texts from the late seventies and the eighties.

The reader will not have failed to notice that these narratives pose the problem from the point of view of the upper-caste, middle-class or upper-middle-class woman who is past middle age and is often a grandmother, and whose defining characteristic is that she holds on to her "traditional" and essentially Indian way of life. It is with this figure, who is initially misunderstood but comes into her own as the story works up to its resolution, that the reader identifies. And through this identification the reader embarks on a subtle new education that will rewrite her into the elaborate and demanding dimensions of this conservative-national role, for these stories indicate that it is the moral authority of figures such as Dadi and Bebeji that not only will hold the nation together but will carry it safely into the modern era.

Narratives such as these symbolically house various marginal groups (Muslims, the lower castes, the poor) in a hegemonic architecture that appears to extend itself to accommodate them, yet the same gesture— euphemistically referred to as assimilation—also marginalizes and contains them. An upper-caste Hindu centrality is consolidated and acquires increasingly powerful currency as it edges all other identities to the margins and begins to operate as a national and often "secular" identity.[61] What also takes place almost unnoticed, but extremely efficiently, as this identity is produced and empowered, is a delegitimation of the lower castes (and indeed a delegitimation of caste itself as a problem). Those who are not upper caste or Hindu are written out of

---

[61]This is the genealogy of secular nationalism in India. The history of secularism in its Occidental homeland is similarly battle scarred. The white, Protestant, bourgeois male was set up as norm and his interests entrenched through a brutal process of exploitation (at home and in the colonies) and ruthless homogenization (millions were massacred, their cultures destroyed, their systems of knowledge delegitimated) in what has been wittily described in a phraseology that conflates the economic with the cultural as "propriation—as in proper-ing, as in the proper name (patronymic) or property" (Spivak, p. 91).

the story despite the fact that they comprise the majority of the people in the country. Women, it would appear, are among the principal agents for these transactions through which the social Imaginary is consolidated.[62] And the female subject is required to transmute herself as she measures up to the subtle politics of this crucial function.[63] Shivani, like Ashapurna Debi (b. 1909) before her, and many other contemporary women writers who attempt to manage a shift into the modern without disturbing the old order in any radical way, are among the best-selling novelists in their languages. Many of their works have been made into equally popular films.

Hamsa Wadkar, a singer who became a well-known film star, was born in 1923, the same year as Shivani. But if figures such as the mother-in-law in Shivani's story are the stable central pillars of the new social Imaginary, Hamsa Wadkar's compelling autobiography—which well-schooled middle-class readers have sometimes found ill-formed and exaggerated—documents what it is like to be used and outcast(e) by those powers. Written in the seventies, the autobiography deals primarily with Hamsa Wadkar's life in the forties and fifties. Her yearning for a relationship in which she is valued as a person remains unfulfilled, for each man in her life—her uncle, her husband, and the lovers in whom she places her hopes—relates to her ultimately in a script that is endorsed by tradition and has no room for her new, individualist requirements. When she eventually manages to bring a pregnancy to term and have the baby she has not for many years been allowed to have (since her career would be interrupted and her figure affected), there is no social space in which she can relate to her child as she wants to. Her aspirations for independence and for some control over the money she earned leave her, toward the end of her life, lonely and isolated in a world that seems to have no other way of acknowledging or addressing those desires. If the social Imaginary comes together and holds secure around Shivani's upper-caste family women, for Hamsa Wadkar, who speaks from outside that architecture, nothing

---

[62]We are grateful to R. Srivatsan, who helped us articulate this connection between the "rise" of communalism, the suppression/elision of the lower castes, and the new role of women in that social Imaginary.

[63]For an extremely important discussion of how the poetry of the Bhakti movement was deflected and charged with new energy in nationalist ideologies, see Kumkum Sangari, *Mirabai and the Spiritual Economy of Bhakti,* Occasional Papers on History and Society, 2nd ser., no. 28 (Delhi: Nehru Memorial Museum and Library, 1990).

holds together, not even her self, and sometimes not even her story. The nation has no space in its centers for such women, no patience with their dreams.

Progressive Writers' Associations and the Indian People's Theater Association

From about the mid-thirties onwards Progressive Writers' Associations (PWAs), which were groups of writers with socialist sympathies, were formed all over the country. The literature, drama, painting, film, music, and even dance of every region bear the impress of their ideas. Several writers whose work is represented in this volume were important PWA members, and several others were deeply influenced by them. Among the women whose names appear and reappear in the recently published volumes of documents from the movement are Rasheed Jahan, Ismat Chugtai, Usha Dutt, Razia Sajjad Zaheer, Arpita Das, Sheila Bhatia, Binata Roy, Uma Chakravarthy, Sarojini Naidu (1879–1949), Kamaladevi Chattopadhyay (1903–1989), Siddiqa Begum Sevharvi, and Anil D'Silva, who was the first general secretary of the Indian People's Theater Association (IPTA).[64] Other sources indicate the involvement of the novelists Mahasweta Devi, Sulekha Sanyal, and Anupama Niranjana, while recent studies of women in the Tebhaga and the Telangana struggles record the major initiatives of women in those movements.

In the foreword to his two-volume compilation of the "chronicles and documents" of the Marxist cultural movement in India, Sudhi Pradhan, who was involved in the movement from its inception, describes the association as drawing its inspiration from the anti-imperialist struggle in India as well as from writers and intellectuals in Europe, America, and Asia who had, with the shadow of the Second World War looming large, been organizing themselves on the "basis of resistance to imperialism and fascism and on behalf of

---

[64] Anil D'Silva was one of the principal ideologues and organizers of the movement in its initial stages. In 1945 she wrote a book on women in China and was instrumental in the translation and publication of a collection of stories by Ding Ling. In 1946 she was removed from the post of secretary of the IPTA, apparently on charges of sexual misconduct. A brief sketch of this spirited woman who was considered a problem by the predominantly male leadership is presented in Sudhi Pradhan, ed., *The Marxist Cultural Movement in India*, vol. 1: *Chronicles and Documents, 1936–1947* (Calcutta: Mrs. Shanti Pradhan, 1979), pp. xx–xxi.

peace."[65] The Indian PWA sent a manifesto, signed by such distinguished figures as Rabindranath Tagore, Saratchandra Chatterjee, Munshi Premchand, P. C. Roy, Jawaharlal Nehru, and Nandalal Bose, to the second congress of the International Writers' Association which was held in London in 1936, denouncing the "methods resorted to by Italy in the subjugation of Abyssinia" and declaring that they were "against the participation of India in any imperialist war."[66]

Their program on the home front embodied their commitment to a new literature in India that would "deal with the basic problems of our existence today—the problems of hunger and poverty, social backwardness and political subjection." Art was not to remain a poignant record of suffering: "All that arouses in us the critical spirit . . . we accept as progressive."[67] The range of activities undertaken in different parts of the country by units of the PWA and its sister organization, the IPTA (which was formed in 1943), are an impressive record of the excitement aroused by this important new movement in the arts. In Bengal students and others wrote and staged plays, organized discussions and book clubs, and set up cultural troupes that toured the villages; demands for performances of Bijan Bhattacharya's (1917–1978) *Navanna* (New Harvest), which portrayed Bengali peasant life during the terrible famines of the early forties, came from all parts of the country. The PWA in Andhra held a *sahitya pathasala* (teach-in) in which the entire history of literature in India was critically studied and re-evaluated. Special initiatives were taken to learn and use the traditions of ballad singing and folk drama in each area. Though their own upbringing and social sanctions often militated against their participation, women were actively involved. Kondapalli Koteswaramma (b. 1925) wrote poems for children about the lives of peasants and artisans, while the rich timbre of Ch. Kamalamma's (b. 1926) voice and her emotional rendering of the new songs made her a popular figure in the cultural wing of the Communist party. Moturi Udayam (b. 1924) composed *burrakathas* and acted in them. (Burrakatha is a popular folk narrative of Andhra Pradesh that depicts the lives of ordinary people in song and dance. The *burra* is a clay percussion instrument.)

In Lucknow, Rasheed Jahan and others wrote stories and staged plays

---

[65]Sudhi Pradhan, ed. *The Marxist Cultural Movement in India,* vol. 2: *Chronicles and Documents 1947–1958* (Calcutta: Navana, 1982), p. 6.
[66]Pradhan, vol. 1, p. vi.
[67]Ammended manifesto, adopted in 1938. Pradhan, vol. 1, p. 21.

they had written or translated themselves. The Maharashtrian unit translated and performed the Chinese writer Ding Ling's *Strange Meeting,* and accounts of her cultural troupe and its "Big Drum Singing" were circulated and discussed. K. A. Abbas, a Bombay novelist and playwright, produced a play based on the true story of a young Muslim girl from Kerala, but set in Uttar Pradesh, Abbas's native state. In this play, Zubeida, moved by the dirges sung in the funeral processions that passed her house during the cholera epidemic of 1944, and roused by the songs of volunteers doing relief work, flings her purdah off and joins them. Like the people she tries to help, Zubeida dies because there is not enough cholera vaccine to go around. Performed in many parts of the country, and as popular among male workers as it was among women, *Zubeida* is in many ways emblematic of the kind of space reserved for women's issues in socialist ideology. While the cultural schemes of high nationalism rewrote and contained the questions about the oppression of women that had been raised by the nineteenth-century social reform movements, socialists kept those concerns alive and continued to endorse them. Yet, as the plot in *Zubeida* clearly demonstrates, these issues remained marginal in an analysis that considered the "woman question" a social problem that would be resolved with the overthrow of capitalism. Zubeida can cast her purdah aside in an "inspired" human gesture and move so easily into the public world only because the politics of purdah and its deep-seated roots in the social Imaginary, have been rendered invisible, and indeed mystified, by Abbas's text. As Zubeida's life and death are reworked into the schemes of class analysis, purdah is reduced to an attitude, a habit, a prejudice, social or personal, that will dissolve when more primary questions are posed and more radical commitments made. Socialist ideologies force open the idealist, upper-caste resolutions of nationalism with the question of exploitation. But class analysis of this kind finds little place within the terms of its strict analytic history to acknowledge other histories through which religion, class, caste, gender, and even secularism took shape in India, and has difficulty rendering the contemporary politics of gender intelligible or open for intervention.

An amusing story told by Moturi Udayam about one of their performances speaks volumes about the unacknowledged underlying scenarios of socialism:

> "We did *lambadi* (tribal) dances and collected subscriptions. We used to sing the songs women sang while pounding grain. One of them went like this:

Plant a seed on barren land
The couple is cold and there is no fun
ah-*ha,* ah-*ha,* ah-*ha.*
Who is there to pick the jasmine in the forest?
What can a woman do with a weak old man?
ah-*ha,* ah-*ha,* ah-*ha.*

In Tadipatri, ten thousand people came for a meeting. We had learnt this song and we were pounding away and singing it vigorously. Suddenly Hanumantha Rao roared out like a lion, "Stop that song!" We nearly died of fright! "Don't you have any sense? What do you think? What is that song you are singing? Get off the stage. An old man is of no use. Is that what your *mahila sangam* [women's organization] is all about?"[68]

In Rasheed Jahan's "Woh" (That One), presented in this volume, we witness the crumbling of the secure world of a young upper-middle-class woman as she is confronted with the life of "that one," a disfigured and diseased prostitute in purdah who inisits on claiming her as a friend. It is the nameless middle-class woman, the story implies, who must lift the veil of her consciousness and find the resources to look this figure from the real world straight in the eye. Razia Sajjad Zaheer's "Neech" (Lowborn) also centers its narrative on the privileged middle-class woman and the prejudices she must learn to set aside to relate, in the phrasing of the title, to those "below" her. The education of the protagonist is also a reversal of roles and a revision of the meaning of *neech,* for as the story builds up to its denouement it becomes clear that it is from the ordinary fruit seller that the middle-class woman must draw her strength.

A world of difference lies between these socialist efforts at "connection" and reorientation and the hegemonic schemes for the assimilation of other classes that we find in the writers inspired by a conservative nationalism. Yet we may ask more difficult questions: What are the dimensions in which the working-class woman is imagined in stories such as Rasheed Jahan's or Razia Sajjad Zaheer's? With what tools is this figure being sculpted and to what purpose? The focus of these narratives remains the middle-class protagonist and her moral awak-

---

[68]Stree Shakti Sanghatana, p. 191. Several women activists in the Telangana People's Struggle (1946–1951) were members of cultural squads and speak of their activities in their oral autobiographies. See especially pp. 45–54, 121–137, 180–197. The book also reproduces a rare early photograph of a burrakatha squad.

ening to social responsibility and therefore also to citizenship. The "other woman"—the prostitute, the working-class woman—is a figure cut to the measure of this middle-class woman's requirement that is also, we must not forget, the requirement of the nation. These stories may be about those at the margins, but they are, all the same, stories of the center, told by the center. In distinct contrast to the center that emerges in M. K. Indira's *Phaniyamma* or in stories such as those of Shivani and Ashapurna Debi, in which a heroic protagonist "purifies" tradition and manages the shift into the modern while maintaining the authority of the old order, the center imaged in stories such as those of Rasheed Jahan is one that will have to be radically re-written if its commitments to the people and to social justice are to be fulfilled. Yet the axis of power that their narratives endorse is similar to those upheld by writers such as Ashapurna Debi and Shivani. Not surprisingly, though many of the protagonists in these stories are women, the questions raised pose few threats to a patriarchal order. In fact, there is a sense in which the education of these middle-class protagonists is also an education into the strict paradigms that define gender in the reformist schemes of the progressive writers' movements.

All the same, women of all classes repeatedly acknowledge that their involvement in trade union or peasant struggles transformed their lives and opened up possibilities they would not perhaps have dreamt about outside those contexts. Yet as the oral autobiographies of women involved in the Telangana Peoples' Struggle document, the liberation they experienced was not unqualified. Women were engaged in battle on several fronts. The struggle against landlords was publicly acknowledged and analyzed as political, but there were also many other, never completely articulated engagements in which issues that specifically concerned them as women were thematic.[69] Some of these questions are cleverly broached in Siddiqa Begum Sevharvi's "Tare Laraz Rahe Hai" (The Stars Are Trembling), included in this volume, a rambling, loosely structured story that smuggles several important themes in with its breezy, casual style. The brother who avidly supports his younger sister's education is outraged when he finds his other sister teaching his wife to read, partly because he suspects that the growing friendship between the two women might radically change his world.

---

[69]Stree Shakti Sanghatana discuss this at length in the chapter "Writing the History of Women in Struggles" and in the afterword in *We Were Making History*.

In Deepti Khandelwal's (b. 1930) fiction, the vitality lost by the middle classes can still be found in the people who work the land, though they, too, are systematically being broken down. Though it was written in 1956, Sulekha Sanyal's little-known novel *Nabankur* (The Seedling) reads like a much later text, for it turns the tools of class analysis onto the story of a girl growing up in rural Bengal during the great famine and communal riots of the forties. Sulekha Sanyal not only transforms that analysis but also rewrites the question of class as she frames the issue of gender. It is a compelling novel, hardly in tune with its time.

By the mid-fifties, the PWAs and the active theater movement of the IPTA had declined. While individual artists—poets, novelists, and theater and film people—continued to wield influence in the new world, the progressive *movement* dwindled. Commentators suggest different causes: the setting up of new academies under state patronage and the drawing of many activists into national programs for literature and theater; the Partition and the breakup of the important Urdu contingent in the Progressive Writers' movement; and the lack, after the early fifties, of a clear line of orientation.[70]

Women's Organizations and Liberal Nationalist Feminism

Nineteenth-century concerns with women's "uplift" continue to underwrite government policies and initiatives even in the nineties. These concerns include the fight against such social practices as dowry, child marriage, purdah, and the prohibition of widow remarriage. They also call for an education that would enable women to perform their roles as wives, mothers, and school teachers in an enlightened and socially useful mode. By the thirties, women's organizations at the national level had begun to make their presence felt not only in relation to these issues, but also politically in the demand for equal rights. The question of women's suffrage had been raised as early as 1917, when a delegation from the Women's India Association (WIA) consisting of Sarojini Naidu, Annie Besant, Dr. Joshi, Begum Hasrat Mohani, and fourteen

---

[70]Vasudha Dalmia Ludertz, "Brecht in Hindi: The Poetics of Response," *Journal of Arts and Ideas* 16, 1988, pp. 59–72, provides an interesting critical history of the theater in the twentieth century. She also points to the decline of the progressive movements and suggests that their concerns reemerged in the seventies in the new involvement with Brechtian theater. See also Aijaz Ahmad, "Some Reflections on Urdu," *Seminar* 359, July 1989, pp. 23–29.

others placed a memorandum before the secretary of state, Edwin Montagu, asking that women be enfranchised on the same basis as men. The demand was not mentioned in the Montagu-Chelmsford report of 1918, but the entries in his diary are telling.[71] Women raised the issue again at the provincial and national conferences of the Congress party and the Muslim League in 1917 and 1918 and were able to win a large measure of support. When the issue was finally placed before these groups in the early twenties, the provincial legislatures voted overwhelmingly in favor of enfranchising women on the same basis as the men.[72]

The All India Women's Conference (AIWC), which had initially been organized in 1927 by the Women's India Association as a national conference on women's education, reconstituted itself into a permanent national body. The shift in the emphasis of women's demands from social reforms to franchise seemed to feed straight into a framework of policy and government. The AIWC established branches all over India and entrusted subcommittees with the task of influencing government policy on such wide-ranging subjects as women workers, rural reconstruction, national education, social service, women's health and employment, untouchability, and literacy. The committees studied the questions (often undertaking extensive field visits and consulting with experts), made recommendations to the government, and de-

---

[71]Montagu's diary records that the delegation consisted of "one very nice looking doctor from Bombay" and speaks patronizingly of Sarojini Naidu as a "revolutionary at heart" and of Margaret Cousins as "a well-known suffragette from London . . . a theosophist and one of Mrs Besant's crowd." Later that day he raised the issue somewhat flippantly with landowners from Coorg and was amused at their reaction. Edwin S. Montagu, *An Indian Diary,* ed. Venetia Montagu (London: W. Heinemann Ltd., 1930), pp. 115–116.

[72]Western scholars, feminists included, invariably chronicle these developments dismissively. The Indian support for women's suffrage, Jana Matson Everett comments, "served to increase the self-esteem of Indians interacting with the British. In their advocacy of women's suffrage, the Indian elite were demonstrating that their society was more progressive than British society which had only recently enfranchised women after a campaign of 50 years. The elite were also showing how enlightened they themselves were. . . . Jinnah's claim that Muslim leaders from other countries whom he had met in London also supported women's suffrage suggested he was trying to show that non-Western record on the issue of female emancipation was superior to that of the British." *Women and Social Change in India* (1981; reprint, Delhi: Heritage Publishers, 1985), p. 105.

manded that women be represented in all official bodies in which decisions that might affect them were made.[73]

With the controversy that arose over the appointment of the all-white—and of course all-male, though no one objected to that at the time—Simon Commission in 1927 to draft the new constitution, the question of women's suffrage came up again. Women activists who chose to cooperate with the commission accepted the proposal of partial franchise (which would be even more restricted for women than for men) based on property and formal education, but made what the Congress party regarded as a controversial demand that there should be legislative seats reserved for women. Women's presence in decision-making bodies would be essential for the shaping of educational and social policy, Radhabai Subbaroyan, a member of the Madras legislative council and an active member of the AIWC, argued. Most members of the WIA and the AIWC boycotted the Simon Commission and met to draft a joint memorandum that demanded "1) The removal of all sex disqualifications [in voting, candidacy, public office, or employment]. 2) The immediate acceptance of the principle of Adult Suffrage," and unequivocally refused "to accept special expedients for securing the representation of women in Legislative and Administrative Institutions."[74] As Amrit Kaur, one of its principal architects, pointed out, the memorandum not only endorsed the policy of the Indian National Congress as laid out in the Nehru Report of 1928, but also was in the interests of women, besides being "the only system which would, generally speaking, give a voice in the governance of the country to the poor who constitute India's main population."[75]

---

[73]Perhaps the most detailed account of the work of the AIWC in this period is to be found in Kamaladevi Chattopahdyay, *Indian Women's Battle for Freedom* (Delhi: Abhinav Publications, 1983). Kamaladevi's account is clearly celebrative and was written as a response to what she experienced as the dismissal of the earlier movement by uninformed latter-day feminists. A reader might find that the wide range of subjects taken up and the different positions embodied in the much earlier Shyam Kumari Nehru, ed., *Our Cause: A Symposium by Indian Women* (Allahabad: Kitabistan, 1938) make it a more richly textured document of that period.

[74]Amrit Kaur, "Women under the New Constitution," in Shyam Kumari Nehru, pp. 366–367.

[75]Kaur, p. 367. Gandhi's almost weekly correspondence with Amrit Kaur over the period of three or four years when the issue of franchise was being debated clearly demonstrates the close personal interest he took in the AIWC's discussions. A letter written from Wardha, dated 23 October 1935 reads: "My dear

But others clearly did not think that women would be elected if they simply competed on an equal basis with men, or that the granting of universal adult suffrage would necessarily result in equality for women. Women who did not acknowledge these facts, Radhabai Subbaroyan felt, were "far removed from the realities of the situation."[76] Muthulakshmi Reddi, after years of working with the intensely nationalist WIA, and even after her much-publicized resignation from the Legislative Assembly in 1930 when Gandhi was arrested, continued to hold that there were contradictions between the interests of women and the interests of Congress nationalists. She felt that women were being forced into a situation in which their interests were being subsumed in the designs of the Congress party. Men, she wrote, had actually "welcomed the women into the struggle and honoured them because they wanted their help at this moment, but when women contest for seats in elections, when women come forward to contest places of honour and emoluments, it will be a quite different matter; it will be a fight between the sexes. Further, under our present social system it will be an unequal fight. . . ." Reserved seats for women, she argued, should not be thought of as a favor, or indeed as some vestigial form of undemocratic privilege. They were only a means by which the present inequalities under which women struggled could be acknowledged. Further, "while under the system of adult franchise on equal terms the theoretical equality of men and women might be maintained, the position of women will . . . be rendered wholly unequal." It was not fair, she insisted, "to ask women to wait or to struggle for some more years before they secure their legitimate rights."[77] By that time Muthulakshmi's was a lone voice, for there seemed no options for women if they were not to jeopardize the nationalist project but to accept this legal resolution that ignored all difference and effectively closed off gender

---

Amrit, Your note on the position of women was received yesterday afternoon. I have gone through it. It does not admit of corrections. Your writing is always proper and easy to follow. The argument runs smooth. But it is not what I had expected. . . . When you come here we shall discuss the thing and I will tell you what I would have liked. Then if you feel like it you will write something independently, perhaps for your association. . . ." Raj Kumari Amrit Kaur, Personal Papers, Nehru Memorial Museum and Archives, Delhi.

[76]*Parliamentary Papers,* 1931–1932 [cmd. 3997] 111, p. 98, cited in Jana Matson Everett, p. 120.

[77]Note from Dr. S. Muthulakshmi Reddi, M. B. and C. M., Madras, dated 2 May 1931. AIWC, Franchise File, Nehru Memorial Museum and Archives, Delhi.

as a political question for several years, as it conferred an electoral "equality" on women.

If, despite the generous accommodations that had been made, women continued to remain unequal, it could only be their fault. In 1942 as the country prepared for an attack from Japan, Jawaharlal Nehru wrote, "Women should address themselves to local programmes of self defence and self sufficiency. . . . Public morale depends greatly on how women feel and act. . . . I am against treating women as helpless human beings who cannot look after themselves and who must run away from the danger zone. . . . So the only way to tackle the problem is to make women realise they have to and can face it."[78] Earlier he had lamented women's "long habit of relying on others' goodwill rather than on their own efforts,"[79] and retorted sharply to a complaint that the convention of nominating women to the Congress Working Committee had been broken, saying that the move "would ultimately be good for women themselves," for they had to fight as equals and not "imagine that your rights will be given to you or that they will drop down from somewhere, if you simply sit at home."[80]

Nehru's aggressive impatience is a revealing document of how totally invisible the subjugation of women had been rendered in the ideology of liberal nationalism. The roots of this impatience are deep and its branches appear even in literary texts with explicitly feminist concerns. The AIWC became largely inactive after the late forties, but liberal nationalist ideologies continued to dominate women's writing in the years that followed Independence. These ideologies, as well as class privilege, underwrote the remarkable self-assurance of that literature, its ambivalence towards the women's question, and its peculiar impatience with women themselves. In "Vivahangal Swargathil Vecchu Nadattapedunu" (Marriages Are Made in Heaven), translated in this volume, K. Saraswathi Amma pits her protagonist's more-than-equal wits against a group of elderly men, filled with their own self-importance, who have been sent to look her over as a possible bride. Given half a chance, women like her can beat the system single-handedly, and with humor, the author seems to suggest. The story is

[78]Nehru to Maulana Azad, 5 March 1942. Quoted in B. R. Nanda ed., *Indian Women: From Purdah to Modernity* (1976; reprint, Delhi: Radiant Publishers, 1990), pp. 12–13.

[79]Nehru "On the Women's Movement," press statement, 6 July 1936, *Selected Works of Jawaharlal Nehru,* vol. 7, pp. 313–314, quoted in Nanda, p. 61.

[80]Nehru to Ammu Swaminathan, 2 September 1936, quoted in Nanda, p. 61.

a gem in its genre, but the narrative is predicated on a worldview that places such confidence in the individual and her essential humanity and good sense that it cannot acknowledge the depth, power, or material hold of ideologies that underwrite the subjugation of women. It is not surprising, therefore, that even this courageous feminist author could argue in the early fifties in a radio talk entitled "Nan Oru Barthav-ayirunankkil" (If I Had Been a Husband) that no small part of the blame for the oppression of women must be laid on women them-selves. By comparison, her story "Premabhalam" (The Fruit of Love) is a savage piece, but there, too, the scorned woman plans and takes her revenge, singlehandedly upholding what she regards as true justice. In "Premabhalam" the agenda is revenge for the pain and humiliation that the woman has endured, and involves an articulation and vindi-cation of her experience. Wajeda Tabassum's "Utran" (Castoffs), which is included in this volume, is also a revenge story which, though it involves two women, actually deals with revenge taken in response to class humiliation. Here, too, the act is an individual one and involves the vindication of personal honor. The protagonist in this story is more controlled, more patient, more subtle, than the one in "Premabhalam," but is equally ruthless. Necessarily in such fictions, the world is struc-tured with such delicate balance that the countergesture of revenge can match and offset the initial humiliation.[81] Redress is in the hands of the individual. A great many of the stories in Chudamani Raghavan's oeu-vre occupy a world with a similar algebraic poise but are structured not so much to provide the act of revenge with the valence of reso-lution as to show up the double standards inherent in most social in-stitutions.

The female protagonists in Ismat Chugtai's most brilliant stories, some of them written in the fifties and sixties, may be broken by pov-erty but not by patriarchal oppression or male chauvinism, for the latter appear there as pomposities that may be ridiculed out of exis-tence. In "Lihaf" (The Quilt), which is presented in this volume, for instance, there is nothing that comes in the way of the abandon with

---

[81]In some ways "Utran" is a prototype of a great many popular stories and films of the eighties in which the woman victim takes it on herself to wreak revenge. In these works avenging women take on the task of reestablishing order and decency in a world where the state can no longer be relied on to preserve law and order or guard a woman's honor. What was a liberal fiction is rechanneled to firm up a conservative world.

which the landowner's beautiful wife welcomes her woman servant into her bed, and nothing to subdue the antics of the quilt once she is there, not even the young narrator's amazement. Krishna Sobti (b. 1925) locates an authenticity that has been "lost" by the middle classes in the bold, outspoken protagonist of *Mitro Marjani* (Damn You, Mitro) who may be attacked by everyone but will brook no curbs on her freedom.[82] The first-person narrator in Nabaneeta Dev Sen's witty, quick-paced, and extremely popular stories and travelogues begins with no conspicuous aspirations to independence or daring. She does not go looking for trouble, but when she is precipitated into situations that demand unusual independence and exceptional daring, such as that involving the rescue of the neighborhood tomcat from a third-story ledge, she takes to it naturally and with verve.

By the seventies the cracks were beginning to show. Words shift and slide to reveal other meanings as the protagonist in Abburi Chaya Devi's "Srimathi—Udyogini" (Wife—Working Woman), translated here, tries to answer the apparently simple survey questions asked by a young sociologist. The young woman departs, her requirements (and those of her academic discipline) apparently satisfied with the data gleaned for her research, but the encounter leaves the protagonist disturbed by the gaping distance between the positivist confidence of the interviewer's questions and the complexity of her own untidy life. In "Umr Qaid" (Life Sentence), also included here, Hajira Shakoor tells a story that is usually not told in the liberal-reformist accounts of heroic men and women who have the honesty and courage to stand up to tradition when they feel it is corrupt. This is the story of what happens after those admirable acts of heroism, of their cost. In "Umr Qaid" the narrative is cast as the reminiscence of an old man who in his youth had on an impulse stepped up and volunteered to marry a bride who waited while the intended groom's family argued about the dowry. We reach out to this silenced woman across the distance of a lifetime, and even then only through the screen of the man's growing consciousness, toward the end of his life, of what *he* has lost. It is a finely etched story that probes some of the treacherous depths beneath the question of reform.

---

[82]Sobti's novel is among the most energetic and formally well-wrought works in this genre. Unfortunately, English translation does not convey it adequately and we had to abandon the attempt to include an extract in this volume.

The New Curriculum and the Literature of the Fifties and Sixties

The writers represented in this volume inherited a culture in which many of the authorities that had administered the lives of women like themselves in the nineteenth and early twentieth centuries had been questioned and reconstituted. Yet surprisingly, neither the women's texts that emerged around the middle of the twentieth century, nor those of their male contemporaries, bear marks of those political encounters. Significations won, in the thick of battle as it were, are drained of the drama that attended their birth and of the history that shaped them. The new world is cleared of the detail, not only of the Imperial conquest begun in the eighteenth century and in many ways continuing into the post-Independence period, but also of all resistance to domination, as it becomes the setting for universal rituals of self-realization. The rigors of colonialism are peeled off like prison uniforms, and writers seem only too ready to forget them. The truths of the nation would seem to have displaced the myths of empire and to have made the land and its waters available once more as free and neutral ground on which artists, who are curiously historyless and universal but at the same time essentially Indian, might once more pursue eternal verities. The sense in the literature is of ground so well and truly consolidated that to go over it again would be tiresome, of questions so totally resolved that even the memory of struggle can be set aside and the real human business of living and of standing up to mortality—which, the implication is, is finally also the real business of art—can be resumed. In the most highly estimated of this poetry and fiction, the social, and even the psychological, are only media through which ceremonies of the spirit can be rehabilitated in an avowedly secular and universal space. The writer who had earlier staunchly refused to accept the housing offered by a colonial authority, in the fifties and sixties slips only too smoothly back into the "human" family.[83] For the solitary heroine (or hero) in search of herself, the outside world fuses with the one inside. The world may be a homemade one, as it so

---

[83]Frantz Fanon interprets such developments in Algerian literature as marking a definite phase in the emergence of a national culture, in *Wretched of the Earth,* trans. Constance Farrington (Harmondsworth: Penguin, 1967). See also Edward Said's reading of Camus in "Narrative, Geography and Interpretation," *New Left Review* 180, March/April 1990, pp. 81–100; and Susie Tharu, "Tracing Savithri's Pedigree," in Kumkum Sangari and Sudesh Vaid, eds., *Recasting Women: Essays in Colonial History* (Delhi: Kali for Women, 1989), pp. 254–269.

clearly is in Indira Sant's poetry, but her pain—and apparently the pain of the human condition itself—is ontological. As in the Partition texts we analyzed earlier, contradictions created and orchestrated by nationalism are transfigured into the paradoxes of the human condition. The mode, in both poetry and fiction, is lyrical.

Needless to say, questions of form, which were debated in the abstract and with great intensity, dominated literary criticism and became the guiding principles for the literary histories that were produced. Questions of form seem to have determined which authors and works were to be honored by a place in the new canons that were being set up. By chance,[84] as it were, tendencies of New Criticism and Modernism, both of which were dominant in Western literary circles at the time, suddenly appeared to be ideally constituted for many Indian artists and for Indian critics, who continued to speak of an "authentically Indian sensibility" while embracing a universalist metaphysic.[85] It is useful to recall that while New Criticism presented itself as a formal enterprise and apparently underwrote its readings with purely aesthetic claims, it also took on the task of setting up a national literature and building nationalist concerns into curricula in the United States. In Britain F. R. Leavis renewed the Arnoldian project for a national culture. The rigorous disciplines of Modernism welcomed other cultures with such profound courtesy that it would be many years before its empires were discerned or its uncompromising Eurocentrism challenged.[86]

Literary movements with these configurations emerged in different parts of India. One might cite, for example, the Nayi Kahani movement in Hindi, Navya in Kannada, the Digambara Kavulu in Telugu, the Navkavya and Navkatha movements in Marathi, and, though it

---

[84]We take *chance* here in the sense in which Michel Foucault develops the idea in "Nietzsche, Genealogy, History," *The Foucault Reader,* ed. Paul Rabinow (1984; reprint, Harmondsworth: Penguin, 1986), pp. 76–100.

[85]See for example K. R. Srinivasa Iyengar, *Indian Writing in English* (Bombay: Asia Publishing House, 1973); and C. D. Narasimhaiah, *The Swan and the Eagle* (Simla: Indian Institute of Advanced Study, 1970).

[86]See Francis Mulhern, *The Moment of Scrutiny* (London: Verso and New Left Books, 1981) for a fascinating study of the involvement of F. R. and Q. D. Leavis in the project of building English nationhood; and Susie Tharu, "Government, Binding and Unbinding: Alienation and the Teaching of Literature," *Journal of English and Foreign Languages,* Special Double Number, *Teaching Literature,* 7–8, 1991, pp. 1–29 for a more detailed analysis of the politics of literary studies in India during this period.

made an appearance somewhat earlier, the Kallol group in Bengali. A substantial number of the poets and novelists writing in English in the fifties and even the sixties can be regarded as part of this trend. The significance of this "moment" was writ even larger because the canons of most Indian literatures were consolidated and their curricula shaped (and charged with ethical responsibility for shaping the new citizen) in these years. Indian writing in English, for instance, was first set up as an area of study in this period (in the face of stiff opposition from those who thought that only literature from Britain should cross the threshold of an English literature department). For many years the principal question confronted in critical debate was whether an authentically Indian literature could be written in English, with the forces on one side insisting that no alien tongue was adequate to the task, while the other side went so far as to argue that the only truly national literature would be written in English. Across the country, "alienation," "exile," "authenticity," "Indianness," and "form" were the key words in critical debates, while the hidden agenda was nationhood and citizenship. As a mainstream Indian tradition was authoritatively enshrined, many other traditions, including feminist ones, were delegitimated. Works such as Muddupalani's (ca. 1730–1790) *Radhika Santwanam* (Appeasing Radhika), included in volume 1 of *Women Writing in India,* were totally forgotten. Further, these canons were so powerfully underwritten both by the complex resolutions of nationalism and by the universalist claims of literary and critical tendencies dominant in the West that even the influential literature that came from the socialist movement could be designated as a *trend* and contained within its schemes, just as Marxist literary criticism was, and now feminist criticism is, studied as one of many critical schools.

The "Eleventh among Ten"

How did women writers relate to this new universalism? As the biographical headnotes in this collection indicate, many of the woman writers of the fifties and sixties are formally accomplished artists, and have been often admired and singled out for praise even by orthodox critics. Kamal Desai, Krishna Sobti, Sajida Zaidi, Qurratulain Hyder (b. 1927), Kabita Sinha, Madhavikutty, Rajee Seth, Sugatha Kumari, Gauri Deshpande, and Anita Desai (b. 1927) are well-known names in both national and international literary circles, as are some of the accomplished younger poets—Saroop Dhruv, O. V. Usha, and Nidamanuri Revati Devi. In many senses their well-crafted writing does not seem to be disputing the ground laid out for it any more than the mainstream writing we discussed in the previous section. But it is also possible to read the women's writing of this period as engaged in a bitter and difficult debate about women and the kind of hospitality gender received within the universalist claims of the post-Independence years. Of being, to use an image from Hema Pattanshetti's poem, included in this collection, "the eleventh among ten." Further, it is possible to read these texts as heightening and displaying the configurations of that imaginative geography in their often barely articulated dis-ease with its terms. Indira Sant's chiseled verse draws, as did much poetry from the Swadeshi period, on the *ovi* meter of Marathi folk poetry, but the stances the form now underscores are strangely private. The rural landscape of her poems admits no trace of having been inhabited in the past, and is even today only occasionally peopled. Despite Indira Sant's acknowledged formal virtuosity, the shift is uneasy. As in the poetry of many of her contemporaries, an uncompromising loneliness is the poet's "constant companion." Yet as the empty domestic interiors turn weighty and become symbolic of the unhoused soul, there is also an undeniable excess that seems to insist on marking the familiar settings for these traumas of the spirit as female.

The world of Kabita Sinha's poetry and fiction is by contrast noisy and peopled, but the jostle and chatter of city streets fade respectfully into silence as Eve, lone woman on earth, claims her status as an existential archetype, for she is also "rebellion / first / on . . . earth." In "Adavi Dagina Vennela" (Moonlight Locked in the Woods), Achanta Sarada Devi's deliberate, sparse prose quivers as it negotiates the tension between the social setting in which the plot develops and the narrative focus on the elemental powers that undergird and surround that domesticity. It is a difficult translation the writer attempts as she probes recognizable figures from the nineteenth-century reform movements—the child widow, the child wife—in the language of archetypes. The interest of the story lies as much in the way this translation opens up those earlier questions as in the pressure those concerns exert on the new language. What could be more emblematic of the cultural history of India than a production of *The Barretts of Wimpole Street* in a small-town college? Yet in Kamal Desai's elaborately worked story, "Tila Bandh" (Close Sesame), presented in this volume, the rehearsals and indeed the script itself shed their social and historical dimensions to become the background for another drama in which the protagonist seeks to come to terms in an uncompromisingly absolute way with the meaning of a life that is caving in on her—not least because she is a woman.

Writers (both men and women) in almost every Indian language also return repeatedly in the fifties and sixties to the emblem of the primitive, in which their aspirations to freedom are condensed. In contrast to literature that deals with the somber traumas of the inner world, these works are exuberant, playful, irreverent—concerned more, it would seem, with the rehabilitation of the world and of the sensuous body than with the alienated soul. Yet both these literary modes participate in a universalist cultural economy that refuses any concourse with history. If the agony of existence is marked by a timelessness, the return to the primitive is actually an attempt to posit an authenticity that is prior to culture or history, and therefore unmarred by their corruptions. Both these schemes make difficult demands on women, who are required to step into redemptive roles and are often bitterly blamed for what is perceived as their failure to do so.[87] Either way it is an uneasy housing. In *The Strange Case of Billy Biswas,* Arun Joshi (b. 1939) conjures up a tribal woman whose uninhibited contact with the primal forces of life restore a lost power to Billy Biswas's jaded city body and his tired middle-class soul.[88] When Meherunissa Parvez reconstructs a primal world in "Tona" (Black Magic), translated here, the results are not therapeutic or redemptive. The power women had always depended on, the power of their black magic, is now failing.

---

[87]"Repulsed by the squalor and depravity they see around, a present reality that in no way matches the perfection of an imagined past, and disturbed because for all their nationalistic fervour they are left clutching the bloated particulars of a decadent culture and remain as exiled as ever from the lives of the people, writer-intellectuals withdraw. . . . And women? If we were the heralds of a vision yesterday, today we are the betrayers, for the dream has failed. One holds instead yesterday's soiled underwear . . . [and is] lost in a half light. . . . Mothers extend clawed hands, love is only a sort of relief. . . . The misogyny begins to match the one we are familiar with in Western literature but its roots and its meanings are not identical" (Tharu, in Sangari and Vaid, pp. 254–265).

[88]Arun Joshi, *The Strange Case of Billy Biswas* (Delhi: Orient Paperbacks, 1973). "Even more striking . . . is Mehboob's [film] *Mother India* (1955), where it is the suffering of the woman yoked to the earth, churning it, and the terror both procreative and destructive of the mother that flows out into nature and social conflict. The mother becomes the grim defender of tradition, meaning patriarchy, . . . and [social imbalance can] be righted only when the son's blood is sacrificed to the soil." Ashish Rajadhykshya, "Neo-Traditionalism—Film as Popular Art in India," *Framework* 32/33, 1986, pp. 20–67.

As the story draws to a close, the protagonist, defeated and depressed, drinks herself into a stupor with the very *mahua* wine that had earlier filled her with strength. In different ways, P. Vatsala's "Oru Tadavu-chatatinde Kadha" (An Escape) and Sarah Joseph's "Mazha" (Rain), both included in this volume, gesture towards the female as the source of certain incorruptible human responses (such as the desire for freedom) that are associated in the narrative with nature itself. However, even forms that would erase their history and camouflage their politics are historically constituted and political. In post-Independence India, these spiritual rituals of self-realization and the fictions of the primitive are liberal configurations developed in counterpoint to the conservative regimes of "tradition." And in Indian history, as in the history of Europe, the locating of an alternative tradition for the nation or rationale for the self in nature or in the human condition is a strategy with a radical edge.

Other women writers of the same period, often writers not so highly regarded by mainstream critics and less enamored with the high art of the spirit, deal with the social world. Female figures who rarely appear in the annals of contemporary literature acquire a new centrality in these works. The protagonist in Illindala Saraswati Devi's unusual story "Anaswasita" (The Need for Sympathy), included here, is an older woman, impatient with the pulls of the family and of domesticity. Had she been a man, at that stage in her life, in the traditional Vedic scheme, she would have been allowed to leave the life of a householder—if not physically, at least spiritually—and withdraw into the ascetic life of a *sannyasin,* or "spiritual wanderer." As a woman in the contemporary world, she would be expected to immerse herself in the life and the needs of her children and grandchildren. But neither of these well-made options, both socially sanctioned and eminently reasonable—one traditional, the other modern—measure up to the protagonist's need. Physically she enjoys her body and feels in her prime and is far from wanting to become an ascetic. Emotionally she has no patience with the quite justified but endless and petty demands of the family who would, if she allowed them, swamp her with their expectations. When she announces, unreasonably and much to her family's surprise, that she is leaving, she is indeed going on *sannyas,* but it is a sannyas she now will define anew. Subtly, yet surely, the narrative negotiates these liminal regions—between masculine and feminine, tradition and modernity, the body and the spirit—as it establishes the legitimacy of this older woman's personal quest and its need for our sympathy.

Mannu Bhandari brings yet another female figure to the foreground in "Saza" (The Sentence), presented here, as she depicts the inhumanity of the courts and of the legal system from the point of view of the young girl whose father has been accused of fraud and is suspended from work. In each of the many high dramas that ensue, she is only a minor character. Her life crumbles too, but the poignancy of the story lies in the fact that her life crumbles unnoticed and unmourned. Hers is a figure, and her fate a sentence, that can never aspire to heroic proportions in the world she lives in—except, of course, if the narrative chooses to step in on her side, as it does in this moving story.

The Late Sixties and Early Seventies:
A New Generation of Political Engagement

By the late sixties the scientifically planned, centralized edifice of the Nehruvian mixed economy began to collapse. The stress on the development of heavy industry and capitalist agriculture generated a host of contradictions. In the metropolitan cities India seemed to be well on the way to the twenty-first century. But away from those centers promises of social and economic justice remained largely unredeemed. After the extremely encouraging results of the first two five-year plans, economic growth slackened; during the third plan (1961–1966) per capita income did not increase and large sections of the population remained below what the Planning Commission called the "poverty line." Internationally the country had to cope with the increasingly unequal terms of trade and was being forced to accede to a growing multinational capitalism that considered the world its market and was impatient with the protections provided for national commerce and industry. On the domestic front, urban unemployment remained high and the prices of essential commodities rose by an unprecedented 32 percent. The food shortages and the price spiral led to starvation deaths in drought-hit parts of Bihar, and food riots broke out in Kerala and Bengal. Despite extremely progressive legislation, plans for the redistribution of agricultural land were never effectively implemented, since land reform was resisted by powerful interests whose hold seemed, if anything, strengthened. Clearly the main benefits of independence were restricted to a small urban and rural middle class.

This was the context in which what might be thought of as a totally new generation of political engagement (of which the women's movement was an important part) emerged in the late sixties and early seventies. Even groups conventionally regarded as quietist and conservative began to protest: engineers (in Punjab), teachers (in Kerala), doctors (in Orissa, Bihar, and Delhi), and civil servants (in Bengal, Maharashtra, and Uttar Pradesh). Lightning (and illegal) strikes for enhanced wages took place in several industries. Students protested over outmoded curricula and fee increases. The earliest and most spectacular of these protests were the agrarian movements in Naxalbari in the Darjeeling district of Bengal, Srikakulam in Andhra Pradesh, and Wyanad in Kerala. Inspired also by the developments in China, the Naxalites drew on the history of earlier struggles (such as the Tebhaga and Telangana movements and the Mappala Rebellion) to develop an armed resistance to the landlords and to the government.[89] Since students from the cities had played a leading role in the uprisings these struggles also left their mark on the universities, and recent studies have begun to document the participation of women from all classes. In Hyderabad the Progressive Organization of Women, a student group begun in 1973, ran popular campaigns against the harassment of women students on buses and on the roads (a practice often euphemistically referred to as "eve teasing"), against the giving or taking of dowry, and against the obscene portrayal of women on cinema hoardings. *"Jo dowry mangega woh kunwara rehjayega"* (Those who demand dowry will remain bachelors) was one of their slogans. News of the women students' campaigns spread into adjoining districts, where branch units were started up, and within months the young activists were addressing meetings ten thousand strong.[90] Though this was one of the few groups concerned specifically with gender-related issues, women organized and took active parts in many other movements. The anti–price-rise agitations of 1972 and 1973 were organized and led by women—prominent among them Mrinal Gore and Pramila Dandavate. In Bombay and then in several other cities large marches were

---

[89]Sumanta Banerjee, *In the Wake of Naxalbari: A History of the Naxalite Movement in India* (Calcutta: Subarnarekha, 1980) is still the most detailed and readable historical account of this movement. But see also Mahasweta Devi, "Mother of 1084," in *Five Plays,* trans. Samik Bandhopadhyay (Calcutta: Seagull Books, 1986), pp. 1–36, and "Draupadi," trans. Gayatri Chakravorty Spivak, in Spivak, pp. 179–196.
[90]For a more detailed account of this movement, see K. Lalita, "Women in Revolt: A Historical Analysis of the Progressive Organisation of Women [POW] in Andhra Pradesh," in *Women's Struggles and Strategies,* ed. Saskia Wieringa (Aldershot: Gower, 1988), pp. 54–68. K. Lalita was president of the POW from 1973 through 1975.

led by women beating their *belans* (rolling pins) against empty *thalis* (metal plates).[91] During the railway strike in 1970, which almost brought the day-to-day running of the government to a standstill, mothers, daughters, wives, and sisters of workers lay down on railway tracks to prevent trains from moving, picketed offices, and organized marches. When the strike was broken, women took more than their share of what were some of the most violent reprisals in recent times. Around the same time, in the Dhulia district of Maharashtra, people from the Bhil tribes launched a struggle to reclaim forest and agricultural lands that had over the years been usurped from them, and to demand their rights as human beings and as citizens. At the initiative of the Dhulia women, a conference attended by about seven hundred women was organized in Pune to discuss the questions relating to women that had emerged during the struggle.[92] In Bihar, the Mahila Sangarsh Vahini, the women's wing of the movement led by Jayaprakash Narayan, began to organize the *antimjan,* the poorest of the poor, to demand basic economic and social rights.[93]

Activists, both women and men, from these campaigns were among the first to be arrested and imprisoned when the Emergency was declared in 1975. The government, headed at the time by Indira Gandhi, claimed that it was driven to take extreme measures, as efforts to ensure social justice had been systematically resisted by vested interests, even in the courts. But the massive, cold-blooded programs of slum "clearance" in which "inconvenient" and "unsightly" urban settlements were razed to the ground overnight and the people left with no legal avenues for appeal or protest, as well as the compulsory sterilization drives that were taken up, suggest a far less benign relationship between this authoritarian state and the people. The new dispensation did not go unchallenged, and in 1977 the Emergency was finally lifted.

---

[91]See Nandita Gandhi, "The Anti–Price Rise Movement," in *A Space Within the Struggle,* ed. Illina Sen (Delhi: Kali for Women, 1990), pp. 50–81 for a careful and imaginatively researched account of this movement.

[92]See Nirmala Sathe, "About Stri Mukti and Shramik Sangatana," mimeo, 1981; and Maria Mies, "The Shahada Movement," *Journal of Peasant Studies,* 3:4 (1974), pp. 472–482.

[93]See Govind Kelkar and Chetna Gala, "The Bodhgaya Land Struggle," in Sen, pp. 82–110.

"Shishu" (Children)

Mahasweta Devi's "Shishu," translated in this volume, is one of the most powerful fictional explorations of the historical "moment" discussed in the preceding section. Set in 1977, in the months after the post-Emergency elections in which the Congress party had been defeated for the first time since Independence and the Janata party had come into power, the story presents a dedicated young relief officer's traumatic confrontation with the century-long ravages of government in Lohri, a region inhabited by the Agaria tribals. The climax of the story, which is also a narrative of self-understanding, comes with his realization that he is also implicated in the expropriation and that the ordinary height of the ordinary Indian could be a crime. This account of the Agaria tribals and the history of their involvement with empire and nation can also be read as allegory of the marginalization of women by those awesome powers.

A major theme is the violence of representation. The story opens with a long and tightly constructed section in which the old block development officer (DBO), a cynical but kindly representative of the old order, discusses the region with the young man who has been sent out by the enthusiastic new government to oversee relief operations and to address the problems of this "underdeveloped" area. In the process, the narrative displays the many ways in which the story of the Agarias has been written by various agencies of empire and nation, and the debilitating effects those representations have on their present-day lives. The BDO's account is that of an administrator who is scientific and rational—except when the "otherness" of the place unnerves him. The sources of his knowledge are the respectable disciplines of anthropology and geology, and his charge is the growth of Indian industry, the development of the country, and the welfare of its subjects (which includes lining his own pockets whenever possible). By the time the BDO is through with his story, the reader has been introduced to an array of other institutions and discourses that have made the Agarias their business: the police, administrative schemes, medical care systems, upper-caste superstition, middle-class sentiment and prejudice, mainstream Hinduism, missionary Christianity, Sarvodaya nationalism, and even the Hindi film. The narrative contests each of these representations, playing one off against the other with wry humor. But we are left with no doubt about how these people have been ravaged and silenced, why their bodies are stunted, and how their land has been stripped bare. This is the story that the Agaria myths also relate: the story of their fall from power and their suffering. In a startling and quite savage ending the young officer is pushed beyond the safe boundaries of the national institutions that house him and give him his authority into fearsome regions of insanity, where the Agarias who have been hounded into the night write their sentences onto a mainstream Indian body with the only instruments they now possess.

Toward Equality

If the oppositional movements of the late sixties and early seventies and the resistance to the 1975–1977 Emergency mark one beginning of the current phase of the women's movement in India, the publication in 1974 of *Towards Equality: Report of the Committee on the Status of Women in India* is, one could argue, another.[94] The well-documented report revealed exactly how unequal (despite a national constitution that is a "social document embodying the objectives of a social revolution")[95] women's access to development and to education and health, their political and economic participation, and their status under the law, among other things, continued to be in post-Independence India. The report was an eye-opener, its detailed analyses as powerful and effective an indictment of the nation's priorities in its first quarter century as any of the protest movements had been, its influence tremendous.

By the late seventies, issues related to women were being raised in a range of forums, and women's groups had emerged all over the country. Initially, city-based autonomous women's groups such as the Forum against the Oppression of Women in Bombay, Vimochana in Bangalore, Stree Shakti Sanghatana in Hyderabad, and Saheli in Delhi took up issues that were principally directed against the state. The feminist journal *Manushi,* started in 1979 by a group of women in Delhi, provided an important voice for the emerging movement. Though their focus was typically on local issues, women's groups coordinated campaigns at a national level and made spectacular advances. In 1979, in one of the earliest nationwide efforts, women's groups and

---

[94]Histories of the women's movement in the United States often cite Betty Friedan's *The Feminine Mystique* (New York: W. W. Norton, 1963) as the book that set the women's movement in that country going. The contrast between these two "founding texts" is perhaps as good a measure as any of the contrast between the two movements and their constituencies.

[95]Committee on the Status of Women in India, p. 3.

individual activists from all over the country protested against a Supreme Court judgement that had acquitted two policemen who, while on duty, had raped a sixteen-year-old girl in a police station. Women's groups demanded a reopening of the case and, later, a change in the rape laws. Equally important for the movement, however, was the ensuing debate on women's sexual rights in general, the relevance of "sexual history," biases in medical examinations, and the rights of women (over and above those of men) at the time of arrest.[96] The rape laws were changed. The debate had also managed, however marginally, to change popular attitudes toward rape, and in addition, the women's movement itself acquired a self-confidence and a sense of solidarity that made it a presence to be reckoned with in national life.

Questions raised by the women's movement soon made it clear that women as producers, consumers, and principal sustainers in an increasingly pressurized social architecture have little to gain and often are among those who pay the cost of the nation's economic "progress."[97] When land collectively used by peasants or by tribal peoples is taken over for mines, industries, or large dams, women lose their share in the community holdings. Yet whatever compensation comes by way of other lands or jobs in the new industries accrues to men, though women bear the main burden of displacement, homelessness, and poverty. When farming is "modernized" or mechanized with little thought given to the implications for agricultural labor, the first workers to be laid off are women.[98] When forests are cleared—by commercial con-

---

[96]Sudesh Vaid, Amiya Rao, and Monica Juneja, *Rape, Society and State* (Delhi: People's Union for Democratic Rights, 1980) is the best account of the initial campaign and the debate that followed. But see also *Report of the Commission of Inquiry into the Rameeza Bee and Ahmed Hussain Cases,* (government publication, Andhra Pradesh, 1978), for an idea of the impressive achievements of those legal initiatives.

[97]The issue of women's labor in the unorganized sectors is discussed in Nirmala Banerjee, *Women and Industrialisation in Developing Countries* (Delhi: Orient Longman, 1984) and in Maria Mies, K. Lalita, and Krishna Kumari, *Indian Women in Subsistence and Agricultural Labour* (Delhi: Vistaar Publications, 1986). Both the extent and the implications of largely invisible women's labor for the national economy and for women is extensively documented and analyzed in *Shramshakti* (The Power of Labor): *Report of the National Commission on Self-Employed Women and Women in the Informal Sector* (Delhi, 1988).

[98]Bina Agarwal, *Agricultural Modernisation and Third World Women* (Geneva: International Labour Organisation, 1981). Vandana Shiva, *The Violence of the Green*

tractors for wood to be used in the cities, or exported to feed the Western world's huge demand for paper, building, and furniture—the lives of people who have lived off these forests and tended them over decades are disrupted. Women who traditionally manage the domestic water and food economies are worst hit by droughts and food shortages. Yet the lives of these women are strangely invisible in the schemes of the nation. The National Commission on Self-Employed Women reports:

> During sessions with Government officials and representatives of voluntary organisations, [we] often heard reports from the officer like, "in our state women work very hard—even more than the men. . . ." Despite these reports, the Commission was also firmly told, "As far as our programmes are concerned we do not differentiate between men and women except if there are specific targets to be met for women." . . . Two lasting, disturbing impressions from the Commission's tour stem directly from these kinds of conversations and their contradictory realities. . . . The first is the insensitivity the Commission encountered time and again on the part of Government officials towards poor working women. The second is how invisible these women are at all levels.[99]

Since the late seventies middle-class feminists in the cities and feminist scholars in the social sciences have taken up issues related to family violence, the law,[100] the household, health care,[101] education,[102] curricula, the media,[103] and women's work and working conditions, and have set up ground-breaking critiques at every level, effectively

---

Revolution: Third World Agriculture, Ecology and Politics (Penang: Third World Network, 1991) extends this argument.

[99]National Commission on Self-Employed Women and Women in the Informal Sector, p. i.

[100]See Vimal Balasubrahmanyan, *In Search of Justice: Women, Law, Landmark Judgements and the Media* (Bombay: S.N.D.T. Research Centre for Women's Studies, 1990).

[101]For an overview of the many initiatives in this area, see Padma Prakash, "Women and Health: Emerging Challenges," *Lokayan Bulletin* 4:6, 1986, pp. 77–83.

[102]The whole question of women's unequal access to education has been extensively discussed in Committee on the Status of Women in India, pp. 234–282. Two very interesting new books that develop a critique—which is also, importantly, a feminist critique—of literary studies in India are Svati Joshi, ed., *Rethinking English: Essays in Literature, Language, History* (Delhi: Trianka, 1991); and Rajeswari Sunder Rajan, ed., *The Lie of the Land: English Literary Studies in India* (Delhi: Oxford University Press, 1991).

[103]See Vimal Balasubrahmanyan, *Mirror Image: The Media and the Women's Question* (Bombay: Centre for Education and Documentation, 1988).

relocating political practice.[104] Feminist scholarship in history, ideology studies, literature, and popular culture is relatively more recent but has made critical contributions to each of these fields.

Powerful streams collide in the political and cultural life of the post-1977 period. The eddy and rush underlie years as tumultuous, difficult, and important for the women's movement as they were for the nation. The battles of the seventies gave birth to a radical new generation of political awareness and engagement. Various silenced and expropriated groups articulated their grievances and made their claims on the nation with a new confidence. For middle-class liberals who had taken democracy for granted and had believed that for all its inadequacies, the state did represent the interests of the people, the Emergency was a critical turning point.

Middle-Class Dominance

These trends mark a shift toward a more radically conceived egalitarianism and democracy. But they are accompanied also by the rise of a powerful new middle class that is impatient with the welfare commitments of the Nehruvian era and ready to locate the roots of all India's current difficulties in its "soft" welfarist policies. Socialist daydreams, they assert, have ruined the nation. They have devalued merit and weighed down economic growth. Economically and ideologically this middle class is supported and underwritten by powerful international interests. Yet it is also a class that aggressively—and somewhat desperately—draws on nationalist sentiment to reshape a social Imaginary in which the nation is consolidated. In contrast to the earlier nationalist struggles in which the nation was consolidated in opposition to an Imperial power, these struggles over India involve an internal restructuring of the nation under the sign of this upper-caste and masculinist middle class. Organized political campaigns, such as the widely publicized 1990 attempts to displace the Babri Masjid (a mosque built by the Mughal emperor Babar) and reclaim Ram-Janmabhumi (the birthplace of Lord Rama) that set up a Just Cause and aroused a righteous desire to avenge what is portrayed as national humiliation, have now

---

[104]Vasantha Kannabiran and Veena Shatrugna, "Women's Activism and the Relocation of Political Practice: Some Reflections on the Experience of Stree Shakti Sanghatana," *Lokayan Bulletin* 4:6, 1987, pp. 23–34.

been analyzed.[105] The more subtle and deep-reaching hegemonic initiatives through which middle-class authority is endorsed, however, are located in systems (or logics) of representation that seem to be shared by the political right and the political left and are broadly accepted across caste, class, and gender divides. These systems structure the field of intelligibility in which autonomous, agentive selves (the lynch-pins of liberal humanism) and plausible worlds are set up.[106] Narratives of various kinds are among the principal tools with which the new Indian and his/her world is sculpted, and a new social Imaginary secured, though the increasingly popular genres that purport to deal with "facts"—the documentary film, the news magazines, and indeed history itself—have also played surprisingly important roles.

The new forms in which the nation is being constructed and circulated address the challenges that have emerged from the women's movement, from peasant and working-class struggles, and now, increasingly, from the dalit and *bahujan* (both "lower" castes) movements, but rewrite them into conservative, bourgeois-individualist terms. Though the authorities these narratives invoke are presented as "traditional," and "Indian"— categories that now seem to blend into the "natural" and the "human"— their redeployments of nationalism are aggressive *contemporary* efforts to consolidate power and win consent. Crucial to the appreciation of women's writing since the late seventies is an understanding of the tensions between this new middle-class nationalism and other, more egalitarian currents. Take, for example, the reappearance of the Hindu widow.

---

[105]See for example, Pradip Datta et al., "Understanding Communal Violence," *Economic and Political Weekly* 25:45, 1990, pp. 2487–2495 and Gopal Guru, "Hinduisation of Ambedkar in Maharashtra," *Economic and Political Weekly* 26:7, 1991, pp. 239–242.

[106]Speaking about the media coverage of the Falklands War, which he and others have argued played a crucial role in establishing the hold of a conservative, Thatcherite ideology, Stuart Hall comments: "Journalists of very different views and dispositions can tell the same kind of story. I often say to radical friends, 'I am not interested in what the person's politics are; what kinds of stories do they tell?' Because I know many radical journalists in the media who tell exactly the same stories: they construct events with the same kinds of language as the people who disagree with them profoundly. So there is a kind of stabilisation in the institutions and in the available discourses which are sustained in a set of known practices inside those institutions. Those stories write the journalists" ("The Narrative Construction of Reality," *Southern Review* 17:1, 1984, p. 7). See also the essays in Francis Barker et al., eds., *Policing the Crisis: War, Politics and Culture in the Eighties* (Colchester: University of Essex, 1984).

The Widow: A New Incarnation

The central female figure of nineteenth-century fiction, the young Hindu (or, less frequently, Muslim) widow, was commonly presented either as prematurely widowed or otherwise sexually constrained and ill-treated by a society that refused her the right to remarriage and to happiness. She was depicted as urgently in need of an education designed to transform her (and since the hand that rocked the cradle would rule the world, also her nation) ethically and equip her with the range of domestic and social skills essential for the new companionate marriages and for efficient motherhood. Such figures rarely appear in the fiction of the first decades of the twentieth century, in which women are depicted not as victims or as urgently in need of correction or reformation to be of use to society, but rather as strong, powerful, and central to the social architecture. They are mothers, sustainers of the social order, and indispensable resources in the national quest for liberation. In distinct contrast to the earlier fiction in which women's pathetic lives were an indictment of a culture whose values and mores those stories displayed, the lives of women in the later fiction endorse, and indeed celebrate, the authority and legitimacy of their culture. A feminist reader will not fail to notice, however, that, while the question of reform would appear to have been set aside because the new women are portrayed as "traditional," these women are "naturally" endowed with the bourgeois virtues that the nineteenth-century reformers sought to inculcate in women.

Consider Nirupama Devi's (1883–1951) popular novel *Didi* (Elder Sister), 1915.[107] Suroma, the principal character, is deserted shortly after marriage by her educated young husband, Amarnath, who, while away in the city completing his education, becomes involved with a young girl who has been left destitute by the death of her mother. He later marries the girl. Saddened, but not destroyed by Amarnath's desertion, Suroma remains behind in their country home living a traditional life. She quietly takes on the responsibility of caring for her ailing father-in-law, runs the household with an efficiency that wins her both affection and respect, and gradually becomes involved in administering their lands. No loud demands for equality or for power disturb the peace, but over a period of time she becomes the person

---

[107]See Tharu and Lalita, vol. 1, pp. 366–378, for a translation of excerpts from this novel.

everybody at her father-in-law's estate (including Amarnath and his wife Charu) turns to for direction and help. The narrative presents Suroma as a woman who respects tradition and wins its respect. But the mapping of a bourgeois world onto the traditional one is also clearly apparent: Suroma's authority is a moral one, acquired through the strength of her character and her steadfastness in the face of a bad situation; her power is personally won, not simply ascribed to her by virtue of her status. The everyday texture of Suroma's life is rich, the interactions between people humanly fulfilling. Her status as wife and as daughter-in-law is not changed by Amarnath's actions, and the narrative does not portray her life as restricted to, or as defined by, her relationship with a man. It is also interesting that, while there is no space for Suroma or for his old world in Amarnath's new life as an educated man with reformist enthusiasms, Suroma's world is large enough (and warm enough) to include both Amarnath and Charu, with whom she develops a surprisingly tender relationship. For all the poise that the narrative exudes, and despite its apparently confident resolution, this work is an embattled one. Tradition has to demonstrate its superiority; Suroma's authority is gradually *won,* and the narrative tracks this process.

The contrast with post-Independence incarnations of this figure is striking. The protagonist of M. K. Indira's award-winning novel *Phaniyamma* (a chapter which is included in this collection), is a widow. Published in 1976, the novel addresses questions raised at that time by the women's movement and by movements concerned with the lives of peasants and the rural poor. Phaniyamma's story, we are told, is based on the life of the author's grandaunt and is both fiction and "a little history."[108] The opening of the novel takes us back to "around 1840," when Phaniyamma was born into the Anchemane, or Postal House, the family-run center that for years governed the exchanges that held the community together. Those were days when tradition had become corrupt and people did not "have the courage or the intelligence to question the right or wrong of traditions handed down to them." The only authentic thing was the silver of the coins with which temple officials were bribed: "as soon as a few genuine silver coins were nestling in the folds of their dhotis the poor widow's fate

---

[108]M. K. Indira, *Phaniyamma,* trans. Tejaswini Niranjana (Delhi: Kali for Women, 1989).

was sealed."[109] But Phaniyamma's birth heralds a new era, for her life will reveal anew, and in turn restore the authority of, the true, humane face of tradition.

As the writer sketches out Phaniyamma's world with deft, minimalist strokes, tradition is cast in the dimensions it had acquired in the Swadeshi movement, and though it is not explicitly glorified, the detail of that life is evoked with such tenderness that it is celebrated. "No one knew what it meant for a woman to have a difficult birth, or not to have milk for her baby. Perhaps one in a thousand died in childbirth. People in those days could face any difficulty. They had a great deal of strength, courage and patience. . . . In this atmosphere, like a plant of jasmine, Phaniyamma grew quietly."[110] Though not all is right with this world and there are things that must change, the most humane and the most admirable of the lives portrayed in the novel is that of the protagonist, who observes the strictest austerities demanded of an upper-caste widow, but is in no way diminished. In fact, the narrative takes care to demonstrate that she quietly, almost secretly, revises the harshness of tradition without affecting its "essence" or disturbing those around her. Phaniyamma is able, with the power of her personality, to make tradition more humane, or rather, to bring out tradition's humane face, as she embraces it. As surely as in any of the great foundational fictions or histories in which nationalist thinkers carved out a tradition for the nation, and perhaps more effectively, M. K. Indira turns to the Swadeshi movement as she rewrites that tradition, cutting it to the measure of the mid-seventies.

The episode excerpted for this volume can be read as a blueprint for the consolidations of nation that were newly at issue in those years, and, as the novel's continuing popularity indicates, continue to be thematic into the early nineties. When the need arises, Phaniyamma's ascetic, ritual-framed, upper-caste life immediately extends its scope to attending at a difficult childbirth in a lower-caste household. Sinki, Hasalara Baira's daughter, has been in labor for four days. The midwives are in despair. Only Phaniyamma, whose hand is "small and smooth like a sweet yellow plantain," can save the mother and child, Jabina-bi, a Muslim midwife, decides, and rushes off to call her. The elders in the family are aghast at the request. Childbirth itself is ritually impure and polluting; so is the touch of a lower-caste person. But

---

[109]Ibid., pp. 6, 3.
[110]Ibid., pp. 16, 20.

Phaniyamma does not hesitate: "I'll be with you in a moment," she says. The narrative carefully sifts out the "good, mature" rewriting of tradition in the larger interests of society and of the nation, from the selfish or self-centered "immature" rebellions, just as it distinguishes between the harsh and superstitious practice of ritual and a deep, rational adherence to tradition. The plot makes it quite clear that others may rebel, but that rebellion has no value until it is endorsed by this inspiring and truly (as against falsely or mechanically) traditional Indian woman (who is, the reader would have by now realized, also a "natural" feminist). M. K. Indira's aunt's life may have been lived unnoticed in the heart of rural Karnataka, but in her niece's best-selling re-creation, this traditional figure from a small village that has shed none of its rural and ethnic tone becomes a truly "national" figure, and a feminist at that. The novel draws its emotional capital from powerful and deeply embedded cultural formations and is emblematic of the way Swadeshi formulations of gender, nation, and indeed feminism have reappeared and are renotated in the literature of the late seventies and the eighties.

In an interesting refiguration of the widow stories we have discussed, Binapani Mohanty's "Asru Anala" (Tears of Fire) places the responsibility of restoring order and decency to a society in which "the father is drunk and reeling at home" on a lower-caste widow and working woman, Ketaki. If she is to preserve her hard-earned dignity and independence, Ketaki has little choice but to take over and rise to the tragic proportions that the narrative demands of its hero(ine). Drawn together and implicated in her terrible act of revenge are not only those who toil like her, but also an old brahmin who braves the summer sun to provide water for poor passersby and a young middle-class woman activist.

Suturing the Rural-Urban Gap

The suturing of the rural-urban gap (which is also in many ways a caste gap) is one of the principal agendas not only in *Phaniyamma* but in many other important novels, written by both women and men, and in the popular realist films of the late seventies and the eighties. It is not insignificant, therefore, that Phaniyamma's birth in the late 1830s coincides with the time "that the post began to be delivered to every house in every village," or that as the narrative approaches the later years of her life, she is referred to as Ancheyatte (Post Mother). Intercut, in the opening chapter, with the account of Phaniyamma's birth, is a brief critique of the corruption that had by then crept into tradition, and an extraordinarily detailed description of the postal system that is, we soon realize, emblematic of the changes coming over the village. The reader is taken through a postman's working day and told exactly how addresses were composed in those days. She is provided with an example of the quaint (and to the modern reader, gawky) contents of a typical postcard as well as a complete list of the fifty-three villages for which the Tirthahalli Anchemane was the postal center. The postal system meshes Tirthahalli (and many more remote villages with even more traditional names) into a national (and international) system of address. The identity of both addressor and addressee are fictions of that system of address and as the letter arrives safely at its destination (in fact the danger that it might go astray determines the form of the address), it endorses those fictions. But if the postal system is one form of national address, the story of Phaniyamma's life is another. Both write Tirthahalli into the fictions of the nation, and of the world, and as they do so, they also rewrite those fictions.

In many of the stories and films of the seventies and eighties, the protagonist, sometimes a woman, is from a rural area and is often from the lower castes. It would appear that the urban, upper-class, upper-caste author is seeking an authenticity in these people who are somehow the real Indians, just as the village is the real India. This axis emerged at a time when the insufficiencies of the Nehruvian mixed economy had been laid bare. What we find in the seventies is the village-as-Indian-reality ideology of the forties reincarnated with a new twist as the village is rewritten, this time into a multinational world economy in which the Indian state is only a mediator. The films of this period have a clear brief: "to assimilate the political divide between the rural and the urban into the consciousness of urban mass culture," which was also the educational role envisaged when the national television network was established in 1972. As with the literature of the period, the internationalization of markets demanded of film and television of the invention of "new definitions of indigenism" and a new identity for the national bourgeoisie and for the state.[111] That this was also based on new definitions of gender goes without saying.

---

[111]Ashish Rajadhyaksha, "Beaming Messages to the Nation," *Journal of Arts and Ideas* 19, May 1990, pp. 33–52. "Running parallel to the boom in the advertising industry, we saw a cinema that sought to make a slightly different kind of

What has taken place since the seventies in television is paradigmatic of important developments in narrative languages and forms of address. It is a cultural politics that may be discerned as much in the televisual reworkings of the *Ramayana* and the *Mahabharata*[112] and the new historical novels and films as in the aggressive advertising directed to the new middle classes. It is significant that many of the most successful filmmakers—Shyam Benegal, Girish Karnad, Vijaya Mehta, Sai Paranjpe, Govind Nihalani—have worked also for television, as have the most influential of the serious writers of those years—Mannu Bhandari, Vijay Tendulkar, Dhiruben Patel, Jeelani Bano, Shivani. In other words, though overtly and thematically these stories and films appear to be about rural India, and about social unrest and protest, their visual and narrative languages work as a sort of translation device through which the rural is inducted into the national mainstream, which is itself being rearticulated as the hegemony of the middle class is consolidated and markets become internationalized. In the process, of course, the political energy of protest, like the political energy of feminism in *Phaniyamma,* is dissipated.

Television, Rajadhyaksha comments, firms up the individuated space of the new bourgeois viewer, regardless of the sizable nonbourgeois audiences. "The bourgeois *male* viewer, his property, the spaces he surrounds himself with, and the 'rest-of-the-world' that is a sort of appendage to this identity is reflected physically around him. . . . Nalini Malani's earlier paintings—the *His Life* series—actually articulate this kind of space. . . ."[113] Malani herself tracks the development of her

---

vindication of the state. . . . At the very moment when the advertising industry was speaking of 'rural advertising' and 'public interest advertising' and invoking various kinds of developmental rhetoric, Benegal was making *Manthan* [a film about the milk cooperatives that were developed in Gujarat]. Nihalani made *Aakrosh* [a film about the tribals and their resistance] a little later" (p. 41). The connections of this sort of development rhetoric with the opening up of the domestic rural market, reinterpreted in the language of contemporary marketing as promoting "affordable units" (i.e. multinational brands of toothpaste, shampoo, or cough syrup, in small sachets, accompanied by massive advertising on the national television network) should not be overlooked.

[112]The difference between Irawati Karve's existentialist interpretations of *Mahabharata* characters in *Yuganta* (The End of an Epoch) (Delhi: Orient Longmans, 1969) and Lalithambika Antherjanam's nationalist reading of thirteen characters from the same epic in *Seetha Muthal Satyavathi Vare* (From Sita to Satyavathi; Kottayam: Sahitya Pravartaka Co-operative; 1972) is a salutary measure of these changes.

[113]Ashish Rajadhyaksha, "Beaming Messages to The Nation," p. 50.

critical method as a movement from the extreme close-up, "where even the pores are gaping holes," to midshot, where she was contained in an interior of which she was only dimly aware, and finally to a wide-angle lens. The environment that houses the women in this bourgeois-male-defined space is not merely the "suggestion of a bed or a chair or a room. It includes other people, each supporting the other, held together by the stretch and pull of relationships, embodying a history of its own."[114]

Two powerful stories in this collection collaborate in Malani's critical excavation of this disturbing new space, as they view women edged and confronted by the bizarre requirements of its sexuality. Varsha Adalja tells the story of a young girl, Champudi, who, wanting to earn a few more rupees and encouraged by the men who gather round, begins to sing and dance. Soon the crowd moves in, pawing her and throwing her around, thrusting rupee notes into her torn blouse while they laugh wildly at jokes she cannot understand. Confused, she continues to dance, searching all the while through a wild medley of images her culture has provided, all singularly inappropriate, to understand what is happening to her. Adalja orchestrates to a disturbing pitch the tension between Champudi's understanding of the situation and her own young sexuality, and the reader's understanding of the responses she receives from the crowd, but provides no resolution.

Saroj Pathak's "Saugandh" (The Vow), is in some ways more puzzling. Written in a working-class dialect of Gujarati, with a large admixture of Hindi, the story is set in the growing outskirts of a metropolitan area. It explores the unusual and tender relationship between Poorbi, who, "sick of abuse, blows, and male smells," has escaped from her husband, and Sambal, who has left his wife and children behind in the village to work in the city. Sambal watches over Poorbi, providing her with much-needed protection. She cooks for him. Both of them regularly send money back to their former homes. Some of the most moving exchanges in the story document the growing friendship between this middle-class woman who has come down in the world and this rough-mannered man from the village. When Poorbi finally decides she would like to get married, he quickly agrees—but only if he can keep the vow he has made to his wife in the village that

---

[114] "A Conversation between Yashodhara Dalmia and Nalini Malani," Exhibition Brochure, Pundole Art Gallery, Bombay (March 1979). The cover illustration for the U. S. edition of this volume is a detail from one of Malani's works.

he will never sleep with another woman. Poorbi is overwhelmed by his steadfastness. They must—and will—make a life together. Poorbi turns the pages of her imagination but can find no ready images for what lies ahead. There is no known script for this relationship, but it has room for the other commitments in both of their lives.

Pathak's "Dushchakra" (Vicious Circle) explores, with similar sensitivity, the pressures exerted on men by the new urban culture as it takes us into the world of ladies' tailors who are obsessed with the shape and touch of the women for whom they sew. The story focuses on one whose infatuation with one of his customers reaches such a point that he cannot bear to sew the sari blouses for her wedding, cannot bear it if anyone else sews them, breaks down, and gives up the job.

"Avala Svatantrya" (Her Independence)

Many of the stories and poems translated for this anthology are influenced by, or engage directly with, issues that have emerged in Indian society since the mid-seventies. Jaya Mehta's poetry has a political edge rarely found in the poetry of the early Independence years, which seemed primarily concerned with the spiritual agony of the human condition. Much of Mahasweta Devi's powerful fiction is set at the time of the Naxalite movement and deals with the many questions it raised.[115] Malini Bhattacharya's play *Meye Dile Sajiye* (To Give a Daughter Away), which deals with dowry murders and family violence, was written to be performed by a women's theater group as part of their campaign on those issues. The protagonist of Bankimchandra Chatterjee's well-known early nationalist novel, *Devi Chaudhurani,* one of the most powerful female figures in Bengali literature, appears as one of the characters in the play. She charges the nation, of which she is a founding mother, with callousness and neglect of its women. As she lays claim on this Swadeshi figure and draws her into the imaginative repertoire of the contemporary women's movement, Malini Bhattacharya also battles with other contemporary uses of that past and enters into a long-running argument about the constitution of the nation. Veena Shantheswar's "Avala Svatantrya" (Her Independence) asks what independence women have forty years after the country won its freedom, as she takes us into the life of a new middle-class family

---

[115]See Spivak, pp. 179–197 and 222–240 for important analyses of two of Mahasweta Devi's stories.

and shows what it means to be a working woman. Anupama Niranjana, too, asks new questions of marriage and sets up new measures for relationships in "Ondu Ghatane Mattu Anantara" (The Incident—and After), in which a woman who has been raped suddenly discovers in her husband a man she never expected to find. Chhaya Datar revives and rewrites the concerns of writers such as Rasheed Jahan in the thirties as she attempts to build new connections between women of different classes. Her story "Swatahchya Shodhat" (In Search of Myself) treads a thin line between autobiography and fiction, rehabilitating in its intense focus on the drama of the self an autobiographical voice that would seem to have disappeared from women's writing after the nineteenth century.

Feminist concerns emerge in other contexts too. Ambai's "Anil" (The Squirrel) has a lightness of touch that sets it apart, but it also has an unusual new fictional protagonist: a woman researching women's history, figuring out for herself as she reads through old journals what that new discipline might consist of. The characters on musty, crumbling pages come alive and slip into the lunchtime chatter of the women who work in the building, not very different in many ways from those in the journals. Vaidehi returns to the most highly regarded of Indian plays, Kalidasa's fifth-century classic, *Shakuntala,* to retell it, in a style that measures up to Kalidasa's own lyricism, from Shakuntala's point of view, bringing into focus not only her feelings, but also the world of women's friendship. Panna Naik makes space in her poems for emotions that would have found no legitimacy in earlier times. The recent poetry of Shanta Shelke and Anuradha Potdar, and the entire oeuvre of Vijaya Dabbe, Kamala Hemmige, Jayaprabha, and Vimala is self-evidently feminist, as is the recent fiction of many older writers.

In a powerful post-Emergency story, *Hum Safar* (Fellow Travelers), Mrinal Pande resurrects the widow. In sharp contrast to the widows in the novels of the reform movement, and those who are later drawn upon to sustain an entire social architecture, the widow in this story has become a psychologically rounded character, a *person* we sympathize with. Cornered, harassed and totally powerless in a world that finds her irrelevant and even ridiculous, she can only turn, in a pathetic, displaced outburst to her son, the person around whom her life revolves and the only one who will recognize her presence. The story is set in the early eighties. If this widow is an icon at all, she is an icon of a new and terrible dispensation—and an equally terrible indictment of it. The novels from the eighties that we have excerpted for translation here, Dhiruben Patel's *Sheemlanan Phool* (Flowers of the Silk-

Cotton Tree) and Kundanika Kapadia's *Sat Paglan Akashman* (Seven Paces in the Sky), extend the diagnostic critique of the family prefigured in the tragic, feminist-before-its-time writing of Rajalekshmy and Ratakonda Vasundhara Devi, and the popular fiction of Triveni. Rajam Krishnan's richly textured and inspiring story, "Kaipidite Kadaloruvanai"—the title of which is a difficult-to-translate line from the revolutionary Tamil poet Subramanya Bharati (1882–1921), rendered here as "Lending a Helping Hand"—takes up the theme of alliances that we first met in the socialist literature of the thirties. As the young daughter-in-law struggles to piece together her life as a working woman and as a wife and mother, she finds herself reaching out to her mother-in-law, who sees her own life anew in the mirror held up to her by her young daughter-in-law. When they finally manage to go off together, on what is for the younger woman a vacation and for the older woman a long-desired pilgrimage, it is clearly a major victory. The connection made here is one that challenges many powerful traditions, including the enmity between mother-in-law and daughter-in-law, and forges new political alliances, this time within the family and against patriarchy.

Conclusion

Our still rough-cut analysis of the forces at work in women's writing and in the politics of gender is offered here as an initial step in the writing of a new cultural geography of India. We have tried to map the imaginative worlds in which women wrote. We have read their literary initiatives as attempts to engage with the force and the conflict of the multiple, cross-cutting determinations of their historical worlds. Literary criticism, in its authoritative, New Critical mode focuses on the internal structure and aesthetic achievement of what is taken to be a self-referential, hermetic text. In contrast, our readings have treated women's texts as engaged in negotiation, debate, and protest, invariably in areas that directly concern, or are closely related to, what it means to be a woman. These texts address real tasks in a real world, and are therefore documents of historical struggles over the making of citizen-selves and nation-worlds.

We began with the forties and early fifties, when the very idea of nationhood underwent a significant alteration, and the means and modes by which ideological unities were effected and dominance was exercised were profoundly transformed. Those decades marked the end of a long and grossly unhappy epoch of imperial dominance, but they were also crucible years in which new authorities were fashioned and consolidated, and new repertoires of Indianness were composed and circulated. A whole set of deeply embedded historical discourses, including ones that embodied a nation-people's visions of freedom and of equality, were renotated as they were translated into the schemes of an ascendent nationalism. Literary texts—and women's texts were no exception—often endorsed and elaborated the protocols of government in the domain of the Imaginary, but also resisted and undermined them. We read the hegemonic initiatives of the nation not only along their grain to appreciate the resolutions they proposed, but also against that grain to investigate their composition. In the central sections of this introductory essay, we chose to excavate three strains in the cultural politics of twentieth-century India in some detail: the high nationalism of the Swadeshi movement, the liberalism of national women's organizations, and the socialist commitments of the Progressive Writers' Associations. These configurations allowed us to chart the narrative and symbolic prefiguring of what became a new executive centrality and its constituency. Over the half century that followed, women's texts have fed into and elaborated the course of dominance and the investments of gender in it, but they have also deflected and refigured that course. We hope this anthology will also provide the reader with a sense of the difficult but challenging terrain that the women's movement of the seventies inherited and continues to work on in the nineties.

Rasheed Jahan

(1905–1952)   *Urdu*

After her short story "Dilli ki Sair" (A Tour of Delhi) and play *Parde ke Piche* (Behind the Veil) appeared in the Urdu anthology *Angare* in 1931, Rasheed Jahan shot into prominence. *Angare* was edited by Sajjad Zaheer, who was to become a leading figure in the progressive writers' movements after 1936, and contained ten short stories and plays: five by Sajjad Zaheer himself, two each by Rasheed Jahan and Ahmed Ali, and one by Mehmood-uz-Zafar. These writers were young and charged with the desire to change the world, and the anthology was an attempt to shock the reader into a new awareness.

Angare was principally concerned with social and economic justice, but the treatment of sexuality, as well as its discussion of issues that were always pushed "behind the veil", to use Rasheed Jahan's phrase, was also provocative. Structured as a conversation between women in purdah, *Parde ke Piche* discussed the tyranny of husbands who threatened to reject their wives for trivial reasons. It also spoke of abortion and of other unacknowledged problems affecting women's health. Traditionalists in the Urdu-speaking world were outraged. The Aligarh weekly *Sargushizt* wrote fierce editorials against *Angare* and criticized Rasheed Jahan's family. Though Aligarh was the center of the controversy, reverberations spread through the country. Religious leaders protested against the irreverence and "obscenity" of these hard-hitting pieces, preached sermons against "Rasheed Jahan, *Angarewali,*" and passed ordinances against her and the others. Sibte Hassan, a writer and contemporary, recalls that warnings were issued in the newspapers saying that if Rasheed Jahan did not retract, she would be kidnapped. He suggested that she should have a bodyguard and not move about alone. "Impossible," she retorted. "I am a doctor. How can I work if I have to take bodyguards around with me?"

Rasheed Jahan was born in Aligarh. Her father, Sheikh Abdullah, was a pioneer in women's education and the editor-publisher of a women's magazine, *Khatun.* Their home is remembered as a center for debate and discussion on women's issues. Two of her sisters became college principals, a third an actress. When she was sixteen, Rasheed Jahan entered Isabella Thoburn College in Lucknow, where she studied for two years (her first story, "Salma," written in English, was published in the college magazine) before she went on to the Lady Hardinge Medical College in Delhi. Disturbed by the lives of women who "could keep track of time only by pregnancy and childbirth," Rasheed Jahan organized her fellow medical students to help run literacy classes and free medical clinics.

In 1931 Rasheed Jahan graduated from medical school, and in 1934 she married the writer Mehmood-uz-Zafar, who was the vice principal of a college in Amritsar. Hajira Begum, who has written a biographical introduction to a posthumous collection of Rasheed Jahan's writings, regards the years between 1934 and 1936 as crucially important. It was in Amritsar that Rasheed Jahan met the poets Faiz Ahmed Faiz and Mohibbul Hasan Qasi, and came into contact with the important Lahore-based group of Marxists thinkers and activists led by Miyan Mukhtar-ud-din. A collection of her writings, *Aurat aur Dusre Afsane wa Drame* (Woman and Other Stories and Plays), was published in Lahore in 1937.

Several writers, including Faiz Ahmed Faiz and Ismat Chugtai, have acknowledged Rasheed Jahan's influence on their lives. While they were in Amritsar, Rasheed Jahan used to chide Faiz, sometimes quoting his own lines, for writing about unimportant things when poverty, illness, and slavery abounded. It was Rasheed Jahan, Faiz acknowledges, who introduced him to Marxism and drew him into the Progressive Writers' movement. Rasheed Jahan, Ismat Chugtai said in a 1986 interview, "Shook me up. I stored up her work like pearls. . . . The handsome heroes and pretty heroines of my stories, the candlelike fingers, the lime blossoms and the crimson outfits all vanished into thin air. The earthy Rasheed Jahan simply shattered all my ivory idols to pieces. . . . Life, stark naked, stood before me." The heroines of some of her own stories, Ismat Chugtai added, were modeled on Rasheed Jahan. The writer Siddqa Begum Sevharvi recalls having accompanied Rasheed Jahan through the dingy back streets of Aligarh to visit a patient. They walked into the dark hovel of a room where the sick man lay, and Rasheed Jahan not only examined him, but gave his relative money for medicine. She is remembered as a charismatic figure, the center of any group she worked with.

In 1937 Rasheed Jahan and Mehmood-uz-Zafar moved to Dehra Dun, where she became involved in the activities of the Progressive Writers' Association. She also edited a political monthly called *Chingari* (Sparks). From all accounts she led an extremely busy life: as a doctor, "never refusing a call from a patient in need of her"; working for the Communist party; writing, producing plays, and organizing other events for the PWA; and running a household where many writer friends and party workers found a welcome. With the beginning of the Second World War, her husband and many other party activists were arrested or went underground. Rasheed Jahan took on still more political responsibilities and, in addition, helped to provide support for the families of those who had been imprisoned. In 1944 exhaustion prevented rapid recovery from a thyroid operation. In 1949 she was arrested, along with other Communist party workers, but continued with her work after her release, until her untimely death in 1952.

Though Rasheed Jahan is better known in the late twentieth century as a writer of short fiction, she herself considered drama a more forceful medium and was among those who laid the foundations of the progressive theater movement. She wrote and directed several plays, including adaptations of works by Anton Chekhov, Munshi Premchand, and James Joyce, and moved back to fiction only when failing health and lack of time restricted her involvement in the theater. Her thirty short stories and fifteen plays have become "classics," Hajira Begum comments in her introductory essay to *Woh aur Dusre Afsane wa Drame* (That One and Other Short Stories and Plays), published in 1977, twenty-five years after Rasheed Jahan's death.

◆

WOH
(That One)

I first met her at the hospital. She had come there for treatment and so had I. Seeing her, the other women turned away. Even the doctor's eyes strained shut in disgust. I felt repulsed too, but somehow managed to look straight at her and smile. She smiled back, or at least I thought she tried to—it was difficult to tell . . . she had no nose. Two raw, gaping holes stood in its place. She had also lost one of her eyes. To see with the other she had to turn her whole neck around.

A little later we ran into each other at the medicine counter. In her odd, nasal voice she asked me where I lived. I gave her my address. She collected her prescription and left. Immediately, even without my asking, the pharmacist began, "That one is a scoundrel, a whore, a filthy whore. She's been rotting to death, that one, bit by bit. And now she thinks of treatment! The doctor has no sense either. Just hands a prescription over. Ought to be thrown out, she ought, that slut!"

I was working at a girls' school. I was still fresh from college. The future was a garden where no flower fell short of a rose or a jasmine blossom and the world lay stretched out at my feet. Life was a stream in a moonlit night, rippling gently here, cascading into a waterfall there. I was happy. I had no idea what the wrench of pain might be. Even my job as a teacher was only a pastime then. For me, existence was an expectancy.

The bamboo curtain rose. She entered the staff room. I started up from the chair in surprise and said in a kind of involuntary response, "Do sit down." She hesitated for a moment but then sat down. Clutched in her hand was a single jasmine blossom. She laid it on the table before me. As I picked it up, I felt deeply repulsed, but forced myself to tuck it into my hair. She smiled, got up and left immediately.

Soon it became a daily affair. Every day, at break time, that one would lift the curtain and come into the room. I would mutter, "Do sit down," and she would. She always brought a flower and placed it before me on the table.

The other young teachers started teasing me about her visits. Nobody would sit in the chair she used. I don't blame them. It wasn't their fault. She looked so revolting. I couldn't bring myself to touch the chair either.

Even Naseeban, the old sweeper, grumbled and complained, "A fine new teacher we have! What a friend she has found herself! Disgusting stinky woman. Why should I dust the chair that one sits on?"

The principal was annoyed too. Eyebrows raised in a haughty arch, she asked, "Must you invite her into the school? I'm sure our parents will take exception to a loose woman like her entering the premises."

But come the next day, she was back again. "Do sit down," I would mumble, and she did. She began to stay a bit longer. She kept staring at me, but we never talked to each other. Did she think I knew nothing about her? I wondered. There she sat, just gazing at me with that crooked eye and that ghastly noseless face. Sometimes I thought I saw her eye fill. What was passing through her mind? I wondered. I felt like asking her, but where was I to begin?

As soon as she entered the room, the other teachers often would get up and leave. "Safia's admirer—that one—has come!" they would quip in English. "We'll go away and sit in the library."

"Just look at that face. It's so odious!" one would say. "It quite takes my appetite for lunch away, Safia. I feel sick."

"But she's made a careful choice alright. You really are the most charming, Safia!"

"Tut, tut. You ought to observe purdah before that one," the portly, venerable teacher of Islamic theology pronounced.

I continued to work and she continued to sit and stare. I felt very uncomfortable. What was she staring at? What was she thinking about? Had she once been like me? I shivered at the thought.

Again. Why does she come here? Can't she see that people despise her? That they shudder when they see her? Often the two raw holes in her face were running.

Every day I would decide to put a stop to it all. The principal was right. Of late the students had also started grumbling. All the same, when she came the next day I would offer her a chair and mutter, "Please sit down."

Doesn't she have a mirror? Doesn't she know she's reaping the fruit of a sinful life? Why doesn't anyone tell her? Does she have a family? Where does she live? Where does she come from? Does she actually believe that I consider her only another sick person?

I felt awkward and humiliated. I was being made into an object of ridicule in the school. Still, whenever she placed a flower before me, I would tuck it into my hair and her face would once again crease into that horrifying smile. Why does she stare at me like this? Who is she? What had she been? Where did she come from? How had she become like this? What does she feel when she comes to the school? Pain? Or relief?

One day as she was leaving, she blew her nose and wiped her fingers on the wall. Old Naseeban, who had always nursed a smoldering grudge against her, was cleaning the kindergarten slates with wet clay. Up Naseeban sprang, remarkably youthful, and hit the woman hard in the back with a slate. That one froze. Terrified.

All the good breeding culled from twenty years of working in the school, all those many times when she had pleaded with the girls to behave—Naseeban forgot all of it that day. Once again she was her old back-alley self.

"You bastard, you whore, who do you think you are? Yesterday you were loitering at the street corner, and today as your flesh falls rotting apart, you parade here like a lady," she screamed.

A kick. Another kick. Yet another blow. I rushed out and pulled Naseeban back. "What do you think you're doing?" I yelled. A big crowd of girls had gathered, and several teachers were running to-wards us.

Naseeban had lost all control. "It's all because of you. You are the one who encouraged her!" she burst out at me. "You scooped this scum out of the gutter and set her up here. And now look! She's messed the whole wall up. I've worked here twenty years. I've never seen whores come to school before. I won't work here anymore. I won't. Find another woman who . . ."

Naseeban took another lunge, but the others held her back. I bent down and lifted her up. Sobs shook through her. I led her slowly to the gate. Blood trickled down her temple, but she didn't seem aware of it. She hid her face in her hands and a moment later said, "Now you know everything," and left.

Translated by M. T. Khan.

INDIRA SANT _____

(b. 1914)   *Marathi*

"So often, when I have been deep in thought about an experience, an act, a decision, one of her poems has come and stood unobtrusively behind me, like a point of reference. And suddenly, things have become clearer to me," writes Vasudha Ambiye of Indira Sant, a highly regarded contemporary Marathi poet.

Indira herself considers her poetry to have been born out of moods and emotions and not influenced by events or even social experiences. What happens in an event, she says, "is limited to a certain geographic context. Why can we not move beyond geography? It is my inner landscape that absorbs me." Creativity for her is a pruning, an excising. As she puts it in the preface to *Shelah* (Stole), 1950, a poet's success depends on her ability to "forget extraneous considerations and conventions, to drive away encroaching emotions and thoughts and to adhere to the original experience." Intensity, both in image and emotion, is what she strives for. She admires the poetry of the sixteenth-century saint poet Mirabai, for instance, not because of her *bhakti* (spirituality) or because of her rebellion, but because of her passion. "It was her passion that gave her the strength to break through the impossibly rigid conventions of those days."

Indira Sant, born Indira Narayan, studied in Pune and is by profession a teacher. She was married and widowed young, and has since lived a quiet and private life in the southern Maharashtra town Belgaum. Her first poems date back to 1931, but long before that she had begun collecting the work songs and lullabies that form the rich oral tradition of women's literature. Their musical rhythms, colorful diction, and homely imagery continue to influence her work, which, like these songs, deals sensitively with many dimensions of women's lives.

Commenting on the years after her marriage, when she wrote very little, the poet observed, "It is not true that I did not write because I was engrossed in my family life. . . . I guess it was because my mind was not stretched enough. I did not seem to need relief from my day-to-day life."

Literary historians tend to place Indira Sant within the Navakavi (New Poets) movement that established itself in the post-Independence years, though they point out that the trees, leaves, and rivulets of rural Maharashtra—which are such an insistent presence in her work—connect her to the earlier Romantic poets. If love is her principal theme, nature is a close second. Fellow poet and critic Dilip Chitre includes her work in his important anthology of the major poets of the fifties and sixties. There is certainly a sense in which the well-crafted, gossamer form of her poetry and its intense concern with inner experience make her a kindred spirit to these poets. Yet as we read the poems today, the "four walls"—and sometimes "four windows and two doors"—that she returns to obsessively are not, as has often been suggested, so much an image of the metaphysical alienation of the human condition, as of the limited scope of women's lives. Sadly, within the world of her poems there is no escape from this restriction. What is possible is only an intense longing that turns inward to find riches unavailable in the world outside. Though she says she doesn't believe in God, she feels "there is certainly a power greater than us, beyond us." In the best poems from *Mehndi* (Henna), 1955, and *Mrigajala* (Mirage), 1957, the immediate is suffused with a presence that seems supernatural. *Rangabhavari* (Lover of Colors), 1964, and *Bahulya* (Dolls), 1972, move toward more social themes.

Vasudha Ambiye feels that in Indira Sant's latest book, *Garbhareshim* (Pure Silk/Silk of the Womb), 1982, there is an altogether new sense, a new mood: "Loneliness. The earlier loneliness always existed in the context of companionship. This new loneliness is a different experience altogether . . . as in the 'you' in 'Mist-like.' " The "you" in that poem, Indira Sant explains, is death: "I find the presence of death both inspiring and peaceful." Two of the poems translated here, "Dhukysarakha" and "Shapit," are taken from *Garbhareshim;* "Kanav" is from *Mrigajala.*

◆

KANAV
(Compassion)

The cold earth
beneath the feet;
the oppressive roof
above the head:
four high walls
surround me
on the four sides.

When will it end,
this lifelong imprisonment?
I do not know;
my tired, heavy eyes
cannot make out
if it's night or day.

In a room
twelve feet by twelve feet
I count
thousands of miles;
a window two feet wide
shows me the whole sky;
a gap in the roof
reveals to me
the play of sun and shadow:
the house, showing such compassion,
makes my heart
cry in silence.

Translated by Vilas Sarang.

DHUKYASARAKHA
(Mistlike)

He came walking through the mist of knowing and unknowing
Mistlike.
Even before the fragrance in his hand could reach me
He was there, in my head.
I spoke to myself, "Who . . . and such flowers . . ."
Sitting by my side, he covered me, flower by flower,
Saying all the while,
"For you, for you alone.
Because you are going."
The cool touch of those flowers, kept seeping, drop by drop.
The rich, aching timbre of those words
Resonating
Through the blood.
How new it was. Never before experienced. And you—
A stranger.

Stemming the flow of tears from eye to temple
With a flower, he said,
"Stranger?
No, not me. I am yours from birth. Bonded anciently."
And, as I looked at him, the mist
Had long since faded. And with it he.
But I was no longer alone.

Translated by Shanta Gokhale.

SHAPIT
(Spellbound)

A four-walled house. A house with four windows.
Two doors. But no way out.
If you walk to the door, the threshold rises
And rises
To fill the frame.
So what does one do? Scour this. Dust that.
Adorn this. Change that. Do this. Do that.
And when you're sick of this, flit—
From that window to this.
Outside this one
A jackfruit tree has littered.
Outside that spreads a vastness of wire mesh.
Raindrops on the wire
And birds.
Outside the third,
The neighbor's family life.
And if one's eyes grow sick of this as well,
One paces about, placing foot before foot.
From this wall to that in straight lines, squares, at angles.
One might think it's a tale
Of a spellbound princess. The prince will come
Will take her away. But many monsoons
Have come and gone
The sound of hoofbeats has never been heard.
And the princess will not sleep.
Slowly, slowly—
Windows disappear. Walls vanish.

But the pacing goes on and on—
In straight lines
In squares, at angles.

Translated by Shanta Gokhale.

Ismat Chugtai ————————————————

(1915–1992)   *Urdu*

While still at school she used to write and tear up what she had written,
Ismat Chugtai said in a 1984 interview with the feminist journal *Manushi*.
"When I began to earn, I got the courage to send my writing for publication. I wrote a play, *Phisaddi* (The Laggard), about a girl who is sexually
teased by her cousin during summer vacation. This kind of thing does go
on, but is not spoken of or written about, especially not by women."
Around that time she wrote a story about a young servant girl who becomes pregnant. The girl is badly beaten up, while her employer's son,
who is responsible, is quietly sent off to Delhi. Both the play and the story
caused a sensation. People were scandalized. No woman could have written such "indecent" work, they said then, and continued to say for many
years to come. "I used to receive dozens of insulting, abusive letters. I still
receive them. I just tear them up."

Fortunately, that is only part of the story. Her work has also met with
well-deserved acclaim. Ismat the novelist, Krishan Chander declared,
"captured the soul of woman" as no one had done before, while the literary historian Muhammed Sadiq considers her mastery of the spoken
language and of dialogue unparalleled, and praises the economy of her
form. To that we would add her iconoclastic wit, her fine eye for the
detail that opens out onto a secret world of woman's experience, rarely
spoken about, and her passionate commitment to freedom.

Born in Badayun, a small town in Uttar Pradesh, into a well-to-do
family, Ismat grew up insisting she would do what the boys did; she
refused, she says, to do embroidery or play with dolls. Her early years
were passed in Jodhpur, where her father was a civil servant. When he
retired, the family returned to their ancestral home in Agra. It was there,
among the dingy, tortuous lanes and low-roofed houses, that Ismat, experiencing urban middle-class existence, was appalled by its unhealthy
meanness, its sham and duplicity. She saw the "hunched, half-consumptive
girls who panicked at the flutter of their own heart," and was later to
bring them alive on the pages of her sharp, incisive stories. A major early

influence was her brother Azeem Baig Chugtai, a well-known humorist and fiction writer. He taught her English and history and later the *Quran* and the *Hadith* (the Prophet's recorded sayings). Through him she "discovered literature."

Her friends were "the washerman's daughter, the sweeper's daughter, and the watchman's daughter" who lived in the compound of Ismat's family's rambling official bungalow. Not surprisingly, her aristocratic family did not approve. She must have been a *chamari** in her last life, they taunted. Ismat was quick to reply, "Yes, I was a chamari in my last life and I will be a chamari in my next life. It is only in this one that something has gone wrong!"

Despite her elite background and the freedom she had managed to win for herself at home, she had to fight for her education. The Muslim middle class considered education unnecessary, even harmful, for girls and, when Ismat was fifteen, her parents set about arranging her marriage. She managed to avert what she clearly saw as a catastrophe by the cheeky ruse of getting engaged to a cousin she "never intended to marry." Her friends, she says, "were married off around the age of twelve and I saw their lives. They told me that terrible things happen on the wedding night and after. They warned me never to get married because it was a painful business. I was terrified. I knew nothing about these matters. Neither did my parents tell me, nor was there any literature available. Also the whole business of marriage seemed to be dreadful—sex, cooking, beatings from the mother-in-law and all the other in-laws."

It was another battle to persuade her parents to let her study (the "persuasion" included threatening to run away to a mission school and convert to Christianity) for her bachelor's degree at Isabella Thoburn College, Lucknow. After a brief stint as a teacher at a girls' school in Bareilly, Ismat went on to Aligarh Muslim University to train as a teacher. However, she and six other women had to lobby for admission and were allowed to register only if they would sit in purdah, behind a curtain at the back of the class, a common practice in the 1920s and 1930s in universities where Muslim women studied. "If we could get what we wanted by sitting in purdah we would sit in purdah. We were interested in studying. If they had told us to wear *burqas,* we would have agreed," she says.

It was at this time, while Ismat was a student, that she started writing secretly, her head full of Majunun Gorakpuri and Niaz Fatehpuri, the popular and widely read authors of the time. From 1939 to 1941, she taught at the Raj Mahal Girls' School at Jodhpur. This was followed by an assignment as inspector of municipal schools in Bombay, which she

---

*A *chamar* is an untouchable leather worker; *chamari* is the feminine form of the word.

gave up in 1943 for a career in writing, including script writing for films. In 1941 she married Shahid Latif, a filmmaker, with whom she had two daughters. Of their tumultuous relationship she says, "I was twenty-eight when I got married. Well, we stayed together until he died, though we fought and quarreled all the time."

The person who by Ismat's own account influenced her most and completely changed the course of her thinking and writing, however, was Rasheed Jahan, a leading writer and political revolutionary of the time. "After seeing and hearing her," Ismat records, the candlelike fingers, the lime blossoms, and the crimson dresses of her stories "all vanished into thin air. The earthy Rasheed Apa simply shattered all my ivory idols to pieces. . . . Life, stark naked, stood before me." Her heroines, she says, have been modeled on Rasheed Jahan.

Ismat was part of the group of progressive writers of the thirties and forties to which Rasheed Jahan also belonged and in whose hands the Urdu short story came of age. Though she is impatient with organized movements of any kind ("no association could dictate to me what I could or could not write"), like the Marxist writers she is avowedly anticapitalist and has a deep sympathy for the oppressed. The novel *Ek Qatra Khun* (A Drop of Blood), 1975, depicts the Prophet's grandsons, Hassan and Hussain, as champions of oppressed humanity, confronting a tyrannical government.

Ismat's themes are drawn from life in the middle-class household. She knows its intricacies, its drabness, its bright spots. She explores the oppressions of family life and the workings of sexuality in the middle-class home, its inhibitions and its unsuspected little freedoms, with a subtlety still unrivaled in Urdu fiction. Among what might be regarded as explicitly feminist fiction are the novels *Ziddi* (The Stubborn One), 1941, and *Terhi Lakir* (Crooked Line), 1943, and the short stories "Dayin" (Witch), "Saas" (Mother-in-law), "Chattan" (Rock), "Chui Mui" (Touch-me-not), "Uf Yeh Bacche" (Oh, These Children), and the classic "Chauthi ka Joda" (Trousseau of the Fourth Day). Many of these were published in the popular collections of her stories, *Choten* (Wounds), 1943; *Kaliyan* (Buds), 1945; and *Chui Mui*, 1952.

In 1941, Ismat wrote the brilliantly conceived story that we have translated for this volume, *Lihaf* (The Quilt). The piece was to bring her special notoriety. A lesbian relationship between the beautiful wife of a wealthy landlord and her servant maid is presented by a child narrator who sees it all, yet concludes little and makes no judgements. The style achieves a superb balance of reticence and suggestiveness. As might be expected, however, the story outraged many, as it did even when an English translation was published decades later. Ismat was charged by the then British government with obscenity, but she won the case, she reports, because her lawyer argued that the story could be understood only by those who already had some knowledge of lesbianism.

In an autobiographical piece she contributed to a special number of the literary journal *Nuqush* (Marks), Ismat speaks of meeting with her mother after everyone else in the family had left for Pakistan. "I looked at her age, I looked at her loneliness. After having given birth to ten strong and healthy children, she was lonely. A flood of love rose in my heart. I looked at my mother, then I looked at my daughter and found myself imprisoned between the two."

◆

LIHAF
(The Quilt)*

Every winter when I pull the lihaf over me, and the shadow it casts on the wall sways like an elephant, with a sudden bound my mind begins to race and scour over the past. What memories revive in me!

I don't propose here to tell you a romantic tale about my own lihaf. Indeed, no romance can be properly associated with a lihaf. Come to think of it, a blanket may be less comfortable, but its shadow is never so frightening . . . as the rocking shadow of a lihaf on the wall. My story dates from the days when I was very young and used to spend the whole day getting into fights with my brothers and their male friends. I sometimes wonder why the devil was I so quarrelsome in those days. At the age when the other girls were securing admirers, I was busy fighting every boy or girl that came my way.

That was the reason why, when Mother went on a visit to Agra, she left me for a week in the care of her adopted sister. Mother knew very well that there wasn't a single child, not even a mouse of a one, to quarrel with in that house. A nice punishment for me! Well, so it came about that I was left with Begum Jan, the same Begum Jan whose lihaf has burnt itself into my memory and is to this day preserved in it like a scar from a red-hot iron. Begum Jan's poor parents had given her in marriage to the Nawab Sahib because, although somewhat "advanced" in age, the Nawab was a very pious man. No prostitute or street woman had ever been seen in his house. He had gone on the hajj pilgrimage to Mecca himself, and had helped many others to perform this holy service.

But the Nawab had a mysterious hobby. It is common for people to

---

*Urdu has at least two words for *quilt: raza'i* and *lihaf.* A lihaf is thick and heavy and is made of velvet or colorful silk or cotton prints. It connotes wealth.

have a craze for pigeons or for cock fights and so on. The Nawab detested such silly interests. His only pleasure was to have students around him, young, fair-faced boys with slim waists, whose expenses were generously borne by the Nawab Sahib himself.

After marrying Begum Jan, and installing her in his house along with the furniture, the Nawab Sahib totally forgot her presence, leaving the frail young Begum to pine in loneliness.

It is difficult to say where Begum Jan's life begins; at the point when she made the first mistake of stepping into this world, or when she became the wife of a nawab and was tethered to her canopied bed; or when the boys invaded the Nawab Sahib's life and sumptuous dishes and rich sweets began to be prepared for him, and she felt she was rolling on a bed of live coals as she watched from the chinks in the drawing room door and saw the boys in their translucent *kurtas,* their well-formed legs in tight-fitting *churidars,* their willowy waists . . . or, does it begin when all her prayers and vows, her vigils and charms failed to move the Nawab? What's the use of applying leeches to a stone? The Nawab didn't budge an inch. When this happened Begum Jan was heartbroken. She turned to books. But this too failed. Romantic novels and sentimental poetry left her even more dejected. She lost sleep and became a bundle of regret and despondence.

To hell with all those clothes! One dresses up in fine clothes to catch another's eye. But here, neither did the Nawab Sahib have any time to spare from the boys to look at her, nor did he let her go visit other people. Ever since she had been married, Begum Jan's relatives had come to visit her, staying for months, while the poor lady herself never escaped the confinement of her house. Those relatives made her blood boil. They all came to enjoy themselves, eat the rich food that the Nawab Sahib served, and have their winter needs provided for, while she would lie in the cold, feeling chilly even under her lihaf, freshly stuffed with cotton which had been teased out into a fluff. As she turned in her bed, the lihaf threw ever-changing shadows on the wall, but not one of these held any hope or solace for her. Why should one live then? . . . Well, one lives as long as life lasts. It was in her stars that she should live, and live she did.

It was Rabbu who pulled her back from the brink. And then in no time, Begum Jan's dried-up body began to fill, her cheeks glowed, her beauty burst into bloom. The massage of a mysterious oil brought back the flush of life to her. And the best medical journals, if you ask me, will not give the prescription for this oil.

• • •

When I first saw Begum Jan she must have been forty or forty-two. How elegantly she reclined on the *masnad*, with Rabbu sitting close and kneading her back and her body! She had thrown a purple shawl across her legs and looked as grand as a queen. I was quite enamored of her looks. I was happy to sit near her and look at her for hours. Her dark, luxuriously oiled hair was neatly parted, and so immaculately set that not a strand of hair could be found straying. Her eyes were black and her carefully plucked eyebrows were like drawn bows. Her eyes were a little distended with heavy eyelids and thick lashes. But it was her lips, often reddened, that were the most amazingly attractive feature of her face. She had a downy upper lip with the faint suggestion of a mustache. Her hair grew long at her temples. Sometimes watching her face you had the queer feeling that you were looking at the face of a young boy.

Her skin was white and smooth as though someone had stitched it tightly on her body. Often when she uncovered her legs below the knees so that she could scratch them, I would cast sneaking glances to see how they glistened. She had a tall figure and, being well clothed with flesh, she looked large of build. But her body was perfectly molded and beautifully proportionate. She had large, white, smooth hands and a well-formed waistline. Well then, as I was saying, Rabbu used to sit with her, scratching her back. She sat for hours doing it, as if scratching the back was one of the basic necessities of life, perhaps even more than a basic necessity.

Rabbu had no other job assigned to her. She sat all the time with Begum Jan, on the canopied bed, massaging her legs or her head or various other parts of her body. It bewildered me sometimes to watch the endless kneading and rubbing. I can't speak for others, but I can say that my body would have disintegrated under so much pounding. And this vigorous daily massaging was not all. On the day Begum Jan took her bath the ritual became more elaborate. God, to think of it! For two full hours before she entered the bath, she would have her body rubbed with all kinds of oils, perfumed unguents, and lotions. That would go on so long that the very thought of it made my imagination race. The doors of her room were shut, the braziers were lighted, and the massage would begin. Generally only Rabbu was in the room with her. The other maids stood by at the door, murmuring and handing in whatever was required.

The fact is that Begum Jan suffered from a permanent itch. Hundreds of oils and unguents were tried but the poor woman could not get rid of it. The doctors and hakims said there was nothing they could diagnose. The skin lay clean, without a blemish. If there was a disorder below the skin they wouldn't know. "Oh these wretched doctors, they are so stupid! Who would believe you have a disease? Your blood, God bless you, is a little heated, that's all," Rabbu says smiling and looks at Begum Jan with her eyes screwed into a slit. As for this Rabbu—she was as dark-skinned as Begum Jan was fair, as flushed in her face as Begum Jan was snowy white. She seemed to glow like heated iron. There were faint pockmarks on her face. She had a robust, solid body, small, nimble hands, a small, taut belly and fat, always moist, lips. Her body exuded a distracting odor. How quick her small, plump hands were! This moment you saw them at Begum Jan's waist and in a trice they were at her thighs and then racing down to her ankles. As for me, I used to watch those hands whenever I sat near Begum Jan, intent on seeing where they were and what they were doing.

Winter or summer, Begum Jan always wore fine-spun Hyderabadi lace kurtas, foamy white over her dark colored pajamas. The fan was kept going as a rule. Begum Jan habitually draped a light shawl over her body. She loved the winter months. I enjoyed staying with her in winter. She avoided exertion. One always found her lying relaxed on the carpet, munching dry fruit, while her back was being scratched. The other maids in the house held a bitter grudge against Rabbu. The witch!

She ate with Begum Jan, was her constant companion, and even slept with her! Rabbu and Begum Jan were a topic of amused conversation at social functions and gatherings. There were bursts of laughter the moment their names were mentioned. Innumerable stories had been coined about the poor lady. She, on her part, never stirred out, never met anyone. It was just herself and her itch, and the world could go by! As I was telling you, I was a small girl at the time I am talking about and was quite enamored of Begum Jan. She, too, was very fond of me. And that is why, when Mother went to Agra, knowing that left by myself in the house I would run wild and start up a war with my brothers, she left me for a week with Begum Jan. It delighted me and Begum Jan alike. After all, she had declared herself my mother's sister.

Where was I to sleep? Naturally, in Begum Jan's room. So a small cot was placed for me next to Begum Jan's bedstead. On that first night, Begum Jan and I chatted and played "Chance" till ten or eleven. Then I went over to my bed to sleep. When I fell asleep, Rabbu was still with Begum Jan, scratching her back as usual. The low woman! I thought.

Sometime in the night I suddenly woke up, feeling a strange kind of dread. The room was in total darkness, and in the darkness Begum Jan's lihaf was rocking as though an elephant were caught in it.

"Begum Jan—," I called out timidly.

The elephant stopped moving. The lihaf subsided.

"What is it?—go to sleep—," came Begum Jan's voice, from somewhere.

"I feel frightened—," I said in a scared, mousy voice.

"Go to sleep—what's there to frighten you—just say the 'Aayat-al-Kursi.' "*

"Okay." I started repeating the 'Aayat-al-Kursi' hurriedly but got stuck in the middle although I knew it by heart quite well.

"May I come over to you, Begum Jan?"

"No, daughter,—get back to sleep." This a little sternly. And then I heard two people whispering. Dear me! Who was this other one? I felt even more scared.

"Begum Jan—do you think there is a thief around?"

"Get to sleep, girl—what thief could there be?" This was Rabbu's voice. I quickly pulled my head back under my lihaf and went back to sleep.

By next morning the whole frightening scene had vanished from my mind. I've always been of an apprehensive nature. When I was a child, I had nightmares. Muttering in my sleep, waking up suddenly, and bolting from the bed were daily occurrences. People said I was possessed. The previous night's incident, therefore, quite slipped from my mind. In the morning the lihaf looked absolutely innocent.

When I awoke on the second night, I felt as though a dispute between Rabbu and Begum Jan were being silently settled on the bed. I could not make out anything, nor could I tell how it was decided. I only heard Rabbu's convulsive sobs, then noises like those of a cat licking a plate, lap, lap. I was so frightened that I went back to sleep.

One day Rabbu went off to see her son, a perverse lad. Begum Jan had done a lot to help him. She had set up a shop for him, and tried to settle him in a village, but he was amenable to nothing. For a time, he too took up the service of the Nawab Sahib and received many gifts of clothes from him, but then, no one knew why, he fled and never

---

*The "Aayat-al-Kursi" is a Quranic verse repeated to ward off evil.

turned up at the house even to see his mother. So Rabbu had to go to see him at a relative's. Begum Jan was unhappy about that, but Rabbu had no choice.

The whole day Begum Jan was disconsolate. Her body ached at every joint. She didn't want anyone to touch her. She didn't eat anything and was dejected the whole day long.

"Shall I scratch your back, Begum Jan?" I asked with eagerness, shuffling a pack of cards. Begum Jan looked at me intently.

"Shall I? . . . Really?" And I put the cards away.

For a while I did the scratching, and Begum Jan said nothing. She just lay quiet. The next day Rabbu should have returned, but she didn't. Begum Jan grew irritable—she drank several cups of tea and gave herself a headache.

Once again I sat scratching her back—smooth like a table top . . . I kept on gently scratching. One felt so happy doing something for her!

"A little harder—undo the buttons," Begum Jan told me. "This side—ah me, a little below the shoulder, here—yes—there's a nice girl!—ah!—ah!—," she sighed with pleasure.

"Further, this side." Begum Jan could have easily reached the spot with her own hand, but she was making me do it, and instead of resenting it, I felt important.

"Here," she said. "—Oi,—you're tickling me."

"—You!—" and she giggled. I had kept talking to her while I scratched.

"Tomorrow I'll send you out shopping," she continued. "What will you buy? A doll that opens and shuts its eyes again?"

"No, Begum Jan, not a doll. I'm not a child now."

"What are you then, an old woman?" she laughed. "All right, buy a babua*—make the clothes yourself. I will give you lots of cloth to do it with." She turned as she spoke.

"Fine," I said.

"Here," she took my hand and placed it where she felt the itching. She kept guiding my hand wherever she wanted to be scratched, and I, lost in thinking of the babua, went on scratching mechanically while she kept up her chatter.

"Listen, you don't have many frocks left. Tomorrow I'll get the tailor to make a new one for you. Your mother has left some cloth with me."

---

*A babua is a male figure, the female counterpart of which is a gudia.

"I don't want one of that red cloth . . . it looks cheap . . ." I was prattling and did not notice where my hand had wandered, nor that Begum Jan was now lying on her back, supine. "Oh my . . . !" I hastily withdrew my hand.

"Dear me, child! Watch where you're scratching—you're tearing up my ribs," Begum Jan said with a shy, mischievous smile, making me blush.

"Come here, lie down by my side." And she made me lie down with my head resting on her arm.

"Dear, dear! How thin you are! All your ribs show." She counted my ribs.

"Oo-oo!" I mumbled.

"Oui?—I wouldn't gobble you up, would I?—What a tight sweater! You haven't even put on a warm vest."

I began to fidget.

"How many ribs does one have?" She changed the tenor.

"Nine on one side and ten on the other," I said, haphazardly recalling hygiene lessons learned at school.

"Let's see, take off your hand—right—one—two—three!" I wished desperately to escape but she held me tight and pressed me to herself.

"Ouh!" I protested—Begum Jan began to laugh loudly. Even now when I think of how she looked that day I feel quite distraught. Her heavy eyelids had grown heavier, the down on her upper lip darker, and, in spite of the chilly weather, tiny drops of sweat glistened on her lips and nose. Her hands were cold as ice but so soft that it felt as though the skin on them had been peeled off. She had taken off her shawl, and in her thin kurta her body gleamed like dough. Heavy gold studs that had come undone were swinging to one side of her open front. Dusk had fallen and the room was in total darkness. An unknown dread took hold of me. I felt bewildered. Begum Jan's eyes had deepened. I began to weep inwardly. She hugged and squeezed me like a plaything. The warmth of her body drove me to distraction. But she paid no attention, she was like one possessed. And I could neither scream nor cry.

After a while she lay back exhausted. Her face grew dull and unattractive. She started taking long breaths. She is dying, I thought, and jumping up, took to my heels.

Rabbu, thank God, was back in the evening, and as I got into bed still nervous, I quickly pulled the quilt over me to sleep. But sleep wouldn't come and I lay awake for hours.

Why was Mother taking so long to return? Begum Jan so scared me now that I passed the whole day with the servants. The mere thought of setting foot in her room was enough to drive me out of my wits. There was no one I could speak my mind to. And what could I say, after all? That I was scared of Begum Jan, the Begum Jan who, everybody knew, was so fond of me?

Rabbu and Begum Jan had fallen out again, to my ill luck. This had me worried, for suddenly it occurred to Begum Jan that I was too much out of doors in the cold and would certainly catch pneumonia and die.

"Young girl!" she said. "Do you want that my head should be shaved? If anything happened to you, I'd be held responsible." She sat me down near her. She was washing herself in a basin placed before her and the tea was ready on a small table.

"Pour a cup out for yourself, and give me a cup too," she said, drying her face on a towel. "I'll get changed in the meantime."

I sipped tea while she dressed. Whenever Begum Jan called me to her when her back was being rubbed, I would go, but keep my face averted and run back at the first chance. Now when she began changing in my presence the gorge rose in me. Looking away, I kept sipping my tea.

"Oh, Mother!" a voice within me called out in despair. "Is quarrelling with one's brothers such an offense that you should cause me all this . . ." Mother was always against my playing with boys. As if boys were carnivorous beasts who would eat up her dear one. And what boys were they after all! My own brothers and a few of their rotten little friends. But Mother thought otherwise. For her, womankind had to be kept under lock and key. And here I was, more scared of Begum Jan than of all the loafers in the world. I would have run into the street that moment if I could. But I sat helpless.

After she had dressed, Begum Jan went through her elaborate toilet. When the makeup was over the warm scent of the perfumed oils she had used made her glow like an ember, and she prepared to shower her affection on me.

"I want to go home," I repeated in reply to every proposal she made. And I started crying.

"Come, sit beside me," she coaxed. "I'll take you to the bazaar—listen to me . . ."

But I would have none of it. "I want to go home" was my one response to all the toys and sweets that were being offered.

"Your brother will hit you when you are home, you little witch," she said, slapping me affectionately.

"Let him beat me as much as he will," I thought to myself and remained withdrawn and stiff.

"Unripe mangoes are sour, Begum Jan," Rabbu offered acidly. And then, suddenly, Begum Jan had a fit. The gold necklace which a moment before she had wanted to put around my neck flew into pieces, her fine lace *dupatta*★ was in shreds, and the neat part in her hair, never for a moment disturbed, was all roughed up. "Oh!—Oh! Oh! Oh!" she began to scream. Her body shook with convulsive jerks. I ran out of the room.

It was a long time before Begum Jan could calm down. When later I tiptoed into the bedroom, I found Rabbu sitting with her, massaging her body.

"Take your shoes off," Rabbu said as she scratched Begum Jan's ribs. Like a frightened mouse I crept into my bed and pulled the lihaf over me.

Sr—sr—phat—kitch . . . In the darkness, Begum Jan's lihaf was swaying again like an elephant. "My God," I murmured, my voice faint with fear. The elephant leapt inside the lihaf, and then lay still. I was quiet. But the elephant was on the rampage again. I trembled from head to foot. I decided that I should gather all my courage and switch on the light at the head of the bed. The elephant rose, agitated. It seemed to be trying to sit on its legs. I heard noises, slop, slop—as if someone were eating something with great relish. Suddenly I understood the whole affair. Begum Jan hadn't eaten anything that day and Rabbu—Rabbu had always been a greedy glutton. Surely something delicious was being gulped down under the lihaf. I sniffed the air trying to catch the aroma. Only the warm scent of attar, sandalwood, and henna reached me.

The lihaf was swelling again. I did my best to lie still and ignore it. But the lihaf began to take on such strange, outlandish shapes that it sent shivers down my spine. It seemed like a huge, bloated frog inflating itself and about to spring on me. I plucked up the courage to make some disturbing noises, but no one took notice and the lihaf entered my skull and began to swell there. Hesitatingly I brought my legs down on the other side of the bed, groped for the switch and pressed the button. Under the lihaf the elephant turned a violent som-

---

★A *dupatta* is a long scarf thrown across the chest.

ersault and collapsed. But the somersault had lifted the corner of the lihaf by a foot—"Allah!" I dived for my bed!

Translated by Syed Sirajuddin.

M. K. INDIRA ———————————

(b. 1917) *Kannada*

Though she did not start writing until she was forty-five, M. K. Indira has, in her lifetime, achieved the status of a major Kannada writer. She received the Karnataka State Sahitya Academy Award four times between 1964 and 1976—for *Tungabhadra,* 1963; *Sadananda* (Eternally Happy), 1965; *Navaratna* (The Nine Jewels), 1967; and *Phaniyamma,* 1976. The verdict returned by a popular readership has been equally remarkable. Her novels—she has written more than forty—run into multiple editions, and *Gejje Pooje* (The Initial Performance), 1966, and *Phaniyamma* became major motion picture hits. The film *Phaniyamma,* directed by Prema Karanth, also won several national and international awards.

M. K. Indira's first novel, *Tungabhadra,* was a pioneering work. It portrayed the struggles and aspirations of rural women, and was able, through its use of evocative detail and regional dialect, to create a rural world with unprecedented realism. With *Gejje Pooje,* Indira moved on to a more controversial theme—that of the hopes of a young girl born to a prostitute. Like any other girl she wants an education, marriage, and a family, but traditional society forces her back into prostitution and eventual suicide.

Phaniyamma, which is both fiction and "a little history," is based on the life of M. K. Indira's great-aunt, who was widowed when she was thirteen. Phaniyamma leads the austere life of a widow and never complains or rebels, but she does question tradition, and even go against it, when its irrational demands hurt others. Much to everyone's surprise, she supports a younger woman who refuses to have her head shaved when she is widowed.

The novel has been attacked by some feminist critics for glorifying the traditional life of a widow through the admiration it evokes for Phaniyamma, while others feel that the author "strips bare the hypocrisy and sham of a society that sanctions inhumanity in the name of tradition." It is true that Phaniyamma emerges as a powerful and attractive figure and that the reader is struck as much by what becomes possible, even in the traditional life of a widow, as by the atrocities she is victim to. In fact, the novel works both as a critique of tradition that is followed mechanically because people do not have "the courage or the intelligence to question the right or wrong of [what is] handed down to them," and as a reassertion of the value of humanely and rationally practiced tradition.

M. K. Indira was born in Tirthahalli, a small town in Karnataka, and had seven years of formal schooling before marriage. She has read a great deal of classical Kannada poetry and is one of the few writers in South India with a good knowledge of modern Hindi literature.

The extract translated here appears toward the end of the novel. Phaniyamma is "about eighty-two" and has, over a long life, stored up merit by undertaking several fasts and going on a difficult pilgrimage to Kashi (Varanasi). But all that is suddenly placed on the balance in this episode, when she is called upon to help with a difficult childbirth in a lower-caste household. The elders in Phaniyamma's family are aghast at the request, but she does not hesitate: "I'll be with you in a minute," she tells Jabina-bi, the Muslim midwife who has summoned her, and prepares quickly to leave.

◆

From PHANIYAMMA

[Chapter 10]

Phaniyamma quickly wrapped a *tundu** around herself and followed Jabina-bi.

"Latch the outside door. You can open it when I come back." Without waiting for a response, she hurried out. Baira, who had been waiting silently at a distance, walked ahead, the lantern in his hand.

Back at the house, each one turned to look at the other. Phaniyamma's brother's daughter-in-law burst out, "Just before she died, Mallakka wanted to eat some fish. It's just like that. I really wonder why such a thought entered Ancheyatte's mind. She's gone on pilgrimages, she's done the *rishi panchmi*** regularly—why is she going into that untouchable area now? What were they doing these four days that woman's been in labor, those sons of foolish widows? Eating mud? And now they've come to call her—at this odd hour of the night! And

---

*Tundu means "piece," and suggests that Phaniyamma used an old piece of cloth rather than a whole sari, probably because she is going to an "unclean" place and will have to discard her clothing when she returns.

**The *rishi panchmi* is a special ritual performed by widows on the fifth day of the new moon, in which they worship the *rishis* (sages), not the gods. Widows are usually debarred from religious ceremonies.

she—ready to go when they call. There's little to choose between them if you ask me—them that ask and them that go! And now tomorrow she'll have to undertake the *panchagavya*★ ceremony to purify herself."

This was the first time that the people in the house were displeased with Ancheyatte, or Post Mother, which is what they called Phaniyamma. They lowered the wick of the lantern, and as they went to sleep each one had something to say to the other.

The darkness seemed impenetrable. Phaniyamma followed the path lit by Baira's lantern. They walked several hundred yards before they reached his hut. A part of the veranda had been curtained off with a blanket. Inside, on the mat, Sinki lay in an exhausted sleep. When they saw Phaniyamma enter the hut, the women stood up, dumbstruck. Phaniyamma went straight to Sinki and sat down by her side. The girl had closed her eyes. It was difficult to tell whether she was dead or alive. Poor child, she looked so tired. Baira's wife began to howl. "Phaniavva, save my daughter somehow! Who knows, she might already be dead!"

Phaniyamma placed her hand on Sinki's forehead and felt the warmth. She beckoned to Jabina-bi and said, "Tell me what it is that I have to do now, quick. I've nursed hundreds of women after they've given birth, but have never delivered a child before. Tell me quickly." Jabina-bi put the lamp close to Sinki's feet, then placed the pot of castor oil in front of Phaniyamma and said, "Here, smear this oil on your right hand. Cover it completely. Then bunch all five fingers together tight. Ease your small hand inside, grasp the child's head firmly, and pull it out, slowly. I'll push the baby down from above. Let the burnt-out cinder of a son die if he wants to, but Sinki must live." Jabina-bi began massaging Sinki's abdomen downwards lightly with slow, sure hands. The other women gathered round to help. Sinki's mother continued wailing loudly. Phaniyamma turned to her and chided softly, "Why do you have to cry like that, you left-handed lout, when so many of us are struggling to save her?" The woman fell silent. Phaniyamma's little hand eased into Sinki's body, and within two minutes it emerged holding the baby! A torrent of blood gushed out. Pha-

---

★*Panchagavya* is a mixture of the five bovine products (urine, cow dung, milk, curd, and ghee) mixed in specified proportions. A spoonful is taken to purify oneself after one has come in contact with impure or unholy things such as childbirth or death.

niyamma trembled and went cold. Oh God, how terrible creation is! I don't mind having been widowed. I'm glad I've been saved from all this . . . filth, this sort of life . . . Suddenly she remembered Putta Jois and Paddi's secret love affair and the glimpse she had had of it. She thought, How funny! For this? Is this why one lives in human form? If I am to be born again, God, please give me the life of a flowering plant. In this life I have done nothing sinful. I don't want to be born again, if I can help it.

This was her daily prayer. There were some who believed in heaven, hell, rebirth, punishment, expiation and so on, and others who didn't, but pretended to believe in them all the same. Why? As Phaniyamma turned all these things in her mind, Jabina-bi was working hard to make the baby breathe. She slapped it on its bottom, but it wouldn't cry. She then held it up by the feet, with its head down, and swung it briskly from side to side two or three times. It suddenly let out a feeble cry. Jabina-bi handed the baby over to Sinki's mother and told her to wash it and put it to sleep. Then she kneaded Sinki's belly and pushed the afterbirth out. Along with it came another gush of blood. "Water," Sinki moaned. They gave her a little water to drink. The others bustled around. Thank God, both the mother and the baby were safe. Sinki's mother bowed before Phaniyamma with hands joined in deference. "You have a hand of gold, Mother," she said. "You have saved my child . . ."

Phaniyamma cut her short. "Stop this nonsense now. Take care of the baby and the mother. Give me some soapnut powder and water to clean my hands. When I reach home, I'll send you some musk and medicinal balm for the new mother. Send Baira with me. But listen, don't let any of my people know that I delivered the baby. I'll tell them that Sinki had already delivered when I arrived." Phaniyamma washed and scrubbed her hands. She felt revolted by the sight of the blood and afterbirth. Oh God, how ironic that in spite of all this pain and this disgusting filth, women still go to their men! What strange forgetfulness! How can they simply bear ten or fifteen children—one after another, like that! No, God, I am sure I don't want to be born as a human being in my next birth, certainly not as a woman, no!

She scrubbed her hands thoroughly, and saying "Take good care of the mother and child," she left, warning them again not to let the news spread that she had performed the delivery. They promised not to say a word. Baira picked up the lantern and led the way out.

"Baira, let's go to the farm first. I'll bathe in the pond there before we go home."

Baira hesitated and said, "A bath in this bitter cold? And at this hour of the night? It may not be good for your old body to bathe in such cold water. Surely someone at home will give you hot water."

Phaniyamma laughed at him. "Do as I tell you. For eighty years I've been bathing in cold water. Why should I use hot water now?"

He could not argue with her any more, so he retreated and waited for her a little distance from the pond. It was nearly three in the morning. The big clock in the house could be heard striking even at that distance. Swiftly Phaniyamma dipped herself eight times in the water, rinsed her mouth out, began softly muttering the purificatory mantras, and made the customary propitiatory offerings of water to the gods three times.

Wrapped in the same wet tundu, she walked home and asked Baira to wait near the gate. She knocked on the door. As her sister's son opened it, he asked, "Why did they send for you? Has Sinki delivered?"

Phaniyamma walked in and said, "Tell Baira to wait. Useless fellows! They really have nothing better to do. It was for nothing that they sent for me. The woman had already delivered by the time I arrived. Nanji*—the midwife—was looking after her. Anyway, what do I know about deliveries and all that? I stood outside the house the whole time. I felt so unclean. So I had to have a dip in the pond. I'll send some food and medicine for the new mother now."

Surappa had asked Baira to wait. Phaniyamma gave Baira the medicine and then went and changed her clothes. She lay down on her bed, but sleep would not come for a long time. The first cock crowed. So it was morning already! She rose and set about her routine. When the others awoke, they all asked her about Sinki. She repeated the story she had told Surappa in the night. Once again she went to the pond, took a dip and, still in the same wet clothes, swallowed the panchagavya.

When Baira's wife came at ten in the morning, Phaniyamma turned to her brother's daughter-in-law and said, "Will you ask her if both the baby and the mother are well? I can't come out and speak to her because I've already had a bath. I've brewed some clove tea for the

---

*Phaniyamma changes the name to cover up the fact that she had not only gone into an untouchable's house, but had worked with Jabina-bi, who is a Muslim, thus breaking two strict taboos. Nanji is a gowda and not an untouchable, and therefore is more acceptable.

woman. Take it out and pour it into a mud pot for her to carry home."
Both mother and baby were well, Phaniyamma was told, and the tea
was handed over to the woman. Then Phaniyamma said, "Tell Baira's
wife not to give the new mother any rice for at least two days. Give
her some wheat and jaggery so they can make some gruel for her. We
should help them as much as we can. After that it's left to them."
Because Phaniyamma had ordered it, Baira's wife got some wheat and
jaggery from the house.

"I'll come back, Amma," she said before leaving. In that big house,
that big family, there had of course been many births, but Phaniyamma
herself had never been present at even a single one. Usually some
gowda midwife and some old woman would sit in the dim light with
the woman in labor. Childbirth was not such a problem in those days.
Within an hour everything would be over. Phaniyamma, however, was
always in charge of the supply of medicines, herbal teas, and hot water.
Except for actually attending to a delivery, she could manage just about
everything. Now she had also seen an actual birth with her own eyes,
even if it had been just once. For two whole days she was not quite
herself; her mind was troubled. As she sat to count her beads and
meditate, she felt her slimy fingers slip inside Sinki's body and was
overcome with a great disgust. She even doubted whether the panchagavya had really purified her. So she took a dose every day for two
more days just to be sure.

But to herself, she thought, "Grandmother often used to say that
attending at a single birth is as good, as meritorious, as making a pilgrimage to Kashi. Well, what is done is done. After all, a living thing
is something precious. If I have saved two lives, it should be even
more meritorious. I should stop thinking about it." And so Phaniyamma tried to find comfort for herself and put the event aside in
her mind.

All the same, while going about her work, she often wondered about
the mysteries of creation and birth. Poor old woman! She had, after
all, never been exposed to the real world except for that single trip to
Kashi.

A woman becomes untouchable every month when she sees her own
blood, and must sit apart for three days. On the fourth day she is
supposed to have become pure. Many women, even in Phaniyamma's
family, bled for eight days. But that was not considered foul. Widows
who had been shaved by untouchable barbers remained pure. But an
unshaven widow, even if she is not touched by a man, is impure.

Hundreds of such puzzling thoughts plagued Phaniyamma again and again.

Translated by Pushpa Desai.

RAZIA SAJJAD ZAHEER ————————————

(1917–1979)   *Urdu*

Though her family came from Uttar Pradesh, Razia Sajjad Zaheer was born in Ajmer, where her father was headmaster of Ajmer Islamia High School. While in Ajmer and still in purdah, she earned a bachelor's degree, and after her marriage in 1938 to the renowned writer, Marxist thinker, and revolutionary Sajjad Zaheer, she received a master's degree from Allahabad University. Razia shared her husband's views, and their married life was as much one of love and mutual trust as it was of common interests and concerns. As she says in a touching essay written after Sajjad Zaheer's death, nearly half of their thirty-five years of married life were lived in separation, for her husband was often either in jail or away on political work.

Writing was Razia Sajjad Zaheer's chief occupation. Her youngest daughter, Noor, records how she typically found her mother seated in an armchair, bent over pad and paper, with her legs folded under her, a cigarette in her left hand, and a mug of tea to her right. She worked hard writing and rewriting her stories, many of which were published in the leading magazines of her time. In 1953 she published a novella, *Sar-e-Sham* (At Dusk). The novel *Kante* (Thorns), a children's book, and a collection of Sajjad Zaheer's letters to her, entitled *Nuqush-e-Zindan* (Impressions from Prison) came out in 1954, and another novel, *Suman,* in 1963. She translated over forty works, including Bertolt Brecht's *Caucasian Chalk Circle* and *Galileo;* Bhagvati Charan Sharma's biography of Maksim Gorky; *Aurat* (Woman) by Ram Saran Gupta; and *Alvida Gulsari Jamila* (Farewell, Gulsari Jamila) by Changiz Emui. Two collections of her short stories, *Zard Gulab* (The Yellow Rose), 1981, and *Allah De Banda Le* (God Gives and Man Takes), 1984, from which the story translated here is taken, were published posthumously. Razia Sajjad Zaheer received the Nehru Award in 1966 and an Uttar Pradesh State Sahitya Academy Award in 1972.

Razia Sajjad Zaheer and Sajjad Zaheer belonged to the group of writers who formed part of the progressive movement in Urdu literature. Along with Rasheed Jahan, Ismat Chugtai, and Siddiqa Begum Sevharvi, she represented the new woman who questioned social restrictions and began to assert herself in a male world. She wrote in the cadenced Urdu of upper-class women of Uttar Pradesh (especially Delhi and Lucknow), but she also had a remarkable mastery over the dialect of the working people. Her principal contribution is to the Urdu short story.

◆

NEECH
(Lowborn)

Looking at Shyamali, Sultana was reminded of rough twigs which, in themselves, looked so shapeless, but which, arranged well, produced amazingly beautiful patterns.

There was nothing special about her face. Her complexion, in fact, was dark. But on the very first day, when Sultana alighted from the rickshaw, entered her doorway, and saw Shyamali sitting in front of the servant's quarters, she felt there was something worth looking at again and again. Shyamali noticed Sultana, but instead of folding her hands in a respectful greeting, she only looked up and smiled briefly. Then she bent her head again and began to clean rice on a gleaming brass plate.

This manner of hers pleased Sultana, who believed she loved the common people. Whenever she saw a poor person cringing before a big man, addressing him as *maibap,** she disliked the poor man, which is why she was drawn to Shyamali.

Coming in from the gate, her mind went back to many things she had heard in her childhood. Those low-born women—they were un-reliable, she had always been told. She thought of the stories she had heard from her grandmother about girls bought during a famine who ran off with some man the moment they got enough to eat. These women picked up husbands and dropped them with equal ease. They had no feelings about such things. Sultana wondered who Shyamali was. How did she feel, living alone in the servants' quarters? Sultana took off her watch, went into the bathroom and turned on the tap. She wanted to have a bath. No water. Looking out, she saw Shyamali washing the rice at the outdoor tap. Irritated, she opened the window. "Hey, you! Turn that tap off." Seeing Sultana, Shyamali understood what the matter was, and, swiftly turning off the tap, said, "Bibiji, I

Maibap, "my protector," literally means "my mother and father."

arrived here just yesterday. I didn't know that turning on the tap out-side would stop the water coming into the house."

"Don't worry!" Sultana said. Her anger had vanished. Shyamali's voice was so pleasant. There was something very attractive about her manner of speaking, too.

Next morning, the large outer portion of the house, which had been empty, was rented out. The hall in the middle and the big rooms on either side were to be used as a business office. The smaller rooms were to be occupied by the secretary, the head clerk, and others. The rest of the building was now filled with attendants, sweepers, and watchmen. Shyamali's room and another small room were part of Sultana's portion of the house.

One evening, three or four days later, when Sultana returned from the college where she taught, and was looking through her mail, she heard the sounds of laughter outside. It sounded like Shyamali. Quietly, she opened the bathroom window. Sultana's young daughter was chasing Shyamali around. Shyamali ran into her little room and shouted, "Enough for now! I've lost. Now I must cook, dear child. We'll play tomorrow." The servants and others from the neighborhood stood around laughing.

The child began to pout. "I don't care what you have to do. Give me my turn."

Laughing, Shyamali came out. She changed her tactics. "Come, child, let's light a fire. You take the dough and make a bird. We'll have fun roasting and eating it."

The child sat on a brick while Shyamali arranged a few cow dung cakes in the stove and began to blow into it. Sultana closed the window. Shyamali's unrestrained, innocent laughter and vitality pleased her. Still, had those office attendants and watchmen not been standing around, it would have been better. Under the eyes of so many males to be a . . . Of course Shyamali had not even glanced in the direction of any one of them. Still, it may have been a bit of wantonness. But was it wantonness? Sultana looked up suddenly to find Shyamali standing there. Meeting Sultana's eye, Shyamali grew so shy that Sultana could hardly believe that this was the same woman who, a moment ago, was bursting with laughter, as if her whole body would strew itself like petals into the air. Was it that she did not feel free to laugh in Sultana's presence?

Softly, Shyamali said, "Bibiji, I need a couple of chillies. I would have gone to the market, but it is already dark and it won't look right if I go out now."

"What need is there to go out? Sit down! I'll get them for you." Sultana called out to the cook and began to think of questions she would like to ask Shyamali. Shyamali sat down and, in answer to Sultana's questions, told her that her husband was dead and that she worked in the yellow bungalow next door as a nursemaid for the Major Sahib's child. As she mentioned the child, she laughed with great affection once or twice, and it was evident that she loved him.

The cook brought the chillies and stood looking intently at Shyamali, but she took the chillies without even a glance in his direction. He nodded at Sultana in greeting and went out without speaking. Later, after Shyamali had gone, the cook observed, "Begum Sahib, you should not allow that woman into the house again."

"Hmm. You go and take care of your work," Sultana said, a little put out.

But the old servant, who had spent sufficient years with the family to establish some authority, was not prepared to give in so easily. He continued, "That one has left her husband. She has run away from her home. And she has flung herself on Ram Avatar. She is not a good woman." Sultana felt as if someone had hurled a stone at her.

"Ram Avatar, who is he?"

"The one who works as a watchman for the tenants."

Sultana recalled him. It was as if Ram Avatar came and stood before Sultana wearing his khaki government uniform, carrying a thick stick and a torch [flashlight] in his hands, with heavy boots on his feet.

Sometimes in the night, hearing the sound of Ram Avatar's cough, or the sound of his boots and his call "Ha, ha, *hoshiyar* ha, ha," she, too, would call out to him, "Ram Avatar!"

From the other side of the wall, he would reply, "Don't worry, *sarkar,*★ I'm awake." He was not her watchman. Yet he was considerate and he gave her a sense of security.

She was startled out of her thoughts. The cook was saying, "She has left her man and run away. Ram Avatar—poor fellow—is of a respectable caste. He is a Rajput Thakur. And she is a low-caste woman. She must have drugged him."

Sultana was annoyed. "Don't talk rot. You just have to hear one thing to start your gossip off. Go. That's enough of your stuff." The cook picked up the basket of chillies and left, muttering. Sultana could dismiss him, but not the thoughts he had left with her. She had to

---

★*Sarkar,* "boss," literally means "government."

admit that she was shocked by the cook's tale. Why had Shyamali done such a thing? She had left her husband, run away from home, and worse, was here having an affair with Ram Avatar. Well, be that as it may. She had also lied to Sultana. She had said her husband was dead. Why did she have to do that? She should have trusted Sultana to understand. Perhaps these women of low birth—no, no—what difference did it make whether the caste was high or low?

The next day at sunset Sultana was returning from a women's meeting. It was almost dark; the day and the night were embracing. Smoke was coming out of Shyamali's room, but no light. In the glow of the fire, Sultana could see Shyamali's hands working the dough for the *rotis*. Only the tip of her nose was visible beneath the yellow sari, edged with red, that covered her head. As she baked the rotis, she wiped her tears with the corner of her sari. Ram Avatar sat near her on a few piled up bricks. He was not wearing his usual khaki uniform, but looked especially handsome in a white dhoti and kurta. It suddenly occurred to Sultana that Shyamali and Ram Avatar would indeed make a fine pair.

Ram Avatar saw her and stood up. He bowed in greeting and moved to the side. Sultana walked up slowly to Shyamali and stood near her. She looked at her for a minute in silence. Then she said softly, "Shyamali, the cook says that your husband is alive. You said he was dead."

Sultana was confident that Shyamali would say, "No Bibiji, what does the cook know? He is dead." Then she could go in and scold the cook. She would tell him that folks like him should not slander poor innocent women. But Shyamali raised her eyes and looked at Sultana sardonically. Then she said softly, "What if he is alive? For me, he is dead."

Sultana felt as if she had received an electric shock. Good Lord! Could one speak of one's husband like that? Shyamali smiled at Sultana's silence. She said, "He thought that he could order me around, just because he gave me food and clothing. Am I a prostitute to be bought with money? My limbs are sound. I can work. I have the courage to feed ten like him." Then pouring some water into the basin that had held the flour, she began cleaning her hands, wringing them vigorously, almost as if they were her husband's ears.

Sultana turned and walked quietly towards her door, but her mind was in turmoil. No doubt Shyamali had great courage to think such thoughts. But how could she *say* such things of her husband—how did she have the heart? A husband was so precious, he was a woman's honor, her god on earth. Ah, she thought, with a jerk of her head, the low born. What was that? And she jerked her head again to drive away the thought, again, this obsession with the low born. Did she not know, had she not accepted it for a fact, that marriage in this society was nothing more than legalized prostitution? But today, when this idea appeared before her in all its nakedness, she was frightened. The cobwebs of inherited belief confused her. Had she accepted principles of equality merely to convince others? Had she learned principles by rote without assimilating them? Grandmother used to say, there it was only a matter of spurning food and clothing. But a husband, a woman's dignity, love, but, but . . . She panicked and called out to the cook to bring tea.

Three days later it was Holi, the festival that marked the end of winter. Her daughters had gone outdoors and were playing with the servant's children, smearing each other with color. The cook shut himself up in his room, not wanting to be caught by them. Sultana was sitting alone writing some letters when she heard the music of anklets and the sound of footsteps in the corridor. Shyamali's shadow appeared in the doorway. She was wearing an artificial silk sari with huge red and blue flowers, and a yellow satin blouse. Her lips were red with betel, her eyes darkened with kohl. Between her thick eyebrows she wore a large golden *bindi,* which flashed with every toss of her head like lightning among dark clouds. She held a brass plate. As she stood before Sultana, it was as if a princess from the Ajanta caves had come to life. On the plate small heaps of colored powder glittered with specks of mica. In one corner of the plate, wrapped in fine pink paper, were some sweet yellow *laddus.* Without warning, Shyamali looked up, picked up a pinch of color, and smeared it on Sultana's forehead. Sultana backed away nervously. Then Shyamali picked up a laddu and held it up to Sultana's mouth. Sultana's eyes filled with tears. She covered her mouth in a quick gesture and said softly, "Shyamali, I don't eat sweets . . . I have taken a vow, you know! I can't eat any sweets. When Sahib . . ."

Shyamali understood in a flash. She put the laddu back, took up the plate, and said softly, "Bibiji, don't lose heart. If God wills, all will be well and Sahib will return." Then she laughed and added, "Then all of us will offer you sweets, but . . ." Her eyes began to sparkle with tender mischief, "But then why would you want sweets from anyone else's hands?"

Sultana blushed. She wanted to change the subject, and as she reached into her bag for coins, Shyamali stopped her gently and said, "Please don't give me anything." As she turned to go, Sultana gathered her courage, cleared her throat, and in a hesitant voice asked, "Shyamåli, you are so good—why did you have to leave your husband?"

Shyamali lowered her eyes and began to prod the ground with her toe. The red tint on her soles danced rosy shadows in the gleam of her silver anklets. The next minute she raised her eyes. There was a touch of despair and irony in them. She said softly, "Let it pass, Bibiji, you wouldn't understand." And with her anklets chiming and her toe rings tinkling, she left. Sultana stood stunned. It was as if an electric wire had touched her.

As soon as Shyamali left, the cook arrived. He placed a tray containing the provisions for the meal before her and said, "Bada Sahib's attendant says that Ram Avatar is going to be dismissed."

"Dismissed! But why?" she was startled.

"It's like this. The sweeper, the head clerk, the gardener, and some other clerks have complained about wicked goings on here in the servants' quarters. We're family men with children. There are young daughters and daughters-in-law in our houses. And this woman is of loose morals. The Bada Sahib thinks that Ram Avatar's conduct is also undesirable. Did you hear the noise last evening?"

Sultana remembered that at dusk the evening before she had heard raised voices and had opened her window to listen. She had noticed only that some people were sitting on a cot and talking loudly. She had not understood their words. Ram Avatar had stood there like a criminal, and near him, a man leaned over a bicycle. Another man, wearing a coat, said something in the manner of one issuing a warning. Shyamali was nowhere to be seen, although this dispute had occurred in front of her house. Then Sultana had shut the window.

"Those were people from Ram Avatar's community, Begum Sahib. His uncle's son was also there. Ram Avatar is a man of high caste. His parents have arranged his marriage within the community. But now he is entangled with this woman and . . ." He paused, feeling that Sultana was not even listening to him. Abashed, he said, "Shall I cook the gourd with the mutton, Begum Sahib?"

Sultana awoke as if from a dream. "Huh? Yes."

The cook picked up the tray and left the room in silence. Sultana had just begun arranging her papers again when she heard a knock at the door. She opened the door and was startled to see Ram Avatar standing there. Of course, sometimes when Sultana's letters had accidentally gone to the main office, Ram Avatar had come over to give them to her. But today, looking at him, she felt strange. So this was that lover of Shyamali, about whom there was such commotion! Shyamali liked him—Shyamali, who had said to her, "You wouldn't understand, Bibiji!"

"Bibiji, here's a letter. It's just come for you. The Bada Sahib gave it to me."

Sultana reached out her hand, took the letter, and said, "Ram Avatar . . . this . . . this . . . what is this we hear about your job?"

Ram Avatar looked down. He was silent. That irritated Sultana. A sudden desire to scream at Ram Avatar took hold of her. She wanted to say, For God's sake, why don't you understand that I am your friend? This wall that stands between you and me, knock it down, Ram Avatar. Tell Shyamali not to keep away from me. Let her give me a chance to understand. That both of you were born in the servants' quarters and I in the main house—is it my fault? But controlling herself, she said, "Why? Is it because of Shyamali? Did someone complain about you two?"

Ram Avatar said only this much, and said it very softly: "It is nothing, sarkar. What can I say to you?" He salaamed and left—as if he, too, thought, "What's the use of speaking to you? You wouldn't understand." Sultana grew still more furious, not from anger alone, but from the strength of her determination. She had accepted the challenge that Ram Avatar and Shyamali had thrust toward her. Tomorrow she would confront the Bada Sahib. She would say why not only he, but *no one,* had the right to come between two innocent, honest, hardworking people and their love. If Ram Avatar lost his job, then she would shelter them both in her house. She would herself look for a job for him. Who were these self-important people of the community? Who had given them the right to give him a beating! She would see!

For a long time she planned what she would say, considering the turn of phrase she would use and rehearsing her confrontation with the Bada Sahib and the elders of Ram Avatar's community. She would prove to Ram Avatar and Shyamali that she was their friend, that she also could understand everything. She would go first thing in the morning.

The next day she dressed early, and was ready almost an hour before she customarily left for work. She could be certain that at this time the Bada Sahib would be available in the house and that Shyamali would be sitting in front of her house minding the manager's child. She usually brought the child to her house and kept him with her for hours. Sultana felt a secret happiness that Shyamali could never imagine that Sultana would fight the Bada Sahib on her behalf.

As she stepped out, she noticed that Shyamali's door lay wide open.

Her cot, bedding, pots, and other things were nowhere to be seen. The stove had not been lit. The lamp in the alcove had tumbled over. Sultana was shocked. The sweeper's wife, who was sitting on her cot picking lice from her child's head, promptly gave Sultana the news: "Bibiji, Shyamali has run away!"

Sultana felt as if someone had slapped her across the face.

"When?"

"I don't know, Bibiji. She was here till last night."

"And Ram Avatar?"

The sweeper's wife laughed. "Ram Avatar will stay. He is weeping at his bad luck. What do you expect from whores like her, Bibiji? Today one man, tomorrow another, the day after a third—they are from a low caste, after all." And she squashed a louse between her nails viciously, as if it were Shyamali she was crushing. Sultana's feet began to falter. There was no point going to the Bada Sahib now. How could she face him? What could she say? She walked slowly toward the main gate. Ram Avatar was sitting on a stool next to it. He saluted Sultana as he did every day. Then he stepped forward and opened the half-closed gate. But he did not smile at her. He went back and sat on his stool, lost, sad, lonely.

Sultana cast her eyes down and walked on. She could not find the courage to meet Ram Avatar's eye because, after all, she was a woman, and it was a woman who had deceived Ram Avatar and run away. Yet Sultana noticed that the attendants and the gardeners, who for some time had stayed aloof, were sitting near Ram Avatar today, their faces beaming with unspoken joy. And they were trying to comfort him.

As she reached the street, Sultana was filled with hatred for Shyamali. Poor Ram Avatar! So it was so, that low-caste women . . . Oh, no, she tried to shake the thought off. As she walked along, she wondered about all the women she saw on the way—were they also low-caste? And if they were, did they also deceive the ones who loved them and run away? She had wasted her love on Shyamali. She had pampered her pointlessly. Shyamali had turned out to be worthless, low-caste! She spat angrily on the ground and moved on.

After so many days and at such a distance it seemed unlikely that she would recognize Shyamali at once. But at the very first glance she suspected that the woman wearing a yellow sari and carrying a basket of guavas on her head, who turned into the Sikander Bagh gate, was probably none other than Shyamali. She asked her rickshawallah to follow the woman and draw up beside her so she could take a proper look. Hearing the ricksha behind her, the woman turned and looked in Sultana's direction, and again there was that flash among many clouds. It was Shyamali.

Sultana had thought, as she urged the ricksha forward, that if it turned out to be Shyamali, she would give her such a talking-to that she would remember it for seven lives. She started berating Shyamali right away: "How wicked you are, Shyamali! Why did you run away? Poor Ram Avatar is so broken. He's only half his self now. Everyone is laughing at him. You did a wicked thing. Should you have behaved this way?"

"But he did not lose his job, Bibiji," Shyamali said in reply to the tirade. Before Sultana knew what to make of this, Shyamali began to lift the basket to her head. Astounded, Sultana exclaimed, "But Shyamali, what do you mean?"

Shyamali put the basket down on the ground. She placed her hands on her hips, as if she had taken up Sultana's challenge. She said, a note of anger in her voice, "But what, Bibiji? Ram Avatar kept saying that he was going to lose his job because of me. He made me feel he was doing me a favor. You tell me this—did I tell him that he should or should not take that job? Was it his job that I loved? All the time it was, 'If I lose my job, how will I give you a living?' If I had stayed on in his house, I would have heard the reproach all my life. And what is this fuss about making a living? I have the courage to support ten like him."

Saying this, she lifted the basket to her head and was silent for a moment. Then she glanced at Sultana and her eyes filled with tears. She said softly, "How is Ram Avatar, Bibiji? Is he all right? Give him my—my good wishes."

Sultana bent her head. She said in the same soft tone, "I'll tell him. I'll certainly tell him." Shyamali smiled as if to say, "This time you have understood me."

Translated by Vasantha Kannabiran and Rasheed Moosavi.

ILLINDALA SARASWATI DEVI ⸻

(b.1918)   *Telugu*

The main character in Illindala Saraswati Devi's widely read and much appreciated novel *Darijerina Pranulu* (Lives That Have Reached the Shore), 1963, is a woman who, despite the anguish she feels at not having gotten what she desired, decides to spend her life in a meaningful way, running a nursing home for women. Each patient who comes there has a tragic story to tell, and the novel becomes a detailed account of the problems women face in society. Saraswati Devi is perhaps one of the best known Telugu women writers of her time. She has published several plays, twelve novels, and many short stories and essays. She has also written for children.

Saraswati Devi grew up in the eastern coastal region of Andhra Pradesh, and used its colloquial dialect to write her first stories in the early 1940s. When she showed these stories to her husband, he criticized her nonstandard language and informal style, so she did not submit them for publication until many years later. In the 1950s, after her children had grown up, she took a course in journalism at Osmania University and also expanded the ten-minute talks she had given on Deccan Radio into full-length articles and published them in the journal *Krishna Patrika*. She published several short stories in journals such as *Bharati* and *Sujata*. Saraswati Devi is a voracious reader, and once claimed that for every story she had written, she had read a hundred. Among her important works are the novels *Muthyalu Manasu* (Muthyalu's Heart), 1962; *Tejomurtulu* (Icons of Light), 1976; and *Akkaraku Vacchina Chuttamu* (A Helpful Relative), 1967; and the short story collections *Raja Hamsalu* (The Royal Swans), 1981. She won the national Sahitya Academy Award in 1982 for her collected short stories, *Swarna Kamalalu* (Golden Lotuses), 1981.

Saraswati Devi was a founding member of the Andhra Yuvathi Mandali (Young Women's Association), and from 1958 to 1966 was a nominated member of its legislative council. She won the Gruhalakshmi Award for best woman writer in 1964 and the Andhra Pradesh Sahitya Academy Award for literature in 1974. She is also a member of regional and national film awards committees.

The story we have chosen to translate here, taken from *Andhra Katha Manjusha*, 1958, is one of the few we found to deal with the theme of aging. The sparse realist narrative takes on symbolic resonance as it sets the protagonist on a journey that is also a passage from the life of the *grihasta,* or householder, which she finds claustrophobic and in which she has never been at ease, to that of the sannyasin, or spiritual wanderer. The passage involves a symbolic death, of which the woman crushed beneath the wheels of the train is a prefigurement, but also a release and a coming to life, not only of the protagonist, but also of her sick grandchild.

◆

ANASWASITA
(The Need for Sympathy)

Bangaramma had been looking out through the window since daybreak. She had ordered some coffee, but though the train had passed through two stations, the vendor had not yet brought it. She fell asleep waiting. The compartment was not crowded at that hour, so she could lie down, stretching her legs a bit and resting her head on her arm.

She dozed, disturbed every now and then; a mild headache reminded her that the coffee had not yet arrived. Then, rocked by the speeding train, she fell into a deep sleep. She lost count of the stations the train had passed through. When she woke at last, she realized that several other passengers had entered. The compartment was filled with chatter. She could hear one conversation quite clearly.

"How old do you think she is?"

"About twenty-five?"

"That's what she looks like, but I am quite sure she is much older than that."

"True. It's hard to guess a person's age these days, when most people dye their hair and lavish their skin with creams to prevent wrinkling."

"But even fifteen-year-old boys have gray hair nowadays. What do you think about that?"

She wasn't quite sure whom they were talking about, but she was eager to listen in on what they had to say, so she pretended to be still asleep. They must have noticed her stirring, for they dropped their voices and began to whisper.

At that moment, the coffee vendor finally arrived. She sipped the coffee, and, taking care not to glance up, took out some betel nut shavings from the pouch in her handbag and started chewing them. She noticed that there were four other passengers in the compartment, all men. One wore a suit, while the others were dressed more traditionally in dhotis and shirts. When she sat up, they quickly straightened themselves and behaved like polite, respectable people.

Without raising her head, she looked at her own body. She was firm and taut like a full-blown bicycle tire. Her complexion blended perfectly with the gold bangles round her wrists. She definitely looked much younger than her age. Suddenly she remembered with a sharp thrill of joy the conversation she had overheard. Without betraying her emotion she turned and looked out the window.

It was past eight o'clock. The train was running very fast. The passengers grew stiff and stopped talking. The atmosphere was suddenly oppressive. For want of anything better to do, she had just taken out a few more bits of betel nut and had begun to chew when the train abruptly came to a halt. Several passengers got off and rushed toward the engine. Two of them were from her compartment. There were still people rushing towards the engine while others had begun to return. They were saying, "Poor thing. She was quite young. Her head is badly crushed. She doesn't even look poor."

About an hour later they managed to remove the body, and the train began to move once more. The passengers returned to their seats.

One of them said, "Poor woman! Who was she? How did she fall under a moving train? And why, I wonder." As he had not gone up to the scene of the accident himself, he was asking others for details.

"How can we tell? We just took a look. Her head was badly crushed," one of them answered.

"How old was she?" the first man asked, suggesting perhaps that some clue to the problem lay there.

"I can't really say. It's quite difficult to guess a woman's age. She was neither young, nor old." Suddenly he became aware of Bangaramma's presence and felt awkward.

Noticing his embarrassment, another added, "It seems she had children too. It's really difficult to tell what drove her to forsake them like this and jump under a moving train."

There was a sudden lull in their conversation. The train had stopped at a side station. Two women entered the compartment. Within a couple of minutes one of them started chatting with Bangaramma and asked her where she was going. Bangaramma told her.

"Who are you going to see?"

"My daughter," Bangaramma replied tersely, without even looking up as she spoke.

"What does your daughter do there? Is she married?" She seemed really eager to know.

"My daughter has a child. I'm visiting her only because I want to be there for my grandson's birthday feast," Bangaramma said reluctantly.

The other woman showed surprise. "Your grandson's birthday feast! Looking at you, who would guess that you are a grandmother?" With the air of one who had made a real discovery, she looked at the other people in the compartment with a meaningful smile.

The men also betrayed their astonishment. One of them looked at the others triumphantly, as if to say that he had already guessed as much and had told them so. Suddenly they seemed to relax. Shedding their earlier inhibitions, they began to speak more freely, and even made a few crude jokes. They tossed the newspapers around, making no attempt to keep them in order. Bangaramma sensed the change. She found their behavior nauseating.

She continued to sit in that compartment for another hour. Then she got up and put her baggage together. As soon as the train reached her station, she stepped off and waited on the platform. A young man entered the carriage and picked up her baggage. As the train was pulling out of the station, the woman shouted out to Bangaramma, "Is he your son-in-law?" Bangaramma turned her face away.

When the cart stopped in front of the threshold, her daughter ran out and led her into the house. The place was already bustling with relatives. The boy was out playing somewhere, but her daughter found him and brought him to Bangaramma. Without saying a word, she gave him a tin of biscuits.

He wanted to run back, taking the tin with him, but his mother held him by the hand, and said, "This is your grandmother. Don't run away."

Bangaramma began to feel uneasy. After lunch she lay down and slept till five in the evening. As she was sipping a cup of coffee, her daughter came and sat beside her. The birthday celebrations were to be held the next day. There would be a feast. Several guests had yet to arrive. She gave her mother all the details, and said, "Your son-in-law is very keen on celebrating on a very grand scale. There is no way I will be able to manage it. You will have to take charge of everything."

Bangaramma listened to her without saying a word. Just then the boy came in. He had eaten as many biscuits as he could, and had given the rest away to his friends. They were delicious. He decided he wanted to make friends with his grandmother. His mother expected that the grandmother would reach out for the boy and fondle him. But Bangaramma did not even look at him.

"Why have you come to Grandma once again? Do you expect her

to give you another tin of biscuits?" his mother scolded. "Look, Mother, see how naughty he is," she said.

Bangaramma smiled, but didn't respond.

That night the daughter said to her husband, "My mother has changed quite a bit. She remains distant most of the time, and doesn't seem to talk to anyone with enthusiasm. I sat near her for a while in the afternoon and spoke about the arrangements for tomorrow's function. But she didn't say a word."

"Perhaps she finds it miserable living all alone in that large house. Why don't you ask her to come and live here with us?"

Bangaramma overheard the conversation. She was still tired after the journey, but she grasped the significance of those words quite clearly.

She rose early the next morning, and moved about briskly. Looking enthusiastic, she personally checked on all arrangements. She gave her grandson some more gifts, and hugged him in the presence of her daughter.

Bangaramma had had only one child—this daughter. When the daughter had left her parental home to live with her husband, Bangaramma had felt quite lonely. Her husband had then been her sole companion, and they had looked like a newly married couple. Motherhood had not left any visible scars either on her appearance or on her mental attitude. Her husband's job involved an annual transfer from one place to another, and it suited her well. Wherever they went, people said, "See, how young she looks." Those words were music to her ears. They braced her. Later, even after she became a widow, this pride in her appearance persisted. She continued to wear her ornaments, and continued to look pretty and youthful.

Bangaramma put on a georgette sari that morning. She went round looking gay, welcoming the guests warmly and chatting with them. The celebration went off very smoothly. Soon the guests began to leave. Then she heard one of them asking her daughter, "You said that your mother would visit you. Hasn't she come?"

Her daughter introduced Bangaramma to the guests. "Oh, so you are the boy's grandmother! We never realized it. Your grandson does look a lot like you. Pardon me for saying it, but it is really difficult to guess that you are a grandmother."

The daughter burst into peals of laughter. The guests were surprised, but Bangaramma was deeply disturbed by the remarks. She felt a certain heaviness in her heart.

After dinner Bangaramma sat in the backyard to get some fresh air.

Her son-in-law's parents spotted her and came to sit near her. They talked about the party.

Just then the boy came out carrying a large Japanese toy. He began to prattle sweetly.

Bangaramma was delighted to see him. She looked at him affectionately and stretched her hands out in his direction.

His grandfather said, "Young fellow, will you give that toy to me?"

"No. I'll give it only to my grandma."

Bangaramma was troubled. She pulled her arms back, as though she had been stung by an insect.

The next day all the guests left, but her daughter did not allow Bangaramma to leave.

A few days after the birthday party her grandson suddenly fell ill, and was bedridden with a high fever. The temperature did not come down even after four days. Though there was a doctor attending him, the boy's parents were really frightened.

One night he grew quite restless. It was a difficult task to pacify his mother. Bangaramma was disturbed about her daughter. She wanted to hold her, to console her. But when Bangaramma went out to be with her, the boy called out, "Grandma!" and so she had to rush back to his room. When her daughter came to the boy's room, she hugged her and wept. Her daughter had not eaten a proper meal or slept for over a week. Bangaramma felt anxious.

One night the doctor said to her, "Don't let the boy's mother sit up with him. Otherwise she, too, will fall ill." Bangaramma couldn't bear to see her daughter's suffering. Somehow she managed to control her feelings, and she continued to sit near the boy. He was fast asleep. It was time to give him a dose of medicine. She looked at the clock, and wondered whether she should wake him up.

The boy muttered feebly, "Grandma," and that troubled her too.

During her visit, Bangaramma had begun to enjoy the child's chatter, and had felt happy watching her daughter fondle him. She felt sad that her husband had not been able to enjoy all this. But the word *grandma* was something quite unbearable. Many people would consider the prospect of holding a grandchild in their arms a great blessing, but not Bangaramma. It made her burn within. The boy cried pathetically, again, "Grandma!"

Bangaramma was startled by the sound. She looked at herself from top to toe. Every time the boy called out "Grandma" she felt that the sound had the power to destroy her strength and her youth. Many things began to trouble her. It was as if her firm body had suddenly shrunk. Were wrinkles appearing on her smooth skin, and gnarled veins jutting out of her arms? Were her cheeks growing hollow? Her strong clean teeth falling out? Was her black, gleaming hair turning a little gray? Was her straight spine slowly bending? These thoughts flashed through her mind one after another. Her hands gave way, and the medicine bottle fell crashing to the floor.

Hearing the crash, her daughter and son-in-law rushed into the room. Seeing her trembling, her daughter led her out of the room.

Two days later, the boy showed signs of improvement. One morning his parents were sitting by his bed, chatting casually. The daughter was waiting for her mother to fetch the coffee. It was past eight, but there were no signs of her having awakened. The daughter went round the house, calling out to her mother. Then she noticed a letter on the bed in her mother's room.

> Dear Daughter,
> I didn't want to disturb your sleep. So I am leaving without telling you. I have grown weary of the bonds of the family. For a long time now I have been thinking of serving as a nurse in a hospital. I don't have to execute a separate will and testament. Your son will inherit all my property.
>
> Bangaramma

She read the note. And wiping her tears, she said to her husband, "Really, my mother has no courage at all."

Translated by Adapa Ramakrishna Rao.

AMRITA PRITAM ⸺⸺⸺⸺⸺⸺⸺⸺

(b. 1919)   *Hindi*

"Society attacks anyone who dares to say its coins are counterfeit, but when it is a woman who says this, society begins to foam at the mouth. It puts aside all its theories and arguments and picks up the weapon of filth to fling at her," writes Amrita Pritam.* Running through both of her autobiographical works—*Kala Gulab* (Black Rose), 1968, and *Rasidi Ticket*

---

*All the quotations in this headnote were translated by Madhu Kishwar and Ruth Vanita.

(Revenue Stamp), 1976—as well as her account of the experiences of women writers the world over, *Kari Dhup Ka Safar* (Journey through Burning Heat), 1983, is the theme of a woman writer's battle against persecution and her determination to "dare to live the life she imagines." Her writing is celebrated for its sensuous imagery and evocative rhythm and is widely read and appreciated, though it has also been criticized as vacuous and sentimental.

Born in Gujranwala, in what is now Pakistan, Amrita was the only child of her school-teacher mother and the devotional poet Kartar Singh (Piyush), who edited a literary journal. With her father she shared a love of language, and from her mother she inherited the rebel spirit that has marked her life. Her mother, she writes, "never failed in the slightest degree to honor and obey my father's male will . . . [but] collected all the anger from her mind and poured it into my infant being." Her mother died when Amrita was eleven. Perhaps overawed by the responsibility, her father did not allow young Amrita to mix with other children, and she grew up an intensely solitary person. She began to write poems at a very early age, and her first collection, *Thandiyan Kirnan* (Cool Rays), came out in 1935, when she was sixteen. "In this, my sixteenth year, a question mark seemed to have erected itself against everything. . . . There were so many refusals, so many restrictions, so many denials in the air I breathed that a fire seemed to be smoldering in every breath I drew. . . . That sixteenth year is still present somewhere in every year of my life," she wrote in *Rasidi Ticket.*

Also at sixteen, she married Gurbaksh Singh, editor of the Punjabi magazine *Preetlari,* to whom she had been engaged at the age of four and with whom she had two children, Navraj and Kandia. Her husband's family was disturbed by the adverse publicity she often received, and wanted her to stop writing. And over a period of time, she has said in an interview with Madhu Kishwar and Ruth Vanita of the feminist journal *Manushi,* she realized that this marriage had not provided the companionship she had imagined and wanted. When her father died in 1940, she felt "absolutely alone."

In 1944 Amrita met the poet Sahir Ludhianvi. She describes the meeting in "Akhri Kat" (Last Letter), which, she says, was written as a story only because it could not be posted as a letter to Sahir. "My beloved," it ends, "this is the last letter I shall write to you . . . now with these hands kissed by you I will write songs not of silk but of iron. . . . When you read these battle songs remember I am writing them with the hands you have kissed." They enjoyed a long and mutually supportive friendship, but Amrita declared her love for him only in her poetry. The long poem "Sunhare" (Message), for which she won the Sahitya Academy Award in 1953, and many other poems in her early collections were inspired by their friendship.

In 1947, at the time of the partition of India, Amrita Pritam moved to Delhi. She was witness to the terrible atrocities that took place, and that trauma haunts several poems, including the much anthologized "Ai Akan Waris Shah Nu" (To Waris Shah I Say) and other poems in *Lamian Vatan* (Long Distances), 1945. It is also the theme of the powerful novel *Pinjar* (Skeleton), 1950. "I felt as though the whole of womankind had gathered together its mental anguish and molded my soul from it," she writes in *Kala Gulab*. After moving to Delhi she began to write in Hindi. Today Amrita Pritam is best known as a poet in her mother tongue, Punjabi, and as a prose artist in Hindi, the language that brought her a wider readership and the economic independence she has today. From 1949 to 1961 she worked with All India Radio. In 1960 she and Gurbaksh Singh were divorced, and since 1966 she has lived with the artist Imroz.

Her writings after 1960 deal more and more with women who acknowledge their desires and their independence and accept responsibility for their lives even at the cost, as in the celebrated novel *Erial* (Aerial), 1968, of love. Among her explicitly feminist fiction we might also include *Ik Sit Anita* (Once There Was an Anita), 1964, and *Cak Nambar Chatti* (Village Number 36), 1964. She won the Jnanpith Award in 1973 for *Kagaz te Kanvas* (Paper Was [My] Canvas). In the sensational *Aksharon ki Chaya Mein* (In the Shadow of the Alphabet), 1977, she acknowledges the autobiographical core in each of her stories that deal with husband-wife relationships and the loneliness of married women. In 1980, she published *Kacche Akshar* (Raw Letters). But as she explains in *Kala Gulab,* "My story is the story of women in every country, and many more in number are those stories which are not written on paper, but are written on the bodies and minds of women. . . ." Four of Amrita's books—*Black Rose, The Skeleton and Other Stories, Existence* and *Revenue Stamp*—as well as several poems, have been published in English translation.

◆

EK BATH
(A Story)

Like pure milk is my love,
Like old rice of many years.
Scrubbed and washed the earthen pot of my heart.

The world is like wet firewood,
Everything dim with smoke.
The night is like a brass bowl,
The moon's silver coating worn,
Imagination's faded,

Dreams gone rancid,
And sleep turned bitter.

On the finger of life
Memories tighten like a troublesome ring.
As if from the goldsmith of time
Grains of sand have slipped between.

Love's body is shrinking
How do I sew a shirt of song?
The thread of my thoughts is all tangled,
The needle of my pen broken,
The whole story—lost.

Translated by Keshav Rao Jadhav and Vasantha Kannabiran.

JADA
(Winter)

My life shivers,
And lips turn blue.
From my soul's feet
The trembling begins.

Across the sky of this life,
The clouds of past years thunder.
Hailstones cold as law
Fill my courtyard.

Across lanes deep in mire
If you were to come to me,
I would wash your feet
And raising the hem
Under your whole filled blanket
Perhaps warm my hands and feet.

A cup of sunshine
Let me drain in a breath;
A piece of the same sunshine

I shall tuck into my womb;
And in this manner perhaps
The winters of my lives will pass.

Translated by Keshav Rao Jadhav and Vasantha Kannabiran.

K. SARASWATHI AMMA —————————————

(1919–1975)   *Malayalam*

"In the entire history of women's writing in Kerala," the critic Jancy James writes, "Saraswathi Amma's is the most tragic case of the deliberate neglect of female genius." This self-confident and outspoken feminist writer published, in the two decades after her first short story appeared in 1938, twelve volumes of short stories, one novel, a play, and in 1958, a book of essays significantly titled *Purushanmarillatha Lokam* (A World in Which There Are No Men).

Her achievement is all the more remarkable when we consider that she wrote, long before the resurgence in the seventies of the women's movement, without much support from other women, and in the face of a derogatory and dismissive critical reception. Her own extroverted nature, her bold opinions, and her free interactions with men were unusual in her society, especially for a single woman, and caused much resentment. Though K. Saraswathi Amma seemed initially to have weathered it all with a verve diminished in no way by the hostility, she stopped writing after the early sixties and lived the last years of her life as a recluse.

K. Saraswathi Amma was born in Kunnappuzha, a village near Trivandrum, the third and youngest of three daughters of an upper-class family. She received a bachelor's degree in Malayalam in 1941. In a move that was uncommon for a woman of aristocratic parentage, she decided to remain single and earn her own living. She worked as a teacher for two years before securing a job in the government accounts office. People who knew Saraswathi Amma well say that she carried enormous emotional tensions within her, but that her own independent temperament did not allow her to share her problems with others. She always maintained a "spiritual untouchability." Some accounts hint at a love affair in which she was harshly betrayed and suggest that the woman's revenge in the powerful but macabre story "Premabhalam" (The Fruit of Love), 1951, is an account of the author's own anger. All her life she suffered from psoriasis, though it was never conspicuous and seems not to have restricted her.

K. Saraswathi Amma's strained relationships with her family were complicated by her deep attachment to her elder sister's son, Suku, whom she brought up as her own child. Under her guardianship he graduated from college and became a sub-inspector in the reserve police force. When he moved out of her life, seeking professional transfer away from Trivandrum, K. Saraswathi Amma began to withdraw from public life and all but stopped writing. She did not bother to take departmental tests, was not promoted, and retired early. She died in the house she had built for herself, unmourned, and misunderstood by her family and her readers.

K. Saraswathi Amma's stories, as well as her essays and speeches, were marked by humor and a certain lightness of touch with which she analyzes the relationship between men and women. Though the loud defensive reactions from the predominantly male critical establishment would perhaps lead one to think otherwise, her writing is not a tirade against men. Rather, it is directed at women in an attempt to shatter the illusions they nurture about love and about men, and to instill in women a new, independent self-confidence. In a biting attack on female subservience she observes, "Woman does not worship her husband as a person, but as an ideal; the basis of woman's devotion to the husband is not her love for that man but an attempt to boost her own self-importance." The text of the radio talk "Purushanmarillatha Lokam" warns women that a life of equality will require them to give up the pleasures of dependency and coyness. Many of her stories illustrate different aspects of a well-developed feminist thesis. She has been criticized for appealing more to the intellect than to emotion.

K. Saraswathi Amma's novel *Premabhajanam* (Darling) was published in 1944, and the play *Devaduthi* (Messenger of God) in 1945. Then followed a series of short-story collections among them: *Ponnumkudam* (Pot of Gold), 1945; *Strijanmam* (Born as Woman), 1946; *Kizhjivanakkari* (The Subjugated Woman), 1949; *Kalamandiram* (Temple of Art), 1949; *Pennbuddi* (Woman's Wit), 1951; *Kanatta Madil* (Thick Walls), 1953; *Premaparikshanam* (The Experiment of Love), 1955; *Chuvanna Pukkal* (Red Flowers) from which the story translated here is taken, 1955; and *Cholamarangal* (Shady Trees), 1958.

◆

VIVAHANGAL SWARGATIL VECCHU NADATTAPEDUNNU
(Marriages Are Made in Heaven)

Madhavi's parents had resolved that in no case would they use money to buy her a husband. Her father said, "I didn't take a single paisa when I brought a wife home. Just think, we have eleven children. If we begin to buy sons-in-law, we will end up with the beggar's bowl."

Her mother said, "Times have changed indeed! They stood in line and snapped me up before I was fifteen. We don't want a groom who expects money. He may in the course of time even sell the girl. Let her remain here. When the time and the stars click, a husband will certainly come as though drawn here on wires."

But the time and the stars did not click and years passed without anyone's being drawn on wires to her.

Meanwhile, completely ignoring the disquiet of the parents, time worked bewitching changes on Madhavi's sisters as well. There were now four girls past fifteen in that house.

A house that harbors unmarried girls who have come of age will surely catch fire, the old women say. But Madhavi's parents learned from experience that it is not the house that burns, but the hearts of the parents.

And so their noble resolve melted into a decision to give the groom a small amount of money. But in the friction between the two-hundred rupees they offered and the two-thousand asked for, many proposals vanished into thin air.

At last, when Madhavi turned twenty-three, bargaining brought the price down to five-hundred, in addition to the fifty for the go-between, and the matter was settled.

It was only after the broker had settled the terms that the groom's people came to "see" the girl. A rich repast had been prepared to please them. It was Madhavi who, at her father's behest, served the meal, with a prayer from the depths of her heart that her livelihood might be ensured once and for all. They liked the girl. Then her father went to "see" the boy, and both parties were now agreed on all the terms.

It was the marriage of their eldest daughter, and so they celebrated it as well as they could afford to. Three *payasams,* special sweets made of rice, cooked in coconut milk and jaggery, and a *kathirmandapam,* a ritually decorated dais for the bride and groom, were unheard of in that village. So also the *mangalapathram,* a poem of good wishes for the bridal couple, from the friends of the groom.

The mangalapathram began with the line "Marriages are made in heaven" and continued with a liberal sprinkling of romantic words such as *premamritham* (the nectar of love), *parijatham* (one of the five trees produced at the primal churning of the ocean), *kalpavriksham* (the tree of inexhaustible bounty), and others. The bride and groom, who had been hitched in a deal that was purely business, were said to be "wafting into the matrimonial bower burning with the passion of love."

That night in her husband's home, as the golden letters of the mangalapathram hung on the wall gleamed in dim light, Madhavi stepped down from the heaven of the kathirmandapam into the earthly reality of the bedroom.

Her experiences did not stop there. After heaven and earth follows hell, a truth brought home by her mother-in-law.

For a woman who had completely subjugated husband and son, the daughter-in-law was but a puny little prey.

In a way, the mother-in-law's tantrums were not fully unjustified. On the third day after the wedding Madhavi's father had come, apparently to witness for himself the nuptial happiness of his daughter. But Madhavi's mother-in-law, who was listening in, had heard him ask his daughter to return the major part of her ornaments. Dramatically emerging from under cover, she ordered him to carry away not only the jewels, but also his daughter. Taken unawares, the old man turned pale and weak and sat absolutely quiet. Because of her desire to deck herself out with those jewels, Madhavi too did not say a thing in defense of her father.

The old man was now in a sad predicament. He did not want to be saddled with the burden he had divested himself of, and after great expense and effort. At the same time, how was he to face the neighbors from whom he had borrowed the ornaments?

When he returned home, he told his wife everything and felt better. He hoped that a woman's brains would be a better match for another woman's.

After a few days, Madhavi's father came again, this time with her mother. She removed, in the mother-in-law's presence, the old ornaments from her daughter's hands and neck and put new ones in their place.

As she took leave, blessing her daughter and vowing to offer gifts to various temples, she whispered, "If only God would bless you soon with a child! She might dislike her daughter-in-law, but she will surely love her grandchild. Then the child's mother cannot be thrown out."

The child's tiny hands would fix more firmly than the strong hands of the parents the bonds of wedlock.

After some days Madhavi and her husband, as the newly married couple, went on a formal visit to her parents. Pressed by her sisters, Madhavi stayed on for the night. Her husband, however, left, promising to come the next day to take her home.

But the next day stretched into ten or more days and nobody came. On some pretext or other, her husband's coming was delayed. Two months passed. Madhavi's parents now were very upset.

It was then that they heard of a new charge that had been leveled against them. They were accused of having shown the groom's party another girl who was a beauty instead of Madhavi. The charge was promptly denied, and the countercharge made that Madhavi's mother-in-law was trying to extort more money through such tricks.

Gradually the case gathered more and more evidence and became deadly serious. It even threatened to become a lawsuit in a court. At this point some prominent men in the neighborhood stepped in and tried to work out a compromise.

The decision of the mediators was that the case should be tried in a special court of representatives from both parties, and that Madhavi alone need be tried. A day was also fixed for it.

As she sent her daughter off to the trial, Madhavi's mother prayed for help to all the Gods she knew. The family had a terrible dread of the consequences of an unfavorable verdict. If it was so difficult to find a permanent owner for a pure, untouched virgin flower, what chance for a flower impregnated with dew drops? Madhavi's mother said, "If we win the case, we are saved. There is no need to worry about the fake ornaments that I gave Madhavi. We can say that the sly old woman substituted genuine gold ornaments with counterfeit ones. People would believe us."

In addition to Madhavi's father and father-in-law, there were fifteen others, ten representing the groom and five the bride. They all sat in a circle in the front veranda of the house.

The leader asked Madhavi how many people there were in the party that had come to see her.

"Three," she said. She was then asked to point them out.

Madhavi looked at everyone. One of the three was the groom's father. The other two she had not seen since that day, not even on the wedding day. But she could at one glance pick them out.

Somebody said this was enough evidence for a judgement in favor of Madhavi. But the others objected and so the trial continued.

The next question was whether she had noticed anything special about these gentlemen. One of the representatives of the bride objected to the question. He argued that in such a moment that affected one's whole life, one would be more perplexed than a student in the examination hall and would not be able to notice such details. But nobody supported him and so the plea was rejected. Actually Madhavi had no need for any such support.

Hearing Madhavi's answer to the question, everyone was astounded at her sharp power of observation and keen memory.

To the old man who now sat covered with a simple black-and-white bordered shawl, pan juice dribbling down his chin, she said that on that day he had worn, thrown round his neck, a gold-bordered shawl. He confirmed it proudly. (It was his wife's. His wife got it as a present from a relative whom she had helped at childbirth. He alone knew how much persuasion it had taken him to borrow it for a day.) When Madhavi added that through the folds of the shawl, she had also seen a slight swelling on his neck, he looked a little crestfallen. The spectators considered his sudden change of expression an admission of the truth of the statement.

The other old man, feeling ignored, now put his question. "Don't you remember me?"

"Yes, you wore glasses." Then followed a description of the glasses. The gist of it was that there had been a thread binding the earpiece to the frame near the eyes. Since his hair covered it, the thread was not easily visible. She had seen it only when she had leaned forward to serve him.

The owner of the glasses mentally regretted his question. Even the five members of the bride's party had shown no curiosity regarding his friend's swelling. But now all fifteen made him take his glasses out of his pocket, examining them, and even made him wear them, before they convinced themselves of the truth of what Madhavi had said.

At the end of this scrutiny the man with the shawl asked: "Did anything special happen as the food was being served?" Here too, Madhavi's memory did not fail her. She elaborated, without omitting the details, how she had served eggs for all the three and how for the questioner, who was a vegetarian, a new leaf-plate had to be brought.

Somebody then nudged the man with the glasses and asked, "How about him?" Madhavi looked at the man who had asked. It seemed to her a malicious question. Then she looked at the man concerned. There was no threat in her bearing now. At the most it was tinged with pity. But the man dreaded this girl with her keen memory.

Of course Madhavi remembered very well. His eyes had implored her for a very generous measure of rice and the other dishes. But after they were served, he had pretended that too much had fallen on his leaf due to Madhavi's carelessness, and her father had rebuked her. She understood her father's fear that, if she behaved like a spendthrift before her future father-in-law, the marriage proposal might be dropped. But even then she did not try to prove her innocence by denuding him of his mask of respectability. On that day as well as on this, she had only pity for the glutton who tried to appease his voracious appetite without damaging his self-respect. She might have considered that, after all, she too was playing this role only for her livelihood.

However that might be, her pity evoked a response in the old man. Turning to the groom's father and veiling his anger in earnest words, he asked, "If you can't feed one more mouth, why not admit it frankly, instead of disgracing a decent girl? One can see at a glance that she has no guile. You must take her home with you, if you have any shred of honor left."

With these words he looked at all the others. Noticing that his judgement had been accepted unanimously, he turned triumphantly to Madhavi's father. "I am ashamed of being involved in this disgraceful business. I have never seen a girl with so much intelligence and memory. You have let it run to waste. If only you had sent her to school! She would have been the best student in every class. That would have been far better than this humiliating begging."

Later, as Madhavi, with intense relief at the sparing of her life, entered her bedroom, her eyes fell on the mangalapathram on the wall. The words "Marriages are made in heaven" twinkled at her.

Translated by Celine Mathew.

SHANTA SHELKE _____

(b. 1921) *Marathi*

Shanta Shelke was born in Manchar, a small village in central Maharashtra, into a family that was well placed, but which had no long tradition of literacy. However both her mother and father were educated, and it is from her mother, who had read *Manas Geet Sarovar* and *Stri Geet Ratnakar* (rare compilations of women's songs), that she imbibed her love of literature. Her father, a forest ranger, was an unusual man. He did not believe in traditional restrictions and the children were brought up to cherish their liberty. "Consequently I've always lived like a man," Shanta Shelke, who was their eldest daughter, says. When she was nine, her father died and the family moved to Pune. There she joined Huzurpaga, a school that, she says, changed her totally. She read a great deal of Sanskrit and Marathi literature, but most important, she "became fearless." At sixteen (and today she recalls this as a hazy, unimportant event in her life), she was married to a boy of her own caste. The marriage meant little to her, and she left him to live independently and to continue her education. She received her master's degree in Marathi in 1944.

Initially, Shanta Shelke worked at several jobs, including proofreading, writing columns for magazines, translating books from English into Marathi (her translation of Louisa May Alcott's *Little Women, Chaughijani,* is a best-seller), and writing scripts and lyrics for films. Later she taught Marathi literature at a Bombay college. She has lived a bold life, breaking many social conventions—and doesn't regret it. Her life "has been a rich experience, filled with ideas and friendships." But about today's urban feminists who are fighting for equality, and want to "imitate men," she has her reservations. Women should assert their difference, she feels, and never give it up. Shanta Shelke has published four collections of poetry: *Varsha* (Season of Rains), 1947; *Rupasi* (The Beautiful), 1956; *Toch Chandrama* (The Same Old Moon), 1973; and *Gondan* (Tatooing), 1975, from which the poem translated here is taken. She has also written fiction, and among her better known publications are the short story collections *Kaveri* (A River [also a girl's name]), 1962; and *Kach Kamal* (Glass Lotus), 1969; and the novel *Odh* (A Pull), 1975.

◆

PANNASHI ULTUNHI
(Even Past Fifty)

She's past fifty;
yet she's still
a little girl at heart,
for whom the house is a doll's house,
and running the household
a childhood game.

She has traveled a long road; but her little feet
are not yet fatigued.
Catastrophes to her
are still like the evil spirits
in children's stories
whom she fights with blades
of grass; wipes the sweat
from her brow; hits hard;
sometimes wins, sometimes loses,
her sword broken.

Difficult questions
she has simplified for herself;

fitted the tangle
into a simple frame;
on her face
she has made distaste smile,
like moonlight that makes everything smooth.
But sometimes totally in despair,
a flower crumpled in a fist, she
rises again, smiles, or sings to herself,
though hers is not a musical voice.

I saw her the other day
after a long time;
she talked
with her usual, irrepressible intensity;
but I, for the first time,
noted the hair fast becoming white,
noted, for the first time, and with a pang,
the hollowness of the froth
rising above the stream of her life.

Translated by Vilas Sarang.

ACHANTA SARADA DEVI ————————

(b. 1922) *Telugu*

Achanta Sarada Devi published her first short story in the journal *Chitrangi* in 1945, and has now more than a hundred stories to her credit. Although her style is apparently simple, she has been generally acknowledged as a writer's writer rather than as a popular one because of the multiple levels of meaning evoked by her symbolism. There is a bareness and melancholy about the vision of life her stories provide, and her women characters often struggle with an inarticulate grief. In "Paripoyina Chilaka" (The Parrot that Flew Away), the title story of a 1963 collection, she uses the house as a symbol of female imprisonment and is able to explore enclosure as well as escape. The story draws parallels between the life of the protagonist, Kamakshamma, and the caged parrot she tends with great care and affection. There is nothing Kamakshamma can really complain about: her husband provides her with every material need and is kind. Yet an inexplicable restlessness troubles her always.

The story translated here, taken from the collection *Marichika* (Mirage), 1969, also explores the theme of confinement and exposure. Tapati is reared in a prisonlike house, and marries into another. A woman whose innocence glows like moonlight, she manages to eke a minimal existence out of whatever emotional sustenance comes her way. In this story the house, harsh as it is, and the affection of parents-in-law within the household, are also protection against the rapacious sexuality of the world outside. When she is left unprotected and alone in the open, the twist of the rough thread that ties her to life comes apart.

Sarada Devi hails from Vijayawada, and studied at both Women's Christian College and Presidency College in Madras. She is married to the artist and writer Achanta Janakiram who, she says, encourages and influences her. From 1954 to 1977 she was professor of Telugu at the Padmavathi Women's College in Tirupati. Her writing, she comments, is a hobby. As literary influences she names Rabindranath Tagore and Devulapalli Krishna Sastry, a well-known Telugu Romantic poet. She also admires the work of Anton Chekhov and Katherine Mansfield.

Sarada Devi has published five collections of short stories: *Pagadalu* (Corals), 1960; *Vokkanati Atithi* (The Guest on That Day), 1965; *Marichika*, 1969; *Paripoyina Chilaka*, 1963; and *Vanajallu* (A Drizzle), 1989. In 1980 she received the Andhra Pradesh Sahitya Academy Award.

◆

ADAVI DAGINA VENNELA
(Moonlight Locked in the Woods)

Tapati was the daughter of Kamaiya's first wife. She had lost her mother when she was three years old. Tapati could not remember her mother at all. As she grew older, she had longed for some image of her mother and tried to visualize what she might have looked like. They lived such an old-fashioned life in the village that there was not even a picture of her anywhere. Perhaps her mother had never had a photograph taken! Perhaps her mother had always worn a blue sari. Poor thing! Perhaps that was the only sari she had possessed. Whenever Tapati recalled her childhood, she heard a blue sari rustle as it moved, and then come close. That was the only fragment of her mother that remained with her.

After his first wife's death, Kamaiya found it impossible to look after the little girl and manage the household all by himself. He married again. His second wife, Latangi, had no family except a brother, Sarabhaiya, who was a sick man. When his sister married, he too had moved to Kamaiya's house. Latangi managed the household quite efficiently, and her brother helped her with the farm work. Tapati did not grow to like or feel close to Latangi. Latangi was some new person, and Tapati had no idea why she had come or when she would go. She watched her nervously from afar. Latangi was not inclined to draw the child closer to her either. She gave the child odd jobs to do and kept her at a distance with her cold eyes. There was no tenderness in Latangi's makeup. As a child, she had struggled through by herself, with no one to turn to. Though no one could be blamed for her situation, she had grown bitter and treated everyone harshly. The day she stepped into Kamaiya's house, she felt that the place was hers, that she was its mistress.

Tapati was barely nine when Latangi handed over all the household chores to her. Fat now, and covered with jewels, Latangi settled down comfortably on the single cot. An idea struck her. If only Tapati were married to Sarabhaiya, both of them would continue to live with her. Tapati could go on doing the housework. Her brother would settle down, and besides, she would be rid of the burden of having a step-daughter. She promptly conveyed her idea to Kamaiya, who in any case never had the courage to go against anything that Latangi said. Since his first wife's death he was like a living corpse, in terror of Latangi.

The brief ceremony was almost like a make-believe doll's wedding. Tapati herself hardly felt any change in her life except for the yellow thread that now hung around her neck to symbolize her married state. Sarabhaiya looked after her more gently than before, and also exercised his authority more obviously. That was all the difference. But before the year had passed, Sarabhaiya's illness worsened and he died within two days. Latangi moaned. It was all Tapati's ill luck, she concluded. Tapati herself was not yet of an age to understand much. She had not grown fond of Sarabhaiya. But she had not disliked him either. He had simply been like any other member of the household. Now he was gone, and she did not understand why. Everyone around her cried, but she herself sat there and stared. By evening, when things had quieted down, the thought suddenly struck her that she wouldn't be able to comb her hair neatly any longer or put the *kumkum* on her forehead, or wear flowers like her neighbors Vanaja and Lila did. Suddenly she was overwhelmed with grief and wept bitterly, all alone. After a while she fell asleep. The next morning she felt a little relaxed, and forgot the pain of the previous night. Gradually she learned to move around with hair unkempt, and went through the motions of her housework mechanically.

Kamaiya was heartbroken when he saw Tapati come of age. Overworked and tired though she always was—and dressed in drab clothes—there was still something beautiful about her. Like the moonlight, she glowed with a soft radiance. Kamaiya felt extremely guilty. The injustice that he had inflicted on his daughter rankled in his heart. After his wife had died, he had neglected the child in every sense, and had given in to Latangi like a slave. He had not even objected to his own daughter's marriage to his brother-in-law, who was known to be a sickly man. Now he himself was old. What would her life be like after he was gone? What could he do for her now? He spent many sleepless nights with these anxieties haunting him. He would not have any peace of mind until she was married again, until he had found a mother-in-law who would care for her in every way. But it was impossible in his village. He could not show his face in public if he married off his widowed daughter again. In any case, Latangi would allow no such thing to happen as long as she was alive. The truth was just beginning to dawn upon him—that he and Tapati were really her slaves. One day Kamaiya set off without telling anyone what he had in mind. He just said he had to fulfill a vow to some god in Padamatapalli Village and that he had to take Tapati along. Before a surprised Latangi could even question him, he had left, bag and baggage. She noticed him leaving the village in the darkness.

Kamaiya had known Sastrulu of Padamatapalli for quite some time, so he went directly to his house. He explained why he had come. Sastrulu immediately took the whole burden upon himself. He told Kamaiya about a possibility in the same village. The man, Anantam, was the son of a woman called Ramalakshmi.

Ramalakshmi's house stood a little beyond the village. It was more like a small cattle shed on the side of the road to the city. Bullock carts and human beings sometimes passed in front of it, but at night there was nobody around. Behind the house was the wilderness of a thick forest. How far that forest extended and what lay beyond it, Ramalakshmi did not know. She always kept the back door shut after dusk. Occasionally during the day she would leave the door open and sit there staring into the forest.

Ramalakshmi's only son had had little schooling. During the day he kept accounts in a shop in the village, and after that he sat at the counter and played cards the whole night long at Ratnamma's house. He even slept there. Ratnamma did not have a good reputation, and the whole village gossiped about their relationship.

It was years since Anantam had lost his wife, and she had hardly ever lived with him. Her mother's house was in the next village, and since she was sickly and didn't much like her husband or her family life, she had chosen to live with her mother most of the time. They had had two children. When she died, Ramalakshmi had brought both children home and reared them. Anantam was now forty, and both children were over twelve. Yet Ramalakshmi wanted to see her son married again so that she would have a companion, someone to help her, someone to take care of the house after her death. She had told Sastrulu about it. She did not mind who the girl was—it was enough if she was a good person. And it was this proposal that Sastrulu put forth to Kamaiya.

Kamaiya took Tapati to Ramalakshmi's house. Ramalakshmi was drawn by Tapati's innocence and her beauty. Kamaiya did not hide anything from Ramalakshmi—he told her that this would be the girl's second wedding, that she had been married before, but that must have seemed to her like a sort of doll's wedding. Ramalakshmi also did not try to hide anything, and talked about her son and their situation very frankly. She was not well off either. Her son earned very little—barely enough for his card playing and his other pleasures. The family just managed. Kamaiya listened to it all and was still willing. Where would he get a better proposal for a second marriage? Ramalakshmi seemed to be a good woman, and he felt she would cherish Tapati and shelter her; she would wrap the girl into her womb. After all, what happiness did the girl have in her mother's home? Here she would soon have two children and be the mistress of her own family.

They got the wedding over with quietly in Ramalakshmi's house. Tapati had been running a high fever that day—nearly a hundred and four—and found it difficult to sit up on the wedding dais even for an hour. Ramalakshmi did not buy a new sari for her daughter-in-law—she did n ot have the money. Kamaiya asked his daughter whether she would like him to buy her one. "No," she said. She just sat there in her old sari, half-dazed, scarcely knowing what was happening. Then, barely able to keep her eyes open any longer, she fell asleep without even eating. By evening she felt a little better. Kamaiya was relieved and took leave of her, placing her hand in Ramalakshmi's. He started home, feeling freed of a burden and satisfied that he had fulfilled his responsibility.

The marriage did not affect Anantam's life. He came home as usual to eat, as if to a hotel, and if he went out at night, he would return early in the morning to sleep. Ramalakshmi had only two rooms. The first, the largest, was where they cooked, ate, and sat. It had two doors, one of which opened onto the roadside and the other onto the trees in the woods. A little stretch of open space served as the backyard, where they scrubbed the pans, washed the clothes, and dried them. Sometimes other things were put out to sun there. At night the space was enveloped in darkness and the back door was kept tightly shut. Next to the big room was a small one. It had one door and a tiny window, and was stacked with trunks, bundles, and other things. A small folding cot, which stood in one corner, filled the room. The short time that Anantam was at home he spent lying on that cot.

Tapati's fever dropped after a week. Then she simply took on all the work of the house without anyone's asking her to. Ramalakshmi was a supporting presence and the children grew close to Tapati. Anantam didn't disturb her in any way. During the short time he was at home, she was silent and kept her distance, and after he left, when she was with the children and her mother-in-law, she was her usual self. She felt life was much better in this house than it had been in her parental home. Ramalakshmi did not snap at her as Latangi used to, but spoke to her affectionately, and what little she gave her to eat was given with love. Ramalakshmi stayed close to her, as a mother would. Tapati had never known this kind of affection. The tendrils of her young heart curled around Ramalakshmi.

Ramalakshmi chided her son, "Even though this child of gold has come into our house, you have not mended your evil ways. She is so innocent. Surely we will have to pay for this one day." But Anantam's heart was deaf. It had hardened into stone and there was nothing that could soften it. Ramalakshmi wept. Once, when Anantam returned at night, she woke Tapati up. She combed the girl's hair, wiped her face, put vermilion on her forehead, and smilingly told her to go and sleep in the inside room. Tapati crept in timidly. Anantam was sleeping there on the folding cot. He did not seem to have a care in the world. Tapati stood for a while, watching him. Then she pushed some of the bundles aside and made space for herself to sleep. Soon she got used to this routine. Ramalakshmi would wake Tapati up, she would go in, watch Anantam sleeping, and fall asleep in a corner. One day the pattern was suddenly disrupted. Tapati stumbled on a trunk and fell. There was a clatter, her hand was scraped and bled. Anantam woke up. He was furious. "Can't even sleep in this bloody house," he shouted, and flung a dirty pillow onto the floor. Tapati was terrified. She crept back into the other room.

Ramalakshmi heard the scream and saw Tapati's bleeding hand. She felt as though she had done something terrible. She wiped Tapati's hand clean with a wet cloth and smeared some lime paste on it. Never again did she wake Tapati up, or ask her to go in to her son.

Sometime later Govindaiya, one of the village elders, came to visit Ramalakshmi. Govindaiya was a rich man, rich enough to lend money to everyone in the village. He had been away for six months on a pilgrimage with his wife, who suffered from asthma. Each day she thought she was going to die, but was determined she would not do so without setting her eyes on holy places like Kashi and Rameswaram. So when she had insisted that they go on a pilgrimage, Govindaiya had no choice but to go. They were childless, and Govindaiya was both very fond of his wife and terrified of her.

When they got back to the village, Govindaiya heard about Tapati. One day he went to take a look at her on the pretext of visiting Ramalakshmi. Tapati's face seemed to glow like a piece of the moon itself. An ugly glint crept into his eyes.

In some people, the ugliness of the mind can clearly be seen on the face. Even an innocent person is frightened by it. Govindaiya was talking to Ramalakshmi. He inquired about her welfare and joked with her familiarly, but his gaze never shifted from Tapati, even for an instant. Tapati felt as if serpents and centipedes were crawling all over her. She felt frightened. She rose and went into the next room and sat on the folding cot. After some time, Govindaiya left. As he was going, he whispered something in Ramalakshmi's ear. Tapati could barely hear what he was saying. It sounded as though he was saying he would be back.

Tapati went to Ramalakshmi. Her face looked drained. Ramalakshmi knew exactly what Govindaiya meant by his last words. A mixture of anger and sadness churned through her. She was disgusted by Govindaiya. Neither old age nor pilgrimages had changed the man. To think that human nature can change was an illusion, but there was nothing she could do. It was Govindaiya who had helped her when her husband had died. It was Govindaiya who had paid for her son's education. It was Govindaiya who had found him a job. It was Govindaiya who had paid for the funeral expenses when she had lost her daughter-in-law. It was Govindaiya who had given her this house at the edge of the village. Outside the shadow of Govindaiya's patronage there was no life for Ramalakshmi. She must swallow all her hatred as she must swallow both her anger and her pride, and give in. Even so, when her eyes fell on Tapati's innocence, her heart thudded inside her. She grew restless. Somehow, she felt, she must save the child from this danger.

At dinner Ramalakshmi begged her son to stay home that night at least. Anantam threw his plate down and left in a rage. Ramalakshmi was upset. If she had kept her mouth shut, he would have at least eaten properly, she thought. As the night advanced, her fears increased. Tapati was sleeping peacefully. As Ramalakshmi looked at her, a knife cut at her heart. She trembled. What could she do for the girl now? Slowly, she woke Tapati up.

"Are you afraid of the darkness?" she asked her.

"No," said Tapati sleepily.

Ramalakshmi breathed again. "Govindaiya said he would come. Stay out in the backyard until he leaves. I will call you in later," she said anxiously. Tapati did not understand anything. Govindaiya's name somehow reminded her of the *karanam*★ of her own village. When Tapati was a small girl Latangi had sent her to his house on some errand. There was no one at home except the karanam. Eagerly he had called out to her. "Come, my child, come," he had said, and suddenly embraced her. Neither that tone nor the embrace were like ones used to caress a little girl. He had squeezed her. Tapati felt disgusted and scared. She screamed and struggled to release herself from those ironlike hands, and ran all the way home, her body scratched and bruised all over. She was puzzled. Why were these memories coming back now? Tapati started trembling. She got up immediately and went into the backyard. Ramalakshmi shut both the front door and the back door, and waited fearfully, alone, the whole night. Both children were fast asleep.

That night Anantam did not return, and neither did Govindaiya come. His wife had been taken ill. She had had another attack of asthma and would not let him move out. Ramalakshmi did not sleep that night either. She was terrified that Govindaiya might arrive anytime, and was anxious about Tapati, alone in the dark. There was nothing she could do; she couldn't even call her in. She waited, agonized. As it became light she grew relieved, and opening the back door, called out to Tapati. Tapati did not reply. Ramalakshmi was stunned. She stepped out and searched all round. Tapati was nowhere to be found.

When day broke, she walked a little further and looked around. There, huddled under the trees, was Tapati, sleeping. Ramalakshmi walked slowly up to her and tried to wake her. But Tapati did not stir. Neither did she utter a word. Never again would she open her eyes or

---

★A *karanam* is a village accountant and is always a brahmin.

look at anyone. Ramalakshmi broke down and wept. Tapati had gone silently, but she would remain in Ramalakshmi's heart.

No one knows exactly what passed through Tapati's mind as she walked alone into the forest that night when fear gripped her heart.

Translated by Rama Melkote.

SHIVANI

(Gaura Pant, b. 1923)   *Hindi*

When asked who the major influences on her work have been, this prolific and widely read author was quick to reply, "Mahatma Gandhi and Rabindranath Tagore." Many people today consider Shivani to be one of the most influential feminist voices in India. Her books quickly run into several editions and are available in small, out-of-the-way bookshops; she is a member of the Television Screening Committee, and a program adviser to All India Radio. Her Hindi style, simple and evocative, is often held up as a model for students.

Shivani's connections with Tagore can be traced back to the period between 1935 and 1943, when she studied at Santiniketan, the idyllic, ashramlike university and high school that he established. Drama was an integral part of the curriculum, including plays that Tagore wrote for student performances in the beautiful open-air theater at Santiniketan. The young Shivani took an active interest in the theater and in many of the other literary activities there, and soon began to write fiction. Her first published story was written in Bengali. She also has a fluent grasp of Gujarati, Sanskrit, and English. In 1953 she graduated from Calcutta University. She is married and has two children. Her daughter, Mrinal Pande, is a well-known writer and journalist.

Shivani's fiction proclaims a quiet, warm humanism. Characters who might seem pale and uninteresting in real life—an undistinguished, very orthodox Brahmin priest in a village up in the foothills of the Himalayas, his traditional wife, the village idiot, the widowed mother—take on a human glow and their lives an unexpected resonance. It is the small events, little gestures, nondescript people, that suffuse the world of Shivani's fiction with hope, and the future is something one enters with courage. Shivani's feminism is like a gentle humanism that does not stop short when it meets the female. Within the world-view of her fiction, there are few contradictions or problems that cannot be transcended with a little sympathy and a belief in the goodness of humankind.

Of Shivani's forty-five published books, thirteen are novels and eleven are collections of short stories. Her major works are *Pushpahar* (Garland), 1969; *Kariye Kshima* (Be Forgiving), 1971; *Prayas* (Effort) and *Aparadhini* (The Female Culprit), 1974; *Gavaksh* (Window) and *Gainda* (Sheep), 1977; *Darya* (Ocean), 1978; *Kishnuli,* 1979, from which the story translated here is taken; *Manik,* 1981; and two autobiographical works that deal with her life at Santiniketan. She also writes for children.

◆

DADI
(Grandmother)

Dadi's comings were always linked to her departures, which, Ranjana felt, came too suddenly and too soon. So her little heart lay dangling between joy and sorrow whenever Dadi's arrival was imminent. With a child's innate shrewdness, she had guessed long ago that relations between her mother and Dadi were not smooth. Dadi never stayed with them for long, and whenever she came, Mother's mood turned black. Quarrelsome noises arose at night from her parents' bedroom, the raised voices always in English, and then one day Ranjana and her brother would return from school to find that Dadi had gone.

"Mother, is Dadi gone?" they'd ask together.

"Yes, she is gone." Mother's tone would put a total stop to any more queries regarding the grandmother's departure.

So when Dadi came this time, Ranjana clung to her and begged, "Promise us, Dadi, this time you'll not leave suddenly when we are away in school."

Dadi's sunken eyes swam with tears of love. This is why the wise ones say one's sickle will always reap the harvest towards one's own lap, and that blood is thicker than water. "Hai, my beloved ones, can I ever leave you and go suddenly?"

Reassured, the brother and sister hitched up their school bags and left for school. The poisonous sting that her older son's wife had left behind on the old woman's heart as she departed was completely dissipated by the salve of the grandchildren's spontaneous love. This time she had arrived at her younger son's house with the older daughter-in-law and her children. She knew none of them was very welcome in this household, but how could she help it? Jodhpur was no longer a safe city, what with those deadly Pakistani bombs falling from the skies. Her older son had insisted that she and his wife go with the children and stay with his younger brother while this war between India and Pakistan was on.

Both Dadi and the older daughter-in-law knew that living with the younger daughter-in-law was like swallowing a fly knowingly. Dadi, therefore, ruled that the Older One and her children should keep their stay in this house short, and then depart for the Older One's father's house. The older son held an ordinary job; his wife, too, was rather ordinary, and the children were nondescript. The Older One, therefore, grudged the Younger One her affluence, and as is common among women, her animosity towards her sister-in-law would come out clearly once in a while. As it is, the relationship between two sisters-in-law is always so delicate that even if they be blood sisters, their ties always teeter on the verge of breakup. It is like the precarious relationship between India and China, despite all the *"Hindi-Chini Bhai, Bhai"* proclamations of enduring brotherhood. Social opinion would go in favor of the Older One. It was she who had been the traditional daughter-in-law looking after the conservative mother-in-law. The Younger One's husband was a lieutenant colonel, and her nuclear household was a Westernized one managed by a retinue of servants, in which the very old and the very young were not welcome. The children in this house ate eggs and sausage before going to school, and celebrated their birthdays by blowing out candles planted upon big birthday cakes, not by offering the traditional pot of sesame seeds and milk to Markandeya, the god of longevity, and Lakshmi, the goddess of prosperity. The conservative mother-in-law's traditional kitchen had always been out of bounds for those who had not been ritually cleansed. She drew a line with charcoal around her cooking space, even an inadvertent crossing of which by others meant total pollution of such magnitude that the old lady would not eat what she had cooked therein. But each time she came there, the Younger One would, like a cruel and shameless enemy, find an excuse to cross this forbidden territory, and then apologize with a grin, "Hai, Mother, what will you do now? I've crossed into your cooking space by mistake."

What could the poor old woman do? Instead of the soft rotis she had kneaded in holy milk or curds, she'd have to satisfy herself with a few bananas or an apple. There were comparatively few such transgressions in the Older One's kitchen, so the mother-in-law had chosen to stay permanently with her, even though her older son's job was not as lucrative, nor was his house as comfortable to live in. She now cursed, day and night, the suddenly erupted war that had forced her to cross the threshold of the Younger One's traditionless house much against her wishes. To make things worse, this time her soldier son was away at the front, and the old servant had also left. As evening came, darkness descended like a canopy over their heads, and then that son of a cursed mother, the siren, began to hoot its ominous message. Dadi trembled and feared for all of them.

The idols of Dadi's large family of gods occupied a corner of her room. They were to be bathed only with water mixed with holy water from the Ganges. As Dadi returned after borrowing some from the Younger One, the Older One took one look at the wide-bottomed bottle of holy water, and shot with perfect aim a fiery dart at her mother-in-law's heart. She was the daughter of a contractor and knew these bottles very well, and also what kind of "water" they'd originally contained. "Hai, will you put your holy Ganga water in this Ammaji? The Younger One has given you a bottle of her husband's special holy water, hasn't he?" Suppressing her giggles, the Older One busied herself packing her bedding.

If she'd wanted, the Younger One, who stood by, could have performed the last rites of seven generations of the Older One's ancestors and their bottles then and there, but why should she poke a stick at an injured snake? The Older One was leaving in a few hours' time anyway. Besides, whatever she might say, Dadi's coming this time had eased the domestic pressures on her somewhat. Without her husband, going to the club was out of the question. Dadi cooked the vegetables in the evening, and the children ate with their grandmother. She didn't need to worry about them. She herself wanted only a light meal at the end of the day. If she felt hungry, she needed to bake only a few chapatis for herself.

The Younger One missed her husband, though, and also the parties they were so fond of giving. His birthday was coming up, but he was away. Otherwise, each year they had a big party to celebrate the occasion. But no, she must not give way to despair. She must celebrate his birthday, she had decided. So what if he was away fighting the enemy? She phoned and invited a few army wives who were her close friends to an evening party. She hinted lightly that it would not be a feast to match the earlier ones, but a simple get-together before the blackout.

And now there was an early evening meal to handle, and no servant. The mother-in-law, who made excellent chutneys and savories, was fasting today. How could she ask her? To top it all, that spoilt little daughter of hers was getting a rag doll made for herself. The old woman could have cooked a veritable feast had she not been squinting over that miserable bundle of rags! This Ranjana of hers was really the limit. Her father had brought her such a lovely fair-haired doll with blue eyes from Singapore, which could walk and talk. But Ranjana didn't care for her. Well, she had begun kissing and bathing her so often, that she was told the doll had to be put away beyond her reach, unless she promised to handle it with care. At this, the little demon had suddenly lost all interest in the toy. Her ayah's daughter Rahiman had a monstrously ugly but thrice-married rag doll, whose nonexistent nose had been pierced thrice with the bridal nose ring. Ranjana, too, wanted a doll she could give away and fight over and get back and remarry. So, for the last three hours her grandmother had been laboring to deliver into her hands an easily marriageable and remarriageable rag bride. Two large black eyes had already been embroidered upon an oval white face, the nose bridge had been raised with deftly put double stitches, and now only the mouth remained to be formed. But when Ranjana went to her mother to ask for a bit of red thread for the mouth, the mother, who had just accidentally burnt her hand, snapped back, "Get out of here. See, you've made me burn my hand. Always lurking around you are!"

Ranjana slunk back. Mother had already been blowing on her burnt hand when she'd arrived, but she'd not listen to anyone at a time like this. Ranjana thought a bit, ripped the seam from her new purple frock, and extracted a long purple thread.

"Here, Dadi, give her a purple mouth. We can imagine that she has put on purple lipstick like Mother. What do you say, Sanjay?" As usual, the twin brother dared not contradict the sister's statement. He agreed wholeheartedly.

With her glasses perched on her nose, Dadi began to plan with the grandchildren a grand wedding for the rag bride. "See, you'll need four yards of silver *gota,* and half a yard of yellow and half a yard of red satin for the bridal dress. As for the jewelry, I've seen the balloon vendors sell little gilt sets stuck on cardboard for ten paisa. So we'll get one set of those. And I'll fry you some tiny little *puris* for the feast . . ."

The twins, goggle-eyed, saw a fairy-tale wedding take shape before their eyes. "But Dadi, whom will she marry?"

Oho, this was a big problem they had not before encountered. The houses around contained quantities of convent-going children whose dolls were all blue-eyed, fair haired, and female. How was a totally Indian bride, with her brass jewelery and shimmering, satiny bridal clothes, to find a matching, mustached bridegroom for herself?

In the end it was decided that Dadi should also bring into this world a suitable male doll, who could then be sent to the neighbor's house for adoption and subsequent bridegroomhood.

All this, while the poor servantless mistress of the house was struggling with unfinished chores in the kitchen. At this point, as though to test her patience, the lone cylinder of gas breathed its last, the telephone turned out to be dead, and there was no alternative source of energy available on a public holiday. The Younger One thought she would die!

Suddenly, however, the auspicious Bruhaspati, smiled upon her. She found a clean-shaven and competent-looking individual literally standing on her doorstep: "Bibiji, do you need domestic help?" So taken aback was the Younger One that the paring knife slipped out of her hands and clattered to the floor. The strange individual stood politely waiting for her answer, his head bowed, and his hands folded together in supplication. He certainly was too elegant to be a servant. Perhaps he was the runaway son of a well-to-do family.

"Can you cook?" the Younger One asked.

"I have been a chef at a five-star hotel, ma'am," came the answer.

"Can you ride a bike?" The children have to be dropped at school each morning."

"I can even drive a car, ma'am. I am a trained mechanic." His teeth, when he smiled, were dazzlingly white and even.

"What's your name?" The Younger One sensed her mother-in-law's presence in the room. "And caste?" she added.

The smiling stranger extended a sheaf of papers that declared Shri Bholanath Trivedi, the bearer of the certificates, to be a pure *kanyakubja* brahmin who was adept at the jobs of a cook-cum-waiter, driver, and motor mechanic.

Bhola was immediately hired. The Younger One knew she had found a veritable diamond. At a paltry salary of a hundred and twenty rupees a month, plus meals, Bhola was retained and given a room in the servants' quarters at the back.

The children took to Bhola immediately. He was as fair as a European and had green eyes, which closed when he smiled. His easy-going ways and excellent cooking won over everyone but Dadi.

"The eyes, did you see his eyes? Green as a cat's they are," Dadi would say.

The Younger One would retort, "How can you say that, Mother? See how quick he is, and how cheerful! The previous one would sulk if even one guest arrived, but this one doesn't mind, even though the house is like a hotel these days."

Dadi knew why the house was being dubbed a hotel. Since she had come, a lot of her nephews and cousins had been dropping by to see her. But she decided to let that one pass.

"Dear Younger One, tie up my wisdom in a corner of your sari like good money. Always keep a dumb servant. A smart one will eventually shave you with your own razor," she added.

But who listened to her anyway?

Little Sanjay had become an ardent admirer of Bhola. "He is such a terrific shot, Mother," he'd say. "He can toss a coin in the air and hit it with my air gun."

Whenever the radio broadcast the news, Bhola pricked his ears like a rabbit. As the Younger One looked at his worried face while the radio gave the latest about the battlefront, she felt a deep fondness for her patriotic servant, who'd leave a roti on the griddle to keep abreast of the national news.

Then Bhola took to going for long walks at night. Dadi pointed this out to the Younger One, but her previous servant had tendered his resignation at being checked once too often about his nocturnal habits.

"What headache is it of ours?" she asked her mother-in-law, a trifle irritated. "After all, he finishes his job before leaving, doesn't he?"

But inside her the worm of worry began to gnaw. Once, when she got up at midnight to go to the toilet, hadn't she seen Bhola quietly sneak back into his quarters with a hefty stranger with a big mustache?

What should she do? Confide in her mother-in-law? What if he turned out to be merely a fellow villager of Bhola's? What if Bhola felt insulted and left?

The next morning Bhola came in as usual with her tea. "I went to see a midnight film, ma'am," he smiled. "Sorry your tea is a little late." Who could get angry with so polite a retainer?

"All right, Bhola," the Younger One said, completely mollified. "Go and give Ammaji her tea in her steel tumbler. She fasts on Ekadasi."*

Initially, Ammaji had refused to drink tea made by a servant, but when her daughter-in-law underscored the kanyakubja brahminhood of Bhola many times, she had felt her resistance give way.

But on that same evening of Ekadasi, Bhola's mask slipped. The Younger One sat reading, when the children rushed in excitedly. "Mother, we saw Bhola perform a *namaz*.** And Mother, he has many

---

*Ekadasi, the eleventh day of each lunar month, is a holy day for widows.
**The *namaz* is the Islamic ritual prayer.

maps spread on the floor and he and a fat man with a mustache are reading them."

She followed the children and peeped. The room was littered with paper, and a wireless kit stood in a corner. Bhola and his companion were whispering and drawing lines on a map. The Younger One now knew the game. She shut the bolt from the outside and raised an alarm.

Within minutes a crowd began to collect. Rumors changed the sex of the offenders many times, and bloated the numbers of the suspects to twenty. When the room was broken open, the wireless apparatus and foreign maps confirmed that the two were indeed enemy spies whose real names were Hamid and Latif. They were paratroopers sent to collect valuable information.

The fat red-eyed man, who owned the fruit juice shop around the corner, and had lost a son in the last Indo-Pakistani war, came forward with a fat stick. "My friends, today I shall eat my roti with their curried livers."

The crowd stepped back in fear and glee. "Yes, yes, go ahead, Praji," they screamed.

Just then Dadi spoiled things by running into the crowd and clinging to the fat man's arm. "No, my son, no! Your son will not return thus." But the man's eyes were spouting fire. "I don't care, I must have my revenge," he bellowed. Dadi hung on to his arms. She let go only when the police arrived. "Hold on, son, the guilty will not go unpunished," she kept saying.

The police soon took away the culprits and the hitherto awestruck crowd suddenly turned into a loud mass of courageous knights. "How terrible! This old woman spoiled things for everyone. Otherwise what fun we'd have had!"

"Think of it, had we landed in their territory, would they have left us alive? Never!"

"That's right! They'd have fed us to their dogs."

"This is why we Hindus always get left behind. We know how to die, but not how to take revenge."

Dadi rounded up her family like a mother hen and brought them back into the house. The Younger One was still trembling. "Ammaji, for so long I kept a snake in my sleeve—suppose he had bitten us?"

Ammaji's old heart had forgiven the snake long ago. Wasn't he someone's son too? Wasn't he doing it for his country? But her die-hard beliefs demanded a harsher personal expiation.

"On the holy Ekadasi day of the Pitripaksha,* he made me drink his tea; thus he made me forever guilty in front of the souls of our ancestors. I must leave immediately for Varanasi for holy dips in the Ganga." Dadi's cheeks were wet with grief.

The very same night, leaving behind a contrite Younger One, a sobbing pair of grandchildren, and a husbandless rag doll, Dadi left for Varanasi, for a hundred and twenty holy dips to be followed by the gift of sesame seeds and milk and a milch cow to the brahmins, to expiate the sin of imbibing Hamiduddin Khan's tumbler of tea on the holiest day of the Pitripaksha.

Translated by Mrinal Pande.

HAMSA WADKAR ————————————

(1923-1972)   *Marathi*

Hamsa Wadkar was barely eleven when she had to leave school to start acting in films. Her father had begun to drink heavily and the family found it increasingly difficult to make ends meet. It was Hamsa's earnings that pulled them through and made it possible for her older brother to continue at school. Her first film, *Vijayachi Lagne* (Vijaya's Marriages), 1936, based on a play by the famous Marathi dramatist Mama Varerkar, was an instant success and young Hamsa found herself earning the princely sum of 250 rupees a month. But she was quite unconcerned at that time, she says, about what happened to the films, and was thrilled just to be earning the money. When she was married at fourteen, she had already acted in ten films. This exceptionally gifted woman went on to become one of the most sought after and colorful of Maharashtrian film actresses. She had acted in over thirty films, and was not quite fifty when she died, in many ways a lonely and broken person. Yet in her autobiography, *Sangatye Aika* (I'm Telling You, Listen), 1970, narrated to Arun Sandhee, she comes through as a rebellious individual, a brave woman who strained tirelessly for what her heart wanted. Her work was a matter of honor. Through all the vicissitudes of her extraordinary life, she "kept faith with the goddess of theater," she says, never betraying her commitment to her art.

Hamsa Wadkar was born Ratan Salgaonkar, but adopted a stage name

---

*Pitripaksha is the holy fortnight of the ancestors.

because her brother objected to her using the family name. She took the name Wadkar from her grandmother, who came from a *kalavanta gharana,* or a family of courtesans, and was a well-known singer herself but had broken the family traditions by getting married. As Hamsa's elder brother was very ill around the time she was born, she was sent away to be reared by her grandmother in the family home on the Konkan coast. Hamsa stayed there until she was nine and had completed four years of schooling.

Across from her grandmother's house lived a relatively better-off family. There was much coming and going between the houses, and Hamsa was only six when the neighbors' son, Jagannath Bandarkar, who was ten years older than she, made her promise she would marry him. He never let her forget and chased her, she recounts, years later, all the way to Karachi, where she had gone to make the film *Airmail,** when he suspected she was becoming fond of another actor. In 1937, when she was fourteen and was in enormous demand as an actress, she slept with Bandarkar in defiance of her mother and married him when she was three months pregnant. Her autobiographical narrative captures this pivotal event in all its complex uncertainty. He had worn her resistance down; she was tired of acting and wanted a quiet domestic life; she was rebelling against her mother, who had taken to drink and seemed to regard Hamsa as a money machine; she was fond of Bandarkar, who, in an avuncular way had stood by her and helped the family; and she was flattered. However, the marriage changed nothing. It only meant she had to earn for two families instead of one, since Bandarkar grew as exploitative as her mother. After the birth of their daughter, he would not allow her to carry a pregnancy to term, he would not let her stop work, and he became increasingly harsh and suspicious.

Hamsa left home several times, once for three years during which she lived as the third wife of a rich landlord. There, she was confined to the household, but finally managed to send word to Bandarkar, who came to her rescue but was very aloof. In those days, she writes, "no one in the house talked to anyone. No one laughed. I felt suffocated and always feared that I would go mad."

One of her best-known roles is that of Baya in *Ramjoshi,* 1947. The film, which was a colossal hit, tells the story of Ramjoshi, a young brahmin composer of folk songs who is fascinated by the Tamasha dancer, Baya, and finally marries her. The film provided a break for Hamsa from earlier films in which she played straitlaced, domestic women, and was the source of her enduring screen image, consolidated in the classic film of the Tamasha genre, *Sangatye Aika,* 1959. Hamsa Wadkar herself considers *Sant*

---

*Hamsa Wadkar mentions *Airmail* in her autobiography, but in all probability that was the working title for *Modern Youth,* 1936.

Sakhu (Saint Sakhu), 1942, produced by the renowned Prabhat Studios, her best film. Sakhu was a medieval saint-poet and a rebel who was tortured by her husband's family when she joined the bhakti movement.

Hamsa Wadkar was honored by the state with an award in 1971, a year before she died. By then, she was an alcoholic, living a solitary life, never seeing her daughter, much as she wanted to. Her friend in those last, painful days was the young actor Rajan Javale, the last man in her tempestuous life. As the memoir of an independent working woman of the 1940s and 1950s, her autobiography makes chastening reading. More so her comment at the end: "If you are wise and wish well for your daughter, never allow her near the cinema." Her story created quite a stir in Maharashtra, because several well-known, respectable men had been involved with her, although their real names were carefully edited out of her narrative before publication. The award-winning film *Bhumika,* 1977, directed by Shyam Benegal, the opening sequences of which refer back to the film *Sangatye Aika,* was based on Hamsa Wadkar's autobiography.

◆

From SANGATYE AIKA
(I'm Telling You, Listen)
Chapter 8

This time, when I returned to Bombay after the film shooting at Kolhapur was over, relations between my husband and me deteriorated steadily. Financial problems made matters worse.

There was no immediate reason for the deterioration in our relationship. Right from the beginning we had quarreled. Any pretext would serve. It was all becoming quite unbearable for me. I was not at all happy. I was earning a lot of money, but it brought no satisfaction. My work did not give me any satisfaction either. Neither the money I earned nor my life at home helped me to find fulfillment. When Rekha was born, I was eighteen. After that I was pregnant three more times. Each time I was overjoyed because I loved children. But every time my husband suspected that the child was not his. He would think, The way she behaves, it couldn't be my child. Actually I was very strict about such matters. They really were his children. But he was extremely suspicious.

On the third occasion, when my husband brought the medicine, I did not take it. I wanted the child and besides, the effect of those medicines was dreadful. When he learned that I had not taken the medicine, he brought a doctor to the house and asked him to operate on me. It was the fifth month of pregnancy. Each time he forced me to have an abortion I was furious and wept bitterly because I wanted a child. This was the main cause of conflict between us. I came to look upon him as an enemy. Then I deliberately behaved badly. I suppose I did it to provoke him. If anyone suspects me unjustly, I get irritated. I deliberately do what I was accused of doing.

My gold bangles were another cause of persistent conflict. My husband Bandarkar's father was dead, but he had an uncle who owned a house at Sawantwadi that was in front of our family house. That is why I had known him since my childhood. He told me stories when I was a child, so I was very fond of him.

After I married Bandarkar I went for a visit to his family home at Sawantwadi. Whenever I remember those days that I spent in my in-laws' home, my mind overflows with joy. I had taken toys and sweets for the children. The new daughter-in-law, who lived in Bombay and worked in films—how thrilled everyone was to see me!

When I got there, Uncle was ill. He called out to me, "Beti, come here." I went and bowed at his feet. "Tell me a story," he said. "I've forgotten all the stories, I don't know any of them now," I replied. "You *do,* tell me one," Kaka persisted.

My mother-in-law, my brother-in-law, everyone took great care of me. At my in-laws' house I went around in a nine-yard sari and I wore my hair coiled round at the back of my head. At that time my hair was long and thick, so it looked really beautiful coiled round at the back.

On the second day of my visit, Uncle said, "Let's see what you eat in Bombay. Make a typical Bombay dish." *Biryani* was not known there. So I cooked a delicious biryani and served it to everyone. They all were delighted. After the meal, Uncle said, "Now have a wash and come here." I wove a twist of sweet-scented *aboli* flowers into my hair and went to him.

For every daughter-in-law he had had a set of jewelry made—gold bangles, earrings, a nose ring, and a necklace. He gave me my share of jewelry and said, "Wear these." I put them on. I bowed before the family shrine and touched the feet of Uncle and the other senior members of the family. After enjoying myself there for about ten days, I returned to Bombay.

The bangles Uncle had given me were my favorites. I was very fond of them. Whenever I put those bangles on I would remember Uncle, my in-laws, and each little incident in my life there. I would remember the village. There were so many sweet memories interwoven with those bangles.

After some days, our financial situation deteriorated. Bandarkar and I—it would be more accurate to say it was Bandarkar—had started a film company called Kalpana Films. The Hindi film *Dhanyawad* was made by this company. Jagirdar and Lalitabai acted in it. After the completion of the film it was shown to Morarjibai, who was home minister at that time. But it was not possible to release the picture immediately. Even while the shooting was going on, Jagirdar and Lalitabai increased their rates and asked for more money. All the money in the house was spent. Funds had to be raised from a moneylender, and when it was due to be released, the film had to be auctioned.

With this heavy loss there began the sale of jewelry from the house. Everything was sold rapidly. I did not mind at all about my other jewelry. But when Bandarkar asked for my Sawantwadi bangles, I flatly refused.

At last·one day he said, "I will pawn the bangles just for a few days. I will bring them back soon."

Since there was no help for it and he had assured me that he would bring them back within a few days, I parted with them. But those bangles were never brought back again. Most probably they were sold. I asked about them repeatedly, but that always irritated him, and the quarrels resumed.

While my mind was so disturbed, it wasn't as if there were any other kind of domestic happiness. I would return from shooting at odd hours of the night, even at four or five o'clock in the morning. At that time the whole household was fast asleep. I returned strained and irritable. At least my mother should inquire about me, I thought. But no one bothered about me, my mother included. Only my father would wake up when I returned. But he was crippled. Lying in bed, he would say, "My little girl, eat and go to bed." But I never felt like eating. Since my father's death, no one was left to say even that much. Only my two servants, Raghunath and Balu, took care of me. Raghunath was from Madras.

After I came home he would heat bath water for me and warm the food. After my bath I would sit down to eat and he would wait beside me till I'd finished my dinner. I'd be sitting eating alone, like a ghost. Then I'd go to bed at four or five A.M. and get up at eleven o'clock. I'd talk to my father or look at a book for a while, and in no time at all it was time to leave for shooting. There was no conversation with anyone else in the house. So I used to feel, "What sort of a house is this! What sort of domestic happiness is this!"

I was doubly dissatisfied, writhing in agony within. I did not know whether anybody knew of this restlessness of mine. It was under those circumstances that I acted in the film *Shri Gurudev Dutt.*

When I returned from Kolhapur my mental torture had increased. My husband had imposed new restrictions on me. I was supposed to inform him in advance about my hours of work and was supposed to come back at the fixed time. Even if I were slightly late, he would question, rage, suspect.

Mr. Joshi, whom I had met in the hotel at Kolhapur, was living in Bombay at that time, and after my return from Kolhapur I often visited him. Our friendship was growing.

Once Bandarkar and I had a violent clash and I left with my head in a whirl. Immediately I made my way to where Joshi lived. Shrikant Sutar was there too, and we drank a lot that evening. It was too much for me and I lost consciousness. That had never happened to me before.

Next morning, when I recovered consciousness, I was lying on a mat on the neighboring terrace. I could not recollect anything that had happened during the night. As soon as I came to myself I was terrified.

How could I go home? "Where were you all this time?" What would I say? My brain was benumbed. I did not know what to do.

Joshi and Sutar were inside. The three of us sat down again. Though it was morning, we started drinking again, since we couldn't think what to do. That day, too, passed in the same way, and it became even more difficult to go home. Joshi and I went to Poona and lodged in a hotel. Once I thought of ringing Bandarkar to tell him where I was. I used to phone him like that if, suddenly, at the eleventh hour, I had to leave for Poona on some urgent business. But at that moment I didn't have the courage to ring him up. I was torn by guilt. My time in Poona was also spent drinking. I thought that the doors of my home were now closed to me. It was like a state of delirium. I had left out of panic, and because of panic I dared not return. I seemed to be mesmerized by some evil being.

I roamed around with Joshi. Wherever he asked me to go, I went, and got more and more involved in fresh complications. I was going further and further away from home. We reached Bangalore.

We spent some days there, drinking and wandering around. I did not know how much money Joshi had with him, but almost all of it was spent and we were beginning to feel the pinch. What next? was the question before us.

Joshi found a way out. A friend of his turned up. Joshi borrowed some money from him, and we were on our way to Marathwada.

He took me to a small village in Marathwada—his native village. His mother, his two wives, and his children lived there.

I went wherever Joshi took me. Where we were proceeding, what we were doing—I did not ask him about anything at all. Even when I came to know about his wives and children, I did not express any astonishment. I was ready to face silently whatever came my way.

For another three years, I lived with Joshi in that village. That was a section of my life that stood apart from everything else. I passed those three years as if I were existing in a dream.

Joshi owned many fields. Far away from the village and on the other bank of the river his house stood at one end of a field. His mother lived there. One of his wives was dead and two were living. The older of the two had weak eyes. There were many children in the house, but it was only after my arrival there that I learned of their existence.

Both the wives were continually at loggerheads, and with me as a new addition, naturally there was further bickering. The older wife was more considerate, but the younger one was suspicious and quarrelsome.

On my arrival she let loose floods of abuse, looking on me as a vixen who had brought bad luck to the household. But I had decided beforehand that wherever I went I would remain and make the best of things.

I was treated as if I were a newly wedded bride. That is, I had to wake up early in the morning, sweep, sprinkle cow dung in the courtyard, wash a huge heap of utensils, and cook—all these tasks fell to my lot.

Gradually I became adjusted to the ways of the house and won the hearts of the people. They wondered how a movie actress would be able to handle all those household chores. But I toiled wholeheartedly, did whatever came to my lot, and looked after the children of both wives. The younger wife had an infant daughter who always clung to me. She would not go to anyone else. Sewing clothes, keeping the house clean, drawing *rangoli* designs on the floor each morning—I threw myself into all this with great enthusiasm.

Both the wives slowly developed a fond attachment to me. I had gone there with just the set of clothes I had on. Joshi bought me a coarse, thick, nine-yard sari and a blouse. They lasted me a year.

I dragged on in that fashion, but my inmost soul was grieving. On the surface I seemed to be working and behaving enthusiastically, but I kept asking myself what I had done. The memory of my daughter wrung my heart. I felt that I had committed a terrible crime, and was very disturbed at such moments, but there was no solution.

Joshi's house was far away from the village, with a river in between. So there was no contact with anybody else or with the outside world. Sometimes workmen would come to his house or to the farm. Those were the only outsiders I ever saw. When two years had passed, I was desperate. I longed to return home. But how could I?

Joshi kept a strict watch over me. He did not even allow me to move beyond the courtyard. I often thought I should send a letter to my husband and let him know everything in detail. But how could I get money for sending the letter? How could I post it?

Once, in the evening, I took a risk, and seeing that no one had noticed me, I went into the courtyard. I looked all around and reached the gate. But at that very moment Joshi saw me. He came running. He dragged me inside and started hitting me with a burning log of wood. He beat me mercilessly. At last the two wives came to my rescue and he stopped.

An even stricter watch was maintained. I didn't know how long this kind of life would continue. After that incident, my longing for home increased. I seriously planned an escape.

Some women selling goods used to come to Joshi's place, and I gradually made their acquaintance. Once I met them in secret. I gave them whatever money I had been able to put by and asked them to bring an envelope from the post office. I told them, "Please do this for me. And don't tell anyone."

In secret I wrote a letter and gave it to them to post. I watched them till they were far from the house. I was afraid lest they should tell someone.

That letter was to Bandarkar. I wrote in the letter where I was and how I was. The letter also contained directions for reaching that place. And I asked him to bring me some of my own clothes.

After a few days Bandarkar arrived. He himself waited in the distance, but the police, who had accompanied him, came to the house. On seeing the police, everyone started weeping and wailing. They were all afraid that Joshi would be arrested and taken away. I told the ladies of the house, "Don't be afraid. I won't say anything against Joshi." I wanted to go with the police.

Nevertheless, during my stay there, I had become greatly attached to the children and the women, and I was accustomed to having the smallest girl with me all the time. She, too, started crying. I told them all that I'd be back soon. But I took the younger wife aside and said, "I am leaving. Now, at least, look after your husband."

I came out. They had brought a bullock cart, in which I sat with my head bowed. Bandarkar did not even look at me. While crossing the river he just said, "I've brought your clothes."

Afterwards I had a look at my clothes. My old, expensive clothes had been preserved. But so many changes had taken place in me during those years. I was reduced to almost half my size. The clothes did not fit me. When I put on my blouse, it was very loose. I looked as if I had just recovered from a serious illness.

We reached a large village not far away. I had to appear before a magistrate. The office of the magistrate was in the front room of his house. He was old and looked decent and kindly.

Bandarkar said, "I have no complaints against anyone. I only want to take my wife back home." The magistrate sent him out to get someone's signature.

No sooner had he gone out than the magistrate picked up the statement. He said to me, "Come inside or I'll tear up this paper."

I was terrified. He led me inside and locked the door. His wife and children were in the adjacent room. What a degenerate brute! I could not even cry out. He gagged me and beat me.

I came to know that day how a rape takes place.

After some time, when Bandarkar returned, I was sitting on a bench in front of that old man, supporting my head on my hand, lamenting my evil fortune. I was utterly broken in spirit, writhing in agony. It was impossible to speak of what had happened.

I had got into that cart with great hopes, resolved to leave the past behind and begin again. But that old magistrate had destroyed everything, reduced everything to ashes. And my rage against the whole world erupted once more.

We returned to Bombay. I had been away for three years. When I reached the door, Rekha was standing on the steps. She had certainly grown.

I was overcome with emotion. I wanted to run and embrace her. She looked at me with a strained expression. Probably she did not recognize me, as I was changed entirely. But then she recognized me.

She came running and threw herself on me and said, "Mother, where were you all this time?" I entered the house with her, weeping.

That strange phase in my life was thus over. I had been afraid; I had not known what to do. As there was nobody to support and guide me, I had abandoned my home. Family life meant so much to me.

There was a time when I used to express astonishment when a wife deserted her husband. Two or three actresses had actually done so. Some of those people were very close to us, so I had felt it acutely. I used to say, "I'll never do anything like that."

Once, when we were shooting *Parijatak,* Shahurao looked at my palm and predicted, "There will be many transitions in your life. You will abandon your husband."

I said, "Nonsense, that's impossible! I'll put it down in writing if you like."

I had been so certain of myself. And yet I did leave. I had returned after three long years. When I left my home and with it, the film world, I was at the height of my glory, at the peak of my popularity. Why did I leave, why did I stay away, how did I stay, why did it happen? I had no answer, so why should I blame my fate?

I often felt that, if Father had been alive, I would not have left. Only he could have stopped me from leaving. But there was no sense in thinking about it.

Now, though I had returned, my world had changed. The contracts that I had signed were null and void. New actresses were offered the roles instead of me, for many new stars had appeared on the horizon.

That span of three years had changed me so much. At one time the whole of Maharashtra resounded with my talent. I dominated the film world, and I could scarcely believe that my name was on everybody's lips. Now, even if this turned out in the long run to be a temporary phase, my name seemed to have been utterly erased from the slate of time.

Translated by Chandrakant Vartak and Shirin Kudchedkar.

SIDDIQA BEGUM SEVHARVI _____

(b. 1925)   *Urdu*

Though she was born in Lucknow and lived the first ten years of her life there, Siddiqa Begum's ancestral home was Sevhara, a small town in Uttar Pradesh. After the years in Lucknow she went to live in Sevhara before moving to Aligarh, where she met Rasheed Jahan. This meeting proved a turning point in her life, and the beginning of her literary career. It was Rasheed Jahan who helped her understand the roots of social injustice and introduced her to Marxism and to the progressive movement in contemporary writing. "Whatever she taught me is to this day a beacon of light for me," wrote Siddiqa Begum in 1956. Her first collection of short stories, *Hichkiyan* (Hiccups), was published in Allahabad in 1944.

In 1942 Siddiqa Begum moved to Gondia, Madhya Pradesh, where she worked with the Bidi Mazdoor Sabha, a *bidi* workers' trade union. A large proportion of these pieceworkers are women who carry tobacco home to roll into bidis. As in other home-based industries, each woman is isolated and unionization is difficult. While in Gondia, Siddiqa Begum edited and published the magazine *Nauras* (The Mellowing). In 1947 she married the well-known Urdu writer Dr. Ather Pervez. She moved to Allahabad, and from there to Delhi, where she was a regular member of the Progressive Writers' Association. Five years later she and her husband moved to Aligarh, where she lives today.

Siddiqa Begum has published five collections of short stories: *Hichkiyan* (Hiccups), 1944; *Palkon Mein Ansu* (Tears in Eyelashes), 1947; *Raqs-e-Bismil* (Dance of the Wounded), n.d.; *Dudh Aur Khun* (Milk and Blood), 1952, from which the story translated here is taken; and *Thikre Ki Marg* (Engagement at Birth), 1957. Some of her stories have been translated into Russian and Malayalam.

◆

TARE LARAZ RAHE HAI
(The Stars Are Trembling)

Safi flung the books down as she entered the room. She startled me. What's wrong with this kid of a Safi? Just that moment, Mother's voice filled the room like a thunderclap. Her heavy steps shook the floor and my heart.

"Just look at the girl, look! Being in college has turned her head. Just comes and throws the books down, as though one gets them for nothing! Put them away properly on the shelf."

This imperious order given, Mother vanished, but Safi sulked. Her face was so swollen. It was as if bees had stung her. She muttered, "What do they know, those who've never studied? Here I am, all fagged out, no tea, nothing to eat, and all I get is, 'Put the books in place'—as if this were a bookshop."

"But Safi," I said, looking up from the book I was reading, "you were thoughtless too, weren't you? Just throwing them like that as if you really get them for nothing. And these are *books,* mind you."

"Oh, you, you better shut up. You have no right to lecture me so," Safi retorted. She tossed her head and her long, loose hair rippled on her chest. I turned to my book but continued to glance occasionally at her from the corner of my eye. It made her self-conscious. She slowly pushed her hair back and looked thoughtfully at me, a frown on her face.

"Oh, hell!" I said, "What do I care? *I* don't lose anything. It's *you* who will never learn if you ill-treat books." I was put out too. Here I am, I thought, speaking only for her good and this is what I get in return. Why should I take it?

"Oh, keep these outdated ideas to yourself," she dripped back. "I don't want them." Safi's mercury seemed to be touching Everest now. She had a wild look.

In that instant we saw our new sister-in-law drifting in like an ambling breeze. I was relieved to see her. At least that would bring the noisy argument to an end.

"Ah—so my Safi is back," Bhabi* said. "What made you so late today?" I felt my hopes being trampled.

"I went with Zohra, Bhabi. I had to pick some notes up from her."

"Notes? What notes? Had you lent her some money?"

I could hardly contain my laughter. Bhabi turned to look at me.

"Not currency notes," I said. "Study notes, class notes."

"I see," said Bhabi, as if she had understood everything. "How would I know? I've never been to school. Ah well, come let's have tea, it's gotten cold waiting for you." Bhabi put her arm around Safi and walked out with her.

And me, should I rot in this room alone? I don't need tea I suppose! All right, I thought, I'll get them back a bit today. I rose and slipped out through the back door to see Khalida. My name is not Birjis if I don't make 'em pay for it. It's always the same tale. I live in this house too, after all, but it's only Safi she wants. Safi doesn't care a pin for her, but she still runs after her all the time. As long as Safi is away at the college, madam won't stir out of her room, but the moment Safi's voice is heard, there she is.

Bhabi's image flashed before me—her creased dupatta thrown round her neck—mother screaming, "Daughter-in-law, how many times must I tell you to drape your dupatta properly, like a married woman?"

"I've got it on. How else . . ."

"What new style is this? The dupatta lies like a twisted rope round your neck and you run around, bobbing the balls."

---

*Bhabi means "sister-in-law" (brother's wife).

Bhabi lowered her eyes, and slowly pulled her dupatta down to cover her chest.

Khalida came running to me. "Birjis Apa,* I've asked you so many times to cut a blouse for me. And you still haven't done it!" I grew calmer.

"All right, fetch it," I said. "I'll cut one out for you in the latest style."

"Just like the one Safi Apa was wearing."

Safi Apa again. Wherever you go it's Safi. I was bewildered. What does it mean? Is there no one in the world but Safi?

"No, not that kind," I said, "that's a bit too rustic," and busied myself with the cutting.

"Ah, it's the same design as Apa was wearing. Safi Apa's has the same neck."

"Oh, forget it," I said. "If you like it that's enough."

I got up and left. The act was over. That's what I wanted. Back in my room, I lit the stove, and went to the kitchen to get the kettle and a cup. As I passed Bhabi's room, I could see through the window curtain. Safi and Bhabi were locked in a tête-à-tête. Why not listen in a bit to what they were saying, I thought, but I could not pick up the courage to do it. I went to my room and started fixing the tea.

I won't talk to Bhabi again either—why should I? My throat becomes dry from calling out "Bhabi, Bhabi," yet she doesn't have so much as a gentle word for me. I know why she flatters Safi. Safi goes to college, doesn't she? And she sits with Bhabi all the time, talking in whispers, giving her every little bit of news about what has happened out there. For her too I hardly exist. It's only Bhabi for her. Fine, let Safi's exams come. I'll see what she does then. Now she's too grand for me. My eye caught the red and blue flames of the stove, and absently I started humming a verse: "Let the nightingale enjoy itself for a few days more in the garden." The line kept ringing in my mind. I finished my tea, went into the kitchen, and started peeling onions, since I had nothing else to do. From the kitchen I could hear Safi and Bhabi talking. Their voices were clear, and I found I had started crying. The tears came without my knowing why.

"Tell me," I heard Bhabi saying, "do your professors ever scold the girls?"

"They don't say a word even to the boys, let alone the girls," said

---

*An elder sister is addressed as Apa.

Safi. "That's why the boys are up to so much mischief, and with such impunity!"

"Really—are the boys mischievous?"

"What do you think? Only yesterday someone got hold of Kamla's braids and looped them to the desk behind, so when she got up to go they pulled taut like the reins of a horse."

Bhabi's laugh rang out, Safi joined in, and they continued to laugh for a long time.

"Let it be," Bhabi said. "Teach me English. I'm going to go to college too."

And for some unknown reason Bhabi took an interest in learning to read.

"This is not a bird you can just catch," Safi said to Bhabi. "It calls for sweat and blood." As if she, Safi, alone had the ability.

"Why can't I learn?" Bhabi said, "Am I not human?"

"Oh dear," Safi said to her, "you don't understand. It's a brain-wracking business, Bhabi."

And Bhabi fell silent. She looked as if the branch to which she had fastened her swing was giving way.

God! I said to myself, imagine being married when one is so green. Involuntarily my heart went out to Bhabi. Only the other day when she told Bhaiya* about her wish to learn, he had laughed. "An old mare wishing to deck itself with a red saddle," he had said. "Tomorrow you'll wish to go to the club to learn tennis." Such words, and from so educated a man as Bhaiya!

"Does one become an old mare at seventeen?" Bhabi asked.

"That's how it is, Daughter," Mother put in. "The moment a girl is married—she may be only twelve—she is no longer young. These glowing cheeks last only a few days. Then, when something stirs in the belly, it's all up."

A flush rose to Bhabi's face, and her eyes threatened to turn red—what was so upsetting about this? I looked at Bhaiya. He'd gone white, as if the blood had drained from him. Everyone looked stunned. Something had gone wrong. Mother hurled this remark and went away. Bhabi ran for her room. I could just see a flash of her dress before she made it out. I followed her. She was lying face down and crying. And that darned Safi couldn't so much as go up to her and try to calm her. Quite the contrary. She would probably say, "This business of reading

---

*Bhaiya means "elder brother," and here refers to Bhabi's husband.

and writing is not for you, Bhabi." And Bhabi would look at Safi as if she had flung an insult at her. But what did those tears mean?

Then—

"Come what may, you'll teach me or no one else." I peeped in. Bhabi was clinging to Safi. "My Safi will teach me. I'll see that she does," she said.

"Lord! Let go! Really, Bhabi, what an awful habit you have. You crush me so. All my bones are shaken." Safi was struggling in Bhabi's arms. Her face was so comic it made me laugh. And, I don't know why, but the moment she saw me, Bhabi released Safi, as if she had been caught in a furtive act. Safi heaved a sigh of relief.

"Go tell Bhaiya to teach you," said Safi. "He teaches so well. He taught me too, after all."

"I don't want to be taught by Bhaiya," muttered Bhabi. I was amused. She, too, calls him "Bhaiya." I chuckled.

I peeped again. Bhabi was desperately holding Safi tightly in her arms.

"How many times have I told you to stop this. What's the matter with you? My whole body is aching," Safi wailed.

"All right, tell your Bhaiya to send me to a college," said Bhabi. "I'll never trouble you again."

"I'll tell him, that's no problem," Safi said, "but you get your Birjis Apa on your side."

Get Birjis Apa on your side! As if I were the one who would block her plans!

For a few days Bhabi's education became quite a topic in the house. The whole day they argued over it. It irritated me to think that Bhaiya was standing in the way. Why should that be? If she wanted to educate herself, why should he resist it? Safi went out, didn't she? And once Bhaiya had so much wanted to have an educated wife! Why was he so upset now that his wife wanted to educate herself?

"What will you do with it?" Bhaiya asked. "Will you get a job?"

"Are you educating Safi for a job?"

"Safi? Oh, Safi is a different matter. Why do you compare yourself to her?"

"Bhabi, don't bring my name in," Safi cut in. "Settle your own affairs—why drag me into it?"

Bhabi gave Safi a stare as if she would pulverize her with her eyes.

Go on, Bhabi, I thought to myself, go on now and have your long, whispering sessions with Safi, hold her to your heart. Oh, I know the girl, I know every inch of her.

Bhabi's stare made Safi blurt out, "If she is so keen on learning, Bhaiya, why doesn't she ask you to teach her? What's the point of wasting money on it?"

I took Bhabi by the hand and led her to my room. She came without a word and sat down, her eyes fixed on the floor. The tears stood in her eyes; she seemed lost in thought. She blinked, hoping, it seemed, that the tears would shrink back. It felt as though the portraits of Tagore and Iqbal* on the wall were welcoming Bhabi, as if all the books in the room were calling out to her. She raised her eyes to one of the pictures, then lowered them. The tears, which had been waiting only for a sign, started to fall like rain. Despite the thrill of having her in my room, I was sad to see how hurt she was. But the stars were twinkling. We conversed silently like old acquaintances, like brother and sister who, after a quarrel, stare at each other, the past unwinding in their eyes. The silence grew long, but we felt so close to each other that we didn't need words, like a branch that, even after having lost its blossoms, keeps its arms stretched out.

After this we became as intimate with each other as the twin stars in Bhabi's eyes.

Bhabi began to come now, every evening, to take lessons from me. She was scared of Bhaiya. He was such a good teacher—the whole house admired him for it—and yet he had failed to pass Bhabi's test. When she saw him coming, she tucked the book away, under a pillow.

I felt that in the dim dusk of the past there had been a light somewhere, like the flicker of a candle in a graveyard. In this darkness, as if emerging from a stretch of crumbling graves, I walked, panting, taking quick steps, stopping short to glance back, then continuing. In the sky the stars now twinkled, now went out, as though extinguished by a breath.

"What's the book you are reading?"

"It's not *Tilism-e-Hoshruba*,** anyway."

I had a feeling of being pulled by the hair—damn! She's still on such stuff—I'd been through all this in childhood!

Bhabi pushed her book under the pillow.

I said, "You act as if it is *Tilism-e-Hoshruba* that you were reading."

Bhabi smiled, then clasped me in a mad embrace. Safi flashed across

---

*Iqbal Muhammad (1877–1938) was a nationalist poet, scholar, and philosopher.
**Tilism-e-Hoshruba* is a rambling romantic fantasy, generally kept away from the young, especially girls.

my mind, Bhabi hugging her with all her might, and Safi, her breath coming fast, saying, "Oh Lord! Let go. What an awful habit—holding me like this—all my bones are shaken." I too thought of screaming like Safi, but then it was as if someone had put a hand on my mouth, and a delicious agony made my eyes open wide. Safi was a fool to have screamed so loudly. What would anyone who heard her have thought? I blushed. When Bhabi's grasp loosened, she was panting like one who had come running from a long distance.

"I don't want to read this Inglish-Pinglish anymore," Bhabi said. "Give me a magazine with delicious stories in it." She picked up an old issue of a magazine from the shelf and was gone before I knew what was happening. She did not reappear for hours.

"I see! So it's *this* magazine that you are reading now." I was startled to hear Safi's voice coming from Bhabi's room. "It's precisely for the likes of you that Akhter-ul-Iman has written the lines:

> Thus one age departs, another comes,
> While I just stand between two darks.

The Lord protect one from Safi's fault-finding! She'll never let go when she's got it in for someone. On the other hand, Bhabi too is a problem. To get to know her is no child's play. Once she started with the magazines, she did nothing the whole day but read them.

Last night I walked boldly into Bhabi's room. I didn't even bother to check whether she was alone or not. Imagine my going to her like that at ten at night! Surely if Mother had seen me she would have raised a storm. "They won't let Daughter-in-law have a moment's rest, these girls. They are always in her room."

As if Mother cared so much for her daughter-in-law's comfort! She would pick a quarrel with Bhabi over every little thing, but if we went to her room, Mother had to protest. I sometimes feel I should boycott Bhabi and her room. After all, it's not going to make much difference if we don't go to her. But then how was she to blame? Poor thing, she always says with such solicitation, "Do come to my room Birjis, whenever you want. Who can stop you, after all?"

And my steps, of their own accord, led me to Bhabi's room. Bhaiya stood near a cupboard, doing something—I couldn't make out what. Why should I mind him or anyone? It was for Bhabi I had gone there. "But what shall I do," Bhabi was saying, "I've no option. What can these stories do to a person? They can't . . ."

When he saw me, Bhaiya seemed upset, for some reason. He clicked the cupboard shut and fell silent as if he had been bitten by a snake.

Then Bhabi said, "After all, is there harm in reading this?"

"Of course there is," Bhaiya replied. "You shouldn't read this stuff."

"Fine, if it's so, you should stop your sister before telling me to stop."

"Birjis is another matter," said Bhaiya.

I felt as if I had stumbled against a stone. What does it mean? Safi is another matter, Birjis is another matter. Did Bhabi commit a crime by marrying? Is that why she alone is not "another matter?"

And I felt Bhabi's eyelids grow heavy with God knows what unseen dreams, getting caught in them and crumbling to pieces. What chance did those dreams have against reality? Bhaiya left the room. Bhabi got up from the bed and threw her arms around me.

I saw Safi's magazine lying before me in the light. Safi stood on the threshold saying, "Oh Lord! Let go. What an awful habit you have. You hold me so tightly, my bones begin to shake."

Suddenly the light went off, Safi's shadow disappeared, and the two of us were left in the darkness, groping for the sun—.

Tears fell on my cheeks. I closed my eyes very tight. From the other room came Safi's soft humming:

Of light and color the camp is close at hand,
The stars are trembling, the dawn is close at hand.

But the fact was that night still remained and the dawn was far off. There was a camp of tears before one could reach the glittering camp of the stars.

Translated by Syed Sirajuddin.

RAJAM KRISHNAN _____

(b. 1925)   *Tamil*

The prodigious output of this committed writer is, in the world of Indian letters, comparable perhaps only to that of Rabindranath Tagore. Since 1946, when she published her first story, Rajam Krishnan has written forty full-length novels, a couple of hundred short stories, twenty radio plays, and two biographies, and has translated several works, mainly from Malayalam into Tamil. Among the dozen or so awards she has won are the National Sahitya Academy Award for *Verruku Nir* (Water for the Roots) in 1973 and the Soviet Land Nehru Award for *Valaikkaram* (Wrist with Bangles) in 1975.

For one who has achieved so much, Rajam Krishnan's childhood and early adult life were remarkably traditional. Her education was interrupted by her marriage at the age of fourteen. Rajam Krishnan writes that it was "unthinkable that a girl brought up in a conventional middle-class brahmin family in a village would become a writer"—especially in her case, since she was the youngest member of a joint family. "I had to toil with humility and perseverance, obeying all my husband's people, to earn a good name and add to my own family's honor and pride. . . . I was calm outside, discharging my duties in the house, but there was turmoil inside." Things eased a little within the household when, in 1950, one of her short stories was chosen for an international competition. But that was only a first step. It was difficult for a woman with little formal education to have her work published or to be read seriously. Things are easier, she writes, when a woman writer remains within the boundaries that men, over the years, have marked out for her. But as the Bengali writer Nabaneeta Dev Sen also points out, should a woman writer venture beyond the family and the lyrical expression of her feelings into territories regarded as male, there is an immediate outcry. Every obstacle will be placed in her path. One has to struggle, Rajam Krishnan says, "earnestly and with enthusiasm."

Rajam Krishnan's novels are regarded as having set a new trend in Tamil literature. For each volume, she does careful background research. Some of this work is done in libraries, but as most of her writing deals with the lives of people who have rarely been written about or studied—salt pan workers, fisher folk, children in match factories—she also visits and lives among the people to gather her documentary information firsthand. "A novel can also be a social document," she says, and many of hers are.

Her earliest work in this new genre, *Kurunji Then* (Nectar of the Kurinji Flower), 1962, depicts changes in the lives of tribal peoples in the Nilgiri Hills following industrialization. To write *Valaikkaram* (Wrist with Bangles), 1969, which depicts Goa's struggle for freedom from colonial rule, she traveled through the area and interviewed people who had taken part in the freedom movement. Other books written in the same mode are *Kutu Kunjugal* (Fledgelings), 1980, which depicts the lives of the child workers in match and fireworks factories in Sivakasi, and *Alaivaikkaraiyile* (On the Shores), 1978, which deals with the life of fisher folk on the southeast coast.

When she was traveling through southern Tamil Nadu, gathering material for a biography of the famous early-twentieth-century Tamil poet Subramanya Bharati, Rajam Krishnan, heard of the *devadasi* who had, acting on his advice, set aside her traditional profession, and, at thirty-five, married to "lead a life of dignity." The devadasis—women dancers and singers dedicated to the Hindu shrines—can be traced back in Tamil Nadu to the late bhakti period, when many important temples were built. In the early twentieth century, however, the institution came under attack from social reformers who depicted the devadasis as prostitutes and their dance, from which the contemporary dance form Bharat Natyam is derived, as immoral. Efforts were made to "rehabilitate" the devadasis and draw them into "respectable" family life. The feminist sociologist Amrit Srinivasan, writing in 1985, considers the devadasis professional women of independent means, governed by a sexual order radically at odds with that which was emerging among the colonial middle classes. The contradictions for women are presented quite clearly in Rajam Krishnan's book *Manudattin Makranthangal* (Human Pollen), 1984, which was based on the life of the woman she had heard about. It is, she says, "not a fictional account, but written in fictional style." Her admiration for the woman, who wiped away the large *pottu* she wore on her forehead as the "bride of god" and started on a new life, is evident. "Long before the early social reformers turned their attention to the devadasis," she writes, "this lady took up the challenge of foregoing royal patronage and struggled, in penury and against many odds, to bring up her family." During the twenties and thirties this woman took part in the freedom movement. Her son eventually became a high ranking official, but she was never allowed to shake off her past. She continued to be isolated and regarded as disreputable. As Shakuntala Narasimhan puts it, "The novel probes, on the one hand, the changes in interpersonal and intergenerational relationships within a family in a society in transition, and on the other, the 'morality' that sneers at a prostitute's depravity but uses it unhesitatingly for pleasure on the sly, and condemns the same woman to 'respectable' starvation and ignominy once she turns 'clean.' "

C. S. Lakshmi criticizes these novels because the documentary information is not integrated into the fictional structure and often remains merely as background for a conventional plot. She has, however, hailed Rajam Krishnan's sparkling sense of humor, her detailed observation, and her sympathy for those who labor and those who suffer.

Rajam Krishnan does not define herself as a feminist, believing women's issues to be inextricably intertwined with social, economic, and political ones. Some of her fiction focuses on the politics of the family, and the story translated here, taken from *Kalam* (Battlefield), 1985, is from this phase in her writing. *Vidu* (Home), 1978, has been compared to Ibsen's *A Doll's House*. Her interest in these questions has been rekindled by the resurgence of feminism in the seventies. Critic Kalpana Sundaram describes the dominant mood in these works as an "optimistic realism."

◆

KAIPIDITE KADALORUVANAI
(Lending a Helping Hand★)

Unused to working the pestle, Ranjani struggled fiercely to grind the coriander seeds. Her sari slipped from her shoulder, perspiration dripped from her brow . . .

"Why you, what are you grinding? Is it for the *sambar?* Her mother-in-law, Rukmani, had come sharp-eyed into the kitchen. Without waiting for a reply, she asked, "For pity's sake, what are you using the cumin for?"

"For the *rasam,* Mother."

"Then, what's that cooking on the stove?"

"Rasam, Mother."

Nostrils flaring, cheeks quivering, her mother-in-law leapt to point out, "The smell of asafetida is filling the place. Does anyone ever use it for cumin rasam? What ignorance!"

While the daughter-in-law looked back ruefully, Ananth, her husband, came in carrying their whimpering child. Even before Ranjani could wash her hands, the child leaped into her arms.

"Can't you hold the child for a bit?" she asked gently.

"He doesn't like being with me."

"Why wouldn't he, if you played with him a little?"

"Oh, yes," interjected the mother-in-law. "Do you think the child will know a parent if he sees him just once a week? Even the mother, he doesn't get to see for a whole day. Go, go—I will manage the cooking. Just yesterday, HE said he couldn't bring himself to touch the rasam. It will be the same today."

Ranjani by now was hardened to her mother-in-law's remarks. Holding her child, she stood aside, and watched her mother-in-law dissolving tamarind, frying the vegetables, seasoning the food, meticulously measuring out minute quantities of each spice. What energy, for someone in her sixty-fifth year! The troublesome coriander was ground to a fine paste in just half a minute. *Gas*★★ for cooking, and a *pressure cooker* had come into the house only after Ranjani's marriage. Her father-in-law, refusing to accept these conveniences, insisted that

---

★"Kaipidite Kadaloruvanai" is a line from a poem by Subramanya Bharati, who was also a social reformer and champion of women's rights.

★★Italicized English words are in English in the original.

his food be cooked in the traditional way, and rotis baked only over coals. This obstinacy was meant to control not only his diet, but the newly arrived daughter-n-law.

Rukmani would go out every morning for just half an hour, after finishing the cooking by nine o'clock and serving a second cup of coffee to her husband. This was the time of her freedom. She was supposed to visit temples. However, in this short space of time many family matters would be talked about with friends and neighbors—the role of husbands, questions of family prestige, stories about sons and daughters-in-law, dowries for daughters, and their trousseau ... At the same time, she would buy the vegetables for the evening meal, and arrive home by nine-thirty on the dot. Only after her return would her husband start his ablutions and his prayers. At leisure, he would then sit down to eat, slowly and appreciatively, the rotis cooked by his wife over the coals. By the time he had finished, it would be twelve-thirty.

Ananth stayed clear of all this. On holidays he would finish his meal by ten. Even if Rukmani said, "You have a child now, why don't you eat," Ranjani wouldn't eat. She would eat only with her mother-in-law. The food would be cold by then. Leftover rotis, curry, not left over all that much, rasam that had begun to thicken. Rukmani would feed her daughter-in-law, and then eat whatever was finally left over. This Ranjani found pathetic. Father-in-law's orders were that nothing from the morning meal should be left over for the evening. For Ranjani, all this was new and strange.

Today, Rukmani was a little late starting for "the temple." Buvanammbal came searching for her. "Auntie, aren't you coming to the temple? Is the daughter-in-law here?" Obviously she hadn't come just to call Auntie to the temple. Ranjani put the child, already asleep on her shoulder, into the cradle in the front room.

"Yes, she has got *leave*. She has come. Once the *leave* is over, she will go back."

Buvanammbal got up to look at the child in the cradle. "Your grandson is the spitting image of you, Auntie. And just as it should be. Her people have put a bracelet on the child's arm. It's quite heavy too! Must be a *poun*."*

"I never ask about such things," said Rukmani.

---

*Poun, derived from the English word "pound," is a measured weight equivalent to that of an old English gold sovereign coin.

"What does it matter if you don't ask? They know what should be done for the child. He's the firstborn grandchild! And what has she brought for you from her parents' house? A *boiler?* Pankaja had brought her youngest daughter the new, coal-free *electric boiler.* It's so nice and compact!"

Ranjani, startled, looked at her mother-in-law. She hadn't known about these customs. The bracelet was not real gold. It was gold-plated silver.

"She—she doesn't run a family here," Rukmani said. "She goes to *work.* The family just loiters between here and Pondicherry. When the marriage was being arranged, she decided to begin work on a Ph.D. We thought she would get it soon after marriage. It's three years now. A child has also arrived. I don't ask about anything. Anyway, I got them both married properly, with proper dowry, and proper cere-monies. I saw to that. I have also seen my two daughters give birth. After that storm subsided, now this . . ."

Her mother-in-law rattled on. Ranjani was mortified. She had been twenty-eight, and he had been thirty-eight. She was the eldest daugh-ter of a musician, who was gifted but not with a voice, and had to go from house to house to teach music. After many years, he married a person as poor as himself. Her younger brother, after getting a B.A., went to Bombay for a job. She had two sisters. Father was now quite enfeebled, and Mother ran a school at home. Ranjani herself, though not fair, was tall, good-looking, and very clever in her studies. After getting an M.A. in English literature, she had enrolled for a Ph.D. Then she agreed to this marriage. Ananth, though working in a bank, had been very interested in literature. He was present at every literary meeting in the city, and took part in debates and discussions as well.

Since Ananth had refused to get married earlier, his two younger brothers had married first and started their own families. One went to Dubai to earn money. Another left for the all-wealthy America. For Rukmani, who used to wait patiently till ten or eleven at night to feed her bachelor son, and who washed his clothes, it was a comfort that at last he had decided to marry a girl of his own choice—one he had met at a discussion. She wasn't of another caste.* She didn't wear her sari below her navel. She covered herself modestly and did obeisance

---

*From the style of the Tamil dialogue, it is clear that the characters are all brah-mins.

to her future father-in-law and mother-in-law. Ananth had said, "Mother, this is she—Ranjani—whom I told you about."

Ranjani, when she looked up gently, saw that her future father-in-law didn't seem gentle enough to approve of her. From under raised eyebrows, he stared haughtily at her. "You . . ." he addressed his son. "What has she studied?"

Ranjani had replied herself, "An M.A. in literature. Soon I hope to complete my Ph.D." She had hoped he would ask what her *subject* was.

"Ha! What Ph.D.? What are you people going to do with a Ph.D.?" he had snarled.

Afterwards, the mother had asked her son if the girl worked. Yes, he had told her, she was a lecturer at a college.

A simple marriage was performed at Vadapalani Temple. Her father-in-law didn't even talk to her father. Without even eating the wedding meal, he had gone home. A week later, when her leave was over, Ranjani got ready to go. "Is she going away?" the mother had asked her son. "Yes, Mother . . . there's the college . . ." After Ananth saw Ranjani off at the railway station, Rukmani had confronted him. "Where's the need for her to work? You have married late. Shouldn't she stay home nicely and look after you?" He said nothing. If he visited Ranjani one weekend, she would come for the next. Rukmani didn't think of the time when she had waited up for her son to come home. It hadn't mattered. Now it did matter that she waited for her daughter-in-law, even when told not to. At the end of the first year of marriage, in the summer, the daughter-in-law came for the holidays.

Rukmani had suggested civilly, "Why do you need to work? In another four or five months, it will be time for the baby. Father-in-law doesn't like you working at all. Even our Rama and Shamba are educated—but it's not our custom to send them to work." The daughter-in-law said nothing. Later she tried again. "There's no rest for me, you know. There are three different meals to be prepared for the three here. When he was working, my husband was always on the move like his trains. And with five children I had to manage this house alone. At nine at night he would demand that I cook him turnips for dinner. He should want for nothing. Even for a day, the seasoning shouldn't lack in anything. I never had any time even to sit on my doorstep. No time to go to a temple, or bathe in its tank, or go to the *cinema* or *drama.* That's how I ran this house. Now, he says, 'When I worked, I had to eat on the run—now, why don't you give me something tasty to eat?' It's right, isn't it? Just half an hour in the morning, and a little time in the evening to light a lamp to God, that's all the time I have for myself.

Even at this stage, if I have to look after a grown son, his food, his needs, it's difficult." All this torrent was not without its effect on the daughter-in-law, but not exactly as Rukmani had intended.

Ananth heard of this later. The *pressure cooker* came. *Gas,* registered for long ago, also came, at last, after he was victorious in getting a "recommendation." He even started to wash and iron his own clothes.

"How our son has changed! As long as we were the ones working, he didn't bother about a thing. Since the wife came, things are done without a word being said," she told her husband. Inwardly, she was proud.

"Yes, be proud, and do your salaams to her," He had said. "To-morrow she will get transferred here, dump her child on you, and go to work—and you will look on!"

To prevent that from happening, when Ranjani visited her next, Rukmani had stopped her from helping in the kitchen. "It's confusing if two cooks work together. When I went to give him his towel, you had already made the curd chutney. For him, curds should be mixed in only when he is sitting down to eat. Rotis shouldn't be made before the meal. They should be cooked one by one as he eats. Yesterday, I cooked the rice after you cleaned it. He found a stone in it. He pushed the rice aside. Nowadays, they turn off the *current*. It is so humid. We need to fan him. I am accustomed to it. It's the *training* I got from my mother-in-law! Would you be able to be so disciplined?"

Ranjani, though irked, felt sorry for her mother-in-law. While eating, she reminded her about the matter of the *boiler*. "We don't know what all your customs are. The *electric boiler*—shall I buy it in the evening?"

"We know you work—but you don't have to show off immediately. There are customs known to elders. They should have known what they should do when they send you back with your new baby and so on . . . but nothing happens these days according to the customs."

Such a conventional attitude stuck in Ranjani's throat. Instead of respect for a woman's economic independence, there was this harping on her limp dependence on her family—when would it cease?

"I feel sad about Mother's life," she said later to Ananth. "When there is no current, she sits up all night fanning Father. Deep in her heart she is fond of me, but doesn't know how to show it. Poor thing. How frugal she is, and careful in her work. When she draws a *kolam* in front of the threshold, the lines are clean and straight as if drawn with a taut string. She used to sing well, didn't she?"

"So you have become an 'admirer' of Mother's—you can't change her story. It won't work with Father. He is not like me."

"I'm trying to get into City College here. I'm going to get your father's imperial fiat rescinded."

Ananth warned her, "Look here, why get into all this trouble? Mother actually likes being bullied by Father like this. Don't stick your head into that. That's my advice. Later, there will only be misunderstandings and squabbles, that's all."

But Ranjani didn't agree. Despite her mother-in-law's strong protests, she started doing things in the kitchen. "Mother, you look after the child. See if I don't learn cooking." She pushed her further. "Mother, I have heard you sing very well. Though my father and mother are musicians, I have no talent. Do sing a little song." Who doesn't melt at praise? Later, "Mother, with such a lovely voice, and such talent, still you don't sing. Did you ever study music?"

"Beginning when I was ten, they taught me for four years. After coming here, there was no singing or dancing. He doesn't approve. If ever there was a good concert over the *radio,* one longed to listen—but that was never possible."

"Mother, next month there's a festival at the Subramanyaswami Temple in our village. For ten days there will be good concerts. Just come. My mother will look after us. You also need a *change."*

"It is just not possible to go and stay at a place from which a bride has come into our house. Your father-in-law would never allow it."

"Let him come also."

"Aiyo! In the old days it was another type of problem. Now he won't consider leaving home."

"Shall I ask him? It's because he doesn't get a *change* either that he keeps driving you so."

"No, don't, my dear. He will bark at you. From the age of thirteen— since I came here—I have slaved right through. I am used to it now. Let my days end like this. I only pray I should close my eyes before he does, and pass away auspiciously as a married woman." Her eyes glistened with tears.

Ranjani remembered two lines of a poem by Bharati:

The little deep coils of slavehood
with fire we shall burn them through;
Human lives with spirit are endowed—
Only they enslave who truly are insane.

The lines clashed and clanged in her heart. It would be seventy years since the poet sang thus. From one's birthplace to bring a dowry. Despite all sense, blindly to sink deeper into slavish beliefs—and then to call this our custom! This still-prevalent belief—when will we set it aside? When will we trample it down!

When Ranjani was leaving, Rukmani wept. "I pray that somehow you will get posted here. Or else that somehow he should get transferred there—Ananth was telling Father." Her voice quavered.

"Don't worry, Mother," Ranjani said. "I am going to come and live with you here."

Later, her husband said, "You woman. What did she so unctuously fool you about? She is going to come here? And you will wash her saris and send her off to college? Aren't you ashamed? You are old— so I permit you to visit temples—if she comes that will come to a stop also. I have told Ananth to go there, himself. We don't need the money of any son."

Rukmani looked at him angrily for the first time. She felt deep down: she is educated, she works, she is superior. Ranjani had said once, "For Father-in-law, I bought this sweater. It is not too heavy. It will be good for the winter season." He had tossed it aside. All right. Then Ranjani had bought her a fine mustard-colored sari. He had said, "Aren't you ashamed? If your son wishes to, let him buy you a sari with his own earnings. But this girl—this, this dropping found yesterday! When we are here, who is she to buy you a sari? Instead of flinging it in her face, you are displaying it to me." He had flung it at Ranjani. She had picked it up without a word and left. Even when Rukmani pushed her away, the girl had kept calling her Mother, Mother, and had continued to do jobs she wasn't used to. Your own daughters, what do they do for you? Rukmani thought to herself. They wouldn't lift a finger to help their mother. The daughters-in-law, whose marriages had been arranged according to orthodox customs, well, the less said about them the better. They had time only to change their saris, prettify themselves, go with their husbands to the *cinema,* or ride pillion on scooters around town. All their babies they leave for "Mother" to look after. The second son's wife was supposed to come from an important family. If anyone from that family ever came to Madras, they always stayed there. That woman would bring her sisters and run Rukmani ragged for ten days while she made them all meals and snacks.

"Now you are tired, Mother. Sit and rest," says this girl. This girl's affectionate concern touched her for the first time—wetted the throat that had been parched for affection for so long.

Rukmani decided to go away with her daughter-in-law for ten days. The college gave the girl four days' leave. She would take another four days, and with her mother-in-law visit Madurai and Kanyakumari before returning. This was decided when Ananth next visited Pondicherry.

"For ten days serve your father, in your mother's place," said Ranjani to her husband. In the half hour allowed to her in the morning for temple visits, Rukmani got ready for the journey. Ananth was already at the bus stop carrying her bag with a change of clothes. This new freedom took Rukmani back to her youth. At the Pondicherry bus stop, Ranjani was waiting for her with her aged father.

"I thought you might come by the morning bus, so I asked Father to wait here for you. I'm so happy to see you here." With this welcome she led her to their home, an old-fashioned tiled house with few comforts, but with two very affectionate younger sisters. One had earned a B.A., the other an M.A. In the evening she was taken to the beach, to the Aurobindo Ashram. After two days of such welcome, and such hospitality, daughter-in-law and mother-in-law departed. In Madurai, they were received by Ranjani's uncle's son. After two days there, they went to Kanyakumari, the point where the three seas meet. After a dip and divine audience, there was rest in a *hotel room!*

"It would have been nice if Ananth had also come along. Everyone wishes to travel with her husband, but you have brought along your mother-in-law," Rukmani said.

"We will come together some day. It will happen. But you must understand. If one is a slave, and thinks that is happiness, how can the family flourish? First he said he would come. But Father was so *shocked* that I asked him to stay back with him. Father tells me to stop working. It's not just the pay. My education, my status, can I set all this aside, and stand at the kitchen door and gossip about others? The world has changed. One cannot abandon one's responsibilities. If I try my best, and you try your best—what can't we accomplish?"

"You are right, my dear. Even for an anna, I have to ask him. It is very difficult. Just to make sure that we are totally dependent, He doesn't want us to work. Now I understand." Her voice quavered.

In Madras, after their return, Ranjani rode high on her triumph. But Rukmani had only her shyness with which to hold up her head. After all, she was not a little girl. What would He do? It is He who needs her now, she thought, steeling herself.

"We didn't expect you at the station. Hello, how is Father?" asked Ranjani. He said nothing as they arranged for a vehicle to carry them, their baggage, their palm-leaf boxes, and their baskets home.

"Did you cook?" she persisted.

"Come home and see. Father himself cooks."

At the doorstep, they heard voices. Who has arrived, Rukmani wondered, startled.

"Who? Chambu? When did you come from Hyderabad?"

"You should be ashamed of yourself," stormed her daughter. "Leaving Father like this. You went away emboldened by your working daughter-in-law. And this fellow," pointing to Ananth, "stood by silent. I thought as much even then. Even before marriage, the way she got around you! This mother will do whatever anyone asks. I knew she would get around to it. That's how she will dump her child on you and go to work. I have also studied. I was offered a job in the *Reserve Bank.* But in my house I wasn't permitted to work! Father telegraphed me saying he was ill. I came home straightaway, and was so ashamed. This fellow was cooking, and Father dicing the vegetables!"

Rukmani couldn't breathe.

"Wait, wait, Chambu. What has happened? Mother needed a *change.* Father wouldn't let her go—that's why I took her along. What's wrong with that? She is also a person."

"Yes, yes, my girl. How is it you show all the sympathy we don't seem to have? You will have first one, then two children. You need someone to look after the house. You don't have five 'poun' worth of jewelry. Mother has jewels. Such cheek, you, fooling innocent Mother! You have taken her around without a male escort! I had asked for a gold knotted chain of two pouns—will she give it to me now?"

Ranjani stood dumbfounded. Her uneducated mother-in-law could be convinced without great difficulty—but how was one to deal with this woman with a master's degree? Ananth winked as if to ask, "How will you shake this imperial flag?"

Translated by Chudamani Raghavan and Vithal Rajan.

DUDALA SALAMMA _____

(b. ca. 1925)   *Telugu*

Dudala Salamma was a participant in the 'Telangana People's Struggle (1946–1951). Her oral history, reprinted here, is one of nearly fifty that were collected by Stree Shakti Sanghatana, a women's group in Hyderabad interested in seeking out the history of women participants in the struggle. Sixteen of these accounts have been published in the volume *Manaku Teliyani Mana Charitra* (We Were Making History: Women in the Telangana People's Struggle), 1986.

The drama implicit in the writing of all history, always an interaction between a present and a sought-out past, comes alive in autobiographical narratives of this kind. Life stories such as the one Dudala Salamma recounts here can only be told to listeners who have sought them out and appreciate their significance; the narrative itself is not only drawn out, but also shaped by that attention. Stree Shakti Sanghatana began work on the project as a result of the realization that it was necessary to learn what the history would be like if told from the perspective of women participants in the uprising, but also because "their history constituted . . . the basis of our own attempt to recover for ourselves a tradition of struggle." They add, "For us as a women's group searching out our past, oral history has a particular appropriateness. Though women have traditionally been marginalised in written cultures, they have always told stories and sung songs" that never saw the light of day in patriarchal modes of literary production.

The Telangana People's Struggle began as protests against forced labor and other exactions by the nizam of Hyderabad State and Hindu landlords. Each peasant family had to send one person to work on the landlord's farm, to collect firewood, carry mail to other villages, deliver and pick up supplies, and so on. Footwear, agricultural implements, pots, and cloth for the landlord's family had also to be supplied by the peasants. Peasant girls worked as slaves in the landlord's house, and when the landlord's daughters married, these girls were often sent away with them to serve as concubines. When the exactions of the landlords grew to include eviction of the peasants from their lands, the peasants resisted. As their movement took shape, they demanded abolition of all forced, unpaid labor and of illegal exactions, as well as reduced taxes and interest rates and the confirmation of their title deeds to the land.

During this period, women were drawn into the struggle in large numbers, partly out of the conviction that, as half the human race, they too were part of the struggle, and partly out of necessity. In a time of severe repression, the active involvement of women was indispensable. Their presence sometimes provided cover for movement members living and acting as members of a family. But many women also fought actively in the movement's squads. Most of the life-stories in the collection stress that joining the struggle was tremendously liberating for these women. "It was a magic time," one of them declared. Women found it was possible to break with custom, to travel alone (even at night), to carry guns, to act as couriers, to fight in squads. And they grew in ways that would not have been possible outside this important peasant movement.

In 1981, when Stree Shakti Sanghatana began working on a history of the women in this peasant struggle, they heard from many people about the strength and daring of Dudala Salamma, one of the few peasant women who rose to importance in the organizational structure and finally became a *dalam* (squad) leader. One of the most striking features of her account is her self-confidence, her sense that as an organizer and a fighter she stood second to no male leader. Salamma spoke in the dialect used in the Telangana region of Andhra Pradesh, which is commonly considered nonliterary and "inferior" in comparison to the "standard" Telugu of the coastal Andhra. She "drew on conventions of expression, orchestration and elaboration" that were unfamiliar to many of her listeners, but they were struck by her cadenced and dramatic recounting of events and the vivid metaphoric language she so effortlessly used.

But listening to—and reading—women's accounts of their lives also requires, the authors of *Manaku Teliyani Mana Charitra* say, that we "learn, as we read these life-stories, to listen for what another oral historian has called the 'language of silence,' straining to be heard. We need to understand the pauses, the waverings, the incoherence, the questions that are avoided just as much as we need to 'hear' the real import of obsessive repetitions."

The authors describe the meeting with Dudala Salamma in Quila Shapur, a place often mentioned in tales told of the Telangana days, as follows: "It was noon when we arrived there. We went to the fields looking for her and finally saw her standing, hands resting on her hips, near her son's well. We sat there together under a tree, talking until it grew dark."

◆

DUDALA SALAMMA, KHILA SHAPUR
(Dudala Salamma of Quila Shapur)

I have made so many petitions. So many applications. Even to Indira Gandhi. But they didn't send me the money. Where have the papers gone? Where have they thrown them? Two years before the Razakars, my husband passed away; my children were that small. I was there right from the time of the Razakars but not a pie have they sent me. Whoever promised to help, I gave them money. I have become this old and I tell you, I walk with a stick. Why did you all come this far? I know—there are so many (of those who fought) in this district. Who got any money? There is so much to tell—my story: a house, courtyard and all. They looted—looted it all. I had a cot with headboard, woven with cloth tape and a large bed[roll] on it. It was a nice, decent house. I fed the communists and they said, "You fed them, tell us where they are," and tortured me. They hung me up with ropes under my arms, sprinkled water on the ropes and put a spiked board full of nails under me. My feet were split into bits (crying). I was in bad shape. They tortured me so much.

I have one daughter. I got her married to a man from Secunderabad. One son of mine is in Bellampalli. He works in a coal mine. He has three sons and two daughters. He looks after his children. My limbs have been broken and cast in a heap—who will look after me? My younger son is also here. They live their own lives. They find it difficult to make ends meet. If I tell them to look after me, they will say: "Who asked you to go? Why did you go? What did you get out of it?" He died two years before the Razakars. Did I have this much knowledge then? I had just these two sons when the father died. Yadgiri is the younger one. So when they tortured me I felt that rather than suffer this repression here it would be better to go away with the squads. I left one boy in my mother's house. My mother's village is Madaram. Anyway, people will say what they will! One should work in the Sangham [collective/organization] and die. One should be born to live with strength, the strength of our shoulders. How did my wisdom grow out of all this? Do you know how cruel Congress's wickedness can be? Naked as the noonday sun! I kept saving my life from these troubles, escaping them—do you hear? I was caught because I fed them. My mother was here. There was a mustedar [tax collector] called Eddarti Yeraiah. He caught me and said that I should show him where Gujjula Yeraiah and the other communists were. I had sent them all some food. I can't remember the names of the others. This is the result—just look at me now. . . .

You ask why did I feed them? Why have you come here to see me? Why do you roam about, for the Sangham or for women? I too wanted to do the same thing. At least you can read a few letters, but me, I used to graze buffaloes. I lived in the strength and faith that a communist survives on the strength of the shoulder. The struggle for gruel and water—I lived in such strength and power for it. I leaped five feet with Baddam Ella Reddy. Baddam Ella Reddy, Nalla Narasimhulu, Ananthapuram Macherla Yadagiri, Seelam Sarvaiah, Cheetakonduru Rami Reddy, Mukunda Reddy, Siddenki Narasimha Reddy, they were all there. Not one leader had a single complaint to make about me. I roamed about, travelling for the Party. I served it. If you ask what did you do—it will be there in the sufferings of those days. As far as I knew I helped the poor. But I couldn't do anything good. I helped. Where will these brigands let us eat? So I fed them all. I moved with them like a member of the squad. But they had looted my house too.

DUDALA SALAMMA ◆ 219

It would have been a barren life. It was only because I walked along righteous paths that I was able to come back to this village.

My mother-in-law and father-in-law were also beaten to a pulp. My brother, he died because of me, didn't he? He was taken to Nizamabad jail, my brother. Why are you doing this to my sister . . . ? They took him away saying he was a pukka communist fellow. He died of their blows. His record was all covered up in Jangaon—they didn't let it come out. He was called Madaram Balle Ramalingam. Even the people there will tell you. So many sufferings in the story of those days!

Where did I roam in those days? Which villages did I go to? How many years have gone? What can I say now? Akkirajupalli, Bairampalli, Goparajupalli, Madduru, Salakapuram, Pothareddipalle, Bachonna-peta, Siddonki, Ammapuram . . . may these villages prosper! I roamed all the boundaries here. They fly like hawks, don't they? I was in the squads. My life became good for nothing. Unable to see my suffering they took me away with them. "Why suffer this torture here, why not go off to our Sanghams?" they said. I felt the same and went off with our people. Gujjula Yeraiah and I went from Shapuram. I was the only woman who went. We are toddy [palm tree] tappers. I—Salamma. The sound of Salamma was like the roar of a lion. I fought like that—but not a pie has been sanctioned to me so far. I fought in this movement and collapsed. That's all that counts. Nothing else. Not a cow in the herd, not a rupee in my waistcloth, not even a copper chain on my neck. Look at my life. Look at these hard-working hands. I fall on this land and cry. . . .

Our squad had big leaders. Nalla Narasimhulu, Baddam Ella Reddy, Pittala Narayana, Perumandla Yadagiri and others. They beat me up in this Keshav Rao's mansion. He knew English it seems—no Telugu. He did not know our tongue. He threatened that if we did not show them where the Sangham people were, they would put lizards into their underpants. I could understand a little. He's talking like this. What do I say . . . all these lizards, I kept repeating to myself . . . lizard . . . I understood. If they try and grab your head we should be prepared to catch them by the groin. What is it now? As for me I was so good-looking then. I—in my youth—fit to jump four yards! I had two chil-dren then. My household was a fine one, full of pots and pans and cots. So many kinds of things. I had so much hair—such a huge knot. The day they caught me . . . my child wanted to ease himself. The whole place was surrounded by hundreds of military police—it was about ten or eleven in the night. A thousand people from the village can swear to it. We came to know we were surrounded. The children were small—such tiny eggs. I was lying on the cot, a pillow under my head. The boy and I. I had covered him with a sheet. There was no electricity then. All the women, brass pots in hand, going out in the dark to ease themselves, were whispering loudly—"She is going to be arrested; she fed the communists." So I left with the clothes I was wearing. Where did my pots go? And where did my household go? I thought if I fall into the hands of the military it would be like going to hell. My sons will be harassed. At least going into the struggle would give me a name. After being called a communist, I had to go into the forests. I made up my mind—my boy, under one arm, the pot in the other . . . as if to ease myself. I left the doors wide open. Over there was a *madiga* [leather worker's community] house—that far. The child in one hand and a pot in the other—I was marching along. Here there was a *medara* [basket weaver's community] house. I threw the pot into that house. I jumped over the wall there. There was a fellow called Srisailam. He is still alive. He swore he would shave off his moustache if he couldn't hand me over. Oh son, you are not going to catch me, I thought. I jumped across the wall and hid in the niche where the cowdung cakes lay. I sat there, crouching. The madiga family there was a man and wife—extremely poor. They covered me with cowdung cakes. I let down my hair and covered my face with it. I was wearing a good sari—so she took it off and stuffed it in one of the pots used for mixing cowdung with water and gave me an old worn sari to wear. I tied it round my waist. Even if I tell you these troubles, you can't see or feel them. I sat after it was dark until it was almost five. Then at about six they said, "We can't catch this bitch," and left, leaving behind a couple of policemen to guard the place. In the evening again Razakars came. I was hiding in the maize field. After dark they posted some more men to watch. They said: "How can she go out— she is still hiding here in the madiga houses. We must pour some petrol and set fire to them." There was one madiga there, he's dead and gone—Jangirigani Lingaiah. He said, "If you set fire to this—we'll go. That whore is not in this house." Then he started abusing me aloud. He said "That bitch is not here, not in this house or even this village"—and all the time I was hiding in his very house. Do you hear? Well I crept out of that house secretly. I got to the well there. When I got to the well I got a message from Nalla Narasimhulu. They heard that I was caught and shot dead. Then the squad came with machine guns and what not and I left with them. Fifteen days after I left with them, the attack on Bairampalli took place. To tell you all this—all this detail—it is just at the tip of my tongue. I have survived to tell you all

DUDALA SALAMMA ◆ 221

this—you hold the pen—it all comes from my stomach. What is the use of your holding the pen?—my courage stands tall.

Although I suffered all these troubles—I never abused anyone or hit anyone. I walked only on the righteous path. There was one Duddenki Yeraiah. His wife Satyamma said that I had her husband killed—by the communists. Saying this she accused me before the people. I was in the squad. I didn't hold a gun—after all I was a woman. It was all this work that one had in the squad. The work of the Sangham; meet this one, meet those there, tell them how to do this work, what to do with the land, to give the land to the poor . . . [asking] "Why do you need ten acres of land, give this poor thing two acres of your land," and so on. We went against the saukars [traders and money-lenders].

I wandered with the child on my hip. There were so many with us. They all carried him. After all we were comrades. The Party means togetherness . . . ! All of us would go about together. Each would do their own cooking. When we were there in some forest or hill, someone would cook and give us some food. Our folk ran like calves. Where did I cook? Oh fuck! . . . Cooking—no I never cooked. I wore a dhoti like a man, wore a shirt (to cover my tattoos on my arms) and shorts, bound a kerchief around my head. I was disguised as a man. One should serve the people. One marks the day one is born and the day one is dead . . . we make rituals . . . but forget in a few days . . . but to us communism is for several lives. It is like a low fever that never leaves you. It was out of such desire that I entered the forest.

We'd all sleep there together in the forest covering ourselves with a blanket. No, I was never afraid. After all, weren't they all there—our folk? We had some understanding. Even if they split our tongues—we never said that our people were here or there. We observed certain restrictions so that no one would get caught. We couldn't tell—we wouldn't. Twelve whole months I was in the forest. Then what happened was—I told you didn't I that Madaram was my mother's village? My brother had toddy trees. You remember Duddenki Yeraiah, he told my brother—"Ramalingam, I'll give you Rs. 500, you just fetch your sister and her children." He dinned this idea into him. Then he said, "She has children, where will she live in the forest, go and fetch her." And he sent him. My brother walked for a whole month, suffered many troubles and came to me. Here there was a village called Pachapuram. I said to the squad, "Now how is this?" Then he said, "I will give my life for yours. You have sons like Rama and Lakshmana. I'll set you up in your house. You stay in your own house. Your brothers have some land to cultivate. For your expenses and for your children's support—I'll send money. How long will you live in the forest like this (crying)? You must come home definitely." But the squad did not agree. They said, "How can that be?" But I said I'd go. It was two years since I had seen my son. I gave up everything (crying). Let my life go if it must. I gained nothing with this wisdom. A handful of food and cloth—that was all after all. And so I returned . . . my sister-in-law was making rotis . . . she gave me a roti as I sat there . . . I washed my hands and feet . . . put aside my blanket and bag . . . I had a half roti in my hand and I was still eating it. . . . One does not know how long they were watching. The police surrounded us. There is a mango tree here, a toddy palm there. I was near my people's house. They pushed my hands back and tied them to a tree. They tied me with ropes. They used some fibre rope and bound my feet as if they were anklets. They sprinkled water so that the knots would get tighter. My brothers, their wives, the children, and my mother and father, they were all there. There were scores of people. My brother was upset. He said, "Why did I coax her to come needlessly and do her this harm?" Then there were the lashes with the whip. They were so thick—woven stiff by the madigas in the village. Every time the whip was swung, it would go round me thrice. There were so many lashes . . . then they brought me to the landlord's mansion. There were nearly 300 of them—Sikh police and Mussourie police. I was caught by these fellows who came from Mussourie—damn them. I do not know how long back it was. The one they called the Havaldar Sahib. He tied me to a pole. If he hit me the blows would fall really deep, leaving welts on the hands I held lifted up to prevent the blows. There were grooves on my hands. The blood spurted all over the room. This boy was only this high. He kept shrieking aloud. The whole household reverberated with his cries. Then a man came wearing a dhoti. He filled my wounds with coal—you know, the coal used in the railways, not soft charcoal. And he bound them up with a piece of cloth he tore from his dhoti to stop the bleeding. Look at these scars—how yellow they are—all that coal is there in these. How many tortures they put me to! I was kept in that house for three months. This same Keshav Rao's mansion. Then my brothers, my sister, my cousins, all together signed a bond that they were willing to go to jail if I disappeared and I was allowed to go. Then I came to this house. I brought some pounded rice and fetched both the boys and came here. We stayed here. Then this Duddenki Yeraiah was killed. Who knows who killed him or why? His wife said that I, Salamma, had ruined her home—her name was Duddenki Satyamma. "Catch that whore and bring her," they said. By sunrise the military was taking me away. They brought his body there. They cast it before the mansion and said to me—"You whore! You got him killed, this old man who is dead. We will put you also on a bier. I'll put my husband on one side and you on the other. . . ." All this suffering because of her. I just kept quiet. . . . Then, after all this, I was at home. I carried liquor bottles from Jangaon. I pounded paddy. I didn't sit still. I worked for wages. The children were tiny after all. I put the older one through school till the 7th. There is a chap called Ramayya here. I put both my sons to work with him grinding herbs for medicines. They earned a pot of millets as wages those days (crying). I really suffered in those days. I did not go to the Party and earn money.

And after all this, who do I tell my story to? Look how wonderful I am now,—I can't even get up when I want to. I am at God's mercy. I don't tell anyone my story—not to my daughters-in-law, not to any human being.

Translated by K. Lalita and Vasantha Kannabiran.

DHIRUBEN PATEL —————————————

(b. 1926)   *Gujarati*

Gandhian ideals were a formative influence on Dhiruben Patel's household, as they were in so many families in Gujarat, and indeed in the rest of India in the late twenties, thirties, and forties. During those decades women took part in the public campaigns to burn foreign cloth and to support indigenous cottage industries by wearing homespun khadi. Many took seriously Gandhi's call for a program for national reconstruction in which all Indians should learn to spin, and women spent some time each day producing the thread that they hoped would ensure that the poorest person in the country would be clothed. If thread were spun and cloth woven in the household, Gandhi said, women too would be economically self-sufficient. The movement emphasized self-discipline and moral rigor, and women felt that the contribution they could make to the cause of freedom and dignity, however limited, was important. Dhiruben's story "Lipstick" has the Gandhian satyagraha movement as a backdrop.

Dhiruben was born in Baroda and educated in Bombay. Although her mother had very little formal education, she was an active member of the Indian National Congress and a journalist. The family environment was a sustaining one for this girl who began to write stories when she was still in school. All in her family were well read, and, in Dhiruben's words, "Writing was as natural as cleaning one's teeth." It is a tribute not only to this remarkable family, but to the Gandhian movement as a whole, that no pressure was put on Dhiruben when she decided not to marry. In answer to a question from poet and critic Jaya Mehta, she speaks of having had to face the "astonishment" of society, but no opposition. She taught English at a Bombay college for some years. From its inception in 1966, to 1975, she edited the Gujarati weekly *Sudha* and in that capacity encouraged younger writers and provided thought-provoking reading for women. Later she established Kali Prakashan, a publishing company that specialized in books on Gandhian thought.

Although Dhiruben does not call herself a feminist, like the novelist Kundanika Kapadia she believes that the root cause of women's inferior status lies in their own mental conditioning. Change in status, then, must start with a change in consciousness. At the outset of her career as a writer she sought deliberately to depict women's life situations and create a context in which their oppressed status could be discussed. Subsequently her focus shifted to building character and plot, although if the protagonist is a woman, or the theme involves the man-woman relationship, woman's condition and her quest for selfhood do become central to the work.

Dhiruben's first two books—*Adhuro Kol* (The Incomplete Promise), 1955, and *Ek Lahar* (A Ripple), 1957—are collections of short stories, but she is known principally as a novelist. Mention must also be made of her plays and of the popular collection *Vishrambkatha* (The Story of a Secret), 1967, the powerful title story of which has been widely translated. In it the son, who has taken his mother to Benares on a pilgrimage, watches her in animated conversation with an old friend she meets there by chance and realizes with a shock that this suppressed nonentity he has known all his life was once a buoyant, carefree girl. Dhiruben's range may be further illustrated by "Be Dost" (Two Friends), another story in the same volume, in which a child protects his crazy grandfather from a mocking world and even from his own unsympathetic parents. In Dhiruben's first novel, *Vadavanal* (Suppressed Fires), 1963, the heroine is thwarted from childhood by an attractive but vicious cousin who steals the affection of her mother, and later that of her lover and her husband. Critics have praised the novel for the insight with which it depicts the gradual warping of the heroine's mind as every attempt to escape her cousin's clutches fails. Dhiruben's own favorite among her novels is *Vavantol* (The Tempest), 1979, a picaresque novel in which a considerably idealized heroine is involved in a series of exciting and extraordinary events.

Shirin Kudchedkar, however, considers *Sheemlanan Phool* (Flowers of the Silk-Cotton Tree), 1976, to be of greater interest because it is an early exploration of a theme that novelists have begun to explore only recently.

A woman who leaves her husband because of overt cruelty or infidelity would be sympathetically regarded by most contemporary readers. But the novel portrays a marriage that has become intolerable to the wife because over the years there is a lack of communication except in sex and the long-established daily routine. The heroine's certainty that she must leave and her uncertainty regarding the causes of her alienation from her husband or her future course of life are subtly portrayed. Ultimately she returns, but with no illusions and with no regrets about her earlier action. Jaya Mehta criticizes the central character, Ranna, for wanting "to run before she has learnt to walk," as well as the novel's conclusion, for the compromise it makes. But Dhiruben does not present Ranna as an erring wife. Rather, the husband is depicted as incapable of change, though he is passionately fond of her, and by the end of the novel, Ranna has acquired a surer knowledge of herself and the choices open to her in the contemporary world.

◆

From SHEEMLANAN PHOOL
(Flowers of the Silk-Cotton Tree)
Chapter 1

"I still feel you should stay on here."

The words slipped out but immediately Vimal felt he had made a mistake. He shouldn't have said it. Perhaps he shouldn't have returned early that night. If he'd gone to see a film with Pramathesh or Kumar or anyone else, he could easily have dragged out the time till ten o'clock before he got back home. But like so many other ideas, this one had come to him a little too late. Now there was nothing he could do. He'd managed to come back and he'd managed to say what shouldn't have been said. Like a thirsty traveler waiting for the water to settle again after the sharp impact of a stone thrown into a deep tank, Vimal sat still a while. Then he looked at Ranna.

Though there was really no point in looking at her. She would be the same as ever. A very quiet face, the lids always slightly lowered over the large, somewhat protruding eyes. If you saw her you would feel that there could never have been any ups and downs in this woman's life. Nor would there ever be any. The future years would flow on with the same slow, even motion.

But tonight she was leaving home.

It was absolutely definite. Now there could not be the slightest change, yet like an ass he had said, "Stay on."

Vimal began to feel thoroughly ashamed. It would have been much better not to have spoken. But a room is not like a slate. You can't take a wet cloth and rub it clean . . . He suddenly felt exhausted. Closing his eyes he said, "Well, do as you think fit. After all, you must have thought it all out!"

"I *have,* but I'm not sure that I've thought it out properly. Now only time can tell."

"It may be too late then."

"That's possible." Ranna spoke in the same quiet manner. Vimal looked at her. A shapely, slender figure. One year after another had knocked at the door and gone away disappointed. They had not been able to leave the slightest mark on her soft skin or her cloud of black hair. Ranna was just as she used to be twenty years ago. As if life had come to a standstill.

And yet her life had certainly not come to a standstill. She had lived through a great deal that Vimal could not understand. Otherwise this business of leaving home could never have arisen. Suddenly the words slipped out: "If Dipali were alive, you wouldn't leave." This time he didn't repent having spoken. On the contrary, it made him feel better, as if at least some of the burden weighing down on his chest had been lifted. There was no need to look at Ranna's face. She would cry. Vimal knew this, yet he felt good. It was just too much, that Ranna should go off in such a tranquil manner. Unbefitting, unnatural!

After all, they had lived together for twenty years. Well and good if she remembered Dipali and shed a few tears at her departure—Vimal would like that. Without saying anything, he got up to get her a glass of water. On the way back his eyes happened to rest on Dipali's photograph. She must have been about eighteen months old at that time. Dipali had stretched both hands out eagerly to take the red ball he had been holding up behind the photographer's back. Today, too, she was stretching out to him, but there was a wall between them. A wall of glass, a wall of death.

Nothing could penetrate that wall and pass through—neither the scent of the flowers that the gardener had placed before the photograph, nor the tears that Ranna shed. Yet Ranna wept.

Vimal felt it was not enough to give her a glass of water. As he always did he should stroke her head, hold her close and soothe her, wipe away her tears—but now that could not be. Ranna's unsupported physical frame lay between them like a python. He couldn't cross over.

"Ranna!"

"Hm."

"Drink a little water. After all you know—"

"Yes. I won't cry any more."

Ranna gradually wiped her eyes. She picked up the glass and drank the water. But again her eyes filled with tears. Even when she cries the lines of her face scarcely alter, only the pearl-drops shine in her eyes. How beautiful Ranna is! From tomorrow she, too, will be just a photograph in this house. Beside Dipali—no, no, her photograph can't be placed there. Perhaps in the bedroom. Yes, there.

"Ranna!"

"What do you want to say?"

"What is there to say now? Both of us have talked incessantly for the last fortnight—the house still echoes with our words."

"Well then, shall we eat?"

"All right."

The table was laid as always. Thank God she had not cooked anything special as a parting gift. The same simple meal, the same skill in serving the food, never forcing it on one, but always attentive to one's needs. No woman would ever again provide a meal for Vimal as she did.

"What time is the train?"

He asked even though he knew. He knew very well that Ranna wouldn't let him see her off at the station, but he had to ask. Let her refuse.

"It leaves at five to ten. Don't make an unnecessary trip."

"Don't go alone so late in a taxi, Ranna. I'll drop you. What's the harm in that?"

"There's no harm at all. But since I have to leave I might as well leave alone."

The words were out: "I have to leave." Why does she have to leave? Vimal's mind blazed with a hundred flames of rebellion. He felt like screaming, like shaking her violently and saying, "Ranna, why do you have to leave? You don't have to. Stay here! This is your home. Are you listening? Do you understand?"

But the blaze died down as quickly as if it were a bundle of grass that had caught fire. Like a bullock grinding lime, they had gone over the same ground a hundred times. There was no sense in continuing with it. Now her decision was unchangeable. She would definitely go. All right then, let her go alone if she wants to.

With a cigarette and a copy of *Reader's Digest,* Vimal went and sat in his usual chair. One after another all the articles bored him. He read a paragraph of one, two paragraphs of another. Three-quarters of the cigarette burnt away without his touching it. From tomorrow the whole routine of the household will have to be altered. Oh no, he can't face it. Better go out of town himself for a few days. People might think they've both gone together. But as a false coin can be detected the moment one picks it up, this plan struck him as hollow almost before it occurred to him.

Of course people will know. They must have known for a long time. It was a good thing no one had asked him to his face. Otherwise he'd have had to go and live in another city. Anyway, what was there in this city that one should drag on here till the end of one's life?

Vimal was fatigued with the strain of the whole day. As usual, he dozed off. His hair had begun to gray near the temples. In sleep his face looked tender, vulnerable. Holding a glass of milk that she had brought for him, Ranna looked down at him for a while. She could leave the house without waking him. But Vimal would be terribly hurt. He'd be furious. And Ranna wanted to cause him as little pain as possible.

"Vimal, it's almost time."

"Hm? What? Oh, you're leaving, aren't you?"

Ranna held out the glass of milk. Vimal took it and, depositing it on the table, grasped Ranna's hand with both his own. Ranna stepped back startled. Vimal felt a knife had pierced his chest.

"Don't be afraid, Ranna! I just—I just wanted to tell you to look after yourself. I won't see you off."

"Do, if you want to."

"Would you like me to?"

"It's pretty late, it might be better if you came."

If Ranna can change her mind on one subject, perhaps she can also— no, that decision she'll never change. She *will* go. He could refuse to see her off, but Vimal wouldn't behave in such a way. From tomorrow onwards, what was there he could do for her? Gulping down the milk, Vimal went off to change. He always used to leave the car keys lying around. As always, Ranna started looking for them. When she found them in the glass-studded ashtray on top of the cupboard, she was about to call out, "Just look where you had dumped them," when she checked herself. The less said at this moment of departure the better.

Whistling loudly without any reason, Vimal entered the room. "Getting to VT's [Victoria Terminus] no joke—it'll take over an hour. Let's leave. Oh, have you seen the car keys, by any chance?"

"Here they are, take them."

Taking extra care not to touch her fingers, Vimal took the keys. Ranna felt a great impulse to cling to him, like a creeper. She wanted to sob her heart out and make him understand: Vimal, you're a very good man, I've been very happy with you, but—

But what? Then what? No, it was something she couldn't explain to anyone. Not to Vimal, not to herself.

She daren't look round at her things for the last time. She might break down. She hurried out of the house. Vimal was starting the car. Stretching out his arm, he opened the back door. With a spurt of anger, Ranna closed it and came to the front door.

"As you please," Vimal said, opening the door for her, and Ranna got in beside him.

It was like administering oxygen to a patient on his deathbed. For a moment hope lights up in the hearts of his near ones. Then it goes out. That's all, there's no other meaning in it.

There's so much delicacy in Ranna's movements. She's sitting beside him, but is so quiet, so still that one would not notice her presence. But for a faint fragrance in the air, Vimal might have believed himself to be alone and might have started speeding—sixty, seventy, eighty!

"Oh yes, I almost forgot to tell you! Beginning tomorrow, I have arranged for Subhadraben to come in the morning and cook both meals so that—till you make some other arrangement—I mean—"

"Thanks!" Vimal couldn't bear to see Ranna fumbling for words. He looked at her with some surprise. She appeared calm and undisturbed as always. But that little scented handkerchief was being twisted about in her fingers. A small tribute to twenty years of married life. Vimal pressed hard on the accelerator.

"Oh!"

Vimal made no response. There wasn't much traffic. The car sped on as if some devilish presence had entered it. In such circumstances an accident can be fatal. More unfortunate still, one can be maimed for life. One should be sure one's insurance policy is up-to-date. Just think, if that lamppost that's rushing forward were really to dash into the car, what a quick and splendid end there would be to the whole situation! The news would appear in the papers.

"Vimal!"

"What?"

"Nothing."

"Go on, what is it?"

"Please, go a little slower—this frightens me."

What a woman! She's not afraid of leaving home, but let the car go a little fast and she's frightened. But she's always been like that. Her hands must be cold with fear. Without touching her, Vimal can tell.

Still, the intoxication subsided. The car automatically slowed down. In any case they were close to VT.

"Shall I come in?"

"No, no!"

"Just this one small bag? No other luggage?"

Ranna said nothing. The car stopped with a jolt. With a navy blue V.I.P.* bag in her hand, Ranna stepped out. Vimal felt like saying, Ranna, you are a Very Important Person—but he kept quiet.

Ranna got out and said, "All right?"

"OK."

The car started up again. Now there was no one to stop him. He could speed as he liked. Lighting a cigarette near the traffic light, Vimal thought he had used an absolutely inappropriate phrase. When everything was all wrong, wrong side up, just as it should not be, he had said, "OK."

Even though it was a useful phrase, it had a finality about it. A tomb, even if a marble one!

Before Dipu's birth, the two of them had gone on a tour of Delhi and Agra. On seeing the Taj Mahal, Ranna had said, "Shah Jehan couldn't have loved Mumtaz all that much, otherwise how did he live on for thirty-five years after her death?" To tease her Vimal had said, "Then should he have committed suicide?"

"Why would he have needed to commit suicide?" Ranna had said quite seriously, gazing at the dome of the Taj. He had been in a mood to tease. With a dramatic air he had recited some lines from an Urdu poem—

Some people kill themselves with a knife,
Some swallow poison,
Some love so intensely
That with the word "hai," life just passes away.

"That's what you'd like, wouldn't you?"

Ranna had been most offended. It was all he could do to bring her round. Yet today the same Ranna had left him. Poor Shah Jehan had survived after the death of his wife—that wasn't such a great fault. His love must have lived and have kept him alive—while the two of them— Damn it! Love is all humbug! There's nothing to it. For all these years

---

*V.I.P. is a widely advertised line of luggage. The early copy presented a series of Very Important People carrying V.I.P. bags.

the two of them got along together, stayed together, now they don't get along, so they separate. That's all there is to it, as simple as that. Thank God, Dipali is dead! Otherwise there'd have been ever so many more complications. Vimal tried hard to whistle the tune of the latest movie score.

Entering the house, he experienced again the sensation of a mourner returning from carrying a corpse to the funeral pyre. It seemed wrong to touch anything without washing himself clean from head to foot. From the frame on the shelf Dipali stretched out her arms. The person who always responded with tears to her appeal was no longer in this house. Vimal placed a magazine over the photograph. Now all he had to do was to drink a glass of milk and go to bed. He would take a sleeping pill. Tonight perhaps he would need two.

That wouldn't matter—the pills were absolutely harmless. Even if he swallowed four instead of two, no one would have to break open the flat next morning. If he overslept, he'd be late for work, that's all. That didn't matter. Nothing mattered. The train must have left VT.

There is no poetry in the sound of the train's black wheels, dull, heartless, monotonous . . . When they let themselves go, the sound is like the stampede of maddened horses, which will continue till the world ends . . . When they're running down you hear the screeches of iron, the helpless sighs of one who has to bow under the yoke of oppression . . . Finally all is silent. Then it starts up again, silence again . . .

Vimal fell asleep. It was probably the effect of the two tablets.

But Ranna had not taken any kind of tablet. She sat leaning her head against the windows of the first-class compartment. In her wide-open eyes there was no sign of sleep. Perhaps it had been a mistake to set out with so little luggage. But once she had made up her mind to leave she was reluctant even to touch her cupboard. Let the clothes and other things lie there.

Let Vimal give them all away to anyone he pleased. She felt acute shame at taking anything more than a change of clothing. Vimal mightn't have minded at all, but Ranna minded. When the tiny particle is lost round which a pearl has formed, the pearl is worthless. Now she had no rights and no expectations. Now nothing remained. All that remained were the misery and the sense of failure of a lost relationship.

A blast of tiny particles of coal dust blew into the compartment. She would have to close the glass window. That one contact with the outside world would be cut off. The communication was through only one of the five senses, and that, too, was further restricted. Giving a sigh in spite of herself, Ranna wiped her face with her handkerchief.

It was a women's compartment. Opposite sat a mother and daughter looking so alike that it seemed they had been cast in one mold. Very fair, smooth-complexioned, bodies nourished by lavish love and care. Their expensive saris were trailing in the dust on the floor of the compartment, but neither noticed. They were absorbed in their conversation. Perhaps the daughter was returning from her in-laws' home.

Dipali would have been seventeen . . . Ranna's imagination circled round in the blue sky of the impossible and settled back on the branch of hopelessness. She had left home. For good. Now there was no point in carrying around bundles of memories. Perhaps there was nothing precious contained in them. If there had been, she would not have been able to set out like this.

The next day another life would begin. Suddenly Ranna began to feel as if she had committed a crime. Some fault condemned by society such as breaking the queue to get a ticket out of turn. When every human being is given only one life, how could she, before her death, wind up everything and stand on the threshold of a different life? Feeling somewhat ashamed, she got up and prepared to lie down on the upper berth.

Vimal was a very good man. If it had been anyone else, she would not have been able to break with him so easily. People cling fanatically to the corpse of love. To prove that they have not made a mistake. Or perhaps they are faithful—true and faithful. Full of feeling.

Before she realized that she was about to weep, her eyes filled with tears. Not for Dipali, not even for Vimal, but for herself. Why was she so different from everybody else? Callous, incapable of feeling. She had not shed a single tear when she stepped out of the house.

But when the outburst of weeping had subsided, she resumed her train of thought. It was true enough that she no longer loved Vimal at all. She had loved him dearly once. But no more. It was all over and once it was over, it seemed totally wrong to her to remain in his house, spend the money he earned, go by the name of Mrs. Vimal Mehta.

Circulating in her blood like a disease, this deceitful living of a false life had drained her of all vitality. Becoming more and more like a hollow carton every day, Ranna would some day have collapsed and broken up. Much better to have left home. Must every individual be born only on the first day of life?

Putting out the light, with her determination renewed, Ranna fell asleep.

Translated by Shirin Kudchedkar.

MAHASWETA DEVI ─────────────────────

(b. 1926)   *Bengali*

The publication of *Aranyer Adhikar* (Rights over the Forest) in 1977 established Mahasweta Devi's position as the leading novelist in Bengal, and, as her work is increasingly translated into other Indian languages, as one of the most powerful writers in India today.

She was born in Dhaka into a well-known artistic family. Her father, Manish Ghatak, was a leading novelist and poet; her mother, Dharitri Devi, a writer and social worker; her father's youngest brother, the talented film maker Ritwik Ghatak; and her mother's elder brother, Sachin Chaudhuri, the founder-editor of *Economic and Political Weekly.* Mahasweta grew up at a time when the national movement was at its height, and in 1946 she graduated from Santiniketan. It was a time of upheaval and change. The peasant movement in Tebhaga was at its height, and even as she graduated, the Calcutta communal riots were taking place. As one might expect, Mahasweta had close ties with cultural and political organizations in Bengal at the time. The horrible famine of 1943 had called for student involvement in relief work, and Mahasweta, just out of school, volunteered.

In 1947 she married the dramatist Bijan Bhattacharya, whose play *Nabanna* was being performed by the left-wing theater movement. Their son Nabarun was born a year later. Mahasweta Devi took a job at the postal audit office, but lost the job when the new nationalist government found her "guilty" of being a communist. She worked temporarily as a school teacher and began writing regularly for a journal. During the long struggle to keep her head above water, she tried her hand at several jobs, including selling soap dyes and exporting monkeys to the United States. Her first book, *Jhansir Rani* (The Rani of Jhansi), 1956, was a biography of a queen who held out bravely against the British in the battles that followed the Sepoy Rebellion of 1857. Before writing the book, she traveled extensively in the area, collecting documentary information from the people who lived in the area and recording folk songs about the rani.

In 1962 she was divorced from Bijan Bhattacharya and married the writer Asit Gupta. A year later, seventeen years after graduating from college, she received a master's degree in English literature from Calcutta University and began work at Bijaygarh College, a coeducational college in a poor refugee area where she taught until 1984.

Though much of her writing in the late seventies focused on tribal people and the formerly untouchable castes, her work also dealt with the agrarian movements of the late sixties. These had begun in the Naxalbari region in North Bengal and had quickly spread into other parts of India. Students and young intellectuals in Calcutta and elsewhere set aside their studies to move deep into the rural areas and support the uprising, which had as its target landlords as well as the state that aided their exploitative enterprises. The movement was violently suppressed, and by the mid-seventies many of the activists were in jail. The best known of the novels to portray these troubled and exciting times, Mahasweta's *Hajar Churasir Ma* (Mother of No. 1084), 1974, has been translated into several Indian languages.

Aranyer Adhikar, 1979, a novel, based like many of her other writings on extensive research, is about the Ulgulan (Great Tumult) of the Munda tribals, which took place between 1895 and 1900 in the forest regions just south of Ranchi. Under the charismatic leadership of Birsa Munda (c. 1874–1900), the Munda tribals attacked the local British authorities, the missionaries, and the Indian landowners. The distinctive style, now associated with Mahasweta's mature work, in which different registers and dialects of Bengali jostle each other in a text crowded with echoes and voices rarely heard in mainstream literature, first appeared in this book, which the critic Manabendra Bandhyopadhyay has called "savage, fecund and irresistible . . . an experiment in the novel form as an extension of the epic genre." Mahasweta has also published impressive collections of short stories: *Agni Garbha* (Fires Underground), 1978, which includes the well-known story "Draupadi"; *Murti* (Icon), 1979; *Nairete Megh* (Clouds in the Southwest Sky Heralding a Storm), 1979; *Stanyadayani* (The Wet Nurse/Breast Giver), 1980; and *Chhoti Munda Evam Tar Tir* (Chhoti Munda and His Arrows), 1980.

Throughout Mahasweta Devi's varied fiction, women's subjugation is portrayed as linked to the oppressions of caste and class. But in the best of her writing she quite brilliantly, and with resonance, explores the articulation of class, caste, and gender in the specific situations she depicts.

Mahasweta Devi has over a hundred books to her credit, including novels, story collections, children's books, and collections of plays. She has also edited a Jim Corbett omnibus and has written a Bengali textbook series. She was a roving reporter for the Bengali daily *Jugantar* (End of an Era) in 1982 and 1983 and worked as a weekly columnist for the Bengali daily *Bortoman* in the late eighties. She also edits a quarterly, *Bortika* (News), for which tribals, poor villagers, and factory workers write. In 1980 she initiated the bonded labor organization in Palaman, and is now connected with several other tribal and Harijan grassroot-level organizations. She is an activist as well as a writer, and even as writer she is an activist, for she contributes to little magazines, district papers, and journals usually disregarded by the established writers. She tries, she says, to keep a close link with rural Bengal through the district newspapers.

As Mahasweta Devi sees it, her creative writing, her journalism, her active fieldwork, and her personal life are complementary. She is a regular visitor to tribal huts, and keeps an open house for the poor and the needy. Among her many awards are a Padmasri (for tribal work) and a Central Sahitya Academy Award (for her novel *Aranyer Adhikar*, 1979). She is actively engaged in preserving and propagating the people's culture rooted in the soil, which she says is threatened by the onslaught of a debased mainstream culture.

A recent honor, the gift of a *ma sari* (a sari given to the mother of the bride during tribal marriages), has made Mahasweta feel, she says, "very very heavy. This symbol of total acceptance by a number of the tribals has made me conscious of the struggle that lies ahead for them." The story translated here first appeared in *Sharodiya Paromash* in 1978.

◆

SHISHU
(Children)

The place was called Lohri, and it was situated where the three districts Ranchi, Sarguja, and Palamau shared a common border. On the official records it belonged to Ranchi district, but the place was a vast stretch, scorched and burnt beyond reclaim, as if the earth underneath were a furnace. That is why the trees were stunted and dwarfed, the bed of the river dry, and the villages covered with a mantle of dust. The color of the earth was unusual. Even in this area of red earth, one seldom came across such deep brown-red earth, the color of blood before it dries.

The relief officer had been properly briefed before he arrived there. An honest and sympathetic person, he had been chosen for the assignment after much deliberation. He was told that it was a genuine bastard of a place. The residents did not have any way of making an honest living.

"But why?"

"Won't cultivate."

"Do they have land for cultivation?"

The relief officer and the BDO [block development officer] were talking inside the bungalow. Outside it was still hot. The watchman would make their beds for the night on niwar-woven iron cots within the bungalow compound. No one slept under a roof in the terrible summer. The relief officer was posted to this duty for only three months, and even so, he had to be borrowed from the food department. Never had he seen a place so sunbaked and godforsaken. He had come to hate the sight of the people thronging for relief, half-naked and emaciated, their stomachs protruding from worms and enlarged spleens. He had always thought that adivasi [tribal] men played the flute and that adivasi women danced with flowers bedecking their hair. And he had thought of them running, from one hill to another, singing.

Whenever he had had to leave the jeep behind and climb even a low hill to reach the village above, he had quickly become short of breath, and had come to realize that it was next to impossible to run up and down a hill. He had known music to be a part of adivasi life. But now he could hear them singing. The songs were all monotonous, like the keening of an old witch imprisoned in her loneliness. It was all very disappointing. The relief officer had formed his ideas about the adivasis from commercial Hindi movies. If this was song for them, how would they wail for their dead? Their singing was too much like wailing anyway. Ah, how uncomfortable one felt.

"Why are they singing?"

"Outlandish barbarians. They attribute each calamity to the wrath of some supernatural force. They are singing to drive away the ghosts."

The word "ghost" was enough to ruffle the relief officer's composure. The BDO marked his discomfiture, and smiled. "Does it scare you?"

"No, no, it doesn't."

"For them, this drought and famine are a curse from the evil spirits."

"I see."

"A cursed place. The better places have Hindus living there—you can see the holy banner of the great god Hanuman flying from the pinnacles of the temples. This place has nothing, nothing. I'm dying to get a transfer."

"Where am I to go tomorrow?"

"Lohri. That's a bad place. A bad place. Give them land—they simply sell it to the moneylender. Then they place a countercharge on us. 'Where's water? And seeds, the plow, the bullocks? How are we to till the land?' And if you supply them with those, they sell them, too, and say, 'How are we to survive till the fields are harvested? We had to borrow and now we have to pay it back by selling the lands.' "

"Do I have to stay there?"

"Yes. In a camp. There are no two ways about that. Set the camp

running smoothly and you can leave. I'll send help. Don't worry, and
. . . and, don't be frightened."

"Frightened? Of what? Of whom?"

"Of thieves."

"Thieves?"

"Yes. Each time we send relief supplies, there are small children who
come and steal them. One or two bags of rice, milo . . . molasses,
anything they can get hold of."

"Small children, did you say?"

"Yes. And no one can touch them. Some have seen them. Once I
saw them too—with my own eyes. I had a gun."

"You carry a gun?"

"Sure, a licensed one. Lohri is a bad place, you know. Ten or twelve
years ago there was quite an uprising. The whole place was up in
arms."

"What!"

"Well, I hadn't joined the Service then. Have you heard the legend
of Lohri?"

"No." And the relief officer did not want to know, either. He pined
for the bright lights of Ranchi that he had had to leave behind, all
because of his job.

"The ironmongers used to live there, the Agaria tribals. The Agarias,
the legends go, were descended from the *asuras,* the demons. They
mined iron ore and forged implements in their smithies. They drank
fire and bathed in a river of fire. Lohri was their capital, Logundi their
king. The demons under the earth allowed only the Agarias to descend
into the underground caverns to mine the iron ore."

"What happened then?"

"Well, Logundi had eleven brothers and among the twelve of them,
they had only one wife."

"Sounds more titillating than the Draupadi tale."

"Logundi became so inordinately proud that he declared he was
mightier than the sun god. So the sun god himself came and burnt
Logundi, his brothers, and the kingdom of Lohri to cinders. The queen
was in another village, so she was saved. Still burning with fire from
the sun's rays, she escaped to a shepherd's house and, jumping into a
big tumbler of buttermilk, managed to cool her body. There, under a
chindi tree, she gave birth to a son. They called him Jwalamukhi. Jwalamukhi breathed fire, and fire spewed out of his mouth whenever he
opened it."

"What a savage story!"

"When he had grown to manhood, Jwalamukhi went out to fight the sun god. The battle was fought in Lohri, and the heat that rose burnt the soil there. When the battle was over, Jwalamukhi cursed the sun god. 'The moon may be your wife,' he said, 'but you will be able to meet her only on the day of the full moon.' And the sun god said, 'You Agarias will work as ironmongers, but you will never be able to save any money. All that you earn will turn to ash and blow away.' And the Agarias have been poor ever since."

"Another of those barbarian myths."

"Yes. You see what the Agarias are now. They have lost their traditional occupation. They don't work with iron anymore. But it's difficult, really difficult to make them turn to agriculture. They say they are still observing the period of mourning for Jwalamukhi's defeat and are still impure. Lohasur, the demon guarding the iron ore, does not give them iron; Koilasur, the demon guarding the coal, does not give them coal; and Agaiyasur, the demon guarding the fire underground, does not give them fire. But they still believe that some day they will have their day of glory again."

"Tell me about the trouble, their uprising."

"Twelve or fourteen years ago, the Indian government sent a team of geologists and other people to prospect for iron ore at Lohri. The Agarias of Kuva Village were real troublemakers. They said that the hills were the abode of the three asuras—Lohasur, Koilasur, and Agaiyasur—who wouldn't let outsiders violate the sacred territory or allow prospecting there. As far as the Agarias were concerned, those three asuras were already angry with the unhappy tribe. Prospecting for iron ore would only seal the fate of the Agarias. But the outsiders were educated people, who could not be expected to submit to Agaria superstitions. The two officers from the Punjab and the geologist from South India had no fear of the asuras. They blasted the hills with dynamite."

"And then?"

"The Agarias of Kuva Village hacked every one of the team to death. I don't know how many they were, for they escaped into the jungle."

"Escaped?"

"Yes, escaped. And just think of it, Mr. Singh, they simply vanished, God knows where! Lost forever. No one has seen them since. A hundred or a hundred and fifty people wreaked their vengeance and disappeared into the jungle."

"But how strange!"

"It's a mystery yet unsolved."

"No clues?"

"Not a trace, not one inkling of information."

"Didn't the government try to track them down?"

"Sure. They combed the jungle as carefully and minutely as a brahmin's widow picks insects from the rice to be cooked."

"And still no trace?"

"No."

"What happened afterwards?"

"The government conducted a thorough and ruthless combing operation. Apart from the inhabitants of Kuva Village, no one was missing. That proved that the others were not guilty. After a month of searching, the police set fire to Kuva, sowed the earth with salt so that nothing would grow there, and left. The other Agaria villages suffered too. Punitive taxes . . . ruthless oppression . . . terrible persecution."

"And they were never found?"

"No."

"But where could they have gone?"

"Into the jungle, where else! There're so many hills and caves inside the jungle . . . who knows where they went?"

"All this happened in Lohri?"

"Yes, Lohri."

"Why do you carry a gun?"

"I feel scared. It gives me the creeps. So many people! What if they come out of hiding all of a sudden, tell me?"

"Just because of that?"

"No."

"What else?"

"Every time the relief materials are sent—there're thefts . . . earlier it would be four to five sacks of food . . . for the last few years it's been two to three sacks only. And the place is so cursed! Nothing grows there, simply nothing. Once my own nephew tried to till the soil . . . to become a farmer . . . but he simply failed to grow rice or maize or even the sturdier *marwa* or *jowar*. After the first layer of earth, it's rock hard underneath. Plows cannot break it. It's an accursed place. One look'll tell you."

"Do the thefts still take place—?"

"Yes . . . they do. People used to say that children came in at night to steal the food. I didn't believe them. I was convinced that the relief workers were selling off the stuff, that *they* were stealing it, not outsiders. Such things are common. The government understands nothing, you see. They keep sending blankets, clothes, and so on, in the summer as well as in winter. These barbarians have no use for Dhariwal blankets or good clothes or fine sugar. Give it to them, and you'll find the traders or moneylenders trading them cheap battery-torches or packets of matchboxes or mirrors for it. The relief workers know this. So they steal the things and sell them. I don't see anything wrong there, no, I don't really."

"But that's not right."

"These things are common practice. Remember the Bangladesh Liberation War? Oh, mountains of things were sent from Calcutta, from Delhi, and from other countries to the border camps there. Clothes, fancy garments, woolens, blankets, mosquito nets, utensils, stoves, shoes, and what not. Didn't we buy them all at the Ranchi bazaar?"

"That's true."

"Anyway, I was convinced that they stole the food themselves and blamed the children. Then I went myself. I was carrying supplies worth twenty thousand rupees, so I had taken police guards with me. The camp was in Lohri. The night was dark, really dark, like black hair. It was hot too. I was sleeping outside the tent. Suddenly I heard something strange. I got up at once and saw a host of little men, could be children, running away with the sacks."

"What did you do?"

"I fired in the air. What could I do? Can I shoot at children? But the thieves escaped . . . naked kids . . . shoot at them?"

"That's true. You can't."

"But . . ."

"What?"

The BDO frowned and stared at the darkness outside broodingly for a spell. The darkness was hot and molten. A burning liquid darkness that filled up all the crevices with steamy heat. The stars seemed dim and lost in a hazy sky. It was still many hours until moonrise.

He said, "I haven't told anyone about this so far. But you're a good man. The state minister happens to be your uncle, so I'll confide in you and I'll give you a remedy for the danger if it comes your way."

"What are you trying to say?"

"Mr. Singh, that place has a bad reputation. People say that the place is still haunted by the *asuras,* the *bongas*—tribal ghosts and deities with evil power. I saw the children who were running away with the bags. They were not like human children."

"What did you say?"

"Their arms and legs . . . they were different."

"Different? In what way?"

"I can't explain. They had long hair . . . but it was the way they cackled . . ."

"I feel quite frightened."

"Don't be afraid. I canceled my trip to Tahad today just to brief you properly. Your uncle's a state minister . . . I stand guarantee for your life . . . your property . . . I've brought this *prasad** from Hanuman especially for you. Please put it in your pocket. It will save the carrier from all danger."

"But I don't have a gun."

"So what? You'll have people guarding you."

"Guns . . . or the police . . ."

"Can't ask for them now. All right. You're leaving tomorrow. I'll see that some constables go with the batch of supplies that comes the next day."

"Come, let's eat."

"Have a bath first."

The water from the well was divinely cool. As Singh's uncle was a minister of state, the dinner was good. Fine rice cooked with green peas, rich meat curry, pickles, sweets. Sleeping out in the open. The ground had been soaked with water first and then the cots placed there. It was as cool as could be expected. But sleep eluded Singh. A youth battling with the sun god. A hill. Shining axes flashing out of the depth of the darkness. Corpses. Combing operations in the jungle done by the police with the same meticulous care that a brahmin's widow displays while picking insects from the rice to be cooked. The relief camp. In the dark of the night, children, not sprung from human loins, stealing bags. Frame after frame, the images flickered. Heat on the face, Singh woke up and realized that he had fallen into deep sleep, and that the sun's rays had nudged him awake.

In the morning he started for Lohri, and the BDO went back to Tahad. The food bags and tents followed Singh in a truck. The road soon turned into a dirt track, passable only because it was summer. In the monsoon it would be a quagmire. Along the path they came to a mission house where the missionaries had opened a relief center. Hoards of people waited there, dark, lean, and silent.

The jeep driver spat. "Bloody animals! When famine comes they just leave their babies in front of the mission door. And then they explain—

---

*Prasad is food that is offered to a deity and then distributed among the devotees.

'The mission people will never let them perish. They'll save them somehow. With the parents, the children were sure to starve to death.' "

"They are simply not human beings."

"They're being converted to Christianity and are losing their original faith. But they are clever, very clever. They're becoming Christians and worshipping their old gods too."

"Don't the missionaries know this?"

"They do. Yet they look after them . . . treat them when they're ill. Those fair-skinned women take the children of those animals on their laps and even kiss them."

"Shameful!"

"Animals! Just listen to them singing. Could decent people sing like this in such times?" The singing sounded like the wail of lost spirits. It filled the hills and forests and waves of it dashed against the running jeep.

"Why are they singing like that?"

"That's what they are like! Those who can still walk will come to collect relief. Those who can't, the really old, sit in a circle and sing like that. They go on singing until they die. This singing starts in one village, and hearing the song, the old and the dying of the next village send their able-bodied ones to the relief camps and start singing. Then in the next village . . . it's incomprehensible."

Singh felt as if a bed of quicksand were sucking him under to where there was nothing but abysmal despair. He had come from Ranchi, where life was on the move with the dazzle of electricity, motorcars, taxis, and buses. Into what land was he going? Into some place where spectral children defy the gun with ghostly cackling and run away with bags of food? A cursed land, where all one came across on the way were the gray and brooding forests and hills. A land where the old folks did not try to save themselves from starvation but, sitting in a circle, sang weird songs. It was all so confusing.

"Do many die?"

"Many do. Look at the buzzards and kites flying. Sometimes the buzzards devour a live one too feeble to resist. It's an ungodly place."

"How far is Lohri?"

"Well, we've just entered the territory. See how red the hills, the trees, and even the grounds are! They could have been made of copper. Yes, sir, this is Lohri. There's poison in the ground."

In the distance there were a few hills. "That's the campsite," the driver said.

After a while the driver spoke again. "I hope you don't mind my saying so, *huzur,* but there's something about Lohri that's scary. We don't know what it is,yet . . . I hope you don't mind if we have a drink or two at night . . . near the camp. Otherwise we'd feel frightened. Poor Bahadur! He went crazy."

"Who is he, this Bahadur?"

"A driver. Why, didn't the BDO tell you about him?"

"No, he didn't."

"He hasn't done the right thing. Should've told you."

"What happened to Bahadur?"

"No one really knows. Those who were with him said that they were sleeping and suddenly Bahadur cried out, 'Thief! Thief!' and ran after somebody. He was swallowed by the darkness of the night. The others followed him but they heard such dreadful laughter ring through the dark that they were frightened and came back. The next morning Bahadur was found unconscious. He regained his consciousness, but not his sanity."

"Then?"

"Went mad, totally mad. He's now in Ranchi. Ah, we've reached the camp."

The campsite had been cleared. The tahsildar came out of a small, low-roofed, grass hut, and said, "Please have some tea first, sir. There's water too, if you want to have a bath. Water has to be fetched from half a mile away."

The driver asked, "That same natural lake?"

"The same."

The tahsildar turned to explain matters to Singh. "After the trouble of Kuva, a hill was blown up and a deep rift formed. It catches the rains and is a year-round source of water."

They drank their tea. The tahsildar erected the tent, counted the bags of relief material and arranged them in order. He said, "You've nothing to worry about, huzur. I have been doing this every year. I have the lists ready, arranged by village. All you have to do is to distribute the relief from ten to four, and we are free after that."

"How many people do you expect?"

"One thousand, perhaps two thousand, who can tell?"

"A medical unit is coming."

"Here, huzur?"

"Yes. They'll need tents. Put the tents up."

"Very good, huzur, but there've never been medical units before."

"You've never had a government run by the Janata party before and you've never had a special officer to distribute the relief material before either."

The tahsildar swore under his breath, "Son of a pig!" He said, "I'll do anything you ask me to, huzur."

"The unit from Sardoha Mission will work, too."

"Those people? Here?"

"Yes. They have nurses and a doctor."

"As you say, huzur."

"We need men to fetch water to the camp, to keep the camp clean, to scrub the pots for cooking gruel. Select ten boys from the village and write down their names. They'll do all the work. They'll get food and a rupee a day as wages."

"They'd do everything, just for food."

"Have you come to talk, or to listen to my instructions? I'll run the camp. You'd better be here every day."

"How long'll the camp be open?"

"For a month. I'm in charge of this camp. There'll be a camp every twenty miles. And listen, I'll stay in the tent where the stores are kept, because it's very much my responsibility."

"Fine, huzur. I can say for myself that I wouldn't sleep there even if you paid me a hundred rupees."

"Why?"

"Thieves. And they are not human beings either."

"Don't talk rot. There are students from the colleges coming to work as volunteers. They will carry relief to the distant villages. So tell everyone that the old folks need no longer sing their death songs."

The tahsildar left the place greatly astounded. Every year he stole relief materials. He was a crook, but he was also efficient. He appointed ten Agaria boys from the village to do various jobs for the camp. Then he got two men to help him arrange the relief food the first day. From the next day on, there would be gruel for the adults and milk for the babies. The tahsildar told Singh, "These Agaria boys will guard the store through the night. They'll keep you company since none of us will stay here. Otherwise you'd be all by yourself!"

Singh was reassured by his words. The camp began the very next day and was run in a most disciplined manner. Gruel was prepared and distributed. The medical volunteers gave injections for cholera and typhoid. The camp hummed with activity.

Now people started coming from distant villages. Even at night one could see processions of hungry people moving toward the camp with flaming torches. It was impossible to walk during the day in the scorching summer heat. It was easier to reach the camp by night and wait for the day to begin. After a few days, even the old fox of a tahsildar had to admit, "Huzur, the way you've been running the camp, you've given back to these animals a faith that they'll live. Earlier the old folk knew that death was near and so they used to sing. Now they've stopped singing. Why not do something?"

"What?"

"Don't send relief to the villages. The able-bodied ones are getting regular food anyway and they can very well carry their old ones here."

"No, no. You see, hunger dries up the normal human emotions in starving people. If they just leave someone behind, that one is sure to die. And how can they carry another? Even now some are falling down and dying on their way to the camp. Do they have any strength left in their bodies?"

Singh became so deeply involved in the relief work that the scorched earth, the dense forest of dwarfed and leafless trees, and the copper-red and gray hungry hills lost their horror, and the starving hungry populace became top priority. The doctors left for another camp, sure that everyone in this area had been inoculated against cholera and typhoid. Singh brought inspiration to the doctor and nurses from the Sardoha Mission. The book of rules said that it was enough to inoculate the people against cholera and typhoid. Yet Singh defied the protocol and had had antibiotics, baby food, ointment for sores, and soy nutri-nuggets brought from Ranchi.

The ten Agaria boys attached themselves to him with a rare devotion. They didn't let him bathe in the deep lake formed by the blasting of the hills. It was taboo to them, this abode of the asuras. They took him to the hidden natural-rock reservoir on the bed of the river Lohri that they used. As he bathed, Singh listened to their version of the Jwalamukhi story. Jwalamukhi, as an Agaria youth, was their hero, though through him the Agaria had become poor. And it was his curse that would not let the almighty sun god sleep with his moon-wife except on the full moon night. Yes, the Agaria were suffering. But their fate would change the day the three asuras—Lohasur, Koilasur, and Agaiyasur—turned benign. It was usually long past evening by the time Singh finished his leisurely bath and returned to the camp.

At night he slept on the cot placed before the store-tent. He was convinced that the relief workers had been stealing the relief sacks and that the story of spectral children was just an invention to cover their guilt. He tried to figure out how one might truly help the Agaria of Lohri. An honest and sympathetic officer with some initiative was all that was needed. Such a person would be able to coax the Agaria to begin farming. Land, irrigation, agricultural implements, livestock—he would see to them when he went back to Ranchi. It was simply monstrous to keep a people dependent upon yearly relief alone. With such thoughts he always fell into a deep and peaceful sleep. The ten Agaria boys slept around the tent. Singh felt a glow of triumph. These boys had started speaking of him as a *devta,* a god in human form. No mean triumph for an outsider who had been there such a short time. The Agaria of this region didn't trust anyone but themselves. "Devta" from them meant a real victory.

He slept; the Agaria boys didn't. They kept awake and waited to hear something. Why couldn't they? Was it because the camp was so big this year? Too many people, too much noise—was that the reason?

One night at last they heard the sound of footsteps of a host of creatures treading with catlike stealth. There was a soft whistle and another in reply. They were loosening the tent ropes. Then there was silent but quick activity. The young men got up and lifted the tent bottom. There was a sliver of a moon in the sky. Sacks of rice and milo were lifted by the young men and the small hands caught them deftly.

Singh suddenly woke up. He turned on the battery-powered torch to discover that the Agaria had gone. He walked quickly around the tent. The young men were retying the ropes to the pegs. Why? Who had loosened them in the first place? Stunned, confused, and hurt by their betrayal, Singh stared at them. Their faces were those of strangers. The same people, the same faces, but he didn't know them. Why? The question seared his heart but he realized that he couldn't reach their minds. There was no common meeting point between an honest relief officer and ten Agaria tribals. They were citizens of two different planets. The young men bared their teeth in a smile of savage triumph and viciousness and ran into the forest. Singh ran into the tent. Yes, two sacks were missing.

He ran out and gave chase. There they were, the patter of small feet somewhere before him, yet eluding him. He could see the sacks being carried away through the forest. No, not unearthly beings. Children. Children of men. Ah, the cunning, the cunning—they come for relief and, at the same time, engage their children to steal. Yet according to the government records, the Agaria of Lohri never stole, they were not criminals. They did not lie either. Singh had really wanted to help these people. They knew it. Even the young men addressed him as devta. Was it a hoax? Were they pretending? It seemed as if someone had really cheated him and left him a pauper. Their treachery had left him bereft of everything. His blood rose. He was honest and incorruptible and had a genuine sympathy for the adivasis. These were the reasons why he had been especially selected for this job, and he had tried hard, really hard, to justify his appointment. He had worked to get the relief material to the actual beneficiary. He had resolved to try his best to find a way out for these people. A way out—so that they would no longer have to depend on relief. A permanent solution to their hunger. And in return? This treachery. Sending children out to steal! He would catch them and solve this endemic problem of theft, finally and ruthlessly.

He ran forward, goaded by the sheer passion of his anger. The thieves ran too. The forest thinned and he reached the wilderness of stunted grass where, in the legendary past, Jwalamukhi had fought with the sun god. The children stopped and put the sacks down on the ground.

So, they must be tired of running. Singh approached the sacks, which they were guarding in a circle. They stood, Singh thought, like savage animals crouching before leaping upon the prey. And they kept staring at him. Their eyes were silent, unwavering, their figures blurred and indistinct in the wan moonlight.

Suddenly they moved closer. Boys and girls in a group. And fear struck at him, a great fear, leaving him immobile. Moving forward together, they made a circle around him and stood still. But why?

They looked at him and he watched them warily. The circle moved in. Singh turned his head and found that the circle was complete. There was no way to break through the cordon and run. But why should he try to escape? They were human beings born of human parents, not spectral beings. Spectral beings didn't steal milo and rice. Who was it who had said, "That's a cursed place. . . . " And someone had pleaded, "We'll have one or two drinks. . . . " Singh tried to control the hammering, crashing beats of his heart. They inched forward.

Fear—stark, unreasoning, naked fear—gripped him. Why this silent creeping forward? Why didn't they utter one word? Their figures grew more distinct. What was it he was seeing? Why were they naked? And why such long hair? Children, he had always heard of children, but how come that one had white hair? Why did the women—no, no, girls—have dangling, withered breasts?

And the being with the white hair, why was he coming closer, even closer? He screamed silently, "Don't come nearer," then he found his voice and screamed aloud the same words. But the white-haired being, why was he coming closer, and what was he trying to show him? He was lifting his dangling, dry, and shrunken penis and showing it to him.

These were no children. They were adults! Singh could not drag a single sound out of his throat, but the truth thundered in his brain like the megablast of a nuclear bomb. His face must have registered the horror he felt, for the old man cackled with inhuman glee as he watched Singh. The cackling spread. Now all of them joined in, in a savage frenzy. Some of them jumped up into the air, some crouched on the ground. What was Singh's duty? What was he expected to do? Who would tell him? The officer's book of rules did not prepare him for such an encounter, and Singh had thought he knew everything there was to know.

"We are not children. We are Agarias of the village of Kuva. Know the name of Kuva? Heard the name Kuva?"

"No, no!" Singh longed desperately to cover his eyes, but his hands failed to obey because no order came from the brain, which was numb with the savage blow it had received. Who had said, "The prasad from the temple of Hanuman, keep it in your pocket"—who was that?

"We hacked up your people to save our holy hill and escaped to the forest. Neither the police nor the army could catch us—they will never be able to."

Again they cackled in unison.

"No, no, no . . ."

"The Agaria help us to survive. Many have perished, you know . . . living as fugitives . . . starving . . . many, many have died."

"No, no . . ." Singh whispered.

Now the circle was smaller. They moved in closer.

"Don't . . . come . . . near . . ."

"Why shouldn't we? So many sacks of rice and milo you have, and you had to chase us for two sacks—why? Since you've come, you have to see us as we are. Hey! You! Come closer. Show him, show him!"

The men displayed their penises and the women their breasts.

The old man was now closer still to Singh. His penis touched Singh, now in front, now from behind. A dry, unholy touch. Making him impure. Like the touch of a dried, sloughed-off skin of a snake.

"There are only fourteen of us left. Our bodies have shrunk without food. Our men are impotent, our women are barren. That's why we steal the relief. Don't you see we need food to grow to a human size again?"

"No, no, no . . ."

"The Agaria help us survive. And why are we made to suffer so? All for that killing at Kuva. The killing at Kuva!"

"No, it can't be true."

If this was the truth, then the rest was untruth. What was he to believe? Whom was he to believe? If those Kuva Agarias were right, then what plea for civilization? For Copernicus's order of the universe? For the advancement of science? This glorious, glorious century! This independence! These plans after plans to build a better India! All Singh could do was repeat, "No, no, no . . ."

"Can your 'no' make it all a No? Then how have our organs come to be so shrunken? Have a good look and take in the fact that we are not children, we are adults."

They cackled with savage and revengeful glee. Cackling, they ran around him. They rubbed their organs against him and told him that they were adult citizens of India.

The faint moon in the sky seemed so helpless, so impotent, as it shed its weak light on the plain scorched with the fire from the battle between Jwalamukhi and the sun god. Adults no larger than children danced in primitive excitement. They cackled in the vicious joy born out of desire for revenge. They must have rejoiced in the same manner when they had hacked off the heads of their enemies. The same revenge, the same joy!

But revenge against what?

Singh's shadow covered their bodies. And that shadow brought the realization home to him.

They hated his height of five feet and nine inches.

They hated the normal growth of his body.

His normalcy was the crime they could not forgive.

Singh's cerebral cells tried to register the logical explanation but he failed to utter a single word. Why, why this revenge? He was just an ordinary Indian. He didn't have the stature of a healthy Russian, Canadian, or American. He did not eat food that supplied enough calories for a human body. The World Health Organization said that it was a crime to deny the human body of the right number of calories.

But he could not utter a single word in his own defense. Standing still under the moon, listening to their deafening voices, shivering at the rubbing of their organs against his body, Singh knew that the ill-nourished and ridiculous body of an ordinary Indian was the worst possible crime in the history of civilization. He knew that he was condemned, sentenced to death. He delivered the judgement on himself, sentencing himself to death, because he, too, was responsible for the diminutive height of these Agarias. "Yes, the death sentence for me," he wanted to say, and lifted his face towards the moon. They were still cackling, still dancing, still rubbing their penises against him. The only recourse left to Singh was to go stark, raving mad, tearing the expanse apart with a howl like that of a mad dog. But why wasn't his brain ordering his vocal chords to scream and scream and scream? Only tears ran down his cheeks.

Translated by Pinaki Bhattacharya.

SAJIDA ZAIDI ————————————————————

(b. 1926)   *Urdu*

From 1955 until she retired recently, Sajida Zaidi taught education at Aligarh Muslim University. She studied at the same university, though she received her doctorate from the University of London. Aligarh's long history of commitment to modernization and progressive thought has been a strong influence on Sajida Zaidi's thinking and personality, as has been the case for most people educated or employed there. Her father, Mustahsan Zaidi, died when she was only eight, but it was from him that she first heard the verses of Ghalib, Iqbal, and the Persian poet Hafez. Another important influence was her sister, Sabira Zaidi, whom Sajida describes as a sensitive, enlightened, and deeply affectionate person.

Sajida Zaidi's mind has always been, according to her own reading, in a state of restless progression. She names the stages of this journey as religiosity, Marxism, humanism, and, finally, existentialism. She considers her existential position to be a natural development, born of her personal experience and observation of life. Existentialism is, she says, in the West the inevitable result of people's alienation in a machine-ridden society, and in the East, a result of religious and political tyranny and the breakdown of human values and relationships.

She started writing poetry in 1958; her first collection of poems, *Ju-e-Naghma* (Stream of Melody), appeared in 1962. Many of her early poems were published in Pakistani magazines and journals. *Aatish-e-Sayyal* (Liquid Fire), 1972, from which the poems here are taken, consists of poems written between 1965 and 1971. She has also written verse drama and has made a successful Urdu stage adaptation of Federico García Lorca's *Yerma*. A widely read and sophisticated writer, Sajida Zaidi introduces a strong intellectual element into her poetry. Among those who have influenced her work, she cites Friedrich Nietzsche, Carl Jung, Jean-Paul Sartre, and

Franz Kafka. Her themes, like those of many of her contemporaries, are alienation, loneliness, ennui, and the existential predicament. Her poems, the critic Syed Sirajuddin writes, "have a somewhat dry, cognitive quality, and she keeps an incipient romanticism at bay with her intellection." Her latest collection, *Sel-e-Wajud* (Flow of Existence), was published in 1986.

◆

RISHTA
(Kinship)

Every fiery glance once was mine,
Now the gloom gathers.
Mine once the flowers of lips speaking,
Now turned stony seals.
Mine now the whirlpools of your mind,
The unfinished chapters of your life,
The bitterness of your days,
The vehemence of your passions.

The thorns in your path hurt my feet,
The pangs of your heart strike my ribs too,
Every ache you feel,
I feel.

The bitter poisons you swallow
Dissolve and corrode my blood.
The steel-clad walls crack and split.
Every call from you, lost
In the wilderness,
Is my call.

The passion that once kept you tuned
Has turned shadow,
> The kinship of suffering,
> A journey of wounds,
> The meeting of two souls.

Translated by Syed Sirajuddin.

NAYE ZAVIYE
(New Angles)

Why does the night have a bleak soul?
What language does silence speak?
What color does the air hold?
What note sounds the boundless expanse?
What feelings shadow the gray face of the sky?
Where does the soul dwell?
In the fire of a glance
Or in the melting movement of lips?
Where shall we seek for meaning?
In wisdom's court
Or in a life of sorrow?

Translated by Syed Sirajuddin.

ANURADHA POTDAR ————————————
(b. 1927)   *Marathi*

Anuradha Potdar was born into a literary family. Her grandfather, D. K. Ghate, was the well-known Marathi modernist poet Datta, and her father, V. D. Ghate, a writer and an eminent educator. Their home was filled with books, and the young Anuradha read a great deal and began writing when she was still in high school. She wrote a novel during her first year of college, but poetry has always been her major love.

While still in college Anuradha Potdar married a brilliant fellow student: "I admired his intellect and his love of literature," she said. The marriage took place much against the wishes of their parents, for he was a brahmin and she a maratha, and intercaste marriages were rare in those days. She continued with her studies, earning a master's degree in Marathi in 1950 and a doctorate in the same subject in 1957. She taught Marathi at the university from 1957 until her retirement in 1987. The marriage turned out to be a difficult one: her husband was eccentric and suspicious, and what began as occasional attacks gradually developed into repeated battering. "Looking back at my own life and the lives of others I know," Anuradha Potdar comments, "I am convinced that basic attitudes have not changed. The man still wants his woman to be helpless and dependent."

She has published three collections of poetry: *Avarta* (A Completed Circle), 1969; *Kaktas Flawar* (Cactus Flower), 1979, from which the poem translated here is taken; and *Manjdhar* (Mainstream), 1989. She has also written several books of literary criticism, including one on the early-twentieth-century novelist Kusumavati Deshpande.

◆

TUMACHE HE SOJWAL SAMSAR
(Your Pious and Irreproachable Homes)

It's what I want to do—
scatter, with a breath,
your pious and irreproachable homes
like a house of cards:
your escapist crises
that reach the cliff-edge
only to run back in greater haste;
your pitiful storms
that dissolve
in the unachieved ecstasy of copulation;
and the litter of sweet, helpless babies
hatched by the human female—
it's this litter that drives deep
into the soil
the obstinate roots of your homes,
and these houses of cards
become stone mansions
for us to bang our heads on
till they bleed.

Translated by Vilas Sarang.

KUNDANIKA KAPADIA ⎯⎯⎯⎯⎯⎯

(b. 1927) *Gujarati*

A journalist by profession, Kundanika Kapadia has earned a reputation as a highly articulate feminist writer, more so after the publication of *Sat Paglan Akashman* (Seven Paces in the Sky), 1984, which won a Gujarat State Sahitya Academy Award. She was born in the small town of Limbdi in Saurashtra and attributes her early interest in writing to the solitude of her surroundings. It was the seclusion, she feels, that led her to turn inwards. She has, for many years, been editor of the monthly journal *Navneet*. She is married to the well-known Gujarati poet Makrand Dave.

In the preface to an early collection of short stories, *Vadhu ne Vadhu Sundar* (Increasingly Beautiful), 1967, Kundanika Kapadia explains that her stories are centered more on character than on plot. Her prime interest is not in form, but in theme, which is invariably one of quest. Elsewhere she has emphasized that living, for her, is more important than writing, and that life is a constant opening of new vistas. Many of Kundanika Kapadia's books show women gradually coming to realize their own oppression. The novel *Agan Pipasa* (The Thirst for Fire), 1972, depicts strong women who get nothing from life because of the drunken husband, the father, the son, or the lover to whom they are bound by ties of loyalty and devotion. In the powerful short story "Tamaran Charanoman" (Prostrate at Your Feet), which appeared in *Premnan Ansun* (Tears of Love), 1978, a wife who has become increasingly aware of how her seemingly devoted husband has always pressured her to act according to his wishes finally abandons him when a beloved younger sister commits suicide after having been forced by her brother to marry a man of his choice instead of the man she loves.

The strongest and most fulfilled of Kundanika Kapadia's characters is perhaps the heroine of "Punaragaman" (The Return), also in *Premnan Ansun*. Deserted by her lover when she was pregnant, and scorned by her family and community, she leaves home, has her child, and lives with him in a place where no one knew her before. She is happy and in no way restrictive or possessive of her son. When the child's father tracks them down ten years later, he is astonished to find that she has no feelings of rancor or bitterness, but that there is no place for him in her life either. Like her contemporary Dhiruben Patel, Kundanika believes that a change in the condition of women must begin with a change in their own consciousness. She considers women partially responsible for their victimization because they accept their state of dependence and cling to security above all, an impatience evident in many women writers of this period, especially Saraswathi Amma, the celebrated feminist from Kerala.

The preface to *Sat Paglan Akashman*, however, is a scathing attack on the inferior status accorded to women. The standpoint is closely akin to that of a liberal strand in Western feminist thinking, but it is one that is also consistently prefigured in her own writing since the early fifties. At the end of the novel, several characters, men and women, set up a utopian community where there is genuine sharing and respect for one another. The characters are urban and middle-class, the setting domestic. There is no overt violence or visible injustice, but a series of minor encounters drains the joy out of the protagonist Vasudha's life. Gradually over the years she realizes that she does not matter as a person to her husband, Vyomesh, or to his aunt (who is really a mother-in-law to her), and that there is no possibility of what she regards as a human life in that household.

Vasudha becomes a mother, and, years later, a mother-in-law, but her status scarcely changes. Her existence is taken for granted; her wishes do not count. However, younger women—a stranger in the park where she takes her baby son and the niece of that same son's wife when he is a grown man—find in her a sympathetic listener. Friendship with the women in the neighborhood sustains her. Women who seemed to be interested only in superficial matters and appeared reasonably contented with their lot are discovered to be scholarly, artistic, and with griefs far more acute than her own. But Vasudha is powerless to aid her friends. When an older woman, a neighbor, obviously desperate, needs a loan, Vyomesh considers it unthinkable that Vasudha should dare to ask him to lend the money, and when that evening the neighbor's promising young daughter commits suicide and they realize the money was needed for an abortion, he feels no guilt, but rather righteous indignation that his help could have been sought to further what he sees as immoral actions. Ironically, the final break comes when he reacts with indifference to the death of his aunt, who to Vasudha had been an enemy but who had been like a mother to Vyomesh. Vasudha feels she can no longer even nominally share a home with this man.

The novel has been praised for its boldness, but also sharply criticized for what has been called its "extreme stance." It is a tract, not a novel, its critics claim. There can be no doubt, however, that it is a landmark in Gujarati literature.

◆

From SAT PAGLAN AKASHMAN
(Seven Paces in the Sky)
Chapter 3

The days, months, and years that had passed were rolled up like a long Egyptian scroll. Today, she felt like sitting in a secluded corner and going over it all. Slowly she unfurled it and each incident exploded in her face like a mini bomb. The scroll was crowded with writing. But scarcely any bright reds and greens, flowers of a joyous festival, were to be seen. Here and there was a strip of green grass. All the rest was crammed with the gray etchings of work. Crisscross, zigzag, up and down went the endless lines, shapes of incidents extending in all directions, misty, joyless.

It wasn't that she didn't like work, but shouldn't there be some time for work that one enjoys? Shouldn't there be a few moments that one can spend alone with what is dear to one?

From the day she married and came to this place, life was a passage through the dark caves and ravines of work. If only she had occasionally been able to breathe in to her heart's content the clear evening air from her veranda!

The house had a large veranda. Vyomesh was a well-organized and farsighted person. When the house was being built he had bought up two adjacent flats. He would marry, there would be children, they too would get married. Then they'd need the space. But prices would have gone up steeply by that time. He had started earning his living while he was still quite young. Using his savings, some inherited wealth, and some of his aunt's capital, together with other loans, he had bought the place. Alterations had been made as required. Adding half the floor area of a room to a balcony, they had made this large veranda.

When Vasudha came to live in the place there were only two people in the household, Vyomesh and his aunt. She was surprised. Such a large house for just two people? But her eyes lit up when she saw the veranda. "What a lovely veranda," she exclaimed.

Aunt responded with pride. "Yes, we had it specially made. It's so useful to spread out the grain in the sun and to dry *papads,* or mangoes for pickles. We pound our spices here as well—chillies and turmeric."

Vasudha just stared at her for a moment. This was her first acquaintance with Aunt.

Keeping such a large house clean took an immense amount of time. From morning to night she was occupied with an endless round of housework. Aunt's alert gaze pursued her everywhere. Once or twice Vasudha had felt as if a weapon were being aimed at her back, and had looked behind her in fear. It was Aunt watching her. She had been deeply wounded. These people have got me married and brought me here, but they have never cared to make me feel that I belong. What do they think I am? Or do they think I am nothing?

Her friends had said, "You're going to have an easy time. Just two people at your in-law's home."

Just two—it could be even just one. Would that preserve you from persecution?

Even her mother had said, "You don't have a father-in-law or mother-in-law. There's just Vyomesh's aunt. Keep her and Vyomesh happy and that's enough. You'll have no problems. Naturally a daughter feels sad when she leaves her parents' home, but soon you'll be so involved with life there that you won't keep thinking of us."

When you make somebody yours and bring them to your home, why should you ill-treat them so much? What satisfaction do you get from it? Vasudha often used to ponder these matters. Nobody could ever have suggested to Aunt and Vyomesh that when an innocent girl had come to them, leaving behind her old familiar home, her loving parents, the affection showered on her by brothers and sisters, the friends with whom she had played since her earliest childhood, the lime tree in the courtyard, and a whole world of unrestrained laughter and vivacity, surely it was all the more necessary that she should be made to feel at home. Nobody had ever told them, "Care for this girl, cherish her dreams and her hopes." A daughter is always told to win the hearts of her in-laws through love and service. Why are the husband, the mother-in-law, the sister-in-law never told, "Two tender feet have come this way, leaving so much behind, see that thorns are not strewn on their path!"

Aunt would not let her rest for a moment. Just because a woman is a daughter-in-law, can one take it for granted that she never tires? It was true that Aunt was the senior person in the household. It was natural that she should have greater knowledge of housework. But why this craze to issue an endless series of commands? "Vasudha, the sheet is dirty, put it aside for the wash . . . cut the okra only after you have wiped it with a wet cloth . . . when you sort out the lentils check that they are not moldy . . . don't put a wet spoon into the coffee tin . . . when the milk cools, cover the saucepan . . . take care to roll the edges of the chapatis well. They should not get thick . . . ."

I know the sheet is dirty. Even without your telling me I was going to put it aside for the wash. I know one doesn't put a wet spoon into the coffee tin. Aunt, we can get along without all this advice—Vasudha often felt like saying this, but it would have made Aunt furious, and she had been taught from childhood that one must not displease one's in-laws. So she went on with her work with head lowered, responding briefly with, "Yes, Aunt, very well, Aunt."

It's not as if one takes to every kind of household activity. Keeping accounts, for instance. That was something that did not appeal to Vasudha at all. In her mother's home whenever she bought anything she'd say, "Mother, this is how I've spent the money." This was all, and if her mother wanted to make a note of it she might. Her mother had never told her that, whether she liked it or not, she must keep accounts.

But that's just what Aunt demanded. No sooner did Vasudha start buying the daily vegetables than Aunt instructed her, "Vasudha, every day keep a regular record in the diary of what you've spent during the day, right!"

The words slipped out: "Aunt, I don't like keeping accounts one bit!" There was no note of contradiction in her voice, only of appeal.

But Aunt raised her voice. "What do you mean, you don't like it?" She glared at Vasudha as if to say, How could you possibly say such a thing? What you like or don't like doesn't matter in the least. You have to do what we tell you.

Vasudha was cowed by the look on Aunt's face. She felt like saying, You used to write the accounts before I came, didn't you? Can't you continue to do so? After all, I've taken over a lot of your other work!

But she didn't have the courage. From the very next day she started putting down every amount she spent. It was such a bore noting two annas for coriander leaves, four annas for spinach, eight annas for bananas. She made mistakes. But she dared not say she wouldn't do it. In her old home she could say anything she pleased. What was it in this house that forced her to lock up her thoughts?

Sometimes she wondered about Aunt's past. A child widow, she must have been stunted in every way. She must have had so much to endure. She herself did not know the history of that suffering. Each individual has a history comprising every single day, every single night. How many days are soiled with agony, how many nights are soaked through with tears, nobody else knows. After many years she has, for a time, got the reins of empire in her hands. She probably never had a chance to lord it over anyone before. Let her. She'll do it for a while. When she realizes there's no resistance she'll ease off.

But it was Vasudha who realized that it wasn't merely a question of getting a chance to domineer. Aunt had her own view of the creature called a daughter-in-law. There was a blind fear and mistrust: Perhaps this girl will snatch away my empire.

More days passed. She came to understand more about the way Aunt's mind worked. To her, a daughter-in-law was a beast of burden that must be set to work all day long. No questions, no arguments, no likes or dislikes—these were unmentionable.

"Vasudha, do this and do that. Vyomesh doesn't care for savories. But he loves sweets. They must be made at home, though, not bought in a shop. What other work do you have anyway? As you go about the house, make the sweets also . . . The woolen clothes have to be aired. In this house the mattress covers are washed every week. Vyomesh doesn't like things to be dirty or untidy . . . Keep checking on our stock of wheat, it doesn't take long for the grain to mold . . .

Keep count of the spoons and bowls—once we had a new part-time servant who stole a saucepan."

If a person never speaks, it's like the suffocation one would experience on issuing from a dark cave and finding the entrance blocked by a stone. If someone never ceases talking, it's like having one's ears pierced by a drill. Were my ears made just to hear this kind of talk? Don't I need to hear anything better, sweeter, more affectionate?

A hundred times a day she had to hear what Vyomesh liked. Who cared about what Vasudha enjoyed, what she liked to eat? Nobody ever asked, because her likes and dislikes had no value. Vasudha loved the evening, the sky, sunset, and moonrise. They take place silently but have their own music. The silence of night has its music. The early morning light has its music. She loved to listen to this music. And she loved to read. How many books she had read in her youth! Not only the Gujarati classics—Munshi, Dhoomketu, Ramanlal Desai—but translations of Bengali writers—Sharat Chandra and Tagore—even Shakespeare and Ibsen in translation. Whatever she could lay hands on, she read. Her mother was so proud of her passion for reading. "My Vasudha is so keen on reading! When she sits down to read she even forgets to be hungry!"

But this quality of which her mother was so proud was a flaw in Aunt's eyes. "Isn't there enough work in the house that you sit down to read?" Once, when seeing Vasudha with a book, she had snapped, "What kind of a habit is this, sitting down with a book now and again!"

Vasudha was astonished. Does marriage mean that a woman must stick all her tastes and interests up on a shelf? If this house is mine and these people are mine, why can't I tell them frankly, "I like this, I don't like that?" And if they're not mine, why should I slave for them the whole day? Why should I take what they say lying down and struggle to please them at all costs?

But she doesn't have the courage to speak out. She continues with her work without a word. She gets tired. Her hands and feet get tired, her spirit gets tired. Subjected to advice all day long, her ears get tired.

"Vasudha, Vyomesh's uncle's sister-in-law's daughter died, have you heard? Go on a condolence visit this evening. Wear that new white sari you bought. And take off your earrings. It's not proper to wear such things when a young person dies. You can keep your *mangalsutra**

---

*A *mangalsutra* is a necklace of black beads worn by married women.

on. There's no harm in that. And on your way back, drop in at the sweet shop and buy some thickened milk. You're to make Vyomesh's favorite sweet tomorrow, remember. He was talking about it just this morning. . . .

"Vasudha, you must go and call on Vyomesh's other uncle. Finish the visit quickly. The hospital's far off, so coming and going will take a long time. Just ask after his health and hurry back. There's no need to sit for a long time. You need only put in an appearance."

Do this and do that. Why did you do this? Why didn't you do that? Is this the way to do such-and-such? Does it take so long to finish this much work? Why are you in such a hurry to rush off for your bath? Go and call on Vyomesh's paternal uncle . . . There is no need to call on his maternal aunt.

If Vasudha had protested, Aunt would have opened her eyes wide in astonishment and said, But I'm telling you everything for your own good. The house is yours. I don't want your belongings to get spoilt, your pots and pans to be stolen, or criticisms to be made of you by our relations. Otherwise, what's it got to do with me? All I have is you and Vyomesh. That's why I sold my jewelry and brought him up. I handed over all my capital to invest in this flat . . .

Vasudha understands. Aunt had made sacrifices to bring Vyomesh up. A person who makes a sacrifice for another expects something in return. Not only in the form of money but in the form of status, power, the right to demand service. And if she doesn't get it, she'll keep wiping away her tears with the end of her sari and say, I did so much for him. I never spared myself in setting him up. And now he pays no attention to what I say . . . There's no value in doing good to anyone in this world.

If Vasudha could have spoken she would have said, There's great value in doing good, Aunt, but it loses its value when you expect some right in return . . .

There's a lot that Vasudha wants to say: Listen, Aunt, do you know that these sharp scissors of advice are snipping away at sprouts and the buds of my spontaneous gaiety? Because I don't say anything, because I quietly do whatever you tell me to do, you think I'm obedient. You chose a girl from a poor family so that she would keep doing what you wanted and would remain under control. But I'm not obedient, I'm just a coward, that's why I can't speak out. And you don't know that I'm tormented by your never-ending instructions, your keeping watch, your suspicions, your conviction that I must function only according to your wishes.

Aunt, you believe that I'm an understanding, self-respecting girl! I listen to everything in silence, but I don't like it. There's a great deal that I don't like. Why do you always attempt to control me? Who has said that a mother-in-law should always bully and dominate? Why can't you be warmer and more intimate with me? I'm a human being like you. But you are so blinded by tradition that you don't see the questions that surface in me. You don't see me at all. What you see is just a daughter-in-law, the wife of Vyomesh, whom you raised like a son, for whom you made sacrifices, in return for which you now desire a kingdom.

And listen, Aunt, you, too, must have been deeply wounded somewhere. It's those who've been badly wounded in childhood, who are tormented by a profound melancholy or revulsion, who get so much satisfaction out of making others suffer. Come, Aunt, let's sit close to each other and talk freely without any reservations. Tell me, what griefs did you suffer, and when, to lead you to be so harsh to a new, young, unknown girl like me? Who instilled in you the poison of suspicion and fear? How did the desire to domineer to such a degree take possession of you?

But I'm not able to say all this to you since you're in the position of a mother-in-law, and I in that of a daughter-in-law. Traditionally our relationship has been one of distrust and envy, domination and obedience. Our relations are fused with our roles, so it is impossible for us to move out of our roles and enter into a real relationship.

Vasudha often held these long conversations with Aunt in her imagination, but she never dared to express herself in actuality. She had never said a word to Vyomesh about Aunt. Indeed she knew Vyomesh largely through Aunt. How Vyomesh used to laugh or cry when he was little, what he preferred, what he disliked, what made him boil over with rage, what exploits he had performed in his student days and how rapidly he had risen in his job, all this was narrated to Vasudha with great zest. Vyomesh was the center of Aunt's existence. It occurred to Vasudha that Vyomesh was also the center round which all else in the house revolved. Why should one person occupy the central position in a household? True, he had established the household. But that was not quite correct—if Aunt had not helped, had not run the house, the household would not have been what it was. Vyomesh, too, would not be what he is today. Yet Vyomesh is the head of the household. Aunt accommodates herself totally to him and his ways. She wishes Vasudha to do the same. It's not just a wish, it's an expectation that Vasudha will do precisely that. How often: "Vasudha, you are cooking the kind of lentils Vyomesh doesn't care for." "Vasudha, when you go to the market for the vegetables, don't buy bitter gourd, Vyomesh never eats it."

Vasudha would ask, "Aunt, don't you like bitter gourd either?"

Aunt would say, "Oh, I love bitter gourd. But Vyomesh never eats it, so I never make it. For years it's never been cooked in our house."

In her words there was no note of regret at being deprived of what she enjoyed. Perhaps there was a touch of pride. Or perhaps Vasudha imagined it.

One takes pride in giving up something for the sake of another person. Just as there is pleasure in the possession of something, sacrifice also creates its own kind of satisfaction. Did Vyomesh know of Aunt's sacrifices—small and large?

And—

Vasudha hesitated. Then she laughed silently to herself. Even if a person is not free to express her thoughts, she is free to think. She gave free rein to her thoughts and the question arose, Has Vyomesh ever accommodated himself to Aunt's needs? Has he ever given up anything he liked or enjoyed for her sake? If he were asked, he would be sure to shrug his shoulders and say, When did I ever tell Aunt to do something or refrain from doing something for my sake?

There are just two of them in the house. Vyomesh is at work from morning to evening. It's impossible to talk freely to Aunt. What's the point in talking if one can't speak without reservations? But Aunt jabbers ceaselessly and it never occurs to her that Vasudha listens but does not participate in the conversation. She is absorbed in her own tales. Tales of housework, of the house, of Vyomesh. Listening to her, Vasudha remembers incidents from her own childhood. If I tell you about them, Aunt, will you listen? Are you interested in me? Not as a daughter-in-law, but as a person, have you any concern for me?

At first she longed to visit her mother, but couldn't bring herself to say so. She waited. Perhaps Aunt would suggest, Why don't you go back to your mother's home for a visit? You lived there for so long, you must be yearning to go there!

Oh—if only sometimes Aunt knew how she felt. If only she would make the smallest effort to satisfy her wishes.

One morning while she was dusting and arranging some old magazines and journals, Vasudha suddenly took it into her head to pick up an old issue of the Gujarati journal *Navneet,* and she sat down to glance through it. There was a science article, discussing whether the solar system contained a tenth planet. She was reading with eager interest when Aunt turned up. "Vasudha!" Her voice was so hard and so sharp that Vasudha leapt up in fear. "Is the early morning the time to read books? Don't you have any sense? Is this the time to read?" Vasudha hastily put the magazine down and hurried to the kitchen. On the way she glanced in at the sitting-room. Vyomesh was sitting there with his legs stretched up onto the table reading the paper. This was his daily routine. With the teapot containing two cups of tea by his side, sipping his tea slowly, he would relax and read the paper. It would take half to three-quarters of an hour. Then he'd shave quickly, dress, have his meal, and leave for work.

"Is this the time to read?"—the words echoed in her mind all day. Would Aunt ever have said this to Vyomesh? If Aunt had had a daughter, would she have had to hear such words? But Vasudha was a daughter-in-law. The decision regarding what to do and when no longer rested with her.

Vyomesh had uttered similar words: "Is this the time to stand on the veranda?"

After the wedding, Vasudha had gotten into a certain routine. Every evening she would wash and freshen up and stand at the door awaiting Vyomesh's return. Plagued all day by the pricks of Aunt's petty fault-finding, her heart was eager to meet Vyomesh, listen to him, touch him. Seeing him approach at a distance, her face would glow. As soon as Vyomesh arrived, she would take his things from his hands and quickly make tea. As he drank his tea, Vyomesh would chat about happenings at the office. She would listen, laugh. Then Vyomesh would look at his letters and read; Vasudha would cook. After the meal, as soon as she had wound up the rest of the chores, she would go impatiently to their room. Close to Vyomesh, Aunt's nagging would be forgotten. Cooking for Vyomesh, waiting for Vyomesh, sleeping enveloped in his warmth—her young body experienced bliss. Vyomesh had winning ways; in his inviting glance Vasudha found fulfillment. Whether it was a fulfillment of the body or the mind she could not tell. Body and mind were one in that fullness.

In the evening Vyomesh would say, "Today I just couldn't apply my mind to office work. I couldn't wait till I got home. When I come back home and see your smiling face, that's all I want, nothing else in the world matters."

When Vasudha heard this, her heart overflowed with love. She felt she had entered a city glowing with light. She forgot Aunt's world.

She even forgot the attachment to her old home. Colorful lamps shone on all sides.

One day a gray mist spread over those colors. It was July. Aunt was out somewhere. Heavy rain clouds covered the sky. There was moisture in the air. The earth had the fresh scent of rain. Fearing that the clothes drying on the veranda would get wet if it rained, Vasudha hurried out to the veranda and her eyes lighted on the western sky. Through an opening in the clouds, behind the dark curtain of rain, suddenly the crescent of the new moon appeared. Right in the center of the crescent, the evening star reposed as if it were sleeping in the cradle of the moon. She had never seen the moon and the star together like this before. Losing all track of time, losing all consciousness of herself, she gazed unblinking, entranced.

Suddenly she felt a hand on her shoulder. She stared. It was Vyomesh. "Is this a time to stand on the balcony?" Was there affection in his voice, or displeasure? "I returned ages ago. What were you doing here? Don't you know I want to see you standing in the doorway when I get home?"

Vasudha's lips moved, but before she could say anything, Vyomesh said, "It's going to rain—come along inside." Vasudha entered the room without a word. Vyomesh put his arms around her. "It's the first rain of the season, isn't it?" He drew her closer. No—no . . . Vasudha's body stiffened. Putting his hand under her chin, Vyomesh lifted her gentle, fine-featured face. "Are you cold?" He embraced her even more closely. Something hurt Vasudha profoundly. My wishes, my reluctance count for nothing. My time is not my own. I have no right over my own body. Utterly dejected, she surrendered.

Translated by Shirin Kudchedkar.

KAMAL DESAI ⎯⎯⎯⎯⎯⎯⎯⎯⎯⎯⎯⎯⎯⎯

(b. 1928)   *Marathi*

Once every five years or so, between 1955 when she first started writing and 1975 when the classic "Hat Ghalnari Bai" (Woman Wearing a Hat) was published, Kamal Desai has produced a short novel. Though an occasional short story appeared in between, the body of her work is hardly voluminous. Yet she is acknowledged as one of the most intense and sophisticated of Marathi writers today. In a perceptive book-length study, R. B. Patankar points out that the problem that haunts all her work is that of the autonomy and independence of woman, an autonomy sought with unswerving commitment but, within the structure of Kamal Desai's existential world, never found, or perhaps tragically unattainable. Her fiction is focused at the microlevels of inner life, where experience is held together by a compelling, but essentially mysterious, struggle for selfhood and autonomy.

In "Hat Ghalnari Bai," commonly regarded as Kamal Desai's best work, a woman asserts her right to a Promethean venture, just as she appropriates the phallic symbol of the hat. She is making a surrealist film, but abandons the project when she realizes that her creative freedom is tainted by a man's intrusive power. Kailas Shet, a moneylender, helps her build a studio. His is a world in which money can buy anything, but he is disappointed to find that he can purchase the mysterious woman wearing the hat only physically. She, in turn, sees that it is impossible, try as she will, to separate her individuality and her art from her body and impossible to keep them pristine and inviolate while she is compromised sexually. Realizing that he cannot possess her completely as long as she has her studio, Kailas Shet plans to destroy it. But she preempts that assertion of his power by setting fire to the studio and burning herself down with it.

The novel's end is a disturbing resolution to what begins to seem an inevitable antagonism—stated bluntly in the title of an earlier novel (taken from a famous line from the bhakti poet Tukaram), *Ratradina Amha Yuddhacha Prasang* (We Confront the War Day and Night), 1963. Many of the stories in *Rang* (Colors), 1962, from which "Tila Bandh" (Close Sesame), the story translated here, is taken, explore the subtle antagonisms between male and female that Kamal Desai regards as the very basis of community life. In the author's world view there is no transcendence, or even a way out, for men and even less so for women, from the human condition itself, which is intense and unchangeable.

Yet she is equally sure that to be human is also to struggle, relentlessly, to hold on to one's values and keep control of one's world, even though events have their own laws and things happen as they will. Before she can tear down the walls of the temple of the dark sun in "Kala Surya" (Dark Sun), 1975, the protagonist must extricate herself from its pervasive, tenacious hold in the crevices of her self and her world. Though many of the women in Kamal Desai's fiction are lonely they refuse to be objects of pity or compassion. It is a fiction, the literary historian Balachandra Nemade argues, that embodies a subtly felt understanding of the modern way of life.

"Tila Bandh" revolves around the many roles Urmila plays with an almost inhuman precision and efficiency, leaving a finely evoked but uneasy distance between herself and these roles that never meet.

Kamal Desai was born in Yamkan Mardo, a small town in the Belgaum District, into a family of six sisters and two brothers. Her father was a postmaster. She hardly remembers her mother, but speaks of her father as a liberal-minded and just person, religious but not conservative. Even in those days, during their menstrual periods the girls in the family were not required to sit apart from the others. They had many friends and the house was always full of people. Kamal Desai went on to complete her under-graduate work in Belgaum and receive a master's degree in Marathi in Bombay, securing gold medals for both. She has worked as a lecturer in Marathi in several universities in Maharashtra. Talking to Vidyut Bhagwat about her life, Kamal Desai said she never married because she had always wanted to be a writer and if one were a writer, it was necessary to think independently. She has had male friends, but has never felt her freedom curtailed by them.

She has now retired and lives by herself in a small flat in Pune. As a writer, she told us, she has really explored only two subjects—God and womanhood—adding mischievously that when she began to write, only a one-sided, male view of the world, and of sexuality, existed.

◆

TILA BANDH
(Close Sesame)

In the midst of marking the half-year examination answer-books, Ur-mila Raje suddenly gets up. And then forgets why she has got up. Why should one get up in such a hurry? Perhaps she wants something . . . the geometry textbook? Perhaps she doesn't want anything at all . . . who knows?

She wanders all over the room, stops here and there touching things. Then returns to her desk. Perhaps she's tired of marking answer-books. The girls haven't solved the geometry questions. They don't appear to know much about algebra either. That's the kind of batch it is this year. Or perhaps—who knows—she isn't capable of teaching any longer.

She has suddenly become an Egyptian mummy. And, nobody quite knows how, all the stuffing has come out of her. And the body rots.

She pulls the papers roughly towards herself.

Unbidden, one of Snow White's dwarfs appears below her desk. He toddles out from under it and quickly jumps on top. Within a minute he has marked all the answer-books.

She laughs. She pushes the answer-books away and gets up.

The glare of the sun comes in through the window. Her eyes burn. She closes the window to shut out that glaring light.

She will not submit the answer-books today.

The window holds for a moment and swings open again.

Somebody seems to be standing outside the front door, awkward and embarrassed. She catches a rustle of clothes. The whiff of a cigarette scrapes her nostril and passes on. There's uncertainty outside the door. There's doubt. Should one knock or not?

She goes to the door.

Perhaps, when she got up a little while ago, it could have been because of this vague feeling. Perhaps the feeling had barely grown into a scratch upon her consciousness before dissolving again.

She opens the door.

There are three totally unknown men standing outside. Unfamiliar smiles linger on their faces. Urmila, however, only stares in astonishment. She doesn't even move away from the door. Her curt surprise bruises them. All three look abashed. Embarrassed. Drawn in with uncertainty. We should not have come!

Chandrashekhar feels the urge to take her by the arm, move her aside and walk in. He would love to do so if it were possible. But he doesn't do it.

"If you will allow us to come in . . ."

"Please excuse me. I was a little confused because I don't know any of you and this is so unexpected."

She moves away from the door.

Her voice has none of the curtness of her face. Perhaps what she is saying is true. Only, she has not liked this unexpected coming of theirs. And they must be made aware of it. At least that is what Chandrashekhar senses.

"Please sit."

They sit down. And that's all that happens for a long time. It's difficult to know where to start, and Chandrashekhar can never simply come to the point. She could lead with a token question. But that's not in her nature to do. She must grill them with a stare that makes them uncomfortable.

Palms are rubbed against palms. Looks are exchanged. Legs are crossed and uncrossed. And now something really must be said.

He looks at her.

Her hair is short and curly. It is all over the place. Her sari is quite dirty and untidy. The kumkum on her forehead has been rubbed off. It is now no more than a barely visible stain. She would look OK if she put herself in order. One of the pleats of her sari is hanging way down.

She should tuck it in.

"My name is Chandrashekhar. I am Nalini Nadkarni's brother. You may remember Nalini."

"I remember Nalini Nadkarni."

Chandrashekhar has the feeling that she's bluffing. She does not remember Nalini. She should have said she didn't remember her, rather than bluff. He'd have preferred that. And, in any case, it is not like her to be devious. Perhaps this is a new habit. But it makes her seem more self-centered.

"Nalini was in your class. And we all went to the same college."

What's the point in unnecessarily increasing familiarity? Some people have this habit. She doesn't say a word.

But he's here for some work. He's not sure how to begin, though. Is he embarrassed?

His hair is sparse. His nose is a little turned up at the tip. He likes confiding in people—her eyes observe him quietly.

"This is Shrinivas Sathe. And this is our teacher friend. The translator of the play."

She has not quite taken it in. She continues to listen.

"We're doing *The Barretts of Wimpole Street* this year."

So that's it.

Suddenly she understands everything. She rises hastily, takes a currency note out of her handbag and holds it before them.

"I don't understand theater much. Literature's not my sphere. But I'll come to see the play."

Shrinivas Sathe laughs outright. He has noted her haste. He cannot deny that there's a strange attraction in her abrupt gloom.

She also laughs with him, and just as openly, despite guessing that he knows. Proud, perhaps of that very knowledge.

"I've not come to sell tickets for the play."

Her question takes shape without utterance.

"I've come to ask you to play Elizabeth in it."

He's angry. Infuriated with this overhandling of everything, this cynicism of hers, this attitude of being above it all. He thinks, Why bother? Let me leave.

Yet he's convinced that she should play Elizabeth. She is talented. She'll do it well. If only she'd be a little less haughty.

He waits. She's forgotten how to speak. His question is incomprehensible to her, nonexistent in her world. It has dropped down from somewhere to irritate her. She doesn't like to open up, to blossom with emotion.

"I don't think I could act in a play. I've never done it before."

He is a trifle overawed by her. But she must not refuse. He can see only her as Elizabeth in the play that's taking shape in his mind. If she's not in the play it will be quite blank, vacuous. The pain will go right out of it. The blossoming of a personality will be lost. He senses that her "no" is a means of escape.

"You'll do the role very well. You must do it." He is gentle now.

Why should she? Her ego pricks her. She grabs herself tight in her own fist.

"I can't do it."

She grows suddenly still. She lowers her head and instantly her hair covers her face.

Shrinivas Sathe thinks, She has turned into a mathematical formula, unbending and harsh.

After a long pause Chandrashekhar asks her, "Do you have to think so hard about it?"

"Oh I'm not thinking at all. I've already told you—I can't do it."

"You can. You'll do it." He makes her speechless with his trust, his intense intimacy.

"I'll send the script over this evening. And the works of Robert and Elizabeth Browning. Exactly four days from now, a taxi will come to collect you. Directly from school."

That's done.

He gets up without glancing at her, and starts walking. The teacher and Sathe follow, quite bewildered.

2

As soon as they are outside the door, Shrinivas takes out a cigarette. The teacher is lost in thought. He finds it difficult to keep pace with Chandrashekhar. Shrinivas is quietly smoking and walking in step with Chandrashekhar. She is impossible.

He flings his cigarette down and grinds his heel into it.

"You think she'll do Elizabeth's role well?"

"She will. I think so."

"Meeting her, I am confused. She seems a little unstable. Elizabeth might just slip away from her."

"That won't happen. Elizabeth is actually in her."

That doesn't make sense. What do you mean Elizabeth is in her? Shrinivas thinks. But he says something else.

"Why do you feel that way?"

"I can't explain it very well. I studied this play in my third year in college. She had just entered college. She used to come over with Nalini sometimes. As I worked on the play I always saw her as Elizabeth. I had this strong desire to do the play and to get her to do Elizabeth. It's quite foolish really. But I'm very keen to do it all the same."

It is not that Shrinivas Sathe didn't respect his feelings. But this kind of intensity of feeling wasn't going to get them anywhere.

The teacher doesn't say a word. He thinks, She is no Elizabeth. She'll never cope with Elizabeth's frustration, her vitality, her self-control. It'll remain incomplete.

3

They have gone. The room is empty. She's not at all sure she understands. He has decided everything without giving her a chance to speak.

Urmila shuts the door noisily after them. As if the noise will drown this unwanted responsibility.

These unknown people have caught her in a peculiar trap. She can neither reject the responsibility nor accept it. The dilemma alarms her.

She ties up the answer-books, and lights the cooking stove. She pumps it hard and long to help her collect her faculties together again. Her arm aches. The flames of the stove ripple all around her body. And their fatal blue touch sets her trembling.

He shouldn't have trapped her like this.

And she shouldn't have given in. The thing now done, has cut a fault in her ego. Then there's no way to integrate the figure.

4

She returns home from school in the evening. She finds *The Barretts of Wimpole Street* in the original and in translation, along with a whole lot of other stuff on her desk. Curious, she leafs through the whole play. She hovers around the desk for a long time.

It had been a frenzied day at school, and had taken on the pace of her distractedness. The morning had been wiped so unexpectedly clean. And now she is taking shape again. Shrinivas Sathe has rather a nice laugh. Why had he come? And who was the third guy? He didn't seem to quite approve of the idea of my acting. He made such a sour face.

He's probably right, though. Who knows whether I'd manage it—not manage it? One hasn't even read the play . . .

But why had Chandrashekhar asked her to play Elizabeth? This must be explained to him properly. It would be so good if he'd relieve her of this deadly responsibility. She doesn't like even the smallest change in her everyday routine. She has to carry her umbrella and handbag to school everyday. She has to take the same road, the road that is snowed with silk-cotton. That's how it has been—that's how she is. One can't leave out a single step in solving a mathematical problem. It has to be solved in the same way each time. There are no alternative methods.

Perhaps she has a nameless fear that she will simply slip out of her own fingers.

She must tell Chandrashekhar.

And yet she lies in bed reading into the small hours of the morning. Browning comes quietly, pulls up a chair and sits down beside her. She wants to talk about Sordello.

But he reads a different poem. He reads it out loud, bending low. The light from the lamp drips drop by drop into his hair. The drops turn lightly into words—"For ever ride"—that's all she can hear. The pain in them touches her.

Elizabeth falls asleep without drinking her port. She is exhausted and stirs in her sleep.

She dreams: she is walking, bearing an invisible load. But she can't lift her feet. They follow pulled, dragged. As if she has never walked before. But there's no way to tell what she is carrying on her shoulders. Suddenly she sees that house standing on the corner of the road beckoning to her. She has this sudden feeling that she knows it. It is familiar. How strange! How could she know it? But she can't walk. And yet she must get there. And she might even get there now . . . but all of a sudden the house falls, noiselessly, like rain in a picture. The elegance of its falling is fascinating.

It should not have fallen that way. She is restless, and moans in her sleep. On the verge of consciousness she becomes aware of the smell of cigarettes.

5

And when she gets up in the morning she decides, I will forget it all. Obliterate it from my memory. Close sesame. And surprisingly, her tidy little dream, along with its pain, is locked in that mysterious cave. She knows it.

Now I will tell Chandrashekhar once and for all that I won't do it.

She goes to school by the usual road, carrying her umbrella and her handbag and her books.

Nalini is playing with Shalini's braids during morning prayers. Teacher looks on. "Let go of my braid," Nalini says, glancing at Urmila. Teacher looks grim today! Shalini's eyes brim over with deep devotion. For a moment Urmila's feet are not on firm ground. But she has seen nothing.

Mrs. Palsule comes across in her usual bustling way to tell her something, and forgets completely what she was going to say.

"Why? Why is your face looking so drawn today?"

But she knows. She has forgotten now.

Mrs. Palsule chances to touch her hand. "See? Did I not say so? You're not well today. Your hand feels hot."

Nirmala comes over from wherever she was to scold her in righteous anger—"That's the way she is. Pays no attention to us. As if the school will not run without her!"

She thinks she's going to cry. But she doesn't. She laughs. Like sugar candy. Nirmala always talks like that. She knows Nirmala is terribly attached to her, and that she must not do anything that will crack her devotion. And she will not. It has now been settled that this is how she is. There must be no change in that.

The arithmetic lesson in the eleventh standard classroom begins. She is solving a problem on the blackboard in the midst of which, suddenly, she cannot remember a step. The step that was before her eyes has been gently wiped off the surface of her mind. What comes next? What? How can I proceed without that step? And how can I erase a half-solved sum off the blackboard?

"No, I just can't remember the middle step today. I'll complete this problem tomorrow."

And as she leaves the class she overhears—"It's never happened before. Teacher was very strange today and serious!" The girls become serious too. They continue thinking about her.

But she knows there's nothing wrong with her. She forgets all that has happened. Perhaps she has just lost the capacity to teach. Why else would she have faltered as she did?

As she is passing by the science laboratory, she casually, very casually, picks up the thermometer. She locks the eleventh standard syllabus into it, and quietly buries it in a pit in the garden. So, at least as far as this class is concerned, she has managed to put an end to one problem.

She wants to laugh. She enters the teachers' room. Palsulebai rec-
ommends a medicine. Nirmala sulks, angry with her.

6

Chandrashekhar comes to fetch her on the scheduled day, at the scheduled time. But was it decided that she'd be fetched by cab? She can't
remember. Chandrashekhar's face looks unfamiliar. She is a little confused.

Chandrashekhar holds open the door of the taxi for her—a little
embarrassed, a little fearful. Who knows what's going on in her mind?
Perhaps I was too hasty the other day. Elizabeth took a bold and determined shape. But did she like the idea . . . or didn't she?

She remembers that she is Elizabeth in his play. She has not been
able to brush off the responsibility Chandrashekhar has placed on her.
She has never felt, even in the remotest corner of her mind, that she'd
like to act in a play like this. She has always been oblivious to other
people's existence, even in a crowd. That is why she is afraid she won't
be able to do it. Yet she cannot avoid it either. Sometimes something
happens out of the blue and unwittingly one is trapped.

She gets into the taxi and sits down. Chandrashekhar pulls the door
shut without a word. He doesn't even look at her.

Perhaps he didn't like the way she behaved the other day. Perhaps
he isn't much of a talker. Whatever it is, Chandrashekhar must be told
that she can't cope with this. She can't understand Elizabeth. And
Browning has disturbed her. She glances at him. He has disappeared
into the crowd outside the window.

But this is no way to behave. Had Nirmala been here, she'd have
given him a thundering piece of her mind. She's like that. Short-
tempered.

The *kho-kho* team is shaping up rather well this year. With a little
more practice they can make it to the district schools' tournament.
Their running isn't calculated enough, though. Prabha is an excellent
chaser. She's fast, but erratic. She runs as the fancy takes her. Mere
speed is meaningless. And Shalan has this bad habit of faulting—.

"This is where we get out."

She starts. "H'm?"

Her face becomes innocent, like a child's.

"I said this is where we get out."

As she gets out she realizes her legs are aching. Her legs give way
for some unknown reason. Chandrashekhar steadies her gently. She

feels confused, then grows wary and watches him. Perhaps it's just a doubt. She brushes it away.

She steps into the living room. Many people have gathered there. They are all eager to see her. There's a lot of curiosity: What is she like? How does she talk? How does she laugh? People have fixed notions about women who act in plays.

Somebody has been asking Shrinivas, "What is she like?"

Shrinivas is strangely baffled. She's good—bad—it's difficult to decide. She's okay. Surely she's okay! As Elizabeth?

"Who knows? I really wouldn't know."

Though he has seen her, he has not actually seen her. Or perhaps he has wanted to avoid seeing her.

And now there she is in the doorway.

Tired. Bored. She's really too old—with eyes that have burnt out—she's like someone dragged in from another planet.

No—she's much too dry—much too old. All eyes converge on her and wander at leisure over her body. Slowly a bitter irony enters that leisurely examination. Their eyes grow blunt. Her body shrivels up. She feels it. She has understood.

"So this is the woman Chandrashekhar had set his mind on."

She's nothing much. But isn't that what they had wanted? They wouldn't have liked it if she'd turned out to be unexpectedly lovely. Some satisfaction. She's quite ordinary.

And then, quite unnecessarily, they close ranks. A silent pact is made. She will not be accepted. She will be kept at a distance. Everybody in the room grows unaccountably still.

She realizes this. Her eyes narrow. Her thin nostrils tremble. She follows Chandrashekhar into the room with magnificent carelessness.

This is Henrietta, Edward, George. Chandrashekhar moves hurriedly through the introductions. She moves with him without noticing anybody.

"And this is Browning."

She starts. Shrinivas's eyes meet hers. Surely Browning wasn't like this? Who knows?

He halts for a second in the doorway and enters.

"Your room isn't unknown to me. I have seen one exactly like this."

However hard she tries, she cannot become Elizabeth. And he isn't Browning.

She looks palely after him as he goes away. The fresh, soft smell of a just-smoked cigarette stirs her.

"Wilma, I want to forget," she tells D'Silva.

But Sister Wilma says nothing. She makes the sign of the cross and leaves, telling her beads. But the huge balloon of her long robe, floating in the air, stays behind long after she's gone. Urmila wants to get up and catch the balloon.

The play is being read. It is gathering momentum.

"No. I won't drink porter."

She flings the porter away in a temper, and sinks into a chair, exhausted.

The unexpected variation brings on a spreading stillness spiked with inquisitive reproach. Chandrashekhar walks over to her, ensuring that his feet make no sound at all.

"Elizabeth doesn't throw away the porter. She drinks it. You mustn't do that. You've had a tiring day at school. I can understand that. Let's do this just once more. Then we'll stop."

Chandrashekhar speaks to her, aware of the other people's eyes drilling through him. He is hurt. Was I wrong? She is really a sly one.

She rises, holding back with great restraint the unendurable pain within her. Suddenly the scene lifts.

She drinks the porter. Her body heaves with the sobs in the play.

The act ends. She is utterly desolate, as if everything is over. Slowly the others leave. Chandrashekhar is moved.

"You caught Elizabeth perfectly then. Come. You're tired. I'll take you home."

She hasn't quite understood what Chandrashekhar has been saying. She follows him, and sinks brokenly into the taxi that he has called.

She has forgotten Chandrashekhar.

She is home. Chandrashekhar has gone. She sits on her bed benumbed in body and mind. She feels limp. Her sari is crushed. It's sticking sweatily to her body. Her face is also sticky. Her feet inside her sandals are clammy. They burn.

But she continues to sit, still dazed, with the door of the room left open, and the light not turned on.

She walks in through the open door in a long, black, high-necked gown. Her feet are unsteady. Gathering her dress around her, she carefully lowers herself into a chair as if the room is quite familiar to her.

"Elizabeth?"

She shakes her hand.

It makes Urmila laugh. Who knows how they were. Those starched people under the Queen's rule. Not at all my type.

"You threw the porter away."

"To tell the truth, I find that stiffness an unbearable strain. I felt so good when I threw it away. True, so free. Otherwise the whole thing becomes intolerably irritating."

"But finally it's the tension that is the real thing."

"True."

"Even your not understanding me is a strategy. You don't want to understand me. Isn't that true?"

"Perhaps it is. But there are times when life seems to make you grow faint. You drink up the vital spirit itself. I can't reach the source of your faith. I feel confused."

"And wouldn't you like to grow faint with life?"

"Perhaps I might. Perhaps not. I feel afraid of losing consciousness. I don't have the strength for it."

"Your explanation is empty of meaning. It's all lies. You just don't want to admit that you would have loved to be Elizabeth. But the mere thought of it embarrasses you."

She heaves. Trembles. Clouds over. And holds on tightly to the darkness, resting her tired head upon it.

7

Rehearsals for the play fall into the usual routine. Settle down to it quite naturally. Become an everyday thing. But she cannot fit these hectic evenings into the equation of her days. What is her value? She has been flung far away. She is on the outside. The distance stays.

The everyday meetings bring the others very close to each other. They grow intimate. Browning likes weak tea. Henrietta has made a note of that. Barrett always offers Browning a cigarette. Barrett has guessed that Browning has a soft spot for Henrietta. In fact everybody has guessed it.

"You've forsaken Elizabeth, have you? And got a whole new play going here."

Shrinivas glances at Henrietta.

"I want to switch over to the Captain's role. Doing Browning is a strain in any case. She's an inexplicable enigma."

"She acts beautifully though, doesn't she?"

Shrinivas doesn't answer. He flicks the ash off his cigarette.

"She acts well. There's no doubt about that. But she's snooty."

"Is that how she is in school as well?"

"I don't suppose so. My sister is in her school. Not a day goes by without her talking about her. But that's a different thing altogether."

"Maybe she's in the habit of—."

Shrinivas is hurt to the quick. "No. She's not like that. That's an unjust thing to say. She may be snooty. But not that."

"It's beyond me why Chandrashekhar thinks so highly of her."

Elizabeth, however, is untouched. She comes. She does her bit. And goes away. She would like to tell Barrett one day, You are a marvelous actor. She wants to praise Henrietta's playfulness. But she doesn't. And she herself doesn't know why. She's just unable to bring herself to do such things there. There, she is Elizabeth, and nothing more.

On her way to school she meets Wilma. She feels so glad to see her. She is suddenly weeping.

"I needed to see you and you're here. I'll call up school to say I'm coming late—let's sit somewhere quiet."

They go to Wilma's room. Wilma puts a tumbler of cold water before her.

"How did you guess I wanted water?"

"You're looking upset."

"No. I get this feeling of warmth when you're with me. It makes me want to weep."

"Is something wrong?"

She sits still looking into the tumbler and fingering its fluted surface. Wilma waits for her to speak.

"I don't know Browning. I have no idea what he was like. I see only Keshav in his place. Keshav is constantly around me. It confuses me. I can't bring any togetherness into the scene." Suddenly she snaps shut. The secret cave has opened without the password. She grips Wilma's hand and rests her head on it. A loud sob gathers in her. She shuts her lips tight to hold it in. She suffocates with the pain in her chest. She feels sick at heart. She swallows all the water in the tumbler in a single gulp.

"We have a terrific kho-kho team. We'll make it to the district this year."

Wilma strokes her hand. Puts her lips on her palm. Urmila laughs. Her laughter looks pathetic around the corners of her mouth where it lingers.

9

But these days she can't bear the sight of Shrinivas. Yes, she hates him. Hates him with all her being. She wants to scream when he comes close to her. Why does he hold his hands that way—so stupidly? Why can't he walk properly? But it is not like that, really. Actually he is a very skilled and understanding actor. She has told herself this so often. He is Browning. He just is Browning. She has told herself very firmly. Yet, she can't stand Shrinivas. She asked him once, "Why don't you speak like Browning?"

"What do you mean, like Browning?"

What do I mean? Really, what does "like Browning" mean? She doesn't know either.

She means to say, I know what I mean to say.

It's just that she must now get used to being Elizabeth. And that is something she is unable to do.

10

She hasn't turned up for rehearsals for days. Nor is she going to, today. She slips away from school quietly, secretly. Hope Chandrashekhar doesn't catch me on the way out. If a taxi passes too close by her, she suspects that Chandrashekhar might be in it. If he opens the cab door for her, she'll have no choice but to get in.

She gets home. She is filled with a strange contentment. Must make myself a lovely cup of tea.

Chandrashekhar is watching through the door. She's totally engrossed in reading, with a pot of tea on the table before her. She tops up her half-empty cup with more tea. She wants to laugh in the middle of her reading. She puts her cup down and bursts out laughing.

This natural side of her is new to Chandrashekhar. She is relaxed, one of us. She's not like this during rehearsals. She's not in the least aware that she has forgotten something, or done something wrong. Why bruise her happiness!

She happens to glance towards the door. She knew Chandrashekhar would come.

"So, you've come!"

"H'm. You've been missing rehearsals like a child playing hooky from school. You slipped out the back door. What could I do?"

She is greatly amused. She wants to laugh.

"But I'm feeling so good today. I love having tea like this. Care for some?"

She's so much like one of us today!

He takes a sip from the cup she has given him.

"Have you been forgetting to come to rehearsals?"

She doesn't answer for a long time.

"No. Not quite. I decided during the last lesson today. To give rehearsals a miss. I saw my chance. I took it."

He falls silent.

"Also I don't feel like acting."

He stares at her, teacup in hand. He is helpless before her. He has a feeling she has escaped him.

"I won't leave you in the lurch halfway through, of course. Don't be afraid. But I'd rather not come to rehearsal today."

Chandrashekhar doesn't know what to say. He is afraid. Something gnaws inside him. Will he manage to see the whole thing through?

He gets up, near to tears. He goes away, forgetting to say good-bye.

The fun has gone out of drinking tea now. But she continues to drink it all the same, sip by sip.

11

She has made things needlessly difficult. Chandrashekhar wonders how he's going to tell her. He recalls a similar fuss she'd made when they'd talked of having Sunday rehearsals.

"Sunday is my day. Nobody can take it away from me. I wouldn't like that," she had said. Chandrashekhar had pacified her and brought her round. Not because she had agreed, but because she hadn't wanted to create a scene. Why should she be so stubborn? As if she were doing him a favor. She wanted him to feel it was something she was doing for him—because he had insisted. That's why she was making him miserable, to remind him constantly of this.

Chandrashekhar can't understand now why he should have been so insistent either! Quite unknowingly, he has become involved with her. She has wrapped herself around his heart.

He wants to quarrel with her. Have an all-out row. Shake her hard and ask, What's all this snootiness for?

Or else say, quite seriously, Let us forget our deal.

But he knows only too well that forgetting the deal is just what she wants. It will make her laugh, out loud, and say—That's perfect. That's how she is. She won't feel a pang. But he'll tell her, all the same.

And then he remembers. As soon as she knows Browning has arrived, she grows tense with fear. She trembles with joy. She says, "Doctor, it is not easy to write poetry: read Sordello." Her dark despair before the meeting. And her nervous walk. And then, when they meet, the bright, fresh eagerness that springs from every footstep she takes.

Chandrashekhar is lost in confusion. He goes to his usual lonely restaurant. Sits down at his usual table through force of habit.

Shrinivas arrives in great haste. He feels relieved to see Chandrashekhar there.

"I've just been over to your place. I knew you'd go to see her. I went to your place directly from the office. For a moment I thought of going on to her place. But it's best to avoid her."

"What did she say?"

"What else? Just that she won't."

"Is that all?"

"That's all."

"Hmm."

They sit together for a long time, smoking. They drink strong coffee. Sitting together without saying a word.

"I have to tell you the truth. You're not going to like it. But, Urmila is erratic. She won't concentrate. She's wayward."

"I have no doubts about her acting. But I'm totally baffled by her strange behavior."

"You are free to think that. But I personally think she isn't aware of Browning's existence at all. She's looking for someone else in me. I can sense her terrible despair. It throws me off. There's this point where I say, 'Would you like us to send it all up in flames?' And she just forgets her lines. She's wounded by my words. She keeps shaking her head to say no. I almost feel as if she's holding on to my hand very, very tightly."

"But wouldn't that be called good acting? That kind of thing is more effective than speaking."

"The audience would certainly think so. I'd have felt that way too. But I know she's not acting. It's a genuine, secret emotion revealing itself spontaneously. It makes it very difficult for me. I've just about had enough of it now. It scares me."

"I don't quite see."

"You wouldn't. You just can't stand people saying anything about her. You get angry. You lose your temper. You take her side and explain her to us. I'm beginning to think you've fallen in love with her."

The time she stumbled, Chandrashekhar had given her his hand. He had thought for a moment, She has yielded to me. But it was only a thought. He had shrugged it off easily.

"You're talking nonsense."

Chandrashekhar gets up.

12

And today is the last evening of the play. Chandrashekhar is distracted. He'd like to say to her, "You must act well!" But even that might upset her. He'd said to her once, "You must rest a little. You need to, badly." She'd said, "Resting frightens me."

He avoids her intentionally. Glances surreptitiously at her as he passes by. She is more serene today than usual. Her body isn't withdrawn and tense. She's quietly having her makeup done. She smiles delicately at Chandrashekhar. There is reassurance in her smile. A confidence. His tension lessens. He tells himself, "There's no need to worry."

The evening darkens, and with it the play. She drinks her porter.

"Who is that? The girl who's playing Elizabeth?"

"I haven't a clue? But she's wonderful!"

Her entire body shudders with a sob.

"Beautiful. Truly beautiful!"

"What a presence she has!"

She meets Browning. He comes close to her. Holds her hand.

"She's frigid, cold, isn't she?"

"That's not surprising. But she seems to be in an awful hurry to get it over with."

"Poor Browning looks quite confused by the way she's going on. She isn't giving him an inch."

Browning is really quite unsure. Totally bewildered. She continues to act. There's no faulting her there. She speaks her lines with great sincerity. And yet he doesn't find Elizabeth in her. She is somebody else twisted with agony, yearning. Somebody quite different. Shrinivas falters, gropes repeatedly while she forges deftly ahead, speaking with mechanical ease.

The play ends. But she doesn't immediately realize that the play has ended. That the suffocating responsibility is over. She collapses like a stretched thing snapped. There's a crowd milling around. Human voices coming and going. The dragging of shoes and sandals. The smell of cloth and greasepaint mixed with the bittersweet smell of tea.

She's afraid she's going to throw up. She waits, numbly. For nothing in particular.

Chandrashekhar comes up to her.

"Have your tea and I'll take you home straightaway."

She has her tea. But her stomach heaves. She follows Chandrashekhar, trying to steady herself.

"You'll feel better after you've rested," Chandrashekhar tells her softly as they get out of the taxi before her house.

Then he goes away.

13

But, on his way home after leaving her, Chandrashekhar cannot decide at all how the play has gone.

She did act. She acted well. And yet, something was lacking. Always had been lacking.

He arrives home later, weakened in spirit. Shrinivas is waiting for him. Their eyes meet. Both detach their eyes from the other's.

"The play was good!" Chandrashekhar leans back in his chair, eyes closed.

"Maybe it was. But she forced me to grope right till the end. I was stumbling, faltering all the time, trying to reach her. But there was no telling from one moment to the next where she would be, how she would proceed. She was the limit today. The lines came from habit. Otherwise she remained untouched. I'm never going to act with her again. It's such a strain."

"She's never going to act again either."

Chandrashekhar is desolate. He had desired her closeness. Her strangeness had attracted him. Their days together had been ones of futile intoxication.

Shrinivas is aware of this. These things happen. It'll pass. But he doesn't say anything.

They sit together in silence for a long time. They are aware of each other's presence. And yet they have forgotten each other. It is daybreak. Chandrashekhar's wife comes in with tea.

Chandrashekhar starts violently. He feels guilty. It's as if he had forgotten. He smiles at her, abashed.

But she looks at Chandrashekhar with pride. Worries about his health. Complains about him to Shrinivas. And blooms with joy. She snuggles up to Chandrashekhar as they have tea. And Chandrashekhar tries to snuggle even closer to her.

14

She enters her room. She wanders all over the house as if she's looking for something. The greasepaint is still on. It is there, loud and screaming. Stretching, burning her skin. Her clothes still carry the smell of the play.

She lies down on the bed as she is. Presses her feet against the iron foot rails to get her sandals off. She kicks them off. The breeze caresses her bare soles.

The whole play is finished. All the acting is over. But how it hurts. It's not so much the pain of being reminded. It's the darkening of the ego. Even forgetting is no longer such a great thing.

She gets up hastily. She gathers up the script and everything to do with the play, and flings it onto the loft—into the farthest corner. The work leaves her breathless.

It's well out of sight now. But her restlessness has not diminished. Her head is throbbing. Her eyes don't close. They refuse to close.

It is daybreak. The milkman calls and delivers the milk.

She opens her science textbook. Her tired, wearied, red-rimmed eyes lock onto a figure. This is force—this is the fulcrum. Figure 2 appears on the page. Today she must finish off the second and third types of lever.

She has said, "Close sesame," and the cave has closed.

Her eyes are burning. But she straightens her back, blinks and continues to draw the figure.

And, as usual, she goes to school.

Her eyes are very tired. So is her body. But it has been swallowed up by her emotions. Her restless wanderings have made her lose her sense of exhaustion. She is feeling stimulated, excited without reason.

She comes into the teachers' room.

"How was the play yesterday?"

"I didn't like her performance. But there's a lot of talk—she and Chandrashekhar—there could be some truth. He never missed dropping her home it seems."

Mr. Bhosale always avoids mentioning her name when he speaks of her. He is not prepared for her to come in so suddenly.

But she has overheard. The words have meant nothing to her.

"Oh! So you're here today?"

And all the teachers crowd around her. Words of congratulation are dancing around.

Never before have these people gathered around her like this unless they've wanted something from her. Why then this familiarity today? Mrs. Palsule, however, is aloof. She is smiling, but why doesn't she come nearer? It would be nice to hear her warm chatter. Urmila misses hearing it.

And Mrs. Palsule is thinking—She is now a celebrity. I am a nonentity. But she shouldn't have acted that way. The thought scares her. She erases it from her mind. But Nirmala is sharper. She blurts out, "She's a celebrity. She won't bother with us now."

She senses this. She merely narrows her eyes and glances at Nirmala, but doesn't go near her.

She enters the eleventh standard classroom for the science lesson.

"Hey, our teacher acted beautifully in the play!"

"I loved it too."

"Didn't she look lovely?"

Shalini is sitting silently in her corner. Suddenly she says, "But she shouldn't have acted that way." She cannot hold back her tears. She cries luxuriously, with abandon, and all the girls stare at her astonished and fearful. Why should she cry like that?

Urmila ignores Shalini's crying. She begins the lesson abruptly. "The second type of lever. . . . "

She teaches with her usual intensity. That's how she wishes it to be. The girls are very quiet. Bewildered. As though they are not sure what to make of this racing ahead of hers, unchecked.

Shalini is sitting with head bowed. And Urmila is teaching. Exactly as she does every day, though perhaps with even more passion. But ignoring Shalini.

Translated by Shanta Gokhale.

TRIVENI _____

(Anasuya Shankar, 1928–1963)   *Kannada*

Triveni published her first novel in 1953. Though her literary life lasted only a decade, she went on to produce twenty novels and three collections of short stories. Her work, which was in its day regarded as fiercely feminist, instantly became popular. It has been translated into several Indian languages and retains, to this day, a wide circle of readers. Triveni studied psychology at college in Bangalore, and this interest is evident in all her writings.

The central forces of Triveni's novels are women. She explores, with considerable insight, the psychological problems faced by middle-class women at different stages in life, and is particularly interested in societies in which women's social status, their educational backgrounds, and their professional involvements are rapidly changing. Triveni sets the individual against a background of the social forces that determine her experience and investigates the origins, especially within the structure of the family, of women's tensions and behavior.

She writes about the emotional cruelty women experience in marriage, their longing for affection, and their frustrations. Her stories shine a new light on corners of women's lives that have, for centuries perhaps, remained in the dark. In *Sharapanjara* (Cage of Arrows), 1965, her much-discussed last novel (published posthumously), the protagonist has a breakdown, is hospitalized, makes a recovery, but suffers a relapse once she returns home. Though what strikes one about Triveni's writing is its realistic portrayal of the psychology of the middle-class family, she seems in her novels to be making a plea not so much for a radical change in the social structure as for a scientific attitude towards mental illness. She advocates psychoanalysis and medical intervention and suggests that the family and society should help those who have broken down to regain normalcy. Among her better-known novels are *Modala Hejje* (The First Step), 1956; *Sotu Geddavalu* (She Who Was Defeated, But Won), 1956; *Kilugombe* (The Mechanical Doll), 1958; *Durada Betta* (The Distant Hill), 1962; and *Bekkina Kannu* (The Cat's Eye), 1964.

"Though Triveni's attitude towards women's liberation is debatable today," the critic Vijaya Dabbe writes, "in her day, because of its bias in favor of women, her writings were considered full of hatred towards men." The story translated here, for instance, was considered radical and feminist. It was included in *Samasyeya Magu,* 1968.

◆

KONEYA NIRDHARA
(The Final Decision)

The movement of the needle and the fingers kept pace with one another. The long green silk thread slowly arranged itself into a pattern of green leaves on the cloth. The penciled outlines of a few more leaves, drab like an actress without makeup, awaited their turn.

The evening had begun to cast long shadows in the room, drawing a hazy curtain over the surroundings. Eyes blurred with tears.

The once-active fingers were now slow with age. The speed and skill demanded by embroidery were gone. The slim and agile body of a dancer defeated by obesity.

"I can always finish it tomorrow." I laid the embroidery aside and turned on the light.

There was no need to cook again. Not twice a day just for myself.

I put the lessons out to be prepared for tomorrow's classes.

Then came a soft knocking on the door. Who could it be? At this hour?

I glanced up at the clock. It was already half past seven.

The knocking again.

I responded a little sharply, "Who is it?"

"It's me." The voice was gentle.

I opened the door expecting to see the father or brother of one of my students, wanting to enquire about her progress.

A man who seemed to be around fifty stood outside, holding a hat in his left hand. The darkness hid his face.

Opening the door wide, I asked him to come in.

His gait—it seemed to touch an old wound in me.

A familiar gait. Someone used to walk just like this. Who could this be?

He sat down facing the light, and turned toward me.

My heart stopped beating for a moment. The blood ran cold in my veins; dizziness overcame me. Sinking into a chair, I ran my tongue over my lips.

The pictures on the wall and the furniture whirled round madly and came to a sudden halt.

For a second I felt like a coward stepping on a snake in the dark. The next instant I was the snake charmer in full control of the reptile.

I joined my palms in greeting.

Slightly startled, he returned the *namaste*.

"Hmm . . . have I seen you before . . . ?"

He raised his bowed head and asked in surprise, "Don't you recognize, me, Lalitha?"

"I beg your pardon. The name is Lalitha Devi."

My words and tone were intended to convey resentment at his familiarity.

His surprise increased.

"It's me, Lalitha, Venkatesh Murthy . . . Venkatesh"—he stammered.

"Now I know your name. Is your daughter in our school? What's her name? Which class is she in?"

In a stunned voice, he said, "Yes, my Vanaja studies at the high school. But I have come because . . ."

"Look here, Mr. Venkatesh Murthy, is it right on your part to come and plead that your daughter get higher marks? Her paper has been evaluated according to her performance in . . ."

"Lalitha!"

"Everyone calls me Lalitha Devi. I suggest that you do the same."

As soon as he realized that I was deliberately provoking him, he began to shout, pounding the table.

"Enough of this, Lalitha!"

Earlier—a long time ago—I would have quailed under his anger. But now?

I was surprised at myself, surprised at my hard-as-iron heart. My body trembled with emotion, but my mind was firm.

In a voice as musical as a note from the *veena,* I cautioned, "The table is old and rickety."

He got up and began to pace up and down in agitation. "Lalitha, I have forgiven you. Why don't you come back to me?"

There was a time when I had been eager to hear words like these.

Acting on a baseless suspicion, he had doubted my virtue and decided to live alone. If this speech had come in the early days of our estrangement, I would have raised the man onto a pedestal. Such consolations would once have warmed my heart, turned me into a *koel* singing in spring time. I had once dreamed of such bliss. But hope and desire had evaporated in the agonizing wait. All that remained was an empty vessel.

All tenderness had burned away, leaving only ash behind.

Exaggerating the bitter twist my lips had acquired, and raising my left eyebrow, I spoke sarcastically, "Forgiven me? I have done no wrong! And neither do I need your pardon."

"Can't you forget the past, Lalitha?" he asked helplessly.

"I *have* forgotten the past—including my marriage."

"You must remember that I, too, was young then. I decided to leave you when I heard those rumors. But now I'm more mature, Lalitha."

"By my youth's vanished forever. It can't survive the heat of family life any longer. Besides, how is it that you've come to believe in my innocence?"

"I realized—that I had acted on mere rumor . . ."

Again I said sarcastically, "Yes, it's true that you trusted others, and not my word."

"I was a mere youth then, and you were beautiful. When I heard others throw dirt on your character I was ready to believe them, but now I realize how foolish I was."

"Neither of us is beautiful or young any longer. But while age has corroded my beauty, it's improved my mind."

"Can't you forgive my lapses, Lalitha? Will you never live with me again?"

"Set up house—at this age? I'm an old woman now—past forty," I laughed.

"So what? How does that prevent you from coming to live with me?"

The dormant volcano came to life, spewing forth a stream of lava.

"If you'd uttered these words twenty years ago, things would have been different. I still longed for my husband, my home, my family. But the wait has deadened those longings."

"Please think it over before you say anything, Lalitha," he said gently.

My mind whirled back twenty years.

I had just been married. Life always seemed new, fresh and full. Little did I know then that green fields shelter venomous creatures. It didn't take even a year for a drop of doubt to curdle the atmosphere at home.

He did not have the patience to sift through the facts. Besides, I have a lot of self-respect. Why should I even have to make a case for my innocence? I faced the storm brewing in our home.

"I'll stay if you'll believe me."

He had no faith in me. And he was supported by his sister and his parents.

As a result, I had returned to my mother's home.

My husband married again.

Everywhere I went I heard whispers and saw sly smiles and questioning looks. Sarcasm and stinging laughter were wafted to me on the breeze, but I did not lose heart.

I resumed the studies disrupted by marriage.

It helped me create a life of my own.

The small flicker of hope I had nourished within me died out when he married again. I hardened my mind, and learned to live without him.

I learned how to face the insinuating phrases and the crooked smiles.

My attempt did not fail.

Now at this time in my life, after so many years, this man had the temerity to ask me to live with him again. My first reaction had been anger.

"Don't be hasty." His words made me think more calmly.

In a way, what he said was right. Wouldn't a solitary existence be much more painful in old age?

It seemed futile to chase the mirage of married life, yet I could not help but contemplate the mirage with longing.

But something held me back.

The thin cord of the mangalsutra hanging around my neck appeared to have a strength of its own.

I had been victorious in the battle to bring my mind and body under control, but in the process my hair had grown gray. The lines on my face had made me an old woman at forty-two.

Noticing that I was silent, he came forward.

"What do you think, Lalitha?" Again, the tone was ever so gentle. He sensed the softening in my attitude.

Perhaps I should forgive and forget all that happened in our youth. Perhaps I should be happy that he's prepared to admit his mistake and make remedies, that he believes me innocent . . .

"I'd like to come with you. But . . ."

"But what?" he asked anxiously.

"What will your second wife say? Will she agree to the arrangement?"

There was a look of triumph on his face. "Oh, it looks as though you don't know what happened. Actually, she died two months ago, leaving the five children behind. You needn't worry. Nobody will object to your coming."

I blanched, and sat down suddenly.

"What happened, Lalitha?" he asked with concern, coming closer.

So this man had not come to me wishing to make amends for his mistake! There was neither pity nor love in his request.

Of course, he couldn't remarry at his age! All he needed was a woman to run the house. A woman to mother the orphaned children, a woman to be his wife.

He was ready to establish a family again—but had his own reasons for it. Reasons involving himself, his children, his family. It was not a question of my happiness and peace of mind at all.

I stood up and said in rage, "It's getting late. You'd better leave. People might mistake your being here."

His face crumpled.

"You really are a mystery."

"But you don't have to solve it. Please go." I pointed toward the door.

He was like a hunter deprived of his catch, surprised, angry, regretful. "But you had just agreed to come with me . . . ," he began.

"I can neither believe nor respect you. The little respect I had for you has just evaporated. How can you expect me to live with somebody I don't even care for? Besides, I have grown accustomed to my kind of life."

"Lalitha . . ."

"If you don't leave at once, I'll have to call the neighbors."

The determination in my voice did not fail to reach him. Having no other option, he moved toward the door.

"Think about it," he urged.

I slammed the door behind him.

The sound of his footsteps slowly faded away.

Translated by Seemanthini Niranjana and Tejaswini Niranjana.

SULEKHA SANYAL ━━━━━━━━━━━━━━━

(1928–1962)   *Bengali*

The appearance of this talented, feminist writer on the Bengali literary scene, and her sudden death at an early age, went largely unnoticed. Even now, most Bengali readers are unacquainted with the work of Sulekha Sanyal, and her novels are difficult to find. Yet in each of her remarkable books, one is brought face to face with the torment of human beings living through one of the most difficult phases of Bengal's history—the famine of the forties, the partition at Independence, and the consequent disintegration of the society they were familiar with. This is the world Sulekha Sanyal's women live and fight in.

Sulekha Sanyal was born in Korkandi, a village now in Bangladesh, into a decaying zamindari family. Before going to school she was taught by her father and uncle. A childless aunt then took Sulekha to live with her in Chittagong and sent her to school there. Her first writing appeared in the children's section of the newspaper *Yugantar*. In 1942, when Chittagong was bombed, she returned to Korkandi and completed high school there. Later she went to Calcutta, where she graduated from Scottish Church College.

An important intellectual influence on young Sulekha was that of the philosopher Ramtanu Lahiri, who belonged to her mother's family and whose agnostic humanism she eagerly absorbed. But there were other factors that would mold her life. Korkandi was a hideout for revolutionaries and terrorists of the pre-Independence period, and from an early age Sulekha must have been familiar with political activity and brutal police violence. As a young girl she was introduced by her brother and his friends to socialism, and in 1948 and 1949 she actively participated in the political movements in Bengal, even experiencing imprisonment for a time. Her marriage, begun in 1948, ended in divorce in 1956.

Sulekha Sanyal's first story, "Pankatilak" (Marked with Slime), was published in the journal *Arani* in 1944. Her political awareness and revolutionary commitments are evident in all her writings during this period. In 1947, at the time of the partition, she left what would become East Pakistan and came to India. Like the millions of refugees who arrived at that time, she, too, struggled to survive, but as is evident from her published work, she never gave up writing. For some time, she worked as a teacher. In 1957 she was afflicted with leukemia, and although treatment in Moscow was advised, the government of India initially refused to issue her a passport. Some time later she was able to go to Moscow where she underwent medical treatment, returning to India in 1959.

Although she knew that her life was nearing its end, Sulekha Sanyal never lost her passion for it. She continued with her education, receiving a degree in Bengali literature from Burdwan University, and she kept writing until her death in December 1962. After returning from Moscow she deliberately had avoided literary circles in Calcutta, so her passing away went unnoticed and unsung. Among her major published works are the novel *Nabankur,* 1956; *Sindure Megh* (Red Clouds), a collection of short stories written between 1957 and 1961; and *Dewal Padma* (Wall Flower), a novel published posthumously in 1964.

◆

From NABANKUR
(The Germinating Seed)
Chapter 4

On the veranda beside the pantry, Purnasashi is busy feeding the menfolk—Poltoo and Pradip—just back from school, and their fathers, Shukhada and Kulada. Shukhada's two younger boys are there too. There's *murki* and *kheer** today. She doles out handfuls of murki from a big basket into each one's bowl, and tops it with a ladle of kheer.

---

*Murki is sweet puffed rice. *Kheer,* milk and rice cooked together until the milk is thick, is flavored with cardamom and laced with almonds. It is a favorite dessert in Bengal.

Chobi's eyes glisten. She hadn't had any lunch that afternoon. In fact, she'd forgotten all about it. Now, at the sight of kheer and murki, she suddenly feels very hungry. Flinging her books and writing slate to a corner by the door, she gets a bowl for herself and flops down beside them. "Me too, Grandma."

Purnasashi fills Chobi's bowl too, with murki first and then kheer. Poltoo and Pradip hold their bowls out for second helpings. Some more murki, a little more kheer.

Chobi, too, holds out her bowl. "You're giving the others more—give me some more too, Grandma. I'm still hungry."

"There's no more. Look." Purnasashi holds out the empty bowl for her to inspect.

All of a sudden, Chobi's head burns with rage, and she screams sharp and shrill, "You gave everyone two helpings, and me just one, and so little too. When Pholtuda or Monida ask for more, you never say it's gone!"

"Well I never!" Purnasashi is struck dumb for a second, and then she lets off, "Teach her to read and write, and look what happens next! The girl imagines she's as good as these darling boys of mine! Ridiculous! Will you be earning like the boys? All you'll ever be is a shackle on your father's neck. Yes, those days are coming, and pretty soon, when we won't be able to get food down his throat for worrying over how to get you married off . . ." Purnasashi leaves her words hanging in the air, brings some more kheer from the pantry, and pours it into Chobi's bowl.

During her wait, the kheer has dried on her fingers. Just as her grandmother serves that extra bit, the girl goes berserk. "I don't want it!" she yells, and flings the bowl into the courtyard.

How shocking! Purnasashi has never been so shocked in her life. The boys, too, have stopped eating, and are gaping at Chobi in stunned silence.

"Not a girl, no, she's poison ivy!" screams Purnasashi. "At work—bone lazy; eats like crazy; fiery speeches come so easy."

All this shouting has brought people out from all around, but Chobi hasn't even noticed who they are. It is only when her mother comes and pulls her up by the hair and gives her a few hard knocks on her back that Chobi realizes she has done something awful.

Mother says, "You don't have to eat, you greedy girl. You couldn't come for lunch—why the hell did you have to come now?"

Mother's voice is heavy, and her words sound shaky. She tells her mother-in-law in a low tone, "You should have thrown her out by the neck. If you had to feed her, what was the need for so much talk? How would a little girl know the difference between boys and girls?"

Chobi forgets about her aching back the moment she realizes her mother has seen and heard it all. Her backache seems to have instantly disappeared.

Purnasashi looks even more amazed than before, and speaks as if she cannot believe her own ears. "Dear! What did I say to your daughter, that you've come armed for battle? If I've given any offense, do forgive me, Daughter-in-law . . ." Grandma actually joins her palms, begging mock forgiveness. Chobi bows her head and grins to herself in delight.

In the middle of this argument both Father and Uncle have arrived to find out what the commotion is all about. Now Mamata looks embarrassed, pulls her sari over her head, and moves away.

Sukhada has found out from someone what happened. He draws Chobi to him and says, "Come, Chobu. We'll polish off all the kheer Grandma has in the pantry. Won't give, what does she mean?"

Chobi has no time to decide whether the idea is good or bad. Mamata comes forward suddenly, pulls Chobi back by the hand and stands guarding the door. Her voice is serious, though soft. She says, "No, Brother-in-law. Don't distract her so. Let her understand."

Sukhada looks once at his sister-in-law's covered face. His hand loosens, as if on its own, and he lets go. Still he tries to laugh it off. "Why carry on so, Sister—she's just a child, after all! She's asked for something—give her a little—she'll be happy, instead . . ."

"A child!" Mamata sounds angry. "Child she may be, but she's a girl child! She can't understand the difference that makes, like other girls do—that's my problem!"

Through all this, Kulada has not spoken a word. He's been sitting on the cement platform sipping tea. Now he looks around and yells, "And why is this fellow sitting here whimpering, eh? Did you get a few thumps on the back too?"

Chobi forgets everything and looks his way. Pradip is crying! She goes over to him and sees that his bowl is still full. The kheer looks dry and sticky. He's weeping with his head between his knees.

Chobi shakes him with both hands, saying, "Hey, Dada, hey. It's me Mother beat, so why are you crying? D'you know, a whole handful of my hair came out in her hand!"

Pradip says, his voice choking with tears, "They keep scolding you all the time. Mother beats you at the slightest . . . You don't think that hurts me? Why did you have to go and fling the bowl that way? You wouldn't have been beaten otherwise."

Chobi kneels down beside him, and dries his eyes with a corner of her frock. Her expression is serious as she says, "Grandma said all that—or I wouldn't have thrown the bowl, would I? But I didn't cry, not even when I got beaten. Why should you cry, then? Look, Pholtuda, Montu, they're all laughing. Uncle, Father, all of them. Now come, Dada!"

Mamata is sitting quietly in the kitchen. She notices them from there, brother and sister together. She sees the girl looking happy again. Who would say to look at her that only a moment ago, on an empty stomach, she had been scolded and beaten? The last rays of the sun are on her face and hair, bathing her in light. At the sight of the child, Mamata's heart aches with an inutterable pain. She dries a tear from the corner of her eye and gets back to work in silence.

It is very late at night. How late, Chobi can't say. Usually at this time of night if she awakes suddenly, all she hears are the dogs barking in the distance, the lantern in the corner flickering, and the sounds of people breathing. Then Chobi's heart goes cold with fear. Her limbs are frightened, stiff. She doesn't dare open her eyes. Rolling over closer to her mother, Chobi places the big hand on her own body, and puts her own fingers in her ears to stop those breathing sounds.

Tonight, too, she wakes up around the same time. She must have moved a little to get closer to her mother, for suddenly someone beside her whispers out her name, "Chobu."

Mother! Mother is calling her! She doesn't have to feel afraid tonight. She can dare open her eyes. A bit of lantern light has fallen aslant on Mother's face. She forces her eyes open and sees her mother's eyes on her. The breathing sound no longer floats around the room— it whispers to her, "Chobu, darling! You're my one and only daughter, still they won't let me love you even a little . . ."

Chobi, half asleep, feels her mother stroking her back, her cheeks, her hair.

Chobi never feels any sense of hurt, never takes offense. If she feels pain, that sensation, too, never stays for long. With Mamata caressing her this way, she feels sleepy again. The sleep that was broken resettles firmly on her eyes. She clings hard to her mother, puts one leg around her with ease, and with a deep sigh drifts back to sleep. Deep within her consciousness, in that serene posture, one thought floats still—

"Mother, my mother!"—those words seem to bring her complete peace.

But sleep will not come so easily to Mamata's eyes.

Chapter 29

In the kitchen, Mamata has received news of Kulada's arrival, but she doesn't come out. She continues cooking, but is distracted from time to time—What will be will be. She won't think of it any more. She simply can't think any more . . .

Saraswati says, "What will happen, Didi?"

"Has the girl gone off, just check will you?"

She comes back and says, "No, not yet! Shall I fetch her?"

Mamata looks compassionately at the worried face of the pregnant Saraswati. She worries herself sick over Chobi all the time, though she nods in agreement with the rest of them. What a stubborn girl, really— what will become of her?

But Mamata knows that she doesn't speak from her heart. Secretly, Chobi is the one Saraswati loves most, the one she looks at with admiring eyes, the way a proud mother looks at her handsome, healthy son.

To Saraswati this household is like a house of horrors. Every year, year after year, she keeps bearing children, but she hasn't the courage to express the disgust she feels.

Seeing Saraswati's frightened, helpless face, Mamata attempts a smile and says, "Why should you feel so scared? That girl needs a bit of straightening out—she's going too far." But having said that, Mamata still cannot feel easy in her mind. A shadow descends on her face too, and she gives a deep sigh, saying, "I can't bear this any more, Saraswati! I lost two girls at birth, you know. When Pradip was born after that, I felt no joy—I was still mourning for those lost baby girls. Then God gave me a girl at last! And she's nothing but trouble . . . I've thought so many times, let me die and be delivered of this pain!"

Saraswati, shocked and startled, gets up and holds Mamata in her arms. "For shame! How can you even think such things? Are you really so worried? Our child may be a flibbertigibbet, but she's sure to settle down when the business of marriage comes up!"

What can Mamata say? How can she explain to anyone why she is so restless, so disturbed? Mother that she is, she has read on the quiet those letters Tamal wrote to Chobi. She had gone running to Adhir that afternoon. She was really livid, had flung insults right and left—

at their ideology, their ethics, their rules of conduct. She had wept in the end, held Adhir responsible for everything. "You are the reason the boy has left home! And now you've set the girl, too, on the path to ruin. Not only have you brought her out of the house, you're teaching her how to break a home up!"

He listened to her accusations, smiled at her anger, this man who was on his deathbed. He said, "There's a lot you have seen, Sister-in-law. All your life you've seen just one law prevail. Why not let them proclaim a new law now? It is not your happiness, nor society's, but their own that is at stake."

"Even if I personally were to ignore the business of caste say, for the sake of the girl's happiness, why would everyone else accept it? Breaking an age-old tradition like that—and you say it means nothing?"

Adhir had said, "You're the limit, Sis! Is that any kind of a problem at all? People have enough real problems as it is! Holding out against sorrow and pain, for instance, and so many other real questions of life and death? Caste! Is that a serious issue? Well yes, if you choose to go by it! Don't worry so much, I tell you."

"But her father has arranged a match for her—don't you see? We don't want to make her unhappy. Her studies won't be disturbed—why don't you put some sense into her, please, Adhir?"

Adhir had refused to do so. "You cannot force her to do anything, Sister. You've managed to throttle your own faculties completely—must you do that to Chobi too? And besides, if she has any strength of mind, she will choose her own course of action herself."

An anxious Mamata had stayed up deep into the night, studying Chobi's sleeping face, dreading the worst. Do you have to be so very disobedient, Chobi? Chobi . . . will you break my heart . . . and tears had come to her sleepless eyes.

She knows only too well what makes her so fearful, but Saraswati wouldn't understand. Not a single member of the family would, for that matter.

Saraswati, in the meanwhile, had gone and fetched Chobi. "Did you want me, Mother?" the girl asks.

Mamata draws her close, lovingly pushes back some wisps of hair from her face, looking at her all the while with pleading eyes. "Just one request I have—will you fulfill it, darling, please? Don't cause me any more grief, I beg you. I can't bear it any more!"

Chobi's lips quiver. She too has heard the news. And every now and then she feels a cold shiver in her heart. She has kept Tamal's last letter close to her breast.

Mamata says, "He's a fine boy, well-educated, generous, has a fine job too. There's a college over there too, and they've said they'll have you admitted after you've passed . . . they . . ."

Chobi laughs suddenly, "Why all this sales talk? Why don't you come straight to the point, Mother?"

"You don't have to do a thing. They're not so provincial that they'll ask you a lot of questions. You just have to put in one appearance before the boy's father."

"And then?"

"Your father's seen the boy—he's as handsome as a prince. Well-off too. You'll be living in much ease after you get married. He's their only son, after all."

Chobi touches Tamal's letter once, tucked in her breast. He's no handsome prince—he's dark. He doesn't have an excellent job, merely tutors boys in various private homes. He's poor, that's why the rich take advantage of him. But still he's Tamal! Can Chobi forget his pleasant laughter! The promise she had made him—to wait for him, to bear it all! That was hardly a month ago!

No, Mamata's tears have a way of putting Chobi into total confusion. She stares hard at the ground to steel herself, and then says, "See how late it is already? I must rush to the workshop now! The things you people are up to, honestly!" She laughs it all off lightly and makes her way outside.

"Chobi!" Kulada calls out to her.

"Wait!" says Dakshina. Purnasashi is there too, standing behind the two of them.

Chobi looks inquiringly at her father. Kulada says, very gently, "All the preliminary discussions are over. They just need to take one look at you."

"That's not possible for me, Father."

"What's that again?" Dakshina comes forward, raging. He looks towards his son and mutters, "Did you hear that, Kulada? 'I cannot do it, Father.' " He grimaces, mimics Chobi. "Isn't that a wonderful thing to hear, from your own daughter! Brought her up like a memsahib, didn't you! So now you see! You are a stain on the family name!"

"Father!" Kulada squawks in agonized protest at this last insult. His face is red with anger. He now drags Chobi forward by the hand. Chobi looks at him once, surprised, and lowers her eyes again. Her hand inside her father's grip shakes a little. Is that his hand quivering, or her own?

Dakshina has cooled down somewhat. His tone is stern and steady. "Put her under lock and key, if you know what's good for her. What absolute impudence! Won't go, she says!"

Purnasashi comes close•to her now, strokes her lovingly and says, "Now don't be disobedient, sweet! Do what they say. They're doing this for your own good. You might study and do whatever else . . . but for a girl, what else is there but marriage, after all?"

Kulada says, "You've brought enough shame on us already. The things they say about you in the village! I have problems and worries enough as it is—enough to make me go rabid. Don't you dare defy me on top of it all—I won't have it. Will you or will you not go?"

"No." One word, and the girl falls silent again.

Kulada now sees red. Dakshina stands beside him with a sneering smile. Kulada drags Chobi along by the hand to the dark corner room beside Sukhada's. He pushes her in and slams the door shut. No one in the house has the courage to stop him. Purnasashi alone gives a small plaintive cry, "What do you think you're doing, Kulada! That's going to make her even more stubborn. Speak to her nicely, explain to her . . ."

A few of them have crowded in towards the door. Dakshina sternly clears them away. Kulada's high-pitched voice sounds more like a scream of distress. "Don't any of you say a thing to me. I'll show her today. I won't be called a black sheep of the family and take it lying down."

There in the dark room, sitting on a broken rack, Chobi waits and smiles a little to herself. This is the family storeroom. Damp and dismal, nearly pitch dark. Just one thin stream of light comes from a small, high window. Chobi brings the letter out, and reads it once again in that strip of light. She murmurs softly once, "Tamal!" Then she spreads out the loose end of her sari and lies down quietly on it.

So time passes, who knows how long? Chobi has fallen asleep. All of a sudden something small scurries over her—possibly a mouse—and she sits up with a jerk. She remembers about the workshop. Not turning up would upset their schedule, and she doesn't like that, either. They had schemed against her and stopped her from going today. So let them! But this is perhaps the very last time that anyone would be locked up in this house—let no one else suffer such a fate. No one would, certainly—Chobi knows that. At least that is some consolation.

A soft sound comes from the door bolt. Somebody seems to have opened it and come inside, to have lain a hand on her forehead, to be calling her by name.

Chobi clings to her mother silently. Mamata is crying, her tears falling on Chobi's head. "Look what you've gone and done, Chobi! Oh I can't bear it any more! Just one small appearance please. Or God knows what your father will do next!"

Still not a word from Chobi. "Chobi!" Mamata calls her again as of old.

Chobi looks her mother full in the face and says, "Maybe I would have gone earlier, Mother. But you should know, I've made up my mind now. Now it's just too late . . ."

Mamata starts up almost as if she's seen a ghost. Her voice, though suppressed, conveys a deep terror. "Too late? You've made up your mind? Dear God, why am I still not dead!"

Chobi says, "When I was a child, you yourself gave me so much encouragement to study, to be brave. Can't you think of some really great future for me—other than marriage?"

"You'll be married one day, live in peace and happiness—what greater future can a mother wish for her daughter?"

"Can you force that kind of peace and happiness on me? Think of something really great, Mother. Think that maybe your Chobi will lay down her life one day for a noble cause."

"Don't even utter such things, Chobi," Mamata calls out in anguish. She sighs deeply and says, "Well, do as you please. I won't worry anymore." And she leaves the room as silently as she had come.

Having sat up, she keeps sitting. Purnasashi had come in at one point, begging her to come and eat. She hadn't gone, but continued to sit there, picking up the footsteps of all the different people in her family.

The day passes; it's almost evening now. Some people had approached the door once or twice earlier, the bolt had been rattled a couple of times, and they'd gone away.

A sudden burst of light in the room makes Chobi sit up straight. The light hurts her eyes after so long.

Grandfather has come, and Father, and Grandma. But Uncle is missing. Must have kept away on purpose.

Kulada has found himself a thin, sharp cane somewhere. He says in a grave voice, "Go eat and get ready. No dressing up—just change your sari."

Purnasashi looks into her face, a mute appeal in her eyes. Dakshinaranjan says, "Go, do what you're told."

Chobi flares up this time. "I won't go. What can you do about it?"

"What did you say?" Dakshina is now shaking with rage. "Of course, why should you go? Mix around some more with low-class riffraff—those farmers and fishermen and potters of yours! Go, check it out, Kulada, maybe your daughter wishes to marry one of them! Go and bring him along! We're ruined, ruined. Scarred and smirched the family name, that's what you have done."

Kulada steps forward and grabs Chobi by the hair. "So you won't go, eh?"

"No, no."

There's a lashing, swishing sound in the air. Sukhada's youngest boy starts howling and runs away. Yet another lash. Kulada yells out an order.

"Go and dress Sefu up instead! I'm not letting go of such a good match. Whatever money they're demanding, I'll spend for Sefu."

Then he lets go of Chobi's hair and gives her a hard push forward. "Get out, get out of this house. I can't show my face in the village for shame—all because of you!"

Purnasashi has withdrawn from the scene, wiping tears away with the end of her sari. But Saraswati clings to Mamata and weeps, "No sister, I can't allow this. Chobi will get a thrashing, and they will come and look at Sefu instead. I can't bear it!"

So Mamata has the job of consoling her too, making her understand.

All through this Chobi sits stubbornly like a headstrong horse. Shame, insult, nothing, nothing seems to affect her now. Her face is wreathed in silent laughter, and there's a smarting sensation where the cane has left its mark on her arm.

One by one, they have all gone their ways. Dakshina had stood waiting to lead Sefu out himself, and Mamata had dressed Sefu up. But Sefu stands stock still as she hears Chobi, and breaks down, her whole body heaving as she weeps. You can tell by her face that she has no desire to go, but she cannot refuse. Mamata says, "Come dry your eyes now, Sefu. You're not going to start weeping in front of them too, are you? Shame on you!"

Chapter 31

That autumn there was no crop to be harvested. The farming folk sat on the workshop porch watching with wet eyes, stared hard and long at the barren fields ahead of them. Now, eyes dried, they were ready for work again.

The workshop had been served a closure notice. Chobi was sitting there with the letter still in her hand. The men had heard the news already and had just smiled wanly in despair. They, too, wish to stand up on their own again. They want an end to the shame of being on charity. They have seen the rice stored in the godowns, thousands and thousands of maunds of it—and watched it with starving stomachs—but they had not looted the grain, hadn't wrested their due.

They know the humiliation of accepting this charity, this food they despise. But at least it has kept body and soul together. They had dried their eyes and swallowed the millet gruel, hoping for better days to come. Hoping that they would laugh again one day, would plow the fields, would stand together and fight. Hamid and Nagarbanshi say as much. "That is why we didn't quit the village. Our wives and children have shriveled up in hunger, and we still haven't given up trying to make a living. We've stretched out our palms and accepted the relief. This is the day we waited for. We were sure we would find a way."

Better if this arrangement had been continued longer, but the government had notified them that there would be no more relief. The Farmers' Society had put forward demands and got its way, but it was not prepared to make pleas and appeals.

They are busy with their various duties now. Chobi alone sits with a heavy heart from the morning, the only one silent amid all the din.

Dhiren walks in very softly and stands before her. His face fills her heart with some unknown dread. "What's happened Uncle Dhiren? What other news have you received?"

Dhiren turns his face away and says with a quavering voice, "We couldn't keep Adhirda back any longer, Chobi. Go see him for the last time."

"What?" Chobi shouts like a banshee. "But I went and saw him just a day ago. He chatted with me for so long. Tamal was to fix up the sanatorium, write back . . . Uncle Dhiren . . ."

"Tamal's letter has arrived, Chobi. He says if we arrange to send him to Calcutta somehow, they'll take care of all the rest . . . but this disease . . . Chobi please don't cry . . ."

Chobi says, "Lately I was not even able to give him much time—I knew you people were there to look after him. Day before yesterday . . . we talked for so long . . . my studies . . . the future, but what happened so suddenly?"

Chobi runs homewards, her eyes welling with tears. When her grandfather died, she had run back sorrowing—today it is more like terror she feels.

"Uncle, Adhir Uncle!" All the respect, the wonder, the courage Chobi ever held in her life is dying today! A fire is dying, a precious life is on its way out!

The room so quiet on other days is now filled with people. Kulada has come, Sukhada too, all her family is here. Some people are holding on to her great aunt, Adhir's mother, to stop her from knocking her head on the floor in grief. Already her forehead is bleeding from earlier incessant knocks.

All of them are weeping silently, except for one person, Maya. Silent and alert, she wipes the blood from Adhir's mouth, pours some medicine between his half-parted lips. Somewhere along the way she had come and made a place for herself there. They all stare at her amazed, but today there is no need for shame. She has drawn a bit of her sari over her head and is nursing him silently. From time to time you can see her quiver as she sees Adhir's half-closed eyes. It seems as if she would hold on to that last bit of life with all the strength at her command.

Chobi rushes right into the room. She stares fixedly at Adhir's face and calls out, "Uncle!"

Adhir coughs up blood again, and then his breathing becomes normal. Chobi holds his hand tightly and cries, "So soon? Uncle? But Tamal has written for us to take you there. What will happen to me, Uncle?"

Adhir tries to smile with his blood-smeared lips. He says in a whisper, "Your real struggle is yet to begin, Chobi. It's a tough world. Where are they?"

Dhiren, Arun, and Prasanna lean their tearful faces forward.

Adhir says, pointing to Maya, "Look after this girl. Dhiren—my parents, the *samiti* [organization]—consider them yours. So take care. Don't be afraid—. Courage, Chobi!"

Chobi says to herself, No, I won't be afraid, I won't. He's coughing blood again, he has difficulty breathing, but he still whispers on, "Very painful—life itself is painful. But you mustn't grieve—all of you—" and he rests his eyes on Maya.

Maya, at the point of giving him some more medicine, stiffens suddenly, and then falls on his breast with a shrill cry. She sits up and stares fixedly at his face once more, as if she still can't take in the truth. Her eyes are dry—her lips are all a-quiver, but Maya cannot cry.

Grandaunt is no longer knocking her head. She is rolling on the floor weeping. When Chobi goes up to her, she says, "I couldn't even feed him properly these last few days. My only son, and he became a wandering sannyasin—even then I didn't feel sorry. But why couldn't he at least stay alive?"

He had dreamed of making all men happy, he had wanted to live an easy life too, but had died working himself to the bone—with no proper food, no medical care.

Chobi's heart burns with grief; she stands alone in one corner of the room. She can't bear to hear the sounds of weeping—such unbearable sorrow!

Arun comes and stands beside her. "The news has spread through all the villages around—seen that, Chobi?"

Chobi sees hundreds of people. They're coming in groups from far and near.

Arun says, "They want to pay their last respects to Adhirda. Do you see them coming with the Farmers' Society banner? Adhirda built that society with his own hands."

Raisaheb has arrived, and a few other village elders. They sit surrounding Harinandan.

They stare wide-eyed when they hear the proposal. "A brahmin's son! He must have proper funeral rites first—only then should he be picked up on the shoulders as stipulated. How can those low-caste fellows take him along, just like that? Why go on procession with a dead body!"

But these objections are set aside. Harinandan's heart is breaking with pain, but he has not shed a single tear. Just once he said in a broken voice, "Let them take him—he belongs to them—leave him in their hands. He doesn't belong to us—he never even thought of us ever—did he?"

And suppressing his tears, he had walked out of the roomful of elders, never to sit with them again. After that, all the arrangements had been made, some people had taken over. Flowers had been brought, and garlands, and numerous little pennants. They had adorned him with infinite care all day, and now they were bearing him aloft.

Hundreds of bare human bodies, dark, barefooted men—men who'd come crying to Raisaheb for reprieve of their tenants' taxes, men who'd come begging at the zamindar's feet to be allowed to keep even a small part of the harvest, these people seemed suddenly to have gained boundless courage.

Raisaheb looks at them with infinite disdain. A son of their own family had died of a dreadful disease. No proper funeral rites, no priest to preside, a brahmin's son unpurified by fire, and low-caste riffraff just bear him away.

Chapter 32

Purnasashi takes Chobi along to her room one day. With shaky hands she opens up a huge wooden chest and takes out a pair of clove design earrings. She presses them into Chobi's palm and says, "I had kept these for your wedding . . . but since that is not to be . . . you can have them anyway. You might need them for your studies."

Chobi's eyes fill with tears. She is going away to stay with some distant relatives where she will continue her studies. What kind of welcome would she receive there? What wonders, what struggles await her she does not know. But she finds herself unable to take those earrings from Purnasashi's old and withered hands. She puts her own hands into the old woman's and says, "Not for my studies, Grandma—please keep these with you."

Purnasashi tries a smile. "What's the point of putting them away Chobi? I won't be here to see you married—to see your husband. Use them as you think fit."

Chobi strokes those bare, shrivelled hands and says, "Keep them Grandma, your blessings are all I need."

Once again today Mamata's eyes are brimming with tears, but she cannot clasp Chobi to her breast and weep as she did when Chobi was a child. Chobi is grown up now—old enough to defy all family traditions, old enough to go out into the wide world.

So she keeps her tears to herself. She looks at Chobi's face, wishes she could stroke her hair, and her lips quiver as she says, "Moni is a boy, I don't feel so worried about letting him go—but I'm letting you go too, all on your own, Chobu."

Chobi knows what her mother wants to hear, what assurance she would like to have. She wipes Mamata's tears away with her own hands and says, "I will stay on the path of justice, truth, and goodness always. Yes, even at the cost of my life."

Mamata holds Chobi's head close to her breast and bursts into tears. "Don't keep saying things like that, Chobu!"

They come in a body to see her off, walking with her for a long way. Mother, Grandma, Aunt. She looks back again and again, and her eyes keep brimming over.

When all the rest have turned back, Mamata keeps standing still. The wind plays in her hair. The sari slips off her head—her eyes follow her departing daughter and then go vacant in thought. She seems no longer to be looking at the path her girl has taken, but peering misty-eyed far back into a past that speaks of failure.

The *Chatim* tree on the west bank of Bosepukur marks the end of the village. From there on, the road leads to the station. In childhood Chobi used to come and stand at this point sometimes, and stare and stare at the station road. A world stretching out to a limitless horizon seemed to beckon to her then. Chobi couldn't tell then where that road would lead to, or how far.

Today Phulmani, Batashi, and the others are waiting for her by that roadside. They ask her, "You won't forget us will you, when you get to the city? You won't forget the village?"

How can she forget? The smell of the grass, the changing scent of every season has become so much a part of her being . . . This village is a part of everything she holds precious . . . With Tamal's pledge, with Adhirkaka's eager encouragement. How can Chobi ever forget?

Sukhada's friend Umapati, who has a job in Calcutta, has undertaken to escort her there. Pradip has been released from prison—he would be there to meet her at the station. Sukhada has come to put her on the train.

Kulada was not expected to be there, but he had come along anyway. There was something he had wished to say to Chobi. He had hovered around her restlessly up to the last minute, and still held his peace.

When the guard blows his whistle, Kulada suddenly draws close, hesitates a little, and then says, "Tell him, . . . tell Pradip to come home. He left in a huff . . . said he wouldn't come back unless I asked him to. Tell him . . . I asked."

Then he takes out a wad of notes and slips them into Chobi's hands. "Here take this, divide it between yourselves. Write whenever you need anything . . ." Bit by bit all their faces blur. Chobi keeps staring right to the end. At last the station is left behind, and her tears suddenly spill over. She wipes them at the window and sits down quietly.

Now another thought disturbs her suddenly. "Unless you go there, you won't get an idea of the world around"—somebody had told her that one day. Who was it?

What was this world? Would Chobi find a place there? Would she survive in that selfish, ruthless, competitive atmosphere? The agitation she feels—is it joy, or sadness, or fear? What can you compare it to?

Gazing out the window, the likeness suddenly hits her. It is with the pace of the train—the rhythm of movement.

Moving forward, that is the main thing—one must keep going.

And now, a new sense of eager expectancy fills her mind, her whole being.

Translated by Madhuchanda Karlekar.

BABY KAMBLE

(b. 1929)   *Marathi*

In the preface to her autobiography, which describes in detail her life as a woman in her community, Baby Kamble says she has taken care to document everything "to show my grandchildren the *agnidivya,* the immolation by fire, that Mahars have had to perform to gain what little status they have today." Formerly, the Mahars were untouchables and lived outside the boundaries of the main village, which housed the upper castes. They were responsible for guarding the village and keeping it clean. They also carried messages and assisted the village headman. Since they were the principal sources of information about village and family history, they often settled disputes about land. The book concentrates on the period before Independence, and, in distinct contrast to earlier women's autobiographies (such as those by Lakshmibai Tilak, Ramabai Ranade, and Anandibai Karve) that focus on the writers' marriages and their husbands, Baby Kamble deals with the life of her people. She is the first *dalit* woman to have written an autobiography in Marathi.

She was born in Veergao, a village in western Maharashtra, in her grandparents' house, where she lived until she was nine. Her grandfather and his two brothers worked as butlers in European households in the cities around. Since they sent money home each month, their family was somewhat better off than the others around it. Her father, Pandhrinath, was a contractor, and earned much more than he would have had he continued with his traditional work. Baby Kamble speaks of him as a kind man, generous towards his poorer relations. It was from him, she says, that she learned many of the most valuable lessons of her life, such as a disinterest in materialism: "I have never tried to collect wealth, and was happy to earn just enough for my basic needs." But this was only one side of him. As a husband, he was stern and authoritarian, and kept his wife confined to the house, taking pride in not letting her go out. As a consequence, Baby Kamble feels, her mother grew bitter and harsh.

As Baby Kamble was growing up, the movement of the formerly untouchable Mang and Mahar castes started by Babasaheb Ambedkar (1891–1956) was at its height. In December 1927 Ambedkar began a satyagraha to establish their civic rights and confront the tyranny of the upper castes. In what has been called an event of as great significance in the nationalist movement as the first bonfire of foreign cloth and the Salt Satyagraha, hundreds of Mangs and Mahars gathered at the Chavdar Tale at Mahad, drew water and drank it. The Kalaram Mandir Satyagraha was another mass attempt, this time to gain entry into the temple. Similar movements arose all over India and Baby Kamble recalls how inspired she and her siblings were by Ambedkar and the other activists. In her own village the Mahar community forced its way into the temples and eating places, and as a result, the whole atmosphere changed.

Also under Ambedkar's influence, her father sent Baby Kamble to school. In the sections of her autobiography about that period, she describes how fights would break out between the untouchables and the higher-caste Hindu girls. The Mahar girls became very insecure and were forced to form a close-knit group. There was no interaction between the castes, only a great deal of hostility.

Baby Kamble has seven children, most of whom have had a university education. *Jina Amucha* (Our [Wretched] Lives), her autobiography, was serialized in the Pune women's magazine *Stree* shortly before it was published as a book in 1986.

◆

From JINA AMUCHA
(Our [Wretched] Lives)
Chapter 8

On the fourth day [of the wedding rituals], there would be the ceremony of taking off the bridal crowns. This would always be done in the morning. The people from both families gathered for the occasion in the specially built *pandal.* A brass plate would be put on the head of the bride's mother, and the other women held that plate in place. The men sat quietly at one side. Tears would stream from the eyes of the women. Weeping, sobbing, they sang "Zalu."*

> Zalubai zalu, in front of the house
> There was a lovely jujube tree
> Then came a thief, the son-in-law
> He carried it off, for all to see
> But the tree was his, that's how it is
> How my poor love, helpless, weeps.

---

*"Zalu" is a song sung on the fourth day of wedding festivities, before the bride leaves for the groom's house. The women from her household sit by the bride and her mother and sob as they sing the song. The men stay quietly in the background.

Zalubai zalu, in front of the house
There was a jasmine vine
Weep not O poor mama mine . . .

Zalubai zalu, in front of the house
There was a champak white
Weep not O poor papa mine . . .

Zalubai zalu, a flock of birds
Weep not O my poor brother . . .

Zalubai zalu, what's left behind
Is a reflection in the mirror
Weep not O my poor sister . . .

While the women sang this song, everyone around started weeping and sobbing. After the crowns were taken off, the bride and the groom would ultimately be freed from the weight. Marriage for the girl meant nothing but calamity. She went back to her people, but after a couple of days, her father-in-law went to fetch her. He would take with him gram, rice grains, and jaggery. The bride's mother prepared small sweetmeats with the material he had brought, and filled a basket with them. The girl carried this with her to her new home. And thus she would embark upon a really arduous life. She would be such a young child, a baby, still immature, yet the poor thing had to break all the ties of parental love and had to go to her in-laws' place to lead a married life, without even knowing what "husband" meant, or what it was to be given away. What would that child know of these things? Besides, in those days there were no vehicles. When the cock crowed early in the morning, the father-in-law started with his daughter-in-law on foot. It took two to three days to reach home. If the place was close by, they had to walk from morning till evening.

When the bride arrived at the in-laws' place, she would be required to cook *bhakris*. Two basketfuls of them. The child sat down to make them. But she wouldn't be able to pat the dough out into cakes bigger than her palm. When she put them on the pan to bake, they were so thick that they either got burnt in places, or remained uncooked. Then the mother-in-law would call all her friends and neighbors and hold an open exhibition of the tiny bhakris. "Atyabai, come and see what's happening here! Didn't you think that I'd brought the daughter of a 'good' woman into my house? Look at the bhakris this wench has made. She can't even make a few bhakris well. Oh well, what can one expect of this daughter of a dunce!"

The child wasn't even allowed to sleep. When the cock crowed at three in the morning, the mother-in-law would pull her out of the bed, dragging her by her hair, make her clean the handmill in which the grain was ground, put in some jowar, and sit down at the mill herself with the daughter-in-law. But immediately after they had begun, the mother-in-law's newborn babe would wake up and start crying. So the father-in-law would call, "Come here, you. This Dhondya is awake. Come and stop his wailing. Leave the grinding to her. Otherwise when will she learn?"

The mother-in-law would promptly get up and, suckling her baby, go back to sleep. The young girl would have to continue the work alone. Her tiny hands often could not pull the heavy stones, and she had to stop frequently. Her palms would be blistered all over. Later they would harden. After the grinding was done, she would be sent to the river to fetch water, with a small vessel. When that was done, she had to sit down to make bhakris. If the bhakris weren't perfect, the mother-in-law examined the kneaded flour and slapped the girl on the face with the unbaked bhakris, pinched her cheeks, and showered a million curses on her.

Pinching her cheeks, she would say, "What's your mother really? Tell me that! Is she a good married woman at all? Or does she know only how to run after the potmaker's donkeys? Didn't she teach you anything? I pampered you a little, but you took advantage of that. Look what a nice mother-in-law I am! My own mother-in-law was a spitfire. A burning coal! Actually one could hold a burning coal in one's hand, but staying with her was a far more difficult thing." These speeches would be punctuated with loud wails. "In our time one had to be polite even to a dog in the in-laws' house before kicking him out. Where would you get a mother-in-law as nice as me? Is that why you're being such a pest?"

On and on it went. The poor girl had to endure the curses of everybody in the household, including the snotty sister-in-law and the slovenly brother-in-law. By the time she had finished all the work in the house, it would be around one-thirty in the afternoon. Then she could wash. By then all the bhakris in the house would have been eaten up. And she had to eat the leftover blackened, half-baked bhakris. But what could she eat them with? She would steal some salt from the kitchen when the mother-in-law wasn't looking, and hide it in her sari. These daughters-in-law had, however, one comfort. There were no pots in the house to clean and no clothes to wash, because there weren't even any rags to wear. So the problem of washing clothes and cleaning pots was automatically solved. When the mother-in-law's period started, she went straight to the river to bathe, as she didn't have another sari to change into. There she took off half of her sari, keeping the other half wrapped around her. And that she washed first. Then when that portion was dry, she wrapped it around her, and washed the other half. She would dry that in the same manner. And that sari also was never in one piece. It would be patched in several places. It would be afternoon by the time she reached home. Till then, the daughter-in-law had to do everything.

This rigorous punishment at a young age, however, was far preferable to what she had to go through once she became mature. When the daughter-in-law got her period for the first time, the mother-in-law became terribly agitated and kept a close watch on the daughter-in-law and her son. She watched them with the eye of a hawk, and wouldn't let them even glance at each other. The husband of the bride kept hovering around, yearning to talk to his wife. But the mother-in-law was far too clever for him. She would not let them meet. She kept awake in the night for fear of their coming together. She would be terribly scared that her son would be snatched away from her and that he would forget his parents and begin pampering his wife.

Immediately after they went to bed, she would wake up the daughter-in-law to grind the grain. And the other women added fat to fire. "You are such a stupid one. Don't let her sleep with your son for a long time. Your delicate shoot will break. Beware of her!"

Then she would also listen to them and poison the son's mind against his wife. She would be worried all the time about his falling in love with his wife. The daughter-in-law was nothing but an enemy for her. She was terribly jealous of her youth. She would constantly try to poison her son's mind against his wife. When the daughter-in-law finished grinding, she would send her off to fetch water. While she was away, the mother-in-law would grind some glass bangles and mix the glass powder with the flour.* When the daughter-in-law returned, she would be asked to make bhakris with that flour. When one bhakri was made, the mother-in-law would herself put one piece of it in her mouth and spit it out. Then she would go from house to house with

---

*It was not unusual for glass bangles to break when the handmill was being operated. A woman had to take care in that case to pick all the pieces out. A careful worker kept her bangles intact and mentioned with pride that she kept them from one Diwali festival to the next, when the old bangles were replaced with new ones.

that bread, showing it to all. "Just taste this bhakri! It feels as if glass is mixed in it."

The other women also loved such happenings. They would get excited. The whole village gathered in front of her door. "The witch! Wanted to kill off the whole house! Oh, she shouldn't have attempted such a stab in the back." Then the sasubai would moan loudly, beating her breast. She complained to any passers by. "See, master, how this witch tried to do away with my house and the kids as well."

To make things worse, some women would get possessed by a goddess. They started chanting, "Ahhhh, it's because of my blessing that you were saved from this woman. This woman is an evil in your house. Don't ever trust her. But you, too, forgot God. Give away the firstborn baby of your son to the Madmalu."*

A fear that went deep into their bones would grip the women. They would put kumkum and turmeric on the possessed woman's forehead and fall at her feet. In this chaos, the poor daughter-in-law trembled with fear like a leaf. She just lost the power to protest against this injustice. The furious husband would beat her to a pulp with a stick, and drive her out of the house. Anybody could torture her as they wished. When she went to fetch water, the mother-in-law whispered in her son's ear, "Watch her, you fool! Look how she goes out all the time! That Sirangya follows her to the river and whistles at her. Keep her under your thumb. Otherwise you will be disgraced in public."

Translated by Maya Pandit.

SAROJ PATHAK ————————————————
(1929–1989)   *Gujarati*

She may have begun writing, Saroj Pathak once said, in reaction to the conservative, middle-class environment she grew up in, for there was nothing in it to encourage a girl who wanted to write. In fact a girl inevitably developed a sense of inferiority in such a context. Though Saroj Pathak married a fellow writer, Ramanlal Pathak, marriage led to a break in her education. It was not until 1964 that she received her master's

————————————————
*The Madmalu is a local goddess.

degree, in Gujarati. In the meantime, however, she worked for All India Radio and for the Soviet embassy in India as a translator.

While many of her stories revolve around women who have been jilted or trapped in loveless marriages, women's consciousness is not the focus of her writing. She seems more interested in examining the mind in a state of loneliness, isolation, and consequent bewilderment and breakdown. In *Nightmare,* 1969, existence is a nightmare not only for the heroine, who is married to the elder brother of the man with whom her marriage originally had been arranged, but for the unloved husband as well.

Some of Saroj Pathak's most successful stories deal with the loneliness and bewilderment of children or of the elderly. In "Niyatikrut Niyamrahita" (Not Subject to the Laws of Destiny), an elderly couple in a broken-down house welcome a young lodger and talk to him ceaselessly about their son. Soon he realizes that they contradict themselves and each other about the details of the son's life and habits, and are even confused about his name. "Dhvanyartha" (Implied Meaning) is about an elderly couple who pore over letters from their married daughter and son, wondering whether to read the lines as an invitation, an appeal for assistance, or a putting off. The unusual story "Dushchakra" (Vicious Circle) takes us into the world of ladies' tailors. The protagonist is a young tailor obsessed with the body and the touch of one of his customers. He can neither bear to sew the sari blouses for her wedding, nor to have someone else do it. Finally he breaks down and gives up the job. "Saugandh" (The Vow), the story we have translated for this volume, is in some ways an exception to this pattern, for it deals with a relationship in which both characters are strong and find ways to live meaningfully despite their unconventional situations.

Jaya Mehta is critical of Saroj Pathak for always depicting women who are either conservative in their values or too weak to resist the ill-treatment to which they are subjected. The problem, however, lies not so much in her characters but in the worldview her fiction projects. These psychological victims of contemporary society elicit our interest and evoke our pity, but within the novels there is rarely a hoped-for alternative.

Mention must be made also of the narrative mode Saroj Pathak developed. Her stories are often told through broken utterances, fragments passing through the minds of the protagonist, or disconnected recollections of past conversations. It is a technique well suited to enact the breakdown of the human being, and the utter desperation that follows, though as critic Shirin Kudchedkar points out, when stretched to novel length, as in *Nishesh* (Withholding Nothing), 1978, it fails to sustain interest. The novel *Priya Punam* (Priya and Punam) was published in 1980, and her collected short stories, *Saroj Pathak Shreshta Varto,* from which the story translated here is taken, in 1981.

◆

SAUGANDH
(The Vow)

There were few people belonging to Sambal's caste in that town. A tall, well-built, manly fellow, he could easily earn what he needed; he wasn't dependent on anyone. If he was in the mood for it he might go off for a drink with his friends and on the way he might even get involved in a fight. And particularly if some wretch insulted a woman, he was in for it. Sambal would never hold back. It would make his blood boil. And that's how, that's why, and that's the time when, returning home from the bend near the bus stop, he had set himself up as Poorbi's guard.

Amrit and Nanda used to gossip. But Sambal didn't care. Pouring scorn on them all, he would say, "Don't you have mothers and sisters, you swine?"

But Poorbi was impatient. A woman alone, and men were never very trustworthy. If she could once and for all wear the wedding sari that would bind Sambal to her for good! She didn't care about caste or class. The trouble was that she had lost all joy in the red of the wedding sari. There was no other reason why she felt hesitant. In such a large city nobody would get to know about his wife and take it to a court of law. Here she earned her bread, lived and acted as she pleased, and one could always find a lodging. Poorbi had passed the middle-school exam. There had been a time when she had had a job filling and storing water in a children's school, and she had even swept and mopped the floor in a college hostel. One adapted to changing times. The hefty, healthy, officer Surajmal had become a cripple and since then it made no difference whether she was married or not. The henna on her hands and feet came off as she washed the utensils. When she was thoroughly sick of abuse, blows, and male smells, she escaped to the city.

In his distant home Sambal, too, had fields, children, an uncle, and a wife who never minced matters. When his wife took him to task, Sambal, who was otherwise fierce as a tiger, would come with his tail down and a woeful face to Poorbi and, having poured out his suppressed resentment, would grow calm again. Is she a woman or what? Doesn't even let one swallow a mouthful in peace! Always squalling and squabbling and tormenting! You'd think five men's heads had been broken and put together to create a woman like Sambal's wife! She would keep harping on just the one point—Sambal should give up his job in the city and return to work on the land. Working on your land was honorable work, while employment in the city robbed you of self-respect, of manliness. Sambal was a shirker. . . . How dare she! What a tongue she had! Satan's grandmother! He regularly sent home a money order for fifty rupees. Talking to Poorbi, he calmed down. He had gotten his elder daughter married, and now Chutki's marriage had to be arranged. His son had passed only the fourth standard. But that boy had taken to smoking and chewing tobacco. There was no restraining him—he brought opium to his uncle, and he'd even taken part in robberies. A real devil, my Babua! His mother might say, "Like father, like son," but Sambal regularly earned a hundred and fifty to two hundred rupees. No robbery or petty thieving—heaven forbid!

Poorbi realized at the very outset of their acquaintance that this was a decent man, not a womanizer. While fondling and petting, he was like a child, like a suckling calf, but as a guard he was like a fierce watchdog. Nobody dared cross his mistress's threshold heedlessly or sniff around without permission. *Grr, grr*—Sambal would spring on him, tear him to pieces, thrash him. No one could cross the boundary line Sambal had drawn around Poorbi and get away unscathed. Poorbi might scold and scorn his methods, but how else could a watchdog keep intruders out? It was he who had erected an unbreakable barrier round Poorbi.

The lane behind Poorbi's house stank. All the garbage was flung there. One had to walk alongside a gutter. One's foot might slip on a vegetable peeling. Sambal made his way carefully. It might be raining heavily. He might have on a patched pair of sandals, or again he might not. He might have a cold or a fever, he might have had a little too much to drink, but as soon as he reached Poorbi's alleyway he assumed the responsibility of a guard.

Poorbi felt that living in this locality she wasn't always safe going to and from work. Why not make Sambal take the marriage vow? She would shudder. This crazy watchdog should be put on a leash. Suppose he went off to keep watch for someone else who petted and fondled him! Heaven forbid that his shrewish wife should come to the city and upbraid him and carry him off. His uncle might come and fall at his feet and mislead him with false tales of woe. Poorbi had seen her Sambal absolutely defenseless in the face of tears. She could not afford to lose Sambal.

When her officer husband had had a stomach tumor, she had brought him to the city for an operation. That time Sambal had not been able to send his fifty-rupee money order home, as he had helped with the expensive hospital and the expensive medicines. Tears of happiness had filled Poorbi's eyes because she felt gratitude that he truly belonged to her now. But Sambal's eyes, too, were moist with tears. How Babua would cry if he didn't send him five notebooks for his fourth standard. . . ! It was just like Sambal to tell Poorbi all this. On the other hand, his wife had the spirit of a man—there'd be no weeping and wailing in his house even in the presence of death. If Sambal felt concerned about his younger daughter, Chutki, or suddenly remembered his son Babua, Poorbi would ask, "Was there a letter from home? Is everything all right? Babua's going to school regularly, I hope. Have they paid for the bull? Is your wife keeping her temper? Did they send you pure ghee this time?" In this way both of them were thoroughly at ease with each other.

Sambal had a way of laughing and saying on any occasion, "At your command! My life at your service!" Well, what was she waiting for? If she once wore the red wedding sari or even made him take a verbal oath she could safely entrust herself to him. Poorbi did not want to leave matters unsettled. If she spoke up freely, Sambal would be sure to say, "My life at your service! At your command!"

It was Poorbi herself who couldn't make up her mind. O goddess Parvati, fulfill my desires! When Sambal licked all five fingers as he noisily ate the savory rice she had cooked, when he wiped his mouth with his dirty pajamas, Poorbi would remember with regret her officer husband's style of living. How crude this fellow was! When he relaxed and stretched out on the cot in the courtyard with only the sky to cover him, and occasionally dropped off to sleep, she was overwhelmed with tenderness. What could one say? On waking up he might start telling her how he dreamt of Babua or of a sari with the colors of spring. If he had borrowed ten rupees, when he returned it, he'd always thrust some extra money into her fist as if he had won it while gambling or as if he were paying interest. He'd say, "But you crazy woman, this is going to be of use to me too! What's the difference between you and me?"

"Lakkhi! I don't want to eat today. I've gorged on pilau with Dhaniram in a first-class hotel!" As if Poorbi were a little girl, he would lovingly address her as "Lakkhi," "Sweetie," "Kiddie," in a manner all his own. Poorbi adored him. This tenderness made her oblivious to all Surajmal's beatings, his male smells. Now was the chance; Poorbi had only to say, "My simple fellow, there's just one thing"—"One thing, one thing, don't be crazy, tell me ten thousand things. Your servant is ready! Give the command!" Poorbi was sure to hear Sambal's resounding voice that made the walls tremble. It was Poorbi who had to decide.

And she decided.

"Listen, there's something, just see, if we took two days' leave from work and went on an outing—"

That was all she needed to say. Everything was ready. At your command! They came to a rest house outside the city.

In the register Sambal asked them to enter:

Name: Sambal Dharamdas Munshi and wife.
Place of residence: Gangapur.
Purpose of visit: Sightseeing.

Sambal sent for tea from a restaurant nearby. The cup and saucer were dirty. The handle of the cup was broken. What a foul smell, and the tea was so strong—they seemed to have boiled an egg in it! Sambal drank both cups. Poorbi lay stretched across the bed. Carefully covering her feet with a rug, Sambal started searching for his bidis and a box of matches. There were cobwebs on the ceiling and she was afraid that bugs might plague her. The boy brought a pitcher of water. Both doors were open. That must be the stench from the toilet. Her sister-in-law had written. . . . To drive the rest house out of her mind, Poorbi made a mental trip to her hometown. Surajmal would flay her alive— he always wanted tea served properly on a tray. He had asthma but was addicted to smoking, wouldn't listen to anyone. If he could get the *asal cheez,*★ Surajmal would put on his officer's airs! Just the previous year, Poorbi had had new crutches made and dispatched to him. He was so hot-tempered that he had hurled them across the room and they had broken. It would take time to get new crutches made. Poorbi could provide money. But her sister-in-law's son Birju was a cunning rogue. If he had his way, he wouldn't leave even Poorbi alone. It was only Surajmal coughing in his corner that kept him in check. The smell of a male!

"What are you thinking about, Lakkhi?" Sambal startled her.

Sambal had stretched out on the other bed. His chest was exposed. He had taken off his dirty vest and hung it on a nail. A wrestler's powerful body! Watchdog! A dark-skinned chest! When he pursed his lips like a child to say "Lakkhi," he looked so innocent. Was this the same Sambal who abused his wife to his heart's content? Was this the heartless husband and father who had rejected his own family to be able to say "At your service!" in response to Poorbi's slightest wish?

★*Asal cheez* means "genuine article"; probably imported whisky.

In pursuit of what desire had this simple fellow come here, taking leave and forgoing his fifty-rupee money order? If Sambal now tricked her, laid hold of her, demanded satisfaction of the flesh, how could she blame him? He was in the full vigor of manhood. A man could not be blamed if he was attracted by a woman's body when they were alone together. And if Sambal once crushed her in his arms then . . . then . . . Poorbi would not be able to protest about going "beyond." All she wanted was to make him take a vow. But what she found was upright conduct and questions.

"What are you thinking about, Lakkhi?" Sambal was asking sweetly. Poorbi recollected herself. Now it was definitely a matter of going "beyond." No doubt about it. But look out! Test him first! A woman should play safe, then let him do what he pleased. She wouldn't hold back!

"I'm worried. Suppose something were to happen to you in this unknown place, whom would I turn to for help? What name would I go by?" Poorbi had thought out what she would say. Sambal extinguished his cigarette and, coming close to Poorbi, began to play gently with her earrings.

"Death doesn't come so easily. There was a drought in our village . . . the crops failed . . . we still had to pay the debts for our elder daughter's wedding. Babua's mother took an oath. Chutki had a high fever . . ."

Look at that, all over again, his Chutki and his crops and his Babua. When Surajmal had been operated on for the tumor, her sister-in-law had arranged for recitations from the scriptures. Her sister-in-law used to say that if Poorbi would learn midwifery, their family income would increase. Their village now had a hospital, electricity, a school, a movie theater—it was a small town now, not a village. When she got fed up . . . But in the village there was her sister-in-law's burly young son— a real wolf. Her sister-in-law looked after Surajmal's household, kept some control over her layabout of a son, and somehow maintained the tottering credit of the family. She was pleasant to talk to. Poorbi always sent her special oil and the best tobacco from the city, out of affection, not because she had to. She, too, became absorbed in thinking about her family.

Sambal was still playing with her earrings and carrying on about the drought in his village. Ramdasji had sent his family away to Allahabad and Varanasi. And in the village, the government! You stood in line for flour, then in line for kerosene, then for powdered milk . . . the little girl . . . the older girl . . . and Babua's mother . . . nobody dared, what a tongue yet. . . .

"Talk about something else—I'm really very frightened." Poorbi changed the subject. Sambal realized that she had something else in mind and said, "A red sari and a nosering. I have this dream of a bride as pretty as a doll. With a bright complexion like Lakkhi's and a colored bridal sari. The scent of *sindoor*⋆. Oh, Lakkhi, will you come to my village?"

Poorbi was familiar with the tenderness that could come into Sambal's manly voice. Sambal was sliding closer. Before she surrendered to him, she must try and make him take the vows she wanted. She gently took hold of his hand and said, "Will you take me to your village? But your wife will cut you into little pieces. And who will be willing to marry your daughter? Rather than that you could come to my village! In our village we now have brick houses, a hospital, and a much larger and more comfortable rest house than this one. You can go there by train now. There's a beautiful temple . . . When shall we go to the temple?"

"Did you go to the temple with your husband?"

"He was an officer. He didn't believe in any god. What he worshipped were his group of friends and his bottle!" Poorbi laughed.

Stroking the soles of Poorbi's slender, delicate feet with his strong hand, Sambal said, "If it comes to that, I'm also fond of a bottle now and again, but if I once swore by the Lord Shankar . . ."

"Sambal, would you give up drinking?"

Sambal's hand came to rest. For a long time there was silence in the room. The drought, food, the line for powdered milk, work, his bullock cart, rebellion, a red sari, his dream, Chutki's wedding, a brick house, Babua's mother's abuses.

"Oh, oh!"

Poorbi's grip on his hand became firmer. Sambal sat up. Pushing aside the hair falling over Poorbi's eager eyes, he said, "If I give up the bottle will we live together? If I make a commitment, I'm a man of my word. If you'll live with me, we'll have my 150 rupees and your 60, and I'll swear never to touch drink again. No moving around with friends, no wasting money, and a bride as pretty as a doll . . . If Babua comes here any time he'll really dance with joy on seeing you!"

⋆*Sindoor* is a red powder worn by married women in the parting of the hair.

"Not like that. Take a vow." Poorbi affectionately pulled him towards her.

"All right, administer the oaths. At your command!"

Poorbi leaned her head on his shoulder. She began counting off the vows on her fingers. Number one—

"You must do just as I please."

Sambal was in a jolly mood. Burying his face in Poorbi's hair, he kept giving his consent with, "Yes, yes. At your command!" Sometimes he'd say, "Lakkhi, you'll give me good food to eat, won't you?"

"Number two, no unnecessary expenses—which includes the money order for fifty rupees."

"Yes, but then you won't contribute to the payment for the brick house in your village either, will you, Lakkhi?"

"Number three. No gambling, no drink, and no running away every so often to your village. You mustn't be affected by your uncle's problems. Your share in Chutki's marriage expenses . . ."

"Lakkhi, just listen to what I have to say! In our village, too, there's a temple. A very ancient idol. Our group of friends used to smoke the hookah there. Babua's mother once insisted on a vow . . ."

"So we don't want to live together? As you please. Now talk as much as you like about your village. I'll talk about my village. I take back all the vows I asked you to make!"

"Why do you get excited, my girl? A promise is a promise. At your command! Administer all the oaths—gambling, drinking, money orders, temple, village, wife, calf, uncle, uncle's grandfather, Poorb—" Sambal reeled off the lot without pausing for breath and then, breaking off, said affectionately, "You won't quarrel, will you, Lakkhi? We'll eat our meals in peace, won't we? I'll earn a lot, provide for you . . . No, Lakkhi, you can continue to remember the idol in your village temple. You can take me there if you like! But I always keep my word. I want to be worthy to live with you. Pray for that to Lord Shankar, won't you?"

Sambal's loving voice, his trembling fingers, and his concentrated gaze—Poorbi dwelt long on them. Like a child one is putting to sleep in one's lap, she kissed his head and drew him to her. Now she was willing to shed all jealousies and repugnancies. He now had the right to possess her. It was the body of one who had claims by virtue of the protection he offered her. She had never been able to repulse Surajmal. Here was one who was so good, whom she loved so dearly; let him do as he pleased. She had borne a great deal; she would bear this as well. As if she were saying, "Now eat and drink your fill," and were giving him an indication that she was ready, Poorbi let her sari slip from her shoulder.

Sambal touched his eyes with the edge of her sari and played around with it. He hadn't finished what he had to say. As if he were winding everything up and there was only a negligible matter still to be settled, he readjusted the sari on Poorbi's shoulder and said, "One more vow— to be administered by me.

"I mustn't become a wolf, Lakkhi. I'll worship your goddess devotedly, eat the sweets offered at the shrine, but Babua's mother once taunted me so . . . You, too, are another woman, so not you, either. I believe in keeping my word, so help me to keep my vow that I will never enjoy another woman. Administer the vow." Sambal's words left Poorbi speechless. Gradually she recovered herself. Instead of the smell of boiled eggs, she felt she could smell the holy oil-lamp. In the rest house she heard temple bells and she said to herself, Oh Mother Ganga, all my desires are fulfilled. What can I say of him? He is not a simple fellow, he is the Lord Krishna! Very lovingly, Poorbi looked again at Sambal's dark chest gleaming with perspiration. She was overwhelmed with love.

Bit by bit she cast aside the web of illusion created by the vows she had insisted on and she became soft and light like a flower as she said, "Our home! In our home we'll preserve just your one vow. I take back all the vows I insisted on. We'll be together, nothing else matters. We'll cope with everything. We have nothing to fear. The contribution for the brick house in my village and your money order . . ." and she didn't say the rest aloud, but included all—Chutki's marriage and Babua's schooling, your uncle's muslin dhoti, my sister-in-law's tobacco and the crutches and the asal cheez . . . we'll manage it all.

"And Bhola, we'll go to the temple here and your vows . . ."

Sambal was trembling with joy. As Lakkhi rested clasped in his arms her voice sounded even more loving, pure, and tender than usual.

"And I'll get a nosering. You're not afraid now, are you, Lakkhi?"

As Sambal directed his gaze and hers at the surroundings, Poorbi thought of the stage her life had reached, the temple, the vow, and replied, "What should I be afraid of? You're here, aren't you? Now this rest house is like our own house."

Their hands remained clasped.

"Do you mean it?"

"Yes, I swear by your life."

Translated by Shirin Kudchedkar.

ZAHIDA ZAIDI ———————————————

(b. 1930)   *Urdu*

Zahida Zaidi is a scholar, poet, dramatist and translator who has had a distinguished academic career. She traveled to England to study at Cambridge, where she earned her master's degree before returning to teach English at the universities of Delhi and Aligarh. In 1971–1972 she was a fellow at the Indian Institute of Advanced Study in Simla.

As a poet, Zahida Zaidi works with ease in English and Urdu and has published in both languages. She has translated into Urdu the plays of Anton Chekhov, Luigi Pirandello, Jean-Paul Sartre, and Samuel Beckett, as well as the poetry of Eugenio Montale, Federico García Lorca, and Pablo Neruda, working from the original French and Italian as well as from English translations. She has staged many plays, including ones she has translated. Though her field of specialization is drama, she is also a keen student of philosophy and religion, and is widely read in Western, Indian, and Persian literatures. As a student Zahida was drawn to Marxist ideology. Her creative writing, however, is marked by an existential and mystical strain and by a subtle ear for the play of words.

A first collection of poems, *Zahr-e-Hyat* (Life's Poison), 1970, won the Urdu Academy Award in 1971; a second, *Dharti ka Lams* (Touch of Earth), from which the poem translated here was taken, was published in 1975. Two collections of poems in English, *Beyond Words* and *Broken Pieces,* appeared in 1979.

◆

BACHPANA CHOD DO
(Stop Being Childish)

Stop being childish!
How will you build castles
from the ashes
of these blasted cities?

You once made toy houses,
but that was in the sand
of the laughing sea,
tiny mud houses

(the sea laid its treasures
at your feet)
at which you placed
the saucy sunbeams on guard
and bending over them
whispered something playful to the sky.
Still the wanton sea
swept away
your tiny sand dwellings.
That was in the laughing sand
of the blue sea . . .

Stop being childish!
How long will you build castles
in these ash-turned cities?

Translated by Syed Sirajuddin.

RAJALEKSHMY

(1930–1965)   *Malayalam*

Many of Rajalekshmy's unusual stories, which began appearing in the mid-
fifties, are thinly disguised autobiographical pieces. The domineering, exploitative father in "Makal" (Daughter), 1956, was like Rajalekshmy's own
father, a lawyer who, abandoning his family, joined the freedom movement and spent several years in jail. The father in the story is betrayed
and deserted by his friends, and his dream of a new nation crumbles into
a politics in which money is all that counts. The story indicts those who
used and betrayed him, as well as the ambitious father who exploited his
daughter and "destroyed her life." The same autobiographical strain runs
through Rajalekshmy's second novel, *Uchaveyilum Illam Nilavum* (Midday
Sun and Tender Moonlight), 1960, the serial publication of which was
stopped because of the protests of people who found themselves portrayed
there in an uncomfortably realistic light. The remaining chapters still have
not been published.

"I have tried not to write for two years now. But it is almost impossible
not to," Rajalekshmy wrote in 1962. Only a few days before she took her
own life, she wrote again, this time to her sister, "If I live I will surely
write again. But there will be many who will be hurt by that. Let me
leave." Her untimely death came as a shock to other writers, who felt they

were in some way to blame. "A section of society that compassionately understands the dilemmas of the writer, the mental restlessness and complex pains that work as a background for literary creation, did not provide shelter for her. If an artist, either man or woman, who has a heart too tender to be tossed even by a gentle breeze, is forced to write out the last chapter of life, the mercilessness of that section of society which served as backdrop stands stigmatized," M. T. Vasudevan Nair, the well-known novelist, commented. Sugatha Kumari's response to Rajalekshmy's suicide was to write an elegiac poem lamenting the death. The initial guilt, however, was soon replaced by a critical response that transformed Rajalekshmy's suicide into an aesthetic fascination with death. Critics spoke of the "innate self-consuming fire of melancholy" and drew on evidence from her 1963 prose poem "Kumila" (Bubble)—"Oh Death if only I had begun to live in you, / If the embers of trivial hurts, small mercies and impossible longings that I blow hard on and aggravate, / If only they had merged in you and disappeared. . . . "—to suggest that she considered death a sort of formal, aesthetic resolution to the contradictions of life.

People who knew her agree that she was sensitive and talented, but they are reluctant to talk more about the actual details of her life. Rajalekshmy was born in Karakkumari, a village near Ernakulam. The family had a difficult time coping with her father's spontaneous decision to give up his job and join the national freedom struggle, but Rajalekshmy managed to earn a master's degree in physics and taught in a college until her death. It is possible that, like the father in "Makal," Rajalekshmy's father blamed her for his failure and resented her for not having become a lawyer to take over his firm. In the story the responsibility for supporting the family gradually shifts onto the eldest daughter, Sarada, without father or daughter quite realizing it—or at least they pretend not to realize it. Because she has to support the family, the daughter decides not to marry the man she cares for. Gradually the burden of her responsibility for the family and the sacrifice demanded of her kill her love for them. When her father dies, no tears fill her eyes. It is clear that Rajalekshmy longed to write, but what she had to say was too controversial, too critical of hitherto sacred familial relationships, too close to the societal bone, for her time—as perhaps it is today.

Rajalekshmy wrote several stories and two complete novels, *Oru Vazhiyum kure Nizhalukalum* (One Path and a Few Shadows), 1959, and *Jnanenna Bhavam* (I), which was being serialized in the widely read literary journal *Mathrubhumi* when she died in 1965. The last four sections were published posthumously. The story translated here was published in the journal *Mangalodayam Visheshalprati* in 1964.

◆

ATMAHATYA
(Suicide)

"Suicide is a sign of cowardice. Of worthlessness and cowardice—"

"I won't accept that it's cowardice. How can it be cowardice to put one's head before a moving train? Cowardice indeed—"

"Then it must be courage to make up one's mind to die when nothing goes as one wants. If one doesn't have the courage to face life, if one hides from reality, I call that cowardice."

I am one of those who thinks it prudent to keep my own counsel when such arguments break out in a gathering where men dominate. If the men remark, "She's dignified, that one," they are talking about a woman who expresses no particular opinion, who listens to both sides and smiles (if her smile be sweet, so much the better). That's how a woman should be, soft-spoken.

But it wasn't the practical application of these principles that made me sit quiet that day. I've never been able to listen to a discussion on suicide without feeling terrified. If I come across a news item in the paper saying that someone has committed suicide, I am anxious till I know who it is. When my younger brother reads his favorite column—the death announcements—out loud, I feel disturbed and restless.

Would Niraja Chakravarthy's name appear among them one cursed day? Niraja Chakravarthy—with her pale, fair skin, her copper-tinged hair, and a faint feline suspicion in her light eyes.

Niraja—the ill-starred heroine of Tagore's "Malanjo" has the same name. I've never found a suitable translation for the word "Malanjo," either in English or in Malayalam. An older brother who knows Bengali told me the story. He has a talent for telling stories in a moving way, has Kuttettan, though he does not write them. Whenever I see the crescent moon glimmering through silvery clouds, I think of Tagore's Niraja, and glimpse the pale feet beneath her white shawl.

I've known Niraja Chakravarthy for three years.

One Sunday, I was walking through my compound, savoring the delight of not having to go to work.

"Sister, a woman's calling out to you from over the southern wall," my younger brother said. Some people had moved into the big house by the southern wall five days ago. He was a senior officer in the navy, a North Indian. That's all I knew. I went up to the fence and saw their maid waiting there.

"Amma, they want to know whether you can speak Hindi or English."

"I don't know any Hindi. But I do know English."

The maid went in. I had almost lost patience when Niraja came out.

I noticed the beauty of her compact figure even on that first day. She asked me something and I replied in a few phrases of heavily impressive English.

"The medium I studied in was Hindi," she said hesitantly.

I was embarrassed that I had tried to show off to this poor creature. All she wanted was for me to explain to her maid that she should come to work in the morning before eight o'clock.

I told the Muslim maid what Niraja wanted and she assented.

Niraja and I stood there awhile, talking. Her husband usually left the house at eight. The maid left too, by nine or half past nine. She was entirely alone after that. Sometimes, she was afraid to be alone. I told her to come over if she was lonely or frightened, or if she needed anything. I showed her the place where the fence had been broken and a wicket gate fixed.

The people who had lived on the southern side of the house before she came had been our friends. The wicket gate had been repaired when they were there.

She came in the next evening, hesitantly. I had just got back from the office, had had my tea, and was washing my hands. She had some anise seed on a piece of paper. She wanted to know what it was called in Malayalam. I told her, and she wrote the word down in Hindi. She stayed for a while, talking to me, then went away.

I don't remember when we became friends. She began to come over every evening as soon as I got home, and she stayed till her husband returned at six. Most Sundays, her husband was on special duty or something. She would come to my house as soon as he had left.

My younger brothers soon found a name for her: sister's white moth.

My life was an endless rush and bustle, and I had little time to call my own. She found this strange, never having had to work for a living herself. Obviously, she had never seen a woman bringing home piles of papers to work on and sitting late into the night poring over files. Such hard work was new to her. She quickly learned enough Malayalam to call me Chechi (Older Sister).

I hated housework, though of course I had to do it. I had only Sundays to catch up on everything. One day, she saw me sweating away at my ironing. After that, she always came and gathered my saris when I was away at the office, and folded and ironed them for me. Sometimes she took them away to her house and ironed them there. Even if my younger brothers were at home, she took the saris away without saying a word to them.

Amma scolded me about this. "She's the wife of a big officer. It's not right, making her do all this for you."

But if I told her not to, she'd look so sad.

She was not happy with her wealthy, important, middle-aged husband. Naval officers often drank a lot, didn't they? She never said anything about that. She never spoke of her life at all. But one understands things like that without having to be told. I could read sorrow in her posture, in the way she moved, even in the way she drew close to me. I never knew whether there had been a Romeo in her childhood home, in the foothills of Bareilly, where mists hid the mountain tops. Perhaps there had. Perhaps there hadn't.

I wanted to escape from the office work and relax for a while. So I took all the leave that was due me and went to stay with my aunt in the country. I grew fat and brown there and when I came back, I learned that Niraja was going to be a mother. That, I thought, would solve her problems.

In spite of her big belly, in spite of feeling weak and tired, she still came over to iron my saris and help me do my hair.

When she went away to have her baby, her husband did not go with her to her mother's place—it was a servant or an orderly, or someone like that, who took her. The day after she left, the woman who cleaned the house came and told me that she had found a bottle of pills in the dirty-clothes basket. She showed it to me. They were vitamin tablets, fortified with iron. The doctor must have prescribed them for Niraja. She had taken only one or two. Why had she hidden the bottle among the dirty clothes? Not because the pills tasted bad, surely. She had only to swallow them. Then why?

"She's always doing things like this, my Amma. How many times I've seen her pour the medicines they gave her out the window!"

"Don't blow it all up. The poor girl must have just forgotten this bottle of pills."

"If you say so, Amma."

Those tablets that had been hidden away and the medicines that had been poured out into the yard haunted me for some time.

It was my younger brother who brought the news. He had met Mr. Chakravarthy on the road. Niraja had delivered, but the baby was stillborn. She was ill with a high fever.

It was three months before she came back. I was away at the office when she arrived. She came over that evening. She had lost a lot of weight and looked only half her former size. It seemed as if she'd aged ten years. For the first time, I saw her weep.

"I never thought that only one of us would die, Chechi. I'd hoped we'd both go together."

I didn't know how to comfort her. She did not remain my neighbor for much longer. Her husband was transferred.

I went along to help her pack and crate her things, but she would not allow me to do anything for her. "They've sent someone from the naval base. He'll do the packing. Sit down here, Chechi, that's all I want."

I took the day off when they were leaving. I saw them off at the gate, not sure whether her husband would appreciate my going to the station.

She folded her hands to bid my mother good-bye. She gathered my brother's son in her arms, kissed him, and set him on the ground.

She wasn't crying. Only her face looked terribly pale. "Good-bye, Chechi," she said, not looking at my face.

"You mean *au revoir*," I said.

"No. I mean good-bye."

I don't know whether she knew the meaning of the words. A voice whispered in my heart, It's true. You won't see her again. This is the last time you'll part from her.

Her letters came, once every month or so, in a rounded hand. They contained no news of her. They were written in the hope that I would answer.

Those who commit suicide are cowardly and stupid. So they say. My Niraja, my Niraja, who knew so well how to love. My Niraja, who never knew what fear meant.

Translated by Gita Krishnankutty.

KABITA SINHA ───────────────

(b. 1931)   *Bengali*

Few readers of modern Bengali literature would be unfamiliar with the author of the poem "Ishwarke Eve" (Eve Speaks to God). Born in Calcutta, Kabita Sinha spent many happy childhood hours in her mother's paternal home in Andul—a palatial house with a large library. She began writing as a child and was encouraged by her parents, particularly her mother, who has been a continuing inspiration. Kabita Sinha's study of botany at Presidency College in Calcutta was interrupted when she married the writer Bimal Roychowdhury. Years later she resumed her studies and graduated with distinction from Ashutosh College, Calcutta.

The novel *Charjon Ragi Juboti* (For Angry Young Women) appeared in 1956, followed by the novels *Ekti Kharap Meyer Golpo* (The Story of a Bad Woman), 1958, and *Nayika Pratinayika* (Heroine, Anti-Heroine), 1960. Kabita Sinha's first book of poems, *Sahoj Sundari* (Natural Beauty), appeared in 1965, and the well-known collection *Kabita Parameswari* (Poetry is the Supreme Being) in 1976. Two of the poems translated for this volume, "Ishwarke Eve" and "Deho" (Body), are taken from *Kabita Parameswari*. She has since published eight novels, a collection of short stories, and two books of poetry, *Horina Boiri* (The Rebel Deer), 1985, and *Shresto Kabita* (Best Poems), 1987. Her most recent work, *Momer Tajmahal* (The Wax Taj Mahal), 1989, is the story of her grandmother's life, written in nineteenth-century autobiographical style.

Though Kabita Sinha's poetry is more widely read and has received greater critical acclaim, she is also a novelist and a short story writer of some distinction. Critics consider her a modernist since her writing is formally innovative and ponders questions of ontology, but feminists have pointed out that her work also focuses on woman's identity and independence—as in the poems translated here—and that the protagonists in her fiction are nearly always female. In three moving poems written in 1970, one of them included here, Kabita Sinha pays tribute to the women writers Mahasweta Devi, Rajalakshmi Devi, and Debaroti Mitra.

Kabita Sinha worked as a teacher before becoming an assistant editor in the state government of Bengal. In 1965 she joined All India Radio and is now the station director at Darbanga, Bihar. During 1966 and 1967 she edited the poetry magazine *Danik Kabita* with her husband. The novel *Paurush* (Manliness/The Third Sex), 1984, won the Nathmal Bhualka award in 1986 and is due to appear in English translation. Kabita Sinha has won several other awards, including the National Fellowship of the Government of India in 1979. In 1981 she was invited to the United States to participate in the International Writer's Workshop at Iowa University, and was among those representing India at the Frankfurt Book Fair in 1986. Her work has been translated into several Indian and other languages.

◆

ISHWARKE EVE
(Eve Speaks to God)

I was first
to realize
that which rises
must fall
inevitably.
Like light
like dark
like you
I was first
to know.

Obeying you
or disobeying
means the same.
I was first
to know.

I was first
to touch
the tree of knowledge
first
to bite
the red apple.
I was first,
first—
first to distinguish
between modesty
and immodesty—
by raising a wall
with a fig leaf
I changed things
totally.

I was first.
I was first
pleasure,
my body
consoled
the first sorrow.
I was first
to see
your face
of a child.
Amidst grief and joy
I was first.
I first
knew
sorrow and pleasure,
good and evil,
made life
so uncommon.
I was first
to break
the golden shackles
of luxurious
pleasure.
I was never
a puppet
to dance
to your tune
like
meek Adam.

I was
rebellion
first
on your earth.

Listen, love,
yes, my slave,
I was the first
rebel—
banished from paradise,
exiled.

I learned
that human life
was greater
than paradise.
I was first
to know.

Translated by Pritish Nandy.

DEHO
(Body)

What do you want?
Look, there she stands, the sorceress,
an only-body, the magic wand, the paradise tree
—an only-body; still above the magic wand
desires rise,
welcome, unwelcome.

What do you want from her body?
Flesh, fat? prehistoric fire? smell of burnt flesh?
blood wine? or nails teeth hair?
the goddess skull shaped like a rice bowl?
or will you filter the best cocktail
of talent and loveliness? or will you,
like the magic cap releasing a million white birds,
unhinge her body, and press open
an endless supply of babies?

Take whatever you want.
There she stands, with arms akimbo,
things apart, the fire-bright magician,
who, if she wills, will bring forth from her body
the magic wonders, on her palms the prints
of fish lotus pig deer, her feet will create
rhythm, the brush between her fingers
will draw the hieroglyphs on the cave walls.
Still her cleverest game, the last game,
so long as her body stays,

after giving you whatever you want—
is nursing in a secret spot
a secret mole, a turquoise doubt.

Translated by Subhas Saha.

MAHASWETA
(For Mahasweta Devi)

The conflagration's final shade is white.
Not the orange hue of blood, the linseed
    flower's yellow, nor the terrible crimson
    of Kali's tongue,
Fiery vermilion or warm gold.
Can none approach the terror of fire?
There, fire knows no agitation,
Pallor within pallor;
There, Fahrenheit goes off the scale.
You dip your cup into the bushel basket
    and lift up, one by one,
    the queen's doubloons.
There is your own tranquil home.
What woman will enter there? Leaving behind
    duty fortune passion and *release?**
Why have you come three hundred years
Too early to this mistaken world?

Translated by Enakshi Chatterjee and Carolyne Wright.

---

*Duty, fortune, passion, and release *(dharma, artha, kama, and moksha)* are the four
responsibilities or aspects of life that the high-caste Hindu householder must
observe.

CHUDAMANI RAGHAVAN ────────

(b. 1931)   *Tamil*

Chudamani Raghavan's artistic heritage can be traced back to her grandmother, who wrote stories for the family in which she portrayed a woman
as bold and brave, and to her mother, who was a painter. Her family was
traditional, but encouraged the children to be modern and independent.
Her father was an officer in the Indian civil service, and they lived most
of the time in Madras. Chudamani herself has had no formal education,
but was taught Tamil, English, and mathematics by private tutors. Her
eldest sister, she says, who recommended books and introduced her to the
classics, was her first teacher. She liked reading and acquired most of her
education on her own. Even as a child she wrote both in English and in
Tamil, but it was not until 1954 that, encouraged by a friend, she published her first story. Her mother supported her efforts and encouraged
Chudamani, who is physically disabled, to develop a serious hobby. The
death of her mother in 1955 was a major loss.

Chudamani continues to write both in English and in Tamil, and several
of the thirty-one books she has published since 1954 have won awards.
"Nangam Ashraman," translated here, was judged the best Tamil short
story of 1972. It was first published in *Kanaiyazi* in February of that year.
In addition to short stories, Chudamani writes novels and plays, and contributes to leading Tamil literary magazines. Among her better-known
works are *Manattuku Iniyaval* (The Beloved Woman), 1959; *Iruvar Kandanar*
(Seen by Two), 1965; *Codanaiyin Mudivu* (End of the Ordeal), 1967; and
Suvarotti (The Poster), 1985. The Tamil Writers Cooperative Society published a collection of her short stories in 1978. *Amma* (Mother) was published in 1987.

Many of Chudamani's plots explore how, given identical situations,
men and women are treated differently by society. "Avanum Avalum"
(Him and Her), 1975, for instance, is about a widower and a widow who
are about to marry. The widower's mind dwells on the fact that his wife-
to-be has lived with someone else, but he is quite astonished when he
finds that she has had similar thoughts. Other stories treat the theme more
directly. In "Chirippu" (Laughter), 1962, a woman and man from the
same area in the city get married around the same time. Later both are
widowed, but the man marries again. When she attends his wedding, she
is criticized, since a widow's presence is considered inauspicious. She re-
torts, "What about that widower? Isn't he inauspicious? But he's sitting

up there in front. Send him away." People discount her remarks as the raving of a madwoman.

Chudamani's stories are nearly always humorous and well–structured. Despite the polemical intent of her writing, Chudamani feels that a writer must take care to see that her work remains "genuine and is never contrived." She prefers not to go out much, but draws on the experiences of those around her, incidents narrated to her, and her own reading as sources for her fiction. Instances of injustice and discrimination always make her angry, but they also fill her with a sense of helplessness. Only writing gives her keen personal pleasure and satisfaction.

The younger writer Ambai describes how, as a girl, her own fierce admiration for Chudamani was so possessive that she used to resent anyone else's claiming her attention. She dedicates her pioneering book on women in Tamil literature to Chudamani "for being what she is." The story we have included, considered by the writer herself to be one of her best stories, charts a woman's growth through her different relationships to a self-understanding. The *ashrama* are the four stages into which Hindu philosophy divides a man's life: *brahmacharin* (bachelor and student); *grihasta* (householder); *vanaprasta* (one living in detachment in the woods); and *sannyasin* (one who has achieved complete renunciation). In this story the author explores what the stages might mean in a woman's life.

◆

NANGAM ASHRAMAM
(The Fourth Ashram)

I looked up. The gathering clouds had broken up the sky. It grew dark. Was it going to rain? If it did, Shankari would get wet. She had been lying out there in the rain so long. But had I gone mad? She was no living thing out there in the open. For a mere body burnt to ashes and memories on the pyre, what difference did sun or rain make?

These thoughts crept in because I had not yet got used to the fact that she was dead. I must pull myself together, I thought. I must slowly integrate into myself the idea that she is dead.

And yet it was I who had lit the funeral pyre. Though Shankari had had a son, it was I who performed the last rites.

Shankari was dead. Shankari, my wife, was dead. She had fallen from the balcony on the third floor and died.

Was I raising a tomb with these words? Was it that easy to bury her under a tomb? She had had a maturity that demanded completeness, depth and knowledge. She had claimed them as her birthright. She couldn't be caged. She was an independent soul. We create barriers and we create freedom. She was beyond all that.

Was it drizzling?

I looked up. The clouds had cleared a bit. Then why were my cheeks wet?

She had died the day before.

Was I crying for you, Shankari, or for myself?

For whom were the tears?

Was I crying, Shankari, because you hadn't lived longer?

No, I was weeping for myself. It was my own loss I mourned. Where would I ever find such a perfect gem?

I had grown too possessive. Were it not so, it would not have ended like that.

Shankari, my friend's daughter, my student, my wife. She had been twenty years younger than I. Yet she chose to marry me.

"Shankari, do you know what you are doing?"

"I'm fully aware of it, Professor! I never do anything without thinking it through." She had smiled.

She had been thirty-eight then, this woman I had known for so many years. Her face and smile had been familiar. Beautiful? I cannot say. That would depend on the beholder. Each of us interprets beauty differently, such is its poetry. When she had smiled and spoken like that, this woman whom I had known so long had suddenly appeared strange, new, and yet everything that I had been searching for. As she stood before me, I had felt that she was a vision, all pervasive and sacred. Strangely enough, I had fallen in love, I, who until then had been a confirmed bachelor of fifty-eight. It had not been an old man's romance, but a marriage of equal spirits meeting in understanding.

Suddenly I felt drained. My legs went limp. There was a lump in my throat. Did I leave all my strength to burn away with her on the cremation ground at Krishnampet? It was already eleven in the morning, but it wasn't at all hot. One of those cool days in the month of Kartik. But still the sweat was dripping down my bald pate. How far had I walked from the burning ground? This was the bustle of Luz corner. I sat down, weary, in front of a department store.

My heart was heavy. Shankari had fled into freedom like a breeze—why did I feel so heavyhearted?

She had always called me Professor. "I'm your husband now. Am I still just a professor to you?" I had often asked her.

"Not *just* a professor. You are a professor through and through." When she said this, I must admit, I felt a little embarrassed.

It is true that it was as a professor, whose world had always been one of thought and of learning, as an educator, that she had valued me. She made it possible for me to rise to great heights and that had been the basis of her love for me, the basis of our marriage. We used to spend hours together discussing books and philosophy. We were involved in ideological debates and shared likes and dislikes. Often she would listen to me attentively and let me talk on. She had been lavish in her praise. "How lucidly you put ideas across." Then she would add, "You know, I'm so happy with you."

"Hello, Professor!"

I was startled. Then I recognized the figure standing before me and nodded to him. It was Murthy. He worked in the income tax department. He was nearly fifty—about seven years older than Shankari. He had been married to her earlier.

"May I sit with you awhile?" he asked

He sat down. He looked much younger than his age. He had thick, dark hair in which a few strands of gray had just begun to show. Just now his face was deeply troubled.

"I was there at the cremation ground. When I heard the news I wanted to rush to your house, but I just couldn't get up the courage."

"Why not? I would have understood."

"I heard she fell accidentally from the third floor."

"Yes."

"I can't bear even to think how much she must have suffered."

"She did not suffer. Death was instantaneous."

"Oh! That's a relief."

We sat quietly for a while.

"You must be wondering why she still has such a hold over me," Murthy ventured.

"That's not surprising. She was such a lovable person."

"And yet I was the one who let her go."

"It takes a lot of courage—and love—to let another go."

"Professor, I'm not sure if it was out of love that I let her go. Perhaps it was anger I really felt when she asked me for a divorce. If that was the reason I let her go, can you call it love?"

He fell silent and continued. "She told me she wanted to marry you. Just imagine. After a life in which we were so passionately in love. You know how people described our closeness, don't you, Professor?"

"Yes, indeed. Some said it with envy, and some mockingly—that you were like Manmada, the god of love, and Rati, his wife, who was desire and passion personified."

Murthy took a deep breath. "How true it is that one can't make comparisons. It was unbelievable that a woman who had given me such love could ask for a divorce and marry a person twenty years older. It was beyond my comprehension. I was so angry, so jealous! Perhaps that's why I consented to the divorce. Perhaps I felt that living with someone who preferred another man wasn't worth it. It was not love. It was resentment. It was an insult to my very being."

"Perhaps. But she chose someone much older and therefore there was no rivalry, so what insult could there have been?"

"Yes,—only we don't really understand ourselves. But one thing. Whatever I might have felt when she married you a year after we were divorced, whatever other feelings might have crept in, I know I continued to be fond of her, deep down inside. I couldn't bear the news of her death, I couldn't help wanting to steal a final fleeting look at her lifeless body. That is why I was there hiding in the crowd at the burning ground."

For some time we were both lost in our own thoughts.

One of the assistants at the shop looked at us suspiciously. "Do you want to buy something?" It was obvious that he was asking us to clear out.

We started to move.

"Where are you going? Home?" Murthy asked.

"No idea. What's the hurry? Anyway, who's there at home now?"

"I'd like to talk to you about Shankari for a while. I'm feeling low too."

"Oh, by all means."

"Shall we sit in that restaurant there instead of walking around aimlessly? Not that we can eat anything now. But if we just order some food, even if we don't eat, nobody will ask us to leave."

Murthy ordered something. I did not understand what he asked for. I don't know if he himself knew. Plates piled with food were placed in front of us and we stared at them unseeing.

Suddenly Murthy asked me, "You were her literature professor when she was in college, weren't you? Was she in love with you then? Is that why she married you after she divorced me?"

"No, when she was studying under me, she was only a student. She herself confessed that she had fallen in love with me much later . . . 'No one can take your place as my teacher. I have always admired the depth of your knowledge. For me, no one could compare with Professor Gnanaskandan. After all these years, it is those very qualities I need, Professor. Those things that I admired then, I cherish now and I have come to you.' "

"Someone so much older, who was her teacher, her father's friend, how could she suddenly think of him as someone to take the place of a husband?" Murthy persisted.

"I don't think you've understood her at all, Mr. Murthy."

"I still do not understand, Professor. We lived together and loved each other intensely for years, and she was the mother of my two children, yet she wanted a divorce. Isn't it strange? What was the attraction you held for her?"

"She was able to discuss books with me. We used to have very serious discussions. At night—a man and a woman in a bedroom together—we discussed Christ and Nietzsche, and tried to decide whose was the correct perspective on human nature. Do you understand when I tell you that this was the kind of attraction that drew us together?"

He stared at me amazed. He whistled softly, lost in his thoughts, and tapped lightly on the table.

"Now I understand," he confided as if he had only begun to understand. "A little while before asking for the divorce, she had changed. I would return from work, and reaching for her hand, would ask eagerly, 'Shall we go to the movies?' But she would suggest we go to a philosophical discourse at Adyar by some well-known thinker. Suddenly one night, out of the blue, she came to me excited with something she had read, and wanted me to read it too. 'Such a well-written piece. There's such depth to it. Some philosophers have such felicity with language, don't they?' she said. I couldn't understand all this. I couldn't even understand the way she spoke. I knew only that our relationship was no longer the same. Even when her body was in my arms, I often sensed that her mind was somewhere high in the clouds. After the intimacy we had shared, it wasn't hard to sense it. Once, when the moon shone bright it would arouse us. But then? Then Shankari asked, 'People have put a man on the moon. A wonderful achievement. But still there is hatred based on class and race and when we read about such cruelty and hatred, it seems as if it is about the Christians and their Crusades centuries ago. Which of these phenomena, I wonder, reflects humanity? What does progress really mean?' "

"And what did you say?"

"I said, 'Don't talk nonsense.' "

I smiled, filled with pity for him.

"At least, one night, when I went to her eagerly, she said to me, as if she were about to convey an important message, 'They say God is unlimited in his kindness. But when you look at the reality around, it seems as if anyone who is truly kindhearted cannot believe in God. What do you think?' How can I describe the frustration I felt that night? 'If you continue to talk such rubbish, you'll have to be put into an institution,' I shouted. What a look she gave me! Today I realize that with that look, she left me."

He had indeed celebrated the divinity of the body with her. That gift he had been capable of giving. But when she reached beyond, he couldn't keep pace with her. "Professor, with your guidance, my mind grows like a child of light," Shankari would say . . .

And this man wanted to know why she was attracted to me.

"She was a very independent person, Professor!" Murthy said.

"Yes"

"She must have decided to leave as soon as she sensed that we had drifted apart. She wasn't my wife after that. She would never do anything that was repugnant to her. She could never be forced into anything."

"That's true."

"She must have thought of marrying you only after all that. I see that now. And she had the honesty to ask for a divorce."

"And you had the generosity to grant it," I said, thinking of how he had finally agreed to a divorce by "mutual consent." They had lived apart for a year so that it would be legally correct.

"Generosity? I don't think so, Professor. I never forgave her for the past, and never once did I see her again as a friend. I was no different from my children, who rejected her completely after she married you. I was as narrow-minded as they were."

"You, narrow-minded, Mr. Murthy? Had you been so, you wouldn't have married Shankari, a widow, in the first place."

I held my head in my hands, weighed down by the pain of remembering Shankari.

"I never thought of Shankari as a widow when I married her," said Murthy. "Now, I feel interested all over again in her first marriage. You probably knew about it, Professor?"

Slowly I shook myself free of the weight and raised my head. "I was a close friend of her father's, you see, and I knew the family well."

"Tell me about it," he said, eagerly.

"There isn't much to tell. At sixteen, she said she was in love with that boy, Manohar, and insisted on marrying him. Before her father agreed, he consulted me. I advised him to give his consent. I told him it was like an awakening in the first dawn of life, and it would be no use trying to prevent her falling in love with love itself."

"I don't follow."

"She was extremely young. At an age when everything is new, life itself is a wonder, a miracle. It is as though at that age the heart has just gained sight, and the freshness of its view turns everything beautiful and wondrous beyond words. In the intoxication of that joy, each day is like a dream. Her love for Manohar was a projection of that rapture. He was only eighteen. He reflected her joy, for he, too, was in the first stage of blossoming. He embodied her dreams. Actually it was not so much Manohar she was in love with, as her own life and youth, with the light of her awakening sensibilities. She fell in love with a dream, and it is difficult to believe that the marriage might even have had a physical reality."

"The boy died young, didn't he?"

"Yes, of leukemia."

"How old was he?"

"Twenty-one."

"How sad, how very sad."

"In a sense, it seems right that he died before the first flush of youth had passed. It would have been incongruous if he had gone on to age and go gray like everyone else, even after Shankari had lost the freshness of first ecstasy. Dreams should not age, Mr. Murthy."

Murthy settled the bill. We left the restaurant and walked on, down the Luz Church Road.

"Of the three of us, I think Shankari was most deeply and permanently attached to you, Professor," said Murthy, looking at my elderly figure with something like envy.

"No," I said calmly. "Finally she wanted to leave me also, and had asked me for a divorce."

He stood stunned, unmindful of the heavy flow of traffic. I had to caution him to move to the sidewalk.

Standing on the sidewalk, he gazed at me intently, taking some time to get over his amazement. Still incredulous, he asked me at last, "What! She wanted a divorce from you?"

"Yes."

"Whatever for?" For the first time I saw a trace of derision on his face. "To marry for the fourth time at forty-three?"

"What a fool!" I said softly, under my breath.

"Why are you angry with me?" His face was flushed.

"You haven't understood her, that's all."

"Why a divorce at that age?"

"To be alone," I said and paused. "To be herself."

"What's that?"

"She had reached the maturity for final fulfillment, Mr. Murthy." Once again I saw Shankari in my mind. I saw her eyes, large, deep, and calm, looking up from a perfectly chiseled face. Her voice had come up clear and unwavering, confident that I would understand her.

"I want a divorce, Professor. I have to go away and be on my own. I have little more to learn from ties and union. My freedom must gain its completeness in solitude. I cannot stop halfway. Please let me go."

"I don't understand it, Professor," Murthy said. "Can you explain?"

The sun had grown hotter now. I felt the sweat roll down my spine.

I spoke slowly, deliberating. "Every human being is ultimately alone, Mr. Murthy. Shaped through the bonds of relationships, a person develops and matures, but the final release occurs when one finds true liberation in being oneself. Not all of us realize this. Shankari did. She was the kind of person who grows gradually, attaining fulfillment by stages. When she was sensation, dream, when she was pulsating with life, she was with Manohar. Then came the life of the body, beyond the state of mere emotion, with you. Even though she lived a normal conjugal life with all three of us, it is significant that it was only with you that she bore children. Physically, as a woman and mother, she was fulfilled.

"Later, when she went beyond the body, and the intellect took prominence, she lived with me. And when that was fulfilled, and she knew that her supreme fulfillment would require total solitude of self, she broke away from all bonds, including marriage. A total being cannot but reach that stage. Relationships, associations, obligations, marriage, family—she gave up everything, or rather, she experienced and outgrew everything. She wanted to liberate herself in order to be alone. That is why she asked me for a divorce."

"Amazing!"

"Come to think of it, what is so amazing about it, Mr. Murthy? After all, didn't our ancestors decree the code of four ashramams, beginning with brahmacharin? Consider this as the four ashramams a woman experiences. Shankari attained all that had to be attained in the first three. She had become ready for the fourth. She merely asked me to step aside."

"And you would have agreed, certainly. You had the wisdom to understand her."

I answered, but not without a moment of hesitation, "What use is wisdom?"

"Why do you say that?"

"I had grown too attached to her, Mr. Murthy. Whereas she had lived each relationship, discarded it, and gone on, I became totally immersed in the only love I had managed to find, at fifty-eight. My wisdom notwithstanding, my love became a madness. So, even if I understood her, I couldn't let her go, so excessive was my love for her and the greed I felt."

He stood and stared at me.

"Didn't I say that you had the generosity to let her go? Well, I said that because I did not have it and it's a bitter realization."

My body was shrinking with shame.

"I didn't want to lose her. I couldn't let her go. I refused to let her live in the freedom she desired. I stood in the way of her fulfillment. I categorically refused to give her the divorce."

He looked at me, shocked. My distressed voice and trembling body must have told him the rest. He stood petrified, eyes staring fixedly. I looked up at him, my heart heavy with darkness.

"We both know, don't we, Mr. Murthy, that she was an independent soul. Nothing could keep her bound."

Murthy was still silent.

"I wouldn't let her go . . ."

"And so . . . ?" The voice came from a deep hollow.

"Yes. And so she escaped."

I walked on, without stopping to see if he was following.

Translated by Savithri Nataranjan.

MANNU BHANDARI —————————————

(b. 1931)   *Hindi*

"I recently found a diary I used to keep when I was fifteen or sixteen. It's all about restrictions and injustices. I smiled when I read it. I had such sharp reactions to things I didn't like. I felt if something were wrong, it had to be exposed. It is that spirit, I think, that has been channeled into my writing." Mannu Bhandari traces this idealism in part to the influence of her father, Suksampath Bhandari, a well-known scholar who compiled one of the first Hindi dictionaries. The family was not well off, but he did not "think it right to ask to be paid, though he worked on that dictionary for most of his life." He also had progressive ideas about women, she says. The marriage of her eldest sister in the late thirties made the news because the bride did not cover her head with a *ghungat*. Yet, with respect to her mother, Mannu Bhandari adds, he was a tyrant.

Born in Ajmer, Mannu Bhandari grew up when the freedom movement was at its height. In 1946 she helped organize a twenty-six-day strike when two of her colleagues were dismissed for their involvement in the Indian National Army—"We were all inspired. There was something in the air of those times." She began to write when she was a student. Her first story, "Mein Har Gayi" (I've Lost [The Battle]), published in the magazine *Kahani* (Allahabad) was, to her surprise, well received. Readers wrote to congratulate her, and, excited by the success, she tossed off a couple more. Often when she is ready to write a novel, she goes away— to a town in the hills or a room in the college hostel—and works until she has finished. It is almost impossible, she feels, to write seriously in the midst of domestic demands. Her first job, as a lecturer in Hindi, took her to Calcutta, where she worked from 1952 to 1964. Since 1964, she has taught Hindi literature at Miranda House in Delhi.

Mannu Bhandari and her husband, Rajendra Yadav, who is a writer, publisher, and critic, were leading figures in the Nayi Kahani (New Story) movement of the 1950s and 1960s. The group argued that the Hindi literature of the preceding years was too didactic, too romantic, too tendentious. They wanted a fiction that explored a variety of real-life experiences and that had no explicit political commitments. As a group they promoted critical discussion and self-conscious interest in form, such as that evident in *Ek Inch Muskan* (A One-Inch Smile), 1966, a novel jointly authored by Mannu Bhandari and Rajendra Yadav, she writing for the woman protagonist, he for the man. Krishna Sobti (b. 1926), author of the much-lauded *Mitro Marjani* (Damn You, Mitro), 1967, who was also part of this movement, created a radically new prose style—bawdy, colloquial, and totally unihibited.

In 1966, Mannu Bhandari published a collection of short stories, *Yeh Sach Hai Aur Anye Kahaniya* (This Is the Truth and Other Stories), another, *Shresht Kahaniya* (Best Stories), in 1974, and in 1977, *Meri Priya Kahaniya* (My Favorite Stories).

With the novel *Ap ki Bunty* (Your Son, Bunty), 1971, she emerged as a serious writer. The story is written from a child's point of view, and explores present-day pressures on family relationships. It was an instant success, praised by critics for its subtle and in-depth handling of a topical theme. But her best-known work is perhaps *Mahabhoj* (The Great Feast), 1979, in which she moved outside the scope of personal relationships to deal with corruption in public life. The novel is an indictment of politicians who unscrupulously exploit the most tragic of events for personal gain and in the process betray the ethical principles on which the nation had defined itself during the freedom movement. Coming as it did shortly after the Emergency, the novel was read as an indictment of the new ruling elites and their rapaciousness. Mannu Bhandari's novels and stories have been translated into several Indian languages and into English, and a couple of her stories have been made into films. The story translated here was published in *Sarika* in 1965.

◆

SAZA
(The Sentence)

There is a postcard from Father addressed to Umesh Chachaji.* "The date of the ruling is April 16th, and this time there will be a decision for sure; there won't be a stay order again. If you can manage to get some leave and it is not too inconvenient, come down for a couple of days."

Not a line for Munnu or me. No love, no mention of wanting us there. After a whole year this is the first card to come from Father, and there is nothing about us in it—it's as if he doesn't know that we are also here. Has Father changed so much? Maybe he hasn't changed himself, maybe time has done so. It's not only him it's changed, but all of us. Have I not changed a great deal, too? Munnu, is he not different now? I don't know what state Mother will be in! Oh God! Tell me what hasn't happened in these five years!

April 16th, five days from today. I'll go, I'll definitely go. And I will take Munnu with me. After every hearing, Kantmama, Mother's brother, had said that the ruling would certainly be favorable that time. Oh God, please let it be so! But my heart quivers. The first time everybody said the same thing. I was not totally innocent then, but I didn't understand very much, either. Father and Mother always thought of me as a child—perhaps that is why I was such a baby! But how rapidly I have grown and matured! I understand legal matters. I cook two meals a day for seven people. Not only that, I do all the housework. The girls who were with me in school . . . I'll bet you can't get them to do any work at all. But why should they do all this? God forbid that they should have to go through such an experience.

---

*Chachaji means "Uncle," father's brother; *-ji* is a suffix that denotes respect and/or affection.

Will Father really be let off? At the time of the last ruling, Dadi, Baba,* Chacha all came down. Everyone went to the hearing in court, but they didn't take us. They could have left Munnu behind, but I was old enough, I had just completed my ninth class exam. I knew everything about Father's case but still they didn't take me. Munnu and I waited for them with bated breath. I was very nervous, but I kept comforting Munnu. Perhaps nobody else considered me grown up, but he certainly did. At noon Dadi and Mother came back, crying. Baba sat down and hid his face in his hands and wept bitterly. "O Lord, such injustice in your world! My innocent son sentenced for two years!" Seeing everybody crying, we also burst into a flood of tears. Father was not allowed to come home—they took him to prison directly.

I did not go to school for two days. When I did, all my friends began sympathizing with me. But it was not sympathy at all. Does one show one's care by saying, "Hai, Hai, poor thing! Her father has been sent to jail?" Then softly to each other, "Even such well-off people steal. That is why Ashaji had such airs." I would feel like screaming, My father has done nothing. It's just that at this time he is under a bad star. When the stars are in evil conjunction anything can happen. Was Lord Rama a thief? But did he not have to spend fourteen years in exile in the forest? The Pandavas had done nothing, but they too had to live incognito. See then? When the planets are not right, even kings have to suffer. Why don't these girls understand something so obvious? Mother had told me that these were bad times for us. Whatever happens, she had said, you have to bear without lament, and I had understood what she meant. That is why I would never say anything to them. But they never understood. Perhaps one's ability to comprehend things can grow only when times are bad.

Anyhow, just then Kantmama arrived. He had come straight home upon his return from England. He was angry with Baba and Chacha. How could they let such a thing happen? In these times the guilty keep themselves in the clear. They appropriate lakhs of rupees and sit by, twisting their mustaches disdainfully. Files disappear without a trace. And here he is, without having done anything, serving a prison term. He's not guilty of any wrongdoing. Baba listened to this tirade with his head bowed like a criminal. Poor man! What did he know of fine legal points? When he could bear to listen no more, he would cry.

---

*Dadi means "Grandmother," father's mother. Baba means "Grandfather," father's father.

I didn't like the way Kantmama behaved at that time, but nobody could say anything. He was doing the running around for an appeal in the High Court. After he got back from England, Kantmama had begun to think very well of himself. Perhaps he had become worthy of such a self-image.

Besides, he actually managed to get the appeal accepted. Father was released twenty-five days later. I thought, The moment he arrives, Munnu and I will hug him. He will shower his love on us. The cloud under which the house has sat for twenty-five days will be lifted. Good times will return. Nobody had a thought to spare for us ever since all this had begun. There were so many people in the house and Father was not there. We had been the center of the house earlier. Food was cooked to our taste, and we could be taken out when we felt like it. Suddenly, we were nobodies. I did have some sense of what was happening, but not Munnu—he would throw a tantrum on the least excuse. I would try to explain, "These are bad days for us, don't make a fuss over everything." But he wouldn't accept any theory of stars and planets and would continue crying. I thought that our troubles were over now that Father, the one who always wiped our tears and treated every wish as a command, was returning to us.

But nothing of the sort happened. Father came with Kantmama in the tonga. Everybody stood at the door. Father climbed off. Not only did he not speak, he did not even look at anybody. With lowered eyes, he went straight upstairs. Everybody was stunned. What had become of Father! Nobody had the courage to go upstairs. Finally Dadi sent Mother. She came back soon enough. "He won't open the door. When I kept knocking he only said, 'Go away, don't bother me now.' "

Though I had wept with the other members of the family every day, that was the day my heart cried with the pain of the full knowledge of what was happening. What had happened to my Father? He had come back to the house after twenty-five days, and he didn't even look at us! My mind repeated, This is not my Father. He cannot be like this. The people in jail have done something to him. There was a strange fear in my heart—perhaps Father will never love us again. And truly, I have never received any affection from him since, not now, not to this day. In that card, could he not have written one line to us? In a way, I understand his indifference and detachment. Perhaps he does not want to feel attached to anybody. Suppose he gets another prison term?

Everyone went up in the evening. He opened the door then, but did not talk to anybody. He just pushed his face into the pillow. I had a feeling that he had been crying. We were sent back downstairs immediately. How angry I had been! He was our father and all these people were acting as if we were of no consequence. I had the first right to him. He loved me more than anyone else in the world. I wished all those people would leave Aligarh as soon as possible. Surely then Father would care for us as he used to. Perhaps he felt embarrassed before everybody. After all, it was humiliating. Didn't I feel the same at school?

The next day Kantmama and Chachaji did leave. Dadi and Baba stayed—they were part of our household. But Father did not come down. Mother was sent upstairs to sleep. In the morning she said, "Mother, take Munnu with you to the village and put him in the school over there. It will be difficult to pay even his fees here. Asha's in her final year or I would have sent her to her uncle. We'll vacate the ground floor." Then they talked of many things and both of them cried and cried. I used to shed tears without reason if I saw anybody crying. That time there was reason enough. Munnu would go away! How would he live in the village? That school there could hardly be called a school. And he was in such a good one here. Father may have been silent all day, but over this he would never keep quiet.

But he did not utter a word. Perhaps Mother and Father had made this decision together. Munnu went amid much weeping and protest. As he was leaving, Father did hug him close for a long time. I stood beside them. Father's eyes were full of tears. I really wanted to wipe away those tears, not to lessen his grief but to get some of his attention and affection. Munnu was close to Father even though he was going away, but I would probably remain distant always, even though I would be staying so close! But Father did not come down to see him off. Nobody went to the station. And who could have gone? Mother did not go out on her own and, if I went, how would I get back?

After nearly a month we were on our own in our house, but Munnu was gone. Not only that, in a week's time many of our things had gone too. The ground floor had been vacated. Cooking, eating, and sleeping were now to be done on the top floor. I had the small storeroom to study in.

Father had begun to speak a little, but he was not at all like the person I had known. He would lie down all day, or read a little. Sometimes he would write something with the pillow in his lap. I wanted very much to read what he wrote. But I could never gather enough courage. I had read so often that the ones who are courageous in the face of ill fortune are the truly brave—the one who smiles as he bears suffering is the real man. I would feel like telling Father that. But didn't he know it already? Then? It's the one who is a real thief who should hide his face in such a manner. Father should have gone out more. Living like that, he was merely offering proof to everybody that he was guilty. But how could I have said that to him?

My little storeroom was not bad, but it was very hot and there was no fan. The nights would go by somehow, but in the afternoon those rooms were like a furnace. The vacation went by very slowly. I had to desire to go to a friend's place. I didn't even visit the neighbors. Nobody is a friend in bad times. The only firm decision was that, until the bad conjuction of the planets changed, everything was to be borne without murmur.

There was a letter from Baba in July. Munnu had been admitted to the sixth class in school and he was happy. We all believed that he must be happy, because our happiness lay in believing it. Baba also wrote that he had started doing accounts for a shop in the evenings. He would get twenty-five rupees which he would send to Father. Chachaji would sent fifty. I saw Baba with his decrepit frame, bent back, and clouded eyes, working again at his age. Mother said that she had to run the house with these seventy-five rupees.

I stopped taking the school bus. I would walk three miles. Rain or shine, my face would show nothing. Sometimes I would think, It's been two years and three months since Father was suspended. All the savings in the bank are gone, Mother's jewelry has been sold, and God knows what else has disappeared. Lawyers are probably a real swindling lot. Occasionally I would think, Father should have really taken the money from the office. We could at least have kept Munnu with us, and bought a fan also. This steamy heat makes your skin boil. It is not as if we are thriving because of our honesty.

God knows what has happened to Mother—she is shriveling up inside. She used to do no housework, but now she does everything herself. Sometimes Father helps her, and then I feel good. Mother has also become very irritable. She beat me one day over some trivial thing. In my memory this was the first time I had been beaten. And that too at this age! More than my body, my person was hurt. What made me even sadder was that Father just sat there and said nothing. He did not stop Mother, nor did he comfort me.

I sat in my storeroom and wept for hours. O God, send me every grief but make my Father like he used to be. If he works like before, I'll bear anything.

The first date for the hearing had been set for six months. Kantmama had tried very hard to get the date fixed earlier, but the law follows its own pace and not Kantmama's dictates. He had taken on all the expenses for the case. He must have done it by concealing it from his wife, or she would not have let him spend a paisa.

The first hearing went very well. We were shivering in the cold when we heard this, but a wave of warmth ran through from top to toe.

The condition of the house then went from bad to worse. Mother was in particularly bad shape. I used to sense then that she had been gripped by some sickness that was gnawing at her insides. I had studied diseases and their symptoms in hygiene class, and she showed signs of TB. She coughed for four months after catching a chill in the winter.

Then Baba's letter arrived. With desperate helplessness, he had written, "Due to some lapses in the accounting, that job is gone. Now I'll be able to send only fifteen rupees from my pension of fifty. Don't lose heart, son, trouble never comes singly. But times will change for sure. There may be a delay in the court of the Almighty, but justice will be done."

The next hearing was set for April. It was not possible to get an earlier date. Father had been at loose ends for a year, and still there were to be two hearings more. If the gaps between them were as long, then it would all take still another year. My heart quivered in fear. It seemed impossible to carry on this way, Munnu in the village, Father in the bedroom, I in my storeroom, and Mother on the bed.

Only I know in what condition I wrote my school examinations. But still I made second division. Nobody wanted to celebrate. Everybody's spirit was dead, so one felt neither joyful nor sad.

In July there was a fresh problem. The village school was only a middle school. What would happen to Munnu now? What was to become of me? There was no question of going to college. I knew that with a monthly income of sixty-five rupees it was virtually impossible to think of keeping us together and feeding us, let alone consider our education. Baba sent Munnu to Umesh Chachaji directly, and informed us of the move. He knew our conditions. Father quaked when he read this letter and Mother cried, "I would rather Munnu did not have an education . . . Why did he send him there? At least I should have been allowed to see him first. Everyone knows what Lila is like. My child will simply die of fear there." She kept on for two days. Father would sit guiltily silent. Why did Mother do that? If Father could have done something, then why didn't he do it? After two days she said, "I think we should send Asha there also. She can go to the college over there." I did not understand whether Mother was being sarcastic or what, but the next sentence clarified everything. "You know Lila. If Asha is with Munnu, he'll feel a little more secure. He'll at least have a lap to sleep in." And then Mother burst into bitter tears. "Write to Umesh. Whatever he spends, he should count as a debt. I'll repay every paisa. God will turn our luck around or else I'll sell myself and repay him. But he should have some mercy on my children. These poor creatures are virtually orphans. He must spare some affection for them and tell Lila also to be a little kind."

Kantmama had gone to Delhi for his own work. He stopped at Aligarh on his way back. Mother sent me to Allahabad with him. Kantmama did say once, "Send her with me to Calcutta—she can study there." But was I going to study? That was just a notion. I was to look after Munnu. If he cried, I was to offer my lap. And that day I really grew up—I was like Mother. But when the time came to leave, in spite of all my wisdom and maturity, I burst into tears. Because of Mother's condition, I had taken over most of the work of the house. Now what would happen? How would Mother manage all the work in her state? Her chronic fever had reduced her to skin and bone. But to look after Mother, there was Father. She had Father's lap to cry in. Munnu was alone over there. I was needed most by him.

On the way, Kantmama asked me, "Sharda seems to run a fever every day. Has she been taken to a doctor?"

"No." And I cried.

"Don't cry, it'll soon be all right."

"Father said several times that she needs a doctor, but Mother doesn't listen. She says doctors always put false notions into one's head." Kantmama fell silent. Didn't he understand that Mother didn't go to a doctor because there was no money to pay for fees and medicine? The doctor would have prescribed tonics and milk and fruit and would have advised rest and a mind free of care. Tell me, is that possible on sixty-five rupees? He could have asked me—I was managing the money those days. I had it all at my fingertips. But what could I say to him? He was paying for the lawyers, and didn't I know how expensive lawyers are?

As soon as he saw me, Munnu hugged me and cried. I could not hold my tears back either. Chachi* did say something, but in the midst of our weeping we did not hear it. I cannot express what I felt when

---

*Chachi, "Aunt," is the wife of one's father's brother.

I hugged Munnu. I felt he really needed a lap and some support. Talking to Chachi, I realized that she did not like my coming, but I hadn't come of my own will. Munnu had grown quite dark. His face looked pinched and dull and his eyes were full of nervous trepidation. He seemed tense and subdued. He used to be so mischievous at home. Such a young child, how he had changed! His job was to amuse one-year-old Billu. He carried him around all day, when he should have been studying or doing his homework.

At night, as we were going to sleep, he said, "Didi, I want some cotton candy tomorrow. Tillu and Pammi have it every day. Chachi gives them money and tells them to eat it up quickly without letting me see. But they eat it in front of me. One day Tillu was teasing me while he ate, so I took his cotton candy away. He complained to Chachi. She hit me. She really hits hard." And he started sobbing again. I kissed him and promised, "I'll buy my brother cotton candy," but my heart almost burst. I was old enough to understand and bear it all. But how could this poor child understand? He may have understood, but how could he learn to bear it?

The very first night I resolved, I won't go to college. I'll do all the housework so that Chachi gets to rest and her temper remains in check. If she says anything, I won't utter a squeak. If she remains in a good frame of mind, Munnu will be safe. I'll help Munnu with his studies at night.

I would get up even earlier than Chachi and make tea for everybody. Then I would quickly get Tillu and Pammi ready for school and give breakfast to all three and send them off. Chachi would be sure to come to check the breakfast plates. Perhaps the thought bothered her that I might have been giving something extra or special to Munnu. Chachaji would praise me, "You are very efficient, Asha. You do such a lot." Chachi would immediately interject, "When I was her age I used to look after a family of twelve. I used to roll papads and make preserves by the half ton." I kept quiet. I had also taken over cooking both meals.

At night when I made my way to bed, my legs would buckle under me. Sometimes I used to make Munnu stand on them. That used to make them feel a little better, but what of my feelings? Earlier, when Mother occasionally had asked me to do some chores, Father would admonish her. "My Asha is going to be a doctor," he'd say. "I'll send her abroad. Will I let her ruin her life in this, this innkeeping?" This sentence would hang in the air and echo in the room. Slowly, as I got accustomed to the work, my legs ached no more, and my heart also grew numb.

I did not write to Mother that I had not sought admission to college. Chachi had given me four postcards and said that was the number I would get every month. I wrote news of our well-being. That is all.

I worked day and night and kept Chachi's bad temper under control. The rest and leisure made her almost softer towards me, but she would occasionally beat both her children and Munnu. Her children were used to it, so they would just laugh and run away. And though they were beaten, they were also petted and loved. But Munnu would get scared. His heart would weep and he'd look at me with pitiful, haunted eyes. But even though I felt terrible, I said nothing on such occasions. I thought that these beatings would make Munnu either very stubborn or deaden his capacity to feel. Father and Mother had never laid a finger on us. When we were alone, I would hug and console him. "It's a matter of a few more days, Brother. We will go home to Mother and Father—you just wait." I don't know if he believed or understood me. But my feelings were truly wounded when Chachi said in a rage, "Twenty thousand rupees from the office just vanished . . . probably buried somewhere . . . and here they are, sucking our blood. These are supposed to be respected elders. A curse on such elderly wisdom." I would wonder, Does Chachi really think Father had taken the money? If he had, would he have left us there like that? And all the days of the past would come back in a flash. How much did he love us . . . really? Whatever I might have written in my letters, didn't he know what we are going through?

On the thirty-first, when Chachaji gave his salary to Chachi, she said, "Now write to Asha's father that we cannot send fifty rupees. In these times, it is difficult to afford to keep these two. Besides, we have our children to think of. There isn't a gold mine here." What she said was true, but my heart sank. If Chachaji did not send money, how would they survive? What could one do with fifteen rupees a month? That was the rent on the room alone. Mother and Father's stricken faces loomed before my eyes all night, and I cried with them.

There was no letter from Mother for a long time. All day long I carried one worry—What must she have done for money? There was no letter from Kantmama either. I didn't know what was happening there.

The month of August passed. I had used up my four cards, but had received no reply. What had happened to Mother, why didn't she write? In September there was a letter from Kantmama: "Sharda was ill, so I brought her here. She's undergoing treatment. Dineshji has changed his room. His address is. . . . What can I say except that it is destiny or fate that we cannot get a date soon. The third date is at the end of this month. I'll go for the hearing. Don't you worry. God will help us. Something is bound to happen by summer."

Was Father alone there? Mother and Father had lost each other's laps to cry in. And Father's address? I knew every lane of Aligarh. This was a settlement of wage laborers. Dark, damp alleys . . . open drains. Who was cooking for Father? He'd never done all that before. If he ever lit the charcoal stove, Mother would stop him. He would then say, "Sharda, who knows if I'll be freed this time also? If I'm sentenced, then God alone knows what all I'll have to do."

Mother would interrupt sharply, "Why do you ever say such a thing? There may be delay in God's court, but there isn't chaos." This sentence she had learned from Baba and had made her own, like a ritual chant.

And I would repeatedly ask God for one favor: O Lord, let him not be sentenced. Father should be compensated for his penance. What he is going through, is it in any way less than severe penance? Living in a damp, dark, poky room, hiding from everybody. His children far away, his wife somewhere else. Have mercy now. Don't punish him anymore.

The fourth hearing was over in March. Kantmama's letter said that the ruling would be in our favor. The case had been presented very well. The date for the judgement should come soon.

I would sit and count the days. It had been four years since Father had been suspended. What had not happened in those four years? I would pray, God, it's been so long now, don't forget us. The delay is no less than a punishment, but don't do anything worse.

Munnu and Tillu brought their examination results home. Tillu had passed in all the subjects and Munnu had failed in one, but had been promoted. Chachi hugged Tillu while Munnu looked on tearfully. Chachi turned to him and said, "So you failed eh! Put your mind to your lessons, Munnu Sahib. Only then will you pass like Tillu. You can't pass by sitting around crying all day long." His tears rolled down his cheeks. He wiped them with his sleeve, and as he was going in, Tillu began taunting him, "Failu-ram, Failu-ram." That was the first day I found it very difficult to control myself. I felt like saying, "When does he get time to study? All day long he looks after Billu. He is sent to the market umpteen times." But no, I was silent.

Munnu did look at Tillu with burning eyes once. I felt he'd perhaps hit him, but he neither turned nor spoke. How had Munnu become so forbearing? I would lecture him about enduring everything silently.

But I was so pained then when he did bear everything without protest. There was no other way.

Then it was vacation. I thought, If there is any word from Kant-mama or Mother, we will go there, but there was no letter. Father never wrote at all. Mother would sometimes write a couple of lines: "I'm slowly getting better. Don't worry about me. My blessings to Lila and love to the children. Help Chachi and don't make any trouble for her." Every time I'd feel, What a false letter Mother writes.

But the period of our patience stretched to a year. In March there had been a hearing and then it was April of the next year.

I had begun feeling that we'd have to live like that forever, in the very same fashion. I'd never go to college. Munnu would fail every year in one subject and be promoted with difficulty. Mother would always be ill and stay with Kantmama for treatment. Father would stay in his stinking hovel and cook for himself.

And then today there is the postcard from Father—the first note in his own handwriting. I looked at it, read it, touched it a thousand times as if that card would convey something of Father's state.

Father has not called for us. Will Chachaji take us? But we will go this time whatever happens. Should I write to Kantmama and ask him to pick us up on the way?

Tomorrow at 10:00 A.M. we will hear the ruling. Munnu and I have both come to Aligarh with Kantmama. He left us at the *dharmashala* and went to fetch Father. I was hoping Mother would come, but she did not. Kantmama only said, "Her condition is such that . . . When the ruling is through then you can all go there." I wonder how Mother is. My heart quails. Kantmama is concealing something. I've also hidden so much from Mother. Which of us knows the truth about the other anymore? To keep the others free of burden, we are all heavy with our loads.

When Father came, Munnu and I hugged him. Father! Perhaps we seemed as broken to him as he did to us. We all wept. Kantmama too. In the evening Dadi and Baba also came. At night Munnu said, "Dadi, we'll live with Father now, won't we? You pray all the time. Tell your God to release Father."

"Yes, Beta. You will stay with your father. That is what I ask God day and night."

"I'll never go back to Chachi now. What does Tillu think he is? Let him come when I stay with my father! I can beat him in anything, studies or wrestling. I did stand first in class once before, didn't I, Didi?"

My eyes grew moist. I was seeing Munnu in his true form after such a long time. When Tillu teased him, he never said anything, he just sat inside and cried quietly. Perhaps he knew that if he said anything to Tillu it would mean a taste of Chachi's temper. But how awful I felt that day. Where had Munnu's natural childlike envy and rivalry gone? Were we created to endure so much from such an early age?

Munnu slept on Dadi's bed. I couldn't sleep at all. Tomorrow is the day of judgement—judgement for all our lives and our fortunes. Kant-mama seemed assured and confident, but Father's face was expressionless.

The judgement has been rendered. I, too, went to court. Nobody stopped me this time. There was not much of a crowd. Who was interested in Father except his family? Father stood in the box. We sat on chairs waiting for the judge to arrive. When he came, Baba closed his eyes. Dadi's head was bowed. She must have been praying silently. I held on to Munnu's hand tightly. I felt that if there were any further delay I would suffocate.

I understood nothing whatever of the judge's legal jargon, but I heard the last sentence: "The accused is released . . . ". I threw Munnu's hand in the air and almost yelled, "Munnu, Father's been released. Released!" But Dadi and Baba burst into sobs. I trembled with fear . . . had I heard wrong? Last time also, they'd entered the house crying like this. But Baba's maxim came as reassurance: "Didn't I always say, Beta, 'There may be delay in the court of the Almighty but finally there will be justice'? See?"

But what has happened to Father? Why isn't he happy? His expressionless face and dull eyes deep in their sockets, why don't they light up with life and joy? Why is he staring at Baba stonily as if he doesn't understand what Baba is saying?

I run and wrap myself around him. "Father, you've been released. Do you hear? You've not been sentenced . . . No sentence for you!" But Father doesn't move.

Translated by Manisha Chaudhry.

RATAKONDA VASUNDHARA DEVI ____

(b. 1931)   *Telugu*

Though Ratakonda Vasundhara Devi's father did not want to educate her beyond the eighth standard, her unschooled mother, Paripurnamma, and her teachers prevailed upon him to allow her to continue her studies. She went to St. Joseph's Convent in Guntur, a boarding school where the nuns' spirit of sacrifice and strong ethical sense influenced her deeply. Vasundhara Devi wanted very much to study medicine, but her father objected, so she studied chemistry, receiving a master's degree from Andhra University in 1953. She married the writer and critic R. S. Sudershanam the same year. Her husband felt that there was no need for her to work, and that, were she to take a job, it would come in the way of the family's happiness and well-being. She now says that she never thought, in those days, of questioning the restrictions on her life. Nor had she considered other questions about a woman's place in society. Her parents and sisters showered affection on her and her married life continued, apparently, without many crises. She had two children. After her father's death in 1963, she began to question many of her parents' values as well as those of her school years. She was drawn to communism, but later questioned that too.

Vasundhara Devi started writing seriously in 1967. Many critics thought her work that of a man writing under a pseudonym, but, as she has written, "The editor of *Bharati,* the late Sivalenka Sambhuprasad, gave me a lot of encouragement. The regard of someone who was well-versed in international fiction, who was modern in outlook, and who was concerned about the quality of writing that appeared in his magazine helped me a great deal." Her stories appeared in *Bharati, Andhra Patrika,* and *Andhra Jyothi.* Her 1977 collection of short stories, *Gali Radham* (The Chariot of Wind) won the Andhra Pradesh Sahitya Academy Award in 1978. *O Pelli Katha* (Story of a Marriage), a short novel, came out in *Vijaya,* a monthly magazine, in 1977. *Nidalu* (Shadows), another collection of stories (from which "Picchi" is taken), was published in 1982, and *Reddamma Gundu* (Reddamma Rock), a novel, in 1985.

"It seems as though the life of seclusion practiced by my ancestors affected me more than anything else in my life. I always hesitated before taking a new step. In such families all initiative gets crushed in the childhood itself. My self-expression has been limited to my writing and the bringing up of my children," Vasundhara Devi writes. She says that she does not want to consider herself foremost as a writer, since living and searching for the meaning of life are of greater value to her.

Many women writers in Telugu have portrayed the direct and physical violence women experience, but few have dealt with the struggles in a woman's life or even the violence inherent in everyday familial relationships. Vasundhara Devi does so with sensitivity and insight. This feminist writer has also turned a critical pen on what society considers womanly virtues. The characters that emerge in her stories are multifaceted, sometimes self-contradictory, but always realistic. Her first story, "Macchalu" (Spots), 1967, is about a housewife who is terrified of spots that are appearing on her hands. She suspects they might be leperous, but the narrative turns the reader's attention to her irritation with the housework she has to do with these diseased hands. The interior-monologue form in which the story is written takes us through her frustration with her children—she even wishes something would make them disappear—and her dissatisfaction with the family. The causes of the disease, she realizes, are the family, the children, and cooking, each demanding her full-time attention. "Picchi" (Madness), 1968, the story translated here, was hardly noticed when it came out. Vasundhara Devi feels that, if people have not even begun to recognize that a deprived woman can be forced by the cruelty of society to become mad, we cannot hope for much change.

R. S. Sudershanam comments, "Women's rights, their pleasures and pains, and their welfare, are what can be found in her writing. I don't attach such importance to the problems women face." Women's problems, he feels, should be treated among the many problems that afflict society in general. On such opinions and other small household matters she and her husband often have differed, says Vasundhara Devi.

◆

PICCHI
(Madness)

Venkataramana slipped the heavy schoolbag off his shoulder and put it into the cupboard. The newly born calf frisked around merrily in the backyard. He ran eagerly towards it, drawn by its large black eyes and cuddly white body. Then he heard the voices of his granny and his aunt in the kitchen and stopped, moving closer to the kitchen wall, listening.

Papamma Atha was speaking. "She's better now—she asked if the boy was all right. She spoke normally for some time and then . . . the usual thing . . . Her jewelry. It's gone, she said, and cried over it. But at least she is not abusive anymore. If we take the boy to her, perhaps his visit will help her recover."

Grandma Sundaramma lamented, "Recover? I have no hopes that she will. She's been mad these ten years. She's not going to recover now. God knows how we've sinned. We had to get that witch when we married off our only son. We got rid of her, but the second one, Damayanti, has turned out this way. What is it but our karma! The special diet we gave her after childbirth didn't agree with her, but who expected she would go raving mad!"

"What has happened has happened . . . don't think too much about that . . . think of the present. She might get better if she sees the child. After all, she has to be cured somehow and brought home. Who's going to agree to a third marriage after the first two have turned out this way? Things are fine now, but who knows what'll happen? How long will you be able to do all the work alone?" Papamma Atha argued.

Venkatramana lost interest. He sat down in the hall, absentmindedly toying with a pen. There he was, a small handsome figure, ruffled hair falling on his forehead, staring at the pen in his hands.

Granny always said, "Don't fiddle with things when you have nothing to do. It's wrong."

After a while Sundaramma came out to see Papamma off. Spotting Ramana, she exclaimed, "Why, when did you come back from school? You should have called out to me. Wait—I'll get some fresh milk from the cow and heat it for you. Why are you twiddling that pen? It'll be ruined if it falls down!"

Even as she said this, the pen fell to the floor. Ramana quickly picked it up and put it back on the table.

"Look! You've dropped it! Just when I was telling you. You're so destructive! When your father comes home he'll thrash you. The least you can do is take your books out and read something," she scolded as she picked up the pen and hurried back into the kitchen.

Ramana put his legs up on the table. He knew that his father wouldn't beat him. Granny just said these things. Besides he didn't feel like studying. How can one study as soon as one returns from school?

So, that's what it was. They wanted to take him to the mental hospital in Madras and show him to her. He didn't know what to think. She—his mother—that person—would probably have dirty, matted hair and would be wearing tattered clothes. Frightened and repulsed, Ramana thought, "That madwoman, what *is* she to me? I have never even seen her in all my life!"

When Ramana was new at school, Papamma Atha's son Naraidu had told the class that Ramana's mother was mad. The children had burst out laughing. Ramana had felt so humiliated. His mother was in the mental hospital in Madras, that fellow had said.

"No!" he had screamed, "Sundaramma is my mother and she isn't mad." Then he had slapped Naraidu hard. Bleeding from the mouth, he had sobbed, "Sundaramma is your granny. That's what you call her. I'm going to tell my mother you hit me."

When she heard what had happened, Sundaramma had gathered Ramana up into her arms, kissed him and said, "That Naraidu, what does *he* know?"

But Ramana had hated mad people ever since. One day on his way back from school, he had even thrown a stone at a madwoman sitting under a tree.

He was in his first year of school when all this had happened. Now he knew for certain that his mother was in a mental hospital. He'd never seen her, he had never even thought of her. Today after listening to Papamma Atha, he wondered about her. He never thought of her as "Amma" [Mama]. It was not possible to think of her as "that person," so whenever he thought of her, it was just as Her. No name seemed right for his relationship to Her.

He didn't really like Her, or think well of Her. If anything he felt angry and repelled.

Once, Her father—Grandpa Subbaiah—had come to visit. He had just been to Madras. He was an old man, bent and gaunt, with stringy gray hair. He always grinned broadly, baring all his teeth as he spoke. Like a monkey! Perhaps he thought his grin pleased people! He looked like a beggar. He had stayed on and had lunch, evening coffee, and dinner as well before he left. Ramana's father hadn't spoken to him at all. Sundaramma had listened politely for a while, but had soon got up and gone away.

Sitting idly there, he tried to begin a conversation with Ramana.

"Do you buy peppermints?" he had asked. Ramana was puzzled. Did he want to give Ramana money to buy mints, or did he want to know if Ramana's people bought peppermints for him, or did he want Ramana to give him some peppermints if he had them? Irritated and annoyed, Ramana left without answering.

Subbaiah's wife was not Her mother. Everyone in the village knew she was his second wife. People called her Nallachamma. Sometimes Ramana saw her on his way to school. She was thin and dried up. She tied her shiny black hair into a funny little lemonlike knot. She always seemed to be quarreling loudly in public with someone or other. She had a habit of untying her hair, tugging it back, and pulling it into a knot over and over again as she quarreled.

Like the other children, Ramana also jeered at her and called her names. Not only was She mad, but She belonged to a family like this. It all added to Ramana's embarrassment. They were all a mad, good-for-nothing lot, he thought.

Whenever people from the village went on a trip to Madras, they would go to the zoo, take a look at the lighthouse and the Life Insurance Corporation Building, and visit Damayanti in the mental hospital.

From snatches of their conversation, Ramana had picked up a few things. His father's first wife had hanged herself. Then She was given in marriage to him. Before her marriage, She had lived in Nallachamma's house like a slave; She had been beaten and scolded and She had done all the work.

"How does it matter that she comes from a poor family? Doesn't a lotus bloom in murky water? Besides, the girl is obedient and hardworking," Sundaramma had thought when she had arranged the marriage.

In the beginning, She had been obedient and hardworking, but had suddenly changed after the boy was born.

"It must have been the diet they fed her when they took her home to have the baby," Sundaramma said. "It did not agree with her. We brought her back within a month. Who knows, perhaps she was getting worse all the time. She clung to her baby like a monkey and wouldn't let go of him at all. A nursing mother may not eat what she pleases. If she is not on the right diet, the child will not grow properly. 'Let's give him cow's milk,' I suggested. By then the child had developed loose movements. But this woman just wouldn't listen. I sent the baby away for a couple of days to Kishtayi's house. She had already begun to lose her sanity. She lay down, stiff as a board, for two whole days. She wept incessantly. She wouldn't eat, wouldn't work, wouldn't do anything at all. I thought—We'll leave her alone for a while—and kept quiet. Without food, she got worse. On the third day she got up in a frenzy. I had killed all her children, she raved, and caught me by the throat. By the time the others ran up and loosened her grip, I was quite exhausted. We bound her with ropes and took all her jewelry away. There wasn't much—just her mangalsutra and two bangles—that was all. She forgot about her children and started off on her jewelry. The abuses she heaped on me! She used to be so meek and ready to please, and now, madness! That's it, she just went mad. We tried mantras and several home remedies. It was all no good, so we took her to Madras."

Once Sundaramma had told the story to the third grade teacher. The teacher said, "Perhaps all this happened because you didn't allow her to feed her baby. Did you try giving the baby back to her?"

"Oh, no! What would have happened if she had strangled the month-old baby!" Sundaramma had exclaimed.

"Yes, that's true," the teacher said.

Ramana hadn't liked them talking like that about him. He interrupted, saying, "Father asked you to come home soon because he wants to go to the farm."

"Coming—I'm coming," but Sundaramma had continued. "Who breastfeeds babies today except the very poor? They all are worried about their beauty and health, and give their babies milk from cans. Only a madwoman would cry about a thing like that. 'If the baby doesn't drink your milk, why, press it out on the wall,' I said. But she cried as if her heart would break. Everyone learns these things from the movies, I tell you. This crying, this laughing, dancing, singing. I thought she'd reconcile herself to it, but her madness only grew worse."

Sundaramma didn't usually talk of these things in Ramana's presence. These were things he happened to hear by chance. Though he didn't always understand all of it, he tucked it away somewhere in his mind.

They went to the exhibition first. The next day Sundaramma, Ramana's father, and Ramana went to the hospital. From the time they had started for Madras, Ramana's thoughts constantly returned to Her. The person who had been a strange madwoman to him all these days started taking on a hazy new relationship.

He shivered, remembering the madwoman under the tree. He hoped against hope that She wouldn't be like that.

Damayanti looked neat and clean. Her hair was combed. Her sari was a bit dirty, but it was not torn. Seeing Sundaramma, She screamed, "So you have come, have you! Did you bring my jewelry with you, you fiend?"

Ramana stood behind Sundaramma and watched helplessly. Damayanti saw him and frowned. "Who is this boy?"

No one replied.

"Come here, boy," she said.

Sundaramma stopped Ramana from moving forward.

"You're Venkataramana, aren't you? Papamma told me you might come. You're my son, after all—won't you come when I call you? I'm your mother. Remember one thing. The world is full of women, but regardless of whoever brings you up or looks after you, remember, I'm your mother. It was in my womb that you grew. My hands knew all your movements and followed their mischievous twists when I placed them on my stomach. I swear! You have a debt to me and you should repay it. That she-devil has my jewelry. Some day you should bring it back to me, do you understand?" she asked anxiously and looked at him with hope in her eyes.

Ramana was frightened by these words. But despite his fear, he murmured in his heart, "Amma".

Sundaramma said, "Let's go," and as they left, Damayanti shouted, "I'm your real mother—you should get my jewelry back."

Coming out, Ramana asked his granny softly, "Will Amma be all right? Will her madness be cured?"

Sundaramma was annoyed and snapped, "Mother, my foot! I listened to Papamma's advice and brought you here. Her madness will never be cured. What chance is there if she keeps raving like that? What terrible language she used, and before a small boy!"

Poor thing! Ramana thought. Granny will never return her jewelry.

Translated by Vasanta Duggirala and M. Sashi Kumar.

MEENA KUMARI NAZ ─────────────
(1932–1972)   *Urdu*

Meena Kumari became a legend as an actress in her lifetime and has remained one even after her death. At the height of her career, there was no other name in the film world that sprang more joyfully to the lips of millions of fans across the country who watched all her films, followed each incident in her tragic life, and mourned her death. An exceptionally beautiful and talented actress, always dressed in white, she was, and remains, to quote the critic Afeefa Banu, "an object of fantasy and a motif of melancholy."

Meena Kumari was born and reared in Bombay. Her mother, Iqbal Begum, was also an actress, and her father, Ali Bux, a music director. Soon after Meena Kumari was born, her father fell seriously ill and her mother had to support the family and manage the home. The child shared her mother's burden, and grew up with adult responsibilities in an atmosphere of sadness. At the age of four, she acted in her first film, and earned what in those times would have been considered a handsome sum—twenty-five rupees. "Baby Meena" (so christened by the director Vijaya Bhatt) worked in several films before graduating to adult roles. Her films became box office hits and she in turn rich and famous. Among her classics are *Baiju-Bawra* ([The Legendary Love Story of] Baiju and Bawra), 1952, *Parinita,* 1953, and *Sahib, Bibi aur Gulam* (The Master, His Wife, and the Slave), 1962. She won the national "best actress" award for her role in each of these. *Pakeeza,* 1971, a popular film based on the story of a court singer who fell in love with a nobleman was released posthumously.

Though Meena Kumari did not have a formal education, she loved literature, and when she had time, read widely in poetry, taking careful notes in her diary. People are often surprised to discover that this distinguished actress and singer was also a poet who wrote under the pen name Naz. Many of the lyrics from the popular album she released are her own compositions. Their startling images and intimate tone speak of her sensitivity, her warmth, her philosophic disposition. Sahir Ludhianvi, a well-known writer of lyrics for Hindi films, said, in a singular tribute on her death in 1972, "She was an artist with a rare talent, a softspoken woman in white with the soul of a poet which she had to sacrifice to start work. Her youth was spent depicting various tragedies that befall Indian women, with no time to think of her personal tragedy. Her whole life was a sacrifice of her own emotions."

Meena Kumari's personal life, like that of Hamsa Wadkar (an excerpt of whose autobiography is reprinted in this volume) a decade earlier, moved from tragedy to tragedy. According to Ram Aurangabadkar, a film journalist, "She helped several actors to become stars but most of them left her without a backward glance once they took off. . . . Love was the predominant emotion in her life, and she was a hopeless romantic. She loved too easily and let her love destroy her." Of herself, she wrote in her diary, extracts from which were published in *Film Fare* in 1969, "I feel as if I am suspended in a vacuum, a dark void in which my whole being is so cold and desensitized that when thoughts and feelings come to me, they seem to come to someone else, and I watch the inner world of that other person as though I stand at a distance. . . ." A collection of her poems, *Tanha Chand* (The Solitary Moon), from which the poem here is taken, was compiled by S. S. Gulzar and published posthumously.

◆

[Bit by bit the splintered day has ended]

Bit by bit the splintered day has ended,
The night is all in shreds.
To each of us is given just as much
As we can carry.

The spattering, singing drops of rain
Hold poison and immortality too.
My eyes laugh, my heart rains tears,
Such is the monsoon I've been granted.

Whenever I've strained to know myself
I've heard a chuckle,
As if someone within me spoke and said,
In this game you'll be foiled again.

What does defeat mean, or waiting,
When an endless trek is my allotted fate?
When my heart was gifted to me, as companion,
An unrest walked alongside.

Translated by Syed Sirajuddin.

JAYA MEHTA ⎯⎯⎯⎯⎯⎯⎯⎯⎯⎯⎯⎯⎯

(b. 1932)   *Gujarati*

Jaya Mehta was born in a village in Saurashtra and spent her childhood there and in Bombay. As a result of the constant moves back and forth, she tells us, her studies suffered. The lack of girls' schools in Saurashtra and the orthodox attitude of her father added to the problem. Both she and her elder sister acquired their education in the teeth of stiff opposition, but their struggle made matters easier for their younger sisters. Today Jaya Mehta speaks appreciatively of her father's eventual willingness to accept new lifestyles and values. While as a young girl she had to cover her head with her sari when she went out of the house, the time came when she could wear sleeveless blouses without comment from the family. No pressure was put on her to get married and, when a younger sister married a Maharashtrian, her Gujarati parents took it as a matter of course.

Because the family found it difficult to make ends meet, Jaya Mehta had to put herself through college by teaching in a school, and eventually completed her master's degree in Gujarati. Teaching and research were for many years her main occupations. She chooses to live alone, thus ensuring independence, while maintaining close ties with sisters, brothers, nieces, and nephews.

Exposure to the world of poetry and the constant search, as a translator, for the exact word, inspired Jaya Mehta to start writing herself. Her collection *Ek Divas* (One Day), 1982, contains an account she has given of her own poetry, significantly titled "The Struggle to Achieve the Detached Word." While for her contemporary Panna Naik, poetry is the deepest expression of the self, for Jaya Mehta—much as it is for Indira Sant, the older Marathi poet—it is "not a path to lead one from the personal still further into the self, but rather from the personal to the impersonal." Restraint and control are as necessary for the poet as are intensity of feeling or acuteness of sensibility. The poet may have experienced the tempest, but when writing of it, there must be no tempest, but calm, she says. Even her more personal poetry (allowing for the possibility that the "I" in her poems is not necessarily herself), such as "Sangrahastan" (The Museum), 1982, or "Ekoham Bahusyam?" (I Am One, I Can Become Many?), 1978, is not confessional.

Several of her poems contain Sanskrit phrases or refer to Gujarati legends. Because this poet's consciousness is profoundly shaped by myth and belief (although she herself is an atheist), these allusions reflect the way she sees the world and responds to it. Among her published volumes are *Venetian Blind,* 1978, for which she received the Gujarat State Sahitya Academy Award in the same year, *Ek Divas, Akashman Tarao Chup Che* (The Stars Are Silent), 1985, and *Hospital Poems,* 1987. Two of the poems translated here, "Lokshahiman" and "Ekoham Bahusyam" are taken from *Venetian Blind;* the third, "Dushmanu Lashkar Pasar Thai Gayu" is from *Akashman Tarao Chup Che.*

◆

LOKSHAHIMAN
(In a Democracy)

The ocean framed in a picture
Is free to toss its waves.

The lion born in a zoo
Can claim to be called king of the jungle.

Sheep driven by the shepherd
Have the freedom to march in line.

Translated by Shirin Kudchedkar.

EKOHAM BAHUSYAM?
(I Am One, I Can Become Many?)*

My eyes distracted
By my child's trifling illness
—Is that me?

Or
My eyes refusing to see
The child breathing its last on the pavement's edge
—Is that me?

My eyes moistening
At the mere thought of my loved ones aging
—Is that me?

Or
My eyes drowning
In the flooded mine of Chasnala**, yet dry
—Is that me?

Translated by Shirin Kudchedkar.

DUSHMANNU LASHKAR PASAR THAI GAYU
(The enemy army has passed through)

The enemy army has passed through
The city is deserted
Stupefied the tree stands
Leafless and gray in an unseasonal autumn.
Amid the debris of the fallen house
The walls sag, exhausted.
One's breath rebounds
Like the echoes in a ravine.
The man takes the unblinking child in his arms

---

*The well-known Sanskrit phrase *ekoham bahusyam* refers to God and is not a
question.
**Chasnala, Bihar, was the site of a mining disaster in which a large number of
miners were killed.

Four silent eyes drip
Into the woman's empty lap.

Translated by Shirin Kudchedkar.

ABBURI CHAYA DEVI ───────────

(b. 1933)   *Telugu*

"My family never encouraged me to do the things I was interested in,"
Chaya Devi said. All the same, she took the initiative to develop her tal-
ents. While at college, she and her friends Ramadevi and Turaga Janaki
Rani (both writers) put on several plays and gave talks over the radio. She
earned an average of twenty-five rupees a month, which was enough for
her expenses. "When I got married," she said, "I had three hundred rupees
in the bank, and that made me feel happy and proud." When she married
writer Abburi Rajeswara Rao in 1953, there was no dowry paid and the
marriage was, she adds, "in a way not a marriage arranged by the elders."
She had meanwhile earned a degree in library science from Andhra University. Her first story, "Anubhuti," was published in 1953, soon followed by "Swatantra" (Independent) in 1954.

Between 1955 and 1957, she edited a quarterly, *Kavita,* which published
English translations of modern Telugu poetry. With her husband's help,
she published an anthology of Indian poetry written in English and of
Assamese poetry in English translation. In 1958 they moved to Delhi.
There she became deputy librarian of the Indian School of International
Studies at Jawaharlal Nehru University, from which she retired in 1982.
She now lives in Hyderabad. In the late eighties Chaya Devi wrote a
weekly column, "Udayani," for a major Telugu newspaper, *Udayam.* A
collection of twenty-five short stories, *Abburi Chaya Devi Kathalu* (Stories
by Abburi Chaya Devi), appeared in 1991.

Though Chaya Devi is by no means prolific, her stories are subtle, humorous and well formed. They explore aspects of everyday life that are
rarely written about in Telugu. "Mudunalla Mucchata" (Three Days of
Enjoyment), 1973, for instance, is about the upper-caste custom of isolat-
ing menstruating women, sometimes in a place outside the house. The
story, which centers on the humiliation the younger generation experiences, is written in a light vein but touches the heart of those who have
suffered the practice. "Sukhantam" (A Happy End), 1969, is about a
woman who has all her life longed to get some sleep, while "Bonsaibra-
tuku" (Bonsai Living), 1974, depicts the warm, yet complex, relationship

between two sisters, the elder an uneducated village woman dependent on her husband, and the younger educated and independent. Chaya Devi captures the subtle mix of envy, pride, and affection that mark the elder one's responses, as well as the problems they face as a housewife and a working woman.

Talking about why she has not written novels, Chaya Devi says, "One can think of plots for stories on the way to the office or sitting on a bus or even while cooking, and one can put them on paper very quickly. To write a novel you need a lot of time. Moreover, there is a cohesion in a short story that is lacking in a novel." The story translated here was first published in *Andhra Prabha Weekly* in 1975.

◆

SRIMATHI—UDYOGINI
(Wife—Working Woman)

Sunday was the busiest. By the time I was done with my chores it was nearing eleven. I looked for a patch of the sun that was forever eluding my house and, just as I found a corner in which to settle down with the paper, the bell rang. Damn! Must be the paper carrier with the bill, or the man from the shop next door to collect the empty bottles. Reluctantly, a little irritated, I forced myself to open the door.

It was a new face. A young girl—in her twenties. A folder in one hand and a leather bag in the other. Must be one of those girls who come to sell soap or sanitary napkins. My face automatically registered boredom as my words came out. "What do you want?"

She smiled. "I want you." Pretty to look at, too. "You know Mr. R. Rao. His wife told me about you. I hope you can spare me a little time."

Raghava Rao was a good friend of ours. Still! Have I a choice? I thought, as I opened the door, and asked her to come in.

We seated ourselves in the corner, sharing the sun.

"My name is Sujatha. I am at the university—doing research." As she spoke, her eyes sparkled like stars. Young enough not to be married, I thought.

"Oh, in which area?"

"Sociology."

"And your subject?"

"You are my subject," she said triumphantly. "I understand you are a working wife. I have a few questions to ask. I hope you don't mind giving me the answers."

"So . . . ?" Vexation crept into my tone again.

"I'm sorry. I know I may be wasting your time. But I need these answers for the research I'm doing. Only women like you can help me."

She must have read my doubts and the irritation in my eyes, for the next minute she opened her bag, took out a file and gave me a piece of paper to look at. It was a letter of introduction from her department confirming all she had been telling me. I thawed a little.

"Gathering responses from working wives like you is an important part of my study. You know, it is not so common in our country for women to work, and it is useful to know how women are fulfilling their dual responsibilities of being a wife and a working woman, what their problems are, and how they face them." She stopped to catch her breath.

"Fine. It is a good subject you have chosen, Sujatha. I am very happy that you are doing this kind of work," I said, mainly to dispel my earlier displeasure and to give her some confidence to continue. She didn't seem to need any, though.

"Madam, I'd like to ask you a few questions and I hope you will answer them frankly. Of course I won't use your name or embarrass you in any way," Sujatha said.

I was just about to say, "Ready," when I heard my husband call me from the inner room. "Please wait, I won't be long," I told Sujatha and went.

My husband was still lolling in bed. "Who is that?" he asked. "I thought I heard voices."

I told him.

"Oh, come on," he said in a bored tone. "Don't waste your time on her. Make some excuse and come back."

"Sujatha is very sweet. Besides, she is well recommended. The Raghava Raos have sent her. I want to talk to her. Better still, why don't you join us?"

"Hell no!" he said. "You won't catch me ruining my Sunday confessing to some unknown female."

"All right. You think I don't have that much sense. Don't worry. I won't say anything to compromise our family secrets."

"Oh, all right. But come back soon," he grumbled and turned over, pulling up the sheets.

I smiled to myself, closed the door, took a couple of Fantas from the fridge, gave one to Sujatha, and settled back into my chair. By this time Sujatha was ready with her pen and pad and began her assault.

"How long have you been married?" she asked.

"We have completed four five-year plans," I replied.

"Twenty years! How old were you when you married?"

"Never ask a woman's age. But I'll tell you. I was twenty when I was married."

"And he?"

"Let me say he was ten years older."

"Was it an arranged marriage, or . . . ?"

"Neither," I taunted.

"You mean?"

"Some people who knew both of us brought us together. We both agreed and our parents had no objection. We had a traditional wedding."

"How many children do you have?"

"We don't have any."

Sujatha wrote something on her pad and looked up at me questioningly.

"Does anyone else stay here with you?"

"No. Just the two of us."

"How long have you been working?"

"About fifteen years, I'd say."

"Did you work before you got married?"

"No."

"Does your husband like your working?"

". . ."

"You mean he doesn't like it."

"Oh no. In fact he's the one who made me take the job . . . But . . ."

"He doesn't like it any more . . . Is that it?"

"I'm not sure. But sometimes I have this feeling that he doesn't like my working."

"Tell me why you took the job in the first place and why you are still doing it."

"In the beginning it was because I was bored at home with nothing to do. And now I am kind of used to it."

Sujatha smiled, making notes all the while.

"Is that the main reason? To help time pass?"

"I guess so."

"You're sure you didn't take the job because there wasn't enough money?"

"Well, there is never enough money. But I can assure you it was not for the money."

"But the money is useful for the extra expenses, you'd say?"

"I didn't think so when I took the job. But neither can I say that the money has not come in handy."

"Was it to get out of the home—to avoid your mother-in-law or anyone else?"

"No, no. Luckily, I don't have such problems."

"It was to make some new friends—spend some time outside the home with others, I take it."

"Maybe! I got married just after I left college. Five years at home doing nothing was more than I could bear."

"Didn't you want to make use of what you studied at college?"

"Perhaps that was one more reason."

"Didn't you have any ambitions? To achieve recognition? To become somebody?"

"Thank heavens, no. It was mainly to spend some time usefully, not to make a name. But years of working have no doubt given me some stature, a few contacts."

"I take it you are happy with your job."

"Most of the time, yes—but, then, every so often I get a little dissatisfied with things."

"You mean at home, or outside?"

"Both. Sometimes when I am hard-pressed at the office, relatives descend on the house. If I spend some extra time at the office, they don't like it at home. And, you know, women aren't such climbers in their jobs as men are. So sometimes dissatisfaction creeps in."

"Are you satisfied with your husband's job?"

"As far as I am concerned, I am satisfied."

"I take it his parents are alive."

"Yes."

"Do you like your father-in-law?"

"What kind of question is that?"

Sujatha smiled softly.

"It is hard for people to understand the woman's side in many cases. But you didn't answer my question. Do you like your father-in-law?"

"Even if I do, can I say that openly?"

"OK. I'll write here 'Yes' to that. Now, about your mother-in-law. You like her?"

"Oh yes. I like her even more than I like my mother."

"You are very fortunate."

I agreed.

"Well, what about the others? His brothers, sisters? Do any of the other women in the family work?"

"Two of his sisters started working after marriage. One had been working three years when she got married, but then she gave up her job. His elder brother's wife is also working. Another brother is yet to be married." As I said this a thought came into my mind. Sujatha looked away as if she had read my thoughts.

"Perhaps part of your happiness has to do with having no children. Or . . ."

"When we married, my husband's brothers and sisters were quite young. We never had the feeling of being without children. The house was always full of children. Anyway it is all in the mind, I suppose. Happiness or otherwise. Nothing to do with one's wants or hopes."

"Yes. But what shall I write here? That you are happy . . ."

"What do you think, looking at me? Write what you feel."

"OK. Let me change the subject," she said. "Tell me, when you have some free time, do you feel like staying at home, or going out, or both? Or does each of you feel differently?"

"It's a difficult question. But let me see. This is one thing about which we argue. He likes to window-shop. I like to shop. You know— buy things we need. I don't see the sense in tiring my legs and my eyes walking past shops. And then, on holidays I feel like going to a movie or a play or a concert. He wants to eat to his heart's content and lie in bed with a book. After he tires of that, he takes aimless strolls. If I suggest inviting friends or relatives over, he starts arguing, and, finally, we end up going no place and wind up on different sides of the bed, each with a book—"

"Is there anything else you do together?" Sujatha broke in.

"No. I don't think there is anything we do together. No, wait. We write. I dabble in stories. He writes poetry."

"Do you discuss your problems with your husband?"

"Many times. Sometimes he listens. Sometimes he gets into a rage, and I suffer in silence and tell him about it long after the crisis is over. Oh yes, we do discuss our problems with each other . . . As long as I don't hurt him, as long as our arguments don't create misunderstandings between ourselves."

"And does your husband tell you his problems—does he open his heart to you?"

"Yes, he tells me everything about our family affairs, our relatives and so on. But he is silent about his work and his problems there."

"What I mean is, does he confide in you? Are you quite satisfied?"

"Oh yes . . . If anything, he loves me too well and not too wisely. He worries about me all the time. If I have to go out alone, he worries.

I am old enough and can take care of myself, but he won't agree. I often ask him to leave me to myself and do you know what he says?"

"What?" Sujatha asked eagerly.

"Well, he laughs! 'How can I leave you?' "

"Well, I suppose you are quite happy and satisfied," Sujatha wrote. Before I could speak, she asked, "And he? Is he satisfied with your love?"

"You should ask him that," I said.

"But I want you to tell me," Sujatha insisted.

Goodness, this girl is something, I thought. How can I tell her everything—everything in my mind—even if it is for her research?

"Oh yes," I said simply, hoping she'd stop.

"Do you and he have any differences of opinion, you know, on important matters?"

"You might as well ask me whether we eat everyday," I said.

Sujatha laughed and started noting things down again.

"I want some more details—if you don't mind."

Oh God, I thought, What have we been doing so far? Aloud, I said, "All right. Shoot." Maybe this will give me an idea for a story.

"Do you have different views on what you should spend on the house?"

"Oh yes," I said enthusiastically. "I want to buy curtains. He prefers old coins. 'Why waste money on curtains? The ones we have are OK,' he will say."

"What about luxuries?"

"He has none. He can't stand shopping. I've already told you that. And he hates picnics, parties, card games, and the like."

"Maybe he prefers religious functions?"

"No way," I said. "He hates all such ceremonies. The year I was married I wanted to perform the Sravanapuja, and you know what he said? 'You are an educated girl. Don't indulge in such meaningless things.' I like to arrange my collection of dolls for the Sankranti festival. When I was young my parents stopped me because it would interfere with my studies. And now my husband tells me that it is childish. I wanted to have the neighborhood ladies over for Varalakshmipuja and he put on such a face. 'Imagine all those women in this small house,' he said. And that was that. You name it. He has an answer for all my desires."

Sujatha seemed disturbed.

"I am sorry. Am I boring you with our petty squabbles?"

"Oh no," she said, embarrassed.

"And what about friends? Do you agree there?"

"Yes," I said.

Sujatha looked at me eagerly. "Please tell me more. I don't understand," she said.

"I mix with his friends from the office and their wives. But he keeps his distance from mine."

"Why?"

"Perhaps he doesn't want to feel that he is just someone's husband."

"And that hurts you, no doubt."

"Definitely, yes."

"I suppose that means he doesn't accept you as equal to him."

"Of course. What man will accept a woman as his equal?"

"And you agree?"

"No, no. I say we are equal. And he says, 'Look I'm older than you, taller than you. How can we be equal? You have a frog's mind.' And I . . ."

"OK. Do you at least agree on the chores you do at home?"

"Of course not." I shook my head.

"I don't deny that he helps me in the house, more than most husbands I know. When he helps me in the kitchen, he leaves cigarette butts in the sink, dumps refuse all over the place. Costs me more work ultimately, so I let him go. I'd rather he did his own work."

Sujatha abruptly changed the subject.

"What are your views as a dutiful daughter-in-law?"

"Well, we are both happy with my mother-in-law. But when it comes to his . . ."

"You mean?"

"Yes . . . He has this feeling that after marriage I should have broken away from my people. He doesn't say it in so many words, but I know he wants me to keep away from my people. I don't think men will ever change in relation to this, do you?"

Sujatha stopped a yawn—not too obviously. But her fingers were busy taking the notes. And then, "What are your views, I mean both your views, on showing your feelings—your affection towards each other?"

"Well, if he doesn't like the food I prepare for him, I think he doesn't love me. And if I don't like the sari he has brought for me, he gets the same feeling about my love for him."

"No, what I mean is the more physical part of love."

"Oh that," I laughed. "You want me to tell you the truth?"

Sujatha blushed and turned her face away. Before I could answer, I heard his voice calling me from the bedroom. I jumped out of my chair.

"Wait. I'll be back in a minute."

I entered our room. "Oh, you have awakened, finally, dearest," I said sarcastically.

"As if I had been sleeping! One day a week, one day I get when I can lie down and relax. And there you go yackety-yacking, clucking like a couple of birds. God! Is she still here?" he said with irritation.

"Look. Why don't you come and sit with her for a while? I'll make some coffee for you."

"Never mind. I'd prefer you to finish with her. Then we can have our coffee here in peace."

"You know, there's something nice about that girl. I feel that she would be good for your younger brother Srinivas. Shall I broach the subject?"

"God! You are out of your mind. You hardly know her," he said, and settled back in bed.

I returned to the veranda, where Sujatha was fidgeting. As soon as she saw me, she shot out, "Doesn't your husband call you by name?"

"No," I said, "he feels that calling me by name is rather formal. Like between friends."

"But he could call you by some pet name."

"You mean like a cat or a dog? What's in a name, anyway?" I said shyly.

"Yes, of course." Sujatha referred to her notes for the next question.

"Oh yes, I was asking about your love for each other. You have no differences of opinion, I'm sure."

"No," I said briefly, to cut her short.

"Let me ask, when you disagree on something, one of you has to give in—or do both of you stubbornly hold on to your views?"

"It could go either way. Depends on the situation."

She wouldn't give in. "What happens most of the time?"

"What can a woman do except give in," I said resignedly.

"Oh," said Sujatha. "Here, I've listed a few qualities of husbands. All you have to do is check off the ones that correctly describe him."

She gave me a list with a series of items.

1. *Argumentative*
   Right. Of course, I am no less.

2. *Narrow-minded*

   Right. He'll eat only what he likes. If I make something I like, he won't even touch it.

3. *Fault-finding*

   Right. He sits at the dining table like a Supreme Court judge dishing out verdicts.

4. *Frowns all the time*

   Right. But his anger never lasts more than a few minutes.

5. *Spoils the children*

   Doesn't arise. Thank God!

6. *Secretive*

   Not very.

7. *Jealous*

   Right. If I wear the sari my father bought me, he can't bear it.

8. *Chatterbox*

   Only with his friends. He has nothing to talk to me about.

9. *Has a roving eye for other women*

   Which man hasn't?

10. *Lazy*

    Right.

11. *Forgets his promises*

    Right. He tells me at night that we'll go to Kashmir this summer, and forgets it the next morning.

12. *Selfish*

    Right. Sits in the bathroom for hours with the morning newspaper.

13. *Smokes like a chimney*

    Right. He feels that his manliness will suffer if he doesn't.

14. *Suspicious*

    Right. Just now when I told him about Sujatha, he was suspicious of her.

15. *Irresponsible*

    Right. Couldn't care less even if the tap were leaking away to glory. Won't even help me carry the shopping bags.

16. *Doesn't care about children*

    Right. As if he even cares about me.

17. *Not interested in anything but his job*

    Right. That's what he says about me, as a matter of fact.

18. *Impatient*

    If I am ten minutes late coming home, he gets all excited. If I don't answer the doorbell at the first ring, he gets excited.

19. *Doesn't believe in tidiness or order*

    Right. You must see our room. Papers and books all over the place. Cigarette ashes and butts. If I try to clean up, he gets upset because I have "disturbed his books." If I say that the place is like a pigsty, he says that's how intellectuals live. Can't stand my making the beds. If I say, "How'll it look if somebody sees this mess?" he'll say, "Why the hell should others come into our room?" And so on . . . Endless, really.

20. *Gambles*
I don't think he knows how many cards there are in a pack.
21. *Doesn't worry about the home*
Not if he has his friends with him.
22. *Doesn't like to go out with me in the evenings*
Hates shopping. Likes walking.
23. *Comes home late for meals*
Especially when I'm feeling hungry.
24. *Doesn't like me to work*
Won't say it aloud though.
25. *Miserly*
No. Rather the opposite.
26. *Won't open his mind*
What's the use?
27. *Can't stand my talking about the neighbors*
Gossip, that's all women are capable of, he says.
28. *No ambition*
Not even for me.
29. *Uncivilized boor*
Ever since coming back from America, he slurps his food up and belches aloud. It is a sign of satisfaction, he says.
30. *Isn't particularly bothered about the state of his home*
No.
31. *Doesn't treat me as his equal*
Right. How can he? I'm two inches shorter.

"Seems to me you're fed up," Sujatha said. "Quite an exhaustive list."
"I've never been cross-examined so thoroughly before," I confessed. Her next question stopped me short.
"Have you ever thought of separating?"
"Yes. I have often thought of it. But never seriously."
"How many times have you two quarreled this year?"
"I haven't counted, but quite a few times."
"But why haven't you taken the step to separate? After all, there seems to be enough reason."
"Why don't you get married, Sujatha?" I said seriously. "You won't understand this strange chemistry that keeps a man and woman together in spite of all their misunderstandings and incompatibility. Besides, there is room only for two persons in a marriage. Others should

keep out." I didn't mean it as a hint to her, but my words came out in a rush. "You need a sense of humor to make it go."

"Do I take it that you love your husband, or the opposite?"

"Well, a little bit of love, a little bit of respect, I think," I said, mostly to myself.

"And what does he feel for you?"

"Love and authority."

"Is there a difference between the first year of your marriage and now?"

"Of course. Then it was just infatuation. Now it is love born out of understanding and togetherness."

"One last question. If you were to marry again, would you marry him, or someone else, or not at all?"

"Of course I'd marry him. Only him," I said fiercely.

"And what would he say to that?"

" 'No, I won't marry you again,' that's what he would say. Of course, he is a man, you know."

Relief at last, as I saw Sujatha sorting her papers, closing her shop.

"I can't tell you how grateful I am to you for giving me so much of your time and patiently answering my questions. I'm sure it'll help my research a lot."

"That's all right, Sujatha. Actually, all these lurking thoughts and feelings—you and your questions have brought them out of me. Really, it is I who must thank you. I see myself more clearly now. There's something else I want to ask you."

"Yes," Sujatha leaned forward expectantly.

"Never mind," I said. "You'll know of it by and by. I must go now. I think I hear him calling me."

Translated by Srinivas Rayaprolu.

PANNA NAIK ─────────────────────────

(b. 1933)   *Gujarati*

Panna Naik began writing when the personal, "confessional" voice was in vogue in the West, where she had settled. Not surprisingly, this was the aspect of her work that critics immediately focused on, and she was congratulated on the frankness with which she spoke of women's longings and experiences (such as childlessness and menstruation) and the sensitivity with which she rendered them.

Though born and brought up in Bombay, she has for many years lived in Philadelphia. The leading themes of her poems are the emptiness and mechanical routines of modern life; the fullness, but more often the hollowness, of love; her increasing despair at not having had a child; and the longing for home one has in a foreign land. The house forms the setting for many of her poems—the living room, the bedroom, even the bathroom. But in her work, the modern home with its chic decor leaves no space for its inhabitants to be themselves, as in "Diwankhanaman" (In the Living Room), 1975. Home in her poems is not synonymous with protection, belongingness, or the warmth of family affection, but with a mechanical existence and a profound loneliness, even when one is not alone.

In Panna Naik's most successful poems, a state of mind, an experience, or a relationship are conveyed through a vivid image, as when, in "Khulli Bari" (The Open Window), 1975, she sits by the open window allowing the rain to drench her and her beautiful furniture, as it rages like a wild beast through the house. What was dead in her is coming alive, and she is herself an open window. In "Sannidhya" (Nearness), her beloved's presence is like the salty water at high tide, disturbing but desired; and in "Billi" (Cat), she is a tame cat, far removed from any kinship with the tiger, but even her occasional meow is objected to.

Five collections of Panna Naik's poetry have been published: *Pravesh* (Entrance), 1975, from which the poem "Billi" is taken; *Philadelphia,* 1980, from which, "Sishu" is taken; *Nisbat* (Connection), 1984; *Arasparas* (Between You and Me), 1989; and *Avan Javan* (Coming and Going), 1991.

◆

BILLI
(Cat)

Your fingers stroke my neck
I won't yowl,
I'm an absolutely tame beast now.

Cast out all suspicion
That I am a fearful
Kin to the tiger.
Look, look, a cat
Is licking your hand, your cheek, your nose
Stretching at your feet.
Don't you feel the smooth fur?

All I need—
The milk you provide
And a corner of your splendid palace.
You a man—
And I a small (innocent?) cat.

You can lift me and fling me into the air
I won't claw you.
See, here, on my throat, on my mouth, you can place your hand,
You can be quite sure of my gentleness.
Just look, I've become a pet animal.
But you don't want me as a pet.
Far, far away in some forest
Far out of the city you want to abandon me, don't you?
Because it's difficult for me to observe your conditions.
You want a cat that will never meow.

My dear, can there ever be a cat
That never meows?

Translated by Shirin Kudchedkar.

SHISHU
(The Child)

Now a few days
A few hours
And then my life
Bidding farewell . . .
Friends and relatives arriving on the pretext of offering condolences

Will mutter softly
Commenting on my childlessness.
Well, it's true!
How many deserts remained dry in me
And I brooded over them.
How many trees failed to blossom in me
And I kept watching.
Only my womb did not stir
And I wasted away.
Now at this moment of death
Won't someone bring a child to my bed

Causing dimples in my cheeks.
My soul can take leave of the body
Only after kissing this delicate beauty of the earth.
It's I who am going now
To take birth as a child in the womb of long-delayed motherhood.

Translated by Shirin Kudchedkar.

ANUPAMA NIRANJANA ————————

(1934–1991)   *Kannada*

A physician by profession, Anupama Niranjana wrote twenty major novels, eight collections of short stories, and several best-selling books on
women's health.

She grew up fighting the differing ways in which sons and daughters
in her family were treated, and went on to study medicine, graduating
from the Mysore Medical College in 1956. In the same year she married,
against the wishes of her parents, the well-known Kannada writer Niranjana.

Anupama's relationship with Niranjana, who was a demanding critic of
her work, gave "a special impetus" to her writing, and she was also attracted to his leftist ideals. The many different kinds of people she met
every day in the private medical clinic she ran were an important source
for her writing, on which she continued to work systematically. When
her husband had a stroke in 1971 that left him paralyzed, the whole burden of running the house and caring for their two young daughters, Tejaswini and Seemanthini, fell on her. More difficulties were on their way.
In 1978, Anupama had the first of three operations for cancer. "Fighting
against these dreadful diseases has taken so much energy from me," she
said. Yet she continued to write, and was, when she died, editor for a
major project at India Book House, the publication of one hundred books
by women writers.

As a doctor she did not face much sex discrimination, and felt there was
far more of it in the field of literature. Male writers and critics were reluctant to take cognizance of her work, but she overcame her "earlier
feeling of inferiority" and eventually "mustered courage to speak out."
As a result of the new awareness among women writers in Karnataka, she
was asked to speak at various seminars, including ones held by the Karnataka Sahitya Academy, to which women writers were rarely invited
earlier. Given her responsibilities and the social restrictions on free move-

ment, it is always more difficult, she said, for women to collect the information and material they may need for their books. That is possibly one reason why so many women writers deal mainly with themes that center on the family.

Madhavi, published in 1976, is Anupama Niranjana's first major work. The novel is based on an episode from the *Mahabharata* in which the sage Vishwamitra asks his pupil Galva to pay his tuition in the form of eight hundred white horses with one black ear. Unable to find them, Galva approaches King Yayathi for help. Yayathi does not have the horses, but gives away his sixteen-year-old daughter Madhavi for Galva to exchange for the horses. Galva takes her to one king after another, for each of whom she is to bear a son in return for the horses. In Anupama Niranjana's reading of the episode, Madhavi's fate becomes a startling symbol of the experience of women in general. Among her other important works are *Ele* (Thread), 1980, about a community of handloom weavers in a small town, and *Ghosha* (A Rallying Cry), 1985, which deals with struggles between a dictator and the people. Her autobiography, *Nenapu Sihi Kahi* (Bittersweet Memories), also came out in 1985, and in 1986 she published *Manini,* a collection of articles on the situation of women. She won several awards, including the Karnataka Sahitya Academy Award in 1978, the Soviet Land Nehru Award in the same year, and the Nanjanagudu Tirumalamba Award in 1987.

Her eight popular medical books were written to give women knowledge of their bodies as well as of common ailments. They also give advice to teenagers and married couples and discuss mother and child care. *Jayi-Magi* (Mother and Child), 1968, and *Dampatiya Deepike* (Advice to the Couple), 1973, appeared in their eleventh and thirteenth editions in 1987. Asked in 1989 whether she would write these books in the same way again, Anupama Niranjana said she would, because their scientific information was still valid. She was, however, not happy with the advice she gave in *Vadhuvige Kivimatu* (Advice to the Bride). When she wrote the book, in 1971, she advised women to give in and make compromises with her husband and her parents-in-law. "When it was pointed out to me in 1981, I did make a few changes. But if I rewrite it, it will be entirely different. I would give the woman more dignity and stress her individuality," she said. The story translated here was written in 1980 and published in the collection *Pushpaka* in the same year.

◆

ONDU GHATANE MATTU ANANTARA
(The Incident—and After)

He looked anxious as he climbed the stairs, apprehensive that some-body would see him and stop to talk. His friend's wife, chatting with a neighbor, saw him come up.

"Where's your wife? You seem to be alone."

Avoiding answering her, he reached the second floor. What business is it of hers? he thought indignantly. But the recollection that she had seen them go out together earlier in the evening sobered him up at once.

Perhaps I should have said something to her. What if she begins to speculate wildly? Standing there, working away at her gossip loom, spewing out yarn . . . ?

He was drenched with perspiration. Standing by his door, he tried to overcome the breathlessness the climb had brought on. His name—white letters embossed on the door—confronted him. He read it over impassively, and without recognition. Is this me? The faceless fellow that I am? Instead of leading this life, I could just walk away . . . along the sea . . . like the camels there.

Involuntarily, his hand pressed the doorbell. The noise resounded inside, evoking an answering tremble in him. Mother will open the door now. What do I say to her? His tongue darted over lips dry and lifeless. Quelling the beating of his heart, he tried to put on a brave face.

His mother received him with a questioning glance. Unmindful, he took off his slippers, and crossing the hall, entered his room. His mother waited awhile at the front door for her daughter-in-law to join them, and then, seeing that she did not appear, shut the door.

"Where is she, Son?"

Pulling off his trousers, he replied, "She's gone to her friend's place." The tone was even, the telltale quiver suppressed.

"To Sunithi's?"

"Hmm."

His mother went inside. Listening to the clatter of vessels from the kitchen, his agitation surfaced again.

"If she wants to visit her friend, she should go in the morning! Why go at night? Besides, Sunithi's married too! It's disgraceful! Haven't you any sense, leaving her behind like this?"

Haven't you any sense . . . to return . . . leaving her behind? The words reverberated. Assumed a million forms. I left her, and returned.

Where? Not sense, it was courage that I lacked. Draping a dhoti around himself, he rushed to the bathroom—and let himself cry.

His wife had said, "Why take this street? It's already dark. Even if one shouts, there's no one around to come to our aid!"

"Don't be so timid! What's there to be afraid of, when we are on the scooter? Besides, this is a shortcut. In a couple of minutes we'll reach the main road that leads home, wait and see."

What a splendid time they had at the seashore that evening! She was always scared of getting her feet wet, of walking up to meet the waves. "What if I drown?" Her trembling reached me, journeying through our clasped hands.

He recalled how he had felt like lifting her high and smothering her in a shower of kisses. In the distance, a couple had strayed even farther into the water. Boys flirted with the oncoming waves. On the shore, ponies and children played. Their happiness had matched the buoyant murmur of the sea, as if the world were devoid of sorrow. But at last the sun set. Darkness came up on muted feet.

"Let's make a move. But before going,—some *bhelpuri* and ice cream . . ."

As he ate the ice cream, he was floating in happiness. The sight of her wide open eyes and blossoming bosom urged a fast return home. Hence the shortcut . . .

He emerged from the bathroom. Somehow, he felt diffident about facing his mother. Wondering whether she had believed him, he stretched out on the bed.

"Come and eat."

"I don't feel like a meal now, Mother. We stuffed ourselves at her friend's place."

"So you went to Sunithi's too! Why did you not say so? I thought you had met her near the beach . . ."

Mother is not convinced. I can tell by the way she is questioning me.

He got up in a huff and went out onto the balcony. A great many of the windows of the opposite building had withdrawn for the night. On one balcony stood a husband and wife, side by side. With an arm over her shoulder, the husband whispered something in her ear. Standing alone, his body began to quiver. Affection, love, desire, kissing, embracing, then uniting—he had considered these the most significant aspects of creation. But all at once, they lost their meaning, seemed mere shadows, without substance.

He retreated. Shutting the door of the balcony, he tumbled onto the bed. The same bed, once the fount of pleasure, now seemed a smoldering volcano! He hid his face, felt himself burning in that fire.

In the obscure darkness, somebody had stopped the scooter. Heavyset men, with harsh voices. One of them had pulled his wife off. She screamed into the night. "Who is it? Let go!" He had rushed forward. A fist lodged in his face; he slumped as his eyes blurred over. When he came to, he could hear the piteous cries of his wife from a distance. In the background, he dimly perceived the contours of a hutlike structure. He tried to get to his feet, but tenacious arms restrained him.

"Just get on the scooter and scram. Raise an alarm and I'll finish you off!"

His throat felt dry as he saw the razor glint in the stranger's hand. His legs quaked under him.

"Go straight home! If you dare bring the police, we'll stab your wife and leave!"

To go to her rescue would only invite fresh danger. Instead he had rushed home, intent on saving his own skin.

He tossed about on the cot. His mother, having completed her work in the kitchen, was fastening the latch of the window. In a little while she would spread her bedding in the hall and sleep. The next moment she would begin to snore.

I should have gone to the police, he thought. His wife's image stood before him. At the moments when his being was utterly satisfied, life without her had seemed unconceivable. And now, all of a sudden . . .

But if the police had been informed, she might have been killed. Yet, of what use is her life now? Supposing I had rushed forward to save her? Then the sharp point of the razor would have carved my breast. I would have died a martyr's death. But what earthly reason would there have been in both of us dying, making a show of bravery? Still, if survival was guaranteed, one could achieve almost anything . . . His thoughts shamed him, and he felt a momentary contempt for himself.

He turned onto his side. He pictured his wife approaching him for an embrace. How did she get here? At this moment, in the hut . . . He tugged at his hair in despair. He had treasured her kisses and caresses, once. But now all that seemed drained of meaning.

He rose. The light was still burning. His mother's snores were audible from across the hall. He picked up his trousers from the clothes stand. Why not take his friend, go *there* and try to rescue her, he thought. Looking distractedly into the mirror, he failed to recognize the face that met him. What if his friend refused to come? If he is let in on the secret, it's as good as telling the twenty-odd families in the building. And later, how do I face them? Deciding against turning to his friend for help, he lay down again.

Can I continue to love her as before, knowing all that has happened? Impossible, he thought. But why? She has lost her chastity, is that it? And what about me? Hadn't I roamed the streets of this town, in pursuit of flesh? But that was before I got married. I'm a respectable man now. Whereas she's a fallen woman, for no deed of hers.

His eyes grew heavy with sleep . . . I stand on the edge of the ocean. The people are looking for somebody. The waves thunder, rise to the skies, recede. Suddenly, the current throws something onto the sands. "A colossal fish!" The people crowd around. I, too, strain to see, in curiosity. But it's her corpse! I scream—

He woke up immediately, with a violently beating heart. It took him quite a while to return to reality. A novel thought came upon him. What if she commits suicide? What do I say to the others, if it is so? Besides, her father is a police inspector. He would not hesitate to pin the blame on me: "You killed her." Dead or alive, she would pose a problem.

He rose and went to the toilet. "Aren't you asleep yet, Son?" asked his mother, roused by the sounds of the door closing. Sleep had packed sloth into her voice.

"I was. But I woke up. Go to sleep, Mother!" he said, abrasively. Turning off the light, he went back to bed.

His wife had said, "Do you know how much I love you?"

"How much?"

"More than my life!"

What will she say now? She is sure to spurn me. How can I ever face her again? Strange! Our intimacy over the past two years has made us almost inseparable. Yet, now, how this incident wrenches us apart!

"We'll have two children, what d'you say?"

"Will only two do?"

"Hmm. One a boy and the other a girl."

They had had no children in the two years that had passed.

But what if she becomes pregnant now? If so, *it* has to be removed. My friend can give me the information . . . where to go, and so on. The expense does not matter. Only, Mother should not hear of this.

If we feel it's not possible to live together, a divorce can be arranged. I can say she is mentally unbalanced, or even that she's sterile. But what if Father-in-law asks me to get myself examined by a doctor first?

The easiest thing would be to be magnanimous and say, "I have forgiven you." She may even be grateful to me. Then we can put on our masks and continue the deception . . .

Suddenly, his stomach gave a sickening lurch.

It was still early in the day. The world was once again being prodded to life. She got off the scooter-ricksha and walked quickly, to avoid prying eyes. As she climbed the stairs, her legs seemed to give way under her. The ache in her thighs was unbearable. Clutching the banisters, she made her agonizing way upstairs.

When her husband tried to support her from behind, "Don't touch me!" she said. The tone was contemptuous and full of rage.

Sighting their ascent from the balcony, the mother went to the door. Her daughter-in-law's disheveled hair and her soiled and stained sari made her ask anxiously, "What in God's name is all this?"

The daughter-in-law walked by with bent head, without answering. The son replied, "A bull came into the street. I had to brake rather suddenly and she fell off."

"A bull? What if you had lost your lives!"

The daughter-in-law snatched her clothes from the stand and rushed into the bathroom. She turned on the heater and tap. Hot water began to fill the bucket. As she sat down on the low stool to bathe, her tears flowed freely.

Could a bath cleanse her? Could all this water wash away the sin now attached to her? She did not commit it! But this stigma would remain till the very end . . .

All those screams have made my throat hoarse. Why, even a stone would have relented and taken pity on me! And what became of God, the god I worshipped every day? From whom else could I expect help, when my dear husband drove away, without even lifting a finger?

Her sobbing increased. Putting the soiled clothes in a corner, she looked at her body. Is this me? The smooth fair skin was discolored by rude wounds. Her thighs were thoroughly battered. The vaginal bleeding hadn't ceased. The contact of hot water brought a silent scream to her lips. Oh God! Had life a meaning for her anymore? She had eyed with longing from the hut the solace offered by the sea, but had no energy left to cover the distance. Otherwise she could have rested peacefully at the bottom of the sea . . .

She began to dress.

Outside, mother was conversing with son.

"Are you going to work?"

"Yes. I have to, I've no leave to spare."

With her body and mind in tatters, she would have expected her husband to stay home; it was the least he could do. But instead he seemed to be running away. What kind of a man is he, who cannot protect his wife? He could have given up his life, fighting those black-guards—that way I would have retained my respect for him. Even if he had died, I would have lived on with memories of him.

She came out. Her husband, standing before the mirror and shaving, appeared to her a total stranger. He breathed his last near near the hut, she thought in trepidation. The soapy lather covering his face made him look like a rabbit. She flung herself onto the bed.

Surprised that her daughter-in-law did not put in an appearance at the kitchen, the mother came up to their room.

"What's wrong? Aren't you well?" She felt her daughter-in-law's forehead experimentally. "She seems to be running a temperature. Why not consult the doctor?"

Mowing his beard with care the son replied, "There's no need. The hurt must have brought on the fever. She'll be all right tomorrow."

Memories a few months old rushed unbidden to her mind. She had complained of a headache. "Shall we go to a doctor?" he had asked worriedly. "To the doctor for a headache! Just get me an aspirin." He had rushed away immediately for the tablet. "I won't go to the office today," he had said.

And now—how could a relationship break up overnight? Husband, wife, love, the bond—what do they all mean? Of what worth was life if one turned to it only for happiness and sought to slip away when confronted with sorrow?

She drank some coffee—because her mother-in-law insisted. Then she slept. Her body ached, as if she were being dismembered. No, I cannot live with this coward. Did he show any concern? Did he say, "I'm sorry. Please forgive me"? Hell, just looking at his face repels me! Anyway there are no children to tie me down. I could go to my father's home, work and earn a living. This man's shifty eyes disgust me!

He left for work.

In a short while the maid arrived to finish the chores. As she washed the clothes, she suddenly shouted from the bathroom, "Amma, the petticoat's all stained with blood. What happened?"

"I fell."

"Wherever from?"

From the skies to the underworld. She stopped herself just in time . . . I should have washed those stains myself. The maid is bound to tell all the neighbors . . . Could one wash away all the sins as easily as one removes these stains? The maid began to beat the clothes, to make the dirt run. The noise resounded through the tiny house. Those stains are forever, they will not fade . . . She lay back, tired.

The cooking done, her mother-in-law joined her. "If you had come straight home all this wouldn't have happened! Why did you have to go to your friend's place?"

Shall I tell her what really happened? She debated for a moment. Probably she won't believe it, but if she does, she'll be aghast. Her only son! How could this happen to his wife? And what about the family now? She would lament, weep, bemoan her plight. Then it would all be put away for the sake of the son. A decaying life would be dressed up in dignified robes . . .

"Will you have lunch? You didn't eat anything in the morning either."

Hunger. Yes. But the churning hasn't stopped. Mother-in-law, too, looks like a stranger.

She pecked at her food and rose. Another worry began to gnaw at her. What if she should become pregnant? No, never. The doctor would help her remove the lump of sin. But then the whole story would come out. The torn vagina, the swollen thighs—won't he know what has happened? What if he refuses to treat me . . . a police case, you see. Then the entire town will be put in the know. Fine. I'll stand on the rooftops and shout, This is the story of a woman who lived in this respectable town . . . Let them hang their heads in shame—the men, the women, the police . . .

As she was drowsing, her husband's friend's wife came in.

"Aren't you feeling well? Where were you all evening? I couldn't get a word out of your husband!"

She gave a wry laugh in answer.

"The maid just left. She says there were heaps of soiled clothes at your place today!"

Does this woman know? In doubt and apprehension, she lay back, fatigued.

The pool of fear kept widening. What now? Do I put everything behind me and resume this drama of love? If love means only sex, I am sick of it. There is only one way out of all this, the easy way: death. To reach heaven treading on the waves of the ocean, that is the real deliverance!

The sun was wilting when the husband returned. Slipping in like an outsider, he changed his clothes and walked into the kitchen. Sipping his tea, he asked his mother, "How is she?"

"She's lying down, can't you see?"

Mother and son went over the morning's conversation again. He settled down in the hall, with the radio for company.

Tossing about in bed, she mused, I should wire my father. After all, he is in the police department. If he can come here, perhaps those wicked boors can be tracked down and punished. Maybe Father can do what this coward cannot!

Night stole over them. He lay on the far side of the bed and did not speak. She waited, fearing he would fall asleep. Then, stiffening her resolve, she began, "Say something. We've got to arrive at a decision, haven't we?"

"What's there to decide about now?"

"Does this mean that this is the end?"

No reply. Silence slept between them. He had a restless night, but towards daybreak a deep slumber overtook him.

He woke in the morning to her absence.

Perhaps she was in the bathroom. He turned on his side. A quarter of an hour passed, but still no sign. He got out of bed and checked. There was no one there!

His heartbeats quickened. The drawn bolt on the front door confirmed his fears. She had left! Surely she would not have gone visiting at this hour. He was reminded of the sea. Maybe she had killed herself. Relief displaced all other emotions: what a simple solution to the knotty issue! In the next instant: how vile could he get! What would the people think, if he didn't lament the death of his wife? Taking a grip on himself, he looked towards his sleeping mother. Shall I wake her, tell her the news? No. It would be better to think calmly first. Tangled in thought, he sat on the bed.

Her things were still here. Since her clothes were untouched, she could not have gone to Sunithi's place. Or to her father's. Which confirms the suspicion of suicide. Now, the first step would be to lodge a complaint with the police about her disappearance. Next, write a detailed letter to her father . . .

His mind moved listlessly from thought to thought. While his hands played with the pillow, something dark caught his eye. Inquisitively he bent forward and saw the note.

It contained just a few lines: "Yesterday our relationship came to an end. I am leaving to lead an independent existence. Do not look for me."

She had signed the latter with her mangalsutra.

Translated by Seemanthini Niranjana.

BRAHMOTRI MOHANTY ⸻

(b. 1934)   *Oriya*

Brahmotri Mohanty's witty, cleverly constructed poems explore the inner world of her emotions. Since publication of her first poem in 1950, her work has appeared in almost every major Oriya periodical. The first of her three collections of poetry, *Abantara* (Uncoordinated), appeared in 1972; the second, *Drustira Dyuti* (Light of the Eye), in 1985; and the most recent, *Stabaka* (A Spray of Flowers), a collection of 131 tightly constructed short lyrics, in 1988. She won the Orissa State Sahitya Academy Award for the latter in 1983, and has received three Bisuva Milana Awards for poetry. Brahmotri Mohanty has lived in Bhubaneshwar for much of her life, but has now settled in Puri with her husband, who is a writer of fiction.

◆

THARE MO GODA KHASIJIBA PARE
(After My Feet Had Slipped Suddenly, Once)

Startled, I looked around—had anyone seen me?
Perhaps they had, perhaps I hadn't seen them.
A terrible restlessness in my heart; in my mind boundless suspicion,
Even if no one had, they would surely come to look.

And then what would I answer? Some lies would have to be told,
That further inquiry could implicate me was not impossible.
What was the way, then, to save myself?
Sweat warmed my brow, flushed my face, a cricket sang in my ears.

Never, never, did I fall deliberately, knowingly.
Why, then, this flush of shame? Could reason ease the mind?
To know its true form I probed deep into my thoughts,
Yet what I saw was what I could not see.

Clothes torn, legs bruised, something broken—even then I did not
  fall.
When did I fall? Direct lies—I merely leaped as I walked.

Translated by Jayanta Mahapatra.

DARPANA
(Mirror)

That image of mine only a mirror can reveal
amazes me, this majesty of my own being.
So much light, so much radiance,
yet I never recognize myself;
but if everything goes wrong after this familiarity
of praise, this worship of the idol in me
becomes mere habit in the end, the excitement spent.
What use is there in these declarations devoid
of brilliance, meaningless the look in space.

I step away from myself, unable to taste this reality of mine.
How can I experience the essence of an indivisible existence?

Translated by Jayanta Mahapatra.

MADHAVIKUTTY ⎯⎯⎯⎯⎯⎯⎯⎯⎯

(Kamala Das, b. 1934)   *Malayalam*

Kamala Das publishes her English poetry under her given name, Kamala
Das, and her work in Malayalam under the pseudonym Madhavikutty,
her maternal grandmother's name. She started writing, she once said, because she watched her mother, the well-known poet Balamani Amma
(b. 1909), "write her poetry lying on her bed all day long and tried to
imitate her." She considers her maternal granduncle, the scholar-poet
Nalapatt Narayana Menon, and the matrilineal ethos of the aristocratic
Nair family she was born into to be the other major influences on her
work. And it is indeed true that in Madhavikutty's writing her grandmother's house, which is also the nostalgically recreated setting for her
famous poem "Hot Noon in Malabar," 1965, is the poet's imaginative
home. It is a place that sustains life as it does art, unlike the library of the

cold city flat that slowly kills her, as it does the "sunshine cat," found dead there one evening, in a poem with that title (1965).

Kamala Das spent her childhood in Calcutta, where her father was working. She was the only girl among her parents' five children and her education, attended to by a series of governesses and tutors, combined modern subjects with some traditional scholarship. At fifteen she was married, in keeping with Nair tradition, to her uncle K. Madhava Das, an official of the Reserve Bank of India, and, except for brief stints in Calcutta and Delhi, the couple has lived in Bombay. Her first short story collection, *Mathilukal* (Walls), came out in 1955. *Pathu Kathakal* (Secret Stories) followed in 1958, and *Narichirukal Parakkumpol* (When Tender Wings Fly) in 1960. The relationship with her husband, she writes in her autobiography, *My Story,* (1975), was by turns brutal and indulgent. She moved seriously to writing poetry after her husband developed a close friendship with another man. Her first and best collection of poems in English, *Summer in Calcutta,* (1965), was followed by *The Descendants,* (1967), and *The Old Playhouse,* (1973). The brilliant title piece of the last book is a richly evoked autobiographical poem, perhaps unmatched by her later work. Many of her poems deal with the longing to be loved and the inevitable frustration of this desire. Death is the other recurrent theme. During the sixties she published several collections of short stories in Malayalam, among which are *Ente Snehitha Aruna* (My Friend, Aruna), 1963; *Pakshiyude Manam* (A Bird's Honor), 1964; and *Thanuppu* (Cold), 1967.

Kamala Das has three sons, the eldest of whom was the colorful editor of the well-known Malayalam daily *Mathrubhumi.* A heart attack in the early seventies set her back, but she recovered well enough to run in the parliamentary elections as an independent candidate from Trivandrum in 1984. She was badly defeated, though she got extremely good press coverage for her campaign, during which she spoke out against the hypocrisy and corruption in public life. She was awarded the Chimanlal Award for fearless journalism in 1986. In her autobiography she discusses, among other things, her somewhat distant relationship with her parents, her childhood, and her writing. The book gained some notoriety because of her flippant and graphic descriptions of her friendships with men, which she later revealed to be more fiction than fact. In contrast to her poetry, with its sensitive and intense confessional tone, the autobiography is more sensational than candid, perhaps deliberately so. It has been translated into fifteen languages. Brief episodes from her childhood, recreated in vivid sensory detail, were serialized in *Mathrubhumi* as *Balyakala Smaranakal* (Reminiscences of Childhood) in 1987.

Right through the sixties, which were undoubtedly the most productive period of her life as a writer, Kamala Das continued to publish stories and poems in Malayalam, many of which have been translated. Her collected short stories, *Ente Cherukathakal,* were published in two volumes in

1985. *Manasi,* her only novel, which later appeared in English with the title *Alphabet of Lust,* came out in 1978. "Neipayasam," the story that follows, appeared in *Femina* in July 1986.

◆

NEIPAYASAM
(Rice Pudding)

Let us call him Daddy, the man who returned home at night after giving his wife a frugal cremation and, later, expressed his gratitude to his colleagues for their words of comfort, for after all he was called Daddy by the three children who were the only ones who knew his exact value and importance.

Seated on the bus, among total strangers, he tried to relive each moment of that accursed day. The morning had begun for him with her voice calling out to the boys. "How can you lie like this wrapped up in blankets? Have you forgotten that today is Monday?"

After waking Unni, the eldest, she had walked into the kitchen, wearing a white sari. Afterwards she had brought him a large mug of coffee. Then what had happened? Had she said anything memorable, anything significant? However much he tried, he could recollect nothing that she had said afterwards.

"Have you forgotten that today is Monday?"

Only that sentence remained stuck in his thoughts. He repeated it in silence, chanting it with reverence as though it were a mantra. He felt that his loss would become unbearable if he were to lose that sentence.

In the morning he had taken the boys to their school as usual. She had given each a lunch packed into a flat aluminum box. There was a smudge of yellow, probably a touch of turmeric, on her cheek.

Once he reached the office he had stopped thinking of her. He had married her after a courtship of two years, against the wishes of his wealthy parents. And yet, not for a moment had he regretted his decision. There had been the usual quota of minor disasters. Children's illnesses, unpaid bills, promotions denied . . . but she had never displayed dissatisfaction or unhappiness. Gradually, she had lost interest in her own appearance. She laughed rarely. But the neighbors still thought her a pretty woman. He had been proud of her complexion.

They had loved each other. Their children had given them delightful moments. They talked of making Unni an engineer, for was he not always trying to take things apart to see if he could put them together again? Balan, the second, would probably make a good doctor, being so gentle and compassionate. Once he nursed a wounded bird back to health, feeding it with an eye dropper. And five-year-old Rajan, brave even when the lights failed, would make a fine soldier. Oh yes, together they had dreamt of a bright, happy future.

They were living in a tenement on a street where only the lower middle classes lived. She had not hung a curtain on the bedroom window, fearing that such sophistication might offend the poorer people who were her neighbors. But on the windowsill she had kept a potted rose which refused to bloom though she watered it every morning. In the kitchen she had hung her ladles and serving spoons on the yellow walls. Each day she had scrubbed her brass utensils with tamarind and made them shine like gold. She used to sit on a wooden seat near the stove while making the chapatis for their supper. When he got off the bus his knee hurt a little. Would it turn into arthritis? he wondered. He thought of his sons, now without a mother, and all of a sudden tears welled up in his eyes. The tears embarrassed him. He walked towards his house, wiping his face with the back of his hand. He had never used a handkerchief in his life.

Would they be sleeping, the boys, his and hers? Would they have eaten something? They were too young to comprehend death. When he had lifted her lifeless form into the taxi, Unni had stood watching in silence. Only the youngest had cried, but that because he was told he could not ride in the taxi.

No, they would not know death's merciless ways. For that matter, had he foreseen this? Had he guessed that she would, one evening, without a warning, collapse while sweeping and lie there dead and free? Yes, she had released herself from the bondage of her responsibility. He envied her her freedom. Now he was saddled with the young children . . .

He recollected how shaken he was when he spotted her lying near the broom with her mouth half-open, her pale limbs flung out in absolute disarray. He had covered her legs first. Then he had placed his ear next to her breast to find out if she breathed. He had not heard heartbeats, although he could hear his own, thumping like breakers in his other ear. Was she dead? he had asked himself. At the hospital, the doctor said that she had been dead for two hours.

At that moment, blinded by an irrational hate, he cursed the woman who had been his wife. How could she have done this to him? How would he bathe the children? How would he cook their lunches and send them to school? How would he be able to nurse them back to health when they fell ill? No, it was not possible for him to bring them up alone. My wife is dead, he said to himself. It did not sound convincing. "As my wife has suddenly died of a heart attack, I request that you grant me a week's leave to put things in order." He would be justified in asking for leave. His wife was not merely ill, she was dead.

The boss might even call him to his air-conditioned cabin to offer condolences. "I am so sorry to hear of your wife's untimely demise . . . I wish I could do something to help you, perhaps a raise, or would you take a loan from our emergency fund . . . ?"

Well, so much for the boss's sorrow. He had not known the dead young woman. He had not ever seen her grace, her long tresses, her milk-white complexion.

His loss was terrifying. He had lost the beauty of existence.

As soon as he entered the house, the youngest rushed out of the bedroom to embrace him.

"Why didn't you bring Amma with you?" he asked angrily.

"Why didn't Amma return with you?" asked Unni.

How could the ten-year-old have forgotten everything so fast? How could he have imagined that the lifeless form carried away in the taxi would revive in an hour's time and travel home? He felt angry and exasperated. He entered the dark kitchen and switched on the light.

"Balan has fallen asleep," said Unni.

"Let him sleep. I shall feed you."

He removed the lids of the vessels placed neatly on the ledge and peered inside each of them.

She had cooked a full supper for her family before dying. There were chapatis, some rice, and *dal* [lentils]. The curds were set in a crystal bowl. In another bowl he found some *payasam,* the kind she made each Sunday for her children, cooking rice mixed with ghee and jaggery.

Perhaps it would be wrong to eat food touched by death, he thought.

"This food is cold. I can make some hot, savory *upma* for you," he said, smiling at the boys.

"No, Daddy, we'll eat the payasam Amma made for us," said the children.

Eating the payasam, the youngest licked his middle finger and said, "Our Amma cooks the best payasam, this is wonderful . . ."

"Yes, she's the best cook in the world," Unni smiled.

Translated by the author.

SUGATHA KUMARI ─────────

(b. 1934) *Malayalam*

Sugatha Kumari's poetry is regarded as having given a fresh lease on life
to Romantic lyricism in Malayalam poetry. At the center of her work is a
deep involvement with melancholy—nameless, inescapable, but powerful.
"More than the majesty of the snowy hills that beam / Glorious, frosty,
immaculate / I like the grief of the volcano / That scatters its fiery flames
around / From a mighty anger within," she writes in "Ekaki" (The
Loner).* In two poems that take up the legend of Krishna—"Krishna Ni-
yenne Ariyille" (Krishna, You Don't Know Me) and "Kadane" (It Is the
Forest)—the archetypal romance of Radha and Krishna is transformed into
a saga of human longing: "Since this Radha is enshrined within / Life is
an unending quest."

This tragic quest for love is accepted as the feminine condition in many
of Sugatha Kumari's love poems, but she has in her other poetry sometimes questioned the real nature of what has come to be regarded as woman's fortitude. In "Ivalkumathramai" (Just for Her), for example, she
writes,

> As the mother earth in whom the fire burns,
> She, for you to trample on, sometimes to worship,
> To cast derision upon, to desert,
> To hold hands with for support,
> To rear the children on the fluttering breast;
> Just for her, such a life. . . .

In another well-known poem, "Rajalekshmiyode" (To Rajalekshmy), an
elegy written following Rajalekshmy's suicide, she too suffers an inner
death: "In my tears blood-drops crackle; / The new moon that had shim-
mered for a while in my sky, / Shudders and turns a dark red black!"

Within the world of Sugatha Kumari's poetry, every object in nature is
linked with every other in the vast scheme of the universe. The poet explores the external world in deft, austere strokes in order to uncover and
celebrate the mind behind it. The unchangeable, ontological pain expressed in the poetry, however, is sometimes tinted by a more ethical note
of regret as she laments the selfishness of human beings, their incapacity

───────────

*The extracts quoted here have been translated by Jancy James.

for sincere love, the instinct of violence, and the loss of inner freedom. Her interest in ecology emerges in such poems as "Thames Nadiyodu" (To the River Thames) or "Marathinu Sthuthi" (Hymn to Trees).

Sugatha Kumari was born at Aranmula, the second daughter of the poet Bodheswaran and V. K. Karthiayani Amma. Her mother, one of the first women in Kerala to hold a master's degree, taught Sanskrit at the famous Women's College in Trivandrum. Sugatha Kumari was free to develop her poetic talent through reading and discussion at home, especially after her family moved to Trivandrum, where she earned her master's degree in philosophy. In the early part of her life, Sugatha Kumari devoted herself to writing poetry. More recently she has become involved in public life. In the late seventies she led a successful nationwide movement to save some of the oldest natural forests in the country, the Silent Valley in Kerala, from submersion as a result of a planned hydroelectric project. Perhaps as a result, the quiet, lyrical sensibility of her earlier poetry has been replaced by increasingly feminist responses to social disorder and injustice, as for example in the poem "Punjab," 1986. Her involvement with the issues raised by the women's movement of the seventies and eighties is evident in some of her recent poetry. "Amma" (Mother), 1989, retells the legend of Devaki, the mother of Krishna, with the focus on her victimization by her brother, Kamsa. "Penkunju Thonnurukalil" (Girl-Child in the Nineties), 1990, is an ironic exposure of the various levels at which the girl-child is suppressed and exploited.

Sugatha Kumari has several literary awards to her credit, including the Central Sahitya Academy Award in 1978 for the collection of poems *Rathrimazha* (Night Rain), 1977, of which the title poem has been translated here. For *Ambalamani* (Temple Bell), 1981, she won three awards, including the prestigious Kumaran Asan Award in 1984. Among other of her better known collections of poetry are *Padirapukkal* (Midnight Flowers), 1967, *Pavam Manavahridayam* (Poor Human Heart), 1968, *Pranamam* (Salutation), 1969, a cycle of seven poems on Mahatma Gandhi, and *Irulchirakukal* (Wings of Darkness), 1969.

◆

RATHRIMAZHA
(Night Rain)

Night rain,
Like some young madwoman
Weeping, laughing, whimpering,
For nothing
Muttering without a stop,

And sitting huddled up
Tossing her long hair.

Night rain,
Pensive daughter of the dusky dark
Gliding slowly like a long wail
Into this hospital,
Extending her cold fingers
Through the window
And touching me.

Night rain,
When groans and shudders
And sharp voices
And the sudden anguished cry of a mother
Shake me, and I put my hand to my ears
And sob, tossing on my sickbed
You, like a dear one
Coming through the gloom with comforting words.
Somebody said,
The diseased part can be cut and removed
But what can be done with the poor heart
More deeply diseased?

Night rain,
Witness to my love,
Who lulled me to sleep
On those auspicious nights long ago,
Giving more joy than the white moonlight
Which made me thrill with joy
And laugh.

Night rain,
Now witness to my grief
When on my sweltering sickbed
In the sleepless hours of night
Alone I reel with pain,
Forgetting even to weep
And freeze into stone.

Let me tell you,
Night rain,
I know your music, kind and sad,

Your pity and your suppressed rage,
Your coming in the night,
Your sobbing and weeping when all alone;
And when it is dawn
Your wiping your face and forcing a smile,
Your hurry and your putting on an act:
How do I know all this?
My friend, I, too, am like you
Like you, rain at night.

Translated by H. Hridayakumari.

RAJEE SETH

(b. 1935)   *Hindi*

Though she has been writing practically since she was a child, it is only since the mid-seventies that Rajee Seth has published her work. She never felt the urge to publish, she says, until she realized that there is "no growth for a writer unless one learns to peel away creatively ripe experiences to let new ones take shape." Her first story, "Samanantar Chalte Hue" (Treading Parallel), appeared in 1974. Shortly after, she wrote—in one sitting—"Uska Akash" (His Bit of Sky) which is still her favorite work. "Writing has become part of my being. I write in many forms—poems, stories, essays [on contemporary literary problems], reviews, memoirs, and travelogues," she says. Her first novel, *Tatsam* (Pilgrimage), appeared in 1983. At present she is at work on what she feels will be a major book "on the problems that endanger the inner life of [Indian] society." She has published three collections of short stories: *Andhe Modh Se Age* (Beyond the Dark Alley), 1979; *Tisri Hatheli* (A Third Hand), 1981; and *Yatra Mukt* (The Journey's End/The Dawn), 1987.

Rajee Seth was born in Nowshera, a town now in Pakistan. She received degrees in English and Hindi literature from Lucknow University and studied comparative religion and Indian philosophy at the Gujarat Vidyapeeth in Ahmedabad. She now lives in Delhi. She is married to a senior government officer and has one son. The story translated here first appeared in *Naya Pratik* in 1975.

◆

USKA AKASH
(His Bit of Sky)

For him only this much was real: the stretch of sky he can see lying on his bed with his face to the window, and as much air as can enter the door of a first-floor room on that side of the building.

He knows that the sky is not only what he can see, even as life is not just what has been his lot for years in this little room, or this bed, surrounded by rows of medicine bottles, where he grows hot and cold alternately in the sticky dampness of his sweat. But this is all there is, in his lot.

To know its dimensions one has to actually move into the arena of life, just as one has to go out under the sky to feel its entire vastness. Outside—out of oneself, to hold the immense blueness in one's eyes, to gather it into one's arms, to feel it . . . Even if it cannot be held in the arms, it descends into one's eyes, surely.

Arms . . . ? He touches his right arm with his left hand, touches the entire length, keeps feeling it, but there is no throb. Doctors say his right side is dead. Can it happen that a person dies on one side and stays alive in the other? He is half his own person and half a stranger; he bears in one half joy and pain, touch and feeling, and he is half without sensation. As if something is hung upon a peg in the wall and the bustling world beneath sees it a little dead, a little alive . . .

He is reminded of Joseph and of that picture—of that bloodied body hung on a cross. Joseph used to say Jesus was divine because he atoned for the sins of the world. No one has to bear the consequences of their sins, nobody is to make efforts to eschew wickedness and vice. You are free to sin—because Jesus is there to expiate your sins . . . Divine Jesus will continue to sacrifice himself. No, no, he cannot be content to think of himself as a martyr. On the face of his eldest daughter-in-law, Badi Bahu, it is writ large: "This is all a consequence of your sins . . . your sins and some of ours too, that we have to clean up your shit and piss, your snot and spit." He is reminded of Amro.

Sometimes when she was very moved, she would say, "Bless me . . . I should go before you. I should like to die while you are still living, a *suhagan*. My pyre should be lit by your hands." He would bless her then because at times like that she did not appear to be a mother of four children, but was like a young innocent girl whom it was easy to hide in his wings. Then his chest was not soft and yielding like a balloon. Little did he know that her seemingly innocent demand and the blessing did not come so cheap. This feeling of being left alone midway. It's like the test of fire-walking to have to bear half life and half death together, and without her demands and her affection, her negligence, and her love. If she were there, he would not have to face Badi Bahu every day; he would not have to be pierced by the sharp prick of a nameless humiliation. How many deaths, how many deaths can a man live at one time, and why is only a complete cessation of life called death?

Death is what you feel . . . what dies even as you feel it dying, as it had happened to him. His death is continuous—half of him dead. The other half is in the process of dying, and he can clearly observe it taking place. Some random day the whole of him will die and he'll be like a heap of mud—completely without the throb of life, shorn of the ability to experience even the death of sensation. Then what will be left to know in him? That will be the inevitable, the "had-to-be."

Varun, his grandson, hurtles into the room. "Baba, Mother's asking if she should bring your milk." He raises his left hand and wipes his eyes. He doesn't feel the thin stream marking the right side of his face.

"You'll stay with me while I drink it, won't you?"

"Yes, Baba, drink it before I go to school. Mother has a lot to do in the morning."

"Yes, of course." His throat is constricted by some unexplained emotion again. "I'll drink it while you are here. From your own hands, my son!"

At least one difficult moment will pass. With the spearlike sharpness of the eyes, one's entire being is shot through with holes. Poor, unfortunate Badi Bahu.

Varun brings the milk and sits on a stool close by. Spoon after spoon, until the glass is half-empty.

"Baba, when will you tell me a story? Baba, when will you come downstairs?" He cannot answer. He is in a hurry to gulp the milk. Just beneath his navel a rumbling, life sapping emptiness rises in waves, as does the niggling worry about Varun's school rickshaw arriving. He does not reply—he gives nothing back to Varun, no story, no outing, no anecdote or joke, no laughter. One day Varun, too . . . He is afraid. Whomever he cannot give to in return stops giving, even God. He remembers the time he offered fresh, beautiful flowers gotten from a mile away to God. A return to memories always becomes an ocean of sorrow that he does not have the strength to swim and cross—he goes under, the whole of him sinks.

Varun's cycle rickshaw sounds its horn. One-fourth of the milk is still in the glass. Varun does not have patience. Strength is burgeoning in his limbs and before him life runs full of promise and temptation. Hearing the sound, he cannot sit still on the stool—if he had his way he would jump off the roof and get downstairs. "Baba, hurry up . . . my rickshaw—" and after pouring the rest of the milk into his mouth all at once, Varun runs off. The milk runs out of the corners of his mouth, down his neck. A sticky aversion that is now a part of him does not disappear even after he has wiped himself with a towel.

Kamal, his son, enters the room. "How are you, Babuji? How do you feel today?"

He begins to respond but then feels that the one who has asked does not expect an answer because, after saying this, after tossing a little concern for his well-being into the air, he is humming and lacing his shoes, gathering his things together. The question was a tax to be given for having entered the room and broken the silence. It's like a toll to be paid when one crosses a border.

If he doesn't reply and does not say, "I'm all right," as on other days, would it make a difference? Maybe it would. He doesn't answer, and lies inert. His silence really makes no difference. His son picks up his things and goes off. He is deeply hurt when his suspicions are confirmed. It would have been better had he answered. The act of answering is vital to him, absolutely vital. To carry on the exchange is *his* need, only his. It is *his* interest to keep the presence of sound, to break the continuous silence of the long days and dark nights, *his* alone. He could not afford to be egotistical with anyone. With Amro it had been another matter. She would devise novel ways to keep his ill-humor at bay. "You are a rogue," was what she would want to say. Had he been her son, she would have said that, but not to him . . . and when he extracted full gratification out of her constraint, she would happily hide her face in his chest, and say, "Oh you . . ."

It is evening. The days passed with such tedious slowness, as if carrying the weight of stones on their chests, and the nights with an ache, their center touched by the barking exchange of dogs and the metalic tap of the watchman's stick.

Varun enters in the twilight . . . "Baba, Baba, do you know, there's a house coming up on the lot next door. It's all been dug up . . . Where can we play marbles now Baba?"

"Here. Play in this room."

"Here?" His eyes widen with surprise and disbelief. "How will we play here in this tiny room? Pappu, Somu, and Vikki will not all fit in here. Mother says we're not to make a noise in Baba's room."

"No, no, make as much noise as you want, play all you like. I'll watch your game."

"Really Baba? . . . Did you play marbles when you were a kid?"

"Yes, I played marbles too." Joy and self-pity mixed uneasily somewhere inside. He wanted to encircle Varun in his left arm, but his back . . . He gave up and said softly, "I'll stay here and watch which marble has hit the other."

"Great!" Varun jumps and claps. "Now Pappu won't be able to cheat . . . You'll just say that my marble hit his each time, won't you Baba?" He strokes his hollow cheeks with fresh tender palms swelling with young blood.

"Yes, yes." His eyes moisten at this display of affection. He doesn't feel like telling Varun it's not right to cheat. The ones who have to live should carry their own burdens of deciding what is good or what is bad in life.

Two days, four days, the children really create a racket. His days of stonelike heaviness fly on wings of air. The children come only in the evening, but one can at least look forward to that. There's something. At least the curse of nothingness is broken.

But by the fourth day they are bored. Pappu's Mother forbids him to come; Somu's marble breaks when it hits the wall; Vikki resents Varun's cheating and tigerlike aggression in his own house and says, "We won't play in your Baba's room. I'm not going to speak to you." Varun grows apprehensive and looks for fresh pastures . . . two lanes away. People of the same age like to be with each other. He has to console himself and keep quiet.

The room is stiller than ever before. The air is colder. The patch of sky grows clouded.

Down below . . . *thak, thak* . . . the foundations are probably being dug. Good thing he married Mini off when the lot was vacant. They only had to exit from this door to enter the *mandap*.* Otherwise they would have had to cart everything to the wedding hall at the crossing. Though that was not so bad, either. That's what they did for Niti's wedding. Ramnath would say with such enthusiasm, "You really have spirit, Bhai!"

Spirit? He again touched his right hand with his left. Frightened, he

---

*A *mandap* is a sheltered dais in which the bride and groom sit during their wedding.

wished to shut his eyes . . . but you can't shut everything out by shutting your eyes. Every hurt inside still stalks, ready to pounce.

Poles and planks made up the scaffold. *Thak, thak, thak, dak, dhum dhadak* . . . mixed with voices. All his energy is concentrated in his ears as if he is listening to the tale of Satyanarayan being ritually recited. At least something that can be heard is happening somewhere. There are voices and sounds. When Devki enters he says, "Devki, is the house next door being built?"

"Yes, Master, Pirthi Babu's son is coming back from America. They're going to build two stories."

"How much of it is complete?"

"Quite a lot, Master. They're using a machine to mix the cement. You must have heard it. The lower story is almost ready."

"Devki?"

"Yes, Master?"

"Push my bed against the wall opposite the door."

He feels good after it had been shifted. The angle of the room changes. Some things look different. He is reminded of the slug-like drawing master in his small-town school. He would place a stained square pot on a large table and say, "Draw it from your angle." He had hated drawing. Devi Singh had once done his drawing for him and the master let him have it with the cane. He had said, "One person's angle cannot be the same as another's. You must have got somebody to draw it for you." And he had sat in each boy's seat and discovered his truancy. It was just as well that the study of angles was soon over . . . but no, the study of angles cannot end, ever. It sticks with you . . . from a changed angle, the room still looks fresh. To distinguish between the voices coming from next door, to give a name to each one as it tangles with the other, he feels a new happiness, as if he has separated the strands of the thick rope of all this noise with his own strength, with the fine sensitivity of his ears. He feels like swelling his chest by filling his lungs to capacity, but his breath breaks again and again. Tired by the effort he lies still. The voices were there before he was stuck in this bed. They must have been, but then he was in the arena of those who make the voices, not in the backyard of life. The quicksand of self-pity sucks him down again and again.

When the masons and laborers begin work, he begins to feel happier because the activity is steeped in sound. In the hide-and-seek of life and death, life is always identified because some sound is caught by the head. When the foundations are dug, when the scaffoldings are erected, when stones are hammered, when bricks are broken, when mortar is mixed, when the lintels are laid, when pipes spray water, when there is a slow, rumbling dialogue between the cement and the scraper in the iron mixing pan, when the walls are whitewashed, when the carpenters begin work and the doors and windows are hammered in, shutters fixed and electric wires fitted . . . he hears and records it all. When they get to the second story he watches as much as he can the activity of the laborers—sitting in the shade and drying their sweaty bodies, opening their bundles and eating, long burps after pouring water into their mouths from a tin mug and lighting up bidis, Prithvi Singh's brows drawn together in preoccupation, commands that make the ceiling ring . . .

Something keeps happening . . . it carries on . . . growing from small beginnings to a large shape. Something is being constructed somewhere. Not all is in the jaws of death as he is.

He feels hopeful as he sees the house grow, hopeful that there will be a world after him. People will start living in the houses that are being built today and will live for generations just as he has lived in the house of his forebears until now. By the time the high structures of today are about to fall, there will be new houses made, whether or not any living being in the flow of life, sitting or prone, watches them grow. What is the relative position of the observer who watches this flow of life? Each one is granted limited time and passes on, but life moves on relentlessly.

That he is not the only one who watches this stream of life as an observer gives him some measure of satisfaction.

But it lasts only a few moments. He gets restless, thinking the house must now be ready, and all will be silent as before. Once again the long, lonely days and the nights of a heavy heart will pass with painful, halting slowness. Badi Bahu will come rushing as before, open this or that cupboard, and go away. Kamal will give his toll of a few niceties and depart. Varun's friends will not play marbles here but will run off to the third lane. Everybody has to run and rush about as if there is something waiting for each of them downstairs. It's like a contest to see who can get there most quickly. But has anybody spared a thought for the destination? Because in the end, after all this coming and going, it's an icy retreat into a bed like this.

He is disturbed when he thinks that everybody continues to run, though they have no clue to their direction. They are all moving in the same direction. Everybody's future lies in the jaws of death. He feels he should stop and check and hold everybody. "Look at me—I am your future . . ." But because the future never appears as the future, always coming as the present, nobody has time. So people confronted by the future itself cannot see it; they cannot recognize it for what it is. It would be better if he were outside on the road, hung on a peg, half-dead and half-alive, and people would, looking at him, know their futures and stop. They would pay the debt of being alive in their lifetime so that after—if there is an after—nobody would be able to pierce anybody with eyes full of contempt for bearing the consequences of sins committed.

He feels that the way to freedom lies in knowing all this, but nobody wishes to know it until they get to this point . . . or perhaps they cannot know it. Everybody has to be nailed to their individual crosses—nobody can be of use to anybody; you cannot actually be a guru to anyone; no one shares suffering. His heart sinks and he begins to perspire profusely again.

His fears come true. When the house is built, the whole place falls silent again. Now? He is afraid to think further, but there is no security from fear because fear rests in the heart and the heart is within the person. Were it outside, it could be thrown off like a centipede.

There is some activity on the roof opposite. He turns to look. Preparations are being made to carry away the leftover material. Now there will be cleaning, then painting, a house-warming party. People will start living there. They will live, work hard, fall ill, lie on beds rotting with disease, pain, and loneliness. They will die in halves, three-quarters, completely . . . like him.

"Like him"—he wanted to experience that again. With his left hand, he attempted to touch the right. Nothing happened . . . even its death could not be felt . . . Is dying so silent, normal, and ordinary that it can take place in half your body and you don't even know it? Is this death?

When it comes some day, he probably won't even know it . . . Maybe he'll be watching the house opposite, or the sky full of clouds, or sunshine or stars, or maybe he'll be asleep. He hopes he will not die in sleep; he should be able to see death, understand it. The "happening" that he witnesses every moment, every instant, the night watch, the ritual of the curtain dropping, should not be taken from him, this last right left to him in this world. His eyes should be fixed on the sky and he should sink—breath by breath.

Busily he calls for Devki once, twice, three times. When nobody comes, he clangs the steel tumbler on the iron chair. Varun appears. "What is it, Baba? Have you been calling for a long time?"

"No, Son, just send Devki."

He tells Devki to move his bed back to the original place. Devki says, "My hands are not clean, Master. I'll be back."

It's best to shift back there now. It's silent on this side; there is nothing here. The house is ready and the life living in it is walking the road to death. What is the use of pausing on the side of one such death? He lives much worse deaths in himself every day. He carries them within him.

Devki says, "Careful, Master," and shifts his bed to the old place.

He is back, after three months. He feels better, has the pillows changed, the basin shifted to that side. He has the table with the medicine bottles placed against the wall and the tumbler of water put on the end near him.

The novelty in the changed angle strikes him again; again he is reminded of that slug-like teacher and he laughs anew and follows the same chain of thought. He feels freer, as if he has reached the last stop on his journey towards death; lying here, he will watch the sky and sink, breath after breath.

He strokes his eyes in turn with his one good hand as if there is no urgency. Now that the house is complete, whatever there "was" lay in the surviving. Put the bed here ... the sky should remain in his eyes, and until the moment of death he will watch it and sink.

Eagerly he opens his eyes but is left stunned. Between him and the sky in his lot is a rectangular bit of concrete.

He had not suffered so acutely even when he had seen the future of the entire world given over to the jaws of death ...

Translated by Manisha Chaudhry.

WAJEDA TABASSUM _____

(b. 1935)   *Urdu*

Wajeda Tabassum's mother died shortly after she was born, and her father when she was two. The young Wajeda and her three sisters and four brothers were brought up by their maternal grandmother, who had once been a very rich woman but had been cheated of her wealth and property after she was widowed. Wajeda remembers her childhood as one of utter misery, redeemed only by the presence of her grandmother, who was determined that the children should be educated. She sawed off the knobs of her gold bracelets, one by one, to pay for books and fees. The children all did well, and Wajeda was able to earn a master's degree in Urdu from Osmania University. Her early struggles, she feels, account for her hatred of injustice and hypocrisy and for the range of themes she writes on.

Around 1947 the family moved from Amravati, where Wajeda had been born, to Hyderabad. Much of her writing, including the story translated here, uses a Hyderabad locale and the Dakkani dialect of Urdu, over which she has uncommon mastery. Quite a few of her stories are critiques of the decadent life associated with the old aristocracy of that region. In 1960 she married, against the wishes of her family, her cousin Ashfaq. The wedding expenses, she wryly observed, "totalled 170 rupees, and we don't even have a photograph to record the occasion." The couple now lives in Bombay. They have five children. Wajeda Tabassum is a firm believer and feels that her writing is so powerful because a religious force inspires her. Five times every day, when she hears the *muezzin*'s call from the mosque, she drops whatever she is doing to pray.

Wajeda Tabassum has published twenty-seven books. Among the best known of her novels and short story collections are: *Teh Khana* (The Cellar/The Room Underground), 1968; *Kaise Samjhaoon* (How Can I Convince You?), 1977; *Phul Khilne Do* (Let the Buds Bloom), 1977; *Utran* (Castoffs), 1977; *Zakm-e-Dil Aur Mahak Aur Mahak* (Let the Fragrance of My Wound Envelope You More and More), 1978; *Shehar-e-Mamun* (The City of Peace), 1978; and *Zar, Zan, Zamin* (Money, Woman, and Land), 1989. The last is a novel of over 1,600 pages which deals with the victimization of women. Two young girls, one Muslim, the other Hindu, both of whom have been forced into prostitution, are rescued and put into a rehabilitation home, where they build up a strong and mutually supportive relationship. Their troubles continue, however, for in the home they are further exploited, this time by politicians and high-ranking officials who consider the institution a sort of private brothel.

"Utran," the story translated here, is Wajeda Tabassum's best-known piece. When it was published in 1977, she was denounced because of attitudes the heroine displayed that were considered inappropriate for a Muslim woman, but the story was also widely appreciated. It has been translated into eight languages and filmed for television.

◆

UTRAN
(Castoffs)★

"For Allah's sake, don't! I feel so shy."

"Come on, what is there to be ashamed of? Haven't I taken off *my* clothes?"

"Mmm . . . ," Chamki said shyly.

"Will you take them off or shall I tell Anna Bi?" shrieked young Shahzadi Pasha, so used to giving orders that it had become her second nature.

Very timidly, very shyly, with her small hands Chamki removed her shirt, then her pajama★★, and then, at her mistress's behest, jumped into the tub full of soap suds.

They finished their bath and the young mistress, in a voice which was tender yet full of a sense of superiority said, "And now tell me, what are you going to put on?"

"Clothes?" Chamki asked gravely. "These of course, my blue shirt and pajama."

"These again?" the mistress cried out in amazement, wrinkling her little nose. "Such dirty, smelly clothes? What is the use of bathing, then?"

Chamki did not answer. Instead she shot another question back at her. "And what are you going to put on, Pasha?"

"Me?" The mistress said with complacency and pride, "That set, the one grandmother gave me for my Bismillah, when I began to learn how to read, the glossy one, there, that one. But why do you ask?"

Chamki thought to herself for a moment and then, laughing, said, "I was thinking—" she stopped abruptly.

"What were you thinking?" inquired Shahzadi Pasha, greatly curious.

Suddenly, from the other side of the door, Anna Bi's voice rose sharply. "Well, Pasha, you drove me out of the bathroom and now what are you doing there with that useless wench? Come out quickly or I'll tell your mother, Bi Pasha!"

Chamki blurted out, "Pasha, I was thinking that if only you and I become sisters by exchanging our dupattas, as adopted sisters do, then I, too, could wear your clothes couldn't I?"

"My clothes? You mean all those clothes that fill my boxes?"

★*Utran* are clothes that have been taken off; soiled clothes.

★★A pajama is a trouserlike lower garment made of fine fabric and worn by both men and women.

Chamki, a little frightened now, just nodded in reply.

The young mistress doubled over with laughter. "What a foolish girl you are! You are a servant. You should wear my castoffs. All your life you will wear nothing but cast-off clothes." And with affection that was more tinged with arrogance than with sincerity, the young mistress picked up the clothes she had shed to bathe, and tossed them to Chamki.

"Here, take this. Wear these used clothes. I have plenty."

Chamki grew angry. "Why should I wear those? Will you wear my clothes?" She pointed at her own dirty clothes.

Shahzadi Pasha was furious. She called out, "Anna Bi, Anna Bi!"

Anna Bi gave a noisy push to the door which, not being bolted, opened wide.

"So," said Anna Bi with false displeasure, "you too are still standing around without your clothes." Shahzadi Pasha quickly snatched a soft pink towel from the stand and wrapped herself. Chamki stood as she was. Anna Bi looked intently at her daughter for a moment.

"And who told you to take your damned bath here in the mistress's bathroom?"

"Shahzadi Pasha asked me to have my bath with her," Chamki said.

Anna Bi glanced around to make sure no one was looking. Then she quickly pulled her daughter out of the bath. "Now run at once to the servants' quarters. You'll catch your death of cold. Don't put on those sweat-soaked clothes. In the red box there are a kurta and a pajama that Pasha gave us the other day. Wear those."

Standing there naked, the seven-year-old girl was lost in thought. Then, hesitantly, she said,

"Ammanni, if Shahzadi Pasha and I are equals, why shouldn't she wear my clothes?"

"Just wait! I'll go and tell Mama what Chamki said . . ." [said Shahzadi Pasha].

Anna Bi was frightened and lifted Chamki into her arms. "But Pasha, this whore, she's just mad—she's a fool. Why do you want to tell your Mama these silly, trivial things? Don't play with her or talk to her. Just spit on her name and forget her existence."

When she had dressed the young mistress, combed her hair and plaited it, and fed her, Anna Bi was finally through with her chores. Coming back to her room, she found Chamki standing there naked like a leafless tree. Without stopping to think, she began to thrash her daughter. "You quarrel with those who feed you—you whore! If the master throws us out, where will you go with all your airs?"

According to Anna Bi's reckoning, it was a matter of great good fortune that she had been hired as a wet nurse to the young mistress. She was given food and drink from the table of the mistress. After all, she was nursing the nawab's only daughter at her breast. Nobody could keep count of the clothes she received—they had to be clean and fresh for one who nursed the child. And the greatest boon was that her own child received all the clothes discarded by the young mistress. There was really nothing more one could ask for. The beauty of it was that often even silver jewelry and toys were given away as used or discarded goods. And here was this stubborn wretch who, ever since she reached the age of discretion, had obstinately been asking why she should wear the mistress's used clothes! Sometimes she would look into the mirror with a knowing air, and say, "Ammanni, I'm far prettier than Bi Pasha, am I not? Then why shouldn't she wear *my* used clothes?"

Anna Bi felt frightened each time her daughter said such a thing. After all, these were big people. If someone were to hear that the wretched Anna's daughter said such terrible things, they would have their noses cut off and be sent away. And anyway, the days of suckling the child were long over. It was the tradition of that great house that people such as Anna left only when they died. But even an offense can be forgiven only if it is fit to be forgiven. Twisting Chamki's ear, she tried to drive some sense into her. "If ever you say such a thing again, be warned . . . You will have to wear the young mistress's cast-off clothes all your life. You understand, you donkey's child?"

The donkey's child sealed her lips for the moment, but the lava kept boiling within her.

When she reached the age of thirteen, Shahzadi Pasha missed her *namaz* for the first time. She had attained puberty. On the eighth day there was the ceremonial garlanding. Her mother had made her a suit of clothes woven with gold thread so beautiful that it dazzled the eye. Pairs of tiny golden bells had been sewn on the dress, so that when the young Shahzadi Pasha moved, they tinkled like anklets. In keeping with the custom of the house, even this excessively expensive suit was later given away as a cast-off piece. When the overjoyed Anna Bi took this gift to her room, Chamki, who had matured beyond her age, said with much grief, "Ammanni, take these things if you have to, but at least don't be so pleased with them."

"Listen child," the mother whispered confidentially. "If we sell this dress, it will fetch no less than two hundred rupees in British currency. It was our great good luck that we found our way into this palatial house."

"Ammanni," Chamki said wistfully, "you know what I long to do? Once, just once, I want to give Bi Pasha some of my used clothes."

Anna Bi struck herself on the forehead. "Listen, you are now a young woman. Have some sense. If anyone should hear these words, what will I do? Have some pity on my white hair!" Seeing her mother weep, Chamki grew silent.

Chamki and Shahzadi Pasha had started learning to read the *Quran Sharif* and learning elementary Urdu from the Maulvi Sahib together. Of the two, Chamki was brighter and quicker. When they had both finished their first reading of the *Quran,* the mistress, in her generosity, had a simple new dress made for Chamki too. Although later Chamki, as usual, also was given the young mistress's much more expensive cast-off dress, she prized this simple one above her life. She did not feel humiliated in it. The light orange cotton dress meant far more to her than all the lustrous, glittering clothes she possessed.

Now that Shahzadi Pasha had finished the education she needed, and had reached puberty, preparations began for settling her in life. The house became a veritable residence of goldsmiths, tailors, and other merchants. Chamki kept thinking that for the wedding day, amid all the pomp, she would wear only the cotton suit which was her own and not anyone's castoff.

The mistress, who was a truly generous lady, cared for her servants almost as if they were her own children. And so she worried about Chamki's marriage with the same anxiety that she had for your young daughter's. At last, after much talking, she had found a good match for Chamki too. What she thought was that, after her daughter's wedding, while the feasting and merrymaking continued, Chamki's marriage should also be performed.

There was barely a day left before the young mistress's wedding, and the palace was teeming with guests and the voices of girls, swarming like locusts, rose high and filled the mansion. The young Shahzadi Pasha sat surrounded by her companions, who were smearing her feet with henna. Affectionately she said to Chamki, "When you go to your husband's house, I will color your feet with henna myself."

"God forbid!" Anna Bi said with tender affection. "May your enemies touch her feet! Your speaking thus is enough for us. Give her just one blessing, Pasha—may her bridegroom turn out to be as noble as yours."

"But when is she going to get married?" a spirited girl in the company asked.

The young mistress laughed the proud, condescending laugh of her childhood days. She said, "When she gets all my wedding castoffs, her dowry will be ready." Castoffs again—castoffs—castoffs. Chamki felt as if a thousand sharp needles had pierced her heart. Swallowing her tears, she went to her room and lay down silently.

At sunset the girls began to drum ritually on the *dhol*. One risqué song followed another. They had stayed up through the previous night. Tonight they would do the same. On the other side of the courtyard, stoves had been lit and cooks were busy preparing countless varieties of dishes. The house was so bright with lights that it looked like day.

Chamki put on her orange dress, through which her sorrowful beauty glowed all the more strongly. This one set of clothes freed her from all sense of inferiority, and made her feel supremely exalted. It was not anybody's castoff. The dress had been made with cloth freshly bought from the market. This was the only unused clothing she had ever received. All her years she had been wearing Shahzadi Pasha's castoffs. "But Bi Pasha—you don't know just how far I can reach. You kept giving me your used things, didn't you? Now wait and see!"

She picked up a tray of sweets and entered the bridegroom's mansion. It was brightly lit, as was the bride's house, which was also bustling with activity. After all, the wedding was to take place the next morning.

In the huge house, in the midst of all the tumult and confusion, no one noticed her. Inquiring of one, then another, she went straight to the bridegroom's chamber. Exhausted by the lengthy rituals of having turmeric and henna applied the bridegroom lay stretched out on his canopied bed. When the curtain moved he turned to look, and kept looking.

Orange kurta reaching down to her knees. Tight pajamas clinging to her firm, fleshy calves, her plump arms, orange dupatta lightly embroidered with gold, reddish eyes, still moist with recent tears, a wreath of jasmine blossoms in her hair, a murderous smile on her lips—all this was not altogether new for him. But then, a man whose mind has been filled with thoughts of a woman for several nights becomes treacherous the night before his wedding—no matter how virtuous he may be.

Night invites temptation,
Solitude encourages it.

Chamki gave him a look that shattered him. Purposely she stood with her face averted. Unable to resist her, he rose and stood facing her squarely. Chamki glanced at him from the corners of her tilted eyes. He was floored.

"What's your name?" he said, gulping his spittle.

"Chamki" she said, and a bright smile lit up her pretty face to the radiance of the full moon.

"Hmm, the way you glitter—it is but fitting that your name should be Chamki."

He put his hand hesitantly on her shoulder—precisely in the manner of a man who before bringing a girl around to his will talks about this or that. Then, trembling, he removed his hand from her shoulder and caught her by the hand saying, "What do you have on this tray?"

Chamki deliberately encouraged him. "Sweets—for you—we kept vigil last night, you know." Without a rapier, she pierced him to the core. "To sweeten your mouth . . . ," she smiled.

"I don't believe in sweets when I wish to sweeten my mouth. I—you know what—" And he bent forward to sweeten his mouth with the honey of her lips. And Chamki melted into his arms—to loot his virginity. To be looted herself and to loot him.

The day after the wedding, when in accordance with the custom of the house, Shahzadi Pasha gave her used bridal costume to her nurse's daughter, her playmate, Chamki smiled and said, "Pasha—I—I—I—All my life I kept wearing your castoffs, but now you also . . ."

And she began to laugh like one possessed. "Something I have used you will also—for the rest of your life . . ." There was no stopping her laughter. Everyone thought that the sorrow of parting from her childhood companion had temporarily driven Chamki out of her wits.

Translated by Rasheed Moosavi, Vasantha Kannabiran, and Syed Sirajuddin.

BINAPANI MOHANTY ────────────────

(b. 1936)   *Oriya*

Binapani Mohanty was born in the village of Chandol, near Cuttack, and many of her stories are set in the rural locations she grew up in. She graduated from Ravenshaw College with a master's degree in economics in 1959, and began teaching soon afterwards. She now teaches at Shailabala Women's College in Cuttack.

Though Binapani Mohanty is regarded as one of the foremost Oriya short story writers today, she began her literary career as a poet while still at school. Her poetry began to appear regularly in the major periodicals of the time, and by 1960, when she published her first short story in the journal *Prajatantra,* she had already written some two hundred poems. After 1965, finding the medium of short fiction more appealing, she stopped writing poetry.

A first book of short stories, *Naba Taranga* (New Wave), appeared in 1973, and Binapani Mohanty has since published eighteen collections, notable among which are *Tatinira Trushna* (The Thirst of the River), 1972; *Andhakara O Chayi* (Darkness and Shadow), 1976; *Arohana* (The Ascent), 1978; *Madhyantara* (Interval), 1979; *Bastraharana* (The Stripping [of Draupadi]), 1980; *Anya Aranya* (The Other Forest), 1982; *Khelona* (A Toy), 1983; *Drushyantara* (Scene Change), 1984; and *Charitra Hasuchhi* (Inner Laughter), 1986.

Binapani Mohanty won her first major literary award, from the Orissa Sahitya Academy, in 1976 for the short story collection *Kasturi Mruga O Sabuja Aranya* (The Musk Deer and the Green Woods). She has since been honored by most major newspapers and periodicals in Orissa and received the national Sahitya Academy Award in 1990 for her 1987 volume of short stories, *Pata Dei.* Pata Dei, the protagonist of the title story, is a village woman who, like Ketaki in the story translated for this volume, plucks up the courage to rebel.

The characters in Binapani Mohanty's fiction, Jayanta Mahapatra comments, represent a wide range of classes and her fiction deals with questions that press people in their daily lives; her stories still touch the reader as they used to do, twenty-five years ago, with their inherent realism." The story translated here appeared in *Jhankara* in 1989.

◆

ASRU ANALA
(Tears of Fire)

She was one of those who could cover the length and breadth of the town at one stretch, moving from one crossroads to another, from this neighborhood to that, like lightning—anyone could vouch for that. Whatever time of day it was, she'd rattle the latch of the front door and call out, "Green bananas, banana blooms, jackfruit and mangoes!" At other times she would shout, "Yams and pumpkins for you, mistress! Cook them with some dried fish!" Some called her Ketaki, others Keti, still others addressed her as Nani or Apa.* It made no difference to her. If she had her basket on her head, the whole world was in

---

*Nani and Apa are terms of address for an older sister or aunt. Nani is generally used by brahmins, and Apa by the nonbrahmin castes.

place. Her legs were still strong and her arms and feet still nimble. She prayed they would stay that way. What else did she need?

But how times had changed! When she was younger, nobody had ever dared snicker at her or make a passing joke—why, nobody had even dared look at her. Two sons and daughters to bring up, and her husband had come home one evening after a day of toil, flushed with fever. He had closed his eyes and never opened them again. But Ketaki wasn't one to give up. The children had to be kept alive somehow!

In a starving household a widow has no time to bewail the loss of a husband. A hundred people had crowded round Siba Babu's wife to comfort her when he died—and had gone away calmed with tea and sherbet. Siba Babu was a good man and he had gone at a ripe age. Their children had all been well taken care of, so his wife could recount his virtues and droop like a tree in a storm. How would such fortune have come Ketaki's way? She had not even been able to weep till her heart was soothed. But she didn't complain. She had stifled her sobs and tended to the children. The girls would be married one day, and the day the two boys grew up to be government officers, Ketaki would go to the Shiva temple and offer *bel* leaves; then, prostrating herself, she would weep till the heavens burst and floods swept through the rivers and the oceans. On that day she would speak her last words. Right now—well, she couldn't afford to. She couldn't carry a basket of flowers to the temple and wail for two hours, day after day, like Siba Babu's wife. She'd set aside just one single day for the gods. Now was the time for her to tuck the end of her sari firmly into her waistband and battle for life itself. She could feel God smiling faintly in his sleep—and why not? Ketaki was not one to give in as long as she had a breath in her. She was not one to be cowed down.

Pari Bhauja counted the bananas in the cluster Ketaki held. "How long you take, Bhauja," she said. "It's sweltering today and my throat is parched. Do hurry up."

Pari Bhauja was over fifty. Husband, sons, daughter, and a daughter-in-law—she was totally wrapped up in her family. The attendant from the office usually shopped for the groceries, but there was always something or other still to be bought from Ketaki. "Why don't you stop for a while, Keti," Pari Bhauja asked as usual. "What's the hurry? You have only these green bananas today, and who's going to buy many of those?"

"No, I've no time to stop today. Ramu Babu's daughter ordered a dozen green bananas yesterday. Something she read about in a book and wants to try out. I should be off."

Pari pulled her mouth into a sneer. "Well, well, one would think they cooked only delicacies in that house! If you ask me, that girl is a real hussy! Fools around with a bunch of young men—and her parents never say a word. If she were my daughter I'd have torn her to bits."

"But Moti is a wonderful girl, and an accomplished one, too. I've known her since she was born."

"Rubbish! She slipped out of her mother's womb into your arms, I suppose. How would you know of the things that take place inside a household, you who roam the streets all day. Go now, I'll pay you tomorrow."

"No Bhauja, we've no oil in the house. Not a drop to cook with, or to oil my daughters' hair. Don't hold my money back today. You can do it tomorrow if you want."

Pari was clearly annoyed. She undid the knot at the corner of her sari and flung the money down. "Go," she said, "eat your fill of green-banana rolls and chutney at Ramu Babu's house. That girl has already driven men crazy—and now its women who are carried away by her. But not me—I'm not that easy to fool."

She stomped back inside, leaving the bananas on the ground, as if she had bought them only as a favor to Ketaki—no one in *her* house would eat such stuff.

Ketaki had met many kinds of arrogance. Five years ago it would take Pari four days to pay for a meager two bundles of greens and a pumpkin. But now that her husband had become a rich contractor and was bringing in piles of crisp money, what was there to stop her from speaking as rudely as she did?

Ketaki walked on, barefoot, in the scorching afternoon heat. At the corner of one street, an old man had set up a shack with some large earthen pitchers filled with water. He floated mint leaves and chillies in the water and sat there, pouring it out to thirsty passersby. For fear that some high-caste person would take offense otherwise, he had thrown a sacred thread across his shoulder and lined his brow with sandalwood paste. Ketaki put down her load and helped herself to a long drink of the mint water.

"How come you're here this morning?" the old man asked. "Didn't you wait for a drink at the contractor's house?"

"This is where the likes of us should drink. It's only because I usually get to the contractor's house before I pass you . . ."

"Here, take a few chillies and some mint. They'll make a chutney to go with your rice."

Ketaki took the mint and the chillies from the old man's hands and wrapped them in a wet cloth. He added, "Stick to the side of the lane, daughter, and walk in the shade. The tar keeps melting in the main street—besides, nothing is the same as before. Who knows what might happen? You have grown older, that's true, but you are a woman after all—" He stopped suddenly in the middle of what he was saying. Two ricksha pullers had come up to ask for water.

Ketaki plodded on with her load. She went down that street every-day. It was only a few yards to Ramu Babu's house. She would dump the bananas with Moti and rush home, stopping for mustard oil and coconut oil on the way. Why should her sons have to come out in the heat? The eldest had become thin as a reed studying for his final high school exams. Fate wouldn't take it lying down if a fatherless son grew plump. But wait, was it a bee that had stung her?

Ketaki turned around. A number of small whitish stones suddenly landed around her feet. What lunatic was playing with a catapult [slingshot] in the heat of the afternoon? She looked to her left and to her right. No one. Then she heard someone elaborately clearing his throat. Good God! Who on earth were these? Eight or ten toughs posed theatrically in front of the *debighara,** leering at her. One of them stood a little ahead of the group and was holding a slingshot. Some drama, this! Such antics had never been seen in the debighara before! Where had these hoodlums suddenly sprung from? Ketaki's bile began to rise—but this was no time to get provoked. She turned to go, and had barely taken another step when a stone hit her hard on the ankle. She dropped to the ground. As if on cue, the boys burst into a theat-rical guffaw. "Was it because you didn't hear us," they taunted, "that you stalked off like a queen?"

Ketaki rubbed her ankle. "Don't you know me? Ketaki is my name."

"And this the end of your kind of game!"

"Can't you find anyone else to play the fool with?"

"How much do you earn in a day? Nothing less than fifty rupees I'm sure. Why, you're all over the town. Out with the stuff!"

"Why should I pay you? Do I live off you? Do I owe you anything? Who do you think you are, anyway?"

A muscular bull of a man swaggered up to her. "Woman, do you know who you're speaking to?"

---

*A *debighara* is a spacious structure built in a market square or at a crossroads to accommodate the image of *debi,* the goddess Kali or Durga, at festival times. Often nowadays during the rest of the year young men use the premises as a clubhouse.

"Why should I know who you are?" Ketaki asked as she lifted the basket back on her head. "Who are you to stop me? I'm not scared of anyone—not even the governor! You hoodlums, don't you have mothers and sisters at home?"

"Enough of your pious rubbish! Open up that bundle at your waist and put down five rupees if you still wish to ply your trade on this road. Otherwise we'll just take everything you have and make sure you won't step out of your house again."

"Ruffians! Scum that you are! Why should I give you any money? Just because I'm a woman alone? Wait and see. If Durga doesn't emerge from this very debighara and wring your necks, pick a mongrel for a pet and call it Ketaki!"

Ketaki was quivering with rage. The basket kept slipping from her head. What was she to do? The old man would have helped, but the young men had encircled her and were hovering mockingly. It was so hot there was not even a crow in sight. Every door, window, and thatch shutter was down. Ketaki lost courage. She sat down weakly. "Why should I give you any money?" she asked.

"Don't you know that you use this route?"

"Does the street belong to your father?"

"No, but the father is drunk and reeling in the house. Yes, the road is ours; it belongs to us all. After all, you earn a tidy sum on this road. Why won't you share it with us?"

What could Ketaki say? What can anyone say to the young people today? They might humiliate you right in the middle of the street. She had the five rupees Pari had given her for the bananas. She thought it over for a while. "All right. Let me go over and sell these bananas at Ramu Babu's house, and then I can pay you your dues. I have learned today that the street I walk on is yours."

"Don't worry. As far as streets go, you can take your pick. Walk on any road you might want to. Our boys are everywhere. Pay your toll and go your way. Otherwise you'll end up at home cradling those two daughters of yours on your lap, you bitch."*

Ketaki couldn't remember having heard such disgusting talk in her life. It wasn't that long since these boys had been weaned from their mother's breasts, yet they acted as if they owned the world! What terrible times these were! Parents moved aside in fear of their children,

---

*The insinuation is that by the time these young men have finished with them, Ketaki's daughters would be unmarriageable.

and even on the town's main streets the police and the government cowered before these ruffians. Whom could she speak to?

Smarting with shame and anger, Ketaki took out the five rupees she had tucked into her sari at the waist and flung it at their faces. "All you can do is grab a helpless woman's money! No, what you'll eat is not money, but shit, you scoundrels! No one will be there to lift a finger when you are in trouble."

All Ketaki heard in reply was ugly guffaws, as though her words were a sweet-scented shower of sandal-water. The insult burned through her. A moment more and, who knows, they might have stripped her naked. She walked rapidly ahead. Moti would be waiting for her. She had promised to return early, and the children would be expecting her to share the usual *pakhala**** together.

She was still climbing the steps to the veranda when Moti opened the door. "Aren't you feeling well?" she asked. "Why are you so pale? Shall I get you a drink of water? Or perhaps some *torani?*** You look exhausted, and there you are, still walking around barefoot in the summer heat. How often have I asked you to get yourself a pair of *chappals,* or use mine." Ketaki leaned weakly on the pillar. "No, my child, don't tie me up in the strings of your affection. My time is almost up . . ."

"Why, what happened? Why do you talk like this? I hope the children are all right."

"They are well, my child, but fate is against me. Never, never in my whole life have I bowed my head before anyone. I have even fought with God. But now, against these young men, I simply cannot win. If I had stretched out my hands to ask for that money, or if I were simply spending what belonged to my father or my husband, it might have seemed all right. Ten rupees or so is all I get for a hard day's work and if I give away five from that, how can I stay alive?"

"Did those young men at the debighara ask you for money?"

"Who else? I wouldn't have minded so much if they were collecting the money for some worthwhile cause. They're simply going to squander it on drink, the rascals."

"Have you paid them already?" Moti asked in a grave voice. "Or are you going to? As for me, I'm going to tell the police. These men won't let the common people survive. They've been extorting money

---

*Pakhala, a summer meal for many poor people in Orissa, is a fermented dish made of leftover rice mixed with water.

**Torani is the water from the pakhala.

for their club for the last eight days. I didn't open my mouth when they picked on well-to-do people. But when they force money out of poor ricksha-pullers and women like you, how will you survive?"

"Take the bananas, my daughter, and pay me. What can you do? It's no use talking to you of these things. I might as well be munching carrots near a deaf person. You're a woman. If they lift a finger, that will be the end of you. You live here, in this neighborhood. So be careful about what you say or do."

"What are you saying? That I shouldn't do anything? They insulted you on the road. Tomorrow it will be me, and the next day some other father's daughter. What kind of farce is this? What is the country coming to? Of what use are all these laws and regulations?"

Ketaki carefully tied the money Moti had given her into a knot in her sari. "Go inside, child," she said. "This blasted country can choose to go where it pleases. There's no saying when it will come back to its senses."

"Wait, eat something before you go. It's awfully hot. I'll keep a couple of the banana rolls in the fridge for you. You can have them tomorrow."

"No, my dear. The children will be waiting for me. And look, please don't interfere with those rowdy young men. They're berserk . . . When will your mother be back from her mother's house?"

"The day after tomorrow. Why? She doesn't go there often, you know. Grandfather's been ill. You're anxious about me, aren't you? What can those empty-headed boys do to me?"

By then Ketaki had already got to the crossroads with her basket. No one heeded what you said these days. Still, Moti was a smart girl—beautiful, but also clever. And of course that was why Pari disliked her. Besides, Moti was also a good sportswoman and had won many medals in cities like Calcutta and Delhi. May God grant her happiness, Ketaki prayed. And may she have a long life as well.

The sun seemed to have gone down a little. The children would be waiting for their pakhala. She had promised to take some mustard oil and salted fish back with her. The chillies and mint tied in the piece of cloth had begun to wilt. Her mind was seething with resentment. But whom could she speak to? If her husband had been alive, perhaps to him. But would he have been able to do anything by himself? He was so excitable it was a good thing that he was not alive to see such times.

Early the next morning Ketaki went out and bathed in the Sahu's pond. When she got home she found that the wholesaler's wife had already brought pumpkins, banana blooms, and bitter gourds and had stacked them in the basket, ready for her to sell. She usually shared half the profits. Ketaki felt reluctant to step out of the house. But if she didn't, what would the family eat? Yesterday she had missed out on her evening job. Her elder daughter worked in the household of a Marwari businessman and earned fifty rupees a month. The younger one ran odd errands, and that brought in enough for her meals. The younger son hadn't done well in school, so he bought and sold old newspapers and in the evenings he helped out at a grocery shop. He earned enough to take care of both his meals. The elder son had just taken his high school exam. If he did well, he would keep the family name going. Until that time Ketaki would have to sweat it out. And then there were the two daughters who had to be married.

Ketaki walked up to the main road with her basket of vegetables. She would go to Moti's house first and find out what those ruffians had been up to. If they dared come in her way today, she would file a report at the police station. She had been selling vegetables in that neighborhood for ten years—was she to stop just because she was afraid? She would find a way out somehow.

She was already near Pari Bhauja's house before she realized where she was. She had no intention of going in, and was on the point of passing by when she heard Pari's call: "Keti, oh Keti, Ketaki, come here, will you?" Ketaki strode swiftly along the street, paying no heed.

The old man was at his usual corner. Catching sight of her, he shouted, "Don't go that way, my daughter. There is trouble there. The place is swarming with policemen."

Ketaki felt a sudden sense of relief. This is what she had wanted all along. She wasn't going to miss the sight of those young men being taught a lesson.

"Moti asked me to bring her some banana blooms. I'll give them to her and be back in a moment."

"Moti? Ramu Babu's daughter?"

"Yes, her mother is away and she must be waiting for me."

"There is a saying that goes 'The flower you now quarrel over is the very one the gardener plans to sell.' Moti is no more. She was found dead, lying naked in her backyard. Can such things be kept secret? It is those boys who are at the bottom of all this . . . Keep hold of yourself, my daughter!" Ketaki's head reeled. She barely managed to prevent herself from falling. What was it that she had heard? Why had Moti gone over to those young men? Ketaki dropped down beside the pitchers, quite weak.

"I only told you what I overheard. Don't tell anyone I said anything. Those scoundrels won't let me go alive."

Ketaki cupped her palms and gulped down a few mouthfuls of water. Rising to her feet, she asked, "Wasn't Moti's father around?"

"He was, but what could he do? Moti wasn't one to be stopped. She always came out into the open and said what she felt. She was one for provoking women into coming out of their houses and she did that again yesterday. She went around, got a group of women together, and stood there shouting at the debighara. And then the police came and took the boys away. We breathed again with relief. But look what has happened today—look at the havoc they have wrought on her body. They have sucked her blood dry, those murderers!"

"But weren't they taken to the police station? Why do you blame these men? Perhaps a snake or some wild animal attacked her in the garden."

"Taking them to the police station was a mere show. They go in one way and come out the other. Can they ever be held there? If they had been kept back, would the sun and the moon have kept rising in the east? The whole town would have been plunged into darkness, my child. It is they who run the country now. Who can stop them?"

Ketaki's mind had wandered back to the previous afternoon. What monsters they were! What was it that had made an ill-omened woman like her tell Moti everything? Self-reproach burned at her insides, but her eyes shot fire.

"Pick up your vegetable-basket and go back home, my daughter," the old man said.

"No, not yet. Let me leave the basket here with you for a moment. I want a glimpse of the girl. What a learned, lovely person she was. Despite all her father's money she didn't have a streak of arrogance in her."

The old man wiped his eyes. "You should have come earlier. The police ambulance came a while ago and moved the body to the government hospital. It'll be cremated after the autopsy. You'd better go home. You're a woman. What can you do here? Look at that crowd of policemen—and so many young men. As if there's a fair on! Who knows what might happen . . . You have daughters of your own at home."

Ketaki's heart rose and fell in apprehension. Yes, she had daughters. Grown-up ones. Yet Moti was a girl in a million. One would be fortunate to have such a daughter. If Moti could die because of a cursed woman like Ketaki, could Ketaki not fight against all odds? Would she have to carry the burden of this debt for all time? All of a sudden her own life seemed meaningless. She had been struggling alone since her husband's death, but now the children were old enough to fend for themselves.

Ketaki picked up her basket and turned toward home, as if in deference to the old man's words. She didn't even glance at Pari's house. Jealous as Pari was, she wouldn't hesitate to speak ill of Moti. It was a terrible, terrible thing that had happened. The girl had lost her life because of Ketaki. What need was there for her to go on living? Her only wish—that when her sons grew up to be government officers she would weep to her heart's content in the Shiva temple—would go unfulfilled, that was all. She would have turned her world upside down in joy, when that happened. But that was not to be her fate. Ketaki was going to fight. If God was on one side, she would be on the other. She quickened her steps almost to a run and the basket kept slipping from her head.

She rushed into the house and closed the door. Then she began hunting among the old bundles for the little money she had kept hidden, and brought it out. She had put away her earrings the day her husband died. She brought those out too. They were tarnished, but would fast regain their shine when they were polished. She would have turned these into new earrings when her daughters got married, but now a time more portentous than seven such marriages had arrived. Deep inside her heart she continued to smolder as she moved across the darkened room.

As dusk fell she called out to her eldest son, "Fasten the door securely before you sleep. I'll be late getting back today. They're celebrating some festival at the Marwari's house. Your sister won't be able to cope with all the work alone."

Her son latched the door from inside. Darkness had fallen. It was the phase of the waning moon. Ketaki had put a can, an ax, a sickle, and a vegetable knife in her basket. She had also tucked a pinch of opium into the corner of her mouth—a habit she had given up years ago. Her whole being felt uneasy, but she walked firmly on. How would she ever get anything done if she felt so weak? She paused for a minute in front of the Shiva temple on the way. Bowing low, she said, "You are saved, my Lord! Here I am, burning in the fires of my own doing, much before I could weep and my tears could topple that altar of yours and sweep it away. Rest in peace for some time more, Lord."

And then she went, through the darkness of the lane, mingling finally with the darkness of the night. Her dark body and soiled dark clothes and the basket over her head all merged to become one with the night.

It was not yet dawn the next day when a great uproar was heard near the debighara. A fire raged across the structure. The blaze had burned down the outer door, which had fallen to one side, leaving a mocking mouth, now wide open, and still smoldering. Ketaki sat on a boulder nearby, calmly puffing on a bidi. In front of her lay a whole pack of bidis, a box of matches, and an empty can of gasoline. The vegetable knife, the ax, and the sickle lay there too, smeared with blood; Ketaki appeared to be out of her mind. Two men emerged from somewhere and dragged her towards a jeep parked nearby.

People were surging in, creating a stampede. There were police officers everywhere. The fire fighters had also arrived, and were dousing the debighara. Was Ketaki dreaming? She simply couldn't remember anything.

Two onlookers forced their way through the fire and managed to pull out two half-burned young men. Someone commented, "Drunk. One of them was probably lighting a cigarette when it happened. Must have caught them unawares. How tragic! Five strapping young men fight among themselves and get burned alive."

"It's always your own deed that gets you in the end," another added.

The voices cleared Ketaki's opium-induced stupor. Why was no one able to understand? Oh God! The basket, the can, the sickle, the vegetable knife—they were all lying there. The police constable who snapped handcuffs on her wrists as she climbed into the jeep shouted at her, "Come on, you harlot! You've chewed these young men alive. Where do you think you're going?"

And then the truth dawned on Ketaki—that when those young men had had their fill of drinks and dropped down drunk to the floor, she had poured out the gasoline from the can, lighted a match, and locked the door, carefully latching it from the outside. The debighara had barely caught fire when a young man came rushing from somewhere and tried frantically to open the latch. It was then that Ketaki had sliced through him with the ax. The head had rolled away from the man's body and came to rest beside the boulders. She had sat on the boulder and kept chopping. Yes, it was the very same man.

People crowded around and stared at her. The whole area was choked with cars and other vehicles. Suddenly a voice was heard above the din. "Wait! Wait, please! Let me give her a drink of water. You can take her after that. Her throat must be parched."

Startled, everyone turned to look. The old man who had been doling out water at the crossroads paused with the jug he was holding for her. A policeman grabbed his hand and yelled, "Stop! What water is that? Have you put poison in it?"

"What? Poison? What are you saying, sir? Would I give poison to a woman like her? Please let me go."

The old man edged his way to the police jeep. Ketaki looked around in a daze, but climbed down from the jeep and stretched her cupped palms out towards him. Slowly he poured a stream of water into them. Tears from her eyes mingled with the old man's tears in the water in her palms. Drops trickled through the cracks between her fingers and fell to the earth.

The world has been torn many times, has been bloodied too, and been salted and wetted with tears. But who keeps a note of these events as they happen day after day?

The old man moistened the towel on his shoulder with the water left over in the jug, wiped Ketaki's face with the wet cloth, and hurried back. He didn't look at her, but simply turned around and walked on.

Ketaki climbed back on the jeep in a trance. As on every other day, the sun was there in the sky, and the trident on top of the Shiva temple could be seen from afar. But Ketaki went on staring at the earth, which had begun to shimmer in the harsh heat of the sun. Instead of tears though, today her eyes held fire.

Translated by Jayanta Mahapatra.

MANJUL BHAGAT —————————————

(b. 1936)   *Hindi*

With *Anaro,* (1977), Manjul Bhagat came of age as a writer. The novel is about a woman who works part-time as a domestic for several middle-class families. In Anaro's world, "even routine things require a special effort and existing is an achievement," the author writes. There is little about her difficult, routine life or her problems with her alcoholic husband that sets her apart from other women of her class. Anaro herself has traditional desires: she wants her straying husband to return, whatever the cost; she wants a wedding with all the middle-class fanfare for her daughter. What makes her unique is her refusal to be defeated and the spirit with which she survives. And the achievement of *Anaro* is not limited to this character. "Its success," theater critic Rama Jha feels, "lies in capturing several shots of parallel lives lived in the precincts of the Indian middle-class family. Anaro, in her naked confrontation with reality, highlights the psychic and emotional vacuum of middle-class women trapped in their own cocoons. . . ."

Manjul Bhagat wrote her first story in 1970. "Ten years of married bliss was enough to make me break out in print," she comments. The story was about a wedding anniversary: the woman excited, longing for her husband to be the lover he once was; the man withdrawn, insensitive. The enthusiastic readers' response started Manjul Bhagat off on what has become a writing career. Today most of her fiction is first published in leading magazines.

Among her collections of short stories are *Gulmohar ke Guche* (A Bouquet of Gulmohar Flowers), 1976; *Atmahatya Se Pahle* (Before Committing Suicide), 1979; and *Safed Kauva* (White Crow), 1986. Her other well-regarded works include the satirical novel *Ladies Club,* 1976, and *Begane Ghar Mein* (In an Alien House), 1978, a novel set in the servants' quarters of a palatial house in Meerut. In the latter, there are both Hindu and Muslim servants and the author uses dialect peculiar to the region to re-create life in that crumbling feudal household.

Manjul Bhagat was born in Meerut, but grew up in Delhi, where she now lives. The family house was located on Babar Road very close to the main art galleries and theaters. Both her parents were fond of literature, and her father encouraged the children to take an interest in the arts. "We were five sisters and one brother. I am the eldest. We all loved reading, talking, going out, walking, and arguing," she says in an autobiographical note. Her sister, Mridula Garg, is also a well-known writer.

Some of her stories have been published in English translation in *The Search and Other Stories,* 1982. "Bebeji" first appeared in *Femina* in July 1985.

◆

BEBEJI

Bebeji loved it, squatting on the well-swept mud floor in front of the lowly tandur, the humble eating place of the poor. The week before, she had eaten there three times. But Bebeji was not poor. She had cooked her usual supper of buttered maize roti and *sag* of mustard greens. After having cooked it, she just could not bring herself to sit down alone to it. Instead, she found herself pulled to the tiny warm place, the tandur, put together with flimsy bamboo walls. How strong were the walls of the stately house Baoji had built for her. They reminded her of the pillarlike strength and powerful personality of her late husband. Yet, death had snatched him away. The day he died Bebeji had lost faith in the house too. It was no longer secure and indestructible.

"Son, why don't you pickle the big lemons when they are in season?" she asked. The *tandurwala* poked the fire in the deep hole sunk in the earth, slapped the round rotis on the walls of the earthenware oven, and answered languidly, "Why should I bother about the pickle? The curry I serve is tongue-tingling enough."

"Ah! There was a time when it took me days just to slice the raw mangoes, juicy lemons, or fresh cauliflowers to pickle them. I had to fill jars and jars of them, there were so many to eat them!"

The tandurwala brought out piping hot rotis from the homemade oven. He lifted them out quickly, with tongs. Holding one out to the old lady, he coaxed, "Here, have one more roti, Bebeji. Just see how golden-red this one is."

"Yes, it is roasted just right. But I don't want anymore. Bless you though. May your little tandur become a big hotel one day."

Bebeji was touched by the tandurwala's concern. She usually ate only a couple of rotis, but the old lady liked to be pampered while eating. The aroma of oven-fresh rotis filled the hut, while the friendly glow of burning coals in the tandur encircled her with a special warmth. She wrapped the shawl around her a little more snugly.

"Son, I will make a jarful of pickled cauliflower for you. Just watch how the pickle will bring you permanent customers. They will return just for the pickle and want more and more rotis to go with it."

The tandurwala believed Bebeji. She had proven it last winter. She had given him two jars of the delicious stuff. The customers asked for the pickle and the rotis, alternately. They just didn't know how to stop. Licked their fingers to the very bones. The tandurwala cooked less of the dal, meant to go free with the rotis. Instead, he charged five paisa a piece for the pickle. He wanted to pay Bebeji for the pickle, but she would not hear of it. She paid for her meals too, as usual.

The tandurwala could pay back this generosity only with an active and interested participation in Bebeji's conversation. There were prompt and well-timed nods from his side, whenever Bebeji was inspired to quote one of her wise platitudes. She quoted one now.

"Son, in my family it is not the beast of burden which cries out in despair, but the load itself."

"Hmm!" The tandurwala made the appropriate polite noise. Bebeji then elaborated the point. "Now, I asked my younger son to come here and make his home with me. I could have relieved his lazy wife of all the household chores. Can you imagine what he told me? He said his wife was adept at household chores and that, if I closed down my establishment here, and went to live with them, life would be easier for me. Don't I understand their tricks? His wife simply does not want me to interfere with her life. She wants me to live with them as a guest."

The tandurwala guessed there was another platitude coming.

"Ah! The daughters! They were plucked away by sons-in-law. And sons? Possessed by their wives. Only I remain, a barren, old, lonely self!"

The tandurwala never pointed out that Bebeji had no daughters to be plucked. Instead, he consoled her by protesting that, while he breathed, Bebeji could neither call herself barren, nor alone. Wasn't he as much her son as her own two? Why did she think he was sitting there so complacently plying his trade? Because he had Bebeji at his side! He finished with histrionic flourish. Bebeji got up to go only after the last client had left.

What a huge house Baoji had built for her! To shield the interior from the vulgar view of the passersby, he had built a grand veranda, leading first to an empty passageway and then to the rooms, all constructed with discretion in mind.

All his elaborate planning had erred but once. He was powerless against his own death. The day he died, Bebeji became anesthetized against all physical pain, and against all minor pain. Only her heart ached and throbbed, yearned and throbbed inside a wooden body. It made her wander in search of she knew not what. Only the tandur gave her a little respite.

Then one day the tandurwala announced he was leaving for a brief visit to his village. Bebeji wandered about like a tortured ghost inside her lonely house until one night at a late hour, she saw a tiny flicker of light at the tandur. That night she slept for a while. But the break of dawn saw her lifting the bamboo curtain of the tandur hut, which was now covered also by a thick bedspread. The curtain lifted to present a stunning view. The tandurwala was spread-eagled on the tiny cot, a comely young woman cradled in one arm while the other arm lay protectively across a two-year-old boy. Bebeji bolted back, buttoning up her shirtsleeves primly. She covered her head to the hairline as she ran home. Then she smiled as the truth dawned upon her. Why! The tandurwala had brought his family home, bless him.

She began to grate carrots for the sweet *halwa* she wanted to cook for them. She remembered how she had fed Baoji till his dying day. Fifteen crushed almonds and a ladleful of pure ghee in his nightly glass of milk. But his doctor friend gave him such a scare. The rascal told him that she would kill him by feeding him such a rich diet. Bebeji stirred and stirred till all trace of fat disappeared from the milk. Then she ordered Baoji to gulp it all down. But he took it in sips, the milk tasted so divine. Yet, that athletic body turned into dust without warning. Baoji died quietly in his sleep. Bebeji's faith in God's sagacity was shaken. Wasn't Baoji someone? Bebeji's very own? Then why was she not forewarned of his end?

The tandurwala's son Nikka became almost an extension of Bebeji. Always trotting beside her, he learned to reach her house all by himself. When his parents were still asleep, he would toddle towards the big house and clamber onto the old lady's lap demanding his maize roti, buttered generously and sprinkled with sugar.

The child's mother would arrive shortly thereafter, breathless and anxious. But she never forgot to touch Bebeji's feet first. Bebeji was stern with the young woman, always remonstrating with her for neglecting the little one. The tandurwala's faith in Bebeji strengthened as he watched her growing concern for his personal affairs. Once, when the tandurwala had gone to watch a matinee show, Bebeji strolled towards his hut. She saw the young woman slumbering soundly while the tiny child smeared mud all over his body and played on his own. Bebeji took the unguarded child home and reported the matter faithfully to the tandurwala in the evening. He promptly slapped Panno in Bebeji's presence for her careless ways. Thereafter, Panno and Nikka were seen more and more at Bebeji's house. Sometimes, the tandurwala, too, joined his family there. Then they all ate what Bebeji fondly cooked for them.

Bebeji missed her sons whenever she cooked the traditional dishes. The elder one was far away, in a foreign land. The younger one, though in the country, was wrapped up in his own life. He visited once every two years with his family. He came by car and was always in a hurry to leave for other towns, vacationing all over the country, but never in Amritsar. Amritsar was the one town Bebeji yearned to visit. Her sister lived there, but her younger son always managed to talk her out of going.

The tandurwala began to look after the minor repairs of the house. The leaking taps and the fused wires were his responsibility now. Then one day, Bebeji ordered all of them to sleep the nights at her house. It was a good proposal and one promptly acted upon.

After closing down the tandur they all slept at the great house, like one family.

One morning found Bebeji walking about in great agitation. That day, at last, she was to board a train for Amritsar.

Sweet laddus, and *pinnis* filled with dried fruit were all prepared and packed to be taken to Amritsar. The tandurwala was to escort her. They were taking Panno and Nikka, too, lest they should both go astray in their absence. The train did not leave until dusk, and the day had only just begun. Bebeji's fond heart was impatient. Just then a taxi came around the curve and halted beside her. Bebeji's lips formed a perfect O as she saw her younger son Chhote get out of it with agility. His wife and two children followed, each clutching a suitcase. They all touched her feet. She blessed them automatically. Her mind silently took in the fact that this time Chhote had avoided driving his own car, lest Bebeji take up the matter of motoring down to Amritsar again.

Chhote marched inside. Bebeji followed, still stunned by his sudden arrival. Chhote hesitated at the bedroom, now occupied by the tandurwala and his family. Bebeji visualized the intimate scene that her son must now be taking in, the wanton fearlessness of the young woman clasped in her husband's strong arms. Her guess proved right as she saw her son galloping back, an unhealthy red spreading on his cheeks. "Who are they?" he stammered.

"Son, he is the tandurwala," said Bebeji simply.

"Well, why isn't he at the tandur, then? What is he doing here in my house?" Chhote demanded.

"He sleeps here."

"But why?"

"Because I feel scared at night."

"You? Scared? At this age, Mother?" Chhote was incredulous.

Just then, Panno made her youthful appearance. Still warm with sleep and raising her arms to her uncovered head, she yawned and stretched. Chhote's wife blinked at the vision. Spotting the visitors, Panno covered her head respectfully.

"Panno, touch your sister-in-law's feet," commanded Bebeji. Panno obeyed. Chhote's wife retreated a few steps, stung at being called the sister-in-law of lowly Panno. Bebeji now brought out Nikka and ordered him to fold his hands in greeting to the visitors. Still dazed with sleep, Nikka was about to holler for his morning needs. But he obeyed Bebeji.

"Mother, would you please step aside, for a moment?" Chhote scrambled over the sprawling luggage and took his mother aside.

"Why is this entire family of bandits here?" he demanded furiously.

"I told you, they only sleep here at night." Bebeji lost her patience now. To change the scene, she took Nikka over to the drain, prompting him to pee. The boy took up the cue immediately. Chhote was beside himself.

"Will you listen here, Mother?" he persisted. Bebeji addressed Panno in theatrical whispers. "Go child, tell your husband. We shall not go to Amritsar after all, Chhote is here."

For the next two days Chhote raged silently. He saw strangers swarming all over his property. Unable to bear it any longer, he shouted in a loud voice, for all to hear, "Mother, when are these people going to get out of my house?"

"Son, how long will you be staying?" Bebeji countered innocently.

"Never mind that. Why doesn't this vagabond family sleep in their own hut?"

"Son, next time you come, you must wire your arrival in advance."

"Bebeji, listen, let me tell the fellow to get out now!" Chhote demanded.

"Yes, you must let me know in advance. So that you do not find the house locked."

"Why locked?"

"Because, we could be away, in Amritsar." Bebeji finished, firmly and happily.

The "we" in his mother's sentence upset Chhote more than the prospect of the gates of the great house being locked against him. He looked dumbfounded at his mother. Could the old lady have gone mad? Could that be possible? he pondered.

Translated by the author.

JEELANI BANO ————————————

(b. 1936)   *Urdu*

Jeelani Bano was born in Badayun and brought up in Hyderabad. She was one of seven children, but long periods of illness made her a lonely child whose companions were books and music. Her father, Hyrat Badayuni, was a well-known scholar and poet. Among those who visited the family home in Hyderabad when Jeelani Bano was a child were Makhdoom Mohinuddin, Alam Khundmiri, Raj Bahadhur Gaur, Aktar Hasan, and Zeenat Sajeda. In the forties and early fifties this group formed the vanguard of young Hyderabad artists and intellectuals. They supported the peasant struggles in rural Telangana, led student movements that were emerging in the towns, and were active in the Progressive Writers' Association in Hyderabad. The young Jeelani Bano listened, fascinated, to their socialist ideas and to their accounts of the exciting events that were taking place around her. She traces her understanding of exploitation and her sympathy for the oppressed mainly to this group and its influence. Among her principal literary influences are Niyaz Hyder, Maqdoom, Ismat Chugtai, and Rasheed Jahan.

Jeelani Bano's first story, "Mom Ki Mariyam" (The Wax Mary), 1954, caused something of a stir when it was first published. "I was so afraid it would be sent back," she says with a smile, "that I didn't even put my address on it." But the story was published and she received letters of congratulation from established writers such as Krishan Chander, K. A. Abbas, and Ahmad Nadeem Qasmi. Faiz Ahmed Faiz wrote to her from prison in Rawalpindi. She had never thought of herself as a writer, but with the success of this initial effort came requests from editors for other pieces.

Jeelani Bano's writing career spans the last thirty years. First to be published was a collection of short stories, *Roshni Ke Minar* (Towers of Light), in 1958. Two other collections appeared later: *Nirwan* (Deliverance), 1965 (Lahore) and 1966 (Delhi), and *Paraya Ghar* (House, but Not One's Own), 1979 (Hyderabad) and 1984 (Karachi). More recently she published two novels—*Aiwan-e-Ghazal* (Palace of Song), 1967 (Delhi) and 1983 (Karachi), and *Barish-e-Sang* (Shower of Stones), 1984 (Karachi) and 1985 (Hyderabad)—and a collection of short stories, *Roz Ka Qissa* (Everyday Questions), 1987. *Barish-e-Sang*, set in the early forties—the last days of the nizam's rule in the state of Hyderabad—is about the profligate, decadent lives of the feudal aristocracy in the city and the peasant revolt in the villages. Many of the women characters in the novel never leave the palace, which becomes a symbol of violence and corruption. Two of the characters, Chand and Ghazal, a critic writes, "will be immortals in Urdu fiction on account of the depth and vividness with which the author has portrayed them." In 1990 she wrote the script for a well-received television program on the communal riots that took place in Hyderabad in 1989.

Jeelani Bano has received several awards, including the Soviet Land Nehru Award in 1985. Her work has been translated into Hindi, Gujarati, Telugu, and English.

◆

TAMASHA
(Fun and Games)

"Give me a piece of bread. Give me something to eat."

She stood in the hot sun on the rock-hard floor of the courtyard. There was no flesh on any part of her body. With her the mysteries of human anatomy were like an open book.

"Mother, give her a piece of bread. She's been roaming in the neighborhood since yesterday begging for food," young Adil pleaded with his mother.

"Get lost," Mother shouted at the girl. "What cheek, planting herself in the yard, demanding food, as though we owe something to her father."

"Wheat is selling at three rupees a kilo. How can one give away bread to beggars?" chimed in Grandma, seated on her prayer mat and looking for her rosary. "A piece of bread," the girl whined again.

"Will you go, or shall I pick up my shoe to beat you?" Grandma's sequence of prayers was broken.

"Why don't you give her something to eat or find some work for her to do? The wretched girl is starving," Adil ventured, taking pity on her sunken belly.

"That's right. We'll take her on as servant." Mother seemed to brighten up at the idea. "God has heard my prayers. Look, wench, will you work for us?"

"Work? What work?" the girl mumbled, a look of incomprehension on her face. After a moment's pause she started sobbing again. "Give me a piece of bread."

"OK, we'll feed you, but you'll have to work for us." Mother suddenly remembered that there was some cooked rice left over from yesterday that she hadn't felt like throwing away. She was waiting for a mendicant beggar to whom she could give it, bringing down God's blessings on her in the bargain. "Thank God, we have found a servant at last." Azra heaved a sigh of relief. Examinations were around the corner, and all her time at home was taken up with cleaning and cooking. She had to walk a mile to school, and her back felt like breaking, from washing clothes incessantly.

"Listen, wench, can you cook?" If one has to employ a servant, one is entitled to some comfort. Who can pay the salary and feed a servant for nothing?

The girl said nothing. She merely stared at the mother, as though there was no use answering such silly questions. One needed stoves for cooking, and how many houses had stoves? This time the question came from Grandma.

"Can you cook meat?" she asked. She had designated herself the chairperson of the intervening committee.

"Grandma, why mention meat to her? She may be a Hindu," Adil remonstrated in a low tone.

"What? A Hindu?" Mother sat up. "The girl hardly has any clothes on her. How is one to know if she is a Muslim or Hindu? It's good Adil has alerted us. The wretched girl would have robbed us of our precious religious relics."

"Are you a Hindu?"

"Hindu?" The girl's voice seemed to grow fainter by the minute.

"What a stupid girl." Mother couldn't suppress her laughter. "She'll drive me mad."

The talk of the girl's presence in the house seemed to have reached the elder brother in his room. Throwing aside the detective novel he had been reading, he came out in search of the girl. "So thin," he said with disgust, "and much too young. Get your elder sister, if you have one." He turned to his mother and said, "She's very young and is of no use!" He thought to himself that if this girl was willing to do anything for a little food, the elder sister would certainly be of some use!

"My sister?" she asked. She seemed ready to lie down, and go to sleep right there.

"Look at this! This young lady has come to stay here permanently," Azra started laughing, raising her head from her book.

"Give one a little bread," the girl repeated, ignoring all remarks.

"See how clever she is. She doesn't say anything about working. The wretch will disappear the moment she gets something to eat."

"Have you worked anywhere before?" Grandma continued her investigation. She whispered into the mother's ear, "Who knows—she may be a thief's accomplice! She might get up in the night and open the door from inside."

The girl did seem to look stealthily towards the kitchen, where the stoves glowed like the devil's eyes, and from which emerged the appetizing aroma of rice and lentils being cooked into a *kichidi*.

"She's a thief, all right. See how her eyes roam around so greedily?" Azra, being a student of psychology, could claim to read people's minds and their hidden desires.

"*Rooo-t-eee,*" the girl whimpered. She could hardly make her voice heard.

"The wretched girl is dumb. God knows what she is mumbling."

"That suits me fine," the elder brother thought to himself. "That wretched Naseeban had a loose tongue and spread all kinds of stories about me in the neighborhood."

"I'll give you seven rupees a month. It will be a full-time job," Mother told the girl.

"Seven rupees! Have you gone mad, daughter-in-law? Seven rupees to a waif like her? Five rupees and not a paisa more. Stay if you are willing, otherwise get going." She nodded her head in consent. The moment the deal was struck, the elder brother's wife emerged from her room. Then she started in at once. "Wash the baby's clothes. Scour out the pans, and clean the baby's bottle with hot water." The young lady thought that if she listed these duties then, there would be no misunderstandings about the work schedule later.

The girl continued to sit in the hot sun, her head lowered between her knees.

"Mother, tell her to water the plants—I'm so busy with my exams," Azra said, without lifting her eyes from the book.

"When you're through with her, send her to me." Grandma suddenly remembered her aching limbs. "I'll be able to sleep a little if she massages my body."

"I'll never eat anything cooked by her. She's so untidy," the elder brother remarked, probing her body once again. "Ask her if she has an elder sister."

"Where do you live? Where's your house?"

"Get up and sweep the floor."

"How clever she is," Azra raised her eyes from the psychology textbook.

"Mother, give her a little bread," Adil pleaded, and then left the house.

"But listen to me first," the grandmother exclaimed, opening her snuffbox. "Does anyone around here know you? Who'll be responsible if something is lost?"

"If you break a plate or a cup, the cost will be deducted from your pay." The mother issued another warning.

"See how immobile she becomes the moment work is mentioned," Azra remarked. "Do you think she wants to work? Feed her, and she will disappear in no time."

"Get up and sweep the floor."

"Wash the baby's clothes first."

"And never eat anything without my permission."

"See how she pretends to be dying when asked to do a little work? Let's have a little fun now." Azra tossed aside the book she'd been reading, went inside, and returned with some bread in her hand. She waved it above the girl's head. "Here, catch this!" She tried to lift the girl's drooping head. It fell limp in her hand. The show had come to an end.

Translated by Taki Ali Mirza.

P. VATSALA

(b. 1938)   *Malayalam*

P. Vatsala established herself as a significant writer in a relatively short span of time. Her first novel, *Thakarcha* (Decadence), 1968, explored the evils of the joint-family system, while *Nizhalurangunna Vazhikal* (Along the Paths on Which Shadows Sleep), 1975, and *Arakkillam* (House of Wax),

1977, depicted, in moving terms, the agonies of exploited women. In both of these novels, women are humiliated and victimized by men who view their money as a protection against all moral lapses and who deal with love as a saleable commodity. The vision of a world that will recognize the personhood and the freedom of women undergirds her critique.

With the publication of *Nellu* (Paddy), 1972, *Agneyam* (Of Fire), 1974, and *Kumankolli,* 1984, her favorite works, Vatsala's reputation as a novelist with a distinct sense of regional dialect and experience grew. Vatsala used the inaccessible hills of Wyanad and its fertile soil as a symbolic backdrop to present the loves and frustrations of a people untouched by modern civilization. Hidden within those silent hills were sad stories of the exploitation of the virgin soil and of virgin women. No other novelist has captured the unusual topography of Wyanad so accurately. *Agneyam* is a study of the empowerment and the destruction of a bold widow, Nangema Antherjanam, who set out to live in a new town, Kollimala, thus challenging tradition. Her son becomes involved in the revolutionary movement that shook Wyanad in the early seventies. For one who writes about society as a whole, the frames of Vatsala's plots are unusually small, but the characters are of towering proportions and their inner lives insightfully explored in their relation to forces operative in society at large. Because she is a Marxist, the social scope of her fiction stands in distinct contrast to the private, introspective strain of many other contemporary writers.

Vatsala was born into a traditional *taravadu* or Nair household, in Calicut, Kerala. She is married and works as the headmistress of a government school in Calicut. She won the Kumkumam Award for her novel *Nellu,* which was also made into a popular film. *Nizhalurangunna Vazhikal* received the Kerala Sahitya Academy Award in 1976. *Palayam* (Army Camp), 1981, which is set in a large government girls' school, explores the increasingly pressurized lives of teachers, students, and others who work there. Among her collections of short stories are *Thirakkil Alpam Stalam* (A Little Space in the Crowd), 1969, *Uchayude Nizhal* (Noon's Shadow), 1978, *Pazhya Puthiya Nagaram* (The Old New City), 1979, and *Anupamayude Kavalkaran* (Anupama's Guard), 1980. The novel *Arum Marikkunilla* (Nobody Dies) appeared in 1987, and *Chaver,* her latest novel, in 1991. *Chaver* is set in the early forties, against the backdrop of nationalist struggle, and deals with a peasant struggle in Malabar. It explores the wavering commitments of the Congress workers, torn between the peasants and their own middle-class commitments. For the peasants, Independence, when it comes, is disillusioning. The title refers to the legendary *chaver pada* of medieval Kerala, who repeatedly sacrificed their lives to overthrow the king. In Vatsala's novel they become a symbol for the peasants who are involved in a similar, long-drawn-out battle.

The story translated here is taken from *Anavettakaran,* 1982, and deals with a man who, like many others, has left his home in Kerala and gone abroad to earn a living. He returns rich, but trapped by the ever-growing demands that accompany prosperity. The principal character, Janaki, is the poor girl next door, whom he loved but did not marry because he accepted a bride chosen by his family. Janaki remains a close friend but is, in the story, also a symbol for the human fulfillment he has lost, and which no money can buy.

◆

ORU TADAVUCHATATINDE KADHA
(The Escape)

Janaki waited at the path through which Ramachandran would have to pass. Surely he would glance her way as he shot by in his car. These five years would have changed him a lot. Still, she hoped that time would not have created a rift between them.

She watched visitors going into Ramachandran's house, people she knew and people she did not know. They came over the bridge and over the ferry, flocking in from all directions. Thekkumpadikkal, Ramachandran's house, had suddenly become the center of the village. Janaki noticed how passersby turned to stare at it.

Five years ago, when Ramachandran would come back from the city with the application forms he had collected, looking tired and worn-out, no one had even bothered to glance at him. Those who flocked to his house then had been creditors who came hoping to get back the money that Ramachandran's father had borrowed from them for the education of his son. Janaki had often heard Ramachandran's married sisters complaining loudly about the jewels they had been forced to pawn for his sake.

Janaki thought of the days Ramachandran had spent filling out those application forms. Putting the broad, sweat-stained envelopes on the wooden bench running along the front veranda, he would call out to her grandmother, "Now for a dip in the pond!"

He would try to make himself forget his difficulties as he swam in the cool waters of the pond at Janaki's house. He would try to drive from his mind the bitterness he nursed against doors that refused to open to him.

Strange. The Ramachandran who had disappeared from the village one day had come back now. It was rumored that he'd come back with enough money tucked away at his waist to buy up the whole countryside. As a prelude to this, his father had already bought a barren hillock that no one else had seemed interested in. Janaki wondered what

Ramachandran was going to do with this hillock, all covered with rocks and wild castor oil plants.

A cloud of red dust rose up on the horizon. Ramachandran's taxi came into view. She opened the wooden barred gate a little way and peeped out. Her hopes sank. Ramachandran didn't seem to be in the car; it was full of boxes. Huge suitcases and bags. Innumerable packets. Perhaps a young man was sitting imprisoned somewhere among them.

It did not occur to Janaki that many people at Thekkumpadikkal must be waiting impatiently for this heavily loaded cart of provisions.

The red dust on the road settled.

Children ran past her, fascinated with the car, a rare sight in the village. Passersby turned to stare at it.

Janaki turned and went in.

The acacias, which had bloomed for Ramachandran's return, blazed in the afternoon sun. She leaned back against the pillar on the veranda, gazing into their red flames.

Grandmother was cleaning the vegetables. She asked, "Is somebody ill?"

The old woman had always associated the arrival of a car in the village with someone's falling ill.

Janaki glanced at her, but did not answer.

"Who was that, child?"

"Ramachandran of Thekkumpadikkal has come back."

"Thank God, at least one of them has done well!"

She pressed her face into the pillar. It smelt of Ramachandran's sweat.

Streams of people flowed steadily into Ramachandran's house.

Adru, the fisher boy, went by with a big stick in his hand.

Butcher Ahmed's son now brought a packet of meat regularly every day to the village. Before, meat had been bought in the village only for the festival marking the year's end. All roads led to Ramachandran's house.

One day, a crowd of workers appeared by the barren hillock. They began to split open rocks that had been burnt through by the summer sun.

As she washed her clothes by the pond, the maid from Ramachandran's house declared, "They're building a mansion!"

Everyone in the village could see the hillock with [men with] pick-axes swarming over it like moths.

Janaki thought, Surely Ramachandran must be somewhere among the crowd of workers, supervising them. There was no chance of his coming now till the work was over.

The women from Ramachandran's house paraded in the village streets in foreign finery. They went across the river to the movie theater and came back in taxis. Taxis had indeed now become a regular feature of the village.

The children from Ramachandran's house played in the newly harvested fields with their pretty toys. They were the envy of the village children. They boasted about the circus they had seen in town.

The house on the hillside rose higher and higher. In the middle of that barren land. Like a challenge. The villagers often climbed the hill to look at the wondrous structure that glowed like a jewel, transforming the whole village. Careless of the scorching summer sun, they stood around, admiring the skill of the workmen. Retired people with nothing to do could be seen coming down the hill in the evenings, accompanied by their servants.

The days passed like the acacia flowers that fell steadily from the trees. No one came up the gravel path, though grandmother swept up the withered flowers meticulously every day.

One day, Grandmother said, "Do you think he'll ever come here again? He's grown rich now."

Janaki was certain that Ramachandran's family and the visitors who came to the house were greedily sharing every minute of his time at home among themselves like vultures.

Surely he'd come, at least to say good-bye, after he'd given all his belongings away and had only a small suitcase of necessities left? Surely no one could stop him then.

The house on the hillside grew bigger day by day. It seemed gradually to take on the shape of a fearful animal. Steel rods stuck out of it like claws. Inside it, gas lamps replaced the daylight, and there was no longer any difference between night and day. A concrete mixer had been ordered. It clattered over the wooden bridge with a terrifying sound, almost shattering its spine. A retinue of admiring village children followed its progress up the hillside.

Janaki thought, It's almost finished now.

She shuddered with fear as the gaps that had been left for the doors and the windows were at last closed up with heavy iron grills.

Was Ramachandran trapped in this prison house? She imagined him in one of its many rooms, glued to a dark corner like a lizard. His family would be enjoying themselves noisily. Forgotten and ignored, Ramachandran would exist only in the echo of their voices.

She longed for the last day of his leave to arrive. He was sure to go out that day. He'd come up the path, swinging his little suitcase. The flowers on the acacia tree would brush against his cheek. He would catch sight of her and exclaim, "Janaki! I forgot to bring you a gift."

"Oh no, I don't need a gift. I just want to see you again once, that's all I want."

So she dreamed, of Ramachandran coming to say good-bye to her, smiling, walking down the path.

The acacia flowers turned dark red.

A hurricane lantern glimmered like a memory on the crest of the almost-finished building. Moments fell gently from the trees, like leaves.

Janaki waited.

She listened to footsteps in the street. None was Ramachandran's.

A soft breeze wafted in the scent of areca flowers. The flame of the lamp flickered.

The rhythmic thud of the iron pestle could be heard from within. It disturbed her, sounding like the footsteps of a sentry. She listened for the swish of gravel on the path. But she could hear only children's voices, reciting their lessons, from the houses across the fields.

She sat on the front step, her face buried in her knees. A shadow touched her shoulder, startling her awake.

"Are you asleep?"

She got up hastily.

He put his foot on the first step.

She moved aside.

Ramachandran came up. She did not have to remind him not to knock his head on the low roof beam. He sat down in his accustomed place on the parapet, even before she thought to ask him.

Janaki's voice stayed trapped in her throat.

"Where's Grandmother?"

"She's in bed. She must be asleep." She asked, "When are you going away?"

She saw him start.

"I couldn't get out till today," he said softly. "Did you think I wouldn't come?"

"How was I to tell?"

"Even now, I got away only on the excuse that I needed a haircut."

Janaki gazed at his face, with its dense growth of beard. She thought he had the look of a caged bird. There was still a shimmer in the arid desert of his eyes, like a slow trickle welling up from a spring that is not yet completely dry. Janaki found it hard to believe that this lean, wild youth sitting before her was the rich Ramachandran, the focus of attention of the whole village. The glow of the lamp made a feeble effort to light up his rough, dry hair. She raised its wick a little higher. He said to her, "Come and sit here, by me."

He made room for her next to him, on the parapet.

He gathered her wet hair into his hands and said, "I'll never forget the fragrance of the oil you use."

She sat still.

He spoke to her of the emptiness of the deserts he had walked through. He told her of how he had chased death in his car, down endless highways.

Grandmother could be heard snoring gently from within.

When palm torches passed through the lanes, Ramachandran stopped talking. He was afraid of the tiniest movement in the village.

It hurt her, this look he had of a bird that wanted to fly away and be free. She went in and brought him a cup of black coffee.

He drank it. Then he leaned back, his hands folded behind his head. She sat watching his eyelids throb.

"Janaki, why don't you talk?"

"It's you who are news in the village now."

She attempted a smile.

"Say something."

She began to tell him:

About Grandmother's falling ill.

About her learning to sew.

About buying a sewing machine.

About Grandmother's wanting to sell the arecanut grove.

"Sell it? Why?" Ramachandran stared at her.

"For money. For my wedding. There's the jewelry to be made. The feast to be arranged."

His hands tightened on her shoulders.

"Whom will you marry?"

She laughed as if to say, What difference does it make?

His hands slackened and fell away from her shoulders.

They sat together in silence. Across the river some lamps went out. A child was crying persistently somewhere. The big front door of the neighboring house creaked shut. Footsteps rustled in the courtyard.

Janaki said, "Your father's come looking for you!"

His father had put out his torch before entering the courtyard. He came up to his son in the dark.

"Couldn't you at least have told us when you left?" His anger was barely under control. "The workers are waiting."

Ramachandran put his hand in his pocket, drew out his purse and held it out without a word.

His father tucked the purse into the palm of his hand and snapped, "You'd better come for dinner. It's past nine."

When his father had left, Ramachandran asked her, "Will you let me sleep on the parapet tonight?"

Dawn blossomed like the petals of a flower. Ramachandran took off his shirt, flung it on his shoulder, and walked to the grove. He felt like a dandelion wafting on a breeze.

Overgrown palm leaves lay scattered on the ground near the tank. Bees hummed around flowers that were stretching themselves toward the sun.

Looking deeply into the water, Ramachandran asked, "Why did I ever leave all this and go away?"

He slipped quickly into the water and swam across the pond and back. He had a sense of relief: his limbs had not forgotten him. He felt as if a suit of iron armor had been taken off his body. An anthem of freedom seeped in through the very pores of his body. He stayed thus, delighting in the cool feel of the water till every searing memory of the burning tap water running through the city's desert was obliterated. The dry skin on his hands turned moist. He watched the fish shed their scales and disappear. In five long years—

He sighed, pondering the horny nails on his hand.

Janaki looked up, hearing a voice.

"Father," he said, "you are to come home."

He was surprised to see his son.

He climbed out of the water, shook the moisture off his body and asked, "Why?"

"It's time for tea. Besides, the fishmonger and the butcher's boy have come."

He took the keys out of the pocket of the shirt he had left on the stone step, and gave them to his son.

"Don't lose them. Give them to your mother."

The boy twirled the keys around his finger.

"Come here." Ramachandran said.

The boy moved farther away.

He tried to gather him into his arms and kiss him. The child struggled, as if he were in the grip of a stranger, and wriggled free.

"Your face is prickly, it's full of thorns, Father."

The father laughed, but the son did not.

"How is it that father and son are still not used to each other?" Janaki inquired.

"He was already five years old when I first saw him."

The maidservant arrived, to remind him about breakfast.

He gave her his dirty shirt and said, "It's not very old. Wash it and give it to your husband."

The woman smiled her gratitude. "Your tea is growing cold," she repeated.

He wrapped himself in the pure white of the homely dhoti Janaki had given him.

He looked at the full-grown chickens pecking at each other in the yard and laughed out loud.

The servant arrived.

"When do you want the car?"

"I don't want the car."

The companions who had been constantly hanging around him came one by one to see him.

"Aren't you leaving today?"

"No."

"Have you extended your leave, then?"

"No."

"What—?"

Ramachandran laughed. He blew on the black coffee that Janaki had brought him and sipped it.

The last to come was a childhood friend, a serious young man.

"Have you decided when you're going?"

"I'm not going."

"Not going! Are you mad? How can you strike at the root of a tree that bears gold—and that too, knowingly . . ."

Ramachandran laughed again.

"Do you know how many young men long to be in your shoes? Don't hurt your family, Ramachandran."

"I've already given them so much, much more than they need."

"You can come back again on leave in a year's time, after all. And if you have enough money, more than one wife is . . ."

Ramachandran's palm fell squarely on his friend's cheek. The other clenched his teeth and got up.

"You're mad! Completely mad!"

Ramachandran said, "That's when I will be alive."

Translated by Gita Krishnankutty.

NABANEETA DEV SEN ————————
(b. 1938)   *Bengali*

Born in Calcutta of poet parents and named by Rabindranath Tagore, Nabaneeta Dev Sen—professor and former chair of comparative literature at Jadavpur University in Calcutta, poet, scholar, literary critic, and popular writer of travelbooks and humorous short stories—describes herself as "single; two daughters, one dog, two cats." Her mother, Radharani Debi (1904–1989), was a well-known poet of the twenties and thirties who also wrote under the pseudonym of Aparajita Debi. Nabaneeta's 1984 edition of Aparajita Debi's complete poems, which received the state Rabindra Puraskar literary prize in 1986, has been described as a pioneering contribution to feminist criticism in Bengali.

Nabaneeta studied at Presidency College in Calcutta and at Jadavpur University before going to Harvard and Indiana universities in the United States for master's and doctoral degrees in comparative literature. After marrying the economist Amartya Sen, she moved to Britain. Nabaneeta did postdoctoral research at Newnham College in Cambridge and at the University of California, Berkeley. When the marriage broke up, she returned to Calcutta with her two daughters.

Nabaneeta's first book, published when she was still a student, was a collection of poems, *Pratham Pratyay* (First Confidence), 1959. Her rather irreverent account of a lone woman's adventures on pilgrimage to the Kumbhamela, the greatest religious gathering of the Hindus, *Koruna Tomar Kon Path Diye* (The Path of Thy Grace), 1978, made her a best-selling writer. Her other travelbook, *Truck Bahoney Mac Mahoney,* 1984, is about her hitching a ride on a ration truck to the militarily patrolled northeast frontiers of India and Tibet in 1977. She has also published several collections of poems and humorous short stories, including *Monsieur Hulor Holiday* (Monsieur Hulo's Holiday), 1980, the title story of which is translated here. Critic Sanjukta Gupta considers her essays the best of Nabaneeta's prose writing; *Nati Nabaneeta* (Nabaneeta, the Actress), 1983, is perhaps the best-known of this genre.

Her first novel—she has written four—*Ami, Anupam* (I, Anupam), published in 1976 during the Emergency, has as its theme the role of urban middle-class intellectuals in first leading the younger generation into revolutionary action and then debunking them in the middle of the Naxalite movement. Her next novel was about an Indian woman revolutionary who fled to England to avoid the Calcutta police and began writing in

English. The novel traces her return to her own language and culture, as she realizes the futility of writing in a borrowed tongue, under a borrowed identity.

Nabaneeta has also published two novels for children, three collections of poetry, including an annotated translation of twelfth-century Kannada bhakti poetry, and two collections of literary criticism. Forthcoming are *Striparva,* essays on women; and a book of fairy tales illustrated by the well-known film director Satyajit Ray.

Nabaneeta's latest novel, *Shit Sahasit Hemontalok* (Autumnal Abode of Brave Winter People), 1990, deals with the problem of aging and loneliness among middle-class women. Set in an old women's home, the novel brings together a variety of characters from different personal backgrounds and with strikingly varied experiences of life. Among them are housewives, working women, a famous creative writer, a rich woman who was brought up in a red-light area and others, each trying to cope with age and loneliness within the unfamiliar and artificial situation of an old people's home. Although the novel portrays the gradual loss of power of older women in today's urban middle class, in which women have been taught to regard themselves only in relation to the family, it ends on a positive note with the women reaching out toward new meanings in life as they learn to value themselves as mature and free individuals.

Nabaneeta is vice president of the Indian National Comparative Literature Association, and the convener of the Bengali advisory board for the highest literary award in India, the Bharatiya Jnanpith. She has been a visiting lecturer at a number of colleges and universities abroad, including Harvard and Columbia universities in the United States and Oxford University in England.

◆

MONSIEUR HULOR HOLIDAY
(Monsieur Hulo's Holiday)★

I was just about to put my daughters to bed when it happened. The quiet night air was suddenly torn apart by an inhuman wailing. It wasn't very far from us—in fact it was alarmingly close. The sound rose right behind me, or so it seemed. What on earth could it be? A careful, fearful listening gradually revealed the identity of the mysterious presence—a cat. A cat? What? A cat in our house? In this paradise of all rodents? Families of mice live here happily, nesting safely amid the endless books and journals entrusted to me by my dead father.

★*Hulo* is the Bengali word for "tomcat."

Even field rats come in and play about with my friendly, nonviolent dog (the kind that is better termed "doggie") on the living room carpet. Gradually the wailing increased; it became almost human. No. Not a cat. I discarded the thought. It could only be a ghost—and ghosts do not matter. We know, thanks to Poe, that ghosts occasionally develop a weird practice of catlike wailing from within solid walls. I tried to pay no attention and continued with the fairy tale. But the wail took on greater dimensions and became impossible to ignore. It sounded more and more like a vehement protest. This could hardly be a ghost—it had to be a desperately angry tomcat. But where could it be?

"Mother, there is a cat under my bed," announced Daughter Number One.

"Please, may we just peep under the bed?" piped up Daughter Number Two.

"Please, please let's take a look—it's crying," came a joint appeal. "It must be caught somewhere! Let's free it—"

Obviously, fairy tales interested them no more. Far more exciting things were happening in their lives at that moment. In a minute they were up and out of bed, prancing around, opening and shutting drawers and wardrobes, slamming doors and windows, pulling chairs and screaming—

"In here—"

"Over there!"

"By the window!"

"Outside the window—"

The cat remained invisible, but my two daughters were fully and vigorously visible as well as audible. Not unexpectedly, my dear mother appeared on the scene in her wheelchair. An icy voice demanded, "What exactly is going on here?"

"A cat, Grandma!—A lost cat!—It's crying for its Mommy—"

"Where is it?"

"Outside the window."

"In the ventilator—"

"Under the mattress—"

"In the refrigerator."

Excited suggestions kept pouring in. The cook and the maid had joined the crew. Our friendly, nonviolent dog, the first in the family to go to bed, was up too, and had joined the fun, madly rushing around, getting under everyone's feet, whining and barking alternately. The room bustled with activity.

The noise seemed to come from the window. But there was no sill for a cat to rest on. It could be coming from the small, high ventilator above it—but this was a second-floor room—the cat could not be outside. Outside the window, there was a fine stretch of winter sky, infinite darkness strewn with the few dim'stars rationed for us through the dense Calcutta smog. Could a cat be stuck out there? Besides, this ventilator was the traditional family mansion of a line of quarrelsome sparrows. I've grave doubts whether they'd keep quiet if a cat tried to take refuge there. Yet, we all listened intently. The wailing, steadily growing louder, came from outside, almost from the ventilator. The cook brought the ladder and took a good look with a flashlight. Mother insisted that the ventilator was so constructed that only sparrows could enter it, that neither people nor cats might disturb their peace. Nope, the cat wasn't in it. But the noise still seemed to come from there. The flashlight woke the sparrows, who screeched, objecting to the cook's unholy curiosity. He slid down quickly, since the nest contained little babies, and mothers can be quite ferocious when they suspect foul play!

"Must be stranded on the cornice outside the ventilator," announced my mother, who knew there was a cornice on top of the ventilator, since she had had the house built. We had never thought of its existence. But how could a featherless quadruped have gotten up there? Aren't their movements rather restricted?

"Ah! Cats! You don't know what leaps they are capable of! Go and look down from the third-floor balcony. You'll find him on the cornice below," announced Mme. Hercule Poirot from her wheelchair.

A wild dash up the stairs—I, my kids, the cook, the maid, and the dog, each competing with the others to reach the balcony first. Leaning from the third-floor balcony, I found, sure enough, a couple of 20-carat emeralds sparkling diabolically from a bundle of rather solid darkness, darker than the night itself.

"Who is it?" I screamed, rather pointlessly, and the wailing stopped. Instead came a threatening growl—*Meeeowwrr*—Goodness gracious! Not he! Not here! It's Monsieur Hulo the Terrible, no doubt. We all know that famous snarl! Monsieur Hulo is the exact opposite of Madame Khairi, the domesticated Royal Bengal Tigress of the Simlipal Forest Reserve. Children love to play with *her*. She laps up milk from saucers held out to her lips.

There was nothing domestic about this particular domestic animal, formally known as an alley cat. Huge and ferocious, he doesn't care for mortal beings. Raven black, tough as a wild boar, totally unorthodox, independent, measuring about three feet (tail included). Monsieur Hulo walks about like Alexander the Great. What style! What majesty!

What grandeur! One can almost see the army marching behind him, the "Te Deum" (or whatever—it's Latin) playing, the world conquered, bowing to His Majesty. Monsieur Hulo dismisses all humans summarily, as irrelevant. He recognizes only the brown-and-white street dog who rules this block. But pet dogs? Pooh! Recently Monsieur had developed a new habit of strolling over to Mr. Gupta's Great Dane pup, Caesar, and after a calculated display of his fine set of teeth through fiercely trembling whiskers and a blood-curdling *Yeaowrr,* he helped himself to a good portion of poor Caesar's lunch. Caesar was getting thinner by the day. I watched this tragic scene from my window quite helplessly. The other day he had visited our kitchen, jumped on our cook with his chilling war cry—*tchssttt*—and made off with a whole fish, right out of his hand. We are quite sure Monsieur Hulo is the missing link between the common cat and the Royal Bengal Tiger. But how did the Monsieur get there? On that narrow cornice beneath our third-floor balcony? And when?

Eventually the cook disclosed that two days before, when the Monsieur had returned to our kitchen again to catch fish, the cook and the maid gave such fierce chase that the Monsieur had seen no way out but to leap blindly over the third-floor balcony into the vast unknown. Luckily he had landed on the cornice, which was an unchartered territory for cat folk. The cook had tried his best to get him out, but genuine efforts having failed, was keeping him supplied with bread soaked in milk and some fish bones. Surely we don't want a creature of Lord Krishna to die on us? It would be very inauspicious for the house. (Especially so if it happened after a chase!) The cook had decided to keep quiet, expecting Monsieur to leap up onto the balcony some day. But the balcony was just that much higher than his extraordinary high-jump record. So the Monsieur had been subsisting on the food dedicated to him for the past two days and keeping a low profile. But a quiet, secluded existence with a limited food supply was not his idea of life—hence today's rebellion. Trapped on the suffocatingly small space of a cornice over a window, Monsieur Hulo felt restricted, angry, claustrophobic, helpless, and hungry. But above all, he felt deeply humiliated. He had not touched the food rationed out for him since last night. He was on a hunger strike. Next, he sent out furious SOS messages all over, calling for help. However disruptive he might be for human society, Monsieur Hulo had to be rescued.

Suggestions poured in. Shibu announced, "What's the problem? Four of us will hold Aunt's big mosquito net out in the courtyard below under the cornice, and you can push him off with the bamboo pole we use to brush the ceiling. We'll catch him in the net, circus style!"

"Oh, no!" shuddered Shibu's aunt—my mother, that is. "Not that one! It's thirty years old and the cat weighs a ton. It will be the end of both. Use the new bedsheet—that's strong enough, I think!" I was rather scared. What if the cat fell outside the bedsheet? I know they are always supposed to land on their paws. But from such a height? No. I could not push him off the cornice. How about lowering a ladder instead? Cats, unlike cows, do climb stairs. Let the Monsieur come up by himself. A dignified solution for such a figure. Everyone agreed. The ladder was let down and strongly secured, tied to the railings with ropes, so that the Grand Monsieur would be safe. After fixing it all up, we disappeared into the room and lay in wait, barely daring to breathe. The wailing stopped. But no sign of a cat. The clock ticked on. The howling began again—and how! Deep pathos welled from his notes.

"Ma, the cat is weeping," my daughters began.

"It's very bad for the household, you know ma'am," said the maid, "this howling of black cats at night. It brings bad luck, even death, to the house. He must be silenced immediately."

"I know, I know, but how?"

The maid started praying. God is the only savior of Stranded Stray Cats on Hunger Strike in Hindu Households.

"The poor cat is so terrified, he's lost his natural instincts," declared Mother. "He has forgotten the technique of climbing altogether."

"Then someone must get down there and carry him up here," Daughter Number One chirpily suggested.

"But who?" asked the more practical Daughter Number Two.

But WHO? was the question. Monsieur Hulo was no pet tiger in a forest reserve. He was a really tough guy, an enormous, ancient, ferocious, wild animal, now generally extinct. This act called for a master life saver—some wilder creature, a rarer specimen.

Shibu paled, "Me? On that narrow cornice? You want me to fall to my death?" We had forgotten that Shibu had vertigo problems.

The maid calmly ordered the cook to wind his dhoti tightly around his waist and descend carefully. It might be mossy, she warned.

"Why don't you pull your sari around your waist and descend carefully instead?" came the cook's curt reply.

The avalanche the maid let loose through her toothless snarl prompted me to volunteer. I have always been good at climbing trees. A ladder is no big matter. But the Monsieurrrr . . . OK, OK, OK. I'm getting down! No big deal, this! I, once a climber on the south face of the Matterhorn, am I afraid of this puny little bit of concrete? Fixing my sari as advised by the cook, tying my hair up into a tight topknot, I was ready in half a second. Ready and certainly steady. Just waiting for a "go" (or a "no"?) . . . the Monsieur might scratch my eyes out. And bite my nose off. And . . . So, I gravely demanded a safety blanket, in which I intended to wrap him before he could start functioning. As soon as the words escaped my mouth, I found myself heavily weighed down—a daughter dangling from each arm, registering firm and vigorous objections, and making me look like a jackfruit tree in season.

"Mother is sure to slip and fall," they said in a chorus. This naked lack of confidence in me was saddening. My image in their eyes did not seem to live up to my expectations.

"Remember the time I forgot the keys and climbed up the drain pipe?" I tried to promote myself.

"But this is no drain pipe! It's Monsieur Hulo! He'll surely push you off the edge, Mother." Monsieur Hulo's plaintive notes had reached unbearable depths of pathos. What could I do? Poor little me? Should we let the creature die in our very own house—and, during this festive season? Shibu had vertigo and the cook was unwilling. The maid was old and I stood there worthless and immobile, weighed down by two determined daughters clinging to me for dear life. Mother could not go down a ladder in her wheelchair. It was getting late. Already two hours had gone by. It was after the ten o'clock news. Where could I look for help? Whom could I grab, beg, force, entice? Suddenly I had a brainstorm! The fire department, of course! They are the ones who solve such out-of-the-world problems as God can't solve. And what could be luckier? Just round the corner we had the sleepiest fire station in the universe. The bright red vehicles never left their shelters. The men in their grand uniforms sat under the banyan tree all day long playing cards or sipping tea from little earthenware cups. They were bored stiff and would certainly be grateful to have something to do. There were our saviors, for sure. That very day I had read in the newspaper that some cats can have vertigo, and that one such unfortunate feline had perched itself on a factory roof for days on end until the fire department was called to rescue it. Quick as a wink Shibu marched off, but returned shortly with a long face.

"You try to convince them yourself. They won't listen to me."

"What's their phone number?"

"I don't know. They wouldn't give it to me. They simply refused to cooperate. 'Go to the central fire station and get their permission,' they said. Wretched people. Lazybones. Try them for yourself." Shibu was disgusted. I was flabbergasted. I had thought I was doing them a favor finding them a harmless (?) pastime.

But the world seems to work on another set of rules, not on the ones I invent for it.

The silence of a winter's night is shattered by a phone call to the main office of the Calcutta Fire Department. A distressed female voice pleads, "Would you be kind enough to give me the phone number of your fire station at such and such a place?"

"Where's the fire?"

"Well, it isn't fire, really—something else—very urgent . . . ."

"What is it?"

"Well, actually, someone—you know, has slipped and fallen . . . well . . . , it, I mean he, must be rescued—and immediately."

"Who has slipped? Fallen into what? From where? Now look here ma'am, we don't take up cases of drowning anymore."

(Shibu's frantic advice in the background: "Didi, tell them it is tame—they won't come if you don't tell them it's your pet.")

"He hasn't drowned, he's fallen onto the second-floor cornice and is very dangerously perched there."

"How big is the baby?"

(Shibu: "Tell them it's tame.")

"Well, it's extremely tame, you see—"

"What? A tame baby?"

"What baby? A tame cat."

"Now, just a minute—this happens to be a fire station, not a cat-catching center. Call the CSPCA."

"Oh no! Of course! We *do* appreciate all you do for us, of course we know how terribly busy you are—but you see, for the last two days this cat—our very own pet cat, you know—has been stranded on this unapproachable cornice. We can't get to him. He is dying out there."

"I am very sorry to hear that. But one should not keep the fire brigade busy with cats. If it were a person, we would rush there immediately."

"But this does happen in other places. One depends on the fire department for help during accidents like this—"

"Forget about other countries, ma'am. This is India."

"Why other countries? It happens in Bombay! Didn't you see it in the papers? This cat was stuck on the roof . . . and finally they called up the fire station—"

"He must have blocked up a chimney or something. There must

have been some sound practical reason behind it—couldn't have been just human sympathy for cats—"

"Oh please, there is nothing wrong with human sympathy, you know, do it out of pity this time. One can't kill a cat in a Hindu household, it brings bad luck—I would have climbed down myself, only my daughters became hysterical at the idea—"

"I'm sorry, ma'am, but this is impossible for us. This is the season for fireworks, with the Diwali festival ahead—what if there were a massive fire somewhere and our men were busy with your cat on the cornice—would that be right? This is a large city, ma'am. We can't afford such luxuries—we have to be ready for emergencies, Diwali is only a few days away."

"Is Bombay a tiny village? Are London and New York small towns? If they can afford . . . besides, the fire station on our street has quite a few engines—I have never in my entire life seen all of them go out at the same time—and this is hardly a luxury, to save a life—"

"Your house is on a street with a fire station?"

"Right next to it—"

"Then why don't you go over? Or send someone?"

"My cousin went over, but they said they needed the permission of the main office—"

"Look, it is quite impossible for me to give an official order. You can make a request and see if they do you a personal favor. You can ring them up if you wish. Here's their number. . . ."

"Thank you! Thank you very much indeed! I can't tell you how grateful I am!"

"Hello! Is this the fire station?"

"Yes, may I help you?"

A repeat performance of the previous conversation. This officer was more duty-conscious than the other. "I'm sorry, but I cannot risk the life of one of my men for a cat."

"Oh no, of course not. But how does this risk come in? It isn't a fire, you know, only a cat. A very tame . . . pet cat."

"What if our man slips and falls? There is a point in dying to save another human being—but certainly not in trying to save a mere cat . . ."

"Dear me! Why should the poor fellow die? The cornice is wide enough, besides it's pretty clean, and does not have moss on it. However, talking about the cat so lightly—(you know not what you speak of)—"

"I know, I know. A pet becomes pretty much like one's own kid, but even if my man sprains his ankle—I cannot take that risk, you see? Tell me, would you . . ."

"Listen! Can you hear it? The deadly screaming?" I had wildly dragged the receiver to the window. "How long can one stand that howling? I am going crazy. Can you hear it? Can you?"

"Yes! Yes, of course! I can! I can! I can quite understand your situation ma'am, but—"

"Look here—does one call up the fire station at the drop of a hat? Especially if one is a woman? At this time of night? Is it not the last resort? In front of my very eyes . . . in my own house . . . the poor darling, a creature of God . . ."

"Ma'am—er—you don't quite get it. It is not possible to give an official order—"

"What about an unofficial one? On humanitarian grounds? I would have got it down myself, but unfortunately my daughters are scared—and my mother is a rather nervous person—or else I would have got it down ages ago—"

Meanwhile my eyes had truly begun stinging, and my voice choking.

"Don't you dare climb down in a sari, ma'am, that would be extremely dangerous—"

"What else can I do? Obviously there is no gallant, tenderhearted, unselfish young man in your office who would take pity on a cat—and there's none in my house—"

"If you want my honest opinion ma'am, there are hardly any gallant, tenderhearted, selfless young men around anywhere these days. But I'll gently suggest it to my men. Honestly, I do not think . . . anyway, I'll try, but I can't promise anything. You see—animal lovers are quite scarce nowadays . . ."

The fat cat's wailing increased and was coupled with my restrained sniffs. There was a pause, and a determined change in the voice. "Oh all right! Give me your address anyway. Which house is it? Oh that one—it's hardly a couple of minutes from here! Let's see what can be done!"

About twenty minutes passed. It was getting later in the night. The starved feline was wailing away in an alarmingly human voice. Shaking away my obstructive daughters with a final flush of determination, I got ready to climb down onto the parapet. My mother declared, "Not in your sari, my dear—put on some pants if you want to get down there."

The very thought of such a sight, of Didi in pants, accomplished what love for a creature of God had not. It prompted the agonized cook to volunteer hastily, "No, no. Didi—allow me." Who says chivalry is a thing of the past? No sooner had he got down, than the fire engine arrived. Fantastic timing. A joyous chorus of excited voices filled the night air—"Someone is already there! Someone is already there!" Just as M. Uncle, firmly wrapped in a blanket, was placed in my arms, somehow the fire engine's bell rang out loudly, breaking into the hushed night. God knows what it did to the confused, nervous wreck of a cat. He leapt out of my arms and, disentangling himself from the blanket, flung himself wildly out the second-floor window onto a different, quite unapproachable cornice farther off and higher up. This time it was quite impossible to reach him with a normal domestic ladder. Heartbreaking lamentation filled the night air, coming from our room as well as from the street.

All was lost! And then?

In a second they jumped out of the fire engine—not one, not two, but half a dozen gallant, unselfish, philanthropic, tenderhearted, chivalrous young men. The three-tier ladder darted out heavenwards, ready, steady and then the crucial question: Who would it be? After all, this was no fire, which was a simple matter of routine . . . Observing the hesitation, I volunteered, "Why don't I go up? Let me—" and I took a step. Before I had finished my sentence, or my step, someone, just anyone, had made a frantic scramble up, up to the second story.

There he turned, "Does he bite?" "Well, you see, it would be a good idea to wrap him up in a towel or something." Turkish towels were immediately thrown down from various neighboring balconies—all lit up by now, and lined with keen spectators. Our man on the ladder caught one nimbly, and proceeded upwards. Uncle Tom was most perturbed at the weird sight of a human apparition presenting itself out of nowhere in a most unhumanly corner—dark, uninhabited, twelve inches wide, with a straight drop of thirty feet. Visibly shaken out of his wits by an event so unexpected, he started a frenzied rush all over the narrow cornice. What excitement ensued all around! As if this were the football game of the year! The street crowd below and the crowd on the balconies cheered faithfully. All eyes were fixed on our hero conducting the remarkable chase up in the air. And then— gotcha!

Amid the earthshaking applause that followed, the lights went out. A power cut. Warnings rang out from all over, and six or seven fire department battery-powered torches flashed at once.

A voice like God's own rang out in the darkness, happy and proud,

"Got him, ma'am! Got him! Don't you worry, ma'am, I won't let him go till he is safe in your arms, I promise you."

I almost jumped out of my skin! "Thank you, oh thank you so much, sir—but just put him on the roof of the garage. That'll be quite enough."

"Not on my life!" said our hero, rapidly coming down, clutching a grumbling bundle close to his heart. "I'll do nothing of the kind!"

The street sported an unusual social gathering for 1:30 A.M. So what if it was the middle of the night? Retired and bathed ricksha pullers, homing beggars, bored and curious night watchmen, agitated street dogs, sleepy neighborhood cows, and various fun-loving people of all ages had filled the courtyard and spilled out onto the street, blocking it. A flow of anxious advice—contradictory but concerned—was pouring down from the candlelit windows and balconies. The older children were all up and awake and had joined the parents, feeling emancipated. There was an excited mass-scale twittering around, a festive atmosphere. At this precise moment, when most of it was over, our new nextdoor neighbor, an elderly gentleman—Mr. Chowdhury—appeared in his pajamas, rubbing his eyes sleepily. When he finally realized what was going on, he began in the deep, husky voice of someone just awakened, "Oh, I see, so this is that massive, ferocious, black-as-death . . ." Desperate, I grabbed his arm and gave him a significant pinch. A pinch only, not a punch, but that finished Mr. Chowdhury. At least, his sentence. Completely flustered by this sudden, unprecedented attack of romantic exuberance, Mr. Chowdhury was struck dumb. I knew the explosive words that were about to escape his mouth: ". . . that horrid, evil, bad-tempered, bully of a tomcat? The one who steals my fish every day and drinks up my grandson's milk?"

No, that sentence could not be uttered right then, not at that point, not in that situation. Truth and revelation must wait for the right moment. I could not allow it to ruin all. In that warm liquid atmosphere of love and affection for all creatures of God, a sentence like that had to be forestalled by hook or by crook. In that unenlightening pitch dark of the power cut, standing under a three-story-high ladder piercing the smog-hazy sky, in the lawless, candlelit rejoicing that went on all around, Mr. Chowdhury stood motionless, wordless, one arm grabbed and pinched, the other free but frozen. Meanwhile, our hero appeared hugging a struggling, grumbling, lively bundle close to his heart. Down he came, gleefully offering me the towel-wrapped danger, as a doctor offers a newborn baby to its father. Sheepishly, I said, "Just leave him on top of the garage roof—he'll be quite okay there."

"Are you crazy?" said our hero, "Who knows where he'll leap to next? Another heavenly spot—another replay of all this? Come on, hold your baby yourself—lock him up for a couple of days, so he learns his lesson." Like the awkward new father, I held out my arms, smiling uncertainly, and received my fate—come what may—clutching him fast to my bosom. The power came back with perfect timing. There was general rejoicing and a public cheering ensued. The lights exposed me, trembling, with "my beloved pet" struggling furiously in my arms, his fierce roars muffled inside a towel. I started to run.

My intention: to turn the corner (our house is on a corner lot with two entrances), go to the main entrance (as the crowd was gathered at the courtyard and back entrance) and release the Monsieur to his long lost freedom.

I carefully avoided Mr. Chowdhury's eyes. He had lost his wife recently. He knew I was a wild divorcee. He might get ideas. I was running round the corner, with a typhoon welling inside a towel, too powerful a natural phenomenon for me to control. Just as I turned the corner, Monsieur Hulo freed himself (tearing the towel), bared his teeth and nails, and disappeared in a fraction of a second. But not before using them both on my left wrist. Because it was the wrist, the bleeding was bad, but I wrapped my whole forearm up in the towel and, holding my elbow close to my breast like a baby, I heard myself thanking the real princes of the fire station with real tears trickling down my cheek and real pain shattering my wrist.

"What you have done for a creature of God today, dear brothers, I shall never forget—God will reward you for this kindness." My voice was choked with emotion, a throbbing pain in the wrist, and tears.

Deeply touched, the young man began a short speech. "We were only doing our duty, ma'am, no need to thank us for that, and a pet is like a child, don't we know it?"

The bells in the fire engine rang through the night once again, and the real princes—the kind, loving, tenderhearted, generous, fearless, adventurous, dutiful, and beautiful young people—jumped up on it. The winged red horse disappeared into the night, and with it, a group of brave young men.

Monsieur Hulo, I could see, was busy with his toilet, licking himself all over, nonchalantly sitting on our boundary wall. The crowd had magically dispersed, guards, dogs, cows, and all. Only Mr. Chowdhury was still standing dumbfounded, half-asleep, in a nightmare in the center of the courtyard. The balconies were empty, lights were off. Mr. Chowdhury looked at me while nursing the point in his arm where the unkindest pinch of all had hit him, with an expression on his face that even Marcel Marceau would envy.

I had to take fourteen injections in my stomach. The price of kindness to stray animals. My wrist still sports that war memorial. Mr. Chowdhury avoids our family like poison. So does Monsieur Hulo.

Moral: Don't disturb the fire department. The 'bloody' aftereffect is too much to bear.

Translated by Antara Sen.

MALATI PATTANSHETTI ————————

(b. 1940)   *Kannada*

"A woman need not depend on anyone else to make her life a happy one. . . . In spite of tragedies, in spite of disappointments, life is beautiful," Malati Pattanshetti says. "Writing poetry is my hobby." For a living she teaches English at a college in Dharwar. She started writing in 1976 and has published four collections of poetry: *Ba Parikshege* (Come, Face the Challenge), 1976, *Garigedari* (Ruffled Wings), 1983, from which the poem translated here is taken, and *Nanna Avaru* (My People) and *Tande Baduku Gulabi* (You Brought the Rose of Life), both in 1988. A collection of short stories, *Indu Ninnina Kathegalu* (Stories of Today and Yesterday) also appeared in 1988. The dominant subjects of her poetry are nature and love.

"Sambandha" explores the despair of one who finds that her relationship is one-sided. What for the man was simply a natural process like breathing became life's very substance for the woman. "Personal elements have been so completely depersonalised here that the poem extends beyond its man-woman context and tries to explore the tragedy of all unanswered human relationships," the critic Vijaya Dabbe writes, adding, "there is a perfect balance of thought and emotion."

◆

SAMBANDHA
(Relationship)

Having built a citadel of disregard
Smeared with snow that turns into smoke
Inside and out a silent sentry,

Wearing your searching eyes,
Each breath churning every atom of my being
On the path you bid me tread, each step a rose,

Still carrying its warm, raw vessels,
Laughter tumbled down the unknown slope.
Awake, alone, bewildered,

I cry "friendship."

Why do you poke your nose here,
Soundless rage?
Your sentry pacing stops all of a sudden.

This purdah, this pacing, these features
Stride businesslike toward me, who is
Sandalwood enveloping you.
They cling, dig, slash
Through your lost moonlight,
Asking what is
Going on between
You and me.

Translated by Tejaswini Niranjana.

NITA RAMAIYA ⎯⎯⎯⎯⎯⎯⎯⎯⎯⎯⎯⎯
(b. 1940)   *Gujarati*

Nita Ramaiya was born in the town of Morvi, Saurashtra, and despite her
Bombay education and current residence, she still feels connected to her
birthplace. She knows, firsthand, the day-to-day life of rural Saurashtra,
its folklore, customs, and beliefs, all of which find a place in her poetry.
For many years she has taught English at the S.N.D.T. Women's University

in Bombay and has recently been doing research on the poetry of Margaret Atwood, which she has translated into Gujarati.

Nita Ramaiya's poetry has been critically well received and her work appears in well-known Gujarati poetry journals. A collection, *Shabdane Raste* (Along the Path of the Word), appeared in 1989. While many of her poems are personal, others are responses to the world about her. In one, a dramatic monologue, a dying old man composes a letter to his long-departed son. Two explicitly feminist poems reflect an awareness of woman's present role and her potential. In both, the poet rebels against the expectation that woman exists for others, not for herself, yet at the same time, she invites man to share a freer future in which both woman and man jointly explore the world that invites them. Several poems, such as "Treeji Ankhnun Jantarmantar" (The Spell of the Third Eye), included here, revel in natural scenes of rain, cloud, woods, and streams. We need the earth just as the earth needs us, but this earth and its waters can also be destructive.

The poet's mother and young brother were drowned in the flash floods of 1979 that killed half the population of Morvi in a matter of minutes, the subject of "Ognisso-Ognyaeshinun Varas" (The Year 1979), which appeared in *Kavita* in April 1985. "Treeji Ankhnun Jantarmantar" was published in *Kavita* in February 1987.

Several of her poems are songs that successfully capture the lilt and idiom of women's folk songs, but she also writes free verse that reflects the experience of the city and explores personal relationships. Her range is evidence of her versatility and her openness to experience. She received the Gujarat Sahitya Parishad Award for her collection of children's poems, *Dhammachakdi*, 1986.

◆

OGNISSO-OGNYAESHINUN VARAS
(The Year 1979)

This is the year
When my mother looked back at us through the water
Submitting the joys and sorrows of sixty-eight years to the Machhu
  River

This is the year
Of the last scream of my brother
Assigning to the flood his twenty-three years
Which could not be contained in his piercing eyes and shining shoes.

This is the year
That reduced to stammering

Learning literature politics ideology
Understanding intelligence wisdom . . .
How can I explain to my son
Whose each footstep's presence brightens
The courtyard of my parents' home
That each footstep grinds me to dust?
That with each footstep the life is drained out of me

This is the year
Of the invisible scene hanging
Between
My son's ten-year-old's mood
And my face molded by that year

This is the year
Of the shameless thirst
Of the deranged river.

Translated by Shirin Kudchedkar.

TREEJI ANKHNUN JANTARMANTAR
(The Spell of the Third Eye)

It is said, if Shankar opens his third eye,
The earth will be reduced to ashes.

You have two eyes.

Close one eye:
            Half the visible world becomes invisible.
Now close the second one:
            The rest of the visible world becomes invisible.
Close both eyes together:
The whole visible world becomes invisible.

Open the third eye.

Kick hard
At the wall behind the eye
Knock down the wall.

Take seven steps
Along with your white shadow.

Remember:
You must not turn and look back.

Descend upon a swaying hill
In the style of a helicopter
Plunge
                From the top of the hill
                Into the dark.

                Hang upside down
                    In the dark
                        Like a bat.
                In the dark
                        After circling the dark
                        Stand with your head erect
                        Steadying your two feet
                        In the center of the dark.

Then you will achieve
The visible form of the invisible
Seen by your third eye.

After that
                You will not need
The two eyes
                That you have been given.
You are not Shankar, remember.
You have not seen all the deeds of Shankar, real or illusory.

You need the earth.
The earth that holds you yearns for you.

In every vein of yours are all the juices of the earth
                        Reduced to their essence
                        Carrying the weight of life
                        (Ages old)
Buried under the earth
From under the earth you have burst out

On opening your third eye
                (From time to time, generation after generation,
                On any slight pretext every day)
                One two three
                Innumerable

From the earth burnt to ashes
In the flames of terrorism
—Fingers will sprout
To hold your finger
—Milk will gush
To feed you
—The earth will offer itself in love
As Parvati offered herself to Shankar
—Even in the twenty-first century.

You need the earth.
The earth that holds you repeats your name
As Parvati repeats the name of Shankar.

Translated by Shirin Kudchedkar.

VARSHA ADALJA

(b. 1940)   *Gujarati*

Daughter of the famous Gujarati novelist Gunvantrai Acharya, Varsha Adalja was born in Bombay in a milieu that would obviously have been congenial to a future writer. Drama was her first love: she trained at the National School of Drama in Delhi and has produced features and plays for television, including dramatized versions of her own novels. She has a master's degree in sociology. At present she is a full-time writer with many books to her credit. Her widely acclaimed book of short stories with the catchy title *E* (He) came out in 1979. Her novels are often best-sellers, and her popular detective stories include social comment.

Many of her novels depict women's lives and explore the problems they face in the contemporary world, but as is evident from the sensitive story included here, the broad range of life in a modern city is also central to her writings. In several novels she has taken up topical themes and used settings such as the Vietnam War (*Atash* [Fire], 1976), or the life of hill tribes in Madhya Pradesh (*Ganth Chutyani Vela* [The Time When the Knot Is Undone], 1980). Like the Tamil novelist Rajam Krishnan, she researches backgrounds meticulously. Before writing about the hill tribes, for example, she not only read extensively on the subject, but lived for a period among them.

Varsha Adalja's novels often portray women who have consistently been exploited and marginalized but who gain strength and insight through those very experiences. In *Timirna Padchaya* (Shadows of Darkness), 1969, the comfortable wife of a seemingly upright judge longs for emotional warmth and for motherhood. Ghosts from the past enter her life when a woman comes to the judge to plead for her son, who has killed her drunken brute of a husband. The young man is the judge's own son, the woman a former servant in his home who was married off to a drunkard when her pregnancy was discovered. The judge's wife befriends the other woman, but the son spurns his mother and she commits suicide. Devastated and totally alienated from her husband, the wife leaves him. The protagonist in *Retpankhi* (A Bird in the Sand), 1974, is an orphan, slighted by the relatives who bring her up, rejected by the children of the elderly widower she marries. When happiness finally seems to be within her grasp she has to turn her back on it, as a pampered cousin who had eloped and ended up as a prostitute leaves her young daughter in her charge.

The story included here, taken from *E*, 1979, leads us into the world of traditional folk singers who now live in penury in the city. The characters in the story speak a lower-class dialect throughout.

◆

BICHARI CHAMPUDI
(Poor Champudi)

Darsaniyo thumped the tabla with vigor. The sound of the bells tied round his wrists and his powerful voice strove to rise to the full height of the eighteen-story building.

When her brother started singing the latest hit from a new film, Champudi was delighted and began dancing with verve and abandon, twisting her body this way and that. Since not many people had collected yet, her attention kept drifting to her mother sitting in the corner of the compound wall. They were accustomed to dancing in alleyways, but this was the first time the family had come into the compound of a huge building like this one. As she danced, Champudi cast another glance upward. She was in a splendid mood that day. She had often pleaded with her mother and brother to let her dance in the areas where the large apartment houses stood, and that day she had wept and insisted that they come to Walkesar. The new building had dwelt in her mind ever since the construction work began. From the moment they had left home that morning, she had plagued Darsaniyo.

"Now, Brother, today we just *have* to go to Walkesar."

As usual, Darsaniyo had been irritated. "How often must I say no, Champudi? Those rich people have small hearts. You're too young to understand."

Jeevli, their mother, walking behind them, had lost her temper.

"You're always thinking up some new plan. The empty pots and pans move restlessly today. What are you brats going to eat? Your father's started on one of his attacks of asthma and here's little Kaniya full of fever. We'll have to burn up the money on medicine for both of them. Let's go to our own area. That's best of all."

Champudi had glared at Kaniya resting on her mother's hip. That was that. Time and again it was Father's asthma and Kaniya's fever. She loved her little brother, but he was forever falling ill. And all the money would be washed away in the colored water of potions for them. There was a time when Mother had treated them to ice cream, and occasionally they had had a peppermint to suck. But from the day this Kaniya had entered the house—

"Come along now. Make it snappy."

Giving her head a despairing shake, she had run to catch up with her brother.

When they had reached the huts near the railway line, her heart had filled with bitterness, as if she were seeing the place for the first time. Streams of filthy water flowed wherever they pleased. The smell of rotting garbage had sent a wave of nausea through her. She had thrust the end of her torn skirt into her nostrils. Ragged, grimy, messy children, and women scratching their heads and holding babies to their sagging breasts, had appeared on the scene. Some men had turned up as well, smoking cigarette stubs and cleaning their teeth or passing a comb through their hair.

Darsaniyo had burst into song and Champudi had begun to contort her body. Screwing up her face disdainfully, she had looked around. Well, whatever one might say, the people here were simple souls. They enjoyed watching her dance. Sometimes they would give the children food, and the small coins usually amounted to ten or twelve annas.

But today Champudi had been determined to have her way—"Come on, let's go to Walkesar. To that new apartment building."

Fed up, Jeevli had finally given in. "All right, let's go."

After walking for an hour in the sun, when the three reached the new building at Walkesar, poor Jeevli had been half-dead with the heat and fatigue, Kaniya almost delirious with fever, and all of them acutely thirsty. But there had seemed to be no way to get water. So Jeevli had deposited herself in the shade near a garage.

"Hurry up, children. These are all big people around."

The newly painted building looked imposing in the sunshine. Champa forgot her thirst and exhaustion. Springing up, she said to

Darsaniyo, "You'll see, Brother, the coins will rain down on us. There'll be no room in your pockets to hold them."

Darsaniyo, too, recovered his spirits, seeing the shiny cars and the splendid building. "Look here, Champudi, if we make enough, I'll treat you to a Fanta. Let yourself go."

Champudi took her place in the middle of the compound. Darsaniyo's melodious, powerful voice knocked at the closed windows of the tall building: "May our friendship live forever." Champudi recollected the style of acting of the hero in the film as she began to dance. One after another, in quick succession, faces appeared at the windows. Brother and sister grinned at each other. Champudi threw a quick glance at her mother. Today they'd have the medicine for Kaniya and the Fanta. Immediately, one after another, in quick succession . . .

She looked up. The panes of the open windows shone like diamonds in the sun. The plants on the balconies were ravishingly beautiful, but there was nobody to be seen there anymore.

She lowered her tired neck. A few people had formed a circle in the compound, but she still hadn't heard the ring of a single coin falling. Her eyes began to fill with tears. Darsaniyo took up one song after another, but the beat of the tabla was slowing down.

Champudi heard a whistle. Her attention was drawn in its direction. The driver of the car opposite was sitting on the seat, with the door open, and there was something shining in his hand. Champudi's heart leaped up. She ran to him, delighted, and stretched out her hand. The driver jerked his hand back. Champudi was crestfallen. The driver laughed and opened his fist. There was a silver rupee coin smiling at her.

"Take it," the driver said.

Champudi stretched out her hand. The driver grabbed it. Spreading out her palm, he placed the coin in it and closed it again.

Running to her mother and flinging the coin in her lap, Champudi started dancing again. Wasn't she lucky! This was the first time in her life she had ever seen a whole rupee coin. Twirling and twisting, she continued to dance. Quite a few people had collected in the circle around her. Champudi looked up again and her gaze slithered down the smooth wall of the building. Not a single one of those wealthy housewives was watching her. All morning she had been cherishing a secret dream. Today she'd really make a pile. These were all big people. Somebody might throw her an old silk sari or maybe a colorful frock she'd outgrown . . . But now her feet were aching, and all she'd gotten was a single rupee.

A young couple came out of the building and got into a fine, large, bright red car. She danced up to them. The girl was so pretty! Champudi liked her a lot. With luck, they'd give her a whole rupee note. The young man's full pink lips showed as he laughed. Champudi bowed and stretched out a hand.

"Get away, you wretch." The boy angrily started the car. "The watchman is so stupid."

The car turned out of the compound. The bottle of Fanta seemed to be disappearing as well. Like the beat of the tabla, her feet, too, slowed down. The sun seemed to have gritted his teeth, the better to beat down on them. She heard a whistle again, and again her heart bounded. The driver was standing in the circle and there was something shining in his hand. Her eyes were glued to the shining coin as her feet danced on. But she didn't hear the ring of the coin. The hand with the coin in it was raised and waved at Champudi. Champudi ran up, but the rupee wouldn't detach; it seemed to be stuck to the fellow's hand. She wasn't sure if the crowd had increased, but her body was crushed on all sides. Getting hold of the coin, she started dancing once more. Two or three more coins followed, of varying denominations. The life came back into her. Since luck was with her, she again danced with zest. What was that film her brother had taken her to the other day? There was a girl in it dancing exactly like this. She had gone from person to person in the group, laughing, dancing.

Leaving her place in the center, Champudi went round to each person in the circle, smiling and dancing. She started making alluring eyes and gestures just like the girl in the film. From somewhere or other, two- or three-rupee notes were thrust into her half-torn blouse. She didn't care any more about old frocks thrown down by the rich women from above. Her tender breast was covered with rupee notes.

She ran up to Darsaniyo. "Here you are, Brother." She burst into merry laughter and held out the crumpled notes to her brother.

"Give them to Mother." Darsaniyo glowered at her and spoke in such a harsh voice that Champudi wilted. Why wasn't her brother pleased? She flung the money into her mother's lap when she heard another whistle. Without noticing that her mother looked aghast, she ran off. Reaching out for the four-anna coin held high above her, she was caught up in the crowd. The pressure against her breast suffocated her. For a time she couldn't make her way out at all. The driver was near her. "Why are you frightened?" he said, and putting his arm round her, pulled her out of the crowd. Champudi smiled at him with relief. Poor fellow, he was really a decent man. Putting her whole heart into it, she resumed dancing. She whirled round and round, just like the girl in the film. People had plied that girl, too, with money. A little heap of money danced in the air before her eyes. Fatigue, hunger, thirst, all were forgotten. She just danced amid the crowd, smiling at them all. The crowd kept increasing, and every so often she was crushed by it. Each time, the driver rescued her. Her tender breast began to hurt. He would press a shining coin into her palm and Champudi's eyes would shine. She went on dancing . . .

Suddenly, as she stretched out for a ten-paise coin, her hand was roughly pulled back. She was startled, but when she saw Darsaniyo's face livid with rage, she was really terrified.

"Come on, you've made enough money. No more dancing. Get back home."

"But Brother, just a little longer. Tomorrow all of us can go to the movies and have our ice cream as well."

"Can't you understand when I tell you something the first time? Or do I have to hit you?"

Seizing her by the wrist, Darsaniyo started to make his way out of the crowd. With Kaniya on her waist, Jeevli joined them.

"May you live long, both of you, brother and sister. We're not going to huts anymore, only big buildings like this one."

Champudi looked at her brother, who was still dragging her along firmly grasped by the wrist, and said hesitantly, "Mother, it was that dance like the one in the film that pleased them all so much."

"Darsaniyo. Go to some good film tonight together."

Darsaniyo, who had been walking along in dead silence with bent head, suddenly bellowed, "Don't dare ever to suggest coming to this place. I'll break your legs."

Poor Champudi couldn't understand a thing. Still holding her brother's hand, she walked along utterly downcast.

Translated by Shirin Kudchedkar.

GAURI DESHPANDE ─────────────

(b. 1942)   *Marathi*

Gauri Deshpande, a bilingual writer like Kamala Das, writes poetry in English and fiction in Marathi. Her journalistic writing spans both languages. Her mother, Iravati Karve, is a distinguished anthropologist and philosopher, whose fictional recreations of the principal characters in the *Mahabharata* provided a major new interpretation of that text and the period in which it was compiled. Her grandfather is D. K. Karve, a well-known social reformer who, at the turn of the century, married a child widow and founded a widows' home in Pune, and the first women's university in Maharashtra. Gauri Deshpande has also translated into Marathi Richard Burton's sixteen-volume translation of the *Arabian Nights*. Her poetry has been widely anthologized and she has published several books of poetry in English.

Deshpande's fiction is centered on women and their experiences. The male characters are often kindly, protective, and accommodating, but the action takes place in the inner and the outer worlds the women inhabit. She also deals with problems and issues that attend the latest phase in the development of urban society in Maharashtra. Other writers depict the passing away of the joint family, but in Gauri Deshpande's fiction, the nuclear family, too, is a thing of the past. Her characters are individuals who hold on, often fiercely, to their independence. The 1989 novella, *Thang* (The Dive/Discovery), celebrates the woman protagonist arriving at a mature self-consciousness, and is in some ways a resolution to all the searching that marked Gauri Deshpande's earlier fiction, and a celebration of arrival. The protagonist finds her self, her own identity, and her own address. The title contains connotations of each of these quests.

Ahe He Ase Ahe (That's the Way It Is) is the title story of a collection published in 1986 and is in many ways typical of Gauri Deshpande's fiction. Among her other writings are three short novels, *Karawasatun Patre* (Letters from Confinement), *Madhya Latpatit* (Shaky in Between), and *Ek Pan Galavya* (Leaves Dropping One by One), published in one volume in 1980. Her latest book, *"Dustar ha Ghat" ani "Thang"* ("A Difficult Mountain Road" and "The Dive/Discovery"), 1989, consists of two novellas.

◆

AHE HE ASE AHE
(That's the Way It Is)

It has been my belief for a long time that "love" means something done with the mind or the heart. Which means that, while love is an *emotion,* even in my childhood I wasn't so naive as to think that the visible part of this emotion, its expression, had only to involve the mind and the heart. Probably because even then, my parents never made me listen to such ideas as "God, the Loving Father, brought you to us." On top of that, I had an uncle who had a terrible itch for free love. I said to him once, "What is love *but* free? Anybody should love anybody else. Who's to say no?" Since I was then only ten years old, he just looked at me pityingly. From this you'll understand how quickly I got into the habit of differentiating between love as an emotion and its expression. Even though the gap between my uncle's free love and my free love diminished over the years, it never disappeared—even very recently I've enjoyed loving several people at the same time. And because, in my opinion, the emotion of love was related only to the mind and the heart, I'd never felt there was anything wrong about it. To tell you the truth, I used to like falling in love very much. On getting up in the morning, I would spend a great deal of time making plans. Whom would I meet that day? What should I say to her (because I'd fall in love with women, too) or to him? What should I do with her or him? Where should we go, how should we laugh, what should we argue about? Then the day would fly by, fulfilling these dreams, and the night in reviewing just what had happened or why it had not. Owing to this system, first in my mind and then later even in my life, I made a variety of serious blunders. And so I had to accept that my uncle's, my friends', and my own ideas about love were all dead wrong.

In college the professor sometimes said, speaking of Keats, "He died of a broken heart." Because I couldn't hold back the laugh that at once spluttered out, everybody called my cynical, strange, stony-hearted, and other such labels. In fact, I used to like all the Romantics very much, whether English or Marathi. But I'd feel within me somewhere that what they had said wasn't enough. And this feeling would many times express itself in my making fun of their idea of love. I became ever more convinced that the palely loitering knight, dying, sickly, wan from love, was entirely a farce. Because wasn't I myself, though constantly falling in love, eating heartily four times a day and sleeping ten hours a night? And no matter how much I tried, I never lost even one pound. So forget this business of wasting away.

Nothing happened to anybody else I knew to make me any less certain that nearly all love literature was pure fabrication. So many of my friends had fallen headlong in love, married, had kids. They, and I, too, with greater or lesser happiness, set up homes. And all these things, more or less, would in due course have come to an end; but as the days passed, I suddenly seemed to feel that something, you know, had really gone wrong. Shakespeare, Keats's knight, and Donne had understood something that had been hidden from me. While reading P. S. Rege's poetry, I used to feel, Here it is—almost! Just one more turn and I'll see it.

Without my actually realizing it, certain things began to take their places and make sense. A small boy I saw on the street held his dead cat tightly to his chest. Dry-eyed, lips tightly drawn, he was fighting with his parents not to give it up. Just so, at the airport I saw a couple, who were completely immersed in each other, parting. On both their faces was the same dry distrust. After they had turned their backs to each other, they never once looked back. The dog we kept in our home acquired a strange obsession. He fell in love with the neighbor's Alsatian bitch. It was just as tragic as it was absurd, because he was a dachshund! He gave up food and water, and would cry day and night with his face lifted to the sky. Then one day he just disappeared. Finally, the mistress of a recently deceased man came to his wife begging for his shirt. His children tried to get the servant and the watchman to drive her away. But she just sat in the doorway, dumb, until she got the shirt. Then she got up and went away, God knows where.

Now supposing there is an earthquake in California. We only read about it in the newspaper. Of course, who, of her own choice, would like to find herself in an earthquake? And when there is an earthquake right here, what, beyond a little lost sleep, happens? But that there are such things as earthquakes and also that it's always *other* people who suffer from them is indisputable. The same with love; it certainly is something; and compared with me, other people must know a lot more about it, or so I began to realize very forcibly.

When the train had reached this point in my life's journey, it was already time for me to put on *chalisi.** I had entered the store and stood

---

*Chalisi lavane means "to have reading glasses fitted"; *chalisi lagne* means "to enter one's forties," "to become middle-aged." Both meanings are implicit here.

waiting to get my glasses. So without even looking in the mirror, I was saying, "The frame's fine, just fine!" (Even now, after wearing glasses every day for ten years, if anybody were to tell me to paint a self-portrait, I'd paint it without my glasses. And I'm constantly warning my daughter, "Hey! don't read lying down or you'll have to get glasses!")

Just then somebody touched me on the back. I looked and it was you. Now the readers will think that, by suddenly introducing this entity "you" halfway through my story, I've deceived them, but not at all. I've known "you" nearly all my life, and long ago, having decided that there wasn't *that* kind of thing between us, we each set out on our own ways. They say that, when we were very small, our families used to spend the summers as neighbors in Mahabaleshwar and that we quarreled and fought so much, the dust flew. Even if I don't have any childhood memories from Mahabaleshwar, still our relationship as adults should prove the latter half of my above assertion true. "You" means Marston. By birth American, when just a few months old you came with your missionary parents and stayed here. Except for your name, you have nothing at all binding you to your homeland. You even insist on speaking our language.

"Marston! Hello!" I said.

You just smiled. After a moment you said, "Getting glasses?"

I was already feeling bad enough, so now I got irritated and said, "No, a loop."

Then you laughed freely and said, "Come, come—I must get rid of these blues."

So I, too, smiled, gloomily, and said, "Middle age has caught up with us, Marston! We're already facing the question of which college to send the girls to."

"At least you haven't started with weddings yet, so there's no problem. And I, at least, can't see any difference in you at all. You're still just as you were in college when you used to march around ignoring the whole world. You're just as outspoken, quick-tempered, troublesome, argumentative."

I felt a lot better. Still, I said, "And my glasses? What about my glasses?"

"They're no problem. They help give you that 'high-thinking' look."

It may have been because I had just purchased the proof that half my life was over, or perhaps because I was finally convinced that I would have to discard the vague hope of not having completely missed the right way, but I couldn't just get up and start walking away with the usual "OK, Marston." Your company felt so comforting—you who have known me so long, and since my very childhood have seen my tiniest idiosyncracy, you who have always looked at me patronizingly and sarcastically. I felt, "It's not as though I *have* to speak to him about anything." How many times had I become piqued because, from where you were four rows away, you just smiled sarcastically. How many times during the past twenty-five or thirty years had you simply waved from where you were across the street and gone on your way? Then, too, it was never as though we felt obliged to stop and talk. Not only that, but at Nirmala's death, when we came to offer condolences, hadn't we two just stood facing each other, looking at one another, not knowing what to say? What a surprise that just that day you happened to see me in the store and stopped to talk. And in the same way, we set off walking. Suddenly I turned and asked, "How long have I known you, Marston?"

Surprised, you stopped and said, "How should I know? I've known you since you were just this big." And with that you raised your shoe about a foot off the ground.

I said, smiling, "Ha! I was *never* that tiny."

You smiled and nodded your head, up and down, like a heron, and we turned once more and began to walk. Passing by sari shops and shoe and clothing stores, we went as far as the Jehangir Art Gallery. We stopped to see whose exhibit was there. You said, "Huh, there's nothing in that. A waste of canvas." And then turning, unexpectedly, "Are your glasses for nearsightedness or farsightedness?"

"For farsightedness. They're chalisi.

"That's right," you said, "you really do need glasses to see up close."

We were still standing in front of the art gallery. I looked up. You weren't smiling then. You were looking at me with a sad, dejected face. I, too, kept looking at you. I saw that your nose was quite snub. Your skin had tanned dark. Your hair, originally tawny, had become more like salt and pepper. Your eyes were nearly as dark as mine. Thin lips and a very wide mouth—so your smile stretches from ear to ear like the Cheshire Cat. Small ears. Very becoming. Nicely shaped, sensitive, like the pointed ears of a fox.

And suddenly, as I was trying to decide how many years I had known you, I saw . . .

At a picnic once you shoved me into a pond. When I pretended I was drowning, you jumped in, but because you couldn't swim, I was the one who had to save you.

When my youngest daughter was sick with pneumonia, I saw your face often at night through her mosquito net in the hospital.

At your wedding, when we presented you with a frightfully expensive gift, how angry you became! It was the first and the last time you were angry with me. You looked at me angrily, with red eyes, tight lips and finally, because Nirmala poked you, you said Thank you curtly, with great effort.

After that you were at parties thousands of times, the children's birthdays, at ceremonies, on committees. Sometimes I saw you and sometimes not. Sometimes I was aware of you and sometimes I wasn't.

Your eyes suddenly filled with tears, and in the clear sunlight, in the middle of the rush hour, I, who was nearly forty years old, completely oblivious to the world around us, dropped down and sat on the steps of the art gallery. We stopped looking at each other only when you sat down next to me.

After some time you took something out of your wallet and held it out before me. It had been written on a long time before with the large, round, small-girl script I used to use. A yellowed, torn note on which I had written, "Marston, you're stupid. What has Keats's philosophy of beauty got to do with love? Where he *clearly* speaks of beauty, truth, etc., don't you go and force love in unnecessarily. You've a habit of misconceiving and mixing up the different things in life. Can't you put two different things into two different compartments?"

I must have written it in exasperation to you, where you sat four benches away, years ago, while everybody else in class was arguing. But I can't remember that now.

When I looked up, slowly you had begun to laugh, and I myself was beginning to cry. I said, "Why do you laugh? Is this something to laugh about?"

You just kept on laughing. I said reproachfully, "Marston, you knew all about this."

And here all *means* all. I was all wrong; I had missed my way in life. My constant arrogant insistence—"What I say is right!"—had kept me from knowing what it was that others understood about life. I didn't let myself know. All *this*.

Without replying yes or no or anything, you ran both your hands over my hair, saying, "Look, not even one white hair yet." And then your face came so close that, without glasses, I couldn't have seen it.

You said my name and I replied, "Oh no, Marston!"

It's likely a few people may have even stopped to look, but in Bombay nobody has the time to be surprised. After a long while you got up and left. It had become dark. I, too, began slowly, slowly, to walk. I had to submit to facts: if there were an earthquake right next to me, much less in California, nothing was going to happen to me now, beyond a little lost sleep. Just what it was we said or even what we didn't say, I don't remember now. What I do remember—just this somewhat bitter, satisfying thought: Keats and company, after biding their time for so many years, shouldn't have taken this kind of revenge.

Translated by Vidyut Bhagwat, Indira Junghare, and Philip C. Engblom.

MALINI BHATTACHARYA ―――――――

(b. 1942) *Bengali*

All three of Malini Bhattacharya's plays were written in response to issues that were alive in the public mind at the time and were performed by the Calcutta-based women's group Sachetana (Consciousness), of which she is a founding member. *Bandor Nach* (Monkey Dance), 1986, picks up the usual routine of the street musician with the performing monkey and inverts it: the monkeys disclaim all connection with a humankind so unnatural that it exploits and oppresses women in a thousand ways that animals don't. The play uses tunes from popular film songs (movie scores), but recasts the lyrics for satirical effect and is episodically structured and easily adapted to include topical references. Her third play, *Eto Rokto Keno* (Why So Much Blood?) was written after passage of the Muslim Women [protection of rights] Bill in 1986 and deals with the question of women in relation to communal clashes.

Born in Calcutta, Malini Bhattacharya graduated from Presidency College and has taught English at Jadavpur University since 1964. Her first story, "Mrinalini Ghoshaler Shab" (The Corpse of Mrinalini Ghosal) was published in the important little magazine *Ekshan* in 1963. Well-known and well-regarded in feminist circles and in leftist politics, she has continued to publish poetry and critical articles in *Ekshan* and to write for other journals, such as *Anustup* and *Baromash.* In 1985 she adapted Dario Fo's *Waking Up* for Bengali audiences and since 1986 has edited *Neel Kamal Lal Kamal,* a Bengali children's magazine that aims to change the horizons of children's reading. In 1989, and again in 1991, she was elected to the Lok Sabha (the lower house of Parliament).

Meye Dile Sajiye (To Give a Daughter Away), the final section of which we have translated here, was written to help rouse public opinion against the practice of giving and taking dowry at the time of marriage. The title suggests a bride being decked out—with jewelry, but also with all the desirable personal attributes—for her wedding. The principal character is a legendary eighteenth-century figure, well known also as the heroine of a classic nineteenth-century novel by Bankimchandra Chatterjee, *Devi Chaudhurani*. Devi Chaudhurani robbed the rich and distributed their wealth among the poor. In Bankimchandra's novel, as Prafulla, the wife of a landowner's son, she is harassed by her husband and his father who turn her out of their house. But she returns as Devi Chaudhurani, the bandit queen, and takes her revenge on them.

In the extract from *Meye Dile Sajiye*, Devi Chaudhurani is seen presiding over the trial of a twentieth-century bridegroom and his father. There are repeated allusions to Bankimchandra's novel—and the responses of the groom and his father when the Devi finally reveals her face are taken verbatim from the novel.

The play is written in the witty, rhyming couplets of Bengali folk theater, which are particularly difficult to translate.

◆

From MEYE DILE SAJIYE
(To Give a Daughter Away)
Scene 3

Dramatis Personae
  Bride/Devi (girl masquerading as Devi Chaudhurani)
  Groom
  Bride's father
  Groom's father
  Rangaraj, Devi Chaudhurani's lieutenant
  Choruses

Devi Chaudhurani is seated in the court. On one side of her stand the groom and his father, tarred as a mark of shame and with fools' caps on their heads; the bride's father and Rangaraj stand on the other side.

Groom: Call this justice—our names are trash!

Bride's father: I thank thee God, for thou art kind.

Groom's father: Well, it's not fair and we do mind.

First chorus: But you must admit they haven't taken cash.

Devi: That's sheer luck—for otherwise
They'd be in jail. And the one who buys

The mirrors, the safes, the bed, and the bedding
Empties his purse for a daughter's wedding,
That's money too, wouldn't you agree?

Second chorus: Quite true—call a rose by any name—you see!

Third chorus: And what about the gold the bride must bring?
The armlet, the bracelet, the necklace, the ring?
No money might have been taken this time,
But that doesn't at all excuse your crime.

Groom's father: Honestly, ma'am, this is grossly unfair!
I am a poor man and wouldn't dare
To cross you or to go against your will.
But what about those who are richer still
Than scores of me—why are they free?
Why let them go and punish me?

Fourth chorus: Sadhu Khan the businessman
Who has his ways with the government,
His granddaughter wed a big shot's son
And do you know what a fortune he spent?

Fifth chorus: Three hundred grams of gold, and oh!
There was money double that amount.
And the marriage over, they did go
For a honeymoon that could account
For thousands more, and there was talk
That they'd honeymooned in Bangkok.
You pick on us because we're poor—
And they range in safety sure.

Devi: You're really beneath all contempt,
For you're the ones—who attempt
To cow the weak. Before the strong
You bow your heads and go along
With all they say and all they do—
And in their turn when they kick you
Or suck your blood you lose your cool
And take that out on your bride—you fool!

Sixth chorus: Today's new brides in time will grow
Into mothers-in-law who proceed to show
What misery means to other young brides.

MALINI BHATTACHARYA   ◆   479

Generations go, yet each strides
By this cruel law which rules her life.
Mother, daughter, sister, wife!

Second chorus: If the bride and groom agree to marry
It's simple enough! Why tarry?
All this fuss for a dressing table?
A wardrobe with a Godrej label?
Oh come now, sir, she wed your son.
And as for him, why what's he done
That's great enough to deserve a wife,
A girl he's promised to keep for life?

Third chorus: I say, everybody, did you know
In wealthy homes it happens so—
Pretty brides are burned to death
When dowries prove inadequate?
A stove bursts and goes up in flame;
A death a day statistics claim.
It's high time now you stopped those games
Of seeking rich prospects with rich names.
The times have changed and you must, too
Or else these times won't forgive you.

Groom's father: Do you have a son, sir? No? I thought so.
Marry a son and then you'll know
How much one spends on the food at the wedding,
And apart from that there's the bread and the bedding
Of a girl who'll stay with you all her life,
And besides, who's to pay when children arrive?

Fourth chorus: Will surprises never cease?
When you get a horse on a lifetime lease
Do you calculate the fodder cost in years?
This is a woman that you will buy,
Put her to work till she should die,
So she'll pay you back in sweat and tears.

Groom's father: Come now, friends, let's start anew
And forget this ruckus and ballyhoo.
I'm good at heart, don't you see?
I'll take her home should my son agree.

Groom: Though I've always dreamed of a fair-skinned wife
I suppose I must keep this one for life.
Some powder can mend her unfair face.
It's Father who's got me into this mess.

Devi: That's enough now. Where's the bride's father?
You can't decide without him.

Bride's father: O ma'am, you've saved my face.

Devi: I? Your face? And what about your daughter?
Doesn't she have face too?

Bride's father: She's saved too, ma'am.
She'll bless you with all her soul.
Now she'll have her home and husband.
All the money I've spent has been worth it.

Devi: But you haven't been tried yet!

Bride's father: Good God! Why should I be tried?

Fifth chorus: But he's the plaintiff.
Why should he have a trial?

Devi: Because he's brought his daughter up
To believe that her only place is at home—
That her husband is her destiny,
That she mustn't leave the four walls of her jail
Unless fate and circumstance play a cruel trick on her.

Fifth chorus: Is that true?

Bride's father: No, no—I've paid for her education.
She has a bachelor's degree too—
I've never stopped her from going out.

Devi: And why, pray? Because you knew
That a B.A. would help you make a match—
A degree would help you catch a catch.
Today, if she cannot envisage a life
Apart from the parasite's life she leads—
Then you're to blame entirely for it.

Sixth chorus: No, it's the women's fault.
It's the girls who insist on money and jewelry.
Their father is their golden goose.

Behold their tears, should he fail
To lay the golden egg.

Devi: What father, then, for his daughter buys
Poison, since she, wayward, cries?
In spite of her, shouldn't he strive
To save her, to keep her alive?

Rangaraj: To pay in cash can't staunch her blood,
With none forthcoming, her life's at stake!
If marriage kills so many, early or late,
It's foolish to sign and say, "All is fate!"

Devi: Give her a million, she's still a doll,
Sometimes petted, sometimes mauled!

Bride's father: [Kneeling]
Yes, I see it now.
It's for me that my daughter suffered.
Madam, you are a goddess.
Won't you tell us how we can make amends?

Chorus: [Kneeling]
Yes, tell us how we can make amends.

Rangaraj: Man has no divinity
Whatever be his woes,
And no god brings you felicity
Or shows the way to freedom.
[Drops cane and moves aside]

Devi: I am not of today.
I am that which has existed forever.
I am the desire in your heart of hearts.
So many times have I been here and yet
You have forgotten me. So I have come again.
I am not a goddess, nor am I a queen.
I am that I am.
[Removes her mask]

Bride's father: It's my daughter!

Groom: Prafulla—thou art a bandit!
Fie on you!

Groom's father: What! Not Devi Chaudhurani,
But our first daughter-in-law?
Where was she until this day?
Who has she been living with?

Brides' father: She's insane. Her grief—
Her sorrows have made her insane! She wouldn't
Have done something of this sort otherwise.
You stupid girl, aren't you ashamed of yourself?
Go home at once—or I'll
Beat your bones to pulp.
[Rises to hit]

Bride: No!
[Stays his hand]

Chorus: No, you cannot hit her.

Groom's father: Do you see now?
That's not an easy girl to handle.
Look how she's humiliated us,
Her husband, and her in-laws!

Groom: She's a real spitfire!
If she were a good girl,
She'd have sat at home and shed tears.
She wouldn't have come out
And raised such a hue and cry.
Look here, this must stop.
I shall not take you in otherwise.

Bride: Take me in? How many times have I
Been beaten up and starved, just to be taken in!
What haven't I done for that?
Now it's all up to you. You won't
Find me crying to be taken in.

Groom's father: What? Don't forget you're a woman,
My girl. How do you plan to live?
What are you going to eat?
Your father's not going to feed you.
That seems to be his major problem anyway.

Bride: Who says he needs to feed me?
[Pointing to Rangaraj]

These people run a primary school in the village
And he's given me a job there.
That's what I shall live on.

Bride's father: Look what you've done now.
They're not going to take you in anymore.

Bride: That's no longer our care, Father.
It's their problem now.

Chorus: Yes, it's their problem. It's their problem now.

First chorus: Riddle me the riddle of this vanity fair—
You can buy the moon with good cheer,
With gold and money and a tear
And you're pleased as punch when you've given it all away.

Second chorus: And the seller gets it all back anew.

Third chorus: Two hands to work and serve him too,
And children? That's the least she'll do.
And she'd never have it done in any other way.

Fourth chorus: Oh yes, she's ready with a smile
To give herself up all the while.

Fifth chorus: To work to death, to neither rant nor rile.

Sixth chorus: And burst with pride in her home each day.
A woman? A wife? A human being?
A parasite, I'd rather say.

Devi: A woman—a mere human—must turn every stone
To be able to call her work her own,
Or else, she's a ware for exchange
And none can solve this riddle strange!

Rangaraj: Come, let's go now.
[About to go out with the Devi]

First chorus: Wait a minute! It sounds like a fairy tale.
You can't get jobs that easily these days.
Forget about women, even men can't—

Second chorus: Take my younger sister now. She's finished school.
Now she can't get into a college. She's plain.
The prospective groom and his parents take one look

At her and ask for so much money it makes me giddy.
Even if I can't get her married off I'd like to see
Her settled with a job. But where would she get one?

Bride: Yes, you're quite right. It's a fairy tale
You have just witnessed.
Do you want to know what really happened?
Listen to this—

Rangaraj: The bride's father throws her out—
That is the truth without a doubt.
She comes back to her husband's home
And with thrashings for her sin atones.

Bride's father: That's what happened. Yes sir,
That's what happens even today. A girl of our breed
Can't be like Devi Chaudhurani.
They'll leave her alone only when
They've thrashed her wits out of her.
She's looking for trouble if she wants it otherwise.

Groom: [To the bride]
You aren't looking for trouble, I hope.
Come, come, let's not talk big now—we're going home.

Bride: Have I been talking big?
Do I have to go home, after all? Tell me, all of you—
Isn't there any other way out?

Chorus: Isn't there any other way out?

Third chorus: Look at the girl next door. Her brothers spent
Thousands on her marriage—but she was treated so
Badly she hanged herself after six months.
There's nothing for it but to endure.

Bride: Should I hang myself?

Chorus: No!

First chorus: I got my daughter married to a rich man's son
When she was only fourteen. I gave
Them a lot of jewelry and bundles of money.
But my daughter didn't survive.
Year after year they'd pester her for more.
One day she talked back—

And they hit her on the head and killed her.
A million rupees couldn't save her.

Bride: May I not be saved? Will I also be killed?

Chorus: No!

Bride: Well then what SHOULD I do?
It's a fairy tale I've told you—of Devi Chaudurani.
If you can't make it come true, there's no end to this life.
For years we've been pushed back
To a hated life.
For our families, we've been told,
For our children, for love.
Is marriage the only place for me if I want to live?
Would you marry me to a lifetime of shame?
Speak! Speak! Oh, you must speak!

Chorus: My daughter is the light of my life.
She will not be a scoundrel's wife.
I'm not going to give her away.
I gave her a ring and a golden chain,
They took it all and sent her back again.
Oh, that was a terrible day—
She was all laughter, she became all tears,
Lived day and night with unknown fears,
I didn't know what to say.
Now she's going to school, she'll forget her fears,
If I can help it, I won't have those tears.
I won't have her crying away.
I'll have her wed whomever she wants,
There must be real stuff 'neath whatever he flaunts.
No dowry this time, no way—
I'm not going to give her away.

Translated by Chandreyee Neogy and Piyali Sengupta

AMBAI _____

(C. S. Lakshmi, b. 1944)   *Tamil*

Ambai was born into a large middle-class family. Her childhood was a happy one, and she has warm memories of holidays spent with her many cousins at her mother's parents' house in Coimbatore. Her grandmother was self-taught and a scholar of Tamil literature; her mother, a musician, had a great zest for life and spread laughter around her. "My love for Tamil I learned from her and my grandmother," Ambai writes.

Ambai grew up reading the popular Tamil journals that her mother subscribed to. In addition to her rigorous routine of school, dance classes, and music lessons, she read all the Tamil books the family had. "When I began to write at the age of sixteen, as an extension of writing my diaries and school compositions, I wrote in the style of whatever I had absorbed from those magazines. Most of my initial stories had very rigid and orthodox views of sexuality, femininity, and life in general. The widows in my stories, after a speech full of symbolic metaphors, always refused to remarry, and my heroines married idealists who were combinations of Tagore, Ramakrishna, and Vivekananda," she comments.

At nineteen, Ambai left her home in Bangalore to study in Madras. After receiving a master's degree, she "wanted to decide what to do in life," and worked as a school teacher. During this period she hardly wrote. Her novel *Andhi Malai* (Twilight Time), 1964, was being serialized, and she was "vaguely embarrassed by it, although [she] didn't know why." In the beginning of 1967, however, she wrote a long story, "Siragugal Muriyum" (Wings Get Broken), about a sensitive woman married to a crude, insensitive man and the sense of suffocation she felt. She sent it to the popular journals and it was returned by all of them. She put it away, thinking that her style "must have deteriorated due to lack of practice." In October 1967 she went to Delhi to work toward her doctorate in political science. The literary journal *Kanaiyazhi* was published in Delhi at that time. "I sent my story to the editor, asking him for criticism. He wrote back to say that nothing was wrong with it. It was just not a story for popular journals. Through the editor, Kasturi Rangan, I met other writers and critics, such as Indira Parthasarathy and Venkat Swaminathan. Venkat Swaminathan introduced me to the writings of important Tamil writers whom I had not read and encouraged me to write the way I wanted."

Ambai wrote several stories for *Kanaiyazhi* in the early seventies. Around that time she also was part of the Madras-based group that published the journal *Pregnyai* (Consciousness). *"Pregnyai* was a phase of evolution for all of us in the group. We read, discussed, fought, and wrote a lot. After 1976 I wrote nothing until 1980, for no particular reason, although research and teaching took a lot of my time," she says. Meanwhile, she had finished her doctorate. In 1976 she was awarded a two-year fellowship to study the work of women writers in Tamil, and in 1984 published her findings as *The Face behind the Mask: Women in Tamil Literature.* Also in 1976 she married Vishnu Mathur, "a friend who was a filmmaker. Both of us decided to move to Bombay in 1978." Currently she is working on an illustrated social history of women in Tamilnadu. She also writes scripts for her husband's films and assists him in other ways.

Ambai's work shows great promise. Her first novels, *Nandimalai Charalile* (At Nandi Hills), 1962, and *Andhi Malai,* were published when she was a teenager. The short story collection *Siragugal Muriyum* (Wings Get Broken), 1976, was her first mature work. This humorous, moving book was an important contribution to Tamil letters, but it did not receive much attention in Tamilnadu. One of the stories included, "Amma Oru Kolai Seidal" (Mother Has Committed a Murder), deals sensitively with the experience of a young girl when she first menstruates. Her mother is away and she is devastated: "Sitting down, I weep with my head between my knees. Something seems to have ended. Like leaving a theater after the curtain falls, like coming away having left something behind. It is as if this has happened to me alone in the history of the whole world." But when the mother returns, all she says is, "Why did this tragedy happen to you so soon? It's yet another burden!"

◆

ANIL
(The Squirrel)

Old, sprawling bungalows with long verandas that once housed the British government offices. Verandas hugged by meshed windows with angled tops. Ornamental arches spanning the veranda every ten feet. Passing under the arches of that dim veranda where the sun hardly enters, an anticipation that at the end of the darkness awaits a library. No particular reason why. But setting foot on that veranda, the anticipation. A hurried breath. A watering of the mouth. And often enough at the end—a library there, in fact. Lying there yellowed, stretched in iron *almirahs* [cupboards].

Once, during the days when the night falls early, the sun had just set. I stepped onto the veranda and a face suspended in mid-air floated out in front of me. From the owl-eyes and down, the flesh of the cheeks and neck cascaded like a waterfall. I started. The body turned cold. A smile parted the wrinkled hanging folds of skin, revealing a few teeth.

"Were you frightened, madam?"

A light came on. A long veranda took shape. Arch after arch. A feeling as if I were entering a cave. At the end of the veranda behind the iron door checkered with iron rods, a soft red light. Above and below the door a curl of red smoke. Like a shadow door leading into another world. I imagined that the door will open to reveal Urvashi, the divine nymph, dancing with her ankle-bells tinkling. Perhaps they were not even verandas, just narrow passages, but for me they were verandas. I felt that each path would lead to old ripe books, their tongues hanging out, lying on their backs. As I touched them, every now and then a dog-eared fold in the page. Close to the fold, a heavy marking. Painful, so painful. Sometimes books with their spines broken under their own weight. Touch one and you hear a snap. Just touch it, wake it to life—and it is an *Ahalya,* seduced by Indra and turned into stone by her husband's curse, waiting for the touch of Rama's holy foot that she might come to life again. Who can tell in which new epic this event will find a place?

The phantom door stood there in front as a physical reality. He opened it. A small garden path. At the end, a heavily boarded wooden door left open.

"They've all left. I was waiting for you. Here is the book you asked for."

A sudden gust of wind. The pages fluttered frantically. As I pressed a hand on the cover to hold it down and felt the tremor of the leaves passing into my hand. The old man was no longer beside me. Only the light in front is still burning; the others have all been turned off. Open iron almirahs touching the high ceilings. Inside, two lofts with railings. An iron stair to climb. I was alone. My hand rested on the book. In the corner, beside the door, the sound of the fluttering pages set off by the wind mounted into a heavy thud. It was then that it appeared. It sat on a pile of books that had just been mended. Giving me a brief look, it began to lick the glue, enjoying it.

"Don't," I said. "That is *Chintamani.* The women's magazine that was run by Balammal. On the back cover, a fading image in a sari, nine yards long, that is she. My relationship with her has just begun.

We have not yet conversed. I do not yet know everything about her. Only that she does not much like Vai. Mu. Ko."*

The squirrel listened. It looked at Balammal briefly and left. The wind, the fluttering, and the throbbing under my fingers continued.

All this has happened so often before both in reality and in dream that it is hard to tell which is the dream and which the reality. It does not even seem so important. The books crumble and fall as I touch them—that is real. The crumbled powder sticks together—that is real. It is also a fact that, with that crumbling powder, the nymph advertising *Keshavardhini*, a popular hair oil and shampoo, also crumbles to pieces. Many times, in dreams as well as in reality. That is why I do not try to sift them. When I think I am dreaming, the fan might stop and the sweat drip down. Thinking it real, I might raise a book and smell it, and then the raindrops splashing on my face through the window might wake me up. I never take any notice. Might some experiences not extend from dream into reality and might some not be reflected from reality into dream?

On a sloping desk near the window, there is a heavy dictionary, brown with age. When the wind blows, it shakes its large pages. Bend, and they strike your face. Rising like a gentle stroke, the pages roll from *B* to *J*. The wind stops. I turn again to *B*. Caressingly, one page flies up to stroke my cheek and returns, leaving a faint smell.

Moving from one end of the almirah to the other, touching the books. Laying the basis of a relationship. A stroke in the dust. Like caressing a naked child. Do you know I share a relationship with all of you? It was my finger that gently stroked the groove running through the letter Mary Carpenter wrote in the nineteenth century. The letter asking for a school to train women teachers. I was the one who blew off the reddish brown dust that looked like rust. The dust that had collected on the description of the Rani Victoria Kummi** in the *Viveka Chintamani*. A speck flies against my lip and I flick out my tongue, lick my lip and swallow it. An old generation descends into my stomach. If some Jashoda had peered into my mouth, as she did into the young Lord Krishna's, perhaps she would have seen, not the universe, but a Victoria dance.

---

*Vai. Mu. Kodainayakiammal, an early-twentieth-century Tamil author of more than 115 novels, is popularly known as Vai. Mu. Ko. She also edited the journal *Jaganmohini,* which she took over in 1924 and ran for more than twenty years. She was a contemporary of Balammal, the editor of *Chintamani* which also began in 1924.

**The Rani Victoria Kummi, which means "Queen Victoria Dance," was a group dance done in honor of the Queen Empress.

Perhaps Krishna himself had arrived when this library had opened to preach his sermon: "be like water on a lotus leaf detached." Nothing touches anyone.

Knee-high steel tiffin carriers. As the Buckingham Carnatic Mill workers went on their first strike in May 1921, on the third floor, downstairs:

"Is it mutton today, my girl? It smells good."

"Yes, father. I made mincemeat, early this morning. All month long, during Puratasi, we can't eat any, and that makes me feel weak. My husband ground all the spices. It is not yet time. It is just twelve. Let's go and sit under that tree in the corner. We'll take the water pot along."

"The master is coming."

"Well, miss? Talking of food, are you? My wife says I should eat only fruit. It seems I have a paunch. One should have been born a woman. Bear two children and bloat. The blouse should choke your breath."

"Well, sir, you do have a slight paunch. That is probably why she says that."

"Well, in my next life I shall be born a woman. My flesh can then hang around my waist like Elizabeth's."

"Oh, sir! Why do you drag an innocent woman like me into all this? I am without guile or malice. That is why I am not all thin and shriveled up."

"Hey, when you go to buy betel nut-powder, fetch half a dozen fruits for me."

"You mean half a dozen jackfruits, sir?"

"What is this, I say? People coming to work dying of hunger. Doesn't like my paunch, she says, my paunch! Can't I even smell a spoonful of ghee? What's wrong with my being served some onions tossed in butter with chapatis? Don't I toil the whole day without pausing for breath? The lot of you . . ."

"What did we do, sir?"

"Go, get back to your work, girls. Five lakhs of books have to be cataloged. Chatting about mincemeat and husbands grinding spices!"

Laughter.

Squeak-squeak.

It comes and sits on the Factory Act.

Again it makes a sound.

Keech. Keech.

"Look, you are a nut-eater. What business have you here? Aren't there trees outside? Go then. What do you find in this glue? Go climb a couple of trees. What sort of bad habit have you picked up?"

It spreads its four legs out effortlessly on the book and lies flat on its stomach. A sunbeam bending and sliding in through a hole in the meshed window touches it softly on the head. It closes its eyes.

I don't touch the squirrel. Not that I believe in miracles. But I don't feel like putting one to a test. I'm not used to talking to magical princes.

The third floor is a neglected place. In the corner the man who catalogs the Telugu books mutters to himself now and then. The other books—torn and about to tear, pasted together to postpone death—rest till they can be cataloged. An iron-sheeted floor full of holes. One might actually see what is happening downstairs. Once, the book of songs used several years ago in the Madurai Meenakshi Temple to drive away evil spirits slipped from my hand and fell through the hole right on the librarian's head.

For my sake, he had once climbed up onto these open iron almirahs, touching the ceiling, forgetting his paunch.

"I can't reach the top, sir! You look and tell me what's there."

As soon as he had climbed up, he struck the topmost stack of books with his hand. The dust rose in a wave.

Standing with legs planted on shelves facing each other, his head hidden in clouds of dust, one hand pressed to his throat to control an imminent sneeze, he had seemed, as I craned my neck to look at him, a good, obedient genie conjured up with a rub of the wonderful lamp.

"What is there at the top, sir?"

"Dust, dust!"

"No, sir, I mean what books!"

"I'll see, madam. People write many good books without all this climbing. This is rubbish, madam, just rubbish."

"If you like, I'll climb up sir!"

"No, madam! This is my duty." He let fly ten sneezes.

"These are just women's books. Do you want them?"

"Throw them down, sir."

They had fallen with a thud. Volumes of *Penmadhi Bodhini* and *Jaganmohini.* Following them had come others. The sight of them tearing through the roof, sides splitting open—even this grew familiar. For someone who does not believe in miracles, here was an overdose. As my finger touched the spine of a mended, nineteenth-century book, a tremor rose from the sole of my foot, like an orgasm. Anna Sattianandhan on her deathbed, asking her husband to pray, and, on the third floor only the squirrel and me to grieve. The woman who first set out on horseback to spread Christianity broke through the meshed windows of this very third floor. A Bengali girl writing to her father, pleading that he should not sell his only house to meet her marriage expenses, set fire to herself, and the killing flame chased through this room, like a snake. The flame spread through the third floor, its shape visible to the squirrel and me. The Telugu cataloger was not here that day.

What had appeared on the third floor were not mere books; they were whole generations throbbing with life. Stately matrons wrapped in nine-yard saris, wearing shoes, and carrying rackets, playing badminton with the white women. How best can young women please their husbands?—so many sermons preached untiringly on the subject. Addressing her as "my girl," trying to sound kind, these preach the dharma that women should follow. Nallathangal, chasing her son even as he pleads with her to let him go, pushing him into a well, and jumping in herself. A brahmin priest, stubbornly refusing to perform the last rites for a girl because she is an unshaven widow. Knee-length tresses shorn as she lies dead. The devadasis dedicated to the temples, dancing to exhaustion, singing, "I cannot bear the arrows of love." Gandhi addressing the women spinning at the *charka*. Uma Rani of the journal *Tyagabhumi* declaring, "I am not a slave." "Kasini" giving new patterns for bangles in the women's section. The *Ananda Vikatan* cover girl, walks, swinging her arms while her husband carries the shopping bag. Tamarai Kanni Ammaiyar—the lotus-eyed one—saying, "Let us give up our lives for Tamil." Her real name in Sanskrit: Jalajakshi. Ramamrutham Ammaiyar angrily confronting Rajaji, who wrote, "Gandhi won't come unless you pay him money." They are all here. I am also here. Sometimes they are like figures of smoke, weightless, sometimes weighty and impressive. The day the girl widow's head is shaved, a heaviness in my heart. Razors appear all around. Each lock of hair falls with a hard sound. And rubs against my cheek, roughly. It is only when the squirrel taps his tail twice and raises dust that my senses return. It is leaning on the *Kalki* with Ammu Swaminathan on the cover. It has finished eating the glue.

I look down through the hole. The librarian's head is leaning against the chair. On the table, a file titled "Subject: String." His favorite file. Three years ago a shining violet file, now moldy, corners dog-eared. The file began with a letter saying that a string was needed to separate the old magazines, here by month, here by year. It is not the practice to supply string to the library; explain the reason for breaking this precedent, said the letter that came in reply. Then the explanation: The magazines that are not separated by month are mixed and useless. Useless for whom? For the researchers. What researchers? Are they from Tamilnadu or from abroad? The letters piled up. One day, the librarian pulled out a bundle of string from his trouser pocket. Later, he wrote a letter asking to be reimbursed for the string, which set off a series of letters beginning with the query, "Why a bundle of string?" Every evening the file would make its way to the table. He has not yet been reimbursed.

The squirrel chirps. *Keech. Keech.* My only link with reality. And yet my companion in illusions. *Keech. Keech.*

I know. It is late. Your glue is gone. But I don't want to leave these women. A magic string holds us together. I hear them talking. As Shanmuga Vadivu's veena strikes the first note of the octave, the sound leaps to my ear. "Beholding the colorful lotus and seeking it, the bee sings a sweet song—utterly lost," sings K. B. Sundarambal. "Utterly lost," echoes Vasavambal from behind, accompanying her on the harmonium. On the Marina Beach, Vai. Mu. Ko hoists the flag of freedom. With children in their arms, the women who oppose Hindi go to jail.

See, this is another world! That glue should have infused a little of this world into you. A world for you and me.

"Come down, lady." Smiling, he looks up and calls.

"I'm up here."

He comes up.

"The ruling has arrived."

"What ruling?"

"They find all this mending very expensive. Not many people use these books. Just one or two like you. That's all. How can the government spend funds on staff, glue, et cetera? They are going to burn it all up."

"Burn what up?"

"All these old unwanted books."

My mind goes blank. Only at the edge a small thought rises. So the file about the string has finally come to a close. Only the burial is left now.

"Come, lady."

I approach the iron stair and turn back to look once more at the room. The evening sun and the mercury lamp spread a strange light on the yellowed books that are to be burnt. Like the initial flood of fire that spreads over the pyre. He turns out the light.

The darkness mingles with the dull red light changing everything into a magical flame, deep red. The squirrel, with its four legs spread out, lies prone before the window as if in surrender. As I go down the stairs, a little wave of thought. That window faces north.

Translated by Vasantha Kannabiran and Chudamani Raghavan.

CHHAYA DATAR ————————————————

(b. 1944) *Marathi*

It was out of frustration with the life of a housewife, Chhaya Datar writes, that she grew active in social and political movements. Many of her early short stories present the experiences of middle-class women trapped in domesticity. They focus on the tension these women experience between the nurturing and caring demanded by their often affluent homes and professional husbands and their own desires to break out of these constrictions and live lives that are more open to the larger issues in the world around them. After publishing two collections of short stories—*Goshta Sadi Saral Sopi* (A Story, Simple, and Straight), 1972, and *Vartulacha Ant* (End of a Circle), 1977—she moved into what she herself describes as "serious writing" and a systematic study of women's issues.

Chhaya Datar has worked in several youth, trade union, and women's organizations. She is well known in the contemporary women's movement and often acts as a resource person for groups that organize rural and urban women, and takes on research assignments. Among her more recent studies is a monograph titled "Organizing Women Tobacco Workers at Nipani." The report, prepared for the Institute of Social Studies in The Hague, is part of a study of women's organizations and women's movements in Third World countries. The story translated here draws on these experiences.

Chhaya Datar is a founding member of Stri Uvach (A Woman Said), a Bombay-based publishing group whose first publication, *Swatahala Shodhatana* (In Search of Ourselves), 1976, is a collective effort by twelve women. They present in fictionalized form real-life stories of fifteen divorced women. As the group puts it, "the exchange of experiences, the necessity to understand divergent viewpoints, and the awareness engendered of what constitutes good writing," have helped them both as writers and as women. Chhaya Datar's other interest is in making slide shows with commentaries, mainly on issues related to women's employment. The story translated here first appeared in the daily *Maratha* in 1976 and is included in the collection *Vartulacha Ant*.

In 1986, her *Stri Purush* (Men/Women), 1984, which presents feminism in a popular style, won the first Nanjanagud Tirumalamba National Award for the best book on women. She also writes on literary and political issues for several Marathi journals. Her publications include *Stri Vimukthi* (Women's Liberation), 1975, and two collections of literary essays, *Mi Taruni* (Me, A Young Girl), 1979, and *Purush Kendri* (Male Centered), 1984.

◆

SWATAHCHYA SHODHAT
(In Search of Myself)

The dazzling glare of the sun had dimmed. The wind that had blown wildly all day was a little subdued. The dust that had bitten the flesh was at rest. I stood up to my knees in the Tapi. Her waters swirled caressingly round my legs and flowed on. My body still felt the waves of heat from without, but within, the coolness of the water rose all the way into my head. The sun stood to the west, smeared with dust—a circle of dust rimmed with light. Standing alone in the vastness of the Tapi, I shed all social connections.

The beat of a drum rose in the distance, growing gradually louder. A flute joined in, running a high, piping frill around the deep resonance of the drum. The sun sank quickly out of sight, and the river began filling with grains of darkness. The rhythmic shuffle of dancing feet had begun. The camp was coming alive. This was the cultural program before dinner.

I walked from the river to the camp while the darkness deepened. A delicious sadness took hold of me. A sadness of the kind one can never experience in the city, with its noises, its people, and its brash lights. In the morning I had received a letter from my husband. It had confirmed the fear I had had when I took a week off to come here—the fear of being suddenly called back. His sister's son was going to be fed his ritual first solid meal. My mother-in-law was coming down for the ceremony. My presence was essential. I had been asked to cut short my itinerary and leave for Bombay immediately. I was furious. Wandering in these parts for the last four days had made me forget home and family. I had experienced the heady freedom of a kite soaring high in the sky. The letter had brought me back to earth. I couldn't decide what to do. My mother-in-law was a harsh woman. If I didn't heed the letter, my husband would be very angry. Yet I wanted to continue traveling in this district. I was there to see how the adivasi farm laborers had been organized into a union and to write about them if I could. I wanted to discover what drove these ignorant, uneducated people to come together to fight.

I walked down the pitch-dark pathway towards the camp. By the time I reached it, the drum had warmed up. Its beat echoed like the call of the pigeon. A tambourine repeated the rhythm. Women who had grown stiff with the afternoon's lessons had thrown off their tiredness, tucked their saris in at the waist, and now danced in circles of four and five. Their bodies swayed back and forth. Their feet seemed to tap the beat out automatically. The lamp in the center shot long needles of light. The semidark beyond turned the women to shifting shadows which formed flowerlike patterns in dance. The drum beat the same rhythm again and again; feet tapped the same rhythmic pattern. Some women pulled me into one of the circles. I danced round and round with them, feeling quite dizzy. The flute made me feel uneasy; I felt choked. It was like fighting sleep after taking a sleeping pill. I was rising higher and higher like a circling bird.

I had been traveling in the district for three or four days. I had arrived at Nandurbar on the first day, and caught the train to Dhulwad at sundown. By the time I had reached Dhulwad, it was pitch dark. Adchi lay two miles from Dhulwad. That is where my itinerary was to begin. The road, unblessed by the daylight of electric lights, was a dense dark. The stars shone sharp and brilliant. In the velvety darkness that covered all things without and within, speech was an intrusion. It was rare to feel this intimacy with the natural world. Buildings, roads, lights severed one from it. But here one was surrounded by the natural world. It wrapped itself around, cloaking one with its moistness.

They sat eating bhakris and thin watery dal in the light of an oil lamp. My eyes filled with tears. The walls of the hut were made of twigs plastered with cow dung. The cooking pots were of clay. They placed two brass plates before us. That was the only metal in the hut. The dal had been cooked in an earthen pot and the *tawa* [griddle] was of clay. No copper and brass water pots, no trimmings of any kind.

At night the worker who had accompanied me called the women together. They came one by one, many with babies nursing at their breasts behind their saris. Somebody fetched a hurricane lamp. But it didn't light the faces of the women. It was difficult to tell what brought them there, whether it was curiosity, eagerness, or obedience.

I remembered what a friend had said over a cup of Irani tea just before I left. "There's no need to feel so excited about this trip of yours. It's all politics. Some people use money for political power, others use sheep." "But Rajesh," I'd protested, "the mistake lies in thinking of the ignorant as sheep. I know there are people who treat them that way for their own ends. But the workers in the place I'm visiting aren't like that." "Nonsense. All they have to do is to understand mob psychology. These are days of mob politics and slogan-mongering. The voice of the individual has been killed."

I hadn't a clue about how these women who had gathered before me thought and felt. Were they sheep? Was this a flock of sheep? I was asked to speak a few words as a visitor from the city. I spoke in Marathi. My companion spoke in a mixture of Marathi and the local dialect. A woman asked a question. My companion answered with a slogan in a lusty voice. The women raised their fists and joined in. Slogans. Slogan-mongering. I was a little disturbed.

Early in the morning, my hostess had escorted me to the edge of the village for my ablutions. "Go anywhere you like. It's all fields out there." The horizon lay beyond the limits of vision. Vast and spreading black soil dotted by a squat bush or two. At the edge of the expanse stood the ball of the sun, ready to start its day. Two figures walked across its face carrying loads on their heads. I began to feel lost in the immensity of the landscape. A serene land. No sound, no fury. A vast, expansive land, difficult to encompass, where humans moved like busy worker ants. And in the center of the village sat the landlord in his stone house, with nothing to do but give orders. Like the queen ant.

A water pump started up at some far-off well. The landscape shook a little.

It was afternoon in the village, but the men sat around with folded hands.

Why were they not at work?

There was no work.

What about the government scheme?

Hadn't received wages last month.

How many days' wages?

Sixteen.

Fourteen.

Ten.

What work was it?

Road construction.

What were the daily wages?

Five rupees.

That wasn't bad.

But they got only two-and-a-half.

Why?

For one shift.

How many hours was that?

Six.

Impossible to work more in the sun.

What time did work start?

Seven in the morning and went on till one.

Was Somwaribai also working on the scheme?

Who could afford to sit at home?

What about the cooking?

When she left work, she would carry the coarse jowar grain to a village two miles away, get it ground, come home and make bhakris.

Walk two miles to have grain ground?

What was to be done? There was no mill in the village.

What time would dinner be after such a late lunch?

What need was there to eat twice? Once was enough.

And the children? What did they have in the morning?

Leftover bhakri scraps.

And now that the work had stopped?

They had bought grain on credit. But the grocer had stopped giving credit. So the children had been sent out to fetch foreign grass that grew on the embankments of the landlord's vegetable garden. When they got back, she'd cook the grass.

And the firewood?

They've cut it in the jungles.

Didn't the forest officer catch them?

He did, and put them behind bars sometimes. Or sometimes made them carry the wood they had cut to his place.

I had a feeling I was discovering the individuals in yesterday's flock of sheep. And yet how similar they all looked. Their joys and their sorrows all cast in similar molds. Then how could they speak of them in different words? They could speak only in one tongue. Their tales of woe all fell into the sea of slogans.

A march had been planned for the next morning. We were to walk to the *taluka* office. Women were to be in the vanguard. I had watched Bombay processions from the roadside. Here, I was part of one, and felt its differentness. In a sense this was a mob. But it was not a flock of directionless sheep. This mob had been given sharp definition by its goal. There was a vitality in it. Its slogans weren't hollow as they often are on marches. They were vigorous. Closed fists held the very essence of life. The loudest voices belonged to the women, as if this were their only way of asserting their existence. They had been transformed for the time being from ants into full-blooded human beings.

Such were the varied moods and situations in which I had been seeing these people for the last four days. The dancing was still going on. I was exhausted. Even after I decided to call it a day, the others continued. They danced late into the night, and yet, when I woke up the next morning, they were already up and about, gathering on the *maidan* for drill.

My enthusiasm had waned after the letter. To get back to Bombay by the next day, I would have to leave that night. I was seething within, but totally helpless.

The class began. Four adivasi women came, their babies slung on their hips. The babies played in the mud outside. The mothers learned new things within. These women had had no education of any kind before. But they sat through two hours of learning at a stretch, nodding their heads when familiar situations were discussed, each one eager to tell the tale of her village. One by one, individuals took shape out of the mob.

It was twelve noon. Everybody waited anxiously for the end of class and the call for lunch. Just then, a young woman hurried in, panting. Her face dripped with sweat, her feet were bare. In her hand she carried a bag. Everybody looked at her and a whisper went around. "It's Bhuribai, Bhuribai has come." Bhuribai came in and sat on the parapet. The worker asked, "Why are you so late, Bhuribai? The camp started yesterday."

Suddenly the tears that she must have been holding back burst forth. She stretched out both her hands. They bore crackling fresh burn marks. "It's my brother-in-law's wedding today, brother. I had packed my bag yesterday to come here. But my father-in-law wouldn't let me go. I made a fuss. So at night he heated the *tawa* and burnt my hands. The skin was burning all night. I couldn't sleep for a second. In the morning I got up very early and sneaked out before anybody woke. I didn't have any money so I had to walk all the way, four miles."

Bhuribai sobbed all through her story. I felt the tears pricking behind my eyelids. I remembered my letter. Where had Bhuribai found the courage to do what she had done? Why was it so important for her to come to the camp? "Bhuribai, you need not have come. A wedding in the family is an important event. You should have stayed home."

In a sense I understood how her father-in-law must have felt. But Bhuribai was suddenly all fire. "Sister," she exploded, "you are saying I need not come for union work?"

I was taken aback. Here was an ignorant, uneducated woman who had broken her leash and come here. The strength to do that had come from within. She had come, she stayed, and by afternoon she was one with other women from her village.

I felt distressed, still unable to find the springs of my own motivation. For four days I had lived in the midst of appalling poverty and hardship. I had been able to identify individual faces in the mob. I had seen the spark of life springing to light. I had seen bodies grow vital again in the headiness of dance. The steel frame around me cracked. The sparks of this life set my old world on fire and the fire raged unrestrained. The time to leave was approaching. An angry mother-in-law, a sulking husband, a sarcastic sister-in-law. I saw them all in minute detail and around them danced the burn marks on Bhuribai's hands.

There was a dust storm again that day. The wind whistled, the dust bit the flesh. I stood in the waters of the Tapi with my husband's letter in my hand. Carefully I tore it into tiny shreds and threw the shreds into the water. They bounced up and down and then floated away. Once again I shed my social connections. At least for some time.

Translated by Shanta Gokhale.

MEHERUNNISA PARVEZ ————————
(b. 1944)   *Hindi*

"One incident stands out in my memory. It's a small one, no doubt, but it illustrates my character. I was in my third year at school and had just learned how to ride a bicycle. Coming home late in the evening one day, my father found me cycling and called out sharply. I felt quite scared. 'Why do you roam around cycling, day and night?' he shouted—and slapped me. I had never been hit before and the incident shook me badly. I decided to run away to the forest, but the thought of tigers and other wild animals was too much. I crept into the garage and hid myself in the huge oil drum the driver kept his cleaning rags in." Tired and hungry, young Meherunnisa sobbed herself to sleep. She was discovered only in the morning. "My father took one look at me and realized I was made of rebellious stuff."

Meherunnisa Parvez's first short story was published in 1963 in the widely circulated Hindi weekly *Dharmyug*. She is deeply concerned about the problems of the tribals in the forest areas of Bastar in Madhya Pradesh, and has worked among them and written about them as much as she has about women. *Uska Ghar* (His Home), 1972, asks about the rights of women who are not legally married but have lived all their lives with a man, and "Akash Neel" (The Blue of the Sky), 1978, explores relationships that have "gone hard and bitter and hang like a stone around the neck, but which we are forced to carry on with." Most of her stories are about those who are, in one way or the other, exploited and are suffering. The stands she has taken have been controversial, particularly those expressed in two articles, "Gardish" (Travails) and "Talaq" (Divorce). "I was punished for every word I wrote in them," she says. After "Talaq" appeared, the local Muslim community threatened to not allow her a place in the traditional burial ground unless she retracted her stand and apologized. "I was ostracized and treated as an outcast. Wherever I went, there were whispers about me and about the incident. It was a struggle to survive. I've always thought it was a weakness to break down or complain," she says. "So I didn't. I merely told the story of my agony through my characters." As might be expected, her husband's family, who were so orthodox that even the "mosquito-meshed windows were covered with thick curtains," were upset and angry. They asked her father to make her give up her writing. "But my father knew well that to do so was to invite danger. I would have either taken my life or rebelled more openly and strongly. He kept quiet."

Meherunnisa continued to write, holding on to her work as to a lifeline, and has published four novels: *Ankhon ki Dahliz* (The Threshold of Eyes), 1969; *Uska Ghar; Akela Palash* (The Lonely Palash Tree), 1982; and *Korja,* 1977, which won the Maharaja Vir Singh Dev Puraskar from Madhya Pradesh, and the Uttar Pradesh Hindi Samsthan Award, both in 1980. Important among her collections of short stories are *Adam aur Avva* (Adam and Eve), 1972; *Galat Purush* (The Tainted Man), 1978, from which the story translated here was taken; *Antim Chadhai* (The Last Ascent), 1982; and *Ayodhya Se Wapasi* (Returning from Ayodhya), 1991. "People say my pen is pungent and that I am rebellious," she writes, "but I have not as yet written what I really want to write, what I feel within. God knows when that will be possible."

◆

TONA
(Black Magic)

The sun-loving, frisky little goat jumped up, leaped over the wall, and landed on the earth where Kaki, with her dry, cracked soles, was sweeping the front yard here and there.

It was early, early in the morning, and Khodi's heart was still pounding from the dream. What a strange dream! People kept piling thick, thick, logs brought from the forest, while she tried hard to cross the open field to get to the bazaar. But it was hopeless. However much she ran, however hard she ran, she remained where she was—and the pile of logs kept growing! It was a horrid dream! Her heart was thumping like that of a charging cow that had stopped, gasping to draw breath.

Khodi had returned from the fair at Jagdalpur only the day before, with her body tatooed, and now this dream! She had clenched her teeth as the sharp needle pricked her tortured body. Kaki had sat nearby and watched. Khodi had taken her time choosing the flowery design for the tatoo. At last she had agreed to have a marigold tatooed on her back, and small mustard flowers on her arms. The village priest had said, "This is the only writing that will go with you to the house of the gods. Those who have not had it done will suffer in hell. This is the only mark of the body that will survive. No one can recognize a body without a tatoo. After Surajni had her thighs tatooed, marriage proposals poured in, even from faraway places! People were prepared to pay two hundred rupees—in cash! Kaki has had her whole body tatooed. The more you are tatooed, the happier you will be. Kaki has enjoyed having four men!"

Kaki had nagged her every day about it, and at last she had agreed to get herself tatooed. The watchman's wife, Sukhmati, went every day to Jagdalpur market to sell rice. Khodi had gone along with Kaki. On the way, when Kaki sat down to rest, the watchman's wife kept asking about her own husband. Nanka had broken loose like a stray bull and escaped! Four fairs had gone by, and still there was no sign of him. Was it true he visited Kaki on the sly, drowning himself in drink and the joys of the flesh? Well! Even if that were true, Kaki was not the one to tell her—she who went around the village with a thick silver chain dangling from her neck! Once your husband slips out of your hands, you are lost. Well! Sukhmati herself was no innocent. She used to hide behind the haystack and carry on with the Lambadar's son, Nahua, but now, when her husband's eyes roved, she went to pieces like torn mesh! And rice always falls through a torn sieve, does it not?

She had returned from the market the night before, her whole body raw from the needles, and what a dream she had had in the morning! Her hair stood on end like the needles whenever she thought about it. That witch, the watchman's wife, must have done black magic. She was convinced of it. It is a woman's caste, her nature, to destroy other women. No wonder Sukhmati had stared at her new sari—she must have pulled a thread from it to cast a spell.

The other day, Kaki said, when Nahua's wife had delivered, her stepmother-in-law had dipped a thumb in the blood of the afterbirth, and in three days the new mother had kicked the bucket. She would get Kaki to read the rice at night—and all would be known. The rice was bound to collect around the cursed watchman's wife's name—that would be a sure sign.

The cock came closer and began to crow. Khodi looked up. It was already getting dark—her whole day had been spent lying on the cot. She went out and opened the latch of the henhouse. The cock called out to the others, pecked the hens in, and went in himself.

Kaki returned with two men after sunset. Both men sat down on the broken bench on the veranda. Kaki walked into the house instead of going to the liquor pots.

"Khodi! Go put some rice on the fire—quickly! The *Patel* [headman] of Titar Village is here. He's come for you. He is willing to pay a hundred rupees and a goat. Do you hear?"

Khodi felt sharp needles all over her body once again. Her body tensed—besides the dull pain, there was now a tingling feeling all over. Kaki picked up the cot to take it outside, but stopped at the door, and said, "Add the dry *mogri* fish to the dal and cook it."

Khodi got up quickly, and took down the vessel with the dry fish that was hanging over the fire. When the rice fields were ripe and ready, full of water, she had gone out with Surajni to fish in them. Kaki served smoked fish with her brew every day, and paid Khodi for the fish. In this month alone she had sold fish worth two *kowdi*-five.

"How do so many fish get into the fields?" Kaki asked. "One fish drops down from the skies with the rain, and then it gives birth to many. They lay eight hundred eggs at a time. Then the *bhata dagu* fish lose their way and ask the mogri fish where to go." Kaki told such stories about the fish!

She could hear the voices in the front room. The guest from Titar had brought some *sulphi* beer in a gourd. Kaki was emptying cup after cup. Her eyes turned red with drink. Perhaps Kaki would not sell liquor today. She waved away two men who came looking for it. Today she was drunk with joy.

"Who said Khodi was deserted by her husband?" Kaki asked. "The people of this village are jealous of her erect womanhood. That's why they talk to hurt. She left him herself. He could not cope with her raging youth—he was terrified!"

She peeped through the chinks in the thatched wall. Among the crowd she recognized the one who had asked Surajni for some tobacco on that Friday near the river.

"Hope there is no fault in the girl?"

"None—only that her name is Khodi, "unlucky one." None of my children survived, so I called her that. When she was born, we put her on the rubbish heap. Then, her paternal aunt put some money on the heap, picked her up, and placed the girl in my lap. Since then, she's always called her aunt 'Mother,' and me 'Kaki.' Like a *mahua* drink, once it gets high into you, it never leaves you. Such is my Khodi," said Kaki, sinking against the wall.

"Khodi! Have you finished cooking? We are famished—it feels like rats nibbling in our tummies."

Outside, they were squashing mosquitoes with both hands. When she came out to serve the food, she found Kaki lying drunk near the wall. Once Kaki started on her sulphi brew, she drank till she was senseless. She couldn't care less about food.

In the morning when Khodi returned from the canal, they had all left, taking their sticks and their gear with them.

Kaki had slept without eating any food, so her eyes were still swollen. Kaki watched her and said, "They want to take you during the full moon." Khodi sat down on Kaki's cot, and did not reply.

"Kaki, I had a bad dream. Why don't you spread out the rice and see if anyone has done black magic?"

"I'll do it in the evening. I have to go to the temple now. One of the girls there has a swollen stomach—it's black magic, and I have to rid her of it."

"No, do it now. I've felt terrible since yesterday, so restless. It's this nagging doubt I have." She caught Kaki's arms and tried to pull her up. "Come, I'm sure it's black magic that's been done on me!"

"All right, I will. Go and clean the floor first."

Khodi got up to clean the room near the veranda—the room stacked with liquor. That was the room with Kaki's gods in it. It had spiritual power for Kaki, and she could drive away or recall the spirits only from this place. Pots of liquor were piled up there. Kaki said the god that possessed her was liquor. Without that she could do nothing, she could not bring down the powers of black magic.

Kaki sat on the floor, now freshly cleaned and layered with cow dung. She was drunk, and she took out her small wooden box of rice and piled the grain on the floor. She would choose a name, and then, repeating it, keep spreading the rice out and picking it clean. Continuing her chant, she kept spreading more rice out and cleaning it. But the rice did not implicate anybody.

"Here, you silly girl! The rice has not gathered around any name. You've just wasted my time. Everyone is waiting for me in the temple. That girl will get well only with the help of the bigger gods." And she walked out, without pausing to rest. She threw the grain at the chickens and soon they were clucking away with joy. The cock pecked at a grain with his beak, dropped it, and called to the hens. When two hens joined him, he enjoyed pecking at the grain with them.

Kaki watched the birds with joy. She was proud of her cock. He had so far earned another five chickens and fifty rupees for her. Every fair, Kaki herself would take her bird to the cockfights, and he would win every time! After the fair, she would spread out the rice and check to see if anyone had done any black magic. You could never trust village folk. They would do it just out of jealousy. Every time her cock won, she would happily sacrifice a small black chicken to appease the gods.

The full moon shone like a diamond in the nose of the night sky. People were sitting on the veranda, some on the cot, some on the floor. Kaki was pouring the brew for everyone, but the goat tripe she had brought back from the market she served in leaf-bowls only to her old customers, the ones who would stay the whole night.

The night fell silent like a well-behaved child. The noise of the drinkers grew with its stillness. People were getting drunk and the talk grew loud and vulgar. They began pawing and clutching at Kaki. She would give her dark, gleaming, plump body a shake, and twist away from them, mocking, "Don't get fresh—go home—your mother is waiting for you . . ."

The whole house smelled of the fresh sulphi brew made from *mahua* flowers. Not so far away, near the canal, the jackals howled. The chickens in their mud cage near the kitchen fire clucked with the cold. It felt as though Kaki had always sold this brew in this small, prosperous village. Her three husbands had all run away. The fourth time, she had taken the hand of the village policeman and agreed to come and live here with him. He had had no children. Then Khodi was born, like a fig flower. When the policeman died, Kaki began brewing and selling liquor. The house and Kaki's copper body always smelled of ripe mahua flowers. In the whole of this village, and in all the villages around, there was no one like Kaki. No one who knew so much witchcraft and so much medicine.

Today, the Patel of Titar had given Kaki a hundred rupees and a goat. He had also brought her some brewed stuff in a special gourd. Kaki tied the money up in a cloth and pushed it into the stored grain with a long bamboo pole—she always kept her money this way, shoved into the bottom of the grain bins.

When everyone had gone and the veranda was empty, Kaki poured some of the sulphi brought by the Patel into a leaf-bowl. When she was very happy or extremely sad, she would sit by herself and drink. Khodi watched Kaki drink well into the third quarter of the night, mumbling to herself. Soon Kaki lay dead drunk on the veranda, oblivious of the world. Her thighs were half exposed; a swarm of mosquitoes hovered over her bare flesh. When Khodi heard the cock crow, she dragged Kaki inside.

Khodi was met by the Patel's other wives. The older one looked friendly, but in the eyes of the second one—now the middle one—she saw gathering an impending storm of jealousy. This house was much better than hers. It had a large open space around it. The women and children had come over to see her. Unsure of herself, she stood under the eaves near the pots that collected rainwater from the roof. The women looked her over from top to bottom, judging whether she might bear a child for the Patel. They stayed late into the night drinking and dancing.

She awoke in the morning and went outside. There was a dhoti hanging on the door. She picked it up and walked towards the well. All was still. Her body had been clawed at and pummeled all night long. She kept pouring water over it to wash the strange male smell away.

When she returned, she saw the middle one sweeping the house. A cloud of dust enveloped her. She might well have been swept away too!

As the days passed, she tried to make a place for herself in the house. The eldest one lived in there but had no relations with the Patel. She had a heavy, horselike figure, with large, frightening eyes. Probably she was bald, for she kept her head covered with a cloth. She ate like a devil, polishing off two portions of rice at a time. But she took care of the whole house. Even on the first day, Khodi sensed that the Patel was afraid of the eldest one.

The middle one was like Badshah Bhog, the fine, long-grained rice from Nagarnar, beautiful and fragrant. Her smooth, fair calves had beautiful flowered tatoos. She kept admiring herself all the time, her envious black eyes lined with black kohl. Whenever the Patel stared at the middle one, she slipped away like a mogri fish. On those nights he was sure to go to her. Kaki had said such women were no good. Women, like fish, were also of different castes.

When she heard that the eldest one actually had no hair, Khodi shivered with fright. She must be a vampire who left home at night to return before daybreak after drinking the blood of men. Kaki used to say that vampires used ropes let down from terraces to draw blood from the navels of sleeping people. When they couldn't get human blood, they would drink animal blood. The Patel said that there were three or four vampires in the village. They played in the fields after their work was done, their mouths dribbling blood. The thought made Khodi's hair stand on end.

Kamar village was planning to celebrate the Bali festival, and there was going to be a large gathering of people. Bali was coming to Kamar after five or six years. There was excitement in the air. Gods and goddesses from near and far were gathering in Kamar. The marriage of the two gods Bhim dev and Kodini was to be celebrated in low key for a month and a half, to be followed by a big celebration on the last day, when people would gather for the marriage procession. Only after this would sowing start in the fields.

Everyone was talking about this event. Khodi was eager to go and see the Bali. It was a rare opportunity. The eldest one had left many days earlier. Khodi pleaded until the Patel agreed to let her go with the middle one. She was overjoyed and got ready to wash her best clothes for the event.

When they reached Kamar it was at the beginning of the third quarter of the day. The village center was overflowing with people. They were all collected near the big pipal tree, where the god Bhima's marriage was to be celebrated. The marriage procession had not yet arrived. Khodi followed the middle one towards the place where the gods had been resting; the procession had already begun by the time they reached the spot.

Eight or ten girls, twelve or thirteen years old, were singing and dancing. They wore white saris and had let their long hair fall in loose ringlets over their faces. They were obviously possessed by the goddess. Two men, balancing large brass pots on the ends of bamboo poles at least twenty feet long ran forward. The priest, who was leading, wore a silver crown and carried a pot of burning incense. The virgins, possessed by the goddess, followed, still singing, dancing, and swaying. Ahead were some young men with bows and arrows, and one boy with a wooden sickle. Right in front of the procession was Bhima's chariot, covered with white and orange flowers. Another man carried an idol, also possessed by Bhima. A woman, with a full water pot on her head, was swaying, and a man followed her, spreading burning incense around. Pipes and drums filled the air.

Many smaller gods were also present in the procession. From every home, the household gods had been brought out and the women, swaying and dancing, carried these in small baskets behind the main procession.

When the procession reached Bhim kut, where all were gathered, it was already the end of the third quarter of the day. The god was placed on a wooden chair, draped with a black velvet cloth, and decorated with peacock feathers. The two young men with long bamboo poles came up, touched the god, and began to swing the poles, while the young, unmarried girls danced on the dais.

The atmosphere was charged with romance. Young girls and boys drew flowers from the chariot, exchanged garlands, and were thus married. In Bastar, it is customary for young people to pick up flowers that have fallen from the god's chariot during the Dussehra festival and to give them to each other as tokens of their love. People were drinking and dancing, and the air was heady with sensuality.

The young men from the city were enthusiastic about this festival. They were flirting and roaming around.

Khodi wanted to taste these moments of joy, but she suddenly realized that someone was following her. Upon turning around she saw a youth wearing *full-pants** and shirt, with a *machine* slung round his neck, watching her. He followed her wherever she went. The middle

---

*Italicized English words are in English in the original.

one smiled when she saw this. Khodi was upset by the middle one's smile.

She did not like it. She went straight to the village priest and complained about the youth.

The priest smiled. "That—that babu is taking pictures. He's come from the city to film this event. Perhaps he likes you and is taking your photograph. There's nothing wrong with that."

She was comforted by this reassurance. The festivities continued throughout the night, and people kept dancing till the early hours of the morning.

From the time she had stepped into the Patel's house, she had not gone back to visit Kaki. She met the watchman's wife, Sukhmati, at the celebrations. The middle one was tired and went to rest at her mother's sister's place, while Khodi roamed around the whole night with Sukhmati.

Sukhmati told her that Kaki had fallen while drunk, after which she could not walk without a limp, though she still sold her brew, hobbling around. Recently, she had begun to wear a chain made of gold around her neck.

That man was still following her, but now she smiled every time she saw him watching her.

In the morning there was going to be a great feast for the whole village after the goat sacrifice. But they did not wait for it. The middle one insisted on returning home.

The whole village got to know that Khodi was going to be a mother. The Patel was pleased. The older one was also happy. Only the middle one was like a wet log of wood smoldering away the whole day.

Then the goldsmith, Chamru, was murdered. There was a commotion in all the homes. The police took many people away. The Patel went with Chamru's wife to the city every time there was a hearing in the big court. From the time Chamru was murdered, the Patel had to visit Jagdalpur City frequently to attend court hearings.

One night, birds were still calling out, and the lantern had just been hung on the veranda. The light shone through between the slats in the door. The Patel had been away in the city for two days. The mango tree had started bearing fruit, and the fragrance of little raw mangoes hovered in the air. The house inside was filled with the smell of stale maize rotis. Khodi liked this smell. Kaki's house had been filled with the scent of raw mahua flowers. She turned and took in a deep breath.

"The small one—is she asleep?" The Patel had returned and his voice could be heard from the veranda.

"Yes, she was feeling sick and heavy, and has gone to bed." She heard the older one's voice from some nearby corner. The heavy steps came up and stopped near the door. After some time he opened the door, the fresh air rushed into the room, and the old smells of maize rotis stung her eyes and nostrils.

"Choti!" He banged the door shut.

She got up slowly on her elbows, confused. The Patel had the lantern in his hand—now it was dark outside, the room lit. His shadow was now tall on the wall. "Have you eaten?" she asked.

He did not answer. He sat down on the cot in a rage. "Did you go to Kamar to see the Bali festival?" She stared at him, surprised. He stood up. "As I was returning from Jagdalpur, they were showing a government film in front of the palace. I went to see it with the others. Your *photo* was there—you were laughing, chewing pan, and walking about with gay abandon. Speak up—did you go there to see the gods, or work in the government *cinema?* You spent the night with that babu, didn't you? The middle one told me everything—and now you want to place the babu's child on my head! Speak up! You bitch!" He kicked her in the stomach with rage. She lost her balance and fell from the cot.

The Patel was still shouting out to everyone as he left. The other two wives came up to him, and he kept cursing Khodi loudly. The edge of the cot had hurt her head and it was aching. What had happened so suddenly, she wondered? She didn't understand a thing.

Oh! This was the work of the middle one—she had kindled this fire. And now the evil magic of suspicion would never leave the Patel's eyes. It was as if someone were hammering nails into the fresh mud walls of her heart. She pulled herself up. The cold feel of the wet earth seemed to reach her heart and she felt as if the slow poison of a festering wound were spreading through her whole body.

Wearily she leaned against the wall and splayed her legs out—like this . . . like this . . . It was like this when Kaki, after drawing out the power of black magic, would lie back exhausted against the wall.

Translated by Veena Shatrugna and Vithal Rajan.

PRATIBHA RAY ———————————

(b. 1944)   *Oriya*

Daughter of a school principal, Pratibha Ray says that as a child, she absorbed her spiritual values from her father. Through him she learned to face her life; through him, too, she developed the quiet maturity that has come into her writing today.

Pratibha Ray's first book was a novel, *Brasha Basanta Baisakha* (Rains, Spring and Summer), 1974. Other books followed at regular intervals. In 1983 she published the novel *Shilapadma* (The Lotus of Virtue), which was a journey into the realm of the Orissan temple. *Yajnaseni* (Born of the Sacrificial Fire), 1985, a voluminous novel, depicts the story of Draupadi through a series of letters. In general, Pratibha Ray's stories exhibit a freshness, whether she is describing a mango tree or an old woman's prayer room.

Pratibha Ray lives with her engineer husband and her three children in Cuttack. She has a doctorate in education. She has also studied the ways of the Bondas tribes in a remote forested region of Koraput in western Orissa. The story translated here is taken from *Shreshta Galpa* (Best Stories), 1984.

◆

KAMBALA
(The Blanket)

That was Mother-in-law's memento. She used it those last few days before her death. Her son, Manmath, had bought the blanket with his scholarship money and had given it to her as a present while he was studying in college years ago. The blanket had been folded carefully with mothballs placed between layers. Then, it had been wrapped in a much-washed white sari and stored in an old trunk. Even during the cold winters, the blanket never saw the light of day. In the exotic aroma of mothballs, huddled against a corner of the trunk, the blanket reposed sleepily, savoring the warmth of the trunk's inside. Mother-in-law would go through even the most bone-chilling of winters with her hand-sewn, patched old cotton sheets, but she would never dream of taking out that costly foreign blanket of hers. Her younger cousin would at times taunt her with, "Don't be so stingy, Sister! Do you think Manmath will not buy you a more expensive blanket when he gets a job? Is that why you hold on to this one? Can't you foresee what Manmath will grow up to be? The first leaf of a basil plant has an aroma. If he could get you an English blanket while he was studying, can there be any doubt that he'll bring you a silver-embroidered one when he starts working?"

Nirmala would then, in a gesture of reverence, put both her palms together and look up at the skies. In a voice tinged with melancholy, she'd say, "Is he man as yet that I should think of such things? Let the gods grant him a long life, let him grow up to be a man first."

And Sebati would counter, "Oh yes, but you know how severe the winter is this year. The English blanket should be just right. A blanket is meant for the winter chill. Did Manu bring it all the way from Cuttack so you could stack it up somewhere?"

Nirmala would open the trunk. She'd lift the blanket with great care, as though it were a sleeping child. As though she were afraid the child would awaken and cry out in distress. How touchy and churlish her Manu had been when he was a child! Even today when he came home on a holiday, he behaved in more or less the same irascible manner. Nirmala would let her hands move softly over the layers of the folded blanket, feeling it tenderly, caressingly. As if its small, warm sleep would be upset were she rough with it! Then, with a shy smile, she'd gingerly, slowly, stroke its silk binding and announce with pride, "Sebati! Have you noticed how exquisitely the border has been done! Look at the way the strands of silk have been woven together—like a garland of jasmine buds! Or a row of chubby children playing leapfrog. Whichever way you look at it, it is ingeniously beautiful! And look at its color. How soft and sleek it is, with the flushed hues of an onion skin! As though it would leave a mark if you simply touched it. Have you seen another like this, where the rose tint of the body complements exactly the mauve of the intricate silken binding? Really, I can't stand those other blankets—hairy, shaggy things that only chafe the skin!" She grimaced and went on, "And if you pull one of those over your body, how suffocated you get! To top it all, the awful smell. As though it were bear or sheep skin! But this one—this has a baby-skin scent. Perhaps it is the only one of its kind. Look everywhere, I'm sure you won't see one half as good in the whole village! Take my word, there's no one to surpass my son Manu when it comes to choosing something. His choice is absolutely the best!"

And Sebati would quip with an amused smile about her lips, "Ah,

Sister! You speak as if Manu had woven the blanket himself," and burst into laughter.

Nirmala would put the blanket back carefully in its place. "Will such a thing ever be available again?" she'd ask. "My son bought it with his scholarship money, for me to remember all my life. If I use it, it will surely be spoiled and torn in the long run. After all, what good does an English blanket do in the penetrating cold around here? One needs quilts, the warmth of a fire. When my Manu becomes a man, I'll ask him to buy me a quilt. A quilt is said to be warmer, cosier. Yes, I'll have one made for my later days."

Indeed, Nirmala had never used a quilt in her life. Who did in those days? Especially for a woman, a quilt was unheard of. Usually old, worn-thin saris were pressed together and stitched one over the other to make a thick, flat sheet. It was an art, making those. And one lasted an entire lifetime. Winter never came to a standstill for the lack of a quilt or a blanket. Nirmala was truly adept at stitching these sheets. For she could also embroider pretty designs on them—parakeets and elephants, pitchers and lotuses and the sun. And new clothes slowly became old, and when the old sheets tore, they were replaced by newer ones. Every year after the long rains, Nirmala's blanket stole its warmth from the sun, silently through the hours. Winter came and went, not caring for blankets or quilts or old sheets, and, with the passage of time, Nirmala became a mother-in-law at last.

Mira came to the house as a new daughter-in-law. As usual, Nirmala took out her old clothes along with her precious blanket to be aired in the autumn sun. And Mira helped her mother-in-law to spread them in the courtyard. Mira's gaze fell upon the onion-hued fleecy blanket and froze. As, wide-eyed, she watched her mother-in-law gently unfold the blanket and flatten it out, the wonder was unmistakable in Mira's eyes. Even though she tried her best to hide her feelings, her covetousness seemed to break through the evening sky of her eyes like shimmering stars. Strange, but this blanket seemed totally out of place among the assorted clothes in the trunk! How could such a fabulous imported blanket come to be in the possession of her mother-in-law?

Nirmala asked Mira to hold on to one edge of the blanket while she kept brushing the other end, and began passionately, "You know, Manu bought this with his scholarship money. It's seven years old already, and I haven't ever used it. Day by day, the blanket seems to look brighter, doesn't it? Anyone who sees it is fascinated by it. Is there another like it? Manu, too, was such a delightful child that passersby would stop and stare at him. I haven't seen another child with the looks Manu had as a baby. With all his studying, and now with this responsible post which makes him travel the year round, he's really lost those looks. What was the necessity, after all, of taking this important job? Where does he get time to settle down, relax a little, have a single meal in peace? You know how his father left us homeless all of a sudden. But Manu studied brilliantly, got a scholarship, and climbed from rung to rung. And now he doesn't get an hour to rest."

Eyes flushed with tears, Nirmala hung the blanket up with painstaking care and caressed it with her palm. She gently brushed off an almost invisible speck of dirt, imagining perhaps that she was wiping the drops of sweat on Manmath's tired forehead.

Mira found it hard to appreciate Nirmala's sentiments. She could merely stare at the blanket and think, What good is such a blanket if it is merely stored away in some old trunk? Even if her mother-in-law covered herself with it, who would realize the value of such a blanket in a remote village? And then how would this blanket look beside the patched-up sheets on Nirmala's old-fashioned rosewood bed? On the other hand, such a blanket would adorn a modern bedroom, would enhance its looks. People would notice it, know it was a foreign one, talk about its unique color and workmanship. Why, *she* had never seen anything resembling this in her life! And the newly wedded Mira had begun to think highly of her husband's tastes.

But the next moment she couldn't see the sense of it all, of a gift that was given away by her husband without thought. Was it appropriate to have presented his mother with such a blanket? A handwoven sari or images of the Lord Jagannath, perhaps an appliqued canopy from Pipli that she could place over the gods in her prayer room, could easily have satisfied. And even had he decided on a blanket, couldn't he have chosen a more usable one? His mother might then have put it to proper daily use. He could have kept this blanket for himself!

Mira was straightening out the folds in the blanket when she said, "What good is it if you put away such a marvelous thing inside a trunk? Only if you use it, will it be noticed, talked about. Why don't you use it this winter? It will be ideal for the chill. This will never chafe your skin. So silken and smooth. Really I've never seen one like this."

Nirmala was ecstatic. "You haven't seen one, have you? I knew it! Like Manu, this one has no parallel in the world. That is exactly why I lay it aside in mothballs. Can you ever replace it?"

Mira's outburst was spontaneous. "Better things than this are available today. Will this blanket wear away so soon? Can't we get another for you if it tears?"

Nirmala brushed the blanket tenderly with her palm once again. Her throat felt a little constricted. In a voice thick with emotion, she said, "Yes, you'll get everything. But then you won't be able to buy one with Manu's scholarship money, will you? Can't you just get me a quilt for my use right now?"

Mira said eagerly, "A quilt isn't a big thing. If you don't want to use this blanket, please use the quilt that I brought along in my trousseau."

Mira had a feeling that her mother-in-law would give her the blanket in exchange for the quilt. For surely Nirmala would consider her daughter-in-law to be the fittest person for the use of her blanket. A quilt, Mira thought, could be procured at any time. But it would never be possible to buy a blanket exactly like this one. A better one, maybe. But not one like her mother-in-law's.

Mira's heart fell when she saw her mother-in-law carefully fold the blanket. She heard her say, "But why should you part with your quilt? My days have gone with these cotton sheets. If you could make me a quilt, it should last until my death. Isn't a quilt warmer? For whether the heart wants it or not, this aging body longs for a little comfort. But I want to keep my blanket as it is. Such a blanket was never meant to be used, you know. Besides, your children will see it some day and understand that their father studied on a scholarship."

Nirmala pushed the mothballs between the folds, wrapped the blanket in an old white sari, locked it in her trunk—and thus shut the door on the secret hopes of Mira's craving.

Mira remembered the affair of the blanket for many years. There always lurked in her heart some unfulfilled need, even in the midst of the luxuries with which she had surrounded herself. She even bought a couple of imported blankets. Nevertheless it was hard to shake that old feeling off. As thought there really had been only one such blanket made in the whole world, just as her mother-in-law had insisted. At times she would needle her husband, "Why does your mother store that blanket of hers? She should be using it at her age. It's truly a marvelous thing! One could never get another like it today!"

Manmath would respond with a broad grin, "That's why I gave it to her. Isn't it fabulous? I once thought that all the world's beautiful things were made for my mother alone! Who else was there but Mother for me to think of?" And he would give Mira an amused smile.

Once Manmath suggested to his mother, "Why do you lay the blanket aside, Mother? Don't you feel chill in these old cotton sheets of yours? Your son holds a good job now, but you never let go of your old things!"

Nirmala smiled and answered, "Do the days stop moving because of this? Do you remember how you'd curl your skinny body against mine and snuggle into the warmth of these sheets—all those years till you passed your high school exams? And what is this high job you hold today that you can't sleep well at night?"

And Manmath thought to himself, Truly what comforting days those were! Of course the chill seeped in through the flimsy cottons. If one were somewhat careless in his sleep, the body turned to ice. But he would pull the sheet off his mother's body in his sleep and lie till dawn in restful warmth. When he awoke, he would feel guilty for having used the sheet himself while he let his mother shiver through the night. He would tell himself to be more careful in the future. But, strangely, the same thing happened every night. It was only much later that Manmath realized that it was his mother who covered him up to ward off the cold. His tender heart went out to his mother for her concern. He promised himself he would buy her a really good blanket when he got his scholarship money. Manmath kept his word. But his mother treasured the blanket in her old trunk. And Manmath told himself it was hers, so she could do with it what she wished.

Nirmala noticed her son's serious demeanor. True, her daughter-in-law had advised her often to use the blanket. But how could they understand that such a blanket was not meant to be used by a common villager? Had he forgotten, too, that he had bought it with his scholarship money? If they wanted to, they could buy her a quilt, which she would use until her death.

Manmath said somewhat absentmindedly, "Well, if you want one, we'll have a quilt made for you next year."

He instructed Mira to send her a quilt next year before the winter.

Mira answered, "I've thought so too. But it slips my mind. We'll send her one next year."

But when the mild breezes of spring begin to blow, one forgets the chill of the winter months. And in the heat of the scorching summer, one literally begins to pine for the cool touch of winter. Effortlessly, today's matters are lost when tomorrow comes. And every year, when the chill became severe, Mira recalled that a quilt had to be made for her mother-in-law. But by then the winter had half gone. Had she ordered one then, it would have taken not less than three weeks for the quilt to be delivered. It would be best if the quilt were sent to her next year before the advent of winter, so she'd be able to use it for the entire season.

So each year around the middle of winter, Mira or Manmath would remember the quilt they had promised Nirmala. Each accused the other for being negligent. Their plans for the quilt were left for the following year. Gradually, Mira consoled herself with the thought that the quilt was not that essential for her mother-in-law. Otherwise, wouldn't she herself have reminded Mira about it? Then, one day, some thought made Manmath exclaim, "Oh, let it be! If the winter is that severe, Mother has her blanket to cover herself with. What use is a quilt when the night is drawing to a close?"

In reality, Manmath sensed that the night was nearing its end. Mira felt that too. Manmath and his wife brought the old lady from her village so she'd be with them when the end came. Nirmala had not forgotten to pack her blanket along with her other belongings when she left her village. How could she have parted with it in those final days, when she had lavished such motherly care on it through the years?

Nirmala often shivered from the fever that attacked her. She suffered from the extreme cold that seemed to enter her bones. Her patched-up cotton sheets were useless. One day, Manmath took the blanket out of Nirmala's trunk and covered her frail and trembling body. "Why do you treasure it, Mother?" he asked. "You never used it even for a day." His voice was choked with emotion. A mist formed in front of his eyes. Eagerly, Nirmala pulled the blanket close to her and answered, "If you feel unhappy, my son, then here you are. I'll use it from now on until my death. But you are here beside me. What harm is there if the blanket goes with me to the burning ground? Let all your ills, troubles, and dangers rest in this blanket. Let them be mine. I have prayed for this all my life. Let God be your refuge from this moment on. It's time for me to rest."

Nirmala closed her eyes and let the warm caress of the blanket seep into her aching bones. A calm entered her heart, and she asked herself, Who said a quilt was more comfortable? If I'd known earlier that Manu's blanket would be so warm, I would have used it long ago. But I feel my winter is coming to its end . . . From her closed eyelids two tears silently trickled down her cheeks in contentment perhaps, or in pain.

Mira felt satisfied that her mother-in-law had, at last, made use of the blanket. But for how long? The doctor had predicted fifteen days, or a month at the most. Everyone admired the blanket Nirmala used, and friends and relatives were convinced that the son and daughter-in-law had not ill-treated her. Mira recalled how her mother-in-law had spoken of the blanket being taken to the burning ground. For according to ritual, all the dead person's possessions—mattress, pillow, and sheets—were taken by the *dhobi* [washerman] before the pyre was lit. Would such a remarkable blanket end this way? The thought totally upset Mira. The impending loss of the blanket was greater torment indeed than the death of Nirmala. No one could go against the laws of the world, but one could certainly prevent the blanket's falling into strange hands.

A solution occurred to Mira at last. She reasoned that there was no harm in it. She pulled a clean white cover over her own quilt and covered Nirmala with it when she was asleep. She removed the English blanket. Let the quilt go with the dhobi, she told herself. Making another was no problem at all. But to replace this matchless blanket was quite impossible!

Nirmala awakened from sleep with a start. The first thing she noticed was the missing blanket. Distraught, she began to rave, "My blanket! Where's my blanket?"

Mira caressed her mother-in-law's feet. "So often you have asked us for a quilt. But we haven't been able to make you one through sheer negligence. This one is my own. Your English blanket will not be enough to suppress your shivers and keep you warm. So I have stored it away carefully in your trunk."

Nirmala asked, "Where's Manu?"

"He's here in the house. He took leave from the office because you're ill. He doesn't go out of the house," Mira explained indulgently.

Nirmala felt relieved. She went on weakly, "Well, if Manu is here, why do I need the blanket? Let it be where it is. But what will you do in this winter chill? You gave away your own quilt just because I asked you for one long ago!" The old woman's voice sounded worried.

Mira's answer came through faintly. "The winter is almost over. I can manage somehow. But you need the quilt more than we do now. What spasms keep racking your body!"

Nirmala stretched out her hand and fondly patted Mira's cheek. Blessings seemed to pour forth from her weakened eyes. "How very thoughtful you are, my child. Your goodness of heart will never go unrewarded. God will bless you always."

Tears shone in Nirmala's eyes. Inside her feverish palm, Mira's hand was bathed in sweat. It seemed to be growing weaker.

That night, Manmath wanted to know why Mira had given away

her quilt. She repeated the words she had said earlier to her mother-in-law. But her voice was barely audible as she spoke, the words unclear. Somehow all her excitement about the blanket had diminished. One single thought kept fouling her mind—that she had lied to her mother-in-law while she lay on her deathbed, that she had succumbed to the temptation of a mere blanket! And Mira had received all her blessings from that simple, truthful heart, despite her own deceitful words.

Nirmala's life came to an end a few days later. She used the quilt until her death. She would point to the quilt when relatives came to visit her and say, "A present from my daughter-in-law! Who knows what she is using herself in this chill! What a generous, thoughtful girl, my Mira!" And there was praise for Mira all around.

The blanket was totally Mira's after the old lady's death. Mira had at first wanted to place it in her bedroom, where it would look grand. But strangely, she, like Nirmala, aired the blanket in the sun, packed it with mothballs, and stored it away on the lowest shelf of her cupboard. Manmath laughed at her actions. "Women are all of the same mind. And you were the one to accuse Mother! For whom do you treasure it now? Mother laid it aside all these years, and whom does it serve now?"

Mira's voice grew soft, trembled. "Well, that's all we have left of Mother." Mira's eyes clouded with tears. And Manmath was amazed by his wife's esteem for his mother; why, he never had had an inkling of it when she was alive! How little he actually knew of Mira, he thought, even though he had been living with her all these years!

At times he told her, "If you would use that blanket, Mira, I'd sleep better perhaps."

"Why?" Mira asked, and Manmath answered, "Even though Mother used it for only a few days, every strand of it exudes the scent of her body. When it's aired in the sun, the unmistakable scent is everywhere. One doesn't feel she is dead, but is here, moving around the house. If you use it beside me at night, Mother's presence will put me to sleep. Somehow, with increasing age, I haven't been able to get to sleep lately."

Mira tried often to use the blanket. She tried to erase certain thoughts from her mind. But when her eyes closed, the blanket's weight lay heavy upon her chest. A choking sensation gripped her at times. The words of her mother-in-law as she lay close to death, like a benediction, became more oppressive and burdensome with the days. And she thought, A simple deceit, a single lie I uttered once—for that, do I have to pay such a terrible penalty? Why hadn't she thought of that before? Now it wasn't easy to express her agony before her husband or children, or even her friends. Her unspoken anguish began to torment her. How petty she would appear were this known! All the years she had nursed her mother-in-law would vanish into nothingness at the admission of that single lie. She could imagine people pointing their fingers at her, saying what a small mind she had—to have pulled a mere imported blanket off her mother-in-law's wasted body! And how the dying woman had to bear the harsh winter with a torn old quilt!

When the blanket was aired in the sun, the neighbors admired it and spoke of its exceptional quality. And Mira remarked with a dismal look in her eyes, "That's the only memory of Mother we have." But her throat dried up, her vision blurred. They withdrew, talking of Mira's love and respect for the dead lady. But Mira's heart cringed inside in her grief.

In time, Mira's repressed sorrow increased even further. Then, one day, she fell ill with a high fever. Her fever continued and she began to shiver. Her body slowly weakened. The doctor failed to diagnose her malady. The blood tests showed nothing wrong. One day Manmath came home early and found her lying nearly unconscious. He felt her forehead, found it was burning. Her feet were clammy and cold to his touch. She trembled a little in her sleep. He thought she might be feeling a chill. The thick winter quilts were in locked trunks in the storage room, so he took his mother's blanket off its shelf in the cupboard and covered Mira with it. He had a feeling that his mother's blessing would soon see Mira to recovery. Mira slept on for a long time. When she awoke and noticed her mother-in-law's blanket on her body, she began to scream. She flung the blanket to the floor. Her body shook. "How did this blanket get here? Who covered me with it?" she cried. Manmath saw the look in Mira's eyes and suddenly felt afraid. Perhaps her fever had shot up, perhaps she was hallucinating. Gently, he sat her down. He picked the blanket up from the floor. His voice was soothing. "You were shivering from the cold. There was nothing else I could find. I thought that if I covered you up with Mother's blanket, you'd get well soon. Why are you upset about this?"

Mira's voice was unsteady. "Please, for God's sake, don't ever cover me with that blanket."

"But why?" Manmath's surprised voice echoed in her ears.

"That is all we have of Mother, that memento," she mumbled. "With what care she preserved it all those years." Tears started flowing from

Mira's eyes. She could not restrain them. But she could not say anything. Manmath's eyes brimmed too as the memories flooded in, feeling the love and regard he perceived in Mira's heart at the moment. He held her close and added, "Let it be as you say. We'll keep the blanket with care. If you'd like to keep Mother's memory alive, why should I destroy it?" A moment later he said, "Mira dear, how generous you are! Really, how much you have cared for my mother!"

Mira's eyes grew hazy again with tears. She said incoherently, "Oh, don't ever say that please. It pains me a lot. Please. Wasn't she my mother as well?"

Manmath sat, overwhelmed by Mira's words. Mira felt she would rot inside in agony. How could she get a little peace? How could she free herself from this torment once and for all?

When one takes a nap on a winter afternoon, a chill seems to envelop the body. Mira's fever had persisted through many days; it had not ever completely left her. She suffered from shivers in her bones whenever she rested, especially during the afternoon, when the thought of the blanket would bear down upon her as a load on her mind. She'd think of her mother-in-law and the graces she had showered on Mira, and her mind would turn to her own deceit—to be swallowed up again, in unbearable agony. One day Mira grew restless. She suddenly seemed to hear someone's call, poignant and faint, outside the house. Must be the beggar woman, she thought. Mira usually felt irritated when she heard the old woman's voice. But on this afternoon, she walked up to the veranda and asked, "What is it you want? Haven't I told you often that there would be no rice left if you came this late in the afternoon?"

The old woman said piteously, "I'm not begging for a bowl of rice today. But if you could kindly give me something to cover myself with, something torn and old, anything you have, God will bless you, my daughter. The old man will not last long in this chill. One can live without food for three days, but this merciless cold will not let us survive. It turns the bones to ice." She dabbed at her eyes. "If you won't let me have something, the old man will surely never live through this night. And he's had a fever for the past four days."

Mira simply stood there, motionless, for a long while. She didn't know what to say. Could the old man possibly survive with a thin cotton sheet? Mira turned round abruptly and went in, opened her cupboard, and brought out her precious blanket. With firm steps, she walked to the front gate and placed the blanket in the old woman's outstretched hands. Her own heart seemed to open out, expand. Her voice was husky when she said, "Here, this is my mother-in-law's memento. I am not being generous. But if you are going to bless me, say a prayer for my mother-in-law, that she may rest in peace."

The beggar woman was stunned. She couldn't believe her eyes. Was this real or all a dream? In a frightened voice, she pleaded, "I am a mere beggar. What will I do with such a thing? I wanted only a torn, tattered sheet."

Mira was firm. "I cannot take back what I've given you already. It is a blanket. Do use it. I am sure your old man will recover. Take it and go your way."

Manmath had just come back from his office. The disbelief in his voice was obvious. "What have you done, Mira! Our only memento of Mother—and you gave it away! You could have given something else. But to hand over Mother's memory . . . I find it hard to understand you."

Mira asked the beggar woman to leave and shut the gate. She walked into the house ahead of Manmath. Without looking at him, she said, "It's our only memento of Mother, but it doesn't necessarily mean that it should be kept under lock and key. I think I've used Mother's memory in the best possible way. Every year, do you remember, Mother used to give away her hand-sewn cotton sheets and old clothes to the poor? I gave the blanket away so that Mother's soul would rest in peace. I feel certain that the woman's blessings will fall on her in that other world . . ."

Manmath reached for her hand. He touched her forehead and said excitedly, "You don't have a fever today, Mira! I feel so relieved."

The intense tone of Mira's voice softened Manmath. "No, I don't have fever. But there's a pain inside me, a pain that persists somewhere."

Manmath's heart melted in sympathy. He said, "But the doctor insisted there was nothing wrong with you. If one could only·look into the heart . . ."

Pale, he began searching for the pain in Mira's heart.

Translated by Jayanta Mahapatra.

PRATIBHA SATPATHY ————————

(b. 1945)   *Oriya*

The first five years in Pratibha Satpathy's life were spent in the picturesque and idyllic surroundings of Koraput, Orissa. Her father was Gopal Chandra Praharaj, a famous writer and the founder-editor of the monumental Oriya encyclopaedia. In 1950, when Pratibha was five, she moved with her parents to the village of Satyabhamapur on the coast, so that she might attend a proper school. As a child, she studied Odissi, the classical dance form of Orissa, and soon gained enough expertise to perform. She went on to study science in Ravenshaw College at Cuttack. After marriage, she received a master's degree in Oriya in 1967 and started working as a lecturer at a local college. In 1980 she earned a doctorate in Oriya literature from Utkal University.

Pratibha Satpathy began writing poetry while still in school. Her themes are ones familiar to any reader of modern poetry—nature, love, impermanence, and loneliness. Writing about her work, she says she is in search of a world different from the one she inhabits, a world free of hatred, envy, cruelty, and violence. The poem translated here is one of many that augur another place, even as the poet remains immured in the ordinary world.

Her first book of poems, *Sesha Janha* (The Last Moon), was published in 1962. Five more collections have appeared, the most recent, *Nimishe Akshara* (Fleeting Letters), published in 1985. Pratibha Satpathy has also published two translations: Pearl Buck's *The Hidden Flower* and a monograph of Kalhana, the twelfth-century poet-historian.

◆

KAKARA TOPA
(Dew Drop)

The tender green grew around me;
a pure dew-drenched scent
drifted over my moth-eaten body.

The star-written sky
grew dark;
someone was wiping it clean
with quick hands.

Today, with no walls or roofs,
my fate smolders, like a log,
unconcerned.
It is dawn already now,
but darkness clings.

I don't remember
having worn fresh flowers last night.
How can I account then
for this garland round my neck?
Where has it all gone?
The lovelessness and disbelief,
and that impatience
I have known so well?

Strange words fall from my lips
like some shy smile or pearly drop;
a tryst with the wind
lightens this body.
Can one be reborn
in the course of a single night?

My oil-slick hair falls loose,
what is it that sways
in the breeze over my right arm?
A peacock feather? Whose is it?
Where has it come from?
Will I call out to time?
Entreat the night not to end,
for an hour's wait
will not make the earth motionless;
I will implore the sun
to dry, just for once,
the truth and dream lines on my palms.
I'll implore my lover not to smile
nor to eye me with mistrust.

But what strange room is this,
with neither walls nor roof?
What unearthly touch,
possessing neither body nor voice?

What strange dream
that can neither be explained nor resolved?

No common souvenir,
this—
a drop of dew, pellucid,
waiting for sunlight.

Translated by Jayanta Mahapatra.

VEENA SHANTESHWAR ─────────────

(b. 1945)   *Kannada*

"Until the late seventies, the heroines of my stories were rebels against
established society and conventional morality, but the heroines in the more
recent stories are women who are compelled to compromise with life,
perhaps because of late I have a feeling that however independent and
aggressive and powerful an Indian woman may be, she has still to go a
long way before she is liberated in the real sense. At present a liberated
woman is an outcast in our society, a miserable creature, with no sympathy or support from anywhere . . . perhaps this is a transitional period.
She is yet to emerge as the truly New Woman who can defy everything
that binds her and yet be happy. It's a slow, painful, trying, and uphill
task," says Veena Shanteshwar, who is among the most highly regarded
of writers in Kannada today. She continues the new wave of women's
writing started by Rajalakshmi Rao (b. 1934) who, after publishing a collection of twelve short stories, *Sangama* (Confluence), n.d., withdrew into
a religious life. Rajalakshmi Rao's work explored the inner life of women.
Her focus, the critic Kirthinath Kurthakoti writes, was on the subtlety of
formal exploration rather than on plot. Although Veena Shanteshwar's
fiction is more realistic than formalist, her stories also reveal the work of
a careful artist. She has a sure sense of dialogue and is able to reach,
through the few words spoken by her characters, into a complex fabric of
the unsaid.

Veena Shanteshwar was born and educated in Dharwar in northern Karnataka. She studied English literature in college and now teaches it at the
University in Dharwad. She began writing when she was seven. Romance
and adventure mark her juvenilia, and the themes and the style of her
writing changed as she came in touch with the progressive literature
movement in Karnataka and, later, with the feminist movement.

Her first book of short stories, *Mullugalu* (Thorns) appeared in 1968. It was followed by *Koneya Dari* (The Last Way) in 1972 and *Kavalu* (Crossroads) in 1976, which was awarded the Karnataka Sahitya Academy Award and from which the story translated here is taken. With the publication of the short novel, *Gandasaru* (Men) in 1975, a bold attempt at depicting the exploitation of women, Veena Shanteshwar came to be known as a feminist writer. In 1984 she published a collection of short stories, *Hasivu* (Hunger), and a novel, *Soshane, Bandaya, Ityadi* (Exploitation, Revolt, and So On). Her latest novel, *Adrishta* (Luck), appeared in 1990. She has also translated stories from English into Kannada and has published a large collection of women's writings in Kannada, *Lekhakiyara Kathasankalana* (A Collection of Stories by Women Writers), 1983. Her own fiction has been translated into several languages and adapted for television.

◆

AVALA SVATANTRYA
(Her Independence)

Saturday. She had been feeling heavy in mind and body since afternoon, and kept gazing impatiently at the clock. She heaved a sigh of relief when it was at last half past five, and rose hurriedly, gathering up her bag, her small umbrella, and her lunchbox. She rushed out without waiting for her companions, automatically smoothing down her hair before the mirror that hung by the door. Worrying that she would be late for the six o'clock local train, she looked at her watch and walked more quickly. As she stepped onto the main road, a bus bound for the station came to a halt before her. She was naturally tempted. But wiser counsel prevailed, and she reasoned that she could buy some spinach for the thirty paisa she would save. The station was not even a mile away. She could walk the distance in less than fifteen minutes. Her spirits lifted; it was Saturday, and Shankar would be home. He loved anything with spinach in it.

She still had a couple of hundred yards to cover when she thought she heard someone hailing her. She walked on resolutely. But the voice reached her with renewed vigor. "Hey, Vimala!"

She stopped and looked back. It was Shashi Kulkarni, who taught at the Girls' Training College. There were three other women with her, all wearing white khadi. Vimala supposed that they were members of Bhagini Seva Sadan, the women's group just started by Shashi.

"My goodness, Vimala, how fast you walk! At this rate, why do you need to take a train from Hubli to Dharwad? Even on foot you could reach your house in Malamaddi in ten minutes!"

Managing a tired smile, she asked, "What's the matter, Shashi? Why do you pursue me so relentlessly? Look, be quick. I can't afford to miss this train."

"Why should I delay you and invite the wrath of your husband and children? Actually, we wanted to meet you at your office, but you'd already left. That's why we're running after you like this. We at Bhagini have our annual meeting tomorrow and . . ."

"I'm sorry, Shashi, but you know it's impossible for me to leave the house on a Sunday."

"I know, but this is no ordinary program. Since this is International Women's Year, we want to make it a very special affair. The collector himself has agreed to preside. You, you will be one of the guests. You must speak—for about fifteen minutes . . ."

"Shashi, you must understand—I haven't done that for ages. Besides, I've neither the inclination nor the time now."

A look of surprise mingled with regret crossed Shashi's face.

"How strange to hear you speak this way, Vimala. I can't believe you are the same person who used to talk about working for women's upliftment, women's emancipation not so long ago! Surely you don't think of our work like some others do—as propaganda or a passing fashion. You know that women, especially middle-class women like you and me, face thousands of problems. . . . In all of Hubli or Dharwad, there's no better person than you to talk about these things."

"Please Shashi, don't force me to speak." She sounded a little desperate.

"I won't take no for an answer. You simply must show up. It's at the town hall tomorrow evening. You can even appear just at six."

"Look, you know my husband's been transferred to Belgaum. He's home only on the weekend. How can I . . ."

"Oh, come on. Married for a decade, mother of three, and yet not ready to miss an evening with your husband? No wonder men get so swollen-headed. You must come tomorrow."

[They arrive at the station.] The train whistled shrilly. Vimala jumped and collapsed onto a seat without having said a word to Shashi and the others.

Having reached home, she washed, changed her sari, and was making tea when the baby began to wail. Raju, too, had raised his voice in protest: "When I say I won't give it to you, I mean it. Mother got this ball specially for me." Her tired body demanded a cup of tea, and she made no move to console the kids. She proceeded to strain her tea, hoping that her father-in-law would stop his chant of "Hare Krishna,

Krishna Hare" and attend to them. Nothing like that happened. The child's wailing reached the skies. In a fit of anger she rushed out, wanting to silence the three children with blows. Just then, Shankar entered. She checked herself. The children stopped screaming when they saw their father. She tried to smile as she bent to pick up his briefcase. With a touch of impatience, he said, "What the hell's going on here? Their rumpus could be heard down the street. Here you are—educated, a graduate—I had thought you'd be able to bring up the children well. I even agreed to a small dowry. But you've done nothing for them— they're so undisciplined and unruly!"

Picking up the youngest child and the briefcase, she went in without saying a word.

Having given everyone something to eat and drink, she sat down in the kitchen. It was nearly eight. As she kneaded the chapati dough, she suddenly remembered: there had been three memos from the Life Insurance Corporation. The premium on Raju's policy was also overdue. She never found the time to do it on working days. Perhaps Shankar could help. Also, the baby needed to go to the doctor for a checkup. She wondered how the child had spent the days with his grandfather . . . Also, Neelu needed cloth for her uniform . . . This could be done in the evening. Maybe in the morning Shankar could go to the depot and get some firewood. Kerosene had become scarce lately. Besides, the monsoon was about to begin.

"Vimala Bai, could you get me some water?" The weak voice of the father-in-law. She was reminded of the doctor's words: "These repeated attacks of stomachache could mean appendicitis. Why don't you ask your husband to bring him over to the clinic? I'll give him a thorough checkup. An operation might be necessary." At least this Shankar must do.

It was half-dark in the kitchen. She started suddenly as a pair of arms encircled her. "What are you doing? The children . . ." she remonstrated.

The arms drew her closer. While her body responded half-heartedly, she extricated herself. "There's the cooking to be done. We mustn't keep Father-in-law waiting for his meal."

Releasing her, he said complainingly, "It's always children, Father-in-law, cooking—Have I no place in your life?"

The children, the father-in-law, the cooking—Whom are they for and whose—she pushed back the retort and bent over the chapatis.

After dinner the kids began to clamor for their bedding. Reclining in a chair and smoking, Shankar said, "For heaven's sake, can't you see to what they want? They're giving me a headache."

She attended to the children, closed the main door, spread out the mattress for her father-in-law, and went to finish the chores in the kitchen. Shankar followed her in, yawning widely, "Now don't sit scouring the dishes for hours. Just leave them aside. I'm already sleepy." She continued her work, pretending not to have heard.

Lack of space forced them to sleep in the kitchen. When Shankar worked in Dharwad, they had had roomy and comfortable quarters. There the mice did not trouble them at night. There they did not need to rise before dawn to fill the buckets. But ever since Shankar's transfer, the problems had piled up. The salary he drew as a supervisor was insufficient to keep them going—ill-health, growing children, the loan to buy a plot of land, the marriage of his sister—no, it was not enough. So she held fast to her clerical job in a bank in Hubli. And the law that says working couples have a right to live in the same town? Shankar, too, was seeking a transfer to Dharwad—or was he? Perhaps he had forgotten. Must remind him . . .

Yes, I must confide in him. I cannot bear these responsibilities alone. I've been crumbly lately both in body and in mind. Please come away here. Soon . . . I've had enough . . . But I can't stop my tears. It doesn't matter, even if I trouble him.

It was late when she went to bed. He did not give her a chance to speak . . .

When she could breathe again, she said in a low, tired voice, "Shankar . . ."

"There you go again—'When will you get your transfer?'—isn't that it?"

All of a sudden she wondered whether he was really trying to get a transfer. Perhaps he was reluctant to come back to all these problems, perhaps he did not want a transfer . . . She turned again to him, and held him by the shoulders.

"Shankar . . ."

"I'm awfully sleepy, Vimala. Let's talk in the morning. I promise to listen to you. Only, don't disturb my sleep."

She was silent. The husband's snores, the father-in-law's groans from outside, the scrabbling of mice, the blowing wind . . . She could not sleep.

Somewhere a clock chimed two. Another two hours. Must fill the buckets. The dratted taps go dry before six in the morning. The baby wakes at six. Sleep after that is impossible. Father-in-law would want his tea by half past six.

Turning, she looked at her husband, stretched out on the mattress. He seemed content. He still looked young except for a slight graying at the temples, and he had not lost his zest for life. And she was six years younger, but already an old woman. The past two years had been extremely trying—housework, the office, looking after the children, shuttling between Hubli and Dharwad . . . Yet the mirror tells me I'm no longer the old Vimala. The lined face, the gray hair, the tired body and mind. All my energy is gone.

She rose at dawn to turn on the taps. Shankar stirred. "What the hell are you up to at this hour?" he grumbled.

She was reminded of the early days of their marriage, of how he used to come help her draw water at the well. They had gone to visit his parents in their village . . . She smiled . . . He got up abruptly and joined his son, who was sleeping in the outer room.

Shankar rose only when the others had eaten their breakfast. Serving him tea, she said, "Please go to the firewood depot later. With the monsoon approaching, we must have a stock of fuel. Later, you must go see Dr. Athavale. Your father's having a lot of trouble with his stomach."

"Isn't there a doctor next door? Why can't you find some time and take him there? Some women are so very efficient, but look at you. You never get anything done."

"What shall I do?" she burst out helplessly. "There's the insurance money to be paid, the uniforms to get, the baby's health to be seen to, pending accounts at the office to be completed . . ."

"That's enough. I come here only on the weekend, and even then there's no peace. I'm more at home in my room at the Belgaum lodge." He got up in a huff.

From outside, she heard the soft voice of her father-in-law. "Why are you so edgy, Son? She's all alone, poor woman, working both in the house and outside. As for yourself, you live away from all this. Why don't you help a little, at least when you're here? Tomorrow's Monday. Nobody will object if you go a bit late to your office. Just finish that insurance work before you leave."

Shankar did not speak.

In a little while, Patil dropped by in search of his friend Shankar. As Vimala served them tea, Patil implored, "Please let Shankar come with me. There's a good English movie showing this morning. It's been ages since we went out together."

"Oh, sure. Who am I to object?"

The others finished their afternoon meal and Vimala sat down to wait for her husband. She remembered Shashi's invitation. No, better get some work done in the evening. After that, if he's free, we can take the children out, she planned.

Shankar rushed in. "Isn't lunch ready yet? Be quick. Our junior engineer's car is leaving for Belgaum at two o'clock. I want to join them."

Vimala halted in her tracks.

"What's the hurry? Can't you stay till morning?" her father-in-law asked.

"And stand for more than two hours in line just to get a bus ticket? Anyway, the car's empty. I might as well go in it."

He ate in a hurry. Picking up his briefcase, he took leave of his father. Vimala followed him outside. "Next week there's a holiday— it's the second Saturday. Will you come down on Friday then?"

He said in an offhand manner, "Let's see. Even on a holiday there's always work to do." He added sarcastically, "What do I come and do here the whole day? Even you aren't interested these days."

He waved to the children. Vimala watched till he turned the corner.

She thought of her father-in-law's remarks: "Lives alone . . . far away . . ." Belgaum, the lodge, who knows how he lives, what he does . . . The insurance policy, the monsoon, fuel, the baby's fever, Father-in-law's stomachache, cooking, office, the local train . . . She sank down, momentarily overwhelmed.

"Our country has been free for a quarter of a century now. And yet we find our women bound in slavery. The causes: 25 percent tradition, another 25 percent circumstances, and the remaining 50 percent men (applause). This is International Women's Year. The year in which women must awake to self-consciousness. We must open our eyes to the realities around us. We must protest against the injustices we suffer. At no time and for no reason must we give in. Only then. . . ."

Hubli's town hall was filled with women that Sunday evening. They listened to Shrimati Vimala Shankar with curiosity, and with admiration.

Translated by Seemanthini Niranjana and Tejaswini Niranjana.

VAIDEHI

(Janaki Srinivas Murthy, b. 1945)   *Kannada*

"Her writing is a new milestone in Kannada literature," writer Vijaya
Dabbe says of Vaidehi's fiction, which began to appear in Kannada periodicals in the mid-seventies. Today she has three collections of short stories—*Mara Gida Balli* (Tree, Bush, and Creeper), 1979; *Antarangada Putagula*
(Pages from Deep Within), 1984; and *Gola* (Globe), 1986—an award-
winning novel, *Asprushyaru* (Untouchables), 1982, and a book of poems,
Bindu Bindige (Drop Pot/Droplet), 1990, to her credit. Her finely etched
portraits of inner life are always unusual and sometimes startling, and give
a reader the sense of having had a new and genuine experience. She gives
the impression that she does not argue for or against anything, but explores the complexity of human life. "However much we understand, we
are thrown into a world of mystery—that is Nature. And that is the nature
of the individual also. . . . I feel that the domineering old faiths are withering away and my inner voice begins to be audible, as if from a distance. . . . What a long journey it has been just to hear one's inner voice!
I may have traveled long to get to the source of this voice . . . but the
quest has been as good as the quest for the knowledge of the whole universe," she writes.

Vaidehi was born in Kundapura, a small town in Karnataka, and grew
up in a very large family. Her mother, "sensitive and intelligent, truthful
come what may, but at the same time kindhearted," was her father's second wife and the focal point of the family. "For us she was a strict dis-
ciplinarian. Like all mothers in the world, she taught the children how to
preserve the dignity of the family and uphold its reputation." Vaidehi's
father, a busy lawyer, wouldn't touch his food until he had recited the
prescribed number of verses from the writings of the bhakti poet Tulsi-
das. He was never harsh or violent with the children, but there was such
an aura around him that he had only to ask, "What's all this?" and tears
would rise to their eyes. "Whenever I think of my father, it is the picture
of my mother—leaning against a pillar, hungry, eyes heavy with sleep but
trying to hold it back, waiting for Father to finish his daily routine of
recitation before they could eat—that comes to my mind," Vaidehi writes.

It was in this large, traditional house, teeming with children, servants,
guests, relatives, and family friends that Vaidehi grew up. Nobody worried about the children's studies. After school and lunch, it was time for
play. The *bimbla* tree with its short spreading branches, the swing on the

mango tree, the dark corners of the room stacked with hay, the attic where the huge old vessels and the trunks were stored, the cows, the calves, and the water-buffaloes made up the children's world. The cradle, "ever-swinging and almost nonstop, the secluded room meant for girls on 'monthly leave' (and it was always occupied by two or three in turn) . . . the guests, the festivities . . . this house of mine, was it not a specimen of the whole world? A miniature, typical world?" she asks. "As I look back, I feel proud of this house—an abode of all the *rasas,* bound together by love and affection, bigger than any big house . . . but with a difference."

As a little girl growing up in this large, rambling family, Vaidehi was "always stricken by a restlessness and filled with emotions that are difficult to explain." She was an introvert, apprehensive about her capabilities, always whispering to herself. Her brother A. S. N. Hebbar helped infuse confidence into her. When she wanted to go to college, her mother first made her promise not to have an "affair" there. " 'Oh, Mother, you can't understand,' I seemed to say—but she understood more, really, than what I thought I understood."

However, the "real vision of the plight of Indian women came to me during the thirteen years I spent in the house of my parents-in-law. I was fortunate, though, to have a husband who allowed me the freedom to have pen and paper as my closest companions," she says.

Vaidehi has translated two important feminist books from English into Kannada: Kamaladevi Chattopadhyay's *Indian Women's Struggle for Freedom,* 1983, and Maitraiyee Mukhopadhyay's *Silver Shackles,* 1985.

The story translated here, first published in *Taranga* in 1986, was written after an open-air performance of what is perhaps the best-known play in Indian literature: Kalidasa's fifth-century Sanskrit classic, *Shakuntala.* The characters and incidents in the story here drawn out of Shakuntala by her sympathetic (feminist?) visitor from the twentieth century all are from the original play. But as Vaidehi recreates it in a language meant to echo Kalidasa's own much-acclaimed lyric prose, the perspective shift and insight gained with each episode reveals its secret, untold story—and Kalidasa's partisan interests.

In skeletal summary, the plot is commonplace: Dushyanta, a powerful king out hunting in the forest, meets Shakuntala and her two close friends *(sakhi),* Anasuya and Priyamvada, who live in the forest *ashram* (hermitage) of Kanva, a renowned hermit/scholar and foster father to Shakuntala. Dushyanta steps forward in response to an involuntary cry for help from Shakuntala, who is attacked by a bee. They are instantly attracted to each other. He uses a trivial excuse to call off the hunt, and remains at the ashram. Their romance, exquisitely portrayed by Kalidasa, is the most celebrated in classical courtly literature. Dushyanta asks that Shakuntala marry him and promises that she will always be his supreme love. But an unexpected summons arrives from his kingdom and he must return. Shakuntala is loath to accompany him without bidding farewell to Kanva, who is away on a journey. Dushyanta goes reluctantly, and leaves behind a ring as a token of his love. Lost without him, Shakuntala wanders through the forest in a daze. She offends a visiting hermit, Durvasa, who curses her. Shakuntala is with child and—encouraged by Kanva, who has returned and foretells that Shakuntala will give birth to a son who will rule the world—she decides to go to Dushyanta. But because of the curse of Durvasa, Dushyanta no longer even recognizes her. She has lost the ring, and there is no way she can prove her claim. Shakuntala is carried away to heaven, but meanwhile a fisherman finds the ring in the belly of a carp. With the sight of the ring Dushyanta's memory is restored and he is stricken with remorse and lovesickness. Indra, king of the gods, sends a messenger to bring him to heaven, where he is reunited with Shakuntala and his son. Reconciled, they return to earth.

SHAKUNTALE YONDIGE KALEDA APARAHNA
(An Afternoon with Shakuntala)

Sitting on the mud-floored veranda of Hemakut, Shakuntala continued, ". . . 'Tell me,' you say. What should I tell you? Where can I begin, and how?

"Well . . . Kanva was away that day. And Dushyanta came. He came like the very splendor of spring. Who was he? I did not know. But the moment I set eyes on him, it felt as if I had known him for eons. Shall I say that was the first illusion? I just floated away. As if I had been made only for him.

" 'Don't dream. Dreams will only turn to ash.' Who was this speaking? And from where? I traveled, searching through my heart, finding no one, but hearing only the voice. It grew fainter and fainter, and finally faded away. I became a canvas, waiting for the painting, a canvas beginning to glow with color. Who was he? Why did I allow him into me? The colors blended with one another and new shades emerged, new, deeper and denser shades. He painted on, never asking for meaning, just gazing at me. He closed his eyes and stood away. Then opened them and drew closer with a smile that would steal . . . I gave myself away. I was joy itself in the thought that I had offered my being to a supreme artist. It was not a dream, but something so real. So palpable.

"And then the bee buzzed and hummed and flew around me, weaving enchanting circles. I still remember that moment. Why did that bee appear there that day? To weave a snare of illusion around me? The people ascribed stories after their own heart to it, but was it the bee that circled around me or did I circle the bee? What matter. I was ensnared of my own will. That is an irrefutable truth.

"I needed him. Why? Not for his genius, not because he was the brightest jewel of Puru's dynasty, nor for himself. No—it was for myself that I wanted him, for my own sake. With all the natural sweetness, with all the warmth that suffuses the flower blossoming on a tree, the bird that sings to its mate, the deer that prances and frolics . . . But why all these trivial details? 'Do you know, my dearest,' I said to the *vanajyotsna* plant that I had nourished, 'do you know how purely, how intensely, Shakuntala loved Dushyanta the moment she saw him?' Shall I say it was a bond formed lifetimes ago? That thought comforted me, made me feel secure.

"Do I hear you exclaim, 'The foster child of Kanva, an innocent girl who grew up under his eyes, one who thought she would go, most willingly, wherever he bid her, small wonder she lost herself the instant she set her eyes on that hypnotic figure, strangely fascinating in the simplicity of the ashram!' Well, why should I hide anything from you?

"They were countless—the kings and emperors who came to visit my father, Kanva—countless, with eyes that moved with the wont of their age. This innocent Shakuntala, For whom has she been made? the whole world wondered, but not Shakuntala herself. She was not drawn to anyone. She had never felt a passion that overwhelmed her, made her want to lose her self and become one with another being. Even Kanva had not encouraged those who hinted at such things. 'My Shakuntala's husband,' he had once remarked, 'will be someone incomparable!' Feeling that I could not bear a separation, I said, 'Shakuntala will never leave you.' His smile turned serious in an instant. 'You should not say such things, my dearest,' he chided in a voice that was ever so soft, almost like one's inner voice.

"Do you suppose that an ashram—with its atmosphere of ideals, penance, self-control, and a hundred rituals—is inviolable? That everyone there is absolute master of himself, has conquered his mind and his body? No, no. It is not that easy to conquer the self. There was no dearth of young noviciate rishis who, despite their awe of Kanva, cast glances at me when he was away. But all they met was my indifference. Was there somewhere deep inside me a pride that even though my parents had both deserted me, I was, after all, the child of Vishwamitra and Menaka*? Now when I look back, I feel it must have been so. Days rolled by, in the warm company of my Vanajyotsna, the deer, Anasuya, and Priyamvada, in the soothing care of the compassionate Gautami, and showered with Kanva's fatherly affection—until Dushyanta arrived.

"He arrived . . .

"Everything else ceased to exist.

"The deer, the forest, the friends, Gautami, Kanva . . . and my own self too, my dearest self! I will not try describing the fire of that love, a fire unlike anything else, a fire that no words can ever wear out. Is there any need to describe the glow that quickens and sets a soul aflame?

"I saw Dushyanta before me.

"Did he see me too? No question.

"I imagined he did. Without a gesture, without any proof, I lost myself in him, as if all the softness and sweetness of nature and I were one. And he?

"I missed the lost, faraway look that abruptly clouded his brow. I was in no mood to notice it. But then one afternoon, when the earth, the sky, and the woods had faded away, an afternoon that was sloping toward evening, there was a warm shade. He sculpted the whole world into just me and him. His words shone like crystals. It was as if my appetite fed on itself and grew, as if my thirst slaked on itself and begged for more . . . Then . . ."

"Why? What happened then?"

"Dushyanta turned cold, rudely cold. Frozen like an immense, icy mountain. And I? I turned my face towards him like a little valley, cradled in his arms. 'It is not just one valley that the Himalayas cradle. They never cast a second glance at the valleys . . .' Voices, nameless voices kept edging in. This voice was silken, warm, brimming with motherly care. But I pushed it aside. It was all so true. I knew I should believe it, but could only turn away as if it were a lie. The voices went on—discordant, disturbing that secure repose. What could I do?

"He thawed as if with the sunshine. Did the waters cool the valley? An indolent anklet tinkled. Not a word was uttered. Passion spoke. The iceman lay back in my arms. A soft breeze wafted in. I questioned his closed eyelids. 'Asleep?' They did not quiver, but seemed to stand witness to something within.

---

*Menaka, an *apsara,* or divine nymph, seduced the royal rishi Vishwamitra, bore Shakuntala, and abandoned her.

"He murmured a name. I listened. Once more, the same name. Who is this Neeharika? Who is this who would not unclasp him even in his dreams? Whoever she be, she is not before me. Is she not? Really? I gazed upon his eyes again. They darted within, this way and that, capriciously. He was not to be awakened, he would wake himself.

"He did awaken, by himself. 'Oh,' he said, 'such a dream!' What kind of dream? But I said, instead, 'Dreaming of state matters?' He smiled. A smile that glowed with the warmth of just having kissed someone. Sakhi, he suddenly seemed a stranger to me.

"I gripped his hand, unable to bear it. He pulled it away, perhaps involuntarily. So, then? A thin, sharp fear pierced me. A faint clamor rose somewhere within me. I did not pay it heed. It is only now that I realize that I had paid it no attention at the time.

"The sun dipped to the west. I wanted only to be free of care.

"Anasuya was wiser. She questioned him directly. And did he not reply, 'I hold none dearer than Shakuntala, who will bring honor to my family, and Vasundhara, who has the very ocean as her girdle'? (Those words at least should have warned my senses against the man with many wives.)

"He shook my immersed self and asked me, 'And if what your friend asked that day is true? What will you do if you come to learn that I have loved many others?' Words choked my voice. Struggling free, I heard myself say, 'They are not there when I am with you, are they? And you haven't brought their memory here, have you? That's all I desire.' He laughed, a little too loudly. Why? A tender moonlight flooded in on us before I could find the answer. He encircled me. Like the bee, weaving circles of illusion.

"Or was it I who bound myself secure in those circles?

"Sweet moments dripped, drop by drop.

"How many?

"Not for me the burden of counting—let it be the world's.

"All measures are a chain of moments.

"My soul longs only for Dushyanta . . .

"The moonlight still played its intoxicating rhapsody. 'This is no sin,' he said. Conquered, I lay back against him. I gave . . . and I received. Was there even at 'that' moment a shrill, bitter voice trying to cry out amid all that sweeping sweetness? 'Child, isn't it probable that he is only trying to find someone else in you? Perhaps you are only a substitute?' a *shakuntala* bird seemed to ask tenderly. With a harsh wave of the hand, I banished the bird that I had raised with my own hands.

The bond with the land of my birth, the home of my growth, snapped suddenly. And I scaled the honeyed peaks.

"If only one could put time off, flicking it forward with one's little toes! He was to leave the next day. The duty of guarding the sacrificial rites was over. If only that night could have lasted forever. If only the whole world had ended that very day. Sakhi, how dark are the nights that follow the full moon!

"He was about to leave.

"I clasped him to me, ever so tightly. I said I would not let him go. Steeped in the passion of youth, I could see nothing else in the world.

"Did I say I clasped him tightly? He did not try to free himself. Nor did he press me closer. He stood silently, as if waiting for me to free him myself. I waved that flicker in my consciousness away. I laid my heart open: 'I cannot live without you, it would be like this forest without water. . . .'

"My voice poured out, deep and intense. And his voice seemed choked with venom, like Shiva's when he swallowed poison from the churning of the ocean. 'No, he can't be shared'—where did the voice come from? Did Neelakantha smile at someone even with Ganga in his arms? The soft smile playing on his lips told me the story of the many, so many, he had already given himself to.

"Listen to me, shakuntala birds! You should never grow up in an ashram! Listen to the pathetic story of Shakuntala's love, the story of one who was a nymph's blossom, a child of royal lineage who grew cradled in Nature's arms. After the glitter of the city, the jungle seemed barren.

" 'I know,' I said, 'You will forget me as soon as you go back to your capital.' He did not deny it, but promised he would send for me.

"He went away, leaving me his ring. The earth circled the sun, I do not know how many times! Dushyanta hid himself behind a veil of forgetfulness. My calls went unanswered. No message. No news. Not once did the yogi's eyes blink. The whole world seemed a huge, vacuous nothingness. 'You have too soft a heart. You should steel yourself,' he had said while leaving, when I had cried out, 'I cannot live without you. I shall lose my mind, my life.' But I did learn to steel my heart, to bear it all!

"I was alone.

"Should I have felt that loneliness so keenly? Kanva had not yet returned. Anasuya and Priyamvada could only banter, 'Oh, so you are lovesick! How could you deign to speak to us, O Empress!' They seemed to dance even on still feet. 'O my friends, may you, too, feel the soft caress of love, and suffer too its stinging shocks. And by the time you can recreate yourselves, renew your life, being stunned by the agony, all your young laughter, all this banter, will have vanished into darkness.'

"Have I, a young girl, grown so old that I should talk this way? Anasuya and Priyamvada are still children and they are the happy ones, the chirpy, cheerful birds.

"No, no. It is I who am really happy.

"I could already feel the tender feet of my daughter, Daushyanti, pushing against my womb.

"The hot, distracting air in the ashram rang with unwholesome words, sickening sneers—

" 'Whenever Dushyanta goes out hunting. . . .'

" 'What is she to the emperor? Sixteen thousand such. . . .'

"Why heed those I had only indifference for? I thought. Yet the words bruised my ears. His affairs, this one, that, and that . . . I would not believe any of it, but . . . but his silence mocked my faith, choked me with an inescapable conclusion.

"Hamsapadika—the tribal girl he had loved, the countless other Hamsapadikas who had adorned his youth, the Vasumathis of his palace, the Shakuntalas, and who was that Neeharika that he dreamt of? Whose was the name that he had whispered? And the wonder of it all was that there grew in me a love for them all, a wish to see them all, if only because Dushyanta had desired them.

" 'But'—the primeval word. Around it revolves all passions, weaknesses, vices, don't you agree? O heart, do not go seeking. Do not forget that you loved Dushyanta for himself. The difference between loving those he loves and loving him is enormous. One is natural, native to a human heart, and the other demands hard preparation.

"You, man with many wives, did you forget this Shakuntala who does not know how to forget? Say no, please say no.

"But he—he is the one who does not say no. One who, when I, torn with torture, yet affecting only a suspicion, said, 'You will forget me,' replied, 'Yes, of course,' as in playful love-talk. One who whispered, 'Why all these thoughts? You should give them no voice,' and smothered all my misgivings with a kiss.

"You who are a descendent of Puru, a king dedicated to truth, why did you tremble and sweat so when you kissed me? (There were tears in his royal eyes. He seemed so much a human being, not an emperor then.) I was so immersed in my love that I believed it was all for me. Why, then, did that dark-veiled fear, squatting silently in my heart, leave its corner and move ominously forward? It stood there and howled in my face, 'He has forgotten you.' When the light in my heart seemed to lose its life, I tried to console myself: 'Where love is, darkness is not.'

"Gautami was there. She understood my soul and nursed my body.

"Disconsolation struck at the very root of my life. I longed to talk, to unravel slowly the gossamer knots I had twisted myself into with someone who had gone past all depravities, to loosen and lose the chafing clasp around me, to release my old self and be reborn.

"I was waiting for this enlightened person.

"Where are you Kanva, my father?

"I sat rooted at the door of the ashram, gazing at the skies and beckoning to the clouds. They all sailed past uncaring. Then I heard the footsteps of Durvasa.

"Didn't the poet write his story as if I had never heard those feet approaching? The whole universe believed him. A universe that thirsts for the fires of falsehood but not the waters of truth, for the painted glitter of love but not its white purity. And the poet—he was a peerless talent; one who could afflict the world with his poetic lie! Will the world today believe Shakuntala as it does Kalidasa? Dushyanta's behavior can be explained away. But Shakuntala's heart? I can only say that this is a heart the worldly minded can never understand.

"Why would Durvasa have cursed me? He was an extraordinary sage, respected and admired for his anger against all injustice. He came often to our ashram. As a baby I used to climb into his lap with the baby deer. Caressing me, he would say, 'Can I find place for another cub beside you?' He gave his most earnest attention to my feelings. 'My child,' he had once said in the presence of Kanva, 'it is a rare life that knows no pain. May you be blessed with one such!' At these words Kanva had drawn me to him and had patted my back, a memory so fresh that even now I can feel his warm breath caressing my cheeks. Could he, who knew my heart to its last fathom, have known that I would tread such a path and plunge into such grief? (I would not say I was deceived. How could one point an accusing finger at Dushyanta?)

"Durvasa arrived when everybody was away.

"I did not leap up and run crying, 'Grandpa, my respects,' as was my habit. I sat still, watching him come. It did not occur to me that I should rise and speak and offer him due veneration. How long I had been without my senses! But the instant I saw him, a deep sigh heaved through me and I felt a great relief.

" 'My, my! What's wrong? My little Shakuntala bird seems so anxious!' he said with a strained laugh. I couldn't smile, either. He closed his eyes, fixed his inner vision on something, and blazed with wrath. My senses rushed back to me even as his lips quivered with speech.

" 'No, no, not that, Grandfather! He should live long as a protector of virtue,' I cried out, and he fell silent. It took a while for his anger to subside. He stroked my forehead gently. How clearly he could see my frozen grief! 'He is a master of clever forgetfulness,' he muttered, as if to himself. And then aloud, 'Child, you have with you the ring with his royal seal, don't you? Should it come to that, hold it to his face.' I felt an overpowering urge to climb into Grandfather's lap, rest against his shoulder, and cry myself out like a child. But where had my childhood run away to?

"Those in the ashram who watched his arrival from afar, saw him speaking to me, turning fiery, and departing abruptly, painted the scene with their own garish colors. No bridles held their fancy in check. With some story of a curse, the poet hid man's careless debauchery. And for all those men who are experts in selective memory, what an appealing tale it is, this tale that shelters you in its arms. A tale of forgetfulness, concocted by a man. Poetry swims in such temperate fancies that keep it warm.

" 'Karu priya sakhi vrittim sapatni jane,' Kanva pronounced.* It was then that grief overwhelmed me. The world sees the tears that well up at parting from one's beloved people. But what was to be my fate? To stand before the forgetful king and say, 'Remember me?' Why did Father, who knew all, pronounce this? Perhaps that, too, was a line that came easy on a tongue that spent the whole day in contemplation and chanting, 'Sahanavavatu, Sahanoubhunaktu.'** Is it a foolish desire I have, that I should drink life to its lees? I hope not. I looked at Kanva. Why was the sage so sad? Unable to share a thought with anyone, I hugged and kissed the deer. At least it would understand the mute language of misery.

"Before me was the promised shelter of Daushyanti.

"I stepped towards my husband's home.

---

*"Be friendly to women [they are your sisters]" (Kalidasa, *Sakuntalam*, act 4) is the advice Kanva gives Shakuntala before sending her to her husband's palace.

**"*Sahanavavatu, Sahanoubhunaktu*" are lines recited before and after studying the Upanishadic text. These go with the *Katha Upanishad* and read "May Brahman protect us both—teacher and disciple / May we relish the fruit of learning together."

"Gautami, Shargarava, and the others traveled the whole road with me talking endlessly. Not a word from me. The path seemed to grow longer with every step. This path is going to end, and, at the end, he will be there. Certainly? Yes, certainly. I comforted myself. 'The capital at last,' said Shargarava. I gazed around, wide-eyed. 'Is he here? Can I see him?' My soul laughed as it stealthily listened to my heart's yearning. 'You foolish girl,' it chided me, 'he is the king of kings, and doesn't show himself everywhere.' I joined in the laughter, replying, 'The heart that loves sees nothing but the loved one. If this be illusion, let that be my portion.' An excited warmth began to fill my senses.

"How did I cross the main gate, how did I enter, where did I reach him? I remember nothing.

"I remember only this, Sakhi.

"That moment when he, sitting on his throne, stared at the blank walls of the court, and said, with a casual wave of his hand, 'I've never seen this girl in my life.'

"What? What is it that happened to me?

"I became fire itself.

"The fire that struck at the very root of creation.

"O Goddess of Fire, you took birth from the turbulence seething within me.

"I was overwhelmed by a desire to shoot out fierce tongues of flame and burn him down to ashes, to cry, to howl, for all three worlds to hear. To stoke with my sorrow the suppressed grief of separation, and burn the whole universe down . . . so that life itself could never sprout again.

" '*Anarya!*'*

"Sakhi, the word stuck in my throat!

"Not a single word could find breath. Speech had burnt itself to dusty ash. I was struck, dazed.

"Why did that happen? In the blazing light of my wrath I quickly cast a searching eye into myself.

"And my dearest, beneath that raging fire there was still the cool stream of love flowing by itself ever so softly. With a timeless beauty, untouched, as if love were the only thing in life.

"I was not Menaka's daughter, nor offspring of a royal rishi, not even Kanva's foster child. I was Nature herself. I could only stand and stare in shock and stunned disbelief. No, no . . . What more shall I say

---

*Anarya means "non-Aryan; unworthy, inferior."

about a forgetfulness that can plunge the entire world into darkness? Words would lose all meaning.

"Dushyanta spoke as he did.

"Shargarava's response was scathing.

"Gautami grieved. 'Show him the ring,' she coaxed. But am I one so self-denying that I would beg love with the show of a ring? It would be impudence to refuse to hold the ring to his face. I pretended, duly upset, that it had been lost. Would a ring ever be an antidote to a memory so conveniently erased?

"(Memories of my father, Vishwamitra, and Menaka, my mother. Is the mother's fate revisiting the daughter? Will I, too, have to abandon my child in the thick of the forest . . . ? No, no! It shall not be. It is not only Menaka's blood that flows in me.)

"Yet, I kept searching his eyes.

"Sakhi, was I there in his eyes? I could see only the crafty art that had looked drunkenly on many like me and enticed them. What a chasm between this Dushyanta and that! That day, it was the man who was predominant over the king, and with such glory. But today, it was a mere emperor under a crown, without the faintest gleam of the human being, that I saw. This, probably, is how it has to be! Is it to give life to the man hidden deep within him that he leaves the capital so often and takes to the woods to hunt?

"I gazed intently at him. Had his mustache grown whiter? With light-hearted speech and joyful little gestures, affectations designed to obscure, he made as if his mind were without qualm. Did you say I'm imagining it all? That, I am not. You did not look so carefully and so long at Dushyanta that day. The mind that loves has a strange sensitivity. It picks up and scrutinizes every tiny tone, but once in a while with unseeing eyes it looks past things that loom large before it.

"As I turned my back on my husband's home, I found that convention had barred the path towards my father's ashram too. (Even had it not been so, I would not have claimed it.) I found refuge at Maricha's ashram. What is township or wood or hill for a solitary soul? And one that has denuded itself at that! In the womb, a joy grew that spat defiance at the very world. It anointed the cracked walls of the broken heart with a sublime thrill. I learned to live. I would not desert my little darling in the deep woods. I would not cry out for the earth to scream and swallow me.

" 'I shall lose my mind, my life, without you,' had I not said something like that, as I cried? He probably knew how stupid that all was. But I realized it only later. Life is something that eludes the grasp of thought, that blossoms just as it seems about to fall, dry and dead. Why hadn't I realized all this before? And, if you go searching, who is there who is not alone? Perhaps Dushyanta is a lonely being too. No, my soul, let me not hang limp on another's shoulders. I am grateful to him that he made me love so selflessly. I shall not tease or twist moments that have gone by.

"To down all bitterness, to live out all pain. To keep an equipoise of mind. Not at a single stroke, but step by step, living to the full every single tithe of life's cruel intensities.

"I became my own teacher, and my own pupil.

"My child, Sarvadamana, was born. Did his birth ease my pain? No pain can be avoided by mere resolve—it can only diminish as it subsides beneath one's consciousness, with the passing of time.

"I thought the pain had gone.

"But it rose up again, stirred and disturbed. It came along with the moonlight.

"Dushyanta came!

"Did he come? Was it indeed he who had come? Is it Dushyanta himself? I asked the trees and the plants, the boughs and the blossoms, the birds and the deer, the yard, the walls and the fence of the ashram . . . without uttering a sound. Oh! And my Bharata was already riding astride his shoulders. I hoped only that at least Maricha (he who had been witness to the earth cooling itself by pressing down all its seething rages) would not take my tear-laden eyes for a vain onrush of sentiment. Let the world that can never look truth in the face take care of itself. It is no concern of mine.

"Was it for me that he had come?

" 'To assist Devendra . . .'

"Why such searching questions, my heart? The flower of bliss stands on a frail stalk, ready to droop.

" 'Do you remember . . . me?' I breathed out softly.

"Remember—the very nature of the word seemed to throw him into an absentminded state.

" 'Well, why shouldn't I tell you the truth?' Profound scholar that he was, he held forth meticulously, so that I could comprehend the complexities of human relationships. And his paramours, his bedchamber, the oddities of love, affection and sex, all became examples of that great philosophy. Was he saying that everything should be savored at the moment of its fleeting existence and then forgotten?

"I had grown mature enough to understand all his words. But I felt unable to love anymore. Yet love tortured me all the more, strength-ening itself, defying my commands and pleas. It is not as simple as saying that Vishwamitra's daughter, one whose soul was blasted at its very roots, speaks like an adolescent. There is nothing so unpredictable as love.

" 'Come,' he said in a honeyed voice. That very Dushyanta!

"Shall I go? Should I go?

"Maricha wore a mantle of silence. I had to make the decision.

"I stood and pondered the edge of the truth that I need not be indispensable to him, just because he was to me. But until I was (and that may be impossible, no one will ever be indispensable to anyone, but all truths have exceptions), I thought to myself, I should not go to him.

"I often used to boast that it was royal blood that flowed in my veins. But what a hollow boast it all was! That diamond-studded throne had no power to draw me.

"I did not go.

"It became known that the emperor was worried about an heir to his throne. Bharata received the blessings, grasped his father's hand, and climbed onto the chariot.

"Bharata had found his home, and I felt unburdened. I grew heavy—did I? Before I could say so, I became unburdened and regained my peace. We are never all this or that, even while we feel so. We only flee hither and thither like drifters between this bank and that. Don't you agree?

"Dushyanta disappeared, holding Bharata in his arms. Always happy? All his contradictions may be found in poetry, to appreciate and contemplate, and to justify his existence to the whole world. Not to protect truth.

"Did you say truth needs no protection?

"I cried out to him, 'I never shall be jealous of your loves . . .'

"My voice certainly could not have reached him as the chariot wheels swerved and hastened back towards matters of state.

"Life is never drab or dreary so long as it keeps rising in ever-new hues before one's eyes."

The afternoon at Hemakoot had turned to evening, spreading its dusky tone on all.

On the mud-floored veranda of the ashram, Shakuntala sat talking, on and on. She closed her eyes and leaned back. Here and there, on either side of the parting of her hair shone strands of silver.

I sat gazing, unwilling to rise abruptly.

Who is she? Lover? Loner? Or yogin?

Or the essence of all three?
Or is she pure nature?
The sun disappeared behind the hills.
I rose softly, descended the steps, and crossed the front yard. Then
I turned and looked back.
Nothing was visible under the dark sheet of night.
Only the wind blowing like a billowing breath.

Translated by Jaswant Jadav.

MRINAL PANDE ——————————————

(b. 1946) *Hindi*

Mrinal Pande brings to her writing a broad intellectual background as well
as the atmosphere she grew up in as the daughter of the popular Hindi
novelist Shivani. She studied English and Sanskrit literature, ancient Indian
history, and archeology, and received her bachelor's degree from the University of Allahabad. During the seventies she also trained in classical music
and the visual arts.

She published her first short story in the influential and widely-circulated
Hindi weekly *Dharmyug* in 1967 and has continued to write regularly since
then, expanding her repertoire from the short story to the novel and then
to musical drama. Her work, which is marked by fast-paced dialogue and
a humor that heightens even a tragic situation, has been extremely well
received. Her first collection of short stories, *Darmiyan* (Between Horizons), 1977, won an Uttar Pradesh state award, while *Shabdavedi* (The
Blindfolded Archer/One Who Can Hit a Sound Target), 1980, was judged
the best work produced by a young author that year. Among her other
collections of short stories are *Ek Neech Tragedy* (A Low Tragedy), 1982,
and *Ek Stri Vidageet* (The Farewell Song of a Woman), 1985, from which
the story here is taken. Mrinal Pande has written two novels, and in the
eighties she began to write plays. Several musical comedies and farces,
produced by prestigious repertory companies in Delhi and Bhopal, include
Jo Ram Rachi Rekha (The Line of Fate), produced in 1980 and published in
1983, and *Chor Nikal Kar Bhaga* (The Absconding Thief), produced in
1985. She also writes for radio and television and is researching the Hindi-
language Parsi theater of the late-nineteenth century.

As a professional journalist, she writes on Hindi literature, art, film, and
on women's issues. From 1984 to 1987, she was editor of the popular
women's magazine *Vama*. She was appointed to the government's Na-

tional Commission on Self-Employed Women and has been responsible for inquiring into the conditions of work, the experience, and the contribution to the national economy of self-employed women, such as hawkers, business women, rag pickers, and domestic helpers.

◆

HUM SAFAR
(Fellow Travelers)

The train started from here and Big Brother had reserved a seat for her. But even so, as usual Father had sent Nirmala to the station an hour ahead of the scheduled time. The unlit coaches were still standing in the railway yard. Nirmala stepped into the compartment diffidently. Always hesitant and scared, she could neither tell her father that there was no need for her to get to the station so early, nor could she ask Big Brother to check the reservation number on her ticket against the list being pasted outside her carriage, just to make sure that she had the right seat.

Of late, Big Brother had been complaining of acute gastric trouble. He had acidity and a burning sensation in his chest, and belched constantly. Perhaps this was why he had become so irritable. She was about to ask him to doublecheck her reservation, but, looking at his sour expression, she restrained herself. Wasn't he an old railway servant? Wouldn't he know whether he had escorted his sister to the right seat or not? And hadn't he said, before he left, that he would also tell the ticket collector to take care of her? What if he forgot? No, no, why should he? Wasn't he an old railway man? She was used to all this, to being abandoned in the midst of unanswered questions in ill-lit carriages with no ventilation, upon hard old benches. Slowly Nirmala buried the hard knot of fear deep inside her heart, and sat staring out.

"Ei, ei, what are you doing?"

She scolded her son, Munna, in a low voice. Munna was trying to stick his arm out the window. He paused and looked at his mother with his sad, yellowed eyes and withdrew his hand slowly. Then he got up and sat at the edge of the row with his shoulders hunched, and began drawing lines on the dirty floor with his toes. Nirmala sighed and looked out. Without the lights, everything around them appeared sad and somewhat ghostly and unreal. There were very few people in the carriage so far. Passengers were also sprawled on the platform outside waiting for other trains. No one seemed to be in a hurry. A newly married girl in a bright pink sari stood eating freshly fried *bhajies* out of a paper cone, while her middle-aged husband sat on his new steel trunk and puffed at his bidi. Maybe she was his second wife, or maybe it was her father come to escort her to the station. Who knows? When Nirmala's husband was alive, people often had mistaken him for her father. This had angered him always and left him a bitter and sour man, given to large, moody fits of silence. Now those three years, when she thought of them, came to her like a dream. The last two saw her husband wrecked more and more by his incurable liver ailment. Pain, medicine, retching, this is all she remembered of his last days. His liver had turned to stone with drinking too much, the doctor had said.

The only consolation was that the end, when it came, was peaceful. It came during an evening hour like this, when he had asked to be propped up. As they had helped him, he coughed up a large clot of blood, and that was the end. Just like that.

Her husband's father and older brother had helped her close her household, and had brought Munna and her back with them. Slowly, all her possessions drifted into her sister-in-law's care and became hers. Her own brother had done nothing, but what could he have done? Hadn't he done his duty by marrying her off? Nirmala sighed and draped her sari tightly around her shoulders. Her colored saris and blouses, her silver anklets and nose ring, all had slowly found their way into her sister-in-law's boxes. Well, she had only a son to bring up, but her sister-in-law had several daughters to marry off. Wasn't her need greater than Nirmala's?

Suddenly the carriage was jolted into motion. "They've connected the engine," Munna said to no one in particular. Her son's thin, timid face and his hesitant speech slashed through her soul like a scalpel each time. Like an animal brought up on leftovers and castoffs from others, he was quiet and diffident, without any of the trusting cheerfulness of a child. He never threw tantrums or raised his voice. Her sister-in-law would glare at him and call him "Ghunna"—one who knots up and stores his anger and revenge inside. Could she be right?

Had Nirmala been childless, she'd have done something to herself. She would have swallowed poison or just gone off. But where could such a woman go? Perhaps she'd still have been exactly where she was now. One doesn't know, does one? Nirmala sighed. Slowly the bulbs on the ceiling began emitting a pale and weak light. She joined her palms and did a *namaskar* to the light. May the gods protect her little one.

"Will you eat something, Munna?" she asked the child gently.

Munna shook his head. He ate very little, but living on the charity of others, could he have developed an appetite? And could a mother, who is bringing her child up on leftovers from someone else's kitchen, plead with him to eat more within their hearing? In the beginning, sometimes her father-in-law asked Munna if he'd like to have some milk, but before the child could reply, her sister-in-law would point out that rich milk for a child with a weak liver like his father's might not be good at all. Nirmala, feeling the old man's compassionate glance, would add quickly that her son truly hated milk or cream. But upon Munna's return from school each day, when she handed him a cup of weak and watery tea, she felt something acrid and dark choke her chest. No, no, she must never be thankless. At least, thanks to their generosity, she and her son had a roof over their heads, didn't they? Many were deprived even of that, were they not?

The train had now crawled up to the main platform and hordes of passengers were pouring into the compartment accompanied by porters shouldering their trunks and bed rolls. The carriage was suddenly full, as though by magic.

"I'm hungry," Munna whispered. Nirmala opened her little bag and took out their dinner wrapped in a greasy piece of newspaper. There were only six puris for the two of them. She handed four of these to Munna. Was this all that had been packed for both of them? Well, who wants to eat too many greasy puris anyway?

"Will you have some?" Munna was asking her. She shook her head. He would need the remaining two in the morning. Her eyes caressed Munna as he ate. The train should be leaving anytime now, and once it began to move, one could fall asleep without much effort and not feel hunger or the heat anymore.

Just then those two rushed in. While the other travelers entered chanting their seat numbers like a holy mantra, those two just stood coolly surveying the scene. One was tall, dark, and amazingly hairy; the other was short, fat, fair, and almost totally hairless. The Tall One had a deep voice, while the Short One's voice was squeaky and thin. Their clothes were expensive and well-tailored, and they wore a great many rings.

After having surveyed the scene, the Tall One and the Short One went and sat down on the bench facing Nirmala's, and began combing their greasy hair with plastic combs. They also began humming lewd film songs. A little away from them, a cluster of young college girls sat chatting. Perhaps they were returning home after their examinations. They caught the attention of the two newcomers.

"It's hot, no?" The Short One winked at the Tall One conspiratorially.

"Wha—? Yes, yes, the heat!" The Tall One laughed. He spoke slowly, as though chewing his syllables before they came out of his mouth. On his index finger was a heavy ring set with precious stones, and his skin was badly scarred with acne. He pulled out a colorful handkerchief from somewhere, and folding it carefully, placed it behind his neck, underneath his collar. "How one sweats in here!"

"Forty-four? Forty-four? Here it is,"—the new arrival was dressed in a superfine muslin dhoti and kurta, and held a box of betel leaves in one hand. "Brother, thish ish my sheet." He spoke with his betel-juice-stained mouth puckered up. Nirmala pulled her pallav a little further down her forehead. The ticket collector had already checked her ticket and pronounced it to be valid. So she was safe.

"This seat belongs to him," the Short One said.

"What? It belongs to him?" the Tall One pretended to be shocked.

"This is what he says. Why, what's the matter?" the Short One winked at the Tall One.

Silence fell over the compartment. The girls' chatter turned into whispers.

"Yesh, yesh, sho it ish. See, here'sh my ticket." The dhoti-clad one swallowed the betel juice and fluttered his ticket under their chins.

Just then the ticket collector materialized upon the scene. He was a thin man, and beneath his chin there hung a goiter as large as a jackfruit. It had almost twisted his face to one side and when he smiled he appeared to be smirking. The Tall One and the Short One jumped up and greeted him with alacrity.

"Good evening, brother," the Tall One boomed.

"Good evening," the twisted neck replied. "So we have the pleasure of your company today after a long time, no? Shall I tear out one for the usual route?"

"Tear out whatever you like. If you say so, we shall even tear out our lungs. No?" The Short One laughed long and screechingly. At this point the train emitted a long sigh and began to edge forward.

"Sir, look—they're occupying my seat, and when I ask them to get up, they start clowning around." The dhoti-clad one was indignant.

The ticket collector's hand entered his pocket, paused, and came out. He made a great show of wetting a finger with his spit and turning several pages from the sheaf of papers held in the other hand—"All right, Big Brother, the seat is yours. But these two sahibs need to travel just a little distance. It's only seven o'clock now, and by midnight they'll get off. You need only make some *adjustment*."*

"Ha, ha, what a term! Nothing like English for terms, no? *Adjustment!*" The Short One's face was suffused with merriment.

The dhoti-clad one was truly angry now—"What kind of joke is this? For fifteen days we've lined up for reservations, paid an additional amount to you for confirmation, and now you ask me to *adjust?* What about these two, who have neither tickets nor reservations and will not release my seat?"

The travelers' sympathy was now focused on the dhoti-clad one! "It's true. They're bullying the poor man needlessly." Grumblings rippled down the rows. He became more confident. But the ticket collector maintained his studied patience. "Just three *ishtations*, Big Brother. After that you'll have the whole berth to yourself."

"Right, Grandfather," the Tall One bellowed. "We don't want to cause any discomfort, do we, now?" "Oh, no," the Short One disclaimed any such intention. The Tall One pulled himself up to his full height and hitched up his trousers. The passengers suddenly noticed the gleaming handle of a lethal Rampuri knife protruding from his hip pocket. For a fraction of a second, the Tall One's fingers barely fluttered over the knife, then they went back to smoothing his hair. "We'd like to talk of love, but," he let his glance travel toward the silent group of college girls—"if some people do not want to talk of love, maybe we can then talk of war, no?"

The ticket collector quietly moved on, as though his responsibility were over. Others followed suit. Some hid their faces behind glossy magazines or with great concentration began drinking water from tumblers. The girls developed a sudden interest in the landscape outside.

The train had gathered speed by now. The dhoti-clad one finally gave up with a sigh, and sat down at the edge of Nirmala's seat. The Tall One and the Short One were reclining on his berth as unquestioned owners. Like potatoes in a sack, they now sat rocking gently together as the train hurtled along. Nirmala signaled Munna to make room for the defeated warrior. Why fight? After all, they were not going to be there till eternity, were they?

"How is this lot?" the Short One motioned towards the girls with his chin, and winked at the Tall One. Once again, he was picking up

---

*Italicized English words are in English in the original.

where they had left off. The Tall One screwed up his eyes and examined the girls.

"The one in the red dupatta appeals to us, the green one is also all right, the rest are just so-so."

The dhoti-clad one had fished a religious text out of his bag and was pretending to be immersed in holy ideas far away from these ugly words. "Son, tell Grandfather that there is not enough light in the compartment. His eyes might begin to hurt," the Tall One growled to Munna. Munna's small, thin hand clasped his mother's a little more tightly.

"Their generator is weak," the dhoti-clad one mumbled.

"Generator? What isn't weak or not working on this train? The people in the yard send these trains out without checking them. No one cares whether we get to where we are going"—this was the Short One.

"Yesterday this train was late by four hours," a small, dark man said softly, eating his supper out of an aluminum lunch box. "At each station before it gathers speed, the train is stopped at least four times by people pulling the chain. The scheduled time of arrival is in the afternoon, but it never makes it before dark, when you can get neither a ricksha nor a porter. Dear Brother, this son-of-an-outcaste route is just not worth taking."

"This is why we asked you to *adjust*," the Tall One boomed, and then he and the Short One burst out laughing, as though they had cracked a super joke. "Ah, it's so hot!" The Tall One pushed up the window, but the air that came in was warm and stale. The overhead fans were not working.

"This time we must buy a refrigerator to chill our beer in. No?" The Short One moved closer to his hero.

"Well, yes, I should imagine it would cost only a paltry ten thousand or so." The Tall One cast a sly glance in the direction of the girl in the red dupatta. "See, we are royal by temperament. If our heart says, 'Spend thousands,' we'll throw thousands down the drain."

"Right you are," the Short One screeched.

"And now we think we should also buy a car. Dilawar of the corner garage has been urging that for sometime, saying, 'Boss, you must have a car.' "

"Yes, yes, why not?" The Short One pushed a fistful of salted gram into his mouth. As though by magic, bottles of liquor had materialized in their hands. The Tall One took a long swig and laughed, "We are free birds, see. No one dares tie us down. What will a bird do with an ugly car? What?"

"Right, sir, right!" the Short One agreed. "We just appear and disappear. Remember how we tricked the policemen at Dadar?" They both guffawed at the memory. "The son of a whore's intestines hung out, remember?" They were delighted by the repulsion they had triggered among the dainty college girls and laughed long. The whole carriage reeked of their cheap liquor. Nirmala was reminded of her dead husband. When he crept towards her, his mouth had smelled the same. She thought she was going to be sick. The Tall One belched and pushed some more fried gram into his mouth, and a smell of stale oil and spices was added to the stench. Nirmala felt a sour flood gurgle up inside her chest—"Munna, take care of the luggage," she said, and rushed towards the toilet. The way to the toilet was blocked with countless pieces of luggage, and water sloshed in the spaces between them, but at least the overpowering stench of liquor had lessened. Nirmala washed her face with cold water that felt full of coal and dust, and wiped it dry with her sari. For a while she stood near the door, holding the iron handle and staring out vacantly.

Dhadak, dhad! Dhadak, dhad! The train was crossing a bridge. Iron hitting iron resounded below. It sounded like an enormous dumb beast howling in the dark. Here and there a few huts flickered, as the train passed small villages. The hills looked like huge prehistoric animals sleeping, heads resting on their paws. *Dhad, dhadak!* Is there truly such a thing as a soul, something that remains after the body has turned to dust? Nirmala could never believe it. How could she believe unless there was someone to answer her questions first? She had never been able to ask such questions, but they churned within.

Shoon! Shoon! A sudden wave of light broke upon the scene. Another train was passing, going in the opposite direction. Nirmala stared wide-eyed at the human forms suspended within squares of light that were the coaches of the other train, carrying hundreds home. Some passengers were lying down, some squatted, a few hung out of the doors, holding on to handles like hers. Do nameless, friendless stars pass each other thus in the heavens above? The engine emitted smoke and cinders that glowed like fireflies. The air smelled of dust and coal. Nirmala felt her pulse near her temples.

Chi! Chi! Why did she always think such unholy thoughts? That, too, about the holy souls in the heavens above. Truly, she was a sinner and that is why the gods had decreed that she carry this widowhood upon her back for the rest of her days. She wiped her eyes. Dear God, do forgive me. Do forgive these strange thoughts that are always flying upwards like sparks, no matter how hard I try. I am sure there are souls. Yes, certainly there are. Didn't Mother say that the sinless ones turn into stars and glow in the heavens above?

Nirmala looked at the sky. It was cold and dark and so far away. A few stars had come out, but they were hard and distant. Each stood burning in its own darkness. Why was everything she wanted to clutch so far off? And surrounded by so much dark? Dear God, dear Shiva, forgive me these thoughts. Nirmala turned back. Thank God Father had given her some money when she left. That would pay for the ricksha. Each time she had to ask her sister-in-law for money to pay someone, her face closed like a fist, and her eyes spewed unsaid curses upon Nirmala and her son.

Oh God, where was Munna? Nirmala's heart skipped a beat. The child was not in his seat. Where could he be? She looked around like a demented woman. Suddenly, she spied her son sitting next to those two, staring at their faces with devotion in his eyes. His hands held a paper bag of spicy goodies which he munched with obvious enjoyment, shaking his legs and putting fistfuls of the stuff into his mouth. The son of an outcaste!

Suddenly, as though a forest fire had burst within her, Nirmala caught hold of her child's shoulder with one skeletal hand, and began slapping his face hard with the other. "You beggar! You eat food borrowed from others? Here, take this, and this, and this, and this. Is your stomach a bottomless pit? Haven't you had all of four puris just now? You son of a beggar! Now you beg food from others, do you? Here!" The bag had fallen down on the floor. Stamping over the food, the ever-obedient and silent Nirmala lashed out at her son as though possessed by a demon. Her hair had come undone; the end of her sari had dropped from her shoulder, and lay on the floor. It was as though the top of a manhole had suddenly blown open to spew forth acid that had been boiling for years. The whole carriage lay submerged under the stinking stream. "Here, take this, and this." The child was so shocked by the sudden onslaught that he couldn't even utter a cry. Like a mute, limp rag doll, he was flung from side to side.

"I had, after all, given him just a little bit of these savories, Sister-ji"—the Tall One's voice had lost its deep timbre. He and the Short One could not meet the accusing eyes of the others. The Short One also tried to smile, but failed. Then the college girls bestirred themselves. Some of them gently detached Munna from his mother's mad grip and took him to their corner.

Nirmala sat spent in her corner, with her sari pulled over her face. The train hurtled along, slashing through the dark night, emitting fire and smoke. An enormous darkness rose like a giant wave and beat against the walls of Nirmala's heart. Why? Why? Why?

No one noticed when the train slowed down and the two companions got off. Munna now lay fast asleep next to his mother, but every now and then a tiny sob still shook his thin frame. Nirmala covered his thin ankles lovingly with her old shawl and sat staring at him. Her mind was empty of all emotion, as though a sharp knife had pared it clean. There was a deep darkness around her, and within her an unending fatigue.

Then she noticed the tear, still suspended like a dewdrop on the pale, colorless cheek of her child. Her ugly, calloused fingers began tracing the features on her child's face with an uncontrollable urgency. She thought her heart would burst, torn apart by sorrow and love.

Once again, all was peaceful within the coach. Having regained his seat, the dhoti-clad one had quickly spread his mat on his bench, and now lay fast asleep on it, snoring gently.

Translated by the author.

SAROOP DHRUV ────────────────────────

(b. 1948)   *Gujarati*

Saroop Dhruv, who was brought up and educated in Ahmedabad, was a rather solitary child who was most at home with her maternal grandparents. Hers could scarcely be called a sheltered childhood, however, since among her earliest recollections are of the rioting, shooting, broken glass, and tear gas in the streets outside her home during the agitation for a separate state of Gujarat during the sixties, events that have left a deep impression on her mind. At present she teaches Gujarati as a foreign language. She uses drama as a method of teaching, and her students have toured villages with some of the plays they have created together.

Folk literature has been of continuing interest to her, and was the subject of her doctoral dissertation. The Kannada playwright Girish Karnad's use of folktale and legend inspired Saroop Dhruv, but she now feels that literature incorporating folk dialect and legends has become frozen and stylized. She is widely read in Gujarati, Hindi, and Urdu, and her range includes Sanskrit as well as European classics in translation. The works of Dostoyevski and Urdu poetry have, she says, influenced her writing. Another important influence is the surrealist movement in Gujarati poetry, represented by the work of Sitanshu Yashashchandra, a poet she particularly admires.

Jaya Mehta once commented that Saroop Dhruv does not write consciously from a woman's point of view, and does not deal with typically feminine experiences. Jaya Mehta attributes this to the fact that Saroop Dhruv was never discriminated against as a girl or made conscious of her femaleness, and goes on to add that this is also true of her own poetry. The tensions Saroop Dhruv has undergone, she has undergone as an individual, not specifically as a woman, Jaya Mehta argues, and there is no markedly feminine element in her personality. Because of her desire to remain free to develop in any direction she wishes, she has not married and she does not regret it.

Both the poems translated here are taken from *Mara Hathni Vat* (Here's What I Can Do/Within My Reach), published in 1982. Since then, many of her poems have appeared in leading poetry journals. If, as she says, her main preoccupations have been attempts to understand the self and the relationship between the individual and the world, the world appears in the form of mountains uprooted and taking off, tearing loose, dashing, bashing, clashing, speeding, fleeing ("This Is a Cave") or in the form of a train speeding on the track from which there leap out cities full of streets, books full of letters, theaters full of people ("My One and Only Garment"). The individual in this world is disoriented, often at a loss, sometimes grotesquely distorted. Her feet grow larger and larger; hooves emerge. Bruises appear on her hands; her skin turns from yellow to red. The poem asks how she can claim to be a "descendant of the sun" unless she experiences the "burning pain of her ripped-off skin." She may achieve nothing, she may understand nothing, but she never experiences suffocation ("My One and Only Garment").

The diction in Saroop Dhruv's poetry is often that of colloquial speech, and there are allusions to children's rhymes, to traditional beliefs and myths, to legends. Patternings of word, sound and meter, difficult to recreate in translation, also contribute to the verbal enactment of the poetic experience.

Over the last few years there has been a marked shift in Saroop Dhruv's interests. She has become involved in the activities of Chingari, a feminist collective in Ahmedabad, which works closely with women workers and with other marginalized groups. Distanced now from the more formalist concerns of a few years ago, she is exploring folk and other popular forms and recreating them as songs and poems that express the grievances and aspirations of the people she works among.

◆

SAROOP DHRUV ◆ 557

EKNUN EK VASTRA
(My One and Only Garment)

As I write this
It's as if in the solitude of my island
Seeing a ship
Approaching in the distance
I start waving
The one and only garment I have on.
I stand by the opened window.
And opposite me the crocodile turns over on its other side.
The water flowing below my window
Changes color.
It breathes in—breathes out.
Stretching its legs, it settles down again.
A crack appears in the window frame.
Stretching forth from it are five fingers
Which I like to watch.
My inclination to gaze
At the hand known—unknown
Is permanently extended like a mushroom.
I like watching the three primary colors
As one watches the three colors of traffic lights.
I like watching them
Replace each other
Again and again.
The yellow between the red and the green
Can fill me with wonder.
The longing for something to happen
Turns into a yellow leaf and flutters before me.
The leaf will fall, it'll fall, it'll fall!
I've taken that hand in my hand.
I seize the searchlight
Of the lighthouse speeding far off
Over the water spread under my window.
I caress the soft, soft back
Of the light circling around.
With each touch there springs up
The train speeding on the track.
From the train descend
Cities full of streets

Books full of letters
Theaters full of people.
I begin to enjoy it all.
I begin to feel it belongs to me.
To whom shall I say
That I don't feel suffocated?
I don't like suffocation.
I never am suffocated.
That's why it thrills me to see
The creases in my palms.
The thrill of opening the window.
My fingers have become
The goat's kid bounding
After it has fed on the fresh green grass by the stream.
It bounds and the bells round its neck tinkle.
It sniffs the fresh grass and whispers in my ear
That something is going to happen.
What is this something?
The needle on a disc?
The indecipherable alphabet of touch
Decoded from someone's finger tips?
Breath melting and uniting in the darkness.
Someone did say that this happening
Was existence without being . . . !
And without experiencing the scalding pain of my ripped-off skin
How can I claim to be a descendant of the sun?
If one wants to turn over in bed,
One has to stretch one's legs.
And one cannot melt without agitation.
I don't know—I can't make out anything.
This is all I can make out—
The skin on my palm;
The softness under my feet turning from green to yellow;
From yellow to . . . ?
Why is everything merging?
A searchlight is white—can whiteness be so rough?
I don't know—I can't make out anything.
All I can make out is
The yellow skin of my palm dyeing into red
Again and again.
This green grass

Threading my fingers—
Are these newborn wrinkles or are they
The scratches left by the claws of the setting sun?
Why do they suddenly charge at me,
This railway track, this train, these books, these people, these
    theaters
That were all circling round?
But they still don't get caught,
They don't call me . . . they don't speak to me . . .
I want to ask
I want to touch
I want to approach—
But the searchlight has slipped from my grasp.
The black rocks are not smooth.
The crocodile turns over on its other side.
Always . . . always . . . after turning over, the crocodile
Swallows up that ship.
My one and only garment
Fluttering in my hand
Turns to shreds.
This is how whenever the time comes for me to talk about myself
I have to speak of my claws
Ripping up the sun's reflection.
Again and again.
No, then the ship won't be seen . . .
The goat-bells won't be heard . . .
    And I have to close the window.
    Have to clench my fist.
    And entangling me is the thread . . . the thread . . . the thread . . .
    Which I myself have become . . .
I weave a garment, once more . . .
Just one garment . . . my one and only garment . . .
The crocodile will turn over
And once more a ship . . .

Translated by Shirin Kudchedkar.

FLAPDOORNI ARPAR
(Beyond the Flapdoor)*

For what I want to tell you,
I cannot find the words.
The wretched words have become the flapdoor of the family room
And I am repelled by the sight
Of the feet of the rabbit peeping under the fence.
I feel a peculiar sensation below my navel
At the sound of the tender carrot
Crunched by sharp nails and tiny teeth
And I can't stop what's happening.
Because when the thousand-armed one**
Is providing the nine hundred ninety-ninth garment
Before him he sees the luscious sugarcane glimmering.
And although he knew all about it
When the waiter went to wipe the tables this morning
He saw that
Between the rings made by the glasses on the table
In the midst of the field thick with sugarcane
Lay a half-length sari and an anklet . . .
Now you tell me!
If I want to tell you this, is there any way I can?

Translated by Shirin Kudchedkar.

SARAH JOSEPH ⸻⸻⸻⸻⸻

(b. 1948)   *Malayalam*

Sarah Joseph's short stories began to appear in leading literary journals in
the mid-seventies. Relatively quickly, she established herself as a writer
with a feminist perspective. The characters in her richly evoked, symbolic
stories are victim to a haunting, intangible sense of alienation—from so-

---

*In old restaurants there is often a separate little room where a family or a couple
  can sit in privacy behind half doors commonly known as "flapdoors."
**The "God who provides for all" is often referred to in Saurashtra as "He with
  the thousand arms."

ciety, family, personal relationships, and even from life itself. Marriage is experienced as claustrophobic, and the women characters invariably have loftier and more imaginative minds than their partners. Domestic chores bore them, sexual involvements seem routine and evoke revulsion. Story after story speaks of woman's craving for fulfillment beyond the mediocrity of a conventional domestic framework. The music of the wild rings in their minds, suicidal impulses haunt them, but they are drawn back each time in compromise. Sarah Joseph pursues these themes in the short story collections *Manassil Thi Mathram* (Only Fire in the Mind), 1974; *Snehathinte Niram* (The Color of Love), 1976; and *Kadinte Samgeetam* (The Music of the Wild), 1979, from which the story in this collection is taken. As a poet, she is able to bring a rich texture into her prose, creating a psychic dimension even out of seemingly trivial details.

She was born in Mullankunathukara, a village near Trichur. She trained as a teacher and taught in a school at Tirur while continuing her own studies. She passed the examination for her master's degree with distinction, ranking third in Kerala, and now works as a lecturer at Malayalam Government College at Pattambi. She is also an activist and has, with the students and other teachers in the college, started a women's organization called Manushi.

◆

MAZHA
(Rain)

At noon, when all of a sudden there was a heavy downpour, she closed the door and pulled shut the windows of the little room in front. She left open a panel of the window looking out on the west and gazed at the rain that roared down. In the distance she could hear the suppressed sobs of the rain bursting out over mountain passes.

"Oh God!" she muttered, pressing her hands hard against her breast. "I want to cry, cry like this screaming, tearing rain." She pressed her cheeks hard against the iron bars of the window. Then she fell back, helpless, on the broad windowsill and sat there, her head pressed against her knees.

Lying back in a rattan chair in the front room, her husband was reading the newspaper. As the clouds gathered and the sky darkened, he switched the lights on. The rain came tearing down. When the wind began to spray the doormat and the curtains, he rose and shut the front door, but the curtains still fluttered in the wind. Lest they get wet, he put on the shelf the books and magazines that she had scattered on the floor beside the sofa. Then he picked up the newspaper again and lay back in the chair.

His children fetched some scratch paper, and sitting on the floor beside him, began making paper boats. "Accha*, open the door for us," they said, shaking him roughly.

"Uh, uh," he said, and continued reading.

"Please open the door," his son whimpered, holding his trousers up with his left hand and clutching a paper boat in his right one. The boy tugged at him again. "Accha!"

"What is it?"

"The door . . ."

"The door?"

"Open it for us, please."

"What for?"

"We want to set our boats afloat . . ."

"Boats! What nonsense! You'll get wet and catch fever. Boats indeed!"

He had not taken his eyes off the paper. Discouraged but angry, the boy looked at his elder sister. Should he try crying?

She was not putting together a crude boat like the boy had made, but was taking great care to make a fine one. "There's nothing to worry about," she signaled with her eyes, and continued to work at her boat. She folded it meticulously. Running the paper between her fingers, she pressed it together into a fine edge, making sure there were no creases. He watched for a while but got irritated. "She and her boat! The rain would soon stop, and how would she float her stupid boat then?"

"Come on, Chechi!"**

"Wait a minute, it's almost finished!"

They quietly climbed up onto the iron grill on the window. Stretching their arms out, they dropped the boats into the water in the front yard.

His boat swayed once in the water pouring down from the eaves, and came to a standstill. Trim and light as a feather, her boat quivered a little and then glided smoothly down the current.

"What a clumsy boat you've put together. Little wonder it doesn't float!" she remarked.

"You'll get wet in the spray. Get away from the window, both of you," the father called out, without lifting his eyes from the newspa-

---

*Accha means "father."
**Chechi means "elder sister."

per. Signaling to her to keep quiet, the young boy remained where he was, holding on to the grill.

Then a dark torrent of rain came howling down. The western sky was heavy with clouds. A deep haze covered the hills in the distance. The downpour left her helpless, unnerved. There was nothing to be done about it, she consoled herself.

"Why am I crying? Why?" she asked herself.

All of a sudden, she saw a nestling, barely the size of an egg, fall from the branch of the *suppotta* tree in the yard. For a second it dipped into the swirling waters at the foot of the tree and was washed away. She choked. She felt it was dying. On an impulse she opened the door and stepped into the front room, through the front door and out into the rain. The nestling was rolling around near the basil plant in the yard. Bending down, she picked it up. Muddy water swirled round her legs. It was wet and shivering and had almost no feathers. She felt disgusted—more disgusted, really, than sorry—at the sight of the birds circling the suppotta tree, their wings flapping. Disgust, but also contempt for herself because she felt that way.

"What's wrong with you? Why do you stand out there, getting soaked?" He was at the door, black with anger.

"Don't let yourself get so wet, Amma!" her son shouted.

Taking the god-sent opportunity, he slipped past his father's knees, picked up the boat that had been marooned, and threw it back into the water. But the paper had soaked through, and the boat just rolled through the water like a ball of paper.

"What sort of a boat have you made, you stupid fellow?" his sister teased. Belittled and angry, he made faces back at her. Just as he was about to step up on the veranda, she called out, "Accha, look! Suresh is in the rain. Serves him right. His hair's dripping wet."

"Let him be. There's nothing can be done. Children'll always take the lead one gives."

Something in her blew up. Holding the nestling fast in her left hand, she rushed up to Suresh and spanked him, "Go in, get out of the rain!" she shouted.

He screamed. It was the sudden change in his mother's attitude rather than the pain that hurt him. She added, now beside herself, "You will kill me, all of you together, you will kill me."

"Do you intend to come in out of the rain?" her husband asked, raising his voice in anger.

"No, I want to get wet."

"So that's it, is it?" Perhaps it was his sarcasm, perhaps his contempt, she did not know what, perhaps it was all she hated in him, that made her step out into the middle of the yard.

"What's wrong with Mother?" the daughter asked, quite unable to bear it all.

"Ask her just that. I've seen many types of madness, but this is in a class by itself."

She fixed her daughter in a stare. Embarrassed, the child added, "What do I care if you catch a fever? You are the one who will have to suffer."

She remained silent. The women who were weeding the field had stopped for lunch. They passed by, sheltered under palm-leaf umbrellas. When he realized that they were looking at her, he said, insistently, "Come in, Padma, will you?"

She didn't answer; didn't even turn or look at him. Pressing the nestling hard to her breast, she stood in the courtyard, her head drooping in the mad rain. Every time a passerby turned to look—she was undoubtedly an object of curiosity—he hissed fiercely, "Whore."

She felt her heart swell with anger and hatred as though it would burst. She crushed the little bird in her left hand. Hearing the tender bones crack, she started. He slammed the door. The bird fluttered a few times in her pale hand, its eyes staring out. She shook it off, suddenly fearful. It fell limp on the grass under the hibiscus plant. The other birds dived down from the suppotta tree and flew around it, their feathers wet with rain stuck close to their bodies, their cackling louder than the rain itself. A murderer's frenzy overwhelmed her. It seemed to her that the wet plumes were stuck to her palm. Disturbed, she rubbed her hands together. The birds flew around her, agitated. She recalled her revulsion. It disturbed her, that response. It was not what she wanted. Deeply pained, she lifted her hands and covered her face. Suddenly she wanted to hug Suresh—her little child—the one she had spanked a moment ago for no reason. She ran into the front room like a madwoman, and fell back against the closed door, panting. She had tripped on her wet sari and almost fallen two or three times while running. Water was streaming down from her hair; her clothes stuck fast to her body; she was shivering from head to foot.

"So, you've had enough, have you?" he taunted, hatred frothing in his scorn.

She muttered something vaguely to herself, something like, I wouldn't have suffered your scorn but for this longing to see my child. But she said in a low tone, "Open the door, please." Her weak voice drowned in the howling rain, but he understood what she was saying perfectly. He stood up, and, opening the door, said, "Such arrogance doesn't become a woman. Understand?"

She did not reply. Neither did she pay attention to him. She just walked into the inner room. Even after she had dried her hair, changed her clothes, and gone into the bedroom, she ignored him.

Suresh had cried himself to sleep. She stood by him for a long time, looking. She stopped herself as she bent down to kiss him and suddenly straightened up. His face seemed almost unfamiliar. What's wrong with me? she wondered sadly. Her daughter had followed her into the room. Her face was clouded over. She remembered the nestling with a shudder as she looked at her daughter. In as tender and affectionate a tone as she could muster, she said, "Come Sudha, get into bed."

The child obeyed silently. She lay down, but her big eyes still wandered over her mother's face, as if to say that she would never understand her. She pulled a blanket gently over the children and fell back into the armchair, exhausted.

The children!

It's their unlucky lot to have me as a mother. I feel I don't love them, don't truly love them. Dear God, tell me, do I not love them?

You do, you don't, you do; no, you don't.

Yes, Lord, I love them, I do. I love them more than I love my own life. But they deserve a far better mother, they are such dear children. Still, I love them. I love them truly. Softly she kissed them on their cheeks.

Their sleeping faces brought back memories of the nestling. She felt that she had twisted Suresh's neck and crushed Sudha's tender bones. Again, she rubbed her hands together in distress.

In the front room, her husband had switched the record player on. It was the pop music he loved and a rhythm she hated. Now again he was taunting her. She knew that.

"I do not have the strength to bear this mocking disregard," she murmured. "I'm nobody here. God, I'm so alone here, all alone."

She lifted up her hands. "You will die," she thought. My children! They have nobody!

All of a sudden, she flung herself down on the coir mat and burst out crying.

Translated by Anitha Devasia.

O. V. USHA

(b. 1948)   *Malayalam*

O. V. Usha is considered the most gifted among the younger women
poets writing in Malayalam today. Her poems are short mood pieces that
capture the shades of emotion that savage her introspective mind. A disturbing sense of gloom haunts her work. In his introduction to her book
of poems *Dhyanam* (Meditation), 1976, the writer G. Sankara Kurup wonders how this "strange melancholic shade" could have pervaded the poems
of such a young woman. No specific experience in her life seems to account for it. Usha points to the silence and loneliness of her childhood,
when the natural world was the major influence on her mind.

O. V. Usha is the youngest child in her family. Her father worked for
the Malabar Special Police. Her mother's interest in Malayalam classical
poetry induced young Usha to read poems and learn them by heart when
she was a child. The well-known novelist and cartoonist O. V. Vijayan is
her brother. After completing her master's degree in English literature, she
joined one of the leading publishing houses as an editorial trainee and later
became editor-in-chief. She is now director of publications at the Mahatma Gandhi Open University in Kottayam.

Usha started writing poetry when she was thirteen. She contributed
regularly to the "Children's Corner" of *Mathrubhumi Weekly*. When she
outgrew that, her poems continued to be published in the same magazine
till about 1973. She wrote little for ten years, but began again in 1982.
The poem translated here appeared in *Mathrubhumi Weekly* in February
1987. The same vaguely felt, silent, and unnamable grief still haunts her
work. Most of her poetry has not yet been published in book form.

◆

MRIGAYA
(The Hunt)

It burns
  White hot are these sands;
  Coils brand the body,
  In crushing embrace.
Who has hurled me alive
On these burning sands?

With growing clarity
I see the strangeness of it all
And the approach of a beast of fierce resolve.

Large, wrought of fire,
With a slouch and a smothered roar,
It runs a bright flame tongue
Slowly over its ember lips.
  In its gaze,
  Poised for a throw
  Is a thunderbolt
  That would cleave my soul!

Now the beast pauses
  Not close and not far!
Cry for help?
  Stilled is my voice
  And there is no one
  Within the throw of human voice.
Has the beast put
A slow burning step forward?
Have those fearsome teeth
Splashed white liquid fire?
  Yes it draws close,
  Lets out a roar;
  Puts out its flaming tongue
    and licks those ember lips.
  It bends over me.

Mercy?
  There is no patch of cloud
  In the spread of its wild fiery eyes
  The skies catch fire
  The world burns!
The beast scoops out my heart and devours
And now in one sweep
It catches
The little bird, encaged in my frame
And it growls and rolls
In awesome play.

Translated by the author.

SHASHIKALA VEERAYYA SWAMY ⎯⎯⎯

(b. 1948)   *Kannada*

The impression that the most promising of women's writing in contemporary Kannada literature is in the field of poetry probably owes its origin
to the work of Shashikala Veerayya Swamy. "The woman writer today,"
the novelist U. R. Anantamurthy says in the preface to her collection
Gubbi Mani (Sparrow's Nest), 1979, "has of necessity to be a rebel and an
iconoclast. The value of the poetry lies in the sincerity of expression."
Shashikala Veerayya Swamy's poetry is marked by a powerful use of North
Karnatakan dialect and a sharp dramatic mode of narration which heightens the satirical edge of her critical comment. In "Menabatti" (Candle),
the protagonist compares her traditional life to that of the medieval bhakti
poet Akkamahadevi, who rejected her husband's control, broke traditional
bonds, and wandered naked in search of spiritual fulfillment. The hovering
between convention and rebellion that is a special feature of Shashikala
Veerayya Swamy's poetry has been acclaimed by many as realist, but
the critic Sumitra Bai considers her poetry the expression of an uncertain
mind, caught between the graces of a traditional life and the need for
liberation. Shashikala Veerayya Swamy has published four collections of
poetry. *Prasne* (Question) appeared in 1982, *Jiva Savugala Naduve* (Between
Life and Death) in 1984, and *Henge Helale Gelati* (What Shall I Say, Friend)
in 1989. She is a college lecturer in Kannada. The poem translated here is
taken from *Gubbi Mani*.

◆

MENABATTI
(Candle)

Sister mine,
you're the lucky one
you gained a virtuous, deathless
husband
and grew strong.

You became bold
leaving naked
both body and mind.

Look at me,
in the quilt Grandmother made,
a slave to his desire
a shell whose pearl shatters
when he sows.

In his palace
like a candle
I burn
I'm aflame inside
I melt in the heat
I'm freezing over.

Your neglect
your disregard
is a lit match
to my breast's dynamite—
never forget!

Translated by Tejaswini Niranjana.

HAJIRA SHAKOOR ⸺⸺⸺⸺⸺⸺

(b. 1950)   *Urdu*

"Though my brothers and sisters are all interested in literature, only I
have become a writer," Hajira Shakoor notes in a biographical fragment.
Her father, Abdul Shakoor, was a well-known critic, and Hajira grew up
reading the major Urdu writers. Qurratullain Hyder, Ismat Chugtai, Jo-
ginder Pal, Krishan Chander, Jeelani Bano, Faiz Ahmed Faiz, Kazmi, Ahmed Faroz, and Bashir Badar are the writers she feels have most influenced
her. A sociologist with a doctorate, Hajira Shakoor is a lecturer at Jamia
Milia University in Delhi. "Since I am interested in social work," she
writes, "my stories reflect the problems faced by women. They ask questions about tolerance, equality, and human rights." Most of her fiction
deals with the lives of middle-class women.

She has published widely in Indian and Pakistani journals. Her first
collection of short stories, *Gardishen* (Vicissitudes), came out in 1970, and
the second, *Band Kamron Ki Khuli Khidkiyan* (Open Windows in Closed
Rooms), in 1987. A third collection, *Barzach* (Purgatory), appeared in 1991.
One of her best-known recent short stories, "Bhedion Ki Basti" (Neigh-

borhood of Hyenas), deals with the anti–Sikh riots that took place in 1984 after Indira Gandhi's assassination. The story translated for this volume, "Umr Qaid" (Life Sentence), was first published in the journal *Subeh Adab* in 1977. It deals with the question of dowry, a major concern of the nineteenth-century social reformers (and indeed of the women's movement today), but picks up where reformers leave off. She takes the reader into the lives of two people involved in a heroic gesture and subtly unwinds the invisible private experiences that hold those spectacular public events in place.

◆

UMR QAID
(Life Sentence)

There's a record playing in Suresh's room. Such a funny song:

"Come, beloved, come,
Let's go beyond the moon."
"I'm ready, come!"

I never see films, but it's impossible to escape film songs. And what sort of a song is this? As if you can go to the moon as you go from one room to another! But it's not just the song . . . It's the accompanying joy of a newly married couple, resonant and boisterous.

It's barely six months since Suresh was married. The honeymoon still seems to linger. Kalpana is a good girl, and so beautiful. There's no real resemblance between her and Janaki, but her quiet seriousness brings so many memories of Janaki back. Both the older daughters-in-law were chosen by my sons, but this one was my choice. There's a strange something about newly married couples. Just to watch and share this sparkle, I spend a lot of time with Suresh and Kalpana. Perhaps they don't like it. But moments like these never came to me in my own life, so I long to suck that joy in.

It is seven years now since Janaki died. When she was here, there was nothing about her to make her presence felt. But now I find it difficult to think of anything that is not linked with her memory. This is the revenge she has finally taken, for that life. There is no moment when I can shed all thought of her from my heart.

Life in our house was like an embroidered shawl. People saw the beauty, the rich hues and arabesques of its outer face. The wearer alone felt the inconvenient knots and tangled threads of the inner side. It was this shawl that the wearer, departing, threw over my shoulders. Caught in its tangled skein and knots, how old I have grown! My person, protected and surrounded once by a wall of attention and care, now feels exposed and shelterless.

Naresh has been posted to Cairo. Ganesh's wife wanted some things from there, but he laughed and replied, "Bhabi! Let me get these things first for myself and my house!" It was as if a knife had sunk into my heart. "My house." When did I build this one? All my life I've prided myself on this—that my house had never grown alien to my brothers, my sisters, and my mother—as have my brothers' houses. But at this last stage of my life, I realize how hollow my existence has been, and it bows my head down. I have nothing left of my own. I am a man lost in the flow of the crowd.

My life with Janaki was flat and uneventful. But my marriage was neither so simple nor so traditional and eventless.

In this strange world, sometimes, contrary to general belief, it so happens that Lakshmi, the goddess of wealth, and Saraswathi, the goddess of learning, choose to shower their blessings together. My father was not only a scholar in his time, but a *jagirdar*★ as well. I was from the very beginning preoccupied with ideas of social reform and the desire to achieve something. In those days the strongest desire of us college kids was to do something truly constructive.

Janaki's father, a man of great decorum and self-respect, was our neighbor. He was a teacher in an ordinary school, but he had educated Janaki very well for those times. She had finished intermediate and could have entered college the next year. When I had finished my M.A. and was studying for my law degree, Masterji, as Janaki's father was called, had to pay the penalty of fathers of girls in this blessed country of ours. He searched hard, and somehow or other, found a groom for her. A little here, a little there, he put some money together and made arrangements to give his only daughter away. As a neighbor, my father was expected to attend the wedding, but he was ill, so I was to go instead. It was with reluctance that I entered the bride's dingy house. In the courtyard a lightbulb—for which a makeshift connection had been taken from somewhere—emitted a sickly light. A few shapeless bits of bunting hung desolately across, and an old record was playing. Those present were mostly silent. The bride's red sari was covered with gold embroidery; she and the groom were seated near the priest, in front of the ceremonial fire.

★A *jagirdar* is a landowner, the lord of a manor.

I had seen a great deal of Janaki as a girl in our neighborhood. I had seen her at every stage, from childhood to youth. There was nothing worthy of notice in her except that she was a very quiet, very shy girl. She was really pretty in spite of being a bit thin, but her whole being was so subdued and unobtrusive that I had never so much as given a second thought to her.

Before they began to go around the holy fire, there was an unexpected commotion started by the groom's party. It was evident that they had planned it in advance. The groom's elder brother, who had assumed the role of guardian, said that the bride's jewelry and the rest of her dowry fell far short of what was promised, so two thousand rupees—in cash—had to be handed over immediately, or else!

It all seemed like a scene from some film to me. The noise was unbearable and so was the commotion. The priest was still sitting in front of the fire, his mouth open. For a single moment the bride's veil somehow slipped off. Her expression of shame and terror struck my heart like lightning. Masterji was speechless. A few others were arguing on his behalf.

Suddenly—I don't know how it happened—with the swagger of a national hero, I walked up to Masterji and said in a deep voice, "Send the groom's party back, Masterji. I am willing to marry Janaki now and at this auspicious time."

For a moment there was total silence, and then a hum of voices arose. After much argument, the bridal party was sent back, although it had expressed willingness to go through with the marriage even without the two thousand rupees.

And I found myself seated in the bridegroom's place!

My two elder brothers were not at home that day. But my sisters, who were on a visit from their husbands' homes, and my mother were there. My father was bedridden. Before I reached home the news had traveled. It is customary for a bridal party to bring a carriage in which the bride leaves for her new home. I had no such thing. Masterji arranged for a car from someplace, and it was decked with marigolds. It was two in the morning when I, feeling like a criminal, reached home with the red bundle of a bride with me. Masterji had bid us farewell with immense sadness. Janaki was trembling from an excess of emotion like one who had malaria.

My parents were quite distraught and agitated. But Masterji was from a very respectable family and was a brahmin of high status. No one could accuse us of having married for love. Everyone knew the facts. All my brothers and sisters were married, so there was no problem about that. My parents were enlightened people who had no greed or desire for wealth. And everyone liked Janaki. So this event passed by without causing much of a problem.

Although the marriage had, after all, taken place under unusual circumstances, I thought the matter was over and done with, but it was not so. My relationship with Janaki was never cold or bitter, yet somehow, perhaps because the wedding had taken place in such a manner, and the bride had come like an unbidden guest, there was no great celebration in my house. I had said to Janaki, "I expect you will never cause my mother any displeasure and will never make my brothers and sisters feel as if this house is not their own. I have faith in your tranquil personality and trust you will always remember to act thoughtfully."

Pained and frightened, Janaki hung her head low in shame. It was only after her death that I began to realize that my behavior on that day had sown in her the seed from which the two white flowers of duty and acceptance sprang. So the rose of love and intimacy was never to be my portion. After twenty years of married life and seven years as a widower I now see what my words must have meant—that the girl who had left her father's house and had given up the position of daughter was to receive in turn neither a husband's house nor the position of wife. The feelings of pity and compassion lurking behind this marriage had become a curse that struck her forever.

Janaki, where are you now? In how many ways did I humiliate you in my ignorance? But by your silence you have turned each thoughtless gesture into an unpardonable sin.

Janaki seized the role of servant and housekeeper so firmly that she never let it slip. There were times when Mother wanted to hand over the position of mistress, but Janaki wouldn't take it. This might have been because of her weakness, or her lack of ambition, or her sense of inferiority, or perhaps it was that the position of mistress was simply of no importance to her. Who will answer these questions now?

There was a long period in which I lived with only Janaki and Mother. Whether Mother was happy with her or not, it is difficult to say. There was no possibility of quarreling with Janaki; even if someone tried a thousand times, it would be impossible. The management of the house was completely in Mother's hands. She bought everything we needed, and in those twenty years Janaki never asked for anything. She was always nervous about going outside the house. Seldom did she even go across to her own mother's house, which was barely a hundred feet away. She stayed at home and busied herself with the kitchen, the pots and pans, and the washing. She had no fine clothes, and always used mother's worn-out saris. Whenever she was given a new sari, she would put it away carefully, and when my sisters or sisters-in-law came, it would be given to one of them as a gift. What I took to be her contentment was really the feeling of being an outsider. This I realized gradually, only after her death. She received no gifts of clothing or jewelry from our house, and stored away even the little she had received from her father.

As our children—Naresh, Ganesh, and Suresh—arrived, one by one, Mother grew very fond of Janaki, but Janaki never took advantage of that regard. Neither did she have any heated moments with Mother. Where there is no wish for privilege, there can be no conflict. The favor I had done her by saving Masterji from disgrace had become a debt Janaki repaid in installments with her servitude. Indian women do not have the power to think. But they have an infinite capacity to suffer. If by chance they acquire the power to think, then suffering becomes intolerable. But in spite of her awareness, Janaki continued to suffer. My brothers and sisters would arrive and there would be elaborate plans for entertainment and outings and other enjoyments, but Janaki would remain at home, cooking and taking care of the household.

I had always prided myself on the fact that in my house Mother enjoyed a position of honor and respect. Because of me, my sisters never felt their mother's house grow strange. They would hold me up as an example and chide my brothers and sisters-in-law. But after Janaki passed away I realized how baseless my pride had been! I had never really made myself a home.

Once, when my younger sister and her husband were visiting us, my brother-in-law, who had just returned from America with an imported camera, wanted to take a picture of the family. He went right into the kitchen and insisted that Janaki should change her clothes and come out. "Come, get dressed for a photograph," he said.

"Me?" Janaki asked. I was a little disturbed at her consternation. She tried to refuse, but Mother asked her to come and Janaki entered our room, where I was lying down. She began to search for some clothes. All the saris in her closet were either frayed with wear or had been washed at home and were not starched or ironed. There were a few new ones, but she had set them aside, to give away as gifts to someone or the other, and none had their edges sewn or a blouse to match. Somehow or other she found a purple sari and a black blouse to go with it, and got dressed. As she let down her long hair to comb and braid it, I realized suddenly that Janaki was very beautiful.

"Listen! Put some makeup on," I urged. The words sounded strange. After all, when did she have any articles of makeup? She looked at me in confusion.

"Don't you see how smartly turned out Munni is? And she was married long before you were," I said again.

A faint smile appeared on Janaki's face. Without uttering a word, she took out some old containers of kohl and sindoor. The deep sadness of that smile sent a cold wave down my spine. The desire to be photographed and to see Janaki dressed well vanished into the air.

Munni was my beautiful and delicate younger sister. My brother-in-law loved her a great deal. He had gone on a six-month business tour of Europe and America, and Munni had stayed with us. Janaki was expecting a child then. Yet to the last glass of warm milk at bedtime, she saw to it that her hospitality did not fall short of her standards. Janaki never so much as mentioned that she was in her eighth or ninth month, or that she herself had any problems. I now begin to understand that she was paying for living in this house. After all, even if you wish to, you can complain only to those you consider your own. In this house, whom could she call her own? She rose at four in the morning because Mother needed hot water for her bath at five. There was of course a maid to do the heavier chores. But often when she had finished her own work, Janaki would help the maid finish hers. Munni ordered Janaki around as if she, too, were a servant. But was it really Munni's fault? If the one who reads the book himself does not care to dust and preserve it, then it is soon fit only for waste and packing material!

I don't even know whether Janaki loved her children or not. She looked after their needs as mechanically as she did the dishes and the washing—as jobs to be completed and done with as soon as possible. But Janaki loved Masterji, though she rarely visited him. As long as Masterji was alive, it was he who came to see her. He never accepted anything, not even a glass of water, in our house. After Janaki's wedding he lived alone. An old woman, distantly related to him, used to do the household chores for him. And one day, Masterji quietly passed away without any illness or fuss. That was the first time Janaki showed distress. When she heard the news, she rushed out bareheaded and barefoot, and ran all the way to her own house. A little later Mother and I got there. There was a sound of loud wailing in the house. Janaki, so quiet by nature, was in agony. "Babuji, in whose care have you left me?" she wailed. She banged her forehead against the cot on which he lay, and howled. Mother went up to her and put her arms around her, but was unable to hold her in her arms. Janaki broke out of her embrace again and again. It was as if there was nothing left in this world for her.

Masterji died seventeen years after we were married. I had four children, and Mother lived with me. She had grown very old but was still hale and hearty. My brothers and sisters or others often came to spend their holidays here. How much money was spent or why it was spent was never any concern of Janaki's, since the expenses were in Mother's control. When a person never asks for her rights, others naturally become indifferent. Often Mother expressed a desire to hand things over to Janaki, but she always pleaded her forgetfulness as an excuse.

After Masterji's death, Janaki fell ill with fever for many days. But as soon as she was slightly better, she would rise and go about her chores, and by evening the fever would return. Janaki seemed more like a mysterious ghost than a human being in those days. Her eyes blazed out of her dry yellow face seeking something. Whose presence was it that those eyes sought so eagerly? I knew very well that before our marriage she had not so much as raised her eyes to look at any boy. So whom did she wait for? Her body kept withering away but her hair reached down to her calves. Surely she was awaiting some angel who would release her from the bonds of duties and obligations. Her life had been mortgaged towards repayment of a debt.

After four months she recovered, though she never really regained her health. She never ate her meals with the others in the family, so no one knew if she had eaten or not. Her sleep, however, was always deep. Sometimes she murmured while sleeping, but I could never catch anything more than "Babuji." Why did she think of Masterji so much? A good household, a noble husband, wealth—what was it that she lacked? But her bowl remained empty. Certainly she, like every other woman, must have desired a house where there were love, anger, pleading, gifts, presents, squabbling over expenses, and all that make up the warp and woof of joy and sorrow. Instead she had entered a strange relationship, steeped in the emotion of pity, where she had come like an unbidden guest. She had taken my first instruction as the final word and had devoted herself to the service of my mother and sisters. My mother gave her no gift of jewelry. Even the five pieces of jewelry she got from her father were given away to my sisters when their children were born.

One winter twenty years after we were married, and three years after Masterji passed away, Janaki caught pneumonia. I don't quite know why, but I realized that this was to be her last illness. She wasted away like a stick that has been eaten by white ants. Mother had gone to Munni's house. Munni used to come to my house for every confinement, but this time the child was to be born in their house, so Mother had gone there to be with her. My children did not grasp the truth of their mother's condition, but I was greatly perturbed. Doctor after doctor was called in, and a nurse was hired to care for her. I sat by her bedside, and when she came to her senses I would talk to her. Earlier whenever she was ill, or in the days after childbirth, if I went near her or spoke to her she would quickly turn my thoughts to something I had to do for my mother or brother or sisters, such as sending the accounts of the income and expenditures of the joint family property to the others, inviting my sisters to visit our house, sending for Mother's medicines, and so on. But this time she did not turn me away. She, too, understood that she would not be able to serve me long. I went to her. She clutched the hem of my garment so passionately that I forgot myself. I felt as if we had been newly married.

The veil that divided us lifted as love shone through, bright and clear. She held my hand, and in the unconsciousness of sleep said strange things. She asked again and again for a pink sari and earrings that dangled like bells. I was bewildered. Coming back to her senses, she would grow silent again. Her lips would be tightly sewn together. Janaki, this simple, artless girl—how many desires had she silently buried within her!

When her delirium grew uncontrollable and both lungs filled with water, I sent a cable to my mother. But Munni was due to deliver any day and Mother could not come. One morning when there was no one else in the house except the nurse and me, Janaki opened her eyes. Her lips were parched, her face ashen, her eyes distracted. In full consciousness, she said, "Come near me. Listen." I hastened to her side. "Remember one thing," she spoke in a low, weak voice. The nurse, too, was all attention. We strained to catch her feeble voice, which turned into a groan.

"It's about Ritu—she . . ." Who knows what she wanted to tell me about our daughter? Her voice became an indistinct whisper and grew still. The sentence was never to be completed. Her eyes lay open. The one whom she had for so long waited had finally arrived.

The frail body of this thirty-eight-year-old woman lay in my arms. With thousands of unspoken words smothered in her heart, she had left me. It was a strange revenge she had taken.

I grieved, then grew reconciled to her death. In the last seven years the three boys and the girl have been married. All my responsibilities, all my duties have been fulfilled. Whether my life has been successful or not I cannot say. Only when I see newly married couples, I yearn to be born a second time and to marry Janaki again. In this life, in attempting to be an idealist I failed to become even an ordinary man. But give me another chance, and I too will sing a song about going beyond the moon with Janaki.

Translated by Vasantha Kannabiran and Rasheed Moosavi.

NIDUMANURI REVATI DEVI ⸻

(1951–1981)   *Telugu*

It is difficult to understand why a person who was so accomplished in many ways and who yearned so ardently for something that could not be achieved, finally asked, "What if I break the bubble?" and ended her life. No one can say why it happened. "She wanted to be a special person, wanted a distinct personality," her husband wrote of her. "She believed there was really no line between life and death, but searched for the thin line—if it existed at all . . . and, without ever making an attempt to explain it to anybody, she left." The thirty-four poems in the collection Nidu-manuri Revati Devi published in 1981, shortly before she died, have a rare intensity and depth, and there seems little reason why her distinguished poetry is not better known.

Revati Devi was born in Tenali into a well-to-do family. As a child she studied music and dance and developed a love for literature. Since her father, a police officer, was often transferred and the family had to move with him around the state, Revati Devi and her two brothers attended many different schools. She went on to receive a master's degree in philosophy, and was working on a doctoral dissertation on Jean-Paul Sartre at Sri Venkateswara University in Tirupati when she died. Her husband, D. Raghuram Reddy, taught at an engineering college there.

Revati Devi's discovery in 1972 of Vaddera Chandidas's *Himajwala* (The Fire on the Ice) changed the course of her life. She had been writing stories and poems, but stopped after reading Chandidas because she felt there was no point "unless one could write like that." In 1975 she met Chandidas, who read her poetry and encouraged her to continue writing, but it was not until 1978 that poetry "poured out of her pen like a stream." The poems she wrote that year were published in 1981 in the book *Silalolita* (The Rock That Sways), from which the poems translated here have been taken. Revati Devi seems to have been haunted by the sense that her work was influenced too much by Chandidas. In the epilogue to her book she writes, "Perhaps the voice is not mine, but the feelings and the heart from which they have originated are entirely my own." It is possible she was responding to the critic Puranam Subramanya Sarma, who said her poetry seemed to have been written by Chandidas. But perhaps what disturbed her more is that critics and readers saw nothing in her work beyond this influence.

Revati Devi's poetry explores many dimensions of inner life and expresses a certain pain, a restlessness, a dissatisfaction with lives "addicted to sleep." It also speaks of social relationships within the tyranny of caste, of corruption and selfishness. A fine poem, "Duram" (Distance), 1981, explores the distances among a whole range of people, including an unmarried mother and her child and a husband and wife—between whom there is a "distance where even breeze cannot enter."

◆

MUGAVOYINA GONTHU
(My Stricken Voice)

All these days
While I babbled
Because I had nothing to say
You listened to whatever I said.

And now
Now that I have something to tell you
Something very deep
Something I like
Something pure
When I have something to tell you
And I begin to talk
There is no one to hear
That is why maybe
This voice is now mute
Because of its intoxication perhaps
Or perhaps its sweetness
Or because anyway you
Won't hear it
This voice is stilled.

No matter
In this silenced voice lie
The stirrings of an awakened heart

Buried this long in
Drunken slumber.

Translated by Srinivas Rayaprolu.

ASAGNI RENUVU
(Embers of Hope)

Long long after my birth
Realizing I am alive
I feel like weeping for the first time
Because there is no way I can live
Not from a strength of will that takes me beyond pleasure or pain
Nor from a numbness that cannot tell the difference
Nor from an ignorance that cannot distinguish the two.

My life like my birth was uneventful
Unresisted actions in which I was not the subject
Physically, emotionally, morally
I am as responsible for them
As I am for my birth
This awakening sprouting forth suddenly
This moment when I am face to face with myself
From this moment of realization that I am alone
I am responsible for all that I do or leave undone
Some longing, desire, pain
Some confusion agony turmoil
A loneliness an emptiness
Imprisoned by my past
My life is not my own
What if I am born this moment
Break free of all these bonds.

Not that I cannot break them
Nor that I cannot rebel
Nor that I am afraid of the world's stings
Having succumbed to a weakness
I am but the spark of the embers of hope.

Translated by Srinivas Rayaprolu.

KAMALA HEMMIGE ――――――――

(b. 1952)   *Kannada*

"What set me to writing was the turmoil and solitariness of being sixteen. Whenever I felt I was collapsing, writing became a crutch. Even today it is the same," writes Kamala Hemmige, whose principal forms of expression are short fiction and poetry. She was born into a conventional family in the village of Hemmige and considers herself as "coming from the middle class, and as acquainted with all forms of humiliation and exploitation." Kamala Hemmige holds a master's degree in Kannada literature. For several years she worked with All India Radio and is now a television executive with Doordarshan Kendra in Bangalore. Her mother, Sarada Hemmige, is also a poet.

When Kamala Hemmige began writing, the Navya (Modernist) movement in Kannada literature was at its height, and she was influenced by the Navya poets Gopalakrishna Adiga and Ramachandra Sharma as well as by the novelist U. R. Anantamurthy. Later she read with admiration Albert Camus, Jean-Paul Sartre, and Pablo Neruda, as well as translations from Bengali and Malayalam. "Now," she observes, "Navya seems stale. Like a ghost. . . . Now I feel that the only 'solid' poets are those who can be read and understood without recourse to the English language and its traditions."

With sympathy and humor, Kamala Hemmige's poetry explores the contradictions in the lives of middle-class women. She has published four collections of poetry, *Pallavi* (Refrain), 1976, from which the poem translated here is taken; *Vishakanye* (Poison Girl), 1983; *Munjane Bandavanu* (He Who Came at Dawn), 1986; and *Nine Nanna Akasha* (You Are My Sky), 1987; a collection of short stories, *Magha Masada Dina* (A Day in the Month of Magha), 1984; and a novel, *Akhyana,* 1982.

◆

GINI
(The Parrot)

Since the door lies
wide open
I can freely fly. Can float
away, easily, like a boat.

Wonder why
I don't. She
doesn't keep me,
like Khanderaya, hasn't
clipped my wings.

I don't complain
that she gives me daily
cashew nuts and guava.
My fault
that I suddenly demanded
ripe tamarind.
My fault
that I remain silent,
knowing how to speak.
Dreaming as I sit; a hundred
colors.
Grumbling into my beak,
weighing, measuring, pouring.
How cool I sit within
this dark green sheen!
Not so.
In the press of these feathers
how many pomegranates
have burst!

Still . . . turning, whirring up,
flopping again—I sit,
dreaming. I suppose she
knows my failing. Always
the door lies open.

Translated by Tejaswini Niranjana.

VIJAYA DABBE

(b. 1952)   *Kannada*

Vijaya Dabbe is among the most promising and serious of poets writing
in Kannada today. In her poetry the present is not an isolated moment but
the outcome of a long historical development, and her concern for the
welfare of women broadens out to include others oppressed or exploited
in various ways. The poem "Miruguva Gorigalu" (Glittering Tombs) takes
us through a woman's life, each phase of which is bound by the dreams
and desires of the others around her, her voice of protest smothered by a
veil of courtesy. Sumitra Bai considers Vijaya's poems to be marked also
by a fine inwardness and a rhythm and tone that vary in subtle response
to her themes.

   Vijaya Dabbe has published two collections of poetry, the award-
winning *Iruttave* (They Exist), 1975, from which the poems "Narimanigalige Ondu Kivimatu" and "Farida Begum," translated here, are taken,
and *Niru Lohada Chinte* (The Worries of Water and Metal), 1985, from
which we have chosen to translate "Miruguva Gorigalu." Well known
also as a critic and scholar of Kannada literature, she has recovered important early classics and has worked on women writers. Among her
scholarly publications are *Shyamala Sanchaya* (Selections from Shyamala),
1989, a collection of writings by the Kannada writer Shyamala Devi (1910–
1943), and *Mahile Sahitya Samaja* (Women/Literature/Society), 1989. She is
an active member of Samata, a women's group in Mysore, and teaches
Kannada at Mysore University.

◆

NARIMANIGALIGE ONDU KIVIMATU
(Advice to Gentlewomen)

Be fearless.
Never worry.
As long as you don't
lift up your heads
men will surround you, guard you
as if they were your eyes.

In case
a Ravana or a Dushyasana is born,
in case they drag you off
and tug at your sari,
there will always be
a Rama or a Krishna,
brave men
who will grant you
superabundance of clothes,
make you pass the test of fire,
and twirl their mustaches.

Translated by Tejaswini Niranjana.

FARIDA BEGUM
(Mrs. Farida)

People have not seen Farida
without her purdah.

Day, night, college, factory
the street, elsewhere, nowhere
have people seen Farida
without her purdah.

Farida's mother
roams the streets in a cotton sari.
The mother's mother wore
an unwearable piece of cloth—
this everybody knows.

Perhaps you can get
a glimpse of Farida's eyes
through the lace in front.

If it flaps a little in the breeze
she sweats and feels faint
as though it had fallen.

The little groups outside hotels and shops
simper as they dream of the fair beauty
behind the black curtain.

Laughing inside the veil
she turns
into another alley.
Translated by Tejaswini Niranjana.

MIRUGUVA GORIGALU
(Glittering Tombs)

Who waits until they're born?
Sacks of dreams atop a fetus
fetuses atop the sacks of dreams—
do you raise an eyebrow?

They waited
for the infant to emerge.
The baby, not seeing the tomb,
breathed deeply
for those who had faith.
Then shrieked and cried
to shatter their faith.

The mother-in-law put
into her lap this woman
born for her son.
Unable to make her cry
the infant gurgles
blinks its eyes.

As warm dumplings
slid down the throat
Mother's promises
stuck
and began to pound.
The mouth opened
but said nothing.

Year after year
a new dress for the New Year
a purse for the arm
a rose for the hair
so it ran . . . without stopping.
Around ten in the morning
people began to throng the streets.

Father in the easy chair
passing his hand over his head
made a vow about family honor
tried to believe.
It wept
two days
in a darkened room.

A thread that cuts
through the friends'
bunch of dreams.
Their life buried in this one
simmering in the woes they embraced
the word-corpse slept.

In front of this nearly-old
woman
who sits splitting
the eyelashes of those
forty bygone springs,
the glittering tomb winks.

Translated by Tejaswini Niranjana.

JAMEELA NISHAT _____

(Jameela Syed, b. 1953)   *Urdu*

"I dream a great deal. I dream my poems—and now this play I've written.
I have been writing poetry ever since I was a child. I had a very close
friend—I loved her—called Nishat. We used to write to each other. Then
there was a misunderstanding between our families and we were not allowed to keep in touch, so I started writing poems and used Nishat as a
pen name," said this young poet from Hyderabad in a warm, rambling
discussion in which we spoke of her life, her love of literature, her poetry,
her experiments in the theater—and women.

   Born in Hyderabad into a family of artists, Jameela Nishat started studying when she was very young because her mother wanted her daughters
to acquire as much education as possible before they were married in their
early teens. Her father was an artist. She did very well in school and
wanted to study medicine, but was not allowed (despite, she says, "all my

father's progressive views") to enter a coeducational college. Since there was no women's medical college in Hyderabad and going away was out of the question, she could not become a doctor, and was married early. "My husband gave me some liberty and I continued my studies," she says, explaining her master's degree in English literature. She now works as a teacher. The theater has excited her, and she has formal training in the theater arts. "Drama has such a wide canvas," she says, "so much wider than poetry. I want to write more plays."

According to Jameela Nishat, she spontaneously writes what she feels. Many of her poems are about sex or death and draw on images in her surroundings. She traces the recurrent theme of death back to her father's last illness. Her nursing him on his deathbed was a traumatic experience for her. "He struggled for twelve days.... I began to think more about death and wrote many poems ... everyone will have to die.... No! One should have eternal life," she adds with a twinkle in her eye that is not just a twinkle, for she is serious. She has a rich life, she says. "Things happen, I make them happen. I love children, so I teach school." But there is also a pervasive sense of something lacking that makes her feel she must write. In one of her poems, Shakuntala waits for her lover Dushyanta to come, but instead the landlord knocks at the door—for the rent.

Jameela Nishat feels she can "write only as a woman." Most of her poetry is written in Dakkani, a form of Urdu commonly spoken in and around Hyderabad but looked down upon in literary circles, where the norm is the Urdu of Lucknow or Aligarh. She also uses many words derived from Sanskrit in her Urdu poetry and has been criticized for it, though others have praised her ear for the spoken tongue and her syncretic language. All her poems, she insists, are "simple." Jameela Nishat published her first poem in 1970, and has since continued to write in *Kitab Numa,* a journal published at Jamia Millia University in Delhi, and in other poetry magazines. The poem translated here appeared in *Kitab Numa* in 1985.

◆

[What fire is this]

What fire is this
that licks the green pasture of my mind
and leaps in my breath?

Who treads
unseen, with muted steps beside me?
I know not.

The crystal palace of my dreams
is turned to mirage.

O that you understand
what I want.

There's a black mound
on the red earth;
on the black mound I stand
draped in white.
Who will ever know
what I want?

Translated by Syed Sirajuddin.

HEMA PATTANSHETTI ——————————
(b. 1954)   *Kannada*

Hema Pattanshetti's major form of creative expression is the lyric poem,
but she has also published a book of short stories, *Musukidi Mabbinali* (The
Encircling Gloom), 1978. The poem translated here is taken from *Virahotsava* (Celebration of Separation), her first collection of poetry, which
appeared in 1983. A second collection, *Hosa Hadu* (A New Song), was
published in 1986. Both collections have won the Ratnamma Heggade
Award. Hema Pattanshetti is a founder-member of the well-known Dharwar drama troupe Rangabhumika and has translated several plays from
other Indian languages.

In contrast to many other younger women poets writing in Kannada,
who question women's traditional place in society, Hema embodies in her
poetry the attempt to realize her self by accepting her womanhood. In the
poem we have chosen for translation, a woman is waiting for her lord.
Her fulfillment becomes an image of the human condition itself. But
though the poetic persona is marked by its difference from others—the
"eleventh among ten," as she puts it—and though the vision held out to
her has a beauty of cosmic proportions, she is not sure she has the strength
to live out its demands. Her poetry is vividly evoked and is marked by
unconventional forms of narration. Hema teaches in a college in Dharwar.

◆

HATTARALI HANNONDAGI
(Eleventh among Ten)

As the eleventh among ten, I won't live
Nothing will match my vagina, my clan-name, my pulse
Born among demons, I stand here praying,
Desiring a god.
He might come to me, god, lord, master
Might bring the umbrella of hope and promise.
In the field cleared by reapers
He will gather the peasants
Will bring me armfuls of little garlands
Will caress my hair and deck it with
Words and flowers and blue oceans.
I wait. Waiting,
My eyes turn into the sky,
My body into earth and water.
The god might come, might bring nectar.
Among my people I sing his praises
Declaim his virtues
I wait for him to come, I ripen for him
On the hill of age-old mountains
A hundred thousand million times heavy.
My mind decays, my gaze patches the world together
My footsteps falter. I don't want to live
Or die as the eleventh among ten
Until the Lord comes.

Translated by Tejaswini Niranjana.

S. USHA ——————————————

(b. 1954)   *Kannada*

A subtle and gifted writer, S. Usha is generally regarded as a young poet
from whom much can be expected. Her poems deal with the task of re-
generating women's spiritual and creative existence and reflect a deep
awareness of contemporary life. Her critics admit that she is aware of the
problems that haunt women and the urgency of solving them, but argue

that, despite the controlled and evocative language she uses, only a dream world is offered as solution. In the poem chosen for translation, the earth is all that is living, creative, and productive in human life, but it also symbolizes women who have been subdued and reduced to being objects of sensual pleasure. Usha's first poem, "Ammanige" (To Mother), appeared in print in 1972. Her first collection of poems, *Togalugombeya Atmakathe* (The Autobiography of a Puppet), appeared in 1981, and her second, *I Nelada Hadu* (Song of This Earth), in 1990. The poem translated here is the title poem of that collection. She continues to publish in poetry magazines, and, since 1973, has taught college-level Kannada. She also helps edit a literary magazine, *Samvada*.

◆

I NELADA HADU
(Song of This Earth)

You did not see the brood
of Krishna that sucked
the breast and grew
calling again and again
Mother! Come!
Did not see
that she has
besides breasts and thighs
a heart
full of dull red desires.
You turn on the one
called mother, fuck her
then cry
that her whole body's womb
She's a Putani* of the graveyard.

My thighs
gashed by a hundred plows
I, my mother, her mother, mothers,
above all my aunt
bearing the pain
the wound drying

---

*Putani was a demoness sent by King Kamsa to kill the god Krishna, who sucked dry her breast and destroyed her.

Husband or son, who knows
who blazed the furrow?
And the hundreds
of lecherous ones
warming themselves at
the light in my eyes
and the vanity
with which they renounce
their bond with this earth
saying they'll live
in caves, in their own light.

Go, go
Where you will go I don't know
The feet that have put down
roots in my chest
are yours
They call me too—
the hundred colors
of the blue sky
the flying birds
Why do you smugly say
mud and slush are magic?
Friend,
have you never seen
the clouds filling with
drops, growing heavy, unable to
wait any longer, pouring
a great flood down on the earth's
suffering bosom
Dryness and water,
the miracle that waits.

Don't you ever feel
I too could bring
color to your dream,
that hearing my dream's song
your heart may grow lighter
that we might, shoulder
to shoulder, turn the
forest paths into highways?

You coward
you shiver at the sight
of the childbearing grave, she
who conceives, who aborts
You bring flowers
worship her from afar
join your palms to her
and run away
without hearing my
voice my breath my cries
You wreck me
and relieve yourself—
triumphant.

No, no
Set aside
your thousand heads
the thousand feet
the thousand arms
Rub off your colors
and come, friend
Touch my body, and my mind
just once
Forget for a second your
old sickness, think with me
of ships and ports and sweet dreams
of the moving river
of the sun's heat
of the pain when there's no food
of the blood of abortions
For a second
let us raise a hand
to wipe this earth's tears.

Translated by Tejaswini Niranjana.

PRAVASINI MAHAKUD _____

(b. 1957)   *Oriya*

Pravasini Mahakud was born in Kokkasara, a village in western Orissa.
She led a nomadic childhood, moving from place to place in western Orissa with her father, who worked as a police inspector. Her childhood was
spent among the scenic mountains for which that region is renowned. She
grew up, fairly independently, in a family of three sisters and developed,
very early in her life, a love of poetry and a fondness for classical Odissi
dancing. She has taught Oriya literature at a college in western Orissa
since receiving her master's degree in Oriya.

Pravasini Mahakud admits she feels emotionally released when she writes
poetry. Although she has not yet published a volume of poems, her work
has appeared in most of the significant Oriya periodicals and is very popular. Love, solitude and a poignant loneliness are her major themes. She
believes that an invisible destiny guides all spheres of her life.

◆

SATARE ETE NISANGATA KEUNTHI THAE
(This Voice of Loneliness)

Where is this loneliness I hear? Where does it live?
Inside my agony?
Beyond, in the possibility of love?
Further on, in a lake of tears?
Or in the fear of death?

Everywhere in this abandoned castle, soft footfalls.
At the heart, vast gray marshes of some desolate forest.
Silence, like an empty sky, only greater, stronger.
A bird circles far off in the ashen sunlight,
Blue ink imprinted on its wings.

All night the moon calls to your roof,
Having drunk to the full the seven scales of music.
How else can so much loneliness fill my ears?
Even in the scent of the *mahua* carried on the breeze
A frail voice reaches me.

A soft dawn raga breaks my sleep.

What is this friendship with loneliness?

How can it disturb me?

Though I refuse another's power,
Yet loneliness binds me.

I ask no questions, yet loneliness seeks answers.

Never have I called out, yet loneliness lies beside me,
Waiting.

I do not speak, yet
I want to know the beginning and the end.

Why does fear rule me?
Why does it rake my memory?
How can it claim intimacy?

Translated by Jayanta Mahapatra.

A. JAYAPRABHA —————————————

(b. 1957)   *Telugu*

Jayaprabha was born in Nagpur, but grew up in Vishakhapatnam, where the family moved after her father's retirement. She is one of five sisters. "I have always felt closer to my mother than to my father," she comments. "My experiences of childhood and growing up were not particularly happy ones. I met Suryanrayana at college, and marriage seemed as good a way of leaving home as any other." They were married in 1975 and published their first book of poems, *Suryudu Kuda Udayistadu* (Even the Sun Will Rise), together in 1980.

"Initially I wasn't very interested in literature. In fact it was only after I began work on my master's degree that I began to read seriously and, through the students' movement at the university, began also to take an interest in political questions. I realized how marginal the women's question was and decided that women would have to take the initiative when it came to problems that specifically concern them. I think I was always a feminist," she adds.

In 1986 Jayaprabha published a second collection of poetry, *Yuddhonmukhamga* (Preparing to Face War), and researched women in Telugu romantic poetry for her master's degree. That study, which was published in 1988 as *Bhava Kavitvamlo Stri* (Woman in Romantic Poetry), criticized the representation of women in the work of major male poets and was a controversial and pioneering work in Telugu feminist criticism. Also in 1988, she published a third collection of poems, *Vamanudi Mudopadam* (Vamana's Third Foot), from which the poems translated here have been taken. Jayaprabha is working on the modern Telugu theater for her doctorate.

In 1981, together with K. Satyavathy, Jayaprabha started the feminist monthly *Lohita*. Her latest publication is a collection of poems written while she was at the University of Wisconsin in 1989 and 1990, *Ikkada Kurisina Varsham Ekkadi Meghanidi* (The Rain that Falls Here, Where Is the Cloud From?).

◆

CHUPULU
(Stares)

Needle-sharp stares
from two eyes
land on these lumps of flesh
and roam freely about.

Liar stares
that do not dare
look into my eyes, but
crawl
like larvae on my body.

Eyes rich and poor
young and old
stare
at women
alike.

Signaling
the hunger of a drooling dog
the ugly grab of a wolf.
They haunt my dreams.

In the dense jungle
I cannot tell
light from darkness.
There is no escape
from these stares.

On the road,
in the bus,
in the classroom,
they chase my step
snapping here and there.
These poison fangs
knife me.

I feel scared.
I wish I could fly
or vanish into the void.

But the earth is mine too.
I've taught my eyes
to stare back,
equally sharp.
Stares for stares,
that is how I wage my war now.

Those cowardly stares
that cannot look me in the eye
flee to the underworld.

How I long for the day when
not only eyes, but
the whole body
of a woman
bristles.

Translated by B. V. L. Narayana Row.

CHITLINA AKULA MAUNAM
(A Split Leaf's Silence)

Silence
may be melodious in song, occasionally.
More often it is a desert.
Desire of the mind,
the desert storm,
both are silent.

Silence, often sad
as a cow's face,

a word unspoken,
builds a cocoon to live in.

Silence
may be beautiful, occasionally.
More often, a jungle,
or chasm, so huge
one cannot see what lurks across its breadth.

So many nights are silent
like the sky wrapped in darkness.
When the clock stops striking,
doesn't life become motion in stone?
The other side
is always noncraving.
It is hard to carry silence
free of desire.

Should silence bloom
with a hundred petals and hues,
or roar as a cannon,
it would be well.
But what if it spreads,
like a leaf split in winter,
or a flower wilting in the blaze of the pyre,
or a sad bird's call?

Translated by B. V. L. Narayana Row.

VIMALA ⎯⎯⎯⎯⎯⎯⎯⎯⎯⎯⎯⎯⎯⎯⎯

(b. 1959)   *Telugu*

Vimala was born in Hyderabad on May Day. Her father had taken part
in the Telangana People's Struggle. "I cannot recall ever being stopped
from doing anything simply because I was a girl. But my mother was
always in the kitchen and I had her in mind when I wrote the poem
'Vantillu' (The Kitchen)." Their house was full of books, and Vimala read
voraciously. "By the time I finished school, I think I had read most of the
important books in Telugu literature," she says. She has been influenced

most by the poetry of Sri Sri (1910–1983) and by Tenneti Suri's historical recreation, *Chenghiz Khan*.

When she was about sixteen Vimala began writing for a magazine published at her college. Also at that time, she got involved in the student movement and since 1980 has been a full-time political worker. In 1983, she joined the editorial board of the journal *Vimochana*, for which she is now the editor. Since 1986 she has been the Hyderabad city convenor of Virasam, the Andhra Pradesh revolutionary writers' association. The poems translated here are from a collection, *Adavi Uppongina Ratri* (The Night the Jungle Rose Up), published in 1990.

Early in 1991 Vimala was involved in organizing women in Karimnagar district in the largest antiliquor campaign witnessed in Andhra Pradesh. Many women regard liquor as a major problem, since men not only squander their wages on it, but beat their wives and children when they come home drunk. However, since excise taxes from liquor form a large portion of the state's income, licensed liquor shops exist even in villages where there is no running water or electricity. Groups of women began by picketing liquor shops and socially boycotting the erring men. Such enthusiasm was generated that over twenty thousand women gathered for a demonstration in Karimnagar Town on 11 January 1991. Vimala said of the state government's response to the protest: "There were about six hundred armed police there that day. They were out to protect the liquor barons' interests. I couldn't believe it. In fact, when I first saw so many of them I thought the police were conducting some sort of training exercise!"

◆

VANTILLU
(The Kitchen)

I remember the kitchen's
flavor upon flavor,
a mouthwatering treasury,
pungence of seasonings,
and the aroma of incense
from the prayer room
next door. Each morning
the kitchen awoke
to the swish of churning butter,
the scraping of scoured pots.
And in the center, the stove,
fresh washed with mud, painted
and bedecked, all set to burn.

We saved secret money in the
seasoning box; hid sweets too,
and played at cooking with lentils and jaggery.
We played Mother and Father,
in the magic world of kitchen
that wrapped childhood in its spell.

No longer playground for the grownup girl
now trained into kitchenhood.
Like all the mothers and mothers' mothers
before her, in the kitchen
she becomes woman right here.

Our kitchen is a mortuary.
Pans, tins, gunny bags
crowd it like cadavers
that hang amid clouds of damp wood smoke.
Mother floats, a ghost here,
a floating kitchen herself,
her eyes melted in tears,
her hands worn to spoons,
her arms spatulas that turn
into long frying pans, and
other kitchen tools.
Sometimes Mother glows
like a blazing furnace,
and burns through the kitchen,
pacing, restless, a caged tiger,
banging pots and pans.
How easy, they say,
the flick of a ladle and the cooking's done.
No one visits now.
No one comes to the kitchen
except to eat.

My mother was queen of the kitchen,
but the name engraved on the pots and pans
is Father's.

Luck, they say, landed me in my great kitchen,
gas stove, grinder, sink, and tiles.

I make cakes and puddings,
not old-fashioned snacks as my mother did.
But the name engraved on the pots and pans
is my husband's.

My kitchen wakes
to the whistle of the pressure cooker,
the whirr of the electric grinder.
I am a well-appointed kitchen myself,
turning round like a mechanical doll.
My kitchen is a workshop, a clattering,
busy, butcher stall, where I cook
and serve, and clean, and cook again.
In dreams, my kitchen haunts me,
my artistic kitchen dreams,
the smell of seasonings even in the jasmine.

Damn all kitchens. May they burn to cinders,
the kitchens that steal our dreams, drain
our lives, eat our days—like some enormous vulture.
Let us destroy those kitchens
that turned us into serving spoons.
Let us remove the names engraved on the pots and pans.
Come, let us tear out these private stoves,
before our daughters must step
solitary into these kitchens.
For our children's sakes,
Let us destroy these lonely kitchens.

Translated by B. V. L. Narayana Row.

NISCHALA CHITRAM
(Still Life)

Birds, stop flying,
may the world's weeping halt too,
sky, stop fading into blue,
ocean, calm those waves
and breeze, those flutters silence.
All still, even time,
and death's shadows.

World, cease motion.
Hold silent and steady!

I want to repaint
this torn, shattered, faded landscape
with the red brush of this age
just once.

I want to plant a kiss
on the brow of the world
with unselfish love.

Translated by B. V. L. Narayana Row.

APPENDIX:
GUIDE TO PRONUNCIATION
OF AUTHORS' NAMES AND
TITLES OF WORKS

System of Transliteration

The literary pieces included in this anthology are drawn from ten different Indian languages and English. A system of transliteration that is capable of distinguishing between the many different shades of speech sounds of these languages with appropriate diacritical marks would turn out to be impractical and hard to use by readers who want only to pronounce certain words as correctly as possible. The problem of devising a suitable system is compounded by the fact that there is extensive social and regional variation in pronunciation in any language. Principally, in order to keep the body of the main text "reader-friendly," but also because it is unlikely that a reader will actually be required to pronounce all the Indian-language words accurately, we have not used a systematic transliteration in the main text (see the Preface). As some readers might be interested in learning to pronounce the names of the writers and the titles of their work, however, we are providing this guide.

The system of transliteration used here is intended to help the reader articulate the names and titles in a way that is as close to the pronunciation of the native speaker as possible. Separate consonant and vowel charts are provided, with examples. We have used the broad transcription notations of the International Phonetic Alphabet (IPA) with several modifications for this purpose. For instance, among other things, we have opted for /sh/ instead of the IPA form /ʃ/, and /y/ instead of the IPA notation /j/. We have not distinguished among dental, alveolar, and velar nasals and have excluded several other vowel and consonant sounds for which English examples could not be easily found. Where an Indian word and an English word have been given as examples, the Indian word is more accurate and the English one a close approximation. The English words are provided for readers who speak only English, as their pronunciation of the Indian sample words will not give the sound indicated.

VOWELS

The order of the vowels in this chart corresponds to that of most Indian languages.

Symbol	As in word
a	but
ā	bar
æ	bat
i	bit
ī	beat
u	bull
ū	boot
e	bet
ē	bake
o	boredom
ō	bore
ɔ	bought
au	bout
ai	bite
ou	boat
ɔi	boy
ei	bait
ṽ (nasalized vowel)	bon (Fr.)

CONSONANTS

The order of consonants in this chart corresponds to that of most Indian languages. Some of the examples and symbols for aspirates and retroflex sounds are only approximations.

Symbol	As in word
k	skate
kh	khaddar, Kate
g	get
gh	ghat, loghouse
c	church
ch	hitchhike
j	judge
jh	hedgehog
ṭ	stick
ṭh	lighthouse
ḍ	drum, hundred
ḍh	adhere
ṇ	vina, button
t	mythology
th	plethora
d	khadi, mother
dh	dhoti, withhold
n	nap, swing
p	spin
ph	phagun, pin
b	bag
bh	bhang, abhor
m	man
y	yes
r	right
l	light
v	very
w	wet
s	see, satem
sh	should
h	house
ḷ	bottle
z	zeal
zh	genre (Fr.)
f	flow

The authors are listed alphabetically by first name. The transliterations of the names and titles follow each name.

Abburi Chaya Devi
abbūri chāyā dēvi
srīmati udyōgini

Achanta Sarada Devi
ācaṇṭa sāradā dēvi
aḍavi dāgina vennela

A. Jayaprabha
jayaprabha
a. cūpulu
b. ciṭlina ākula maunam

Ambai
ambai
anil

Amrita Pritam
amritā prītam
a. ēk bāt
b. jāḍa

Anupama Niranjana
anupamā niranjanā
ondu ghaṭane mattu anantara

Anuradha Potdar
anurādhā pōtdār
tumce hē sōjwaḷ samsār

Baby Kamble
bēbi kāmbḷe
jiṇa āmuca

Binapani Mohanty
bīnāpāni mohanti
ashru anōḷa

Brahmotri Mohanty
brahmōtri mohanti
a. thārē mō gɔḍo khāsijiba pɔre
b. dɔrpaṇa

Chhaya Datar
chāyā datār
swatahacya shodhāt

Chudamani Raghavan
cūḍāmaṇī rāghavan
nāngam āshramam

Dhiruben Patel
dhīruben paṭēl
shimlanā phūl

Dudala Salamma
dūḍala sālamma
dūḍala sālamma, khilā shapūr

Gauri Deshpande
gaurī dēshpānḍe
ahē hē asē ahē

Hajira Shakoor
hajīrā shakūr
umr khaid

Hamsa Waḍkar
hamsā wāḍkar
sāngatye aikā

Hema Paṭṭansheṭṭi
hēmā paṭṭansheṭṭi
hattarali hannondāgi

Illindala Saraswati Devi
illindala saraswatī dēvi
anāswāsita

Indira Sant
indiraā sānt
a. kaṇav
b. dhukhya sārakhā
c. shāpit

Ismat Chugtai
ismat cugtai
lihāf

Jameela Nishat
jamīlā nishat
[untitled]

Jaya Mehta
jayā mehtā
a. lōkshāhimā
b. ekōham bahusyām
c. dushmannū laskar pasār thai gayu

Jeelani Bano
jilānī bāno
tamāshā

K. Saraswathi Amma
k. saraswatī amma
vivāhangaḷ swargatil veccu naḍattapeḍunnu

Kabita Sinha
kabitā sinha
a. īshwarkē īv
b. [untitled]
c. mɔhasheta

Kamal Desai
kamal dēsai
tiḷā bandh

Kamala Hemmige
kamalā hemmige
giṇi

Kundanika Kapadia
kundanikā kāpaḍiyā
sāt paglā akāshmā

M. K. Indira
m. k. indirā
phaṇiyamma

Madhavikutty
mādhavīkuṭṭi
pāyasam

Mahasweta Devi
mɔhasheta debi
shishu

Malati Pattanshetti
mālatī paṭṭansheṭṭi
sambandha

Malini Bhattacharya
mālinī bhaṭṭācārya
meye dilē shajiye

Manjul Bhagat
manjul bhagat
bebejī

Mannu Bhandari
mannu bhaṇḍāri
saza

Meena Kumari Naz
mīnā kumārī nāz
[untitled]

Meherunnisa Parvez
mehrunnisā parvez
ṭōnā

Mrinal Pande
mriṇāl pāṇḍe
ham safar

Nabaneeta Dev Sen
nɔbonita deb shen
muzior hulo'z hɔlidei

Nidumanuri Revati Devi
niḍumanūri rēvatī dēvi
a. mūgavōyina gontu
b. āsāgni rēṇuwu

Nita Ramaiya
nītā rāmayya
a. ognissou-ognyeisinū varas
b. trīji ānkhnū jantarmantar

O. V. Usha
o. v. ushā
mrigayā

P. Vatsala
p. vatsala
oru taḍavucāṭṭatinde kadha

Panna Naik
pannā nāyak

a. billi
b. shishu

Pratibha Ray
pratibhā rē
kamboḷɔ

Pratibha Satpathy
pratibhā satpati
kakɔrɔ tɔpo

Pravasini Mahakud
pravāshinī mahākuḍ
sɔttare ette nisɔngata kyonthi thai

Rajalekshmy
rājalekshmi
ātmahatya

Rajam Krishnan
rājam krishnan
kaipiḍite kādaloruvanai

Rajee Seth
rājī sēṭh
uskā ākāsh

Rasheed Jahan
rashīd jahān
wō

Ratakonda Vasundhara Devi
rāṭakoṇḍa vasundharā dēvi
picci

Razia Sajjad Zaheer
raziya sajjad zahīr
nīc

S. Usha
s. usha
ī nelada hāḍu

Sajida Zaidi
sajīdā zaidi
a. rishta
b. naye zaviye

Sarah Joseph
sārā jōsef
mazha

Saroj Pathak
sarōj pāṭhak
saugandh

Saroop Dhruv
sarūp dhruv
a. ēknū ēk vastra
b. flæp dōrni ārpār

Shanta Shelke
shāntā shēḷke
pannāshī ulṭunhī

Shashikala Veerayya Swamy
shashikaḷā vīrayya swāmi
mēṇabatti

Shivani
shivānī
dādi

Siddiqa Begum Sevharvi
siddikhā bēgam sēvhārvi
tāre laraz rahē haĩ

Sugatha Kumari
sugāda kumāri
rātrimazha

Sulekha Sanyal
shulēkha shannal
nɔbonkur

Triveni
trivēṇi
koneya nirdhāra

Vaidehi
vaidēhi
shakuntale yondige kaḷeda aparāhna

Varsha Adalja
varshā aḍaljā
bicārī campūḍi

Veena Shanteshwar
vīna shāntēshwar
avaḷa swātantriya

Vijaya Dabbe
vijayā dabbe
a. nārīmaṇigaḷige ondu kiwimātu
b. faridā bēgam
c. miruguva gōrigaḷu

Vimala
vimalā
a. wanṭillu
b. niscala citram

Wajeda Tabassum
wājēda tabassam
utraṇ

Zahida Zaidi
zahīdā zaidi
bacpanā chōḍ dō

BIBLIOGRAPHY

Books

Agarwal, Bina. *Agricultural Modernisation and Third World Women.* Geneva: International Labour Organisation, 1981.

Agarwal, Bina, ed. *Structures of Patriarchy: State, Community and Household in Modernising Asia.* Delhi: Kali for Women, 1988.

Agarwala, B. R., ed. *The Shah Bano Case: Plight of a Muslim Woman.* Delhi: Arnold Heinemann, 1986.

Ahmed, Rafiuddin. *The Bengal Muslims 1871-1906: A Quest for Identity.* 2nd ed. Delhi: Oxford University Press, 1988.

Alexander, Meena. "Exiled by a Dead Script." In *Contemporary Indian English Verse: An Evaluation.* Edited by Chirantan Kulshrestha, pp. 23-26. Delhi: Arnold Heinemann, 1980.

Alladi, Uma. *Woman and Her Family: Indian and Afro-American—A Literary Perspective.* Delhi: Sterling Publishers, 1989.

Allen, N. J., et al., eds. *Oxford University Papers on India.* Vol. 1, part 2. Delhi: Oxford University Press, 1987.

All India Congress Committee. *Resolutions on Economic Policy and Programme, 1924-1954.* Delhi: Indian National Congress, 1954.

Ambedkar, B. R. *Thoughts on Pakistan.* Bombay: Thacker & Co., 1947.

Ambedkar, B. R. *Poona Pact: An Epic of Human Rights.* Jallander: Buddhist Publishing House, 1982.

Amin, Shahid. "Gandhi as Mahatma: Gorakhpur District, Eastern UP, 1921-2."

613

In *Subaltern Studies III: Writings on South Asian History and Society*. Edited by Ranajit Guha, pp. 1–61. Delhi: Oxford University Press, 1984.

Amuta, Chidi. *The Theory of African Literature: Implications for Practical Criticism*. London: Zed Books, 1989.

Anantamurthy, U. R. "The Search for an Identity: A Kannada Writer's Viewpoint." In *Dialogue: New Cultural Identities*. Edited by Guy Amurthanayagam, pp. 66–78. London: Macmillan, 1982.

Anderson, Benedict. *Imagined Communities: Reflections on the Origin and Spread of Nationalism*. London: Verso and New Left Books, 1983.

Antherjanam, Lalithambika. *Seetha Muthal Satyavathi Vare*. Kottayam: Sahitya Pravartaka Co-operative, 1972.

Appadorai, A., ed. *Documents in Political Thought in Modern India*. Delhi: Oxford University Press, 1973.

Arkin, Marian, and Shollar, Barbara, eds. *Longman Anthology of World Literature by Women 1875–1975*. White Plains: Longman, 1989.

Armstrong, Nancy. *Desire and Domestic Fiction: A Political History of the Novel*. Oxford: Oxford University Press, 1987.

Arnold, David. *Police Power and Colonial Rule: Madras 1859–1947*. Delhi: Oxford University Press, 1986.

Arnold, David. "Quit India in Madras: Hiatus or Climacteric?" In *The Indian Nation in 1942*. Edited by Gyanendra Pandey. Calcutta: K. P. Bagchi & Co., 1988.

Arundale, Rukmini Devi. "Spiritual Background." In *Bhrata Natyam: Indian Classical Dance Art*. Edited by Sunil Kothari, p. 16. Delhi: Marg Publications, 1979.

Asad, Talal. "The Concept of Cultural Translation." In *Writing Culture: The Poetics and Politics of Ethnography*. Edited by James Clifford and George Marcus, pp. 141–164. Berkeley: University of California Press, 1986.

Azad, Nandini. *Empowering Women Workers: The WWF Experiment in Indian Cities*. Madras: Working Women's Forum, 1986.

Bagchi, Amiya Kumar. *The Political Economy of Underdevelopment*. Cambridge: Cambridge University Press, 1982.

Bagchi, Amiya Kumar, ed. *Economy, Society, and Polity: Essays in the Political Economy of Indian Planning*. Calcutta: Oxford University Press, 1988.

Bagchi, Jasodhara, ed. *Indian Women: Myth and Reality*. Calcutta: School of Women's Studies, Jadavpur University, 1990.

Bala, Usha. *Indian Women Freedom Fighters*. Delhi: Manohar, 1986.

Balagopal, K. *Probings in the Political Economy of Agrarian Classes and Conflicts*. Edited by G. Hargopal. Hyderabad: Perspectives, 1988.

Balasubrahmanyan, Vimal. *Mirror Image: The Media and the Women's Question*. Bombay: Centre for Education and Documentation, 1988.

Balasubrahmanyan, Vimal. *In Search of Justice: Women, Law, Landmark Judgements and the Media*. Bombay: S.N.D.T. Research Centre for Women's Studies, 1990.

Baldick, Chris. *The Social Mission of English Criticism 1848–1932*. Oxford: Clarendon Press, 1983.

Bandopadhyay, Sibaji. "Contemporary Popular Bengali Fiction—Textual Strategies." In *Indian Women: Myth and Reality*. Edited by Jasodhara Bagchi, pp. 1–7. Calcutta: School of Women's Studies, Jadavpur University, 1990.

Banerjee, Nirmala, ed. *Women and Industrialisation in Developing Countries*. Delhi: Orient Longman, 1984.

Banerjee, Sumanta. *The Parlour and the Street: Elite and Popular Culture in Nineteenth-Century Calcutta*. Calcutta: Seagull Books, 1989.

Banerjee, Sumanta. *In The Wake of Naxalbari: A History of the Naxalite Movement in India*. Calcutta: Subarnarekha, 1980.

Barker, Francis, et al., eds. *Policing the Crisis: War, Politics and Culture in the Eighties*. Colchester: University of Essex, 1984.

Bhabha, Homi, ed. *Nation and Narration*. London: Routledge, 1990. See especially his essay "DissemiNation: Time, Narrative and the Margins of the Modern Nation," pp. 291–322.

Bhatt, Ela. *Grind of Work*. Ahmedabad: Self Employed Women's Association, 1989.

Caplan, Pat, ed. *The Cultural Construction of Sexuality*. London: Tavistock Publications, 1987.

Carby, Hazel V. *Reconstructing Womanhood: The Emergence of the Afro-American Novelist*. New York: Oxford University Press, 1989.

Centre for Contemporary Cultural Studies. *The Empire Strikes Back: Race and Racism in 70s Britain*. London: Hutchinson, 1982.

Chandra, Bipan, et al. *India's Struggle for Independence 1857–1947*. Delhi: Viking, 1988.

Chatterjee, Partha. *Nationalist Thought and the Colonial World: A Derivative Discourse?* Delhi: Oxford University Press, 1986.

Chatterjee, Partha. "The Nationalist Resolution of the Women's Question." In *Recasting Women: Essays in Colonial History*. Edited by Kumkum Sangari and Sudesh Vaid, pp. 233–253. Delhi: Kali for Women, 1989, and New Brunswick: Rutgers University Press, 1990.

Chatterji, Lola, ed. *Women Image Text: Feminist Readings of Literary Texts*. Delhi: Trianka, 1986.

Chattopadhyay, Kamaladevi. *Indian Women's Battle for Freedom*. Delhi: Abhinav Publications, 1983.

Chattopadhyay, Kamaladevi. *Inner Recesses, Outer Spaces: Memoirs*. Delhi: Navrang, 1986.

Chugtai, Ismat. *The Quilt and Other Stories*. Translated by Tahira Naqvi and Syeda S. Hameed. Delhi: Kali for Women, 1990.

Clifford, James, and Marcus, George, eds. *Writing Culture: The Politics and Poetics of Ethnography*. Berkeley: University of California Press, 1986.

Coward, Rosalind. *Patriarchal Precedents: Sexuality and Social Relations*. London: Routledge and Kegan Paul, 1983.

Croll, Elizabeth. *Feminism and Socialism in China*. New York: Schocken Books, 1984.

Datar, Chhaya. *Waging Change: Women Tobacco Workers in Nipani Organize*. Delhi: Kali for Women, 1989.

Daheja, Vijaya. *Antal and Her Path of Love*. Albany: SUNY Press, 1990.

Desai, A. R., ed. *Agrarian Struggles in India after Independence*. Delhi: Oxford University Press, 1986.

Desai, Neera, and Krishnaraj, Maithreyi. *Women and Society in India*. Delhi: Ajanta Publications, 1990.

Devi, Mahasweta. *Five Plays.* Translated by Samik Bandyopadhyay. Calcutta: Sea-gull Books, 1986.

Dhanagare, D. N. *Peasant Movements in India 1920-1950.* Delhi: Oxford University Press, 1983.

Diamond, Stanley. *Anthropology: Ancestors and Heirs.* The Hague: Mouton, 1980.

Dube, Leela, et al., eds. *Visibility and Power: Essays on Women in Society and Development.* Delhi: Oxford University Press, 1986.

Eck, Diana L., and Jain, Devaki, eds. *Speaking of Faith: Cross-cultural Perspectives on Women, Religion and Social Change.* Delhi: Kali for Women, 1986.

Ehrenreich, Barbara, and English, Deidre. *For Her Own Good: 150 Years of Experts' Advice to Women.* New York: Anchor Books, 1979.

Ellmann, Mary. *Thinking about Women.* New York: Harcourt, 1968.

Engineer, Asghar Ali, ed. *Status of Women in Islam.* Delhi: Ajanta Publications, 1987.

Everett, Jana Matson. *Women and Social Change in India.* 1981. Reprint. Delhi: Heritage Publishers, 1985.

Fanon, Frantz. *The Wretched of the Earth.* Translated by Constance Farrington. Harmondsworth: Penguin, 1967.

Foot, Paul. *The Rise of Enoch Powell.* Harmondsworth: Penguin, 1969.

Foucault, Michel. *Power/Knowledge: Selected Interviews and Other Writings 1972-1977.* New York: Pantheon, 1980.

Foucault, Michel. "Nietzsche, Genealogy, History." In *The Foucault Reader.* Edited by Paul Rabinow, pp. 76-100. Harmondsworth: Penguin, 1984.

Frankel, Francine R. *India's Political Economy, 1947-1977: The Gradual Revolution.* Delhi: Oxford University Press, 1978.

Friedan, Betty. *The Feminine Mystique.* New York: W. W. Norton, 1963.

Gallagher, Catherine, and Lacqueur, Thomas, eds. *The Making of the Modern Body: Sexuality and Society in the Nineteenth Century.* Berkeley: University of California Press, 1987.

Gandhi, M. K. "Hind Swaraj." In *The Collected Works of Mahatma Gandhi.* Vol. 10: Nov. 1909-Mar. 1911, pp. 7-65. Delhi: Publication Division, Ministry of Information Broadcasting, Government of India, 1963.

Gandhi, Nandita. "The Anti-Price Rise Movement." In *A Space Within the Struggle.* Edited by Ilina Sen, pp. 50-81. Delhi: Kali for Women, 1990.

Gandhi, Nandita, and Shah, Nandita. *The Issues at Stake: Theory and Practice in the Contemporary Women's Movement in India.* Delhi: Kali for Women, 1992.

Ghadially, Rehana, ed. *Women in Indian Society: A Reader.* Delhi: Sage Publications, 1988.

Ghatak, Ritwick. "Subarnarekha: Director's Statement, 1966." In *Ritwick Ghatak: Arguments/Stories.* Edited by Ashish Rajadhyaksha and Amrit Gangar, pp. 78-80. Bombay: Research Centre for Cinema Studies, 1987.

Gilbert, Sandra, and Gubar, Susan. *The Madwoman in the Attic: The Woman Writer and the Nineteenth-Century Literary Imagination.* New Haven: Yale University Press, 1979.

Gilbert, Sandra, and Gubar, Susan, eds. *The Norton Anthology of Literature by Women: The Tradition in English.* New York: W. W. Norton, 1985.

Government of Andhra Pradesh. *Report of the Commission of Inquiry into the Rameeza Bee and the Ahmed Hussain Case.* 1978.

Government of India, Department of Social Welfare. *Towards Equality: Report of the Committee on the Status of Women in India.* Delhi: Department of Social Welfare, 1974.

Guha, Ranajit. *An Indian Historiography of India: A Nineteenth-Century Agenda and Its Implications.* Calcutta: Centre for Studies in Social Sciences, 1988.

Guha, Ranajit, ed. *Subaltern Studies V: Writings on South Asian History and Society.* Delhi: Oxford University Press, 1987. See especially his essay "Chandra's Death," pp. 135–165.

Hardiman, David. *The Coming of the Devi: Adivasi Assertion in Western India.* Delhi: Oxford University Press, 1987.

Harlow, Barbara. *Resistance Literature.* London and New York: Methuen, 1987.

Hobsbawm, Eric, and Ranger, Terence, eds. *The Invention of Tradition.* Cambridge: Cambridge University Press, 1983.

Howe, Florence. *Myths of Co-education.* Bloomington: Indiana University Press, 1987.

Hurston, Zora Neale. *Their Eyes Were Watching God.* Urbana: University of Illinois Press, 1978.

Hutchins, Francis G. *Illusion of Permanence: British Imperialism in India.* Princeton: Princeton University Press, 1967.

Inden, Ronald. *Imagining India.* Oxford: Basil Blackwell, 1990.

Indira, M. K. *Phaniyamma.* Translated by Tejaswini Niranjana. Delhi: Kali for Women, 1989.

Iyengar, K. R. Srinivasa. *Indian Writing in English.* Bombay: Asia Publishing House, 1973.

Jayawardena, Kumari. *Feminism and Nationalism in the Third World.* London: Zed Books, 1986.

Jeffrey, Patricia, Jeffrey, Roger, and Lyon, Andrew. *Labour Pains and Labour Power: Women and Childbearing in India.* Delhi: Manohar, 1989.

Johnson, Richard, et al., eds. *Making Histories: Studies in History-writing and Politics.* London: Hutchinson, 1982.

Joshi, Rama, and Liddle, Joanna. *Daughters of Independence: Gender, Caste and Class in India.* Delhi: Kali for Women, 1986.

Joshi, Svati, ed. *Rethinking English: Essays in Literature, Language, History.* Delhi: Trianka, 1991.

Kakar, Sudhir. *Intimate Relations: Exploring Indian Sexuality.* Delhi: Viking, 1989.

Kakar, Sudhir. *The Inner World: A Psycho-analytic Study of Childhood and Society in India.* 2nd ed. Delhi: Oxford University Press, 1982.

Kannabiran, Vasantha, and Lalita, K. "That Magic Time: Women in the Telangana People's Struggle." In *Recasting Women: Essays in Colonial History.* Edited by Kumkum Sangari and Sudesh Vaid, pp. 180–203. Delhi: Kali for Women, 1989.

Kaplan, Cora. *Sea Changes: Culture and Feminism.* London: Verso and New Left Books, 1986.

Kapur, Geeta. "Articulating the Self into History—Ritwik Ghatak's Jukti Takko Ar Gappo." In *Ritwik Ghatak: Arguments/Stories.* Edited by Ashish Rajadhyaksha and Amrit Gangar, pp. 123–140. Bombay: Research Centre for Cinema Studies, 1987.

Karat, Prakash. *Language and Nationality Politics in India.* Madras: Orient Longman, 1973.

Karve, Irawati. *Yuganta: The End of an Epoch*. Delhi: Orient Longman, 1974.

Kaur, Amrit. "Women Under a New Constitution." In *Our Cause: A Symposium by Indian Women*. Edited by Shyam Kumari Nehru, pp. 366–381. Allahabad: Kitabistan, 1938.

Kaur, Manmohan. *Women in India's Freedom Struggle*. Delhi: Sterling, 1985.

Kelkar, Govind, and Gala, Chetna. "The Bodhgaya Land Struggle." In *A Space Within the Struggle*. Edited by Ilina Sen, pp. 82–110. Delhi: Kali for Women, 1990.

Kosambi, D. D. *Myth and Reality: Studies in the Formation of Indian Culture*. London: Sangam Books, 1983.

Kosambi, D. D. *The Culture and Civilization of India in Historical Outline*. Delhi: Vikas Publishing House, 1987.

Kotari, Rajani. *Democratic Polity and Social Changes in India: Crisis and Opportunities*. Bombay: Allied Publishers, 1976.

Kothari, Sunil, ed. *Bhrata Natyam: Indian Classical Dance Art*. Delhi: Marg Publications, 1979. See especially his essay "History: Roots, Growth and Revival," pp. 23–29.

Lacan, Jacques. *Ecrits: A Selection*. Translated by Alan Sheridan. New York: W. W. Norton and Co., 1977.

Laclau, Ernesto. *New Reflections on the Revolution of Our Times*. London: Verso, 1990.

Lakshmi, C. S. *The Face Behind the Mask: Women in Tamil Literature*. New Delhi: Shakti Books, 1986.

Lalita, K. "Women in Revolt: A Historical Analysis of the Progressive Organisation of Women in Andhra Pradesh." In *Women's Struggles and Strategies*. Edited by Saskia Wieringa, pp. 54–68. Aldershot: Gower, 1988.

Loomba, Ania. *Race, Gender, Renaissance Drama*. Manchester: Manchester University Press, 1989.

Metcalf, Barbara, ed. *Moral Conduct and Moral Authority in South Asian Islam*. Berkeley: University of California Press, 1984.

Mies, Maria. *Indian Women and Patriarchy*. Delhi: Concept, 1980.

Mies, Maria. *The Lacemakers of Narsapur: Indian Housewives Produce for the World Market*. London: Zed Books, 1982.

Mies, Maria. *Patriarchy and Accumulation on a World Scale*. London: Zed Books, 1986.

Mies, Maria, Lalita, K., and Kumari, Krishna. *Indian Women in Subsistence and Agricultural Labour*. Delhi: Vistaar Publications, 1986.

Montagu, Edwin S. *An Indian Diary*. Edited by Venetia Montagu. London: W. Heinemann Ltd., 1930.

Mukherjee, Meenakshi. *Realism and Reality: The Novel and Society in India*. Delhi: Oxford University Press, 1985.

Mulhern, Francis. *The Moment of 'Scrutiny.'* London: Verso and New Left Books, 1981.

Murshid, Gulam. *The Reluctant Debutante*. Rajashahi: Rajashahi University Sahitya Samsad, 1983.

Nairn, Tom. *The Break-up of Britain*. London: New Left Books, 1977.

Nancy, Jean-Luc. *La Communauté désœuvrée*. Paris: Galilée, 1986.

Nanda, B. R., ed. *Indian Women: From Purdah to Modernity*. 1976. Reprint. Delhi: Radiant Publishers, 1990.

Nandy, Ashis. *Traditions, Tyranny and Utopias: Essays in the Politics of Awareness*. Delhi: Oxford University Press, 1987.

Nandy, Ashis. *The Intimate Enemy: Loss and Recovery of Self Under Colonialism*. Delhi: Oxford University Press, 1988.

Narasimhaiah, C. D. *The Swan and the Eagle*. Simla: Indian Institute of Advanced Study, 1970.

Narayan, Jayaprakash. *Nation Building in India*. Varanasi: Navchetana Prakashan, 1975.

Natarajan, S. *Century of Social Reform in India*. Bombay: Asia Publishing House, 1959.

National Commission on Self-Employed Women and Women in the Informal Sector (India). *Shramashakti: A Report*, prepared at the request of the Department of Women and Child Development, Ministry of Human Resources Development, June 1988.

Nehru, Jawaharlal. *The Discovery of India*. 1946. Reprint. London: Meridian Books Limited, 1960.

Nehru, Shyam Kumari, ed. *Our Cause: A Symposium by Indian Women*. Allahabad: Kitabistan, 1938.

Olsen, Tillie. *Silences*. London: Virago, 1980.

Pandey, Gyanendra, ed. *The Indian Nation in 1942*. Calcutta: K. P. Bagchi & Co., 1988. See especially his essay "The Revolt of August 1942 in Eastern Uttar Pradesh and Bihar," pp. 123–164.

Pandey, Gyanendra. *The Construction of Communalism in Colonial North India*. Delhi: Oxford University Press, 1990.

Pollock, Griselda. *Vision and Difference: Femininity, Feminism and Histories of Art*. London: Routledge, 1988.

Pradhan, Sudhi, ed. *The Marxist Cultural Movement in India. Vol. 1: Chronicles and Documents 1936–1947*. Calcutta: Mrs. Shanti Pradhan, 1979. *Vol. 2: Chronicles and Documents 1947–1958*. Calcutta: Navana, 1982.

Qureshi, I. H. *The Muslim Community of the Indo-Pakistan Subcontinent (610–1947): A Brief Historical Analysis*. The Hague: Mouton & Co., 1962.

Ramabai, Pandita Saraswati. *My Testimony*. Kedgaon: Mukti Mission Press, 1917.

Ramamirthathammal, Muvalar. *Dasikal Mosavalai*. Madras: Pearl Press, 1936.

Reddy, T. Nagi. *India Mortgaged: A Marxist-Leninist Appraisal*. Anantapuram: Tarimela Nagi Reddy Memorial Trust, 1978.

Rudolf, S., and Rudolf, L. *The Modernity of Tradition*. Chicago: University of Chicago Press, 1967.

Russ, Joanna. *How to Suppress Women's Writing*. London: Women's Press, 1984.

Said, Edward W. *Orientalism*. New York: Pantheon, 1978.

Said, Edward W. *After the Last Sky: Palestinian Lives*. London and Boston: Faber & Faber, 1986.

Sangari, Kumkum. *Mirabai and the Spiritual Economy of Bhakti*. Occasional Papers on History and Society, 2nd ser., no. 28. Delhi: Nehru Memorial Museum and Library, 1990.

Sangari, Kumkum, and Vaid, Sudesh, eds. *Recasting Women: Essays in Colonial His-*

tory. Delhi: Kali for Women, 1989, and New Brunswick: Rutgers University Press, 1990.

Sant, Indira. *Snake Skin and Other Poems*. Translated by Vrinda Nabar and Nissim Ezekiel. Bombay: Nirmala Sadanand Publishers, 1973.

Sarkar, Lotika. "Jawaharlal Nehru and the Hindu Code Bill." In *Indian Women: From Purdah to Modernity*. Edited by B. R. Nanda, pp. 87–98. 1976. Reprint. Delhi: Radiant Publishers, 1990.

Sarkar, Sumit. *Modern India: 1885–1947*. Madras: Macmillan, 1983.

Sathe, Nirmala. "About Stri Mukti and Shramik Sanghatana." Mimeo, 1981.

Selbourne, David. *An Eye to India: The Unmasking of a Tyranny*. Harmondsworth: Penguin, 1977.

Sen, Ilina, ed. *A Space Within the Struggle: Women's Participation in People's Movements*. Delhi: Kali for Women, 1990.

Sen, Sunil. *The Working Women and Popular Movements in Bengal: From the Gandhi Era to the Present Day*. Calcutta: K. P. Bagchi & Co., 1985.

Sen Gupta, Bhabani. *Communism in Indian Politics*. New York: Columbia University Press, 1972.

Shiva, Vandana. *Staying Alive: Women, Ecology and Survival in India*. Delhi: Kali for Women, 1988.

Shiva, Vandana. *The Violence of the Green Revolution: Third World Agriculture, Ecology and Politics*. Penang: Third World Network, 1991.

Showalter, Elaine. *A Literature of Their Own: British Women Novelists from Brontë to Lessing*. Princeton: Princeton University Press, 1977.

Showalter, Elaine, ed. *The New Feminist Criticism: Essays on Women, Literature and Theory*. London: Virago Press, 1985. See especially her essay "Toward a Feminist Poetics," pp. 125–143.

Sitaramayya, P. *The History of the Indian National Congress*. Vol. 2. Bombay: Padma Publications, 1947.

Sommer, Doris. "Irresistible Romance: The Foundational Fictions of Latin America." In *Nation and Narration*. Edited by Homi Bhabha, pp. 71–98. London: Routledge, 1990.

Spivak, Gayatri Chakravorty. *In Other Worlds: Essays in Cultural Politics*. New York: Methuen, 1987.

Srinivas, M. N. *The Dominant Caste and Other Essays*. Delhi: Oxford University Press, 1987.

Srinivas, M. N. *The Cohesive Role of Sanskritisation and Other Essays*. Delhi: Oxford University Press, 1989.

Srivastava, Mukesh. "The Story of India: The Narrative Production of Humanism in E. M. Forster's *A Passage to India,* Jawaharlal Nehru's *Discovery of India* and Salman Rushdie's *Midnight's Children*." Ph.D. diss., Central Institute of English and Foreign Languages, Hyderabad, 1993.

Stree Shakti Sanghatana. *"We were making history . . .": Life and Stories of Women in the Telangana People's Struggle*. Delhi: Kali for Women, 1989, and London: Zed Books, 1989.

Subbamma, Malladi. *Women: Tradition and Culture*. New Delhi: Sterling Publishers, 1985.

Subramanyan, K. G. *The Living Tradition: Perspectives on Modern Indian Art*. Calcutta: Seagull Books, 1987.

Subrahmanyam, Padma. *Bharata's Art: Then and Now.* Madras: Nrithodaya, 1979.

Sunder Rajan, Rajeswari, ed. *The Lie of the Land: English Literary Studies in India.* Delhi: Oxford University Press, 1991.

Tarachand. *The Influence of Islam on Indian Culture.* Allahabad: Indian Press, 1963.

Tharu, Susie. "Tracing Savithri's Pedigree." In *Recasting Women: Essays in Colonial History.* Edited by Kumkum Sangari and Sudesh Vaid, pp. 254–268. Delhi: Kali for Women, 1989.

Tharu, Susie. "The Myth of Universalism: Feminism and the Problematic of Civil Liberties." In *Indian Women: Myth and Reality.* Edited by Jasodhara Bagchi, pp. Tharu 1–14. Calcutta: School of Women's Studies, Jadaupur University, 1990.

Tharu, Susie, and Lalita, K. *Women Writing in India: 600 B.C. to the Present.* Vol. 1: *600 B.C. to the Early 20th Century.* New York: Feminist Press, 1991.

Vaid, Sudesh, Rao, Amiya, and Juneja, Monica. *Rape, Society and State.* Delhi: People's Union for Democratic Rights, 1980.

Vindhya, U. "The Srikakulam Movement." In *A Space Within the Struggle.* Edited by Ilina Sen, pp. 25–49. Delhi: Kali for Women, 1990.

Viswanathan, Gauri. *The Masks of Conquest: Literary Study and British Rule in India.* London: Faber & Faber, 1990.

Walker, Alice, ed., *I Love Myself When I Am Laughing . . . and Then Again When I Am Looking Mean and Impressive: A Zora Neale Hurston Reader.* New York: Feminist Press, 1979.

Articles

Ahmad, Aijaz. "Some Reflections on Urdu." *Seminar* 359 (July 1989): 23–29.

Ahmad, Aijaz. " 'Third World Literature' and the Nationalist Ideology." *Journal of Arts and Ideas* 17–18 (1989): 117–135.

Bagchi, A. K. "De-industrialisation in India in the Nineteenth Century: Some Theoretical Implications." *Journal of Development Studies* 12 (1975–1976): 135–164.

Baru, Sanjaya. "Market Forces." *Journal of Arts and Ideas* 19 (1990): 53–59.

Bharucha, Rustom. "Haraam Bombay!" *Economic and Political Weekly* 24,23 (1989): 1275–1279.

Chattopadhyay, Ratnabali. "Nationalism and Form in Indian Painting." *Journal of Arts and Ideas* 14–15 (1987): 5–46.

Chhachhi, Amrita. "The State, Religious Fundamentalism, and Women: Trends in South Asia." *Economic and Political Weekly* 24,11 (1989): 567–578.

Datta, Pradip, et al. "Understanding Communal Violence." *Economic and Political Weekly* 25,45 (1990): 2487–2495.

Dube, Leela. "On the Construction of Gender: Hindu Girls in Patrilineal India." *Economic and Political Weekly* 23,18 (1988): WS 11–19.

Guru, Gopal. "Hinduisation of Ambedkar in Maharashtra." *Economic and Political Weekly* 26,7 (1991): 239–242.

Hall, Stuart. "The Narrative Construction of Reality." *Southern Review* 17,1 (1984): 3–17.

Kannabiran, Vasantha, and Shatrugna, Veena. "Women's Activism and the

Relocation of Political Practice: Some Reflections on the Experience of Stree Shakti Sanghatana." *Lokayan Bulletin* 4,6 (1987): 23–34.

Kapur, Geeta. "Ravi Varma: Representational Dilemmas of a Nineteenth-Century Indian Painter." *Journal of Arts and Ideas* 17–18 (1989): 59–80.

Kaviraj, Sudipta. "A Critique of the Passive Revolution." *Economic and Political Weekly* 23–27 (1988): 2429–2444.

Kishwar, Madhu. "Women in Gandhi." *Economic and Political Weekly* 20,40–41 (1985): 1691–1702, 1753–1758.

Ludertz, Vasudha Dalmia. "Brecht in Hindi: The Poetics of Response." *Journal of Arts and Ideas* 16 (1988): 59–72.

Mies, Maria. "The Shahada Movement." *Journal of Peasant Studies* 3,4 (1974): 472–482.

Minault, Gail. "Urdu Women's Magazines in the Twentieth Century." *Manushi* 48 (1988): 2–9.

Mukherjee, Meenakshi. "Reality and Realism: Indian Women as Protagonists in Four Nineteenth-Century Novels." *Economic and Political Weekly* 19,2 (1984): 76–85.

Patel, Sujatha. "The Construction and Reconstruction of Women in Gandhi." *Economic and Political Weekly* 23,8 (1988): 377–387.

Prakash, Padma. "Women and Health: Emerging Challenges." *Lokayan Bulletin* 4,6 (1986): 77–83.

Rajadhyaksha, Ashish. "Neo-Traditionalism—Film as Popular Art in India." *Framework* 32–33 (1986): 20–67.

Rajadhyaksha, Ashish. "Living the Tradition." *Journal of Arts and Ideas* 16 (1988): 73–86.

Rajadhyaksha, Ashish. "Beaming Messages to the Nation." *Journal of Arts and Ideas* 19 (1990): 33–52.

Said, Edward W. "Representing the Colonized: Anthropology's Interlocuters." *Critical Inquiry* 15,2 (1989): 205–225.

Said, Edward W. "Narrative, Geography and Interpretation." *New Left Review* 180 (Mar/April 1990): 81–100.

Saldanha, Indra Munshi. "Tribal Women in the Warli Revolt, 1945–47: 'Class' and 'Gender' in the Left Perspective." *Economic and Political Weekly* 21,17 (1986): WS 41–52.

Sangari, Kumkum. "Introduction: Representations in History." *Journal of Arts and Ideas* 17–18 (1989): 3–9.

Seminar 165 (May 1973). Special Issue: "The Status of Women."

Seminar 300 (August 1984). Special Issue: "The Sexist Media."

Seminar 318 (February 1986). Special Issue: "Purdah Culture."

Seminar 331 (March 1987). Special Issue: "Femicide."

Shatrugna, Veena. "Experiencing Drudgery." *Economic and Political Weekly* 25,16 (1990): 829–833.

Shatrugna, Veena, et al. "Back Pain, the Feminine Affliction." *Economic and Political Weekly* 25,17 (1990): WS 2–6.

Srinivasan, Amrit. "Reform and Revival: The Devadasi and Her Dance." *Economic and Political Weekly* 20, 40 (1985): 1869–1876.

Thapar, Romila. "Traditions versus Misconceptions." Interview with Madhu Kishwar and Ruth Vanita. *Manushi* 42–43 (1987): 2–14.

Thapar, Romila. "Imagined Religious Communities: Ancient History and the Modern Search for a Hindu Identity." *Modern Asian Studies* 23,2 (1989): 209–231.

Tharu, Susie. "The Second Stage from the Third World." *Indian Journal of American Studies* 13,2 (1983): 179–184.

Tharu, Susie. "Third World Women's Cinema: Notes on Narrative, Reflections on Opacity." *Economic and Political Weekly* 21,20 (1986): 864–866.

Tharu, Susie. "Thinking the Nation Out: Some Reflections on Nationalism and Theory." *Journal of Arts and Ideas* 17–18 (1989): 81–91.

Tharu, Susie. "Government, Binding and Unbinding: Alienation and the Teaching of Literature." *Journal of English and Foreign Languages,* Special Double Number, *Teaching Literature* 7–8 (1991): 1–29.

Tharu, Susie. "Decoding Anand's Humanism." *Kunapipi* 4,2: 30–41.

Visvanathan, Susan. "Marriage, Birth and Death: Property Rights and Domestic Relationships of the Orthodox/Jacobite Syrian Christians of Kerala." *Economic and Political Weekly* 24,24 (1989): 1341–1346.

Viswanathan, Gauri. "The Beginnings of English Literary Study in British India." *Oxford Literary Review* 9 (1987): 2–26.

Manuscript Collections

Kaur, Raj Kumari Amrit. Personal Papers. Nehru Memorial Museum and Archives, Delhi.

Reddi, S. Muthulakshmi. AIWC, Franchise File. Nehru Memorial Museum and Archives, Delhi.

PERMISSION
ACKNOWLEDGMENTS

We gratefully acknowledge permission to include the following:

VARSHA ADALJA: "Bichari Champudi" by permission of the author.

AMBAI: "Anil" by permission of the author.

JEELANI BANO: "Tamasha" by permission of the author.

MANJUL BHAGAT: "Bebeji" by permission of the author and the publisher. Translation, by the author, revised for this publication.

MANNU BHANDARI: "Saza" by permission of the author.

MALINI BHATTACHARYA: Excerpt from *Meye Dile Sajiye* by permission of the author.

ISMAT CHUGTAI: "Lihaf" by permission of the author.

VIJAYA DABBE: "Narimanigalige Ondu Kivimatu," "Farida Begum," and "Miruguva Gorigalu" by permission of the author.

624

CHHAYA DATAR: "Swatahchya Shodhat" by permission of the author.

KAMAL DESAI: "Tila Bandh" by permission of the author.

GAURI DESHPANDE: "Ahe He Ase Ahe" by permission of the author.

NABANEETA DEV SEN: "Monsieur Hulor Holiday" by permission of the author.

ABBURI CHAYA DEVI: "Srimathi—Udyogini" by permission of the author.

ACHANTA SARADA DEVI: "Adavi Dagina Vennela" by permission of the author.

ILLINDALA SARASWATI DEVI: "Anaswasita" by permission of the author.

MAHASWETA DEVI: "Shishu" by permission of the author.

NIDUMANURI REVATI DEVI: "Mugavoyina Gonthu" and "Asagni Renuvu" by permission of Vaddera Chandidas.

RATAKONDA VASUNDHARA DEVI: "Picchi" by permission of the author.

SAROOP DHRUV: "Eknun Ek Vastra" and "Flapdoorni Arpar" by permission of the author.

KAMALA HEMMIGE: "Gini" by permission of the author.

M. K. INDIRA: Excerpt from *Phaniyamma* by permission of the author.

A. JAYAPRABHA: "Chupulu" and "Chitlina Akula Maunam" by permission of the author.

SARAH JOSEPH: "Mazha" by permission of the author.

BABY KAMBLE: Excerpt from *Jina Amucha* by permission of the author.

KUNDANIKA KAPADIA: Excerpt from *Sat Paglan Akashman* by permission of the author.

RAJAM KRISHNAN: "Kaipidite Kadaloruvanai" by permission of the author.

SUGATHA KUMARI: "Rathrimazha" by permission of the author.

MADHAVIKUTTY: "Neipayasam" by permission of the author and the publisher. Translation slightly altered for this publication.

PRAVASINI MAHAKUD: "Satare Ete Nisangata Keunthi Thai" by permission of the author.

JAYA MEHTA: "Lokshahiman," "Ekoham Bahusyam?" and "Dushmannu Lashkar Pasar Thai Gayu" by permission of the author.

BINAPANI MOHANTY: "Asru Anala" by permission of the author.

BRAHMOTRI MOHANTY: "Thare Mo Goda Khasijiba Pare" and "Darpana" by permission of the author.

MEENA KUMARI NAZ: [Bit by bit the splintered day has ended] by permission of S. S. Gulzar.

PANNA NAIK: "Billi" and "Shishu" by permission of the author.

ANUPAMA NIRANJANA: "Ondu Ghatane Mattu Anantara" by permission of the author.

JAMEELA NISHAT: [What fire is this] by permission of the author.

MRINAL PANDE: "Hum Safar" by permission of the author.

MEHERUNNISA PARVEZ: "Tona" by permission of the author.

DHIRUBEN PATEL: Excerpt from *Sheemlanan Phool* by permission of the author.

SAROJ PATHAK: "Saugandh" by permission of the author.

HEMA PATTANSHETTI: "Hattarali Hannondagi" by permission of the author.

MALATI PATTANSHETTI: "Sambandha" by permission of the author.

ANURADHA POTDAR: "Tumache He Sojwal Samsar" by permission of the author.

AMRITA PRITAM: "Ek Bath" and "Jada" by permission of the author.

CHUDAMANI RAGHAVAN: "Nangam Ashramam" by permission of the author.

RAJALEKSHMY: "Atmahatya" by permission of T. A. Kuttimalu Amma.

NITA RAMAIYA: "Ognisso-Ognyaeshinun Varas" and "Treeji Ankhnun Jantarmantar" by permission of the author.

PRATIBHA RAY: "Kambala" by permission of the author.

DUDALA SALAMMA: "Dudala Salamma, Khila Shapur" by permission of the authors.

INDIRA SANT: "Kanav," "Dhukyasarakha," and "Shapit" by permission of the author.

SULEKHA SANYAL: Excerpt from *Nabankur* by permission of Abanti K. Sanyal.

PRATIBHA SATPATHY: "Kakara Topa" by permission of the author.

RAJEE SETH: "Uska Akash" by permission of the author.

SIDDIQA BEGUM SEVHARVI: "Tare Laraz Rahe Hai" by permission of the author.

HAJIRA SHAKOOR: "Umr Qaid" by permission of the author.

VEENA SHATESHWAR: "Avala Svatantrya" by permission of the author.

SHANTA SHELKE: "Pannashi Ultunhi" by permission of the author.

SHIVANI: "Dadi" by permission of the author.

KABITA SINHA: "Ishwarke Eve," "Deho," and "Mahasweta" by permission of the author. Translation of "Mahasweta" by permission of Carolyne Wright.

SHASHIKALA VEERAYYA SWAMY: "Menabatti" by permission of the author.

WAJEDA TABASSUM: "Utran" by permission of the author.

TRIVENI: "Koneya Nirdhara" by permission of S. N. Shankar.

O. V. USHA: "Mrigaya" by permission of the author.

S. USHA: "I Nelada Hadu" by permission of the author.

VAIDEHI: "Shakuntale Yondige Kaleda Aparahna" by permission of the author.

P. VATSALA: "Oru Tadavuchatatinde Kadha" by permission of the author.

VIMALA: "Vantillu" and "Nischala Chitram" by permission of the author.

HAMSA WADKAR: Excerpt from *Sangatye Aika* by permission of Dileep Majgaonkar, Rajahans Prakashan.

RAZIA SAJJAD ZAHEER: "Neech" by permission of Najma Zaheer Baquer.

SAJIDA ZAIDI: "Rishta" and "Naye Zaviye" by permission of the author.

ZAHIDA ZAIDI: "Bachpana Chod Do" by permission of the author.

All translations, except of the works by Manjul Bhagat, Madhavikutty, and Dudala Salamma, and of "Mahasweta" by Kabita Sinha, were made especially for this book and are printed by permission of the translators.

ORIGINAL-LANGUAGE
SOURCES:
VOLUMES I AND II

Acchamamba, Bandaru. "Khana." In *Abala Sacharitra Ratnamala,* pp. 76–83. Bezawada: Komarraju Vinayaka Rao, 1947.

Adalja, Varsha. "Bichari Champudi." In *E,* pp. 48–54. Bombay: R. R. Seth, 1979.

Akkamahadevi. [Not one, not two, not three or four], [Would a circling surface vulture], [Don't despise me], and [Brother, you've come]. In *Akkana Vacanaqalu.* Vacana 18, 22, 64, and 295, pp. 52, 65, 70, and 157. Edited by L. Basavaraju. Mysore: Geeta Book House, 1966.

Ambai. "Anil." *Inni,* October 1986, 10–13.

Amma, K. Saraswathi. "Vivahangal Swargatil Vecchu Nadattapedunnu." In *Chuvannapukkal,* pp. 61–70. Kottayam: Sahitya Pravarthaka Co-operative Society, 1955. Reprint. 1965.

Annapurnamma, Darisi. "Gnanamba." In *Marapurani Annapurna.* Edited by Darisi Chenchayya, pp. 123–139. Madras: Darisi Chenchayya, 1932.

Antherjanam, Lalithambika. "Praticaradevatha." [1938]. In *Therengeddutha Kathakal,* pp. 129–140. Kottayam: Sahitya Pravarthaka Co-operative Society, 1966.

Auvaiyar. "What She Said." *Kuruntokai* 28. Edited by U. Ve. Caminataiyar. 3rd ed. Madras: Kapir Accukkutam, 1955.

Auvaiyar. [You cannot compare them with a lute]. *Purananuru* 92. Edited by Auvai C. Turaicamippillai. Madras: Kalakam, 1962. Reprint. 1967.

Bahinabai. "Atmanivedana." Abanga 14–17, 32—35 of *Sant Bahinabaicha Gatha.* Edited by Shalini Anant Javdekar. Pune: Continental Prakashan, 1979.

Bai, Janaki. [I remember the days of love's first flowering]. In *Diwan-e-Janaki,* p. 30. Allahabad: Matba Israr Karimi, 1931.

Bano, Jeelani. "Tamasha." In *Paraya Ghar,* pp. 189–194. Hyderabad: Author, 1979.

Begum, Gul-Badan. *Humayun Nama,* pp. 149–151. Translated by Annette Beveridge. London: Royal Asiatic Society, 1902.

Bhabani. [Knock knock knock]. In *Bangalir Gan.* Edited by Durgadas Lahiri, p. 1043. Calcutta: Natabar Chakroborty, Bengali Year 1312 [1905].

Bhagat, Manjul. "Bebeji." [1977]. In *Kitna Chhota Safar.* New Delhi: National Publishing House, 1979.

Bhandari, Mannu. "Saza." In *Yahi Sach Hai,* pp. 59–79. New Delhi: Akshar Prakashan, 1966.

Bhattacharya, Malini. "Meye Dile Sajiye," scene 3. [1983]. In *Meye Dile Sajiye: O Ekti Abastab Natika.* Edited by Sukumar Bhattacharya, pp. 11–17. Calcutta: Sachetana, 1984.

Chanda, Mahlaqa Bai. [Hoping to blossom (one day) into a flower]. In *Gulzar-e-Mahlaga,* p. 36. Hyderabad Deccan: Nizamul Matabe Press, Mahbubia Agency, 1324 Hijri [1906].

Chandrabati. [After the Black Night comes the Bright Night] and [Back to life she'd brought her husband]. Sections 15 and 27 in *Sundari Malua.* [1923]. Taken from *Prachin Purbo Bangya Gitika.* Vol. 1. Edited by Kshitish Chandra Moulick, pp. 138–140, 190–193. Calcutta: Firma K. L. Mukhopadhyay, 1970.

Chaudhari, Bahinabai. "Ata Maza Male Jeeva" and "Mun." In *Bahinaichi Gani,* pp. 12–13. Bombay: G. P. Parchure Prakashan Mandir, 1952.

Chaudhry, Kamla. "Kartavya." [1933]. In *Yatharth aur Kalpana.* Edited by Viraj, pp. 277–283. New Delhi: Rajpal and Sons, 1968.

Chaudhurani, Sarat Kumari. "Adorer Na Anadorer?" [1891]. In *Sarat Kumari Chaudhuranir Rachanabali.* Edited by Brojendra Nath Bandyopadhyay and Sajani Kanto Das, pp. 135–147. Calcutta: Bangiya Sahitya Parishad, 1950.

Chauhan, Sudha. *Mile Tej Se Tej,* pp. 140–144, 211–220. Allahabad: Hans Prakashan, 1975.

Chauhan, Subhadra Kumari. "Ekadasi." [1932]. *In Seedhe Sade Chitra,* pp. 58–61. Allahabad: Hans Prakashan, 1983.

Chugtai, Ismat. "Lihaf." In *Chotein.* [1943]. Reprint. Aligarh: Educational Book House, 1982, pp. 91–103.

Dabbe, Vijaya. "Narimanigalige Ondu Kivimatu" and "Farida Begum." In *Iruttave,* pp. 11, 44. Mysore: Suruchi Prakashana, 1975.

Dabbe, Vijaya. "Miruguva Gorigalu." In *Nirulohade Cinte,* pp. 32–35. Mysore: Ramya Prakashana, 1985.

Dasi, Binodini. "Star Theatre Sambandhye Nama Katha." In *Amar Katha.* 1912. Taken from *Nati Binodini Rachana Samagra.* Edited by Asutosh Bhattacharya, pp. 33–37. Calcutta: Sahitya Samstha, 1987.

Datar, Chhaya. "Swatahchya Shodhat." [1975]. Taken from *Vartulacha Ant,* pp. 99–106. Pune: Inamdar Bandhu, 1976.

Debi, Ashapurna. "Ja Noy Tai." In *Svanirvachita Srestha Galpo,* pp. 39–47. Calcutta: Model Publishing House, 1988.

Desai, Kamal. "Tila Bandh." In *Ranq,* pp. 59–82. Bombay: Popular Prakashan, 1962.

Deshpande, Gauri. "Ahe He Ase Ahe." [1972]. In *Ahe He Ase Ahe,* pp. 21–26. Bombay: Mauj Prakashan, 1986.

Devi, Abburi Chaya. "Srimathi-Udyogini." *Andhra Prabha,* 5 February 1975, 8–15.

Devi, Achanta Sarada. "Adavi Dagina Vennela." In *Marichika,* pp. 107–120. Vijayawada: Adharsha Grantha Mandali, 1969.

Devi, Homvati. "Apna Ghar." [1933]. In *Yatharth aur Kalpana.* Edited by Viraj, pp. 284–293. New Delhi: Rajpal & Sons, 1968.

Devi, Illindala Saraswati. "Anaswasita." In *Andhra Katha Manjusha,* pp. 371–382. Edited by Tallavajjhala Sivasankara Sastri. Tenali: The Orient Publishing Co., 1958.

Devi, Mahasweta. "Shishu." [1978]. In *Nairete Megh,* pp. 94–112. Calcutta: Karuna Prakashani, 1979.

Devi, Nidumanuri Revati. "Mugavoyina Gonthu" and "Asagni Renuvu." In *Silalolita,* pp. 16, 25. Tirupati: Priyabandhavi Prachuranalu, 1981.

Devi, Nirupama. *Didi,* chaps. 2, 4, and 17. Taken from *Nirupama Debir Granthabali.* Vol 1, pp. 5–8, 11–13, 70–74. Calcutta: Basumati Corp. Ltd., 1915.

Devi, Rassundari. *Amar Jiban,* 3–6 compositions. [1876]. Reprint. Calcutta: Indian Associates Publishing Co. Pvt. Ltd., Bengali Year 1363 [1956], pp. 18–23, 31–45.

Devi, Ratakonda Vasundhara. "Picchi." In *Nidalu,* pp. 53–60. Rajamundry: Author, 1982.

Devi, Shyamala. "Neeleya Samsara." [1936]. In *Shyamal Sanchya.* Edited by Vijaya Dabbe, pp. 7–13. Bangalore: Lekhakiyara Sangha, 1989.

Devi, Swarnakumari. *Kahake,* chaps. 1 and 8, pp. 1–4, 55–59. Calcutta: Sree Chandra Bhushan Sarkar, 1898.

Dhruv, Saroop. "Eknun Ek Vastra" and "Flapdoorni Arpar." In *Mara Hathni Vat,* pp. 71–75, 13–14. Ahmedabad: Nakshatra Trust, 1982.

Gangasati. [Oh, the Meru Mountain may be swayed]. In *Kavyasanchay.* Edited by Anantrai Raval and Hira Pathak, p. 185. Ahmedabad: Gujarati Sahitya Parishad, 1981.

Hemmige, Kamala. "Gini." In *Pallavi,* pp. 5–6. Sagar: Akshara Prakashana, 1980.

"Hindu Vidwanchi Dukhit Stithi: Eka Vidhwa Baine Varnileli." [1889]. *Yamuna Paryatan,* 1857; 4th ed., Bombay: E. V. Padmanji, 1937, pp. 151–159.

Honnamma, Sanciya. [Wasn't it woman who bore them]. In *Satigite.* Edited by K. Narasimha Sastri, p. 21. Mysore: Usha Sahitya Male, 1955.

Hossain, Rokeya Sakhawat. "Sultana's Dream." [1905]. In *Rokeya Rachanabali.* Edited by Abdul Kadir, pp. 575–588. Dhaka: Bangla Academy, 1984.

Hyder, Nazar Sajjad. "Purdah." *Tahzeeb-e-Niswan* 40, no. 9, 1937, 193–195.

Indira, M. K. *Phaniyamma,* pp. 65–71. Dharwad: Manohar Granthamala, 1976.

Jahan, Rasheed. "Woh." In *Woh aur Dosre Afsane aur Drame,* pp. 70–73. Delhi: Rasheed Jahan Yadgaar Committee, 1977.

Janabai. [Cast off all shame] and [Jani sweeps the floor]. *Shri Namdev Gatha.* Abanga 362 and Abanga 219, pp. 972, 937. Bombay: Maharashtra State, 1970. Reprint. 1982.

Jayaprabha, A. "Chupulu" and "Chitlina Akula Maunam." In *Vamanudi Mudopadam,* pp. 3–4, 10–11. Hyderabad: Chaitanya-Teja Publications, 1988.

Jogeswari. [If fortune has brought you my way at last.] In *Bangalir Gan.* Edited by Durgadas Lahiri, p. 186. Calcutta: Natabar Chakroborty, Bengali Year 1312 [1905].

Joseph, Sarah. "Mazha." In *Kadinte Samgeetam,* pp. 96–103. Kottayam: Sahitya Pravarthaka Co-operative Society, 1979.

Kalyanamma. "Suryasthamana." *Saraswati* 5, no. 8, 1926, 17–24.

Kamble, Baby. *Jina Amucha,* pp. 93–98. Pune: Rachana Prakashan, 1986.

Kanitkar, Kashibai. *Palkicha Gonda,* pp. 180–186. [1913]. Pune: Ganesh Mahadev and Co., 1928.

Kapadia, Kundanika. *Sat Paglan Akashman,* chap. 3, pp. 17–29. Ahmedabad: Bhogilal Shah, 1984.

Krishnan, Rajam. "Kaipidite Kadaloruvanai." In *Kalam,* pp. 74–90. Madras: Paari Puthakap Pannai, 1985.

Kumari, Sugatha. "Rathrimazha." In *Rathrimazha,* pp. 3–5. Kottayam: Author, 1977. Reprint. 1982.

Macattiyar, Okkur. [Her purpose is frightening, her spirit cruel]. In *Purananuru* 279. Edited by Auvai C. Turaicamippillai. Madras: Kalakam, 1962. Reprint. 1967.

Madhavikutty. "Neipayasam." [1962]. In *Ente Cherukathakal,* pp. 122–125. Kozhikode: Mathrubhumi, 1985.

Mahakud, Pravasini. "Satare Ete Nisangata Keunthi Thae." In *Muhurta-Muhurta,* pp. 24–26. Cuttack: Friends' Publishers, 1990.

Mehta, Jaya. "Dushmannu Lashkar Pasar Thai Gayu." In *Akashman Tarao Chup Chhe,* p. 19. Bombay: S. N. D. T. University, 1985.

Mehta, Jaya. "Lokshahiman" and "Ekoham Bahusyam?" In *Venetian Blind,* pp. 23, 35. Ahmedabad: Vora & Co., 1978.

Mettika. [Though I am weak and tired now]. No. 34 in *Therigatha, Khuddaka Nikaya.* Vol. 2. Edited by Bhikkhu J. Kashyap. Nalanda Devanagari Dali Series (Bihar Government), 1959.

Mirabai. [The Bhil woman tasted them, plum after plum]. *Mirabai ki Padavalli* 186. Edited by Parasuram Catrurvedi, p. 137. Allahabad: Hindi Sahitya Sammelan, 1973.

Mirabai. [I am pale with longing for my beloved], [I am true to my Lord] and [Having taken up this bundle of suffering]. In *Mira.* Compiled by Niranjan Bhagat, pp. 102, 86. Ahmedabad: Sadbhav Prakashan, 1982.

Mirza, Sughra Humayun. [Who will care to visit my grave when I am gone]. *Ismat,* September 1937. Taken from *Kalam-e-Niswan: Khawateen Ke Urdu Kalaam Ka Benazeer Majmua.* Edited by Mohd. Jameeluddin Barfi, p. 109. Hyderabad Deccan: Ahed-e-Afreen Barqi Press, n.d.

Mohanty, Binapani. "Asru Anala." *Jhankara,* October 1989, 583–588.

Mohanty, Brahmotri. "Thare Mo Goda Khasijiba Pare." In *Adhunika Oriya Kabita,* p. 519. Cuttack: Janashakti Pustakalaya, 1968.

Mohanty, Brahmotri. "Darpana." In *Stalsaka,* pp. 20–21. Cuttack: Rashtrabhasa Samabaya Prakshan, 1988.

Molla, Atukuri. [My father Kesava], [I am no scholar], [As honey sweetens], [Telugu writing], [The sun moved on the sky], and [Are they lotuses]. In *Molla Ramayanam,* pp. 7–9, 35, 45–46. Chennapuri: Vavilla Ramaswamy Sastrulu & Sons, 1917.

Muddupalani. [Move on her lips], [Honey, / why do you think / I stamped on Kali?], and [If I ask her not to kiss me]. In *Radhika Santwanam,* pp. 15–16, 70–71, 56–57. Madras: Vavilla Ramaswamy Sastrulu & Sons, 1910.

Mukhopadhyay, Mokshodayani. "Bangalir Babu." [1882]. In *Bangyer Mohila Kobi.* Edited by Jogendra Nath Gupta, pp. 222–224. Calcutta: A. Mukherjee & Co. Ltd., Bengali Year 1360 [1953].

Muktabai. "Mang Maharachya Dukavisayi." In *Dnyanodaya Centenary Volumes.* Edited by B. P. Hivale, pp. 73–75. Bombay: Wilson College, 1942.

Mullens, Hannah Catherine. *Phulmani O Karunar Bibaran,* chaps. 4 and 10. [1852]. Reprint. Edited by Chittaranjan Bondyopadhyay, pp. 42–46, 133–137. Calcutta: General Printers and Publishers Pvt. Ltd., 1958.

"Mumbaitil Prarthanasamajsambandi Striyanchya Sabheta Eka Baine Vachlela Nibandha." [1881]. In *Yamuna Paryatan* [1857]; 2nd ed., 1882. 4th ed. Bombay: E. V. Padmanji, 1937, pp. 151–159.

Mutta. [So free I am, so gloriously free]. No. 11 in *Therigatha, Khuddaka Nikaya.* Vol. 2. Edited by Bhikku J. Kashyap. Nalanda Devangari Pali Series (Bihar Government), 1959.

Naccellaiyar, Kakkaipatniyar. [His armies love massacre]. *Patiruppattu* 60. 6th ed. Edited by U. Ve Caminataiyar. Madras: Kapir Accukkutam, 1957.

Naidu, Sarojini. "Bangle-Sellers" and "The Temple: A Pilgrimage of Love" In *Sceptred Flute: Songs of India,* pp. 108–109, 211–217. Allahabad: Kitabistan, 1958.

Naidu, Sarojini. "Presidential Address at Ahmedabad Students' Conference 1922." In *Speeches and Writings,* pp. 259–267. Madras: G. A. Natesan & Co., 1923.

Naik, Panna. "Billi." In *Pravesh,* p. 78. Bombay: Vora Publishers, 1976.

Naik, Panna. "Shishu." In *Philadelphia,* p. 29. Bombay: Tripathi Publishers, 1980.

Naz, Meena Kumari, [Bit by bit the splintered day has ended]. In *Tanha Chand.* Compiled by S. S. Gulzar. Delhi: Shama Book Depot, n.d.

Niranjana, Anupama. "Ondu Ghatane Mattu Anantara." In *Ondu Giniya Kathe,* pp. 104–118. Mysore: D. V. K. Murthy, 1983.

Nishat, Jameela. [What fire is this]. *Kitab Numa,* January 1985, 27.

Pande, Mrinal. "Hum Safar." In *Ek Stri Ka Vidageet,* pp. 102–111. New Delhi: Radhakrishan Prakashan, 1985.

Parvez, Meherunnisa. "Tona." In *Galat Purush,* pp. 1–12. New Delhi: National Publishing House, 1978.

Patel, Dhiruben. *Sheemlanan Phool,* chap. 1, pp. 1–3. Bombay: N. M. Tripathi, 1976.

Pathak, Saroj. "Saugandh." In *Saroj Pathakni Shreshtha Vartao.* Edited by Dilawar Singh Jadeja and Ramanlal Pathak, pp. 43–54. Ahmedabad: Shabdalok Prakashan, 1981.

Pattanshetti, Hema. "Hattarali Hannondagi." In *Virahotsava,* p. 34. Bangalore: Kannada Sangha, 1983.

Pattanshetti, Malati. "Sambandha." In *Garigedari,* p. 9. Dharwada: Kriti Prakashana, 1983.

Pentu, Kavar. [You stand and hold the post of my small house]. *Puranuru* 86. 2 vols. Edited by Auvai C. Turaicamippillai. Madras: Kalakam, 1962. Reprint. 1967.

Phule, Savithribai. "Letter to Jotiba Phule." In *Kranti Jyoti Savitribai Jotirao Phule,* pp. 73–74. Kolhapur: Asha M. Mali, 1980.

Potdar, Anuradha. "Tumache He Sojwal Samsar." In *Kaktus Flawar,* p. 19. Bombay: Mauj Prakashan, 1979.

Pritam, Amrita. "Jada" and "Ek Bath." In *Amrita Pritam Pratinidhi Kavitayen,* pp. 27–28, 36–37. New Delhi: Rajkamal Publications, 1986.

Raghavan, Chudamani. "Nangam Ashramam." *Kanaiyazhi,* February 1972, 25–32.

Rajalekshmy. "Atmahatya." In *Mangalodayam Viseshalprati,* pp. 98–101. Trichur: Mangalodayam Press, 1964.

Rajwade, Saraswati Bai. "Pravaha Patite." *Usha,* August 1954, 41–55.

Ramaiya, Nita. "Ognisso-Ognyaeshinun Varas" and "Treeji Ankhnun Jantarmantar." In *Shabdane Raste,* p. 8, 18–20. Bombay: S. N. D. T. University, 1989.

Rami. [What can I say, friend?]. In *Prachina Stri Kavi.* Edited by Ramani Mohan Mullick, pp. 13–14. Calcutta: Sarat Chandra Chakroborty, Bengali Year 1305 [1898].

Rami. [Where have you gone?]. [1896]. In *Bangya Bhasha O Sahitya,* pp. 242–246. Calcutta: West Bengal State Book Board, 1986.

Ranade, Ramabai. *Amachya Ayushyatil Kahi Athawani,* part 3, chaps. 4 and 7 and part 14, chap. 1, pp. 40–41, 44–45, 83–91, 110–115. Bombay: Kashinath Raghunath Mitra, 1910.

Ratanbai. [My spinning wheel is dear to me, my sister]. In *Kavyasanchay.* Edited by Anantrai Raval and Hira Pathak, p. 78. Ahmedabad: Gujarati Sahitya Parishad, 1981.

Ray, Pratibha. "Kambala." *Shrestha Galpa,* pp. 1–21. Cuttack: Nalanda, 1984.

Sabat, Kuntala Kumari. "Shefali Prati." [1924]. In *Utkala Bharathi Kuntala Kumari Granthamala.* Part 1, pp. 70–72. Cuttack: Students' Store, 1968.

Sahasrabuddhe, Indira. *Balutai Dhada Ghe,* chaps. 14 and 24, pp. 117–119, 166–170. Mumbai [Bombay]: Marathe Vasant Balwant, 1931.

Salamma, Dudala. "Dudala Salamma: Khila Shapur." In *Manaku Teliyani Mana Charitra,* pp. 127–135. Stree Shakti Sanghatana. Hyderabad: Stree Shakti Sanghatana, 1986.

Sane, Geeta. *Hirvalikhali,* chap. 4, pp. 19–24. Bombay: Maharashtra Prakashan Samstha, 1936.

Sankavva, Sule. [In my harlot's trade]. In *Ippathelu Sivasaraneyara Vacanagalu.* Vacana 236. Edited by R. C. Hiremath, p. 116. Dharwada: Karnataka Viswavidyalaya Prakashana, 1968.

Sant, Indira. "Kanav." In *Mrigajala,* pp. 63–64. Bombay: Mauj Prakashan, 1957.

Sant, Indira. "Shapit" and "Dhukyasarakha." In *Garbhareshim,* pp. 41, 43. Belgav: Javalkar Asha, 1982.

Sanyal, Sulekha. *Nabankur,* chaps. 4, 29, 31, and 32 [Bengali Year 1362 (1955)]. 3d ed. Calcutta: Manisha Granthalaya Pvt. Ltd., 1985, pp. 45–49, 285–291, 301–304, 311–314.

Saraswati, Pandita Ramabai. *The High Caste Hindu Woman,* chap. 3. [1888]. Reprint. New Delhi: Inter India Publications, 1984, pp. 29–48.

Saraswati, Pandita Ramabai. "Letter to Miss Dorothea Beale, Cheltenham." In *The Letters and Correspondence of Pandita Ramabai.* Edited by A. B. Shah, pp. 136–138. Bombay: The State Board for Literature and Culture, 1977.

Satpathy, Pratibha. "Kakara Topa." In *Nimishe Akshara,* pp. 45–47. Cuttack: Vidyapuri, 1985.

Sattianadan, Krupa. "Saguna." *Christian College Magazine,* 1889–1890, 351–356.

Sen, Nabaneeta Dev. "Monsieur Hulor Holiday." In *Monsieur Hulor Holiday,* pp. 1–13. Calcutta: Karuna Prakashani, Bengali Year 1387 [1980].

Seth, Rajee. "Uska Akash." [1979]. In *Andhe Mod Se Aage*, pp. 33–43. New Delhi: Rajkamal Prakashan, 1983.

Sevharvi, Siddiqa Begum. "Tare Laraz Rahe Hai." In *Dudh aur Khun*, pp. 105–120. Delhi: Azad Kitab Ghar, 1953.

Shakoor, Hajira. "Umr Qaid." In *Gardishen*, pp. 82–95. Delhi: Author, 1979.

Shanteshwar, Veena. "Avala Svatantrya." In *Kavalu*, pp. 83–98. Dharwada: Nirmana Prakashana, 1976.

Shelke, Shanta. "Pannashi Ultunhi." In *Gondan*, p. 62. Bombay: Mauj Prakashan, 1975.

Shinde, Tarabai. *Stri Purush Tulana*. [1882]. Reprint. Edited by S. G. Malshe, pp. 16–37. Mumbai [Bombay]: Marathi Granthasangrahalay, 1975.

Shirurkar, Vibhavari. *Virlele Swapna*. [1935]. Reprint. Bombay: Popular Prakashan Pvt. Ltd., 1986.

Shivani. "Dadi." In *Kishnuli*, pp. 128–140. Delhi: Saraswati Vihar Publications, 1978.

Sinha, Kabita. "Mahasweta." In *Horina Boiri*, p. 42. Calcutta: Navanna, 1983.

Sinha, Kabita. "Deho" and "Ishwarke Eve." In *Kabita Parameswari*, pp. 19, 46–49. Calcutta: Dainik Kavita, 1976.

Sorabji, Cornelia. "The Imprisoned Rani." In *India Calling : The Memoirs of Cornelia Sorabji*, part 2, chap. 4, pp. 99–115. London: Nisbet & Co. Ltd., 1934.

Sumangalamata. [A woman well set free! How free I am]. No. 21 in *Therigatha, Khuddaka Nakaya*. Vol. 2. Edited by Bhikku J. Kashyap. Nalanda Devangari Pali Series (Bihar Government), 1959.

Swamy, Shashikala Veerayya. "Menabatti." In *Gubbimani*, p. 49. Mysore: Nelamane Prakashana, 1979.

Tabassum, Wajeda. "Utran." In *Utran*, pp. 88–98. Bombay: Overseas Book Centre, 1977.

Thottam, Mary John. "Lokame Yatra." In *Kavitharaman*, pp. 47–53. Kottayam: National Book Store, 1929. Reprint. 1983.

Tilak, Lakshmibai, *Smriti Chitre*, part 2, chaps. 1–3 [1935]; part 4, chap. 2 [1936]. Nasik: Ashok D. Tilak, 1973.

Tirumalamba, Nanjanagudu. *Nabha*, pp. 26–30. [1914]. Nanjanagudu: Satihitaishini Granthamala, 1920.

Triveni. "Koneya Nirdhara." In *Samasyeya Magu*. Mysore: D. V. K. Murthy Publications, 1968; 4th ed. 1971, pp. 84–93.

Ubbiri. ["O Ubbiri, who wails in the wood"]. No. 33 in *Therigatha, Khuddaka Nikaya*. Vol. 2. Edited by Bhikku J. Kashyap. Nalanda Devangari Pali Series (Bihar Government), 1959.

Usha, S. "I Nelada Hadu." In *I Nelada Hadu*, pp. 5–7. Malladihalli: Samvada Prakashana, 1990.

Usha, O. V. "Mrigaya." *Mathrubhumi Weekly*, 8–14 February 1987, 23.

Vaidehi. "Shakuntale Yondige Kaleda Aparahna." *Taranga*, 27 July 1986, 22–27.

Varma, Mahadevi. "Lachhma." In *Atit Ke Chalachitra*, pp. 99–109. Allahabad: Bharati Bhandar, 1941.

Vatsala, P. "Oru Tadavuchatatinde Kadha." In *Anavettakkaran*, pp. 158–169. Kottayam: Sahitya Pravarthaka Co-operative Society, 1982.

Venkamamba, Tarigonda. [Gently he lifts me up]. In *Vishnuparijatamu*, pp. 36–37. Hyderabad: A. P. Sahitya Academy, 1965.

Venmannipputi. [What she said to her girl friend]. *Kuruntokai* 229. Edited by U. Ve. Caminataiyar. 3rd ed. Madras: Kapir Accukkutam, 1955.

Vimala. "Nischala Chitram" and "Vantillu." In *Adavi Uppongina Ratri*, pp. 19, 60–63. Hyderabad: Virasam City Unit, 1990.

Viswasundaramma, Tallapragada. "Jailu Gadiyaramu." In *Kavita Kadambam*, p. 208. Visakhapatnam: Mallavarapu Prachunnalu, 1973.

Vitiyar, Velli. [He will not dig up the earth and enter it] and [You tell me I am wrong, my friend]. *Kuruntokai* 130. Edited by U. Ve. Caminataiyar. 3rd ed. Madras: Kapir Accukkutam, 1955.

Wadkar, Hamsa. *Sangatye Aika*, chap. 8, pp. 81–92. [1970]. Pune: Rajhans Prakashan, 1983.

Zaheer, Razia Sajjad. "Neech." In *Allah De Banda Le*, pp. 33–48. New Delhi: Seema Publications, 1984.

Zaidi, Sajida. "Rishta" and "Naye Zaviye." In *Aatish-e-Sayyal*, pp. 22–23, 67. New Delhi: Maktaba Jamia, 1972.

Zaidi, Zahida. "Bachpana Chod Do." In *Dharti Ka Lams*, pp. 40–41. Aligarh: Author, 1975.

INDEX

The Feminist Press at The City University of New York offers alternatives in education and in literature. Founded in 1970, this nonprofit, tax-exempt, educational and publishing organization works to eliminate stereotypes in books and schools and to provide literature with a broad vision of human potential. The publishing program includes reprints of important works by women, feminist biographies of women, multicultural anthologies, a cross-cultural memoir series, and nonsexist children's books. Curricular materials, bibliographies, directories, and a quarterly journal provide information and support for students and teachers of women's studies. Through publications and projects, The Feminist Press contributes to the rediscovery of the history of women and the emergence of a more humane society.

NEW AND FORTHCOMING BOOKS FROM THE FEMINIST PRESS

Anna Teller, a novel by Jo Sinclair. Afterword by Anne Halley. $35.00 cloth, $16.95 paper.

The Captive Imagination: A Casebook on "The Yellow Wallpaper," edited and with an introduction by Catherine Golden. $35.00 cloth, $14.95 paper.

Fault Lines, a memoir by Meena Alexander. $35.00 cloth, $12.95 paper.

I Dwell in Possibility, a memoir by Toni McNaron. $35.00 cloth, $12.95 paper.

Intimate Warriors: Portraits of a Modern Marriage, 1899–1944, selected works by Neith Boyce and Hutchins Hapgood. Edited by Ellen Kay Trimberger. Afterword by Shari Benstock. $35.00 cloth, $12.95 paper.

Lion Woman's Legacy: An Armenian-American Memoir, by Arlene Voski Avakian. Afterword by Bettina Aptheker. $35.00 cloth, $14.95 paper.

Long Walks and Intimate Talks, poems and stories by Grace Paley, paintings by Vera B. Williams. $29.95 cloth, $12.95 paper.

The Mer-Child: A Legend for Children and Other Adults, by Robin Morgan. Illustrations by Jesse Spicer Zerner and Amy Zerner. $17.95 cloth, $8.95 paper.

Motherhood by Choice: Pioneers in Women's Health and Family Planning, by Perdita Huston. Foreword by Dr. Fred Sai. $35.00 cloth, $14.95 paper.

The Princess and the Admiral, by Charlotte Pomerantz. Illustrations by Tony Chen. $17.95 cloth, $8.95 paper.

Proud Man, a novel by Katharine Burdekin (Murray Constantine). Foreword and Afterword by Daphne Patai. $35.00 cloth, $14.95 paper.

The Seasons: Death and Transfiguration, a memoir by Jo Sinclair. $35.00 cloth, $12.95 paper.

Women Writing in India: 600 B.C. to the Present. Volume I: 600 B.C. to the Early Twentieth Century. Volume II: The Twentieth Century. Edited by Susie Tharu and K. Lalita. Each volume $59.95 cloth, $29.95 paper.

Prices subject to change. For a free catalog or order information, write to The Feminist Press at The City University of New York, 311 East 94 Street, New York, NY 10128.